OXFORD TEXTBOOKS IN LINGUISTICS

Series editors
Keith Brown, Eve V. Clark, April McMahon,
Jim Miller, Lesley Milroy

Cognitive Grammar

OXFORD TEXTBOOKS IN LINGUISTICS

General editors:
Keith Brown, University of Cambridge; **Eve V. Clark**, Stanford University;
April McMahon, University of Sheffield; **Jim Miller**, University of Edinburgh;
Lesley Milroy, University of Michigan

This series provides accessible and authoritative textbooks on the approaches, methods, and theories associated with the main subfields of linguistics.

PUBLISHED

A Practical Introduction to Phonetics (SECOND EDITION)
by J. C. Catford

Meaning in Language: An Introduction to Semantics and Pragmatics
by Alan Cruse

Principles and Parameters: An Introduction to Syntactic Theory
by Peter W. Culicover

Linguistic Reconstruction: An Introduction to Theory and Method
by Anthony Fox

Semantic Analysis: A Practical Introduction
by Cliff Goddard

Cognitive Grammar
by John R. Taylor

IN PREPARATION

The Grammar of Words: An Introduction to Linguistic Morphology
by Professor G. Booij

Pragmatics
by Yan Huang

Linguistic Categorization (THIRD EDITION)
by John R. Taylor

Cognitive Grammar

John R. Taylor

OXFORD
UNIVERSITY PRESS

OXFORD
UNIVERSITY PRESS

Great Clarendon Street, Oxford OX2 6DP

Oxford University Press is a department of the University of Oxford.
It furthers the University's objective of excellence in research, scholarship,
and education by publishing worldwide in

Oxford New York

Auckland Bangkok Buenos Aires Cape Town Chennai
Dar es Salaam Delhi Hong Kong Istanbul Karachi Kolkata
Kuala Lumpur Madrid Melbourne Mexico City Mumbai Nairobi
São Paulo Shanghai Taipei Tokyo Toronto

Oxford is a registered trade mark of Oxford University Press
in the UK and in certain other countries

Published in the United States
by Oxford University Press Inc., New York

British Library Cataloguing in Publication Data

Data available

Library of Congress Cataloging in Publication Data

Data available

ISBN 0–19–870033–4

10 9 8 7 6 5 4 3

Typeset in Times and Meta
by RefineCatch Limited, Bungay, Suffolk
Printed in Great Britain by
Biddles Ltd, King's Lynn, Norfolk

Contents

List of figures

List of tables

Preface

This book started life, several years ago, as a short introduction to Cognitive Linguistics. The aim was to offer a compact synthesis of the leading ideas of the main protagonists of Cognitive Linguistics: Lakoff, Langacker, Talmy, Fauconnier, and others.

As the project matured, the focus narrowed to a specific trend within Cognitive Linguistics, namely, Langacker's theory of Cognitive Grammar, to my mind, the most comprehensive, and most fully articulated statement of a Cognitive Linguistics approach. With a narrowing of the focus, the book also grew in size. It soon became apparent that it was not going to be possible to convey the scope and internal consistency of the theory in half a dozen chapters. I also decided early on that it was going to be necessary to address the basic asumptions of the theory, and to show how the theory follows naturally from these. Hence, a good deal of this book deals with methodological and foundational issues. A particular concern was to do justice to phonological and morphological structure, topics which are largely ignored in more semantics-focused approaches within Cognitive Linguistics

In spite of its length, the book still retains its introductory character. Although the 'ideal' reader will have had some exposure to the methodology and subject matter of modern linguistics, as well as, perhaps, to its theoretical controversies, the book does not presuppose any previous knowledge of the discipline. With this readership in mind, I have endeavoured to present the main issues in Cognitive Grammar, exemplifying them, mostly, on the basis of well-known data, usually from English. I am acutely aware of the many topics that could not be included, such as discourse and textual aspects, the application of the theory to languages other than English, as well as more in-depth analyses of the thornier issues in English.

Different readers might use parts of the book for their own purposes. Those with little interest in methodological issues might easily skip chapters 3 and 4, and indeed most of Part 1, while those who want to go straight to the application of Cognitive Grammar can start at Chapter 7. Readers with a special interest in morphology can select Chapters 14–16; those who want to see how phonology is handled in the theory can select Chapters 5, 8, and 13, and so on.

The study questions which follow each of the chapters (except the first one) are intended as suggestions for further investigation within a Cognitive Grammar framework. Many of the questions could easily form the basis of minor (or not so minor) research projects. For this reason, I have not included model answers to the questions. Most of the questions are such that they do not have 'model answers'.

I am grateful to the University of Otago for a ten-month period of study leave, during which time the manuscript was largely completed, and also to Dirk Geeraerts, for arranging a period of residence at the Catholic University of Leuven, Belgium. Thanks also to René Dirven and Ron Langacker, for their helpful comments on earlier versions of the book, and to my wife, for her unfailing support and encouragement. Last but not least, my thanks to the team at Oxford University Press, who guided what must have been a rather difficult manuscript through to publication.

Part 1
Background

The first six chapters introduce Cognitive Grammar against a discussion of general theoretical issues.

Chapter 1 focuses on scope and concerns of Cognitive Linguistics approaches to language study, with special attention on the significance of the word 'cognitive' when applied to a linguistic theory. Cognitive Grammar is the name of a specific theory of language within the more general movement of Cognitive Linguistics. Chapter 2 gives a brief overview of some central concepts and assumptions of Cognitive Grammar, while Chapters 3 and 4 address some of the objections that could be raised against the 'conceptualist' foundations of the theory. Chapter 5 argues that phonology, no less than semantic issues, needs to be incorporated within Cognitive Grammar, while Chapter 6 addresses the status of semantic structure in the theory.

Cognitive Grammar and Cognitive Linguistics

Cognitive Grammar—the subject of this book—is the name which Ronald Langacker has given to a theory of language which he has been developing since the mid-1970s.[1] Initially, Cognitive Grammar occupied a very marginal place in the theoretical linguistic landscape. Over the years, as the theory has developed and become more widely known, it has attracted increasing numbers of adherents and sympathizers. There is now a sizeable literature which has applied the theory of Cognitive Grammar to a wide range of linguistic issues, in a variety of languages.

In this book I make a distinction between **Cognitive Grammar** and **Cognitive Linguistics**.

- I use the term 'Cognitive Linguistics' as a descriptive label for a rather broad movement within modern linguistics. It includes a variety of approaches, methodologies, and emphases, which are, however, unified by a number of

---

[1] In earlier publications the theory was called 'Space Grammar'; see, for example, the title of Langacker (1982). The earlier name probably alluded to the distinctive pictographic representations which the theory still employs. Whatever the appropriateness of the name, Langacker (FCG1: iv) disarmingly remarks that '[a] theory called space grammar can obviously not be taken seriously'. Langacker's two-volume work (published in 1987 (vol. 1) and 1991 (vol. 2)) is referred to as 'FCG1' or 'FCG2' throughout.

common assumptions. Foremost among these is the belief that language forms an integral part of human cognition, and that any insightful analysis of linguistic phenomena will need to be embedded in what is known about human cognitive abilities. Cognitive Linguistics aims, therefore, for a cognitively plausible account of what it means to know a language, how languages are acquired, and how they are used.

- 'Cognitive Grammar' is the name of a specific theory of language, which takes its place within the broader movement of Cognitive Linguistics. Although Cognitive Grammar has its own terminology, descriptive techniques, and pictorial conventions, it shares the basic assumptions of the Cognitive Linguistics movement.

In this first chapter, I set the scene by examining some general features of Cognitive Linguistics, and the relation of Cognitive Linguistics to other current approaches to linguistic analysis. I should point out that the use of the term 'cognitive' in linguistics is not free from controversy, and in this chapter I discuss some of the different ways in which the term has been understood. The situation can easily cause confusion for an unwary reader; it also can cause resentment among linguists who understand the term 'cognitive' in different ways. There are, for example, those who believe that the term is entirely inappropriate, both for the enterprise of Cognitive Linguistics, as I present it here, and for the more specific programme of Cognitive Grammar. On the other hand, there are those who would argue that the term 'cognitive' is valid for a broad spectrum of contemporary linguistics, and that the self-styled 'Cognitive Linguists' and 'Cognitive Grammarians' have no special claim on the word.

Let us begin by looking at the term 'cognitive', and what it might mean for a linguistic theory to be described as cognitive.

1.1 The cognitive turn

'Cognitive' is a fashionable term nowadays. Many of the human and social disciplines like to attach the word to their titles. We have cognitive anthropology, cognitive archaeology, and also, of course, cognitive psychology. Many universities have interdisciplinary programmes in cognitive science, with input from psychology, neurology, philosophy, computer science, and, usually, linguistics.

Cognitive science studies the mind and its workings—such things as memory, learning, perception, attention, consciousness, reasoning, and what, for want of a better word, one can call, simply, 'thought'. Although these look like the traditional concerns of psychology, a number of the human and social disciplines have staked a claim in the cognitive enterprise. The justification for this move is that human behaviour, and the products of human behaviour, in whatever domain, must themselves be treated as the products of the mind, and are ultimately constrained by the potential of the human mind.

Of the various human and social sciences, linguistics lends itself particularly well to the cognitive enterprise. In fact, after psychology, linguistics is probably the cognitive discipline par excellence. For a start, the cognitive basis of language is rather obvious. A language is something that people have to *know*; the knowledge has to be acquired, mostly in early childhood; the knowledge, once acquired, has got to reside in the minds of its users and has got to be invoked in any act of language use. Second, intensive study of diverse languages, by generations of professional linguists, has made available a significant pool of non-controversial and non-trivial facts about languages, their general design features, and their constrained diversity. Since quite a lot is known about human languages, we have a basis for evaluating proposals for the cognitive structures that might support the human language ability.

I think it fair to say that most linguists, nowadays, would at least pay lip-service to the idea that language knowledge resides in the mind, and that what linguists are trying to do, as linguists, is to describe what it is in the mind that enables people to create and understand linguistic expressions. Many linguists might even go so far as to regard linguistic analyses as specific hypotheses about the contents of the mind. To this extent, much of modern linguistics can be appropriately described as 'cognitive'. To be sure, simply to recognize, or to assert, that language resides in the minds of its speakers is not sufficient for a linguistic theory to count as Cognitive Linguistics, as I characterize it in this chapter. At the risk of creating yet more terminological confusion, it will be appropriate to use the term **cognitive linguistics** (with a small 'c') to refer to any linguistic theory which recognizes the fact that language knowledge resides in the mind, irrespective of whether the theory is committed to the view that language knowledge should be embedded in what is known independently about human cognition.

1.2 Non-cognitive linguistics

While most linguists, nowadays, would no doubt agree that linguistics is a cognitive discipline (in the very broad sense described above), there have been important approaches within linguistics which have denied, or simply ignored, the discipline's cognitive dimension. Among these we can identify the formalist and the behaviourist approaches. (A cynic might say that quite a lot of modern linguistics is actually to be located within the formalist approach, with appeals to cognitive aspects being little more than lip-service to a modern fashion.)

- **Formalist** approaches regard a language as a self-contained system, whose properties are encapsulated in a Grammar, i.e. a device which generates, or defines, the set of well-formed sentences which constitute the language. A general feature of formalist approaches is to regard a language as a disembodied object, which is independent, as it were, of the speakers who use it and the purposes for which they use it. Chomsky's first major publication, *Syntactic Structures* (Chomsky 1957) proposed a strictly formalist account of language. Subsequent work by Chomsky and his sympathizers, as well as various offshoots of Chomsky's theories, such as Categorial Grammar and Generalized Phrase Structure Grammar (Gazdar 1987), are very much formalist in orientation.

- **Behaviourist** approaches study language as observed behaviour. In this approach, the only kinds of data that are valid are actual recorded utterances and the observable circumstances of their use, and linguistic analysis is restricted to statements about patterns of occurrence of different linguistic forms. Excluded from consideration are such matters as a speaker's intentions, intuitions, and conceptualizations. The behaviourist approach was codified by American structuralists between the 1930s and the early 1950s; the standard text was Bloomfield's *Language* (1933). Although behaviourism, as an intellectual movement, is now very much discredited, quite a lot of the sociolinguistic research of the past half century, it seems to me, especially that which is concerned with establishing patterns of variation as a function of situation (including such aspects as a speaker's occupation, social status, gender, age, and ethnicity) is essentially behaviourist in outlook and methodology.

1.3 Chomskyan linguistics as 'cognitive linguistics'

It was Noam Chomsky who initiated the 'cognitive turn' in linguistics. As I have mentioned, the emphasis in *Syntactic Structures* (Chomsky 1957) was on the development of a formalized grammar, i.e. a rigorously precise description of the rules that would generate (all and only) the well-formed sentences of a language. Subsequently—and it is this aspect of his work that popularized Chomsky's name in cognitive science circles—Chomsky gave a psychological and biological dimension to the enterprise. This was clear already in Chomsky's next major linguistics publication, *Aspects of the Theory of Syntax* (Chomsky 1965). Here, Chomsky argued that it is insufficient simply to regard a grammar as a device that generates grammatical sentences, the grammar has to exist in the minds of speakers. The question then arises, how do speakers come to 'have' the grammar of their language? Not, Chomsky emphatically states again and again, by any of the generally recognized processes of learning, such as induction or generalization over instances. People are born with (i.e. genetically inherit) a blueprint for language—this came to be known as 'Universal Grammar'—which predisposes them to acquire a grammar of the appropriate structure, after only minimal exposure to linguistic data. In this way, a formal theory of language became a cognitive theory of mind.

Chomskyan linguistics has undergone many internal revisions and upheavals since *Syntactic Structures* and *Aspects*, and it would not be appropriate to review these here. Several enduring characteristics of the Chomskyan approach[2] can, however, be identified:

- **Formalism.** Chomskyan linguistics retains the formalist orientation of Chomsky's early work, in that it seeks to specify with maximum precision the rules and principles which generate all and only the grammatical sentences of a language.
- **Modularity.** From the earliest days it was assumed that the mental grammar constituted a special 'module' of the mind. In any act of language use, there is an interaction of linguistic knowledge with other cognitive capacities, such as memory and perception, general conceptual knowledge, inter-personal and rhetorical skills. But language knowledge itself has always been regarded as a separate cognitive faculty, structured according to its own specific principles and which is independent of other mental capacities.
- **Sub-modularity.** The mental grammar itself has been attributed a modular structure. That is, it is analysed into a number of smaller components, such as the X-bar principle, the Theta principle, and so on, each dedicated to a particular function.[3] The complexities of syntactic structure result from the interaction of these simpler modules.
- **Abstractness.** Over the years, Chomskyan linguistics has become increasingly abstract, in the sense that entities and processes are postulated which have no overt manifestation in actual linguistic expressions. Symptomatic of this trend is the postulation of underlying structures which bear little resemblance to surface structures, of structures which contain invisible entities like 'traces' and 'empty categories', and of movement operations which switch around the linear sequence of elements (some of which may themselves be 'empty').
- **Search for high-level generalizations.** Facets of linguistic knowledge which are manifestly idiosyncratic and not subject to general rules have tended to be pushed aside as theoretically uninteresting. The focus, instead, has been on phenomena which are believed to be subject to a small number of very general principles, such as *wh*-movement (as manifested, for example, in question formation), raising, and anaphora.
- **Restriction to 'core' phenomena.** As the theory has become more abstract and ever more encapsulated from non-linguistic faculties, the focus of investigation has been increasingly restricted to supposedly core grammatical phenomena, i.e. those for which highly general accounts might be viable. The idiosyncratic—and this includes most of what is in the lexicon

---

[2] Within the 'Chomskyan approach' I include, not only Chomsky's own work, but that which has been inspired by, and which has developed, Chomsky's ideas. A good introduction to Chomskyan linguistics is Radford (1988); more recent developments are presented in Radford (1997).

[3] For an explanation of these technical notions, see, e.g., Radford (1988).

(and quite a lot of syntax as well)—is relegated to the 'periphery', and thus falls outside the scope of serious linguistic theorizing.

In light of these general characteristics of Chomskyan linguistics, one might well ask in what sense such an enterprise might legitimately be described as cognitive. Here, we need to bear in mind that there are in principle two ways in which the traditional concerns of the human and social sciences (including linguistics) can interact with the study of the mind as such (the central concern of cognitive science):

- What is known about the mind informs and constrains the kinds of theories that the human and social sciences come up with. Given that the mind is like *this*, we will need a theory of linguistics, psychology, anthropology, or whatever, which is grounded in these cognitive structures.
- Theories about social and human realities feed into a theory of mind. Given that humans are capable of such-and-such, they've got to have minds with properties that can support just these kinds of outcomes.

Chomskyan linguistics has adopted the second of these strategies. The theory has been driven by its own internal logic, not by any considerations deriving from independently established facts about human cognition. Rather than a theory of mind constraining linguistic theory, linguistic theory itself inputs into a theory of mind. It is cognitive science which has to incorporate the hypotheses of linguistic theory, not the reverse.

Thus, Chomskyans have made a point of stressing that a grammar, as conceived within the formalist tradition, could not in principle be learned by any general learning mechanism. For this reason the basic architecture of the grammar has to be pre-wired into the human mind. The evidence for this claim is none other than linguistic theory itself.

1.4 What's cognitive about Cognitive Linguistics?

Cognitive Linguistics (with a capital 'C') approaches the relation between language and cognition rather differently than the Chomskyan tradition. Rather than regard language as an autonomous component of the mind (and then to expect cognitive science to incorporate this perspective), language study is shaped from the outset by what is believed to be cognitively plausible. The basic assumption, therefore, is that language is best regarded as an integral part of cognition, and that it will be insightful to study language in light of what is known about the mind, whether this be from experimentation, introspection, or even common-sense observation. The editors of the monograph series, *Cognitive Linguistics Research*, published by Mouton de Gruyter, characterize the Cognitive Linguistics enterprise as follows.

[Cognitive Linguistics] subsumes a variety of concerns and broadly compatible theoretical approaches that have a common basic outlook: that language is an integral facet of cognition which reflects the interaction of social, cultural, psychological, communicative and functional considerations, and which can only be understood in the context of a realistic view of acquisition, cognitive development and mental processing. . . . It seeks insofar as possible to explicate language structure in terms of the other facets of cognition on which it draws, as well as the communicative function it serves.

This statement makes clear that Cognitive Linguistics is not just psychology, etc., applied to the study of language. It is a fact that Cognitive Linguists study much the same kinds of things as any other linguist—syntax, morphology, phonology, word meaning, discourse structure, and the like. But the general thrust of the Cognitive Linguistics enterprise is to render these accounts consonant with aspects of cognition which are well documented or self-evident, or at least highly plausible, and which may well be manifested in non-linguistic activities. The belief is that such an approach will enable the linguist to go beyond a mere description and formalization of the linguistic facts, and to arrive at a more insightful explanation of the facts.

It will be useful at this point to mention some of the kinds of cognitive capacities that are plausibly involved in language. The following list indicates some of the concerns of Cognitive Linguistics. Many of these topics will be taken up and discussed in greater detail in subsequent chapters.

(i) Categorization. All living creatures, even the most lowly, possess the ability to categorize. At the very least, a creature needs to categorize the environment in terms of edible vs. non-edible, harmful vs. non-harmful. A creature must also be able to recognize its own kind, if only in order to mate and reproduce.

Humans excel at categorizing. We are able to create and operate with literally tens of thousands, perhaps hundreds of thousands of categories, ranging from the extremely fine-grained to the highly general. Moreover, categorization is flexible, in the sense that we can modify existing categories in order to accommodate new experiences, and we can create new categories whenever the need arises. And it is not just things out there in the external world that we categorize. We categorize things that are internal to the mind, as when we talk about *ideas*, *hopes*, *fears*, and so on.

Categorization permeates our non-linguistic cognition. Our ability to function in the physical and social world depends on elaborate categorizations of things, processes, social relations, and other persons. Categorization is also of crucial importance in language, in a number of ways. Most obviously, words can be regarded as names for categories. To know the word *tree* means, among other things, being able to apply the word to anything that can be categorized as a tree. Secondly, language itself is an object of categorization. Acoustically different sound signals get categorized as instances of the same linguistic expression, diverse linguistic expressions get categorized as examples of the same lexical or syntactic category, such as 'noun', 'verb', 'transitive clause', and so on.

Categorization has been intensively studied by psychologists. Major research topics have included the principles according to which categories are structured, how they are acquired, and how they are applied. The theory of prototype categorization, in particular, has had a profound influence on Cognitive Linguistics.[4]

(ii) Figure-ground organization. Visual perception provides the prototype for figure-ground organization. Invariably, some aspects of a visual scene 'stand out' against their background. As you fix your gaze on the page you are now reading, you will be perceiving black marks (figure) on a white background; almost certainly, you will not be perceiving a complex white shape (figure) on a fragmented black background. Figure-ground organization holds for other sense modalities as well, as when a person's voice is heard to stand out against a background rumble.

Figure-ground organization is intimately linked to attention, in that our attention naturally flows to the figure—indeed, a feature of a scene becomes the figure precisely because we focus attention on it. That, no doubt, is the reason why you perceive the page in front of you as black marks on a white background. You would need to do a lot of squinting in order to perceive the page as a complex-shaped white figure which obscures a black background. And if you were to achieve this figure-ground reversal, you would not be paying attention to the linguistic significance of those black marks.

As hinted above, figure-ground organization (like categorization) is in principle rather flexible. Often, we can reverse our figure-ground perception, making the erstwhile ground the object of attention, and can organize a scene in terms of different figure-ground alignments, by selectively focusing attention on different aspects of a scene. For example, in a noisy room full of people, you can selectively focus attention on different speaking voices, making each voice in turn the figure, everything else becoming the background.

Moreover, we can have several levels of figure-ground organization. What is the ground at one level becomes the figure at another level. While reading these words, your attention focuses on a selected sequence of printed marks. This is the 'primary figure', seen against the background of the printed page as a whole. However, the printed page itself constitutes a 'secondary figure' against the background of the wider visual scene at the periphery of your perceptual field.

Figure-ground organization applies not only to matters of sensory perception, whether visual or auditory. It also pertains to the way in which we think of, or conceptualize, a situation. As such, figure-ground organization is crucial

[4] For a review of the psychological research, see Smith and Medin (1981). For the import of categorization by prototype on linguistic theory, see Lakoff (1987) and Taylor (1995a).

to linguistic semantics. The topic has been explored in some detail by Talmy (1983), and is a recurring theme in Langacker's writings. Figure-ground organization manifests itself especially in the manner in which a particular scene is organized for the purpose of its linguistic expression. To take a very simple example, both the following sentences in (1) could describe exactly the same event. However, (1a) presents the scene in terms of what the farmer (figure) did, while (1b) takes the rabbit as figure, and tells what happened to it.

(1) a. The farmer shot the rabbit.
     b. The rabbit was shot by the farmer.

(iii) Mental imagery and construal. Figure-ground organization is but one aspect of a broader phenomenon, namely, our ability to mentally 'construe' a situation in alternative ways. We can structure a scene in terms of different figure-ground organizations; we can vary the amount of detail with which the scene is specified, by including or leaving out particular circumstances, or by characterizing participants in general or specific terms; or we can imagine how a situation might be perceived from different perspectives.

Language is teeming with these effects. The very wording that we choose in order to linguistically encode a situation rests on the manner in which the situation has been mentally construed. The two expressions in (2) might describe exactly the same situation, namely, that of a roof sloping at a certain angle (cf. Langacker 1988b: 62). The difference is that in (2a) the roof is mentally viewed from above, while in (2b) it is mentally viewed from below.

(2) a. The roof slopes gently downwards.
     b. The roof slopes gently upwards.

A special concern in Cognitive Linguistics has been to examine languages from the point of view of the palette of resources that they make available for purposes of construal.

(iv) Metaphor and 'experientialism'. Metaphor reflects our ability to think of (or 'construe') one thing in terms of something else. Metaphor is a familiar figure of speech and is popularly associated with literary composition. An important strand in Cognitive Linguistics—associated especially with the work of George Lakoff (Lakoff and Johnson 1980 and 1999; Lakoff and Turner 1989)—claims that metaphor is much more than a literary ornament, it permeates much of our thinking, and hence our language. Even such prosaic expressions as those in (3) can be analysed in terms of an interplay of metaphor. First, states of affairs are understood, metaphorically, to be locations. Secondly, mental activity is understood as a journey along a path. Putting the two metaphors together it becomes possible to conceptualize an initial assumption as a starting point or source location, the conclusion as a finishing point or destination, and mental activity as a journey along a path from source to destination.

(3) a. We started out from these assumptions.
    b. We came to these conclusions.

Interestingly, the metaphors underlying (3) show up in countless other expressions. Just as you can *be in* a room, so also you can *be in* trouble. This latter expression capitalizes on the metaphor of states as locations; hence, the locative preposition *in* can be used both for literal and for metaphorical locations. Or consider the fact that you can *drive through* the city centre and can *work through* a problem. Here, the mental processing of a problem is construed, metaphorically, as tracing a path through a location. As will be apparent from these examples, a special benefit of this approach is that it provides an insightful way of accounting for the many 'idiomatic' uses that basically spatial terms, such as *in, to, through, come*, may have.

Observe that the metaphors mentioned above construe a more abstract domain of experience in terms of physical, bodily experience. Johnson (1987) has argued that quite a lot of our conceptual world is structured according to a small number of what he calls 'image schemas', i.e. general, recurring patterns of bodily experience which can be instantiated in a wide range of domains. Image schemas include such notions as containment, path, destination, balance, and separation. Johnson's claim (which is further developed in Lakoff and Johnson 1999) is that much of human cognition is based in bodily experience, with linguistic effects that are ubiquitous.

(v) Conceptual archetypes. A major topic in language acquisition research has been the extent to which language builds on pre-existing conceptual structures. We can imagine two maximally opposed positions. The rationalist position—associated with Descartes and, more recently, Chomsky—holds that the mind has a rich inbuilt structure, which severely constrains what is knowable. Rationalism predicts that languages will share much the same structure. In contrast, the empiricist position claims that the human mind is initially a blank slate, and that cognitive development is entirely a matter of learning. Since there are no initial constraints on what is a possible concept, we should expect different languages to symbolize radically different, and incompatible conceptualizations.

The truth probably lies somewhere between the two extremes. We observe both an amazing diversity between languages and with some equally striking similarities. The similarities, though, tend to be at a fairly abstract level. In this connection, Langacker (1999: 9) speaks of 'conceptual archetypes'. One such archetype, which emerges in the first year of life, is the concept of a 'thing', that is, of a spatially bounded physical object which persists over time. It is tempting to assume that the infant's object-concept underlies the subsequent emergence of the universal syntactic category 'noun'. But whereas the notion of 'thing' may be a conceptual universal, grounded in conceptual abilities that emerge in all normal humans, different languages may well differ with respect to the range of entities that are conventionally symbolized by nouns. Other conceptual archetypes include the notion of an event and an action, as well as the figure-ground organization, and its various ramifications. Mandler (1992) surveys evidence for the emergence of early conceptual structures that are comparable to Johnson's image schemas, including the concepts of containment, support, causality, animacy, and so on.

(vi) Inferencing. Humans are smart. Given only a snippet of information, we rapidly fill out the details, supplying missing data, attributing unspoken motives and intentions to actors, inferring causes from effects, and predicting effects from present circumstances.

As a result of our smartness, the interpretation we give to a linguistic expression typically goes well beyond what is actually said. Conversely, when giving linguistic expression to a conceptualization, we do not need to include each and every facet. We mention only a few salient aspects and leave it to the hearer to infer the rest.

One important consequence of this is that the meaning of a complex expression is rarely, if ever, 'compositional'. That is to say, complex expressions nearly always have a meaning that is more than, or even at variance with, the meaning that can be computed by combining the meanings of the component parts.

(vii) Automatization. Humans, especially in their younger years, are good at acquiring complex skills. Practice makes perfect, as the saying goes. We would typically apply this saying to the acquisition of motor skills, as when we learn to play a musical instrument. Initially, we need to pay conscious attention to each posture and movement that we make; our performance is painfully slow, and liable to error. In time, and with practice, whole sequences of movements can be performed as automated routines, rapidly and error free, without our needing to pay attention to the component parts or to their co-ordination. Even motor skills, however, are ultimately cognitive skills. The fingers of the virtuoso pianist are not doing anything that the fingers of an amateur could not, in principle, also do. What the virtuoso has, which the amateur lacks, is the neuro-cognitive routines that control the motor activity.

In language, automatization pertains, most obviously, to skilled control of the articulatory organs. But the effects of automatization go well beyond matters of pronunciation. Quite a lot of our talk consists in running off pre-formed chunks of language. We also see the effects of automatization in the effortless, online construction of complex word forms and of larger phrases, in accordance with well-established and well-practised patterns.

(viii) Storage vs. computation, lists vs. rules. We have big brains, and are able to store large amounts of rather specific information. We are also smart, and are able to perform complex computations by following instructions. Take the case of multiplication. Once we have learned the rules, we can multiply any two numbers of arbitrary length (usually, though, with the aid of pencil and paper). If we follow the rules properly, we can be sure of the correct answer. Equally, we may have learned that $12 \times 12 = 144$, and do not need to apply the rules to get the answer. Recall of the stored product is rapid and effortless, in contrast to computation, which is slow and laborious, and requires our focused attention. In fact, when it comes to multiplying numbers, computation is a 'last resort'—we only perform the computation when a ready-made answer cannot be retrieved from memory, or when we wish to check the correctness of a retrieved answer.

The role of computation vs. storage, of rule application vs. the recall of memorized solutions, is highly relevant to a psychologically plausible theory of language. Many linguistic theories have sought maximally general rules which, when applied in the correct manner to an appropriate input, guarantee the correct output. The fact that such rules can be formulated, and that they can be relied upon to produce the correct output, by no means entails that speakers always do apply the rules. It is conceivable that speakers have simply stored a vast array of complex linguistic forms and that these are accessed, ready-made, when required. In this connection, Langacker (FCG1: 29) speaks of the 'rule/list fallacy'. The fallacy lies in the assumption that knowledge of a rule necessarily expunges knowledge of the instances that the rule accounts for. Take, as a simple example, the question of plural formation. The fact that we know how to form the plural of a noun, and might indeed apply this knowledge whenever we need to form the plural of a rare or newly acquired word, does not exclude the possibility that frequently encountered plurals, such as *eyes*, are simply stored as such.

(ix) Focus on form. An important ingredient in language activity is the pleasure we derive from language itself. Michael Halliday discerned seven 'models of language' in the child's linguistic activity, one of which he called the 'imaginative model':

> Language in its imaginative function is not necessarily 'about' anything at all. . . . It may be a world of pure sound, made up of rhythmic sequences of rhyming or chiming syllables; or an edifice of words in which semantics has no part, like a house built of playing cards in which face values are irrelevant. Poems, rhymes, riddles and much of the child's own linguistic play reinforce this model of language, and here too the meaning of what is said is not primarily a matter of content. (Halliday 1973: 15–16)

Delight in 'pure sound' and in 'edifices of words' will develop, in the adult, into the cultivation of poetry and literature. In this connection, Roman Jakobson (1981) spoke of language in its 'poetic function'.

Language play is symptomatic of a more general human proclivity, which I should like to characterize as 'focus on form'. Just as we derive pleasure from edifices of words, regardless of their semantic values, so also we may come to value the purely formal creations of abstract art. Focus on form also manifests itself in our adherence to rituals, whether these be religious, social, or indeed linguistic. We do certain things in a certain way because, well, that's the way to do them, and we get upset if people don't do them properly. Moreover, we delight in having learned to do difficult things, and derive pleasure from observing a virtuoso performer, whether this be a musician, a gymnast, or a chess player. We admire virtuoso language performers, too, such as a skilled public speaker or storyteller.

Our delight in form is also apparent in the fact that language users seem to treasure precisely those aspects of their language that exhibit considerable formal complexity. Inflectional morphology is a case in point. Consider such things as noun gender, verb conjugations, noun declensions, exceptions to otherwise regular conjugations and declensions, and complex patterns of agreement. These aspects place a considerable burden on a speaker's memory and processing resources, but often add little to the expressive possibilities of a language. (The different verb conjugations of French, for example, or the categories of strong and weak verbs in English, have no semantic significance whatsoever.) These formal aspects are the bane of foreign language learners. 'Couldn't languages be much simpler?', Klein and Purdue (1997) plaintively ask. Certainly they could. As Aronoff (1994: 165) has observed, 'morphology is not necessary'. Some languages get by with relatively little of this kind of complexity (English is one of them), while others (such as Russian and Zulu) revel in a veritable efflorescence of inflectional morphology. Such aspects persist, from one generation of speakers to the next. Clearly, native speakers of a language do not perceive formal complexity to be a burden at all. On the contrary, they vehemently reject any suggestion that their language might be more 'efficient' if inflectional classes were reduced, if exceptions were regularized, and if agreement patterns were streamlined.

(x) Social behaviour. Language supports, and is supported by, many aspects of the human condition. Being social creatures, we have plenty of impulses to use our language in social interaction. We also tend to be rather territorial and cliquish. What better way of establishing and maintaining the clique than speech habits (along with other manifestations of group identity, such as clothing)? And since we are so smart, we have plenty of thoughts on which to exercise the symbolic resources of language.

I have left to last the cognitive ability that is perhaps the most important underpinning of language:

(xi) Symbolic behaviour. There has, in recent years, been much discussion and speculation about what distinguishes human cognition from the cognition of non-human animals.[5] The fact that humans can engage in highly complex thought processes is certainly not a distinguishing feature of our species. The hawk, which swoops down out of the sky to perfectly target a rapidly and

---

[5] See, for example, Bickerton (1995), Jackendoff (1997: ch. 8), Deacon (1997), Dennett (1996), and Carstairs-McCarthy (1999).

erratically moving rabbit, really does need the computational resources of a rocket scientist. The difference is, that the hawk computes its trajectory 'online', as it is actually swooping down on the rabbit, whereas the rocket scientist computes trajectories 'offline', at a time and place removed from their actual implementation, if indeed the trajectories actually get implemented at all. The rocket scientist has to be conscious of the trajectories and their computation, in a way that the hawk (probably) is not.

Bickerton (1995) has argued that it is offline thinking that characterizes human cognition and possibly even the phenomenon of consciousness itself, and that offline thinking is made possible by our control of a symbolic system. A symbolic system, such as language, provides us with the means to represent to ourselves the contents of our thoughts, in a form that is independent of the external circumstances that occasioned the thoughts. A symbolic system thus enables us to reflect on the past, to analyse the present, to plan the future, to imagine fictitious and counterfactual situations, to play with alternative construals of a situation, to work out the possible consequences of imagined courses of action. Further, a symbolic system allows us to communicate the contents of our thoughts to others, as well as (paradoxical as it might seem) to ourselves. The very act of 'putting in words' what we are thinking makes our thoughts manifest to ourselves, it 'fixes' our thoughts by giving them a perceptible form, such that our thoughts can themselves become the object of further processing.

Cognitive Grammar is built on the premise that language is inherently and essentially symbolic in nature. A language provides its users with a set of resources for representing thought, and 'doing' Cognitive Grammar consists, to a large extent, in identifying and analysing these resources. Much of this book is devoted to precisely this enterprise.

1.5 Neurocognitive linguistics

I have listed some of the general cognitive abilities that are intimately associated with the human language capacity. It is to be hoped that this summary account will give some idea of what distinguishes the Cognitive Linguistic enterprise from formalist, behaviourist, (and Chomskyan) accounts of language. Cognitive Linguistics lays claim to the appellation 'cognitive' precisely because it studies language in the context of general cognitive abilities, like those listed above.

It might be objected, however, that a truly cognitive theory of language must be based on a study of the brain, and on the ways in which linguistic knowledge is represented in the neuronal structure of the brain. Sydney Lamb (1998) laments the fact that the term 'cognitive linguistics'—which he claims (p. 381) to have been the first to use in 1971 for the *real* study of language in the brain—has since been diluted and taken over by people doing what he calls 'analytical linguistics', that is, descriptive linguistics in the traditional mould (p.7). Lamb proposes the term 'neurocognitive linguistics' for a linguistic theory that really is grounded in neurological facts.

We need to approach the issue of a neurocognitive linguistics with some caution. Ideally, a cognitively plausible linguistic theory will indeed describe the mental structures that embody a person's linguistic knowledge. The intuitions and introspections of language users are not likely to shed much light on this issue. Lamb himself put his finger very nicely on the problem. He aptly remarks (p. 12) that one of the properties of minds is that they strive to make themselves invisible. If your mind is functioning as it should—that is, if you are engaged in mental activity of some sort—you are not aware of your mind and its workings. You cannot find out about the mind by observing it in operation. Lamb draws an analogy with a pair of spectacles. Spectacles—for people who need to wear them—are an aid to vision. Without their glasses, people who need them simply cannot see properly. But when you are wearing your glasses, and your glasses are doing the job they are supposed to be doing, you are not aware of them—you don't even *see* them. So it is not possible to study the functioning of your glasses by observing them in operation. To be sure, you can take your glasses off and try to study them 'objectively'. But then, without the aid of your glasses, you won't be able to see the object of your study.

Since intuitions and introspections are unlikely to shed much light on the neurocognitive representation of language, we might wish to turn to studies of the neurological foundations of language. There have been impressive advances in recent years in this area.[6] However, it has to be recognized that neurological studies of language tend to deal with very global aspects of language structure and language processing, not with the nitty-gritty details that are the main preoccupations of linguists. Given our present state of knowledge about brain functioning, I think that there would be little point in trying to elucidate constraints on the phonological word in Zulu, the semantics of noun reduplication in Malay, or the distribution of the velar nasal [ŋ] in English, through the study of brain states. Even if we might be able to locate a specific bit of language knowledge somewhere in the brain, this would actually tell us very little, if anything, about the content of that bit of language knowledge.

Lamb's programme for 'neurocognitive linguistics' invites us, rather, to construct a linguistic theory in light of what is known about general aspects of neurocognitive processing. The brain consists of millions of interconnected neurons, and cognitive activity reduces, ultimately, to patterns of neuronal excitation and inhibition. In a structure such as this, there is no place for such things as rules which perform transformations on strings of symbols. The very

---

[6] See, e.g., Bates (to appear). This paper, incidentally, gives an excellent overview of arguments for and against the hypothesis of the innateness of language structure.

idea of rules and transformations raises the spectre of the homunculus—the operator who resides in the brain and who formulates and refines the rules as the data come in, and who sits in charge of their application. If the brain is a network, a cognitively plausible linguistic theory will also construe linguistic knowledge as a network of relations between neurocognitive routines. I suggest that Cognitive Grammar construes linguistic knowledge in just such terms. Knowledge of a language reduces to knowledge of a vast, and open-ended inventory of 'units' (that is, neurocognitive routines), and to the relations that exist amongst these units.

Lamb's polemical distinction between 'neurocognitive' and 'analytical' linguistics is, I think, a false one. Cognitive Linguists, as linguistics, do the kinds of things that linguists have always done, namely, 'analytical linguistics', as Lamb put it. They collect data, they construct theories that account for the data, they examine further data to check whether the theories still hold up. (As a matter of fact, Lamb's own work in linguistics follows just this procedure.) Deane stated the distinctive character of linguistic enquiry as follows:

Linguistics is fundamentally concerned with distributional data. At every level from phonology to pragmatics, linguistic theory is concerned first and foremost with determining (i) how paradigmatic choices are determined, and (ii) how syntagmatic combinations are licensed. Insofar as one is doing linguistics, one must be able to describe distributional patterns, predict them from the tenets of one's theory, and explain why they should be as they are. . . . A theory may draw on concepts from other theories, of course, but to claim to be a *linguistic* theory it must account explicitly for distributional facts. (Deane 1992: 80–1)

My contention is that a rigorous and unprejudiced examination of the distributional facts (the bread-and-butter of analytical linguistics) leads inexorably to a view of linguistic knowledge that is fully consistent with Lamb's neurocognitive programme.

Further reading

On Cognitive Linguistics. Ungerer and Schmid (1996) introduces selected topics in Cognitive Linguistics, including categorization, metaphor, and figure-ground organization. Unfortunately, the book has little to say about phonology, syntax, and morphology. Dirven and Verspoor (1998) covers a broad range of topics from a Cognitive Linguistics perspective. It is available in translation in several European languages, and is aimed at readers with little theoretical background. Dirven and Radden (in prep.) applies Cognitive Linguistic insights to a description of central areas of English syntax. There are a number of collected volumes which give good overviews of the scope of Cognitive Linguistics. See especially Rudzka-Ostyn (1988) and Janssen and Redeker (1999). Rudzka-Ostyn's volume contains four very accessible papers by Langacker. The best introduction to the Cognitive

Linguistic view of metaphor remains Lakoff and Johnson's *Metaphors We Live By* (1980). For prototype categorization, see Taylor (1995*a*).

On the 'cognitive' in Cognitive Linguistics, see Gibbs (1996). For a more sceptical view, see Peeters' (1998) review of Rudzka-Ostyn (1988). Peeters' misgivings have subsequently mellowed; see Peeters (2000).

For the contrast between Chomskyan and Cognitive approaches, see Tomasello (1995). This is a review of Pinker's *The Language Instinct* (1994), a book which promotes an essentially Chomskyan view of language.

Cognitive Grammar: An overview

This chapter gives an overview of the basic assumptions of Cognitive Grammar. It introduces the theoretical apparatus of the theory, and it highlights its salient characteristics. The final section addresses the historical background of the theory.

2.1 Language as a symbolic system

Cognitive Grammar is driven by the idea that language is essentially and inherently symbolic in nature. Linguistic expressions symbolize, or stand for, conceptualizations. I shall refer to this basic assumption as the **symbolic thesis**. Although not uncontroversial (I consider some of the more contentious issues in Chapter 4), the symbolic thesis actually amounts to little more than the claim that language is in essence a means for relating sound and meaning.

According to the symbolic thesis, any linguistic expression, whether this be a single word, a morpheme, a phrase, a sentence, or even an entire text, has the organization shown in Figure 2.1 (p. 21).

Observe that only three kinds of entity are depicted in Figure 2.1: (i) phonological structures, (ii) semantic structures, and (iii) symbolic relations between (i) and (ii). Cognitive Grammar makes the very strong claim that a language can be exhaustively described in terms of these three kinds of entities alone.

(i) **Phonological structure** refers to the overt manifestation of language, i.e. a linguistic expression in its material, or perceptible aspects. Prototypically, an

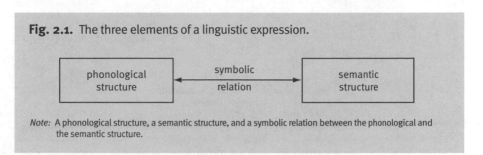

Fig. 2.1. The three elements of a linguistic expression.

phonological structure — symbolic relation ←→ semantic structure

Note: A phonological structure, a semantic structure, and a symbolic relation between the phonological and the semantic structure.

expression is manifested in the medium of sound, in which case 'phonological' is to be understood in the strict sense of the word. Language can be realized in media other than sound, as is the case with signed languages; in principle, therefore 'phonological structure' needs to be understood sufficiently broadly so as to be able to accommodate these possibilities. In this book I shall have little to say about signed languages, or indeed about writing systems (which constitute yet another material manifestation of language), and will therefore be using 'phonological' in its narrow sense of sound structure.

(ii) **Semantic structure** refers to the meaning of an expression. A significant part of the Cognitive Grammar enterprise has consisted in making substantive proposals for the content of semantic structures. Importantly, a semantic structure is taken to comprise not just the propositional content of an expression, but the broader conceptualization that a speaker entertains, including such aspects as figure-ground alignment, construal, and so on (cf. section 1.4). Semantic structure also comprises 'pragmatic' aspects of meaning, that is, the meaning of an expression in relation to situational context. Semantic structure, moreover, is broadly encyclopedic in scope, and can in principle draw on any aspect of a person's conceptual world.

(iii) **Symbolic relations** hold between phonological structures and semantic structures. Observe that the arrow linking phonological and semantic structures in Figure 2.1 points in both directions. This captures the fact that the relation between meaning and sound is a two-way affair, each pole of the symbolic relation invokes the other. Symbolic relations play a pivotal role in Cognitive Grammar. In large part, Cognitive Grammar is a theory of how linguistic expressions are to be analysed in terms of symbolic relations.

An important aspect of Figure 2.1 is that it proposes a *direct* association between phonological and semantic structures. In contrast to many other linguistic theories, Cognitive Grammar denies that there is a distinct level of organization that mediates between phonology and semantics. Most linguistic theories, in fact, take syntax to be the central component of the grammar; syntactic structures receive a semantic interpretation at a syntax-semantic interface, and a phonological realization at a syntax-phonology interface (Fig. 2.2 (p. 22)).

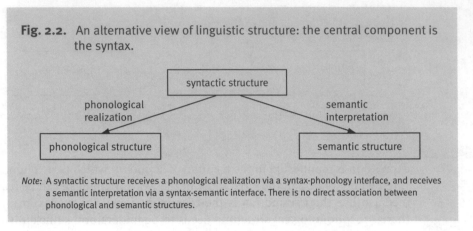

Fig. 2.2. An alternative view of linguistic structure: the central component is the syntax.

Note: A syntactic structure receives a phonological realization via a syntax-phonology interface, and receives a semantic interpretation via a syntax-semantic interface. There is no direct association between phonological and semantic structures.

In excluding a distinct syntactic level of organization, Cognitive Grammar does not deny the existence of syntax. Like any linguistic theory, Cognitive Grammar pays a lot of attention to how larger expressions can be analysed into smaller component parts. What is special about the Cognitive Grammar approach is that syntax itself is regarded as inherently symbolic, and is therefore handled in terms of symbolic relations between phonological and semantic structures. This means, concretely, that patterns for word combination (traditionally dealt with under syntax), as well as patterns for word formation (the province of morphology), are regarded as symbolic units, each of which associates a phonological structure and a semantic structure. Exactly how this is implemented will become clearer in due course.

In brief, then, Cognitive Grammar makes the very strong claim that a language can be exhaustively described by reference only to the three kinds of entities depicted in Figure 2.1. Cognitive Grammar is therefore a truly 'minimalist'[1] theory of language. Obviously, for such a theory to be viable, and to be able to account for the full complexities of natural languages, we will need a fairly sophisticated account of the three kinds of entities. Below, I introduce some aspects that will form the basis of much of the subsequent presentation.

2.1.1 Relations between units

Much of the complexity of human language is handled in Cognitive Grammar in terms of relations that can exist between units, whether these be phonological, semantic, or symbolic. Three kinds of relation are important: (i) the 'vertical' relation of schema and instance, (ii) the 'horizontal' relation between parts and a whole, and (iii) the relation of similarity.

(i) The vertical relation holds between units specified in differing degrees

---

[1] In describing Cognitive Grammar as 'minimalist', I am of course making a tongue-in-cheek allusion to the most recent manifestation of Chomskyan linguistics, namely, the 'minimalist program'.

A note on terminology: 'symbolic'

In this book, I use the term 'symbolic' to refer to the relation between a phonological and a semantic structure. Language is symbolic to the extent that language is essentially a means for relating semantic and phonological structures.

This use of 'symbolic' is not to be confused with another use which is current in cognitive science as well as in some linguistics texts. According to this alternative usage, a symbol is a variable which can stand for an indefinite number of values. The mathematician's x and y, or the logician's p and q, are symbols in this sense. A symbolic operation is one which manipulates symbols, without regard to the values that the symbols can be replaced by.

Pinker (1999: 6) refers to syntactic and morphological rules as symbolic, precisely in the sense that these rules are claimed to operate on symbols, i.e. on category labels such as N, V, NP, which are taken to be inherently devoid of semantic and phonological content. According to Pinker (1999: 119), regular past-tense formation in English is a symbolic operation, whereby a rule operates on the symbol V, augmenting it by addition of the past-tense morpheme, without regard to the meaning or the phonological shape of the actual verbs that the symbol can be replaced by.

As will become clear later in this chapter, the 'symbolic thesis' of Cognitive Grammar excludes in principle the existence of inherently contentless symbols, of the kind proposed by Pinker.

---

of detail. A unit which is specified in greater detail may count as an **instance** of another unit, which is specified in lesser detail, and which is **schematic** for the former (Fig. 2.3 (p. 24)).

The relation depicted in Figure 2.3 can apply equally to phonological, semantic, and symbolic units. Here are some examples:

- Phonological units. Allophones are instances of a phoneme, a phoneme is schematic for its allophones. The phonological structure [dɒg] is an instance of the phonological unit [SYLLABLE]; [SYLLABLE] in turn is schematic for [dɒg].
- Semantic units. The semantic unit [POODLE] is an instance of the more schematically characterized semantic unit [DOG]. The semantic unit [MAN] is schematic for [MAN AT THE BUS STOP]; [MAN AT THE BUS STOP] is an instance of the more schematically characterized unit [MAN].
- Symbolic units. The linguistic expression *tree* (understood as a relation between a phonological structure and a semantic structure) is an instance of the more abstract symbolic unit [NOUN], which in turn is an instance of the even more schematic unit [WORD]. The expression *The farmer kills the duckling* (again, understood as symbolically relating a phonological and a semantic structure) is an instance of the more abstractly characterized symbolic unit [TRANSITIVE CLAUSE].

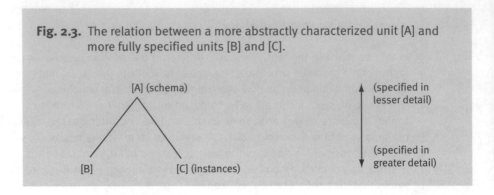

Fig. 2.3. The relation between a more abstractly characterized unit [A] and more fully specified units [B] and [C].

By recognizing vertical relations between schema and instance, it becomes possible to incorporate various kinds of abstract entities into a Cognitive Grammar description, including such things as lexical categories and syntactic constructions. It is important to note that the kind of abstractness involved here is quite different from the abstractness that characterizes formalist, Chomskyan linguistics (cf. p. 7). In Cognitive Grammar, [NOUN] and [TRANSITIVE CLAUSE] are abstract in the sense that they are schematic entities, and subject, therefore, to rather general specifications. To the extent that linguistic expressions can be categorized in terms of such schematic entities, the abstract entities are imminent in their instances. Importantly, these abstract entities, being themselves symbolic units, are not at all comparable to the contentless symbols envisaged, for example, by Pinker (cf. the Box on p. 23).

(ii) The horizontal relation applies to any structure which exhibits internal complexity. We have seen that the phonological structure [dɒg] counts as an instance of a more schematic phonological unit [SYLLABLE]. At the same time, [dɒg] has an internal structure; it consists of three sub-units, each of which is a part of the more complex unit.

The part-of relation applies equally to phonological, semantic, and symbolic structures. Moreover, in an internally complex expression, we often (though by no means always) observe that part-of relations hold in parallel between phonological, semantic, and symbolic units. The past-tense verb form *walked* exemplifies combination at the semantic level, in that it combines the component concepts [WALK] and [PAST TENSE]. Phonologically, the complex form [wɔːkt] contains as its parts [wɔːk] and [t], while the complex symbolic unit is composed of two component symbolic units.

The above example could suggest that a complex expression comes into being simply through the alignment of its parts. In fact, combining parts into a whole is much more intricate, and will be major topic of Chapter 12 and subsequent chapters. At this stage, it is sufficient to note that the part-of relation makes it possible to incorporate into Cognitive Grammar the kinds of topics that are traditionally handled under morphology and syntax.

Fig. 2.4. The relation of similarity.

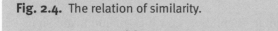

[A] - ➤ [B]

Note: Unit [B] is perceived to be similar to unit [A]; unit [A] is extended to unit [B].

(iii) The similarity relation can cause units that are specified in different, or even conflicting ways to become associated. A family tree is a different kind of entity than an oak tree. Nevertheless, some similarity can be perceived, and, as a consequence, the word *tree* can be applied, not only to trees of the botanical kind (the standard semantic value of the word) but also to genealogical networks. Relations of similarity are thus a principal means whereby linguistic units, whether phonological, semantic, or symbolic, can be extended (Fig. 2.4).

Importantly, the similarity relation makes it possible to handle linguistic phenomena that lie outside of what is strictly sanctioned by the linguistic system. For example, a deviant pronunciation of a word would not, strictly speaking, count as a valid instance of the phonological structure of that word. Nevertheless, listeners have the ability to recognize the word (provided that the pronunciation is not too deviant). A comparable situation obtains at the semantic level, when a word or expression is used to symbolize a conceptualization that lies outside the conventional, accepted value of the expression. In case a person is unable to establish a similarity relation between a novel expression and an established linguistic structure, that expression will be judged ungrammatical, unacceptable, or simply meaningless.

2.1.2 Symbolic units

It will be apparent from the above remarks that a central object of study in Cognitive Grammar is the **symbolic unit**—the conventionalized association of a phonological structure with a semantic structure. There are some commonalities—which I explore in the following chapter—between the Cognitive Grammar notion of symbolic unit and the Saussurean notion of the linguistic sign. Just as, in Cognitive Grammar, the symbolic unit associates a phonological and a semantic structure, so, for Saussure, the linguistic sign associated an acoustic image and a concept.

Saussure illustrated his notion of the linguistic sign on the example of individual lexical items, such as *tree*. A language, though, is not just a collection of words; to know a language you also need to know how to combine words to form phrases and sentences; you also need to know how to create words from more primitive elements. A language is not just a list of word-sized linguistic signs, it also has a morphology and syntax. As already remarked, Cognitive Grammar treats syntax as inherently symbolic. Patterns for the combination of smaller elements themselves have the status of symbolic units; as such, they associate a semantic representation with a phonological representation.

In Cognitive Grammar, therefore, the range of linguistic signs—i.e. established associations between sound and meaning—comprises much more than the word-sized units discussed by Saussure.[2] The inventory of signs is extended from the Saussurean conception, both 'horizontally' and 'vertically':

(i) The inventory is extended horizontally, in such a way that items that are smaller than, and larger than, a lexical item can count as symbolic units. The inventory comprises, for example, bound morphemes (such as the plural morpheme, or the past-tense morpheme in English), as well as fixed expressions, idioms, and common turns of phrase (*How do you do?*, *by and large*, *If I were you*, etc.).

(ii) The range of what counts as a symbolic unit is extended vertically, in such a way that more abstract, schematic entities such as word classes and patterns for the combination of words and morphemes have symbolic unit status. This means that not only is *tree* a symbolic unit, so also are [NOUN] and [WORD]. Likewise, symbolic status attaches, not only to the expression *the tree*, but also to the syntactic unit of which it is an instance, namely [NOUN PHRASE], as well as to the pattern for the assembly of the noun phrase, in this case, [DET(ERMINER) NOUN].

2.1.3 Units

In the preceding sections I have been speaking of phonological units, semantic units, and symbolic units. As a matter of fact, 'unit' is a technical term in Cognitive Grammar, and refers to a structure which has been *entrenched*, or become *automated*, through frequency of successful use. A structure with unit status can be accessed as an integrated whole, without a person having to pay attention to its internal composition.

Unit status is particularly evident with respect to phonological structures. Frequently used words roll off the tongue, so to speak, they do not have to be consciously articulated syllable-by-syllable, segment-by-segment. Rare words (especially if they are long) and foreign borrowings, whose phonological structure may be somewhat deviant *vis-à-vis* the native phonological norms, often lack unit status, and speakers may have to pay special attention to their pronunciation.

Fixed expressions and formulas, of varying degrees of internal complexity, almost by definition, have unit status. (If the expressions did not have unit status, we should not describe them as fixed, nor would they count as formulaic.) For most speakers of English, phrases such as *As far as I'm concerned*, *Take it or leave it*, *I bent over backwards*, and countless more, have unit status,

---

[2] As a matter of fact, Saussure (1964: 173) hinted at the possibility that patterns for the combination of linguistic signs have themselves the status of linguistic signs. See Taylor (1996: 62–3).

not only with respect to their phonological form, but also in their semantic value. On the other hand, novel expressions—again, by definition—lack unit status. Such expressions are acceptable, and meaningful, to the extent that they can be associated with linguistic structures that do have unit status. The novel expression may count as an instance of a more schematically characterized unit; alternatively, it may be assimilated, through the relation of similarity, to an already established unit.

Unit status is a matter of degree, and crucially depends on a person's previous linguistic experience. Take the expression *tree hugger*. If you have never encountered the expression before, you will probably attempt to interpret it in terms of a general schema for expressions of this particular form. Just as a *dog lover* is one who loves dogs, and a *meat eater* is one who eats meat, so a *tree hugger* is one who hugs trees. But hugging trees is a rather bizarre thing for a person to do; consequently, the expression *tree hugger* may generate some puzzlement on your first encounter with it. After several encounters, you may come to realize that *tree hugger* has a conventionalized semantic value—the expression is used quasi-humoristically to designate a kind of environmental activist. The example illustrates an important point, namely, that a linguistic structure with unit status is liable to be associated with specialized values, over and above those that are sanctioned by the schema of which it is an instance.

2.2 Some general characteristics of Cognitive Grammar

In this section I draw attention to some general characteristics of Cognitive Grammar. These follow naturally from the claim that language is inherently symbolic.

2.2.1 Cognitive Grammar is usage based

It is assumed that the input to language acquisition are encounters with actual linguistic expressions, fully specified in their phonological, semantic, and symbolic aspects. Knowledge of a language is based in knowledge of actual usage and of generalizations made over usage events. Language acquisition is therefore a bottom-up process, driven by linguistic experience.

There are several important corollaries to the usage-based orientation:

(i) First, it is recognized that a good deal of a person's language knowledge may consist in rather specific, low-level knowledge, not far removed, in terms of abstractness (i.e. schematicity), from actually encountered expressions. In the limiting case, language knowledge may consist in memory traces of specific instances. Take, for example, the word form *eyes* On the one hand, a competent speaker of English is able to create this form in accordance with a general schema for plural nouns. Equally, a speaker may store the plural form, ready-made, as a result of having encountered it rather often. This last possibility is not an idle speculation. There is psycholinguistic evidence (discussed in Chapter 16) that speakers do store frequently occurring forms, even if these are internally complex and perfectly regular with respect to more abstract schemas.

(ii) Secondly, knowledge of a language is dynamic, and evolves in accordance with a person's linguistic experience. As new expressions are encountered, these may be added to a speaker's store of linguistic units. Conversely, aspects of a language, if not kept activated through regular use, may atrophy, and eventually drop out of a person's language system.

It follows that different speakers of a language may not share exactly the same linguistic system. Indeed, it is an everyday observation that speakers of a language do differ with respect to their familiarity with words, idioms, and phrases. Every practising linguist will have experienced situations in which different speakers offer conflicting acceptability judgements on novel expressions.

(iii) Cognitive Grammar is very much surface oriented.[3] Abstract entities are certainly admissible, but only to the extent that these are schematic for actually occurring structures, and which can be abstracted from actually occurring instances. There is, for example, a general scepticism for underlying structures which diverge from surface structures with respect to their component parts and the sequential ordering of the parts. As Langacker put it:

Cognitive grammar claims that grammatical structure is almost entirely overt. Surface grammatical form does not conceal a 'truer', deeper level of grammatical organization; rather, it itself embodies the conventional means a language employs for the structuring and symbolization of semantic content. (FCG1: 46–7)

It would be inadmissible, in Cognitive Grammar, to analyse a passive sentence, such as *The jewels were stolen*, as deriving from the underlying structure (1) through the movement of *the jewels* from post-verbal into subject position.[4]

(1) *np*   were stolen   [the jewels]

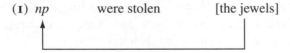

The postulated underlying structure in (1) is simply incompatible with passive sentences that are actually encountered. The underlying structure is not imminent in the passive sentence, and cannot be abstracted by generalizing over instances.

[3] Cognitive Grammar is not alone in its focus on surface form. R. Hudson's *Word Grammar* (Hudson 1990) is one of several contemporary theories that share this focus.
[4] The example is adapted from a recent textbook introduction to linguistics: Radford *et al.* (1999: 334).

2.2.2 The importance of semantics

It will come as no surprise that the study of semantic structure looms large in Cognitive Grammar. Especially noteworthy have been the contributions to lexical semantics. Word meaning has been studied with regard to the ways in which a word's meaning influences the use of the word in syntactic contexts. Polysemy, and the factors which motivate the range of meanings that can attach to a particular word-form, have also been prominent research topics. Some of the earlier achievements of the Cognitive Grammar approach, for example, had to do with the semantics of highly polysemous prepositions such as *over*, *up*, and *out* (Brugman 1981; Lindner 1981).

Semantic considerations have also been important in the study of lexical categories such as 'noun' and 'verb' (Langacker 1987*b*). While these categories are generally defined in purely distributional terms, the Cognitive Grammar approach has sought to identity a semantic content to the categories. Rather than the categories being defined in terms of distribution, it is possible to argue that it is the schematic meaning of the categories that motivates their distributional properties.

A further topic has been the inherent meaningfulness of syntactic patterns and the semantic factors that motivate the syntactic conventions of a language. One of Langacker's first presentations of Cognitive Grammar (Langacker 1982) addressed the issue of the English passive, where he argued that the syntactic form of the passive (*be* + past participle + *by*-phrase) was motivated by the meanings of its parts, and that the pattern by which they are combined was itself inherently meaningful. Subsequent work has addressed topics that generativists have often cited as evidence for the need to recognize an autonomous level of syntactic organization—topics such as the kinds of complements that verbs may take (Achard 1998), various kinds of raising phenomena (Langacker 1995), or problems of anaphoric reference (van Hoek 1997).

It is important to emphasize that the aim of these Cognitive Grammar studies has not been to 'reduce' syntactic phenomena to semantics, in the sense that formal aspects of an expression can be fully predicted from, and are fully determined by, its semantics. It is recognized that syntactic organization will be subject to considerable language-specific conventionalization. The expectation, rather, is that the syntactic (and morphological) facts of a language will be *motivated* by semantic aspects and that they can be exhaustively described by means of symbolic structures.

Although semantic issues have been especially prominent in Cognitive Grammar studies, it would be an error to equate the Cognitive Grammar enterprise with semantic investigations. A symbolic unit needs to be characterized in both its semantic and its phonological aspects. Accordingly, I have devoted a number of chapters of this book to the Cognitive Grammar approaches to phonology.

2.2.3 Blurring of distinctions

In approaching the task of linguistic description, Cognitive Grammar blurs many of the distinctions traditionally made in linguistic theory. For example, syntax (which studies the internal structure of phrases) and morphology (which studies the internal structure of words) are traditionally handled by separate components, or modules, of a grammar. The distinction between word and phrase is certainly a valid one, in general. (I address the status of words in Chapter 9). Nevertheless, essentially the same kinds of operations are involved in the assembly of smaller components into internally complex expressions, whether the complex expressions be words or phrases. Morphology and syntax therefore represent two aspects of the more general phenomenon of syntagmatic combination.

The distinction between the lexicon on the one hand, and syntax–morphology on the other, also turns out to be less than clear-cut. Speakers have learned, not only individual lexical items, but also a vast repertoire of pre-formed phrases. Moreover, patterns for the creation of complex forms—whether these be morphologically complex words or syntactically complex phrases—themselves have the status of symbolic units, and differ from lexical items with respect only to their degree of internal complexity and their schematicity.

Another distinction that gets blurred is that between semantics and pragmatics. Semantics is traditionally concerned with the linguistically determined meaning of an expression, pragmatics with the contextually conditioned interpretation of an expression. Pragmatic aspects can, however, be incorporated into the conventualized meaning of an expression. Because conventualization is a matter of degree, the distinction is a graded one, with no clear cut-off point between the entrenched meaning of an expression and its context-dependent interpretation.

2.2.4 What is a language?

Cognitive Grammar offers a distinctive answer to the question, what a language actually is. A language, namely, is understood as a set of resources that are available to language users for the symbolization of thought, and for the communication of these symbolizations. Acquiring a language consists in building up this repertoire of resources, through actual encounters with usage events. Using a language consists in selectively activating these resources, in accordance with the task in hand.

In contrast to Chomskyan theories, a language is not equated with a device which generates grammatical sentences. It is speakers who 'generate' expressions, not the grammar. Moreover, the distinction between competence and performance, crucial in generativist theories, has little importance in Cognitive Grammar. It is specifically denied that there is such a thing as a narrowly defined linguistic knowledge which interacts in various ways with a person's other cognitive capacities. Given the encyclopaedic scope of semantic structure, language knowledge reaches into many aspects of a person's conceptual world. Any 'errors' that a person may make in using language (and which a speaker may sometimes immediately recognize as such) are not attributed to interference from non-linguistic performance factors, but result from the dynamic aspects of language knowledge itself.

2.3 A bit of history

Since its emergence in the 1970s, there has always been a polemical undertone to the Cognitive Linguistics movement.[5] Cognitive Linguistics developed out of a general dissatisfaction with the dominant Chomskyan paradigm of the time. The feeling was that linguistic theory was becoming so abstract, and so far removed from people's everyday experience of what language is and what it means to know and use a language, that a new approach was needed. A particular concern was the lack of naturalness and conceptual motivation for the kinds of entities that were being proposed, as well as the narrowness of the kinds of phenomena that were being addressed. Langacker (FCG1: v–vi) speaks of his own dissatisfaction with the dominant (i.e. Chomskyan) paradigm:

My own dissatisfaction with the dominant trends in current theory is profound. It reaches to the deepest stratum of organizing principles: notions about what language is like and what linguistic theory should be concerned with. . . . Rightly or wrongly, I concluded some time ago that the conceptual foundations of linguistic theory were built on quicksand, and that the only remedy was to start over on firmer ground. (FCG1: v)

I have already drawn attention to some of the main points of divergence between Cognitive Linguistics and the Chomskyan approach. Nevertheless, it may be useful to fill in some of the historical details.

2.3.1 The descriptivist (Bloomfieldian) legacy

American linguistics between the 1930s and 1950s was dominated by Bloomfieldian descriptivism. Linguistics (especially in North America) was pursued as the study of observable phenomena, i.e. speaker utterances. Language was a kind of behaviour and behaviour was to be studied only in its observable form. Linguistics was conceived as a set of procedures for recording observed utterances, analysing them into their parts, and classifying the parts. The idea was that a language should be described without any preconceptions of what it might turn out to be like. (Even terms like 'noun' and 'verb' were suspect.) One started with a narrow phonetic transcription of a corpus of utterances. 'Discovery procedures' were applied in order to determine the phonemes and

---

[5] The reader may have picked up a polemical nuance even in the characterization of Cognitive Linguistics cited in section 1.4, namely, in the statement that Cognitive Linguistics needs the context of 'a *realistic* view of acquisition, cognitive development and mental processing'. Implicit, here, is the view that other linguistic theories embrace *un*realistic views of these processes.

their distribution, the morphemes and their distribution, word classes and their distribution, and so on. It was considered illegitimate to make reference to mental phenomena, such as speakers' intuitions. Semantic considerations, in particular, were not supposed to cloud the picture.

Bloomfield's great achievement, laid down in his still eminently readable book *Language* (1933), was to have codified the procedures for phonemic, morphemic, and phrasal analysis. These procedures—the essential tools of the trade of any linguist—are still valid today, in their general outline. (I dare say that first-year linguistics courses, at most universities, are still basically Bloomfieldian in orientation, at least with respect to the phonology, morphology, and syntax components.) What was lacking in Bloomfield's approach, however, was an adequate treatment of semantics. In accordance with the thesis that the only legitimate object of study was observable phenomena, Bloomfield equated the meaning of an expression with an objective, scientific account of the circumstances that cause linguistic behaviour, not at all with the conceptualizations that a speaker might entertain:

The situations which prompt people to utter speech, include every object and happening in their universe. In order to give a scientifically accurate definition of meaning for every form of a language, we should have to have a scientifically accurate knowledge of everything in the speakers' world. The actual extent of human knowledge is very small, compared to this. We can define the meaning of a speech-form accurately when this meaning has to do with some matter of which we possess scientific knowledge. We can define the names of minerals, for example, in terms of chemistry and mineralogy, as when we say that the ordinary meaning of the English word *salt* is 'sodium chloride (NaCl),' and we can define the names of plants or animals by means of the technical terms of botany or zoölogy, but we have no precise way of defining words like *love* or *hate*, which concern situations that have not been accurately classified—and these latter are in the great majority. (Bloomfield 1933: 139)

Since most things in a speaker's world are not subject to scientifically validated knowledge—and even if they were, this knowledge would probably not be available to the speaker in question—Bloomfield's position leads to the bizarre conclusion that most people, most of the time, do not know the 'true' meanings of the expressions that they are using. Bloomfield would have us believe that if you say to someone *I love you*, you do not really know what you are talking about.

2.3.2 The Chomskyan revolution

By the 1950s, academic linguistics had settled into a rather cosy self-confidence. All that remained to do was to dot the 'i's and cross the 't's, and to continue to apply well-tried descriptive procedures to hitherto unstudied languages. Chomsky's first major publication, *Syntactic Structures* (1957), radically upset this situation. The locus of Chomsky's attack was not, as one might have expected, the inadequate treatment of semantics, but rather the classificatory zeal of the Bloomfieldians. Dismissing the Bloomfieldian tradition as mere 'taxonomic linguistics', Chomsky made some (for the time) revolutionary proposals:

- A language is not to be identified with a corpus of utterances. A language is a set (infinite in length) of grammatical sentences.
- A grammar is a device for generating all and only the grammatical sentences of a language.
- The major data source for the linguist is not a corpus of attested utterances but a native speaker's intuitions. Introspection becomes a legitimate research method.
- It is conceivable that more than one grammar could be devised for a given language. The grammars would be descriptively equivalent, in that each generates the same set of sentences. Linguistic theory needs to provide criteria for evaluating alternative grammars.
- The ultimate aim must be a theory of grammar which fixes in advance, as it were, the architecture of the grammar of any human language.

There was therefore, from the beginning, a strong universalist orientation to Chomsky's programme. This contrasts with the Bloomfieldian belief that languages must be analysed on their own terms, without any preconceptions gleaned from the analysis of other languages.

We also note the emphasis on syntax as the central topic in linguistic investigation. Moreover, syntax had to be studied independently of semantics:

A great deal of effort has been expended in attempting to answer the question: 'How can you construct a grammar with no appeal to meaning?' The question itself, however, is wrongly put, since the implication that obviously one can construct a grammar *with* appeal to meaning is totally unsupported. One might with equal justification ask: 'How can you construct a grammar with no knowledge of the hair color of speakers?' The question that should be raised is: 'How can you construct a grammar?'. (Chomsky 1957: 93)

Chomsky answers this last question by claiming that a grammar has to be conceived as a device that manipulates inherently contentless symbols, getting them into the right sequence, making sure that certain illegitimate strings of symbols do not occur, transforming one legitimate string of symbols into another legitimate string, and such like.

In spite of Chomsky's flippant remark that meaning is no more relevant to syntax than a speaker's hair colour, it would be an error to suppose that Chomsky rejected the possibility of a serious study of semantics (though Chomsky himself has had little of substance to say about semantics). His contention was that syntax must be studied independently of meaning. Only then might it be possible to investigate the 'points of connection' between syntax and semantics:

[I]t is questionable that the grammatical devices available in language are used consistently enough so that meaning can be assigned to them directly. Nevertheless, we do find many important correlations, quite naturally, between syntactic structure and meaning; or, to put it differently, we find that the grammatical devices are used quite systematically. These correlations could form part of the subject matter for a more general theory of language concerned with syntax and semantics and their points of connection. (Chomsky 1957: 108)

The question whether meaning can be assigned directly to grammatical structure has become a major issue dividing Cognitive Grammar from the approach sketched out in the above passage. Cognitive Grammar does indeed claim that syntactic structures are inherently meaningful.

Chomsky's *Aspects of the Theory of Syntax* (1965) develops the formalism of *Syntactic Structures*, but also introduces some new 'cognitive' (with a small 'c') themes, for example, the distinction between mental competence and actual performance. Competence is the speaker's internalized knowledge of the grammar, which generates the set of grammatical sentences. Performance (what speakers actually say) is guided by competence, but may also reflect various non-grammatical (non-linguistic) influences (e.g. memory, attention). Note here the extension of the modular conception of language. Just as syntax is autonomous of semantics, so also linguistic knowledge (competence) is autonomous of other mental capacities.

At around this time, Chomsky sought historical antecedents for his views. These he found in Descartes, and other rationalists of the seventeenth century (*Cartesian Linguistics*, 1966). *Rationalists* asserted that much of what we know is innate (the doctrine of innate ideas), in contrast to *empiricists*, who asserted that much of what we know is learned from experience. The Bloomfieldians and the behaviourists were decried as empiricists; Chomsky adopted an explicitly rationalist stance.

2.3.3 Controversies

Chomsky's early work sparked intense controversies (and personal animosities) in academic linguistics. The 1960s were a time of university expansion (in the USA and elsewhere), and Chomskyans managed to place themselves in newly founded or expanding linguistics departments. Overnight, the older generation of Bloomfieldians found themselves outnumbered. Some, such as Charles Hockett (*The State of the Art*, 1967), put up a good fight,[6] others vanished into obscurity.

Within the Chomskyan camp there was a particularly vicious controversy between mainstream Chomskyans and the so-called generative semanticists. Chomsky's initial proposals, in *Syntactic Structures* and *Aspects*, had dis-

---

[6] Twenty years later, Hockett was to publish his lifetime's reflections on language (Hockett 1987). Many of the ideas presented there are compatible with the usage-based orientation of Cognitive Grammar.

tinguished between the surface structure of a sentence and the deep structure, from which the surface structure is derived by transformations. Semantic interpretation occurs on the deep structure, while the surface structure gets a phonological interpretation in the phonological module of the grammar. It was assumed that expressions which share more or less the same meaning have a common deep structure. Since the active sentence *The enemy destroyed the city* and its passive counterpart *The city was destroyed by the enemy*, as well as the nominalized expression *the enemy's destruction of the city*, all mean more or less the same thing,[7] the three surface structures could be derived from a common deep structure. The generative semanticists jumped on this idea, and aimed to capture the semantic commonality of superficially very different surface forms in terms of a common deep structure. This led them to propose deep semantic structures which were ever more remote from the surface, and ever more far-fetched transformations that were needed to derive the surface structures. A notorious example was the derivation of the surface verb *kill* from an underlying *cause to become not alive*. Chomsky put an end to these excesses with his 'Remarks on nominalization' (1970), where he proposed to greatly limit the scope of transformations. However, rather than usher in a more surface-oriented kind of linguistics, Chomsky's 1970 paper laid the foundations for ever greater abstraction, with the development, first, of the government and binding theory, then the theory of 'principles and parameters', and, more recently, the 'minimalist program'.

My point in bringing up the generative semantics controversy is that one of the leading promoters of Cognitive Linguistics—George Lakoff—was prominent in the generative semantics movement. (Langacker, too, played a role, albeit more minor, in generative semantics.) Lakoff has since disavowed the formalist trappings of generative semantics, with its abstract underlying structures (which were often expressed in the formalism of predicate logic) and the complex operations which were needed to transform these into surface structures. Cognitive Linguistics does, however, continue to address a basic concern of generative semantics, namely, the centrality of meaning:

The primary function of language is to convey meaning. A grammar should therefore show as directly as possible how parameters of form are linked to parameters of meaning. (Lakoff 1987: 583)

In emphasizing that linguistic expressions link form with meaning, Lakoff is here promoting a version of the symbolic thesis. The focus of Cognitive Linguistics is to give substance to semantic representations, and to show how these are directly linked to formal aspects.

---

[7] At least, it was this view that motivated the postulation of a common deep structure. In Cognitive Grammar, the three different wordings (active, passive, and nominalization) would be associated with three different construals of the situation; the expressions would not, therefore, be regarded as synonymous..

2.3.4 Subsequent developments

In view of this historical background, it is not surprising that Cognitive Linguistics, at least in its earlier days, saw itself in total polemical opposition to the Chomskyan paradigm. In the intervening years, however, the Chomskyan enterprise itself has undergone many transformations and generated many offspring. In particular, a number of scholars closely associated with the Chomskyan enterprise have taken positions that at least in some respects are compatible with Cognitive Linguistics, and more particularly, with Cognitive Grammar. Jackendoff, for one, has offered a critique of what he calls the 'syntactocentrism' of the Chomskyan enterprise (Jackendoff 1997: 15–19), and has paid increased attention to idioms, formulas, and constructional schemas. Likewise, Culicover (1999) has emphasized the role of the idio-syncratic in syntax, and is led to question some of the basic assumptions of the Chomskyan enterprise, concerning, for example, the role of Universal Grammar in language acquisition, and the independence of syntax and semantics. The upshot is that while Cognitive Grammar and 'hard core' Chomskyanism remain irreconcilable on just about all the issues, the con-temporary linguistic landscape is populated with a great variety of individual approaches, which are consonant, in varying degrees, with the assumptions of Cognitive Grammar. In a way, Cognitive Grammar is itself becoming part of the mainstream.

Further reading

The standard text of Cognitive Grammar is the two volumes of Langacker's *Foundations of Cognitive Grammar* (Langacker 1987a, 1991, cited as FCG1 and FCG2, respectively). These are supplemented by two volumes which bring together some of the most important of Langacker's journal articles and other publications (Langacker 1990, 1999). A clear, non-technical introduction to Cognitive Grammar is Langacker (1988a). For a brief overview, see chs. 2–4 of Taylor (1996).

On the first page of FCG1, Langacker characterizes 'language' as follows:

Language is symbolic in nature. It makes available to the speaker—for either personal or communi-cative use—an open-ended set of linguistic *signs* or *expressions*, each of which associates a semantic representation of some kind with a phonological representation. (FCG1: 11; author's emphasis)

Later in the same book, he defines the 'grammar of a language' as follows:

The grammar of a language is defined as those aspects of cognitive organization in which resides a speaker's grasp of established linguistic convention. It can be characterized as a *structured inventory of conventional linguistic units*. (FCG1: 57; author's emphasis)

Langacker goes on to offer a detailed exegesis of the highlighted phrase, starting with the nature of units, then progressively expanding the discussion to cover 'linguistic units', 'conventional linguistic units', and an 'inventory of conventional linguistic units', and concluding with what it means to say that a language is a 'structured inventory of conventional linguistic units'. A close study of this passage (FCG1: 57–77) is strongly recommended.

The rift between Chomsky and Lakoff is beautifully (and reasonably objectively) narrated in Randy Harris's appropriately named book, *The Linguistics Wars* (1993). For an account from a Chomskyan sympathizer, see Newmeyer (1986).

CHAPTER 3

The symbolic thesis

Given the centrality of the symbolic thesis in Cognitive Grammar, I devote this chapter to examining some general aspects of it. I begin by looking at Saussure's conception of the linguistic sign. The symbolic thesis can be seen as a natural development of this aspect of Saussure's thought. I then examine in more detail the notion of the symbolic sign in contrast to other kinds of signs—i.e. icons and indexes—in order to better appreciate the essentially symbolic nature of human language. Finally, I address an important point of divergence between what appears to have been Saussure's views concerning the status of phonological and semantic structures in a language, and the Cognitive Grammar position on these issues.

3.1 Saussurean roots

One of the most important events in the development of modern linguistics was the publication, in 1916, of the *Cours de linguistique générale*, the 'Course in General Linguistics', by Ferdinand de Saussure.[1] (The *Cours* was not actually 'by' Saussure; it was assembled, after Saussure's death, from his students' lecture notes.) The influence of the *Cours* has been enormous, not only in linguistics, but in neighbouring disciplines such as anthropology, cultural studies, and literary theory.

---

[1] The standard reference text cited here is the 1964 edition.

In emphasizing the Saussurean roots of Cognitive Grammar I am not claiming that Saussure was a Cognitive Grammarian *ante litteram*. Cognitive Grammar has probably developed in ways that Saussure himself might not have endorsed. I also do not wish to associate Cognitive Grammar with certain kinds of post-Saussurean structuralism, one of whose basic tenets has been the independence of the language system *vis-à-vis* its speakers.[2] Nevertheless, Cognitive Grammar is driven by a view of language that arguably does have much in common with certain aspects of Saussure's thought. I refer to Saussure's insistence that the basic object of linguistic enquiry is the **linguistic sign**, and to his characterization of a language as a system of signs. Langacker has explicitly acknowledged the affinity with the Cognitive Grammar approach:

> Language is symbolic in nature. It makes available to the speaker—for either personal or communicative use—an open-ended set of linguistic *signs* or *expressions*, each of which associates a semantic representation of some kind with a phonological representation. I therefore embrace the spirit of classic Saussurean diagrams like Fig. [3.1], with the understanding that explicit, substantive characterization is required for the elements they depict. (FCG1: 11, author's emphasis)

Langacker's explicit reference to the Saussurean sign invites us to look more closely at this aspect of Saussure's thought.

3.1.1 Saussure and the linguistic sign

Academics tend to be very territorial people, anxious to defend their disciplinary turf. Saussure was an academic, through and through. One of his preoccupations was the question, how to justify the academic discipline of

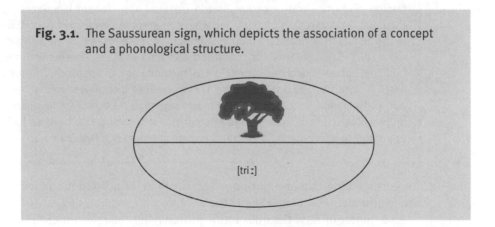

Fig. 3.1. The Saussurean sign, which depicts the association of a concept and a phonological structure.

[tri:]

---

[2] The major exponent of European structuralism was perhaps Eugenio Coseriu. For Coseriu's incisive critique of the Cognitive Linguistic approach to semantics, see Coseriu (2000). For a critique of Coseriu's structuralist semantics from a Cognitive Linguistic viewpoint, see Taylor (1999).

Saussure—the father of modern linguistics

It is fascinating to recall that Saussure (1857–1913) owes his status as the father of modern linguistics to a book that he never wrote.

Saussure had a brilliant career as a young man. In 1878, aged 21, he published his doctoral dissertation on the vowels of Indo-European. After teaching in Paris for a while he was offered, at the age of 34, a chair in his native Geneva. He would have had a hard time in a present-day university, with its annual reports and performance reviews, for, having settled in Geneva, he wrote very little and published even less. There is a touching letter, in which he confesses that he finds himself unable to write even ten sentences on linguistics, because the theoretical foundations of the discipline are so unsound. 'Cela finera malgré moi par un livre' ['I'll end up writing a book in spite of myself'], he lamented in one of his letters (Harris 1987: vi).

The book never got written. However, towards the end of his life he gave three lecture series on general linguistics. These occurred more by accident than by design, in that Saussure was asked to take over the lectures from a colleague who had retired. Geneva was a provincial university, the classes were small, and none of the students went on to distinguish themselves in linguistics. Colleagues, however, got word that something significant was being said in these lectures, and after Saussure's death in 1913 they decided to reconstruct his thinking on the basis of his students' lecture notes. Thus the *Course in General Linguistics* came about.

A modern reader, paging through the *Cours* for the first time, might well wonder what all the fuss is about. The book looks quite unlike what we have come to expect of a linguistics text. There is virtually no syntax in the book, neither is there any of that close argumentation from data which is a hallmark of the modern discipline. In fact, very few data are cited at all in the *Cours*, and the data that are cited—a few examples of sound change, and the like—would have been very familiar to anyone with a background in classical and modern languages. Why, then, was Saussure so influential, and why is he accorded such an important place in the history of linguistics? I think one important reason was that the *Cours* is an 'open' text. Saussure was not concerned with data analysis, or even with theory building, but with questions of principle, of methodology, of approach. He provided a set of schemas which researchers in all manner of disciplines were able to fill out and elaborate according to their own agendas. Structuralist linguists and anthropologists, literary critics and postmodernist theoreticians, have all found it opportune to refer back to Saussure. The same goes for Cognitive Grammar.

Linguistics. How can one mark out a territory in the academic curriculum that can legitimately be called 'Linguistics'?[3]

As a matter of fact, the question is probably just as relevant today as it was

---

[3] Saussure (1964: 20) lists three aims of linguistics: one is the description of languages, another is the discovery of universal laws, the third is 'de se délimiter et de se définir elle-même' [to circumscribe and to define itself].

when Saussure was alive. No one disputes that language is central to human affairs. Language distinguishes humans from all other creatures, and the achievements (and catastrophes) of the human species can be put down, in large part, to the possibility of our transmitting acquired knowledge through language. The centrality of language to human affairs means that practitioners of very many disciplines have had something to say about language, whether these be literature students, anthropologists, philosophers, political scientists, psychologists, educationalists, or, more recently, the cognitive scientists. So there can be no question that language is a legitimate, indeed, a very important object of study.

One approach might be to regard linguistics as simply the grand sum of what all the various human and social sciences have had to say about language. Linguistics would lie at the intersection of various other, well-established disciplines.

Not so, counters Saussure. For linguistics to be a proper academic discipline, there has to be a distinctively 'linguistic' way of studying language. And this resided, for Saussure, in recognizing language as a symbolic system. The primary object of linguistic study had to be the linguistic sign. The sign, for Saussure, was the association of a **concept** (also called the signified) and an **acoustic image** (the signifier). And a language was characterized as a **system of signs**.[4]

The diagram[5] in Figure 3.1 is meant to illustrate the association between a 'concept' and an 'acoustic image' with respect to the word (sign) *tree*. In spite of its simplicity (its banality, almost), the diagram can be deceptive, in a number of ways. To begin with, the diagram might suggest that the linguistic sign associates a 'thing' (i.e. an actual tree growing in the yard) with a 'sound'

---

[4] Cf. Saussure (1964: 32): 'la langue . . . est un système de signes où il n'y a d'essentiel que l'union du sens et de l'image acoustique'. [The language system . . . is a system of signs where the only essential thing is the union of meaning and sound pattern]. 'System' here implies that a language is not just a list of signs, but that the signs bear various kinds of relations to each other.

[5] The diagram in the *Cours* (Saussure 1964: 99) associates a little picture of a tree with the Latin word *arbor*; it also contains arrows, one pointing upwards, from the phonological structure to the concept, the other pointing downwards, from the concept to the sound. I have taken the liberty—as did Langacker (FCG1: 11) when he referred to Saussure's conception of the sign—of 'anglicizing' Saussure's diagram. I also show the acoustic image by means by a phonetic transcription, rather than by the orthographic form.

Harris (1987: 59), in his commentary on the *Cours*, points out that the picture of the tree, as well as the arrows, may have been inserted by Saussure's editors. Saussure himself, it would seem, illustrated his notion of the sign as follows:

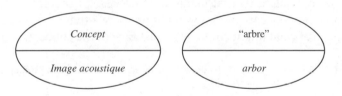

(i.e. an actual pronunciation of the word *tree*). Saussure emphatically states that this is *not* how the linguistic sign is to be understood, and Cognitive Grammar fully endorses his view on this. Both the concept and the acoustic image are mental entities which reside in the mind of a language user.[6] The signified is not to be identified with an entity 'out there' in the real world, neither is the signifier to be identified with an acoustic-phonetic signal, emerging, in real time, from a speaker's vocal tract.

Let us consider these two components of the linguistic sign in more detail.

3.1.2 Concepts

It is not difficult to see why the semantic pole of the linguistic sign cannot be an entity in the real world. There are countless trees out there in the world, each different from every other. If the word *tree* associated a pronunciation with an individual tree, we should have to say that the word has as many semantic values as there are trees. This would be absurd. Rather, we want to say that the meaning of the word is the 'idea' of a tree, a 'concept', a mental entity located in the mind of a language user.

But what is a concept?

The diagram in Figure 3.1, with its little picture of a tree, can be again misleading, in that it might suggest that the concept is a mental image, a little 'picture in the head'. It is certainly true that trees are 'imageable'—we know what trees look like, and we can indeed form a mental image of a tree, should we wish to do so. Yet there are many reasons why we should not want to say that the mental image of a tree *is* the concept [TREE].

One problem with mental images is that they are at the same time too specific and too general. At a pinch, a little picture like the one in the top half of Figure 3.1 (p. 39) might pass for a deciduous tree in leaf and viewed from a great distance, but hardly at all for a leafless tree in winter, a fir tree, a palm tree, or indeed a tree viewed close-up (not to speak of family trees, or the syntactic trees of modern syntax). The image is too specific; it contains too much detail and thus fails to capture what is common to everything that we should want to call a tree. But as we try to make the image more schematic, so as to cover more and more examples, we lose the kind of detail which we want to associate with the concept. The little picture in Figure 3.1 does not portray the leaves and branches—yet having leaves and branches is surely part of the tree-concept.

In fact, to base the concept in a mental image is to get things the wrong way round. It is not the concept that is based in the mental image. Rather, we are able to create a mental image on the basis of the concept. It is because we know the concept—we know what trees are—that we are able to form a mental image of what might count as an instance of the concept, should we wish to do

[6] Cf. Saussure (1964: 32): 'les deux partis du signe sont également psychiques' [the two parts of the sign are equally psychological].

so. But having the concept does not require us to form a mental image. We can use the word *tree* meaningfully, and with full understanding, without a little image of a tree forming in our mind.

Moreover, the mental-image view of concepts couldn't be made to work for the vast majority of words in a language. The vast majority of words are simply not imageable at all. We cannot form a mental image associated with the words *love*, *anger*, *think*, *air*, *good*, let alone *be*, *have*, *the*, and *of*. If the thesis that a language is a system of signs is to have any generality, we will have to allow that these kinds of words also are linguistic signs, each associating an acoustic image with a concept.

What, then, *is* a concept? Saussure was actually rather vague on this point. But I would like to suggest the following preliminary characterization (which we will need to refine in due course). **A concept is a principle of categorization.**[7] To have the concept [TREE] means to know what a tree is. In virtue of having the concept you are able to recognize a tree when you see one, you know what counts as a tree, and are therefore able to use the word appropriately of the object. (You also are able to form a mental image of what might count as an instance of the concept.) Another important aspect of having a concept is that you are able to draw inferences. If you know that something is a tree you can be pretty sure of various things about it, for example, that it has a trunk and branches, that it has leaves (at least in summer), that it grows out of the ground, that it was once a tiny sapling, that it will probably live longer than humans do, that it has roots which penetrate into the earth, that birds are apt to build nests in it, that you can use it, suitably chopped up, as firewood, and much else besides. All these aspects are, I would claim, part and parcel of the concept [TREE].

If we adopt this view of concepts, the way is open for us to say that all manner of words associate a concept with a phonological representation, not just names of concrete physical objects, such as *tree*, but also names of abstract entities, such as *theory*, *language*, *emotion*, and *childhood*, as well as words which belong to other lexical categories, such as the verbs, prepositions, and adjectives.

Take the prepositions *in*, *at*, and *on*. It might seem odd to talk about the meanings of these words as concepts. But consider what it means for a person to know the English prepositions. To know the words means being able to use them appropriately, as when you are describing the spatial disposition of one object *vis-à-vis* another. A person *at* the corner is in a different location from a person *in* the corner; a satellite receiver *in* a building is located differently from a satellite receiver *on* a building. That we are able to make these judgements at all follows from our knowing the meanings of the prepositions. This boils down, essentially, to be being able to make the appropriate categorizations of spatial relations. To know the meaning of the preposition *in* means being able

[7] The view is quite common among psychologists. See the review article by Komatsu (1992).

to categorize the spatial disposition of one object *vis-à-vis* another as an 'in' relation, rather than as an 'on' relation, or an 'at' relation. The same goes for other kinds of words, such as the verbs and adjectives. To say that a person is *sleeping, snoozing,* or *dozing;* to describe a person as *mean, stingy, thrifty,* or *financially responsible,* entails an act of categorization on the part of the speaker, and knowing the expressions in question means knowing the criteria for making the categorizations.

The matter is not so clear, perhaps, with respect to the 'little words' of a language, such as the definite determiner *the*, or the preposition *of*. It is not at all obvious what the concepts symbolized by these words might be, nor even that the words do symbolize concepts. In point of fact, Cognitive Grammar takes the very strong line that even the function words of a language are symbolic units, and, as such, associate a phonological form with a concept. How this is handled will, it is hoped, become clearer later in this book.

Moreover, it is not just the words and morphemes of a language that symbolize concepts. Whereas Saussure had largely restricted his notion of the linguistic sign to the lexical resources of a language, Cognitive Grammar attributes symbolic status to patterns for the combination of words, i.e. to grammatical constructions. Again, this aspect will be explored later in this book.

3.1.3 The acoustic image

I suggested above that concepts can be understood as a principle of categorization. What about the other pole of the linguistic sign, the acoustic image? Actually, we can understand the acoustic image also as a principle of categorization.

Just as the concept [TREE] cannot be a little picture in the head, so the acoustic image cannot be a tape-recording in the head. Just as each tree, the more closely we observe it, is uniquely different from every other, so too each utterance of the word *tree*, if we examine it in sufficient detail, turns out to be phonetically different from every other utterance of the word. The place of articulation of the [t] might be more or less retracted, the [r] might be associated with a greater or lesser degree of lip rounding, the vowel might be articulated with a noticeable in-glide [əi], and so on and so forth. All these pronunciations (and many more besides) count as instances of [triː]. To 'have' the acoustic image [triː] is to know what the word sounds like and how it can be pronounced.

The acoustic image is therefore also a principle of categorization, specifically, a principle for the categorization of auditory and articulatory events. In a way, it is also a kind of concept.

3.2 Icon, index, and symbol

In this section I look more closely at the nature of the relation between the concept and the acoustic image.

Saussure spoke of a language as a system of signs. Following Charles Peirce, the nineteenth-century American philosopher, it is usual to make a broad distinction between three kinds of signs, namely icons, indexes, and symbols. In claiming, in this book, that language is essentially symbolic, I am alluding to the status of linguistic signs as symbols, rather than as icons or indexes.[8] It is therefore important to elucidate the nature of symbolic signs in contrast to the other kinds, in order to better characterize the distinctively symbolic nature of language.

A common approach is to differentiate icons, indexes, and symbols in terms of the relation between the signifier and the signified.[9]

- A sign is iconic if there is a resemblance between the signified and the signifier.
- A sign is indexical if there is a natural connection between the signified and the signifier.
- A sign is symbolic if the relation between signified and signifier is established by convention.

These definitions, as they stand, are deficient, in that they leave out the role of the interpreter. The resemblance between the signified and the signifier—the defining characteristic of an iconic sign—has to be a resemblance as perceived by someone. Likewise, a sign is indexical to the extent that the connection between signified and signifier has been recognized by someone. And what about symbols? Certainly, the interpreter has to recognize (and be familiar with) the convention associating the signifier with the signified. But while the conventionality of the signifier-signified relation may be characteristic of a symbol, it cannot be taken as its defining feature. The point about a symbol is that it is used with the intention of designating a concept. What renders the relation between [tri:] and [TREE] a symbolic relation is the fact that a person who uses the phonological form [tri:] does so to designate the concept [TREE]. A tape-recorder, a speech synthesizer, or a parrot, which produces a sound interpretable to human ears as an instance of [tri:], is not engaging in symbolic behaviour.

---

[8] This does not exclude the possibility that linguistic signs might also exhibit iconic and/or indexical features. As will become clear later in this section, a sign can exhibit characteristics of all three of icon, index, and symbol.

[9] This is the approach found in many introductory linguistics texts, e.g. Dirven and Verspoor (1998: ch. 1) and G. Hudson (2000: 2–4).

3.2.1 Icons

An icon resembles the thing that it represents. In the simplest case, the form of the sign imitates its meaning—the sign 'looks like', or 'sounds like', the thing it is intended to represent. Many public signs (such as traffic signs) are iconic in this respect. For example, a sign warning a motorist of an upcoming railway crossing might display a little drawing of a locomotive straddling the road.

What we might call **imitative iconicity** plays only a marginal role in language. There are, to be sure, the so-called onomatopoeic words—these are words whose pronunciation is suggestive of their meaning, such as *hiss* and *splash*. (Occasionally, iconicity pertains to the written form of a word, rather than to its pronunciation. Consider examples such as *U-turn* and *S-bend*.) The number of imitative words in any language is bound to be quite small, and for many such words the sound-meaning relation is by no means direct. Although the sound of the word *cuckoo* resembles the bird's call, the word does not signify the call, it signifies the bird that makes the call. Moreover, in many cases, words that speakers of a language perceive to be onomatopoeic may not be so perceived by outsiders who do not know the language; the iconic relation is evident only to speakers who have learned the sound-meaning association.

If, in contrast, we pay attention to what we might call **structural iconicity**— whereby some features of the structure of a phonological form correspond to aspects of semantic structure—we may need to accord a more prominent role to iconicity. Consider the fact that in many languages plural nouns are longer (they contain more phonological material) than the corresponding singulars; this iconically reflects the fact that plural nouns designate more things than a singular noun. The length of an expression may also correlate with the complexity of conceptual content. *That house over there on the hill* specifies the concept in some detail, and also gives the hearer instructions about how the referent of the expression can be identified. The very same entity can be referred to by the pronoun *it*, a use which is only appropriate if the intended referent has already been conceptualized and properly identified.

In addition to **iconicity of quantity** we can also identify **sequential iconicity** and **iconicity of proximity**. Consider the question of word order (or, more accurately, constituent order). The three constituents of a transitive clause— Subject, Verb, and Object—can in principle be ordered in six ways, and languages do differ with respect to the preferred order of S, V, and O. Nevertheless, the vast majority have S before O. While SVO, SOV, and VSO are widely attested, OSV, OVS, and VOS are exceedingly rare. The reason for this, evidently, is that the Subject is the conceptual 'starting point' for the conceptualization of a transitive process, and its position before the Object iconically reflects this fact. Sequential iconicity also manifests itself in the order in which clauses are spoken. Generally, when narrating a series of events, a speaker will strive to mention the events in the same order in which they occurred. *They* *married and had a child* would be interpreted as narrating two events which took place in that order. A departure from iconic ordering would need some kind of overt linguistic marking (*They had a child after they married*).

Iconicity of proximity is manifest in the fact that things that belong together conceptually tend to be close together phonologically. Although languages might differ with respect to whether a direct object precedes or follows the verb, the object often has to appear adjacent to the verb, either immediately before or immediately after; intervening adverbials are not permitted. Conceptual closeness often prohibits the insertion even of hesitation pauses or parenthetical expressions such as *I think*. It would be odd to say that the book was 'under the double—I think—bed'. *Double bed* is a tightly knit conceptual unit whose component parts cannot easily be separated.

Although the effects of structural iconicity are widespread (and have been invoked as an explanatory principle by scholars such as Haiman 1985 and Givón 1989), iconicity is in some ways a very problematic notion. First, iconicity is clearly a matter of degree; even onomatopoeic words differ greatly in the degree to which their form resembles their meaning. Paradoxically, though, it is difficult to envisage a fully iconic sign. A fully iconic sign, where the signifier resembles the signified in all respects, would be identical with the thing it represents, and thus would probably not be called a sign at all.[10] Moreover, iconic signs generally exhibit some degree of conventionalization, and to this extent they take on characteristics of a symbol. Even though plural forms, in some (but by no means all) languages might contain more phonological substance than the corresponding singulars, the language user cannot use the iconicity principle to create a plural form; she still has to learn precisely *how* the plurals are formed, in any given instance. Another fact that needs to be borne in mind is this: for every example which can be cited as an instance of iconicity, it is usually possible to cite examples where the same is violated. One might say that the obligatory occurrence of the direct object next to the verb in English iconically reflects the close conceptual relation between a verb and its object; I would say *I like cherries very much*, not *?I like very much cherries*. Yet in French the adverbial has to intervene between verb and object: *J'aime beaucoup les cérises* vs. **J'aime les cérises beaucoup*. Is French, therefore, less 'iconic' than English? One might, in this case, say that in French the obligatory occurrence of the adverbial with the verb iconically reflects the close conceptual association between the adverbial and the verb that it modifies. The dangers in this approach will be evident. Iconicity, at best, can be cited as a factor that motivates linguistic convention, but the conventions themselves cannot be reduced to principles of iconicity.

As we have noted, the very notion of resemblance implicitly brings in an

---

[10] For a putative example of a fully iconic sign, in which a sign, so to speak, symbolizes itself, consider the following, where the noise that the speaker makes is intended to be identical to the noise that the boy made.

(i)   The boy went [NOISE]. (FCG1: 90)

interpreter—the resemblance has to be perceived by someone. Moreover, resemblance has to be the resemblance *of* something *to* something. Traditionally, in linguistics, iconicity is understood in terms of a perceived resemblance between signifier and signified, between phonological structure and semantic structure, between sound and meaning. It is this aspect that I have surveyed above. Understood in this way, iconicity certainly plays an important, though probably limited, role in the language system. But we might also extend the notion of iconicity to the perceived similarity between phonological structures, between semantic structures, and between symbolic structures. An utterance of the word *tree*, in a specific speech event, may not resemble the concept [TREE], but it certainly resembles other utterances of the word. It is through recognizing these resemblances that a person gets to identify the different utterances as instances of the same word.

The recognition of resemblances is the lifeblood of language use. The resemblances are not, to repeat, resemblances between sound and meaning, but resemblances between sound pattern and sound pattern, between conceptualization and conceptualization, and between different uses of one and the same symbolic unit on different occasions. If we extend the notion of iconicity to include these kinds of resemblance, then we shall have to regard iconicity as an essential ingredient of language, and of language use.

3.2.2 Indexes

An index (sometimes called a symptom) stands for something with which it bears some known, or presumed, connection; often the relation is causal, or presumed to be causal. Smoke is an index of fire: smoke, as we know, is caused by fire; thus, if there is smoke, there has got to be fire. Medical signs[11] are an index of the disease—they are caused by the disease, they are the overt manifestation of the disease, and a skilled practitioner can diagnose a disease by observation of the signs. Animals (and humans), when moving around, may leaves tracks—the tracks are an indexical sign of the path that the animal (or human) has moved along, and thus of the presence of the animal (or human) at some previous point in time.

Quite a few aspects of language are indexical, in the sense described above. These aspects may indeed be caused by something else. They are perceived as being subject to the causal relation, and are interpreted as signs of this something else. A state of drunkenness may cause a person to lose control of the articulators; consequently, slurred and imprecise speech may be an index of the speaker's inebriated state. Raised pitch could be an index of agitation; hoarseness may be an index of a sore throat; a person's accent or dialect may be an index of geographical, social, or educational background. Even the fact that you happen to speak language X rather than language Y is indexical—it

---

[11] Medical discourse distinguishes between 'symptoms' and 'signs'. A symptom is what a patient reports, a sign is what the practitioner observes.

conveys that you happen to have been raised in a community that speaks language X, rather than in one that speaks language Y.

Indexical signs can be generated by natural events, by fire, for example, which generates smoke. There is indeed an important sense in which indexical relations have a 'natural' basis. Even when indexical signs are generated by animals or humans, the signs are produced independently of a person's (or an animal's) intentions. If you are drunk, you do not choose to slur your speech—you can't help it. If you have a sore throat, you cannot but speak hoarsely. To this extent, indexical aspects of language are incidental to the conceptual content that a speaker intends to convey.

The status of indexical signs becomes somewhat less clear, however, if a person attempts to manipulate indexical signs in order to convey a conceptual content that is at variance with the indexical value of the sign. Suppose I ring in to the office on a Monday morning, wanting the day off. I attempt to put on a hoarse voice in order to support the claim that I am suffering from a throat infection. In doing so, I expect that my hearer will interpret the indexical value of the hoarse voice at face value, and that they will not attribute devious communicative intentions to me. I assume that indexical signs cannot lie. But my hearer may be smarter than I anticipate, and might suspect that I am merely putting on a hoarse voice. The indexical status of a hoarse voice gets subverted once I consciously attempt to communicate something at variance with the sign's indexical value, and once hearers become smart to this. In such a situation, the indexical sign is taking on attributes of a symbol.

The status of indexical signs becomes more complicated, in another way, if we allow that an indexical relation need not be causal, but can be set up on the basis of frequent co-occurrence. Pavlov's dogs, which were trained to expect food to appear shortly after the ringing of a bell, came to treat the ringing bell as an index of food to come and would salivate merely on hearing the bell. Strictly speaking, there is no causal relation here. The appearance of food was not caused by the ringing of the bell, nor did the imminent appearance of food cause the bell to ring. The dogs associated the two events as components of a frequently occurring scenario.

If we extend the scope of indexical relations to comprise the learned association between two events, such that the occurrence of one causes us to expect the occurrence of the other, we shall have to admit that even the relation between signifier and signified could be indexical. English speakers have learned the conventional association of the concept [TREE] with the sound pattern [tri:]. For English speakers, this is a natural association. Although I can tell myself that the relation is purely conventional, it will feel wrong for me to apply the phonological form [tri:] to anything other than trees, or to call trees by another phonological form. A lifetime's exposure to English has conditioned me to accept the conventional association.

3.2.3 Symbols

As is well known, Saussure saw the essence of a linguistic sign to lie in the arbitrariness of the relation between signifier and signified. The phonological form [triː] means what it does (in English) simply because this is the way it is in English; there is no way in which trees 'cause' the sound [triː], neither does the sound [triː] in any way resemble the concept that is signified. The relation between signifier and signifier has to be learned, the relation has to be respected, and if the linguistic sign is to serve for interpersonal communication, knowledge of the relation has to be shared by members of a speech community.

As a matter of fact, we need to distinguish at least two aspects of arbitrariness. The first concerns the absence of motivation. As Langacker (FCG1: 12) observed, the arbitrary (i.e. non-motivated) character of linguistic signs is easily overstated, especially with respect to units that are internally complex. The fact that *pencil sharpener* means what it does is strongly motivated by the meanings of the component morphemes and the schemas by which they are combined. Imitative, and, especially, structural iconicity also render the association of form and meaning less than fully arbitrary. Moreover, it is possible for a person to exploit non-arbitrary (including indexical) relations for symbolic purposes, as in the case of the person putting on a hoarse voice in order to feign a throat infection.

The second aspect of arbitrariness concerns the conventionality of the relation between signifier and signified. Even though *pencil sharpener* is motivated in its semantic and formal aspects, a speaker of English still has to learn that *this* is the conventional way of naming the device; the device could have been called something else. The conventionality of the signifier-signified relation probably captures the symbolic nature of language better than an insistence on the absence of motivation. Even so, a symbol does not need to be conventional. The person who puts on a hoarse voice in order to deceive the hearer is using voice quality as a symbolic sign. The putting on of a hoarse voice is not the conventional way to refer to a throat infection.

The hoarse-voice example shows that while conventionalization may be a characteristic of symbolic signs, it cannot be their defining feature. What, then, is the essence of a symbol?

Signs, whatever their kind, are signs only for a mind that perceives them as such. In an inert universe, without minds, there would be no signs. But if all signs require a mind to interpret them, it is not the case that all signs have to be produced by a conscious mind. Indexical signs, as we have seen, can be generated by natural events. Symbols have the special property that they have to be used *intentionally*. A sign is symbolic only if it is produced with the intention of symbolizing a concept. A parrot (or a tape-recorder, or a computer) which produces a sound interpretable (to human ears) as *Have a nice day* is not engaging in symbolic behaviour. A hoarse voice may be an indexical sign of a sore throat; it becomes a symbol only when it is used with the intention of deceiving the hearer.

3.3 Language as symbolic

The use of symbols could well be unique to humans. If this is the case, the uniqueness of human language *vis-à-vis* animal communication systems could well lie in its symbolic nature.

This is the view of Noble and Davidson (1996). In their book on evolutionary archaeology, they argue that the crucial evolutionary step that rendered *homo sapiens* distinct from all other creatures was the emergence of symbolic ability. For Noble and Davidson, the 'only viable distinction' between humans and other creatures is that 'humans are unique, under natural conditions, in being creatures who communicate using symbols' (p. 8), further, 'many of the features we regard as unique [to humans] are more or less direct consequences of the emergence of language, of communication using symbols' (p. 7).

A behaviour expressed by a (not so) close relative of modern human beings is the set of vocal utterances made by vervet monkeys in the face of different classes of predators. In response to the sight of snakes heading for them through the grass they make one sort of cry; in response to the sight of eagles flying overhead they make another sort. These calls have the effect of alerting other monkeys to the different sources (and whereabouts) of the different predators. The others look down in response to a 'snake cry' and up in response to an 'eagle cry'. (Noble and Davidson 1996: 5)

The monkeys' cries are not iconic; the snake-warning cry, or the eagle-warning cry, do not resemble, in any coherent sense, snakes or eagles. According to Noble and Davidson, the monkeys' cries are still at the indexical stage; they are an integral part of a tight scenario (sight of predator → cry → flight). They are, as it were, 'caused' by the sight of the predator; if the predator is present the monkey 'instinctively' produces the cry; if there is no predator, there is no warning cry.

Noble and Davidson go on to ask what it would take for the monkeys' cries to become symbolic:

We could call these utterances symbols if only we could be sure that the monkeys used them with intent; that they knew that one call stood for 'snake' and the other stood for 'eagle'. We do not know that; but it looks from all the evidence that the monkeys do not have these cries as symbols. . . . What the monkeys could have is the makings of a symbol system, if they were to *notice*, to *discover*, that the different calls may be made to stand for objects in the world. We suspect that this is not a straightforward discovery to make. (Noble and Davidson 1996: 5–6)

If the discovery of the symbolic potential of their utterances is not a straightforward one for the moneys to make, it is also not a straightforward matter for us human observers to determine whether the vocalizations of other creatures are being used with the intention of representing to themselves, and to each other, objects in the world. Probably, a minimal requirement would be that the monkeys should make the snake and the eagle cries even in the absence of snakes and eagles. (In such a situation, we might be entitled to say that the monkeys were using the signs in order to 'talk' about snakes and eagles.) In order for the threshold to symbolic behaviour to be crossed, the cries would have to be dissociated from the predator scenario and used even if there were no predators around. Whereas indexes are highly context bound, symbols are constrained only by the conceptualizations that their users wish to entertain.

3.3.1 Language development

If the use of symbols differentiates humans from all other creatures, we may ask whether humans display symbolic activity right from the beginning.

There is evidence that early child utterances may sometimes lack symbolic content, and that the symbolic use of language only really gets under way around the age of one. Consider the following report on the way in which a one-year-old child used the word *duck* (which the child usually pronounced [dʌt]):

This word was initially produced by Adam only while he was engaged in the process of hitting one of his toy yellow ducks off the edge of the bath (which is where they were normally kept). He was never observed producing this word in any other situation at this initial stage: he never produced it while he was playing with his toy ducks in other situations, or while he was looking at or feeding real ducks. This behavior . . . tends to suggest . . . that Adam had not yet learned that the word *duck* could be used to refer to either his toy ducks or real ducks. Instead, his behavior suggests that he had simply identified one particular event in the context of which it was appropriate for him to produce the word *duck*. (Barrett 1986: 40)

An adult (especially a parent), observing a young child use the word *duck* when playing with his ducks, would surely be tempted to believe that the child has learned the word *duck*, and is using the word to designate the concept [DUCK] (or, at the very least, to 'refer' to ducks). Barrett's account suggests that this conclusion would be too hasty.

It seems clear from the account that the utterance of *duck* was an integral part of a little game that the child had invented for himself; saying the word was as much a part of the game as knocking the duck off the edge of the bath. Barrett states that the word was never uttered (at this stage) in any other situation. (Unfortunately, we are not told whether the utterance of the word was an *essential* component of the routine, that is, whether the child would knock the duck off the bath rim without the vocalization.) It seems reasonable to infer from this that the utterance of *duck* lacked symbolic content, and that the word was not in fact associated with a duck-concept at all. Rather, the utterance of the word was itself an action, part and parcel of a more complex action routine that the child had invented. Another point is that the child does not appear to be communicating with anyone. In this respect, again, Barrett's report is incomplete. It would be interesting to know whether Adam would perform the routine with the ducks, including saying the word, even if there was no one around to hear him.

Barrett tells us that the state described above lasted only a couple of weeks. Thereafter, Adam used the word while playing with his ducks in other kinds of situation. He also used the word in response to the question *What's that?*; when seeing toy ducks, real ducks, and duck pictures; while approaching a river; and while looking at swans and geese. Here we observe the process of decontextualization (the word is no longer tied to a specific kind of event, or even to the presence of ducks or duck-like things), also the emergence of referential uses (as when the child names an object), and even semantic over-extension (as when the word is applied to a broader range of objects than is sanctioned in the adult language). Although it does not fully conform with adult usage, the child's later usage is more language-like, precisely because it is taking on a symbolic character.

3.4 Symbolic, phonological, and semantic units

Saussure, as we have seen, characterized a language as a system of signs. Moreover, for Saussure, the sign was the only legitimate object of linguistic study. Phonology was of linguistic interest only to the extent that sound patterns functioned as signifiers. Likewise, meanings were of linguistic interest only to the extent that they were symbolized by sound patterns. I refer to this position as 'strict Saussureanism'.

Cognitive Grammar shares with Saussure the belief that language is inherently symbolic (even though, in the last section, I slightly revised the Saussurean notion of the symbol.) In contrast to strict Saussureanism, however, we need to accord a certain degree of autonomy to both phonological structure and semantic structure. Although they participate in symbolic relations, meaning and sound may be subject to their own principles of organization, which are potentially independent of the symbolic resources of a language. Whereas Saussure had recognized only one object of linguistic study, namely the linguistic sign, Cognitive Grammar recognizes three objects of study: symbolic units, phonological structures, and semantic structures.

In this section I expand upon the above remarks. I begin with some of Saussure's statements, and then go on to suggest why strict Saussureanism needs to be abandoned.

3.4.1 Strict Saussureanism

In several passages in the *Cours*, Saussure promotes the linguistic sign as the only legitimate object of linguistic enquiry.

The linguistic sign is a two-sided entity ('une entité à deux faces'); the two sides are intimately linked, in such a way that each triggers the other ('ces deux éléments sont intimement unis et s'appellent l'un l'autre': Saussure 1964: 99). The two sides—concepts and sound pattern—have no existence independent of their role in the linguistic sign. Thought, Saussure proclaimed, was intrinsically unstructured; it was a vague and shapeless mass; it was like a swirling cloud, where no shape is intrinsically determinate. Concepts only emerge through the intervention of the linguistic system. Without the system of signs that is a language, there can be no concepts:

Psychologically, setting aside its expression in words, our thought is simply a vague, shapeless mass. . . . [W]ere it not for signs, we should be incapable of differentiating any two ideas in a clear and constant way. In itself, thought is like a swirling cloud, where no shape is intrinsically determinate. No ideas are established in advance, and nothing is distinct, before the introduction of linguistic structure.[12] (Saussure/Harris 1983: 155)

The same is true of phonological substance. Sound is inherently featureless; it is only through the mediation of the system of linguistic signs that sound acquires structure:

The substance of sound is no more fixed or rigid than that of thought. It does not offer a ready-made mould, with shapes that thought must inevitably conform to. It is a malleable material which can be fashioned into separate parts in order to supply the signals which thought is in need of.[13] (Saussure/Harris 1983: 155)

The linguistic sign serves to structure both thought and sound *simultaneously*:

The characteristic role of a language [i.e. a system of linguistic signs: JRT] in relation to thought . . . is to act as intermediary between thought and sound, in such a way that the combination of both necessarily produces a mutually complementary delimitation of units. Thought, chaotic by nature, is made precise by this process of segmentation. But what happens is neither a transformation of thoughts into matter, nor a transformation of sounds into ideas. What takes places, is a somewhat mysterious process by which 'thought-sound' evolves divisions, and a language takes shape with its linguistic units in between those two amorphous masses.[14] (Saussure/Harris 1983: 100–1)

Saussure appealed to various analogies in an attempt to explain this aspect of his thinking. For example, he compared the thought-sound relation to the two sides of a piece of paper. You cannot cut one side of the paper without at the same time cutting the other side. With respect to language, this would

---

[12] 'Psychologiquement, abstraction faite de son expression par les mots, notre pensée n'est qu'une masse amorphe et indistincte. . . . [S]ans le secours des signes, nous serions incapables de distinguer deux idées d'une façon claire et constante. Prise en elle-même, la pensée est comme une nébuleuse où rien n'est nécessairement délimité. Il n'y a pas d'idées préétablies, et rien n'est distinct avant l'apparition de la langue.' (Saussure 1964: 155)

[13] 'La substance phonique n'est pas plus fixe ni plus rigide; ce n'est pas un moule dont la pensée doive nécessairement épouser les formes, mais une matière plastique qui se divise à son tour en parties distinctes pour fournir les signifiants dont la pensée a besoin.' (Saussure 1964: 155)

[14] 'Le rôle caractéristique de la langue vis-à-vis de la pensée [est] de servir d'intermédiaire entre la pensée et le son, dans des conditions telles que leur union aboutit nécessairement à des délimitations réciproques d'unitées. La pensée, chaotique de sa nature, est forcée de se préciser en se décomposant. Il n'y a donc ni matérialisation des pensées, ni spiritualisation des sons, mais il s'agit de ce fait en quelque sorte mystérieux, que la "pensée-son" implique des divisions et que la langue élabore ses unités en se constituant entre deux masses amorphes.' (Saussure 1964: 156)

Saussure and linguistic relativism

The point is not often made, but it is clear that Saussure's understanding of the linguistic sign must lead to an extreme form of linguistic relativism.

Relativism is a view traditionally associated with Edward Sapir and Benjamin Whorf (the 'Sapir–Whorf' hypothesis), rather than with Saussure. Linguistic relativism maintains that the concepts symbolized in any given language are products of the language system itself, they are not founded in universal aspects of cognition. Since, on this view, there are no pre-linguistic concepts — recall Saussure's statement that thought is inherently shapeless — we should expect that each language will structure thought in different, and very likely incommensurate ways. Since each language encapsulates a unique conceptualization of the world, we should not expect to find similar concepts symbolized in different languages, and translation from one language to another should be impossible in principle. In practice, followers of Saussure have tended not to adopt a position of extreme relativism which is entailed by Saussure's views of the linguistic sign.

While Cognitive Grammar accepts that the conceptualizations symbolized in a given language might be specific to that language, it rejects the idea that, without the mediation of language, thought and sound are inherently unstructured. On the contrary, it is hypothesized that facets of general cognition, such as categorization, figure-ground organization, metaphor, and so on, serve to structure cognition and guarantee the universality of certain basic conceptual and phonological structures.

mean that one cannot segment the phonological structure of an expression without at the same time making corresponding semantic segmentations (and vice versa). The analyst can, of course, choose to focus on meanings, without regard to the sound patterns that symbolize them; likewise, one can study sound patterns without regard to the symbolized concepts. But these, according to Saussure, are not linguistic enterprises—they are 'pure phonology' and 'pure psychology', not linguistics.[15] (Saussure/Harris 1983: 157)

Strictly speaking, then, for Saussure there was only one object of study in linguistics: the linguistic sign, in its two-sided essence. Figure 3.2 (p. 56) shows how strict Saussureanism might be implemented. The Figure shows two component units, A/a and B/b, which combine to form a complex unit C/c. (Capitals 'A', 'B', and 'C' represent semantic units, phonological units are represented by small letters, 'a', 'b', and 'c'. The slash '/' represents the symbolic relation between the units.)

In order to make the example more concrete, you may think of A/a as the noun *dog*, which associates the concept [DOG] with the phonological form

[15] Roman Jakobson adopted a similar view, insisting on the 'indissoluble dualism' of the linguistic sign: "Sound and meaning—both these fields have to be thoroughly incorporated into the science of language: speech sounds must be consistently analyzed in regard to meaning, and meaning, in turn, must be analyzed with reference to the sound form." (Jakobson 1971: 103–4)

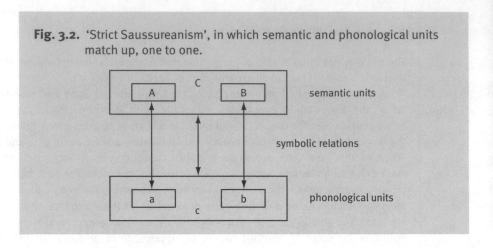

Fig. 3.2. 'Strict Saussureanism', in which semantic and phonological units match up, one to one.

[dɒg], and B/b as the plural morpheme (or, more precisely, a particular instance of the plural morpheme), which associates the concept of plurality [PLURAL] with the phonological form [z]. The semantic units combine to give the concept of a plurality of dogs. The concept is symbolized by the complex phonological structure [dɒgz], which results from the combination of the two component phonological structures. More schematically, A/a might represent a symbolic unit [NOUN], B/b the plural morpheme, and C/c the general pattern for forming a plural noun through combination of A/a and B/b. One could fill out A/a, B/b, and C/c with other contents. For example, C/c could represent the pattern for Adjective–Noun combination, or a specific instance of Adjective–Noun combination, such as *big dog*.

3.4.2 Abandoning strict Saussureanism

Strict Saussureanism, as depicted in Figure 3.2, has to be rejected. Even for such an apparently straightforward example as *dogs* the Figure is misleading. According to Figure 3.2, semantic units, whether these be simple or internally complex, match up, one-to-one, with the phonological units which symbolize them; conversely, each phonological unit matches up with a semantic unit.[16] Now, while it may be legitimate to regard the complex phonological structure [dɒgz] as resulting from the alignment of its two constituents—you get the complex form [dɒgz] by *saying* [z] after [dɒg]—you do not get the complex concept [DOGS] by putting the concept [PLURAL] behind the concept [DOG]. Neither is it a question of somehow 'adding' the concept of plurality to the concept [DOG]. If anything, adding the concepts together would give the concept of a plural dog, which would be absurd. What we need is a mechanism for integrating the component concepts into a single, more complex structure.

---

[16] This situation, in which units at one level match up, one-to-one, with units on another level is sometimes referred to as 'bi-uniqueness'.

Whatever the nature of this mechanism, it operates independently of the temporal alignment of the component phonological structures [dɒg] and [z].

A further problem arises with plural nouns such as *men*. While *dogs* can be segmented, on the phonological level, into its component parts, this is scarcely possible with *men*. Semantically, *men* is analogous to *dogs*. If *dogs* designates a plurality of entities of the kind 'dog', *men* designates a plurality of entities of the kind 'man'. But *men* cannot be chopped up, on the phonological level, into a phonological unit [mæn] and a phonological unit symbolizing [PLURAL].

Moreover, Figure 3.2 fails to represent the fact that a phonological form such as [dɒg] itself exhibits internal structure, in that it is composed of three phonetic segments, none of which, in itself, has any symbolic significance.

How can we accommodate cases like these into a symbolic view of language? We do not want to abandon the central role of the symbolic unit. However, we do want to attribute a certain 'autonomy' to both phonological and semantic structures. The situation we want to move towards is illustrated in Figure 3.3. Pride of place still goes to symbolic units, in that the phonological and semantic poles of the three units A/a, B/b, and C/c certainly contribute to phonological and semantic structures. But the phonological and semantic structures are not exclusively determined by the contributing units, they are subject to their own principles of organization.

I expand on these remarks in Chapters 5 and 6. In Chapter 5 I show why it is necessary to pursue what Saussure had dismissed as 'pure phonology'. Moreover, 'pure phonology' is not at all peripheral, or external, to a theory of language, but must form an integrated part of it. Then, in Chapter 6, I argue that a comparable state of affairs holds with respect to the semantic level. In dealing with semantic structures, we need to pursue what Saussure had dismissed as 'pure psychology'. The combination of semantic and phonological units is addressed in Chapters 13 and 14.

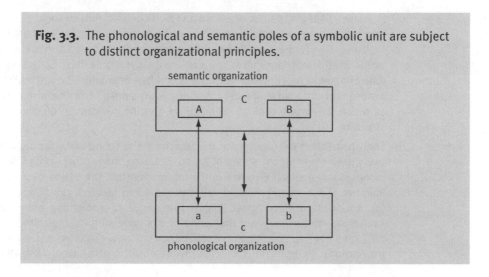

Fig. 3.3. The phonological and semantic poles of a symbolic unit are subject to distinct organizational principles.

3.4.3 A note on autonomy

To propose that phonological and semantic structures are subject to their own principles of organization is tantamount to claiming that phonology and semantics constitute autonomous levels of language. The concept of autonomy enjoys considerable currency in modern linguistic theory. Essentially, a particular level is autonomous if it needs to be described in terms of elements that are specific to that level and which cannot be reduced to elements on another level.

The notion of autonomy is especially associated with modular views of language and the mind (cf. p. 7). My use of the term here might seem to be in conflict with a central assumption of the Cognitive Linguistic approach, namely, that language is not to be located in a special module of the mind, but is grounded in general aspects of human cognition. An autonomous level of organization, however, does not logically entail modularity. It is certainly *not* being proposed that phonology and semantics reside in discrete modules of the mind; the claim is, quite simply, that these levels may be organized in ways that are independent of their role in symbolic relations.

Study questions

1. Onomatopoeia is often cited as a counterexample to the claim that the relation between sound and meaning is arbitrary. However, the number of onomatopoeic words, in a given language, is quite small. Moreover, even words that are felt by speakers of a language to be onomatopoeic often display a good deal of language-specific conventionalization. The following study questions invite you to investigate this possibility.

    (a) In many languages, names of animal and bird cries are felt, by speakers of those languages, to be onomatopoeic. If these words were truly imitative of the sounds that they signify there ought be quite a lot of phonetic similarity between the words in different languages. You can easily investigate this. Collect words in different languages which name the cries of different animals. Do you find that the words in the different languages are phonetically similar? Consider also the extent to which the words conform to language-specific constraints on phonological structure.

    (b) English speakers will often report that, for them, the sound of the word *slap* [slæp] really does resemble the sound of a slap. There are many other words (especially monosyllables) which give rise to the impression that the sound of the word is imitative of its meaning. For example, speakers may feel that *clap* [klæp] imitates the sound of a clap, *bump* [bʌmp] the sound of something bumping into something, and *slurp* [slɜːp] the sound of someone slurping their drink. Design an experiment to investigate whether there is any objective basis for these impressions. (Suggestion: You could invite subjects, who have no knowledge of

English, to guess which out a set of phonetically similar words—e.g. *slap* [slæp], *chap* [tʃæp], *crap* [kræp], *clap* [klæp], *slick* [slɪk], *slump* [slʌmp], *slurp* [slɜːp]—designates the action of slapping.)

Suppose the results of this experiment are negative, that is, non-English speakers fail to identify the supposedly onomatopoeic words with better than chance accuracy. What, in this case, could be the basis for English speakers' very strong intuitions that certain words *are* imitative of their meanings?

2. Traffic signs often have an iconic component. Study the inventory of international road signs. Which aspects of these are iconic, symbolic, and indexical?

3. Gestures often have an iconic and/or indexical component (as well as a symbolic component). Study some gestures from this point of view. You might find it useful to distinguish between gestures that *accompany* speech (such as rhythmical hand and head movements), and gestures that *replace* speech (such as gestures that mean 'Yes', 'Very good', 'I don't know', 'Maybe'). Desmond Morris *et al.*'s *Gestures* (1979) is a mine of information on gestures used throughout Europe and the Mediterranean region.

4. I suggested in section 3.1.2 that the prepositions *in*, *at*, and *on* designate concepts; knowing how to use these words correctly in order to designate spatial relations involves being able to make the appropriate categorizations of spatial relations.

To a monolingual English speaker, the spatial concept [ON] seems both natural and unitary—natural, in the sense that the concept appears to inhere in the nature of things, and unitary, in the sense that 'on'-relations seem to be basically the same. However, Dutch and German do not treat the English concept as unitary; moreover, these closely related languages divide up 'on'-relations in rather different ways.

English	German	Dutch
handle on pan	an	aan
bandaid on leg	an	op
ring on finger	an	om (= 'around')
fly on door	an	op
picture on wall	an	aan
cup on table	auf	op

(based on Bowerman 1996: 154–5)

How could one characterize the concepts designated by the prepositions in English, Dutch, and German?

If you have access to speakers of German and Dutch, extend the database to include further examples of 'on'-relations in these languages. You might also wish to consider data from a wider range of languages, and to contrast 'on'-relations with the relations of 'in' and 'at'.

In order to elicit data on spatial relations, it may be useful to first prepare simple drawings of objects placed in different locations, and then to ask your subjects how they would describe the depicted situations.

5. I suggested in section 3.3.1 that the use of symbols may only emerge at around the age of one. Consider the following report of an eight-month-old girl:

> Jacqueline smiles and says *aa* as soon as the door to her room opens, before seeing the person who enters. She therefore understands by this sign that someone will enter. (Piaget 1952: 195, quoted in Ingram 1989: 124)

   How would you characterize — in terms of its iconic, indexical, and symbolic aspects — the child's utterance *aa*?

6. It has often been observed that the first words that a child uses are typically bound to a particular kind of context. Some examples are cited by Barrett (1995: 365): Adam says *boo* when hiding behind a curtain; he says *sweep* while sweeping with a broom; he says *ball* when looking at and playing with balls (of various kinds), also to request a ball.
   Are these vocalizations symbolic? Why (not)?

7. I suggested (section 3.3.1) that Adam's earliest use of the word *duck*, as reported by Barrett, is not symbolic, it is simply an integral part of a little game that the child had invented for himself.
   We may wonder whether aspects of adult language retain traces of this early non-symbolic usage. We should need to find cases where (i) a vocalization is tied *exclusively* to a particular context or routine, and (ii) the vocalization constitutes an *integral part* of the routine, such that, without the vocalization, the routine could not be said to have taken place.
   Can such examples be found in adult language?

Further reading

A close reading of Saussure's *Cours de linguistique générale* cannot be recommended too strongly to every student of linguistics. Over the last twenty years or so, I must have read the *Cours* half a dozen times, and each reading brings new insights. If you read French, read the French text. For those who cannot cope with the French original, there is an excellent English translation by Roy Harris. A concise introduction to Saussure's thought and influence is Culler (1976). Harris's commentary on the *Cours* (Harris 1987) highlights the salient features of Saussure's thought, as well as the tensions and deficiencies.

On signs and symbolic systems. Ch. 1 of Dirven and Verspoor (1998) gives a good, basic introduction to signs, symbols, and icons, and their relevance in linguistic theory. For more advanced discussion, see Keller (1998) and Ch. 3 of Deacon (1997).

The idea that semantic and phonological structure constitute independent levels of linguistic organization is developed in some detail in Jackendoff (1997). (Note, however, that Jackendoff proposes that syntax also constitutes a separate level of organization.)

CHAPTER 4

The symbolic thesis: Some questions and answers

In the preceding chapters I introduced the Cognitive Grammar claim that language is inherently symbolic. Following Saussure, I emphasized the mental nature of the linguistic sign. The sign does not associate a thing out there in the world with an actual pronunciation. Both poles of the linguistic sign—the concept and the acoustic image—are mental entities, stored inside a person's mind.

In this chapter I address some objections that might be raised against this view of language. Given the centrality of the symbolic thesis to Cognitive Grammar, it is important to address these right at the beginning. Doing so will also provide an opportunity to sketch out some of the demands that a symbolic account of language will have to meet.

The first two objections query the feasibility of building a theory of language on mental entities, such as concepts. The next two are more in the way of problems that any linguistic theory, actually, would have to face, though their treatment within a symbolic approach might appear at first sight to be especially problematic. Finally, I address the status of referring expressions, which, contrary to the mentalist conception of the linguistic sign, do indeed appear to associate an actual acoustic-phonetic event with an entity out there in the world.

4.1 First objection: It is irresponsible to talk about things in the mind, such as 'concepts'

The first objection concerns the mentalist orientation of Cognitive Grammar:

- Cognitive Grammar claims that linguistic units—whether phonological, semantic, or symbolic—are mental entities, located inside a person's mind. However, no one can have access to the contents of another person's mind. It is impossible, for example, for anyone to inspect the concept that a person associates with a phonological form. Does not this initial insistence on the mental status of linguistic units render any kind of linguistic analysis—and more especially, semantic analysis—irredeemably subjective, not to say speculative? Linguistic analysis must surely be based on observable, public phenomena, not on entities that, by definition, are private, and inaccessible to public scrutiny.

Given the subjective nature of concepts, quite a few linguists (and philosophers) have sought to exclude such entities from semantic analysis.

Consider John Lyons' (1977: 112–13) discussion of what he called 'conceptualism'. Lyons used the term to include 'any theory of semantics which defines the meaning of a word or other expression to be the concept associated with it in the mind of the speaker and hearer' (p. 112). By Lyons's definition, Cognitive Grammar would count as unashamedly conceptualist.[1]

While not denying that 'concept' might be a useful construct in psychological theory, Lyons argued that concepts need play no role whatsoever in linguistic theory. Suppose we say that in order to use the word *table* correctly (i.e. of tables) a person needs to 'have the concept' of table. To this, Lyons observes:

it could be argued that what is meant by having a concept of table is being able to identify members of the class of objects to which the word 'table' can be correctly applied when one is required to do so. (Lyons 1977: 113)

What would be the evidence that a person does have the concept? This would be the person's ability to use the word appropriately, i.e. of tables. But if we are able to judge whether a person does use the word appropriately, there is no need to bring in the concept as a criterion for correct use. Concepts become

---

[1] Cognitive Grammar is conceptualist in an even broader sense than that intended by Lyons. It not only proposes a conceptualist semantics. By recognizing that phonological representations are also, in a way, concepts (section 3.1.2), Cognitive Grammar also proposes a conceptualist phonology.

redundant. In fact, 'having the concept' and being able to use the word appropriately turn out to be one and the same thing.

In his later work, the philosopher Ludwig Wittgenstein also argued extensively against conceptualist views of meaning.[2] Suppose we say that the word *toothache* designates a particular kind of pain. Pain is a purely personal thing. I cannot feel your pain and you cannot feel mine. So how can I be sure that when you use the word *toothache* you are referring to the same kind of sensation that I am referring to when I use the word? I might, to be sure, ask you to try to describe what you feel when you have toothache. But in describing your toothache you inevitably have to use language. Now the same question arises. How can I know that the concepts that you attach to the words that you use when you describe your toothache are the same concepts as the ones that I associate with these words? We appear to have an infinite regress.

Wittgenstein's answer was that the meaning of a word is not a concept in the head but rules for the use of the word. How would I know whether a learner of English (a child, say, or a foreigner) has learned the word *toothache*? Not by inspecting the pain that the person associates with the word, nor by accessing the inner feelings of a person when they say *I've got a terrible toothache*. According to Wittgenstein, we determine whether a person knows the word on the basis of whether they use the word appropriately, in accordance with the (observable, and public) conventions for using the word.

More recently, another philosopher, Willard van Orman Quine, made the very same point. Quine rejects a conceptualist approach to language and meaning in favour of a purely observational theory. The meaning of a word *is* its use:

People tend to think of the meanings of expressions somewhat as if they were specimens in a museum of ideas, each labeled with the appropriate expression. Translation from one language into another consists in changing the labels. But John Dewey, and in later years Ludwig Wittgenstein, stressed rather that *there is no more to the meaning of an expression than the overt use that we make of the expression*. Language is a skill that each of us acquires from his fellows through mutual observation, emulation, and correction in jointly observable circumstances. When we learn the meaning of an expression we learn *only what is observable in overt verbal behavior and its circumstances*. (Quine 1987: 130; emphasis added)

As a matter of fact, Quine has packed a number of separate issues into this short paragraph, not all of them relevant to his critique of conceptualism. Quine is critical of the view that each word has a fixed meaning which can be accessed and contemplated independently of its use in a language. Cognitive Grammar would fully endorse Quine's misgivings on this. A major topic of Chapter 22 will be, precisely, the context-dependence of word meanings. But

---

[2] Representative of the later Wittgenstein are the *Philosophical Investigations* (1978) and *The Blue and Brown Books* (1958).

to accept that meanings are context dependent by no means nullifies the conceptualist approach, as Quine implies that it does.

On the face of it, though, Quine certainly does seem to have a point when he asserts that to know a word is to know how to use it. When we evaluate a person's knowledge of a word (and, indeed, their knowledge of any other element in a language) we do so by examining the use that they make of the word, we do not ask the person about the concept that the word designates, and would probably disregard any information in this regard that they might volunteer.[3] But emphasis on matters of use does not obviate the need for a mentalist approach to meaning. To suggest otherwise is to beg two questions:

(i)   What are the criteria for judging whether such-and-such a usage is in fact appropriate?

(ii) How do speakers of a language come to know the criteria for judging that such-and-such a usage is indeed appropriate?

Although the way in which a word is used may well be a public phenomenon, observable to all and sundry, knowledge of how to use a word is not (generally) in the public domain. There are, to be sure, scattered cases where the linguistic watchdogs of our society seek to prescribe, explicitly, how such-and-such a word shall be used. But such prescriptive advice is on the margins of language. Most people, even when they are aware of such prescriptions, are sensible enough to ignore them. In general, rules of usage are no more public than concepts.

We cannot, it seems to me, avoid the conclusion that knowledge of correct usage must also reside in the mind, no less than concepts. True, in evaluating usage, we evaluate publicly observable events. But the evaluation rests on criteria (i.e. knowledge of the rules of usage) that are not, in general, observable and open to public scrutiny. To eliminate concepts in the head—as Quine and Lyons sought to do—does not remove the need to describe the mental structures that condition the use of a word.

There is a more general issue here. Linguists of many theoretical persuasions would concur that the aim of linguistic theory is to *explain* the facts of usage in terms of knowledge residing in a speaker's mind; linguistic theories aim to characterize this mental knowledge by proposing hypotheses about what it is that a person knows. (This is the basic assumption of cognitive linguistics with a small 'c'; see section 1.1.) Different linguistic theories offer different kinds of hypotheses about the nature of this knowledge. A specific assumption of Cognitive Grammar is that the ways in which words are used follow from their role in the conceptualizations that speakers wish to symbolize. To be sure, the conceptual structures proposed in Cognitive Grammar are

---

[3] Wittgenstein (1978: 182) made just this point: If a person *uses* words as we do, wouldn't we be inclined to think that they *understand* them as we do, irrespective of what they say about their understanding of the words?

speculative, in the sense that they are not available to public scrutiny. But the same could be said of just about any construct proposed by a cognitive linguistic theory.

4.2 Second objection: The fixed-code fallacy

A further criticism of the symbolic thesis brings in the role of language in communication. The argument goes like this:

- If people are to communicate using an inventory of linguistic signs (or symbolic units), it is necessary that each member of the speech community has access to the same sign inventory. There has to be shared knowledge of the concepts and of the symbolic relations between concepts and sound patterns; for each sign in the language, each user of the language must associate the same phonological form with the same concept. But if concepts are invisible to public scrutiny, there is no way of knowing which concepts other speakers are associating with each of the phonological forms, let alone of establishing that different speakers associate the same concept with a given form.

These objections have been developed in some detail by Roy Harris.

In the Further readings to Chapter 3, I recommended Roy Harris's *Reading Saussure* (1987) for its sympathetic and insightful commentary on the *Cours de linguistique générale*. In many of his other writings, however, Harris launches into a trenchant critique of Saussure, even going so far as to claim that Saussure's conception of the linguistic sign perverted the whole course of twentieth-century linguistics.

Harris (1981) identifies two related fallacies of Saussure's legacy, the 'fixed code fallacy' and the 'telementation fallacy'. According to Harris, a symbolic view of language, which Saussure promoted, construes linguistic knowledge as 'essentially a matter of knowing which words stand for which ideas' (p. 9). Shared knowledge of the coding relations makes it possible to 'transfer thoughts from one mind to another' (p. 9). Telementation—the transfer of thought between minds—is a fallacy because it rests on the presumption of a fixed code: it requires that all members of a speech community share the same associations of words and ideas. This in turn is a fallacy because ideas are invisible to public scrutiny, so there can be no assurance that different speakers do associate the same forms with the same ideas. Since thoughts are also invisible to public scrutiny, there can be no way of ascertaining whether 'telementation' has taken place successfully.

What are we to make of this? The first point to note is that language can very well function as a means of communication without the requirement that language knowledge is represented identically in the minds of its users. Adults and young children, native speakers and foreign learners, speakers of

markedly distinct dialects, can all communicate with each other with reasonable satisfaction, even though there may be gross differences in the linguistic
system controlled by the conversation partners. But even within a reasonably
homogeneous speech community we can still expect small differences between
the symbolic resources commanded by the different speakers. Langacker,
indeed, regards it as 'self-evident' that no two speakers of a language will ever
share 'precisely the same linguistic system' (FCG1: 376).

Not only this, but the sharing of a linguistic code is only one of many
factors (and perhaps not even the most important one) that contribute to
the success of linguistic communication. Consider, by way of illustration, the
following piece of (constructed) dialogue (Tannen 1982: 224–5).

(1) Wife: John's giving a party. Wanna go?
    Husband: OK.
    Wife: I'll call and tell him we're coming.
    [some time later]
    Wife: Are you sure you want to go to that party?
    Husband: OK, let's not go. I'm tired anyway.

While there are many ways of 'reading' this conversation (or pair of conversa-
tions), one reading has it that both husband and wife end up agreeing to do
something which is contrary to the real wishes of both of them. (Each wants
to go to the party, though they jointly negotiate not to do so.) It would take us
too far afield to examine how this bizarre outcome could be reached, by two
speakers who appear to share the same language system. The point is, the
existence (or otherwise) of a fixed linguistic code has very little to do with how
this outcome is reached.

The idea of a 'fixed code' is misleading. A more appropriate metaphor may
be the one recently suggested by Tuggy. Adjusting, or 'tuning', one's knowledge of a language to that of an interlocutor is seen as a process of
'experimentation'. Every act of communication is a test of whether a speaker's
mental representation of the language conforms to that of an interlocutor:

Every time you use a structure in communication you are conducting an experiment,
betting that your interlocutor is going to understand. If he or she does so, your
hypothesis as to its meaning is confirmed, strongly, to the degree that that particular
structure was crucial to the communication. If miscommunication results, your
hypothesis is disconfirmed to the extent that the particular structure seems to be at
fault, and you will, often even consciously, adjust your hypothesis about its meaning.
Every time your interlocutor uses the structure and what he or she is saying makes
sense, the hypothesis is again confirmed. When repeated experimentation of this sort
starts to produce confirmatory results, you stop worrying about the structure at all
and just use it: you 'just know' what it means; but your continued successful use
continues to confirm the hypothesis ever more strongly. (Tuggy 1999: 353)

Observe that Tuggy's argument is framed in terms of communication and
miscommunication. While Harris encourages us to sneer at the very idea of

telementation, it is surely the desire to transfer thought that motivates quite a lot of linguistic activity. The fact that I say anything at all to other people is surely motivated by my desire to make manifest some conceptualization that I entertain, in the expectation that my communication partner will interpret my utterance as an expression of my conceptualization. It is surely a matter of everyday experience that on hearing another person's utterance we attempt to work out what the person meant. That is, what conceptualization that person was attempting to symbolize, however tentatively and fragmentarily, using the linguistic resources available to him or her.

But what about the more general, 'philosophical' idea that no one can have direct access to another person's mental life? While it is trivially true that I cannot enter another person's mind, I can certainly believe that another person's mental experience is of the same kind as mine. This is because I have a *theory* (Fodor 1980) of human beings, their emotions, sentiments, and mental processes. The theory tells me that other humans are constructed in much the same way as I am, and have minds much the same as mine. This entitles me to attribute to other humans an inner life of concepts and experience on the evidence of even minimal overt behaviour (including linguistic behaviour). What I experience in certain circumstances will be (more or less) what you experience in similar circumstances (so I believe). It would be odd for me to say that my goldfish has toothache, since I do not believe that goldfish have a mental life that is at all comparable with mine. When my computer goes 'eep' as I press some illegal combination of keys I would not for a moment believe that my computer feels a twinge of pain. But when another person says, 'There's a dead cat lying by the side of the road', I certainly do believe that they are reporting a conceptualization not at all dissimilar to the one that I would experience if I saw a dead cat lying by the side of the road.

Our social life is governed by theories of how other human beings are— namely, much the same as we are. Interestingly, Lieberman (1991), a linguist-cum-evolutionary biologist, has argued that the 'uniquely human' ability to *empathize*, i.e. to 'get inside' other people's minds, might have been a precondition for the evolution of symbolic language. It is empathy that enables a person to overcome the 'telementation fallacy', and to attribute to other human beings conceptualizations roughly compatible with their own.

Moreover, linguistic usage constantly reminds us that people do attribute thoughts, concepts, and an inner life to other humans. There is nothing in the least peculiar about my asking a person what they *think* about such-and-such, about my wondering whether a person really *believes* such-and-such, or about asking a person what they *meant* in saying such-and-such. On a purely observational theory of language and meaning, which denies the conceptual nature of meaning, such enquiries would have to be regarded as bizarre, verging on the nonsensical. In our everyday use of language we take it for granted that other humans do have an inner conceptual life, and that they use language in order to symbolically represent (aspects of) their conceptualizations.

Autism

Baron-Cohen *et al.* (1985) raise the intriguing possibility that autistic children's impairment may be related to their inadequate understanding of other minds. They report an experiment in which three groups of children — normal, retarded, and autistic — saw a doll putting a marble into a basket. The doll went off, and the children saw the marble moved to another location. The doll came back, and the children were asked where the doll would look for her marble. The normal and retarded children were able to put themselves into the mind of the doll, as it were, and responded that the doll would look in the basket, which is where the doll had last seen it. The autistic children indicated that the doll would look in the place where *they* had seen the marble go. They appeared unable to dissociate their own understanding of the situation from that of a participant in it. One component of the children's impairment, then, may be their inability to recognize, not so much that other persons have minds, but that other persons might construe a situation differently from themselves. Individuals who have this impairment will presumably lack the motivation to communicate, as well as a sense of what can be appropriately communicated.

The use of language for communicative purposes rests on the belief that other persons have minds much like our own. But we must also believe that the contents of other people's minds are not quite the same as the contents of own minds. We must attribute different states of knowledge, different perspectives, and different construals, to different persons. Unless this were so, there would be no rationale for our ever saying anything to anyone. In fact, the rapid development of language acquisition from around the age of two has been linked to the child's realization of just these properties of other minds.

When the human child [at around two years of age] acquires the concept of other minds, it realizes that other people are unaware of its thoughts and feelings and that it is unaware of theirs. This is the first time that intentional transmission of novel (unshared) information is logically possible . . . It is after the age of two years, then, that linguistic communication begins in earnest. (Locke 1995: 294)

4.3 Third objection: Can we claim that all words symbolize concepts?

Let us assume the general correctness of a symbolic, 'conceptualist' view of language. If we try to implement this approach we quickly run into a number of difficulties. One problem is the following:

- Let us grant that some words in a language (*house, table, toothache*) designate concepts. There are surely many words for which this seems not to be the case. What could be the concepts symbolized by *and, the, of, whenever, anyway*, and countless more? These words are certainly not meaningless. At the very least, it seems that we need two theories of meaning, one for concept-designating words, and another for these other kinds of word.

There does seem to be a genuine problem here. Compare, for example, the words *house* and *anyway*. It seems not unreasonable (*pace* Quine, Lyons, and others) to say that *house* designates a concept. Given my preliminary characterization of a concept as a principle of categorization (section 3.1.2), we might even set about characterizing this concept. We could meaningfully ask such questions as: What is it about an entity that causes us to categorize it as a house? What needs to go into the house-concept, given that the word *house* can be applied to this, this, and this? It would be rather odd, I think, to frame an account of the meaning of *house* solely in terms of how the word is used. (What *is* the use of the word *house*, if not to designate the house-concept?)

It is just the other way round with a word like *anyway*. It sounds weird to talk about the 'concept' of *anyway*. On the other hand, it would be quite natural to describe how this word is used. For example, we could say that the word is typically used when a speaker wishes to return to the main topic after a brief digression: *Well, anyway, as I was saying. . . .* Indeed, the Quinean doctrine, that the meaning of a word *is* its use, that an account of the use of a word exhausts its semantic description, seems particularly apt in this case. With respect to a word like *anyway*, Quine may have had a point.

Yet, even with respect to *anyway*, the situation is not quite so straightforward. For example, the word has other uses in addition to the one I just sketched. Consider the following (from Fauconnier 1994: 114):

(2) If you are good, Jesus will love you, but if you are bad, Jesus will love you anyway.

This looks like a very different use of *anyway*. What is its function? The first half of the sentence (*If you are good, Jesus will love you*) invites the inference that Jesus will love you *only if* you are good, i.e. if you are bad, Jesus will not love you. *Anyway* serves to cancel this inference; Jesus will love you *anyway*, whether you are good or bad.

We appear to have two quite different uses of *anyway*. What to do? We could simply stipulate that *anyway* has two kinds of uses. But this is not an optimal solution; it is, after all, the same word. We should prefer to say that the two uses are somehow related, that there is a reason why one and the same word can be used in two different ways. And the reason, if there is one, will be found in the conceptual content of the word, whatever this may be, and however we may want to characterize it.

What, though, are we to say about words like *the*? *The* is not meaningless. The word does make a contribution to the meaning of an expression in which it occurs. *I like fish* and *I like the fish* differ in meaning, and the difference must be attributed to the presence vs. absence of *the*. But to say that *the* symbolizes a concept again seems weird. Instead, we might want to say that *the* performs an operation on the concept [FISH], i.e. it converts a generalized fish-concept into a concept of a particular fish, or some particular fish, identifiable to speaker and hearer.

Cognitive Grammar takes the very strong position that all words and morphemes in a language are symbolic, i.e. that they are linguistic signs, in the Saussurean sense, and that each associates a sound pattern with a concept. Clearly, if this approach is to be viable, we will need an account of concepts—and of semantic structure in general—that is able to accommodate the meanings of all kinds of words, not just words like *tree*, *table*, *fish*, but also words like *anyway* and *the*.

How this is handled in Cognitive Grammar will become clearer as this book progresses.

4.4 Fourth objection: The problem of conceptual combination

A further difficulty with the symbolic thesis runs something like this:

- Let us assume that words (*all* words) symbolize concepts. What about combinations of words? What happens when we put words together, one after the other? The simple answer would be that combinations of words symbolize complex concepts, formed by combining the simpler word-concepts. But how do we get the meaning of a complex expression from the concepts symbolized by its component words? When we utter a sentence we articulate one word after another. But the meaning of a sentence is not simply a string of concepts, lined up, one after the other.

This seems to have been the problem that Wittgenstein had in mind when he (1978: 181) asked: 'How do the meanings of the individual words make up the sense of the sentence "I still haven't seen him yet"?' The point of Wittgenstein's question, presumably, was to suggest that we cannot arrive at the meaning of a complex expression simply by stringing together, one after the other, the concepts designated by the individual words; this, for Wittgenstein, appears to have been one cogent reason to reject the idea that words symbolize concepts.

How concepts are combined will be the topic of Chapters 12 and 22. In the meantime it should be emphasized that the issue of semantic combination is far from trivial, and is a challenge for any linguistic theory. In order to get the meaning of the expression *red car*, it is not enough, first, to activate the concept [RED], then to activate the concept [CAR]; this will not give us the complex concept [REDCAR]. Take, as another example, the expression *red pen*. The expression looks fairly straightforward—or at least, no more complicated than *red car*—until we realize that it can have two meanings. A 'red pen' could be a pen that is coloured red (on the outside), or it could be a pen that writes in red (and which might be a different colour on the outside). An account of concepts and conceptual combination will need to be able to account for this ambiguity. And what about an 'old friend'? This could be a friend who is advanced in years, a friend who has been a friend for a long time (and still is one), or a person who used to be a friend (though relations were since severed). These different interpretations seem to be built up from the concepts of [OLD] and [FRIEND], but the concepts are combined in different ways.

There is another aspect of complex expressions that has to be borne in mind. Combining symbolic units is not just a matter of combining concepts; combination also takes place at the phonological level. Just as the meaning of a complex expression is not just a string of concepts, so too the phonological structure of a complex expression is not just a procession of word pronunciations. When word forms are combined, all manner of phonological processes—assimilation, elision, liaison, re-syllabification, etc.—may come into play and modify the phonological shape of the constituent words. *Red*, spoken by itself, has the phonological shape [rɛd]. Yet *red pen* may be pronounced [rɛb˺ pɛn].[4]

4.5 Fifth objection: The case of referential expressions

The fifth objection raises the possibility that certain kinds of expressions might have properties different from those discussed so far. On the Saussurean view of the linguistic sign (which I have broadly endorsed), the word *tree* associates one mental entity (a concept) with another mental entity (an acoustic image). The word certainly does not link up an actual tree in the world with an actual utterance of the word. But is this true of all linguistic expressions?

- A noun, such as *tree*, can be incorporated into a referring noun phrase, such as *that tree there growing in the yard*. If uttered in appropriate circumstances, and with an appropriate intention on the part of the speaker, the expression does indeed refer to a real-word entity, i.e. to an actual tree, and the expression's pronunciation is not at all a mental sound pattern but an actual spatio-temporal event. We cannot therefore maintain that both sides of the linguistic sign are always mental entities. It looks as if we need to distinguish between signs proper, which are indeed mental entities, and utterances, which are real-world, spatio-temporal phenomena.

This looks like a valid point. We could address it by extending the Saussurean bipartite sign (Fig. 3.1) along the lines shown in Figure 4.1 (p. 72). The left portion incorporates the sign in its mental aspects, i.e. the concept and the acoustic image, as articulated by Saussure. The right portion represents the sign in its spatio-temporal manifestation, i.e. a phonetic-acoustic event used to

---

4 [b˺] stands for an unreleased stop.

Fig. 4.1. A possible extension of the Saussurean conception of the sign.

concept	referent
acoustic image	acoustic-phonetic event

Note: The left-hand part represents the sign in its mental aspects, the right-hand part shows the real-world entities related in an act of reference.

refer to a really existing entity. The top portion deals with the conceptual-referential aspects of the sign, the lower portion deals with the phonological-phonetic aspects.

Attractive as this approach appears, we need to exercise some caution. Consider more closely the entities to which referring expressions refer.

Common sense tells us that a referring expression refers to something outside the mind. However, Jackendoff (1983: ch. 2) has argued that common sense has it wrong. Linguistic expressions do not refer to things outside the mind; they refer to things as represented in the mind, and by the mind.

We must take issue with the naive position that the information conveyed by language is about the real world. We have conscious access only to the projected world—the world as unconsciously organized by the mind; and we can talk about things only insofar as they have achieved mental representation through these processes of organization. Hence *the information conveyed by language must be about the projected world.* (Jackendoff 1983: 29; author's emphasis)

'Red', for example, is not a property that things in the world actually have; it is a property that the mind ascribes to things, on the basis of how things are perceived by the mind (via the visual system). Even when used 'referentially', *red* still refers to a mental entity.

This, one might think, is just hair-splitting. Does it make any difference, after all, whether we regard 'red' as a property of things, or a property that the mind ascribes to things? As a matter of fact, it does make a difference, and there are good reasons why we need to maintain that even referring expressions refer to things in the mind.

4.5.1 Mental spaces

A useful construct here is the notion of a mental space (Fauconnier 1994). Referring expressions designate things that exist, not in the 'real world', but things in a 'mental space', that is, a situation as conceived by a language user. To be sure, a mental space might be 'veridical'. That is to say, it is taken to be an accurate model of the world as it 'really is'. But mental spaces need not be veridical. If used in the course of a fictional narrative, the expression *that tree there growing in the yard* does not at all refer to a real-world entity, but to an entity situated in the mental space set up by the fictional narrative. Interestingly, there may be no linguistic difference between an expression that refers to an entity in a veridical mental space and one that refers to an entity in a fictional mental space. Linguistically, a narrative which purports to depict events that 'really' happened is indistinguishable from a fictional narrative.

Sometimes, a speaker can juggle several mental spaces within a single utterance. The sentence in (3) would appear to express a contradiction; if the girl's eyes are blue, they cannot at the same time be green.

(3) The girl with green eyes has blue eyes.

Yet, with a little imagination, one can easily come up with an account in which (3) makes perfectly good sense. Suppose someone has painted a portrait, and has named the portrait 'Portrait of a girl with green eyes'. Observing the portrait (which does indeed depict a girl with green eyes), you recognize that the portrait is a portrait of your friend Isabella, and you know that Isabella in fact has blue eyes. You can make sense of (3) to the extent that 'the girl' that is referred to straddles two mental spaces—the mental space of 'reality', as you represent it to yourself, and the mental space of the portrait, as you perceive it. This situation is depicted in Figure 4.2. The circles represent two mental spaces, the 'portrait' (P) and 'reality' (R). Each mental space contains three entities: the girl (x), her eyes (y), and the colour of her eyes (z). The dotted lines establish links between the mental spaces. The girl (x) in the portrait is taken to be identical to the girl (x') in reality. The eyes (y) in the portrait correspond to the eyes (y') in reality. But the colour of the eyes does not

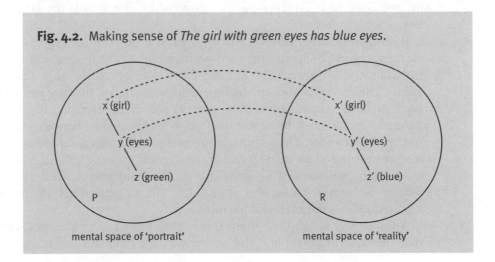

Fig. 4.2. Making sense of *The girl with green eyes has blue eyes.*

x (girl)   x' (girl)

y (eyes)   y' (eyes)

z (green)   z' (blue)

P   R

mental space of 'portrait'   mental space of 'reality' correspond in the two mental spaces. This is not the only interpretation of (3). Suppose that Isabella 'in reality' has green eyes, indeed, she is commonly known as 'the girl with green eyes'. Yet, in the portrait she is depicted as having blue eyes. Other scenarios can be imagined. Interestingly, none of these scenarios has any repercussions at all on the linguistic form of (3).

Linguistic expressions can explicitly introduce mental spaces. *I would like . . .*, *Just imagine . . .*, *What if . . .* are 'space-builders', which set up mental spaces of desire, imagination, and hypotheticality, against a 'base space'. Some adjectives specifically have the function of introducing non-veridical mental spaces. If you say that someone is suffering from an *imaginary illness*, the illness exists only in the mental space of the sufferer's imagination. A *would-be actor* is an actor only in the mental space of their perception of themselves. *Imaginary* and *would-be* are space-builders and signal that reference is being made to entities in the respective mental spaces.

The point of this excursus into mental spaces is to emphasize that the referent of a referring expression is an entity which inhabits a mental space and which is therefore also a mental entity. This means that there are no grounds for proposing a 'second dimension' to linguistic signs (represented by the right portion of Fig. 4.1), existing in the spatio-temporal world outside the mind. Our initial impression, that a referring expression (*that tree there growing in the yard*) refers to a real-world entity, results by default. In the default situation, mental spaces are veridical and are taken to be accurate models of the world as it is. But the default can easily be overridden.

What, then, is the relation between the concept associated with the word *tree*, considered as an item stored in the speaker's mental lexicon, and the word's referent (as determined in a particular act of speech)? The relation—and this is a topic I shall develop in future chapters—is the relation between a **schema** and an **instance**. The schema is a more abstract characterization, whose details get fleshed out in the instance. The concept [TREE] is schematic for the concept [THAT TREE THERE GROWING IN THE YARD]; the latter is an instance of the former.

A similar situation holds for phonological aspects of an expression. The events which make up an utterance—movements of the tongue and lips, perturbations of air molecules, firings in the auditory nerve—are real-world events. These events, however, are linguistic events only if they are perceived as such. In order to count as the phonological pole of an utterance, the acoustic-phonetic events much be conceptualized in terms of the phonological structure of the language. The relation between the phonological representation of *tree*, considered as an item stored in the speaker's mental grammar, and the mental representation of an utterance of the word *tree* is, once again, the relation between a schema and its instance. The more 'abstract' phonological representation is schematic for the utterance.

Another way of thinking about this is as follows. I suggested in Chapter 3 that the concept [TREE] and the acoustic image [triː] can be thought of as principles of categorization. Having the concept means being able to recognize instances of the category, just as having the acoustic image means being able to recognize acoustic events as instances of the image. This is the relation that exists between the left and right segments of Figure 4.1; the elements on the right are categorized by the elements on the left. Both are mental entities, the instances no less that the schemas which categorize them.

Study questions

1. Anyway. Follow up the remarks in the text on the meaning(s) of *anyway*. What are the different meanings/uses of this word? How might they be related? Do the different meanings cluster in a coherent way?

   A good way to start is to examine the account of *anyway* in a good diction ary (preferably, one that cites attested examples, such as the OED or the Collins COBUILD dictionary). Even better, extract some instances, together with their contexts, of *anyway* from a corpus, such as LOB (= Lancaster-Oslo-Bergen) corpus (see Box, p. 77 for details of online corpora). Try to group these according to similarities and establish conceptual links between them. You might also want to include examples of the two-word phrase *any way* in the investigation.

2. Mental spaces. Consider the following story (based on Fauconnier 1994: 36–7):

   Suppose that Orson Welles made a movie called *The Life and Death of Alfred Hitchcock*. The role of Alfred Hitchcock is played by Orson Welles, while (the real) Alfred Hitchcock makes a brief appearance as 'the man at the bus stop'. In the movie, the man at the bus stop (played by Alfred Hitchcock) pulls out a revolver and shoots dead the character Alfred Hitchcock (played by Orson Welles).

   (a) Which mental spaces are invoked by this story? What are the entities that inhabit the mental spaces? Use the pictorial conventions of Figure 4.2 to represent the mental spaces and their inhabitants, as well as the correspondence relations between entities in different mental spaces.

   (b) Consider the following assertions. How can you make sense of these with respect to the above story? Are any of the assertions untrue with respect to the story?

      (i)   Orson Welles shot Alfred Hitchcock.
      (ii) Alfred Hitchcock shot Orson Welles.
      (iii) Orson Welles shot Orson Welles.
      (iv) Alfred Hitchcock shot Alfred Hitchcock.
      (v)   Orson Welles shot himself.
      (vi) Alfred Hitchcock shot himself.

3. Meaningless words. *Of* is often said to be a meaningless morpheme which gets inserted in order to satisfy syntactic constraints. The argument might go

something like this. A verb can take a direct object: *destroy the city*. A noun cannot take a direct object: **destruction the city*. The nominal *destruction* requires a prepositional phrase as its complement, hence 'meaningless' *of* gets inserted to satisfy this requirement: *destruction of the city*.

Other prepositions have meanings that can be characterized with reasonable precision. *On*, in *the book on the table*, designates a specific kind of spatial relation between the book and (the surface of) the table; in this respect, the expression contrasts with *the book under the table*, *the book near the table*, etc. The case of *of* is more difficult, in that its meaning cannot easily be pinned down. Bear in mind, however, that *off* and *of* used to be stressed and unstressed variants of the same word. *Off* had the sense 'taken from'. We can still see a remnant of this sense in partitive expressions:

two of my children, some of the guests, a piece of the cake, hundreds of people

Consider now the use of *of* in the following. What kind of relation is being expressed here? Hint: if someone is a student, then, necessarily, there is some subject matter which they are (supposed to be) studying; if something is a photograph, then necessarily there is a scene which is depicted in the photograph.

a student of Wittgenstein, a photograph of me, a friend of Bob

The following pairs are not synonymous. What is the difference? Is *a friend of Bob* necessarily *Bob's friend*? Why is **a car of me* unacceptable? (Cf. the acceptability of *my car*.)

a student of Wittgenstein / Wittgenstein's student

a photograph of me / my photograph

a friend of Bob / Bob's friend

How would you characterize *of* in the following?

the state of California, the city of Rome, the crime of shoplifting, the idea of going there alone

this bitch of a problem, an angel of a girl, that idiot of a man, that bastard of a husband of mine

(The meaning of *of* is discussed in Langacker 1992.)

Online corpora of English

There are several web sites where corpus data can be accessed online. (Unfortunately, languages other than English are not well served by online corpora.) The following are recommended:

1. The British National Corpus (BNC): **http://thetis.bl.uk/lookup.html**. Up to 50 randomly selected citations are provided free of charge. If you need more than 50 citations, repeat the search.

2. COBUILD web site: **www.cobuild.collins.co.uk/**. A demonstration version is available at **http://titania.cobuild.collins.co.uk/form.html#democoll**. This is especially useful for studying the collocations of words.

3. LDC (Linguistic Data Consortium): **www.ldc.upenn.edu/ldc/noframe.html**. This provides access to the LOB (Lancaster-Oslo-Bergen) and other corpora. It is accessible only to registered users. (The LOB corpus is also available on CD-ROM.)

4. Invaluable also is the electronic edition of the Oxford English Dictionary. This is available on CD-ROM and online (to subscribers) at **www.oed.com/**.

5. It is possible to use internet search engines to obtain sample uses of a word or expression. For languages other than English, for which corpora are not available, this may be the only resource.

Further reading

In the Further reading suggestions to Chapter 3 I urged all aspiring linguists to read Saussure's *Course in General Linguistics* (1964). Here, I strongly recommend another of the classics of linguistics, Edward Sapir's *Language* (1921). (The book—it is quite short—was meant as a popular introduction to the subject.) Sapir fully accepted the idea that linguistic expressions symbolize concepts and he developed it in some detail. See especially his explanation of what it means to say that the word *house* refers to the concept [HOUSE] (1921: 11–13). Later in the book Sapir analyses the various concepts that are present in the sentence *The farmer kills the duckling*. Altogether, Sapir identifies no fewer than 13 distinct concepts in this sentence, including concepts of singularity, present time, definiteness, diminutive, and so on.

Sapir's conceptualist approach (and indeed conceptualist approaches in general) was given short shrift by Ruth Kempson (1977); any statements we make about concepts are 'entirely untestable and hence vacuous' (pp. 16–17). Arguments *for* the mental nature of referents are assembled by Jackendoff (1983).

For mental spaces, see the first couple of chapters of Fauconnier (1994).

CHAPTER 5

Phonological structure in Cognitive Grammar

As I explained in Chapter 2, there are only three objects of study in Cognitive Grammar: phonological structures, semantic structures, and symbolic structures, which relate a phonological structure and a semantic structure. Although our main focus must go to describing a language's symbolic resources, we need to bear in mind that phonology and semantics possess a certain degree of autonomy *vis-à-vis* symbolic associations (section 3.4.2). The phonological structure of a complex expression does not consist simply in the alignment of the phonological structures contributed by each of the component symbolic units. Phonology has its own principles of organization, which may operate independently of the semantic structures that an expression symbolizes.

The main burden of this chapter is to show why it is necessary to attribute a certain autonomy to phonological structures; the next chapter addresses a similar issue with regard to semantic structures.

5.1 Phonology in Cognitive Grammar

There is, I suspect, a widespread misconception about the scope of Cognitive Linguistics in general (and Cognitive Grammar in particular). This is that Cognitive Linguistics is concerned exclusively with semantic matters and with the meaning-bearing units of a language. The misconception probably arises through the equation of 'cognitive' with 'conceptual', and of 'conceptual' with 'semantic'. Phonological units—such things as syllables, phonemes, features— are not in themselves meaningful. Since they have no semantic value, it is easy to claim that they are not conceptual, hence that they do not lend themselves to a 'cognitive' treatment.[1]

Some of Langacker's statements on the opening pages of FCG1 could easily reinforce this view. (I should mention that in the course of *Foundations* this initial insistence on the centrality of meaning is considerably modified.[2])

From the symbolic nature of language follows the centrality of meaning to virtually all linguistic concerns. Meaning is what language is all about . . . Grammar is simply the structuring and symbolization of semantic content. (FCG1: 12)

It is, furthermore, a fact that the bulk of research within Cognitive Grammar (and Cognitive Linguistics in general) has been concerned with semantic matters. Topics such as lexical polysemy, metaphor, the semantics of spatial expressions, and the conceptual basis of clause structure, have no obvious relevance to phonology.

Yet the exclusion of phonology from the purview of Cognitive Grammar would be a grave error, for a number of reasons.

First, the exclusion of phonology would mean that Cognitive Grammar could not lay claim to being a comprehensive theory of language. It is a brute fact of language that phonology is organized according to principles that cannot be reduced to the symbolization of semantic structures. A theory of language has to incorporate these facts. A theory of language which does not do so is only half a theory of language.

Secondly, and more importantly, it is an error to equate 'cognitive', 'conceptual', and 'semantic' (or 'meaning-bearing'). The sound structure of a language is no less a 'cognitive' phenomenon than semantic structure. The phonology of a language is grounded in the human ability to produce, perceive, and,

---

[1] When I first presented an outline of this book to Oxford University Press, one of the Press's reviewers queried the inclusion of chapters on phonology. The reviewer appeared to assume that since phonology is not inherently symbolic, it is not subject to semantic analysis and therefore lies outside the concerns of Cognitive Linguistics.

[2] Whereas, on the first page of FCG1, Langacker had characterized a language as a 'set of linguistic signs', on p. 57 a language comes to be characterized as an 'inventory of conventional linguistic units'. The 'linguistic units' in question comprise phonological and semantic units, as well as symbolic units.

above all, to categorize sounds, and to form mental representations of sounds. And while phonology is not 'conceptual' in the sense that phonological units do not symbolize concepts, phonology *is* conceptual in the sense that phonological units can be regarded as concepts (cf. section 3.1.3)—phonological representations reside in the mind, and are invoked in acts of speaking and understanding. Langacker puts it like this:

Even the articulatory facets of speech sounds are properly regarded as conceptual. . . . Consider the segment [i]. From the perceptual standpoint, speakers can deal with this sound in either of two ways: they can actually hear the sound as a stimulus-driven perceptual event, or they can simply imagine hearing it, i.e. they can activate an auditory image of it (as in silent thought). Moreover, the auditory image is plausibly taken as primary, in the sense that it is used to categorize acoustic input as an instance of this particular sound. Exactly analogous observations can be made about the articulatory representation of [i]. A speaker can actually implement the articulatory routine and produce the sound, or he can simply imagine implementing it, i.e. he can mentally run through the motor routine without this mental activity being translated into muscular gestures. Once again the cognitive presentation is primary, in the sense that it directs the motor sequences but can also occur autonomously. (FCG1: 78–9).

Finally, the incorporation of phonology into Cognitive Grammar is not something that needs to be done grudgingly or reluctantly. On the contrary, once the conceptual nature of phonology is accepted we find that many of the constructs that are needed for the study of semantic and symbolic units can be insightfully applied to phonological units; equally, the study of phonology can furnish us with the apparatus for the insightful study of semantics and symbolic relations. In several places in this book I will in fact be pointing to analogies between the ways phonological, semantic, and symbolic units are structured. Phonology, therefore, is by no means an unwanted, or awkward appendage to the 'real' (= 'semantic') concerns of Cognitive Grammar. Far from detracting from the coherence and elegance of the theory, the incorporation of phonology only serves to strengthen it.

5.1.1 The autonomy of phonology

There is nothing controversial about the claim that phonology constitutes a distinct level of linguistic organization, which is independent of symbolic associations. On the contrary, the autonomy of phonology is one of the firmest results to have come out of the past couple of decades of phonological research. There are two aspects, in particular, which I want to highlight:

(i) The units of phonological structure (segments, syllables, feet, etc.) must be defined and identified in phonological terms, not with respect to their role in symbolic units. It may happen, in some languages, that phonological units such as the syllable or the foot do tend to coincide with symbolic units, such as the morpheme or the word.[3] But the very possibility of establishing such correspondences rests on the prior identification of the phonological units in question.

(ii) The phonological organization of language imposes constraints on what is an acceptable phonological structure. These constraints—which in Cognitive Grammar take the form of phonological schemas—may operate without regard to the symbolic value of the phonological units over which they apply. As a consequence the phonological structure of a complex expression cannot be regarded simply as the sequential alignment of the phonological structures contributed by the component symbolic units. It is as if the phonology has a life of its own, which 'coerces' the phonological content contributed by component units in accordance with strictly phonological principles.

I address these two topics in sections 5.2 and 5.3. First, though, I consider the more basic question of why phonology should be autonomous at all.

5.1.2 Why is phonology autonomous?

If one thinks about it for a moment, there are good reasons why phonology has to have its own principles of organization. Imagine a language in which this were not the case. In such a language each concept would link up to a unique phonological form, and each phonological form would be globally different from every other phonological form. The symbolic potential of such a language would be very limited. This is because the number of elementary concepts that could be symbolized would be constrained by the number of distinct sound shapes that a person could identify, remember, and keep separate one from another. Probably, the upper limit would not be much in excess of a hundred, if that.

Suppose, now, that the number of distinct sound shapes that a person is required to learn increases above this critical value. If the sound shapes are to be kept separate one from another some kind of internal analysis will have to take place. Speakers will try to identify smaller elements that recur within the global sound shapes, and they will look for patterns in the distribution of the smaller elements. Once segmentation has taken place, and once patterns for the combination of the segments have been recognized, the number of distinct sound shapes that can be identified, stored, and retrieved will increase massively. In fact, the number of sound shapes known to a mature speaker of a language will typically run into the tens of thousands, if not into the hundreds of thousands.

Arguably, the primitive language situation sketched out above—in which each elementary concept is symbolized by a globally distinct sound shape—

---

[3] In Mandarin, for example, the phonological pole of the morpheme (nearly always) coincides with a syllable. Even in English (see section 5.2.1) there is a tendency for content words to coincide with the foot.

does obtain during the earliest stages of language acquisition. The first months of acquisition by the child are characterized by a slow, laborious accumulation of global sound–meaning relationships. Then, between the ages of about one and a half and two years, the so-called 'vocabulary spurt' begins. Whereas previously the child may have spent up to twelve months to acquire the first 50 to 70 linguistic units, vocabulary acquisition suddenly takes off, with the child learning as many as ten new words each day. The vocabulary spurt is associated with the beginnings of syntax—the child begins to combine the linguistic units it has acquired into short, multi-word expressions (Bates and Goodman 1999). Although the matter is controversial, it has been argued that the vocabulary spurt is also associated with the beginnings of phonological analysis. Words are no longer unanalysed wholes, but are assigned an internal structure:

When children attain an expressive vocabulary of about seventy words . . . a veritable explosion occurs; suddenly they say four to ten new words a day. This growth in vocabulary entails a reorganization of the systems responsible for representing and producing words. The child's vocabulary is transformed into what is called a *phonological lexicon.*

At the beginning of the second year, the first spoken words are represented in the child's repertoire as units whose construction is relatively unanalyzed. . . . When the number of memorized words increases, this method of representation is no longer sufficient. Such undefined representations do not allow the items of a large vocabulary to be distinguished, stored, or produced. Children must therefore put their lexical house in order, so to speak, by arranging words in a systematic way that guarantees rapid and reliable access to the various elements of their vocabulary. This arrangement involves a more precise analysis of . . . the phonetic segments of words and their combination. (Boysson-Bardies 1999:190–1)

Support for this view comes from the fact that children, once they have discovered the phonological structure of speech, may modify their pronunciations of already acquired words in accordance with their emerging phonology. An often-cited example is the case of a child who, at the early one-word stage, pronounced the word *down* more or less correctly as [dæʊn] (Menn 1971). Subsequently, the word was adapted to the child's emerging phonological system, and pronounced [næʊn].[4]

The matter, as mentioned, is controversial. Ingram (1999) has argued for continuity in the acquisition of phonology, claiming that the units and constraints of phonology are present from the very beginning, albeit in simplified form. But whatever the truth of the continuity theory, the very possibility of acquiring a large inventory of symbolic units clearly rests on the possibility of attributing an internal structure to the phonological pole of the symbolic

---

[4] The child's later pronunciation reflects the emergence of consonant harmony. Consonant harmony is characteristic of child phonologies and stipulates that the consonants in a word have to share some common features. In the limiting case the consonants become identical.

units. The existence of phonological structure may be thought of as a natural, and almost inevitable solution to the problem of how to represent a vast, and in principle open-ended inventory of word-sized units in a form in which they can be reliably identified, stored, and accessed. A large lexicon requires a sophisticated phonology.

5.2 Phonological units

While different theorists might dispute the number and nature of phonological units, there is general agreement that we need to recognize, at a minimum, four units of phonological organization. These are the segment, the syllable, the foot, and the phonological phrase. In what follows, I restrict myself to a few basic remarks about these units. For a more detailed and systematic account the reader is referred to any of the standard textbook introductions to modern phonology.

Perhaps the most salient of the phonological units is the **syllable**. Syllables emerge through variations in sonority, which in turn are a function of the degree of constriction of the vocal tract: more sonorous segments (prototypically vowels) are associated with a relatively unobstructed flow of air through the vocal tract, while less sonorous segments (the consonants) involve some significant obstruction of the airflow. Minimally, a syllable consists of an opening gesture; an obstruction of the airflow is followed by a relatively unobstructed phase. The more sonorous phase constitutes the syllable nucleus, the less sonorous initial phase is known as the syllable onset. Depending on the constraints operating in a particular language, the nucleus may be followed by a less sonorous coda. The nucleus and coda together constitute the rhyme. A template for syllable structure is shown in Figure 5.1 (p. 84).

Speakers of a language usually have very clear and immediate intuitions concerning the number of syllables in an utterance. Even linguistically naive subjects generally have no difficulty counting out the syllables in a word or phrase.[5] Some writing systems (such as Japanese katakana and hiragana) are syllable based. Poetic metre is often defined in terms of the number of syllables per line; such is the case with the twelve-syllable alexandrine of classical French verse, or the eleven-syllable endecasillabo of Italian.

The syllable provides the context for identifying **segments**. Segments can be characterized by distinct packages of articulatory gestures, such as a particular manner of articulation in association with a certain place of articulation, with simultaneous voicing or voicelessness. A traditional phonetic transcription represents speech as a succession of segments. A segmental analysis is also the basis of alphabetic writing systems.

[5] There are, to be sure, some unclear cases. Does *socialism* consist of three or four syllables? (The answer depends on whether the final [m] is considered to be a syllabic nucleus.) Determining syllable boundaries within an utterance is also a controversial matter. *Discuss*, indubitably, consists of two syllables. But where should the boundary between the syllables be placed?

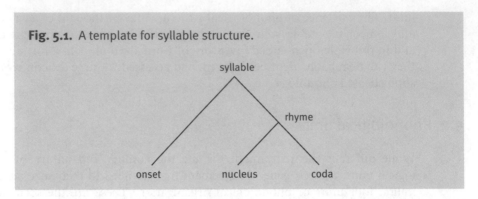

Fig. 5.1. A template for syllable structure.

Languages differ greatly with respect to the syllable structures that they allow and the kinds of segments that can fill the various syllable positions. The acceptable syllable structures within a given language can be represented by an array of **syllable schemas** appropriate for that language. Some languages, such as Māori, Hawaiian, and most Bantu languages, tolerate only two kinds of syllables: CV (consonant onset + vowel nucleus) and a degenerate variant, consisting simply of V (vowel nucleus only). Any utterance, in these languages, must terminate in a vowel, and adjacent consonants are disallowed. Japanese and Chinese permit only nasal consonants in syllable coda position; the schematic syllable for such languages can be represented as (C)V(N), where the parentheses indicate an optional element.[6] English, along with the other Germanic languages, allows a much greater variety of syllable structures, permitting complex patterns for the combination of segments in onset and coda positions.

The number of segments that a person identifies in an utterance is to some extent a function of the syllable structure of their language. Consider the word *Zimbabwe*. For an English speaker, it is clear that the word consists of eight segments, as shown in (1a) below. (The period '.' indicates a syllable boundary.) For a speaker of Shona (the major language of Zimbabwe) the word consists of only six segments (1b). Here, [ᵐb] and [bʷ] are complex segments, [ᵐb] being a pre-nasalized stop, [bʷ] a labialized stop. In a complex segment, two distinct articulations fuse into a single segment.[7]

(1) a. [zɪm . bæb . we]
    b. [zi . ᵐba . bʷe]

Example (1b) conforms with the syllable structure of Shona. In common with other Bantu languages, Shona has a basic CV syllable structure. What appear

---

[6] Actually, Japanese is rather more complicated, in that a syllable may terminate in the first 'half' of a geminate (or lengthened) consonant. (Amongst the Japanese consonants, only the voiceless obstruents may be geminated): *Nippon* 'Japan' [nip . poɴ].

[7] English has complex segments, too, namely the affricates [tʃ] and [dʒ]. Although these sounds can be decomposed into separate gestures (a stop plus a fricative), the sounds count as single segments in the phonology of English.

(to an English speaker) to be sequences of consonants, split over coda and onset, are treated as complex segments in onset position.

Important as the syllable is, the stream of speech cannot be regarded as merely a succession of syllables. Syllables, as they follow each other, differ in their prominence. This gives rise to a higher level unit, the **foot**. In English, a foot comprises a strong syllable, plus any weak syllables that intervene before a following strong. (2) shows an utterance that consists of four feet. Foot boundaries are shown by '|', and strong syllables are underlined.

(**2**) | This is the | house that | Jack | built |

Feet in turn combine to form **phonological phrases**, the domain for intonation contours. While the phonological phrase often coincides with a syntactic phrase, or at least with some kind of syntactic constituent, this need not be the case. (2) could be spoken as a single phonological phrase; alternatively, it might consist of two phrases, as in (3). (Phrase boundaries are shown by '#'.)

(**3**) # This is the house that # Jack built #

In (3), the first phonological phrase fails to correspond with any kind of syntactic constituent.

Phrase, foot, syllable, and segment form a hierarchy, determined by part-of relations: a phonological phrase consists of one or more feet, a foot consists of one or more syllables, a syllable consists of one or more segments. In principle, a phonological phrase could consist of a single segment. The segment would itself constitute a syllable, which would in turn constitute a foot, which in turn constitutes a phrase. (An example would be the utterance *Ah!*)

While the highest level unit—the phonological phrase—may often coincide with a syntactic unit (more so, perhaps, in pre-planned speech), the lower-level units generally do not, of themselves, count as the phonological pole of any symbolic unit. It is evident that the vowels and consonants of English (and indeed of other languages) are in themselves meaningless,[8] while the independence of syllable and foot with respect to semantic structure is easily illustrated. Consider the expression *letter from America*.

(**4**) phrases

feet

syllables

segments   l ɛ t ə f r ɒ m ə m ɛ r ɪ k ə

---

[8] One can, to be sure, cite instances where a symbolic unit has, as its phonological pole, a single phonetic segment: French *eau* [o] 'water', for example. But this coincidence of word form and phonetic segment is just that—pure coincidence. There is no expectation that occurrences of [o] within other symbolic units in French, such as *peau* [po] 'skin', are associated with the meaning 'water'.

The syllables are demarcated on phonological criteria (alternations of sonority, in association with language-specific schemas for syllable structure). As a consequence syllables can cut across word boundaries; observe that the fourth syllable, [mə], consists of the final consonant of *from* and the first segment of *America*. Feet are identified by alternating patterns of strong and weak syllables. Again, feet do not necessarily coincide with word units (or if they do, as in the case of *letter*, this is largely fortuitous); observe that the second foot |frɒ.mə| consists of a word plus a part of a word. It is as if the phonology has a life of its own, which structures sound content according to its own principles, independently of lexical structure.

5.2.1 The word as a phonological unit

I suggested above that phonological structure is organized independently of the symbolic units (primarily: words) that make up an utterance. On this approach, the word would not have any distinctive role in phonology. There are at least three kinds of evidence which suggest that this position may need to be modified.

(i) First, there is the possibility that word boundaries may sometimes be marked in the stream of speech. Consider the pairs of phrases in (5). Even for speakers for whom the pairs are segmentally identical, the phrases can be distinguished, at least in careful speech, through subtle effects of rhythm and timing. Thus, a word boundary may be signalled by a slight prolongation of word-final segments.[9] A comparable situation holds for the French phrases in (6).

(5) gnaw Tinelli's pizzas / naughty Nellie's pizzas
a grey day / a grade A
the grey tissues / the great issues
(Giegerich 1992: 270–2)

(6) le chapeau élégant 'the elegant hat' / le chapeau et les gants 'the hat and the gloves'
(Boysson-Bardies 1999: 98)

(ii) There may be special phonological constraints operating within a word which are different from those which hold between adjacent words. It is quite possible to have geminate (or lengthened) consonants in English—but only if each 'half' of the geminate belongs to a different word. Examples include *this story*, *big guy*, *give Vera*. A lengthened consonant within a word is not possible.[10] This situation is symptomatic of a more general phenomenon.

---

[9] Placement of syllable boundaries may also help differentiate the phrases. For example, many speakers have markedly different allophones for syllable-final and syllable-initial /t/. These differences easily distinguish *grey tissues* from *great issues*.

[10] A lengthened [n] may occur in *unnatural* and *non-native*, but not in *innate*. This fact may be taken as evidence for the 'word-like' status of the prefixes *non-* and *un-*, in contrast to the status of *in-* as a bound morpheme.

English, as mentioned, permits complex consonant clusters in syllable-onset and syllable-coda position. It can happen that the complex coda of one word occurs adjacent to the complex onset of a following word, resulting in an even more complex sequence of consonants, as, for example, in *sixth street*, where we have the consonant sequence [... ksθstr ...]. Such monstrosities never occur within a word. Pierrehumbert (1994) has calculated that there are 8,708 possible sequences of three consonants or more that would result from the concatenation of acceptable codas with acceptable onsets (disregarding geminates). Of these, only 50 (i.e. less than 1 per cent) are attested within words. Facts such as these suggest the possibility of establishing phonological schemas specifically for the internal structure of (polysyllabic) words.

Although (i) and (ii) suggest that the word (in English) possesses a certain status as a phonological entity, it is not at all clear where 'word' would take its place within the hierarchy of phrase, foot, syllable, and segment. It would be incorrect to position the word between the phonological phrase and the foot, or between the foot and the syllable. The word category cross-cuts the units of the phonological hierarchy.[11]

(iii) In discussing example (4) I stated that the coincidence, in the case of *letter*, of the word and the foot was purely fortuitous. Such a conclusion may be too hasty. Cutler (1990) reports a strong statistical tendency for polysyllabic words in English to commence in a strong syllable; the tendency holds both for word types, as they might be listed in a dictionary, and for the word tokens that occur in running text. She found that in running text about three-quarters of all stressed syllables were the sole or the initial syllable of stressed words. Hence, 'a listener encountering a strong syllable in spontaneous English conversation seems to have about a three to one chance of finding that strong syllable to be the onset of a new lexical word' (pp. 108–9).

Cutler's findings again point to the possibility of proposing a phonological schema, at least for the content words in English. The schema would consist of an initial strong syllable followed by an unspecified number (including zero) of weak syllables. Content words, therefore, will tend to coincide with the foot. The phonological schema would not be valid for all content words. But since it would account for the majority, it could reasonably be regarded as the prototype of the phonological form of a content word.

If a content word tends to coincide with the foot, a foot may sometimes be analysed as a content word. A notable example of this, in colloquial British English, is the curious formation *cuppa*. As shown in (7a), the phonological structure of *a cup of tea* has [kʌp] and [ə(v)] combining to form a foot.[12]

---

[11] Anticipating Chapter 7, we can notice an analogy with hierarchies of semantic units. The semantic units [PET], [VERMIN], [WEED] cross-cut the taxonomic hierarchies of plants, animals, birds, and fish (p. 133).

[12] In relaxed speech, the [v] of *of* will typically elide.

Speakers of English—exploiting the phonological schema which identifies the content word with a foot—have made a content word out of the foot [kʌpə].

(7) a. a cup of tea
       ə | kʌ pə(v) | tiː
    b. 'Good morning,' Joyce said. 'Coffee?' 'If it's no trouble I'd prefer a cuppa.' (cited in OED)

The emergence of the word *cuppa* [kʌpə] shows that although phonology is in principle organized independently of symbolic structure, speakers nevertheless may try to establish relations between phonological and semantic units, in accordance with the schema which identifies the word with the foot.

5.3 Phonological constraints, alias phonological schemas

We have seen that phonological units—segments, syllables, feet, and even phonological phrases—do not necessarily coincide with the phonological pole of any symbolic units. A further aspect of the autonomy of phonology concerns the integration of smaller phonological structures into more complex structures. At the phonological pole, a complex expression does not consist simply of the alignment of the phonological poles of its constituents. These have to be integrated into a complex structure, in such a way that phonological constraints operative in the language are satisfied (or, to put it another way, in order that the complex structure is sanctioned by the available phonological schemas in the language). At the very least, the complex expression has to be structured in terms of the phonological hierarchy of phrase, foot, syllable, and segment. As a consequence, the phonological structure of a word may undergo certain modifications as the word is integrated into the stream of speech.

Consider, by way of illustration, a phonological constraint that is operative in most accents of English. This is the **filled-onset requirement**: all syllables must have an onset. The requirement is so powerful that English speakers find it difficult to articulate an isolated vowel, such as [iː], without using a glottal stop to provide the syllable with an onset: [ʔiː]. For many English speakers, [iː] is simply not pronounceable. In order to be able to control the contrasting articulations [iː] vs. [ʔiː], as well as to be able to hear the difference between these, English speakers usually require special training in articulatory phonetics.

The filled-onset requirement conflicts with the fact that a sizeable number of words and morphemes in the language in fact commence with a vowel. Various strategies are used in order to supply these units with an initial consonant. Consider the word *are* [ɑː]. (The following discussion presupposes a non-rhotic dialect of English, that is, a dialect in which [r] can only occur in syllable-onset position.)

Linking 'r' and intrusive 'r'

The account given here ignores the traditional distinction between the so-called 'linking r' and 'intrusive r'.

Standard British English, and British-based accents of English (mainly, the southern hemisphere varieties, that is, Australian, New Zealand, and South African), share the characteristic that they do not allow [r] to occur in syllable-coda position.

The linking 'r' is said to occur when the 'r' is present in the orthography but gets pronounced only when a following word commences with a vowel, as in *for instance* [fə.rɪn.stəns]. The intrusive 'r' is said to occur when an 'r' is inserted without its being present in the orthography, as in *Asia and Africa* [ɛi.ʒə.rə.næ.frɪ.kə].

Phonologically, the linking and the intrusive 'r' are the very same phenomenon: in both cases [r] is inserted between two vowels the first of which is non-high, and in both cases the [r] is inserted for the very same reason, namely, to satisfy the filled-onset requirement.

(i) One strategy involves co-opting an immediately preceding consonant (if there is one). In the sequence *these are*, the final [z] of *these* comes to occupy the onset-position of *are*.[13] We can call this the *consonant-sharing* strategy.

(8)

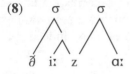

(ii) If a preceding word ends in a high front vowel, such as [iː] or [aɪ], a high front glide [j] functions as the syllable onset. If a preceding word ends in a high back vowel, such as [uː] or [əʊ], the high back glide [w] functions as onset. Thus, *they are* [ðeɪ] [ɑː] comes out as [ðeɪ jɑː], while *you are* [juː] [ɑː] comes out as [ju wɑː]. We can call this the *glide-insertion* strategy.

(iii) If a preceding word ends in a non-high vowel, an inserted [r] functions as the syllable onset. Thus, *where are* [wɛə] [ɑː] comes out as [wɛə rɑː]. This is the strategy of *r-insertion*.

(iv) As an alternative to all of the above, a glottal stop is inserted. If the word is utterance initial, this is, of course, the only option. *Are you* [ɑː] [juː] is pronounced [ʔɑː juː].

When needing to articulate a vowel-commencing word, whether in isolation or in the stream of speech, an English speaker has no choice but to implement

---

[13] In (8) I have shown the [z] of [ðiːz] as ambisyllabic, i.e. the segment functions both as the coda of one syllable and as the onset of the following syllable. On an alternative account, the sequence [ðiːzɑː] would be syllabified as [ðiː]σ [zɑː]σ. The different accounts are irrelevant to the point being made.

one of the above strategies. The strategies are motivated by a purely phonological requirement—the need for every syllable to have a consonantal onset, irrespective of the phonological shape of the word units which make up a complex expression.

There is much more that could be said about the filled-onset requirement. There is, for instance, considerable dialectal and stylistic variation, especially concerning the incidence of glottal-stop insertion as an alternative to the other strategies. There is also the possibility that certain lexical items might trigger one of the strategies rather than another. In my speech, I am more likely to use r-insertion in *for ever* than in the rhythmically and semantically rather similar phrase *for Ellen*. An additional question concerns the appropriate way of representing the different onset-filling strategies within the framework of Cognitive Grammar. I return to this topic in Chapter 13, after some further constructs of Cognitive Grammar have been introduced.

5.4 'Pure' phonology

If phonology is structured according to its own principles, one would expect there to be utterances that are 'pure phonology', as it were. In terms of Figure 3.3 (p. 51), an utterance would consist solely of phonological content (shown in the lower part of the diagram), with no corresponding semantic content. To be sure, such examples would not constitute paradigm examples of linguistic expressions. Nevertheless, examples may indeed be found. Consider the third line of the well-known joke:

(9) To be is to do   (Jean-Paul Sartre)
     To do is to be   (Friedrich Nietzsche)
     Doo be doo be doo   (Frank Sinatra)

Frank Sinatra's *doo be doo be doo* is conceptually vacuous; it even fails to evoke any syntactic schema. But it conforms perfectly with the phonological structure of English. It is made up of segments taken from the inventory of segments sanctioned in English. The segments are organized into a sequence of five well-formed syllables. These combine into three well-formed feet, which in turn combine into a phonological phrase, which can be spoken with any of the sanctioned intonation contours of English. The point of the joke (at the risk of dissecting the obvious) lies in phonological resemblances between elements of the (meaningless) refrain and elements of the pithy aphorisms which are meant to synthesize the thoughts of those weighty cultural icons, Sartre and Nietzsche.

Quite a lot of language play exploits phonological organization, with little regard for its conceptual import. Nursery rhymes, nonsense verse, tongue twisters, even cryptic crossword puzzles, all play on phonological structure (and even orthographic structure, in the case of crossword puzzles). *Hickory dickory dock* (from the nursery rhyme) has no more conceptual import than the Sinatra refrain. To be sure, tongue-twisters such as *She sells sea shells on the sea shore* and *The Leith police dismisseth us* do conform to the syntax of English and the expressions can certainly be said to 'mean' something. But when cited as tongue-twisters, the symbolic content of these expressions is irrelevant. They are cited merely as plays on sound structure.

Halliday (1973—see Chapter 1, p. 14) drew attention to the child's delight in plays of pure sound. The child's fascination with phonological structure develops, in the adult, into more serious enterprises, such as poetry, where principles of phonological organization—patterns of rhyme, assonance,[14] and various rhythmical effects engineered by the succession of feet of various kinds—are systematically exploited. It is worth noting, in this connection, that the linguistic terms 'rhyme' and 'foot' are borrowed from poetic theory.

To emphasize the phonological aspects of verse and other kinds of word play is not to deny the possible semantic resonances of phonological patterns. On the one hand, it is a phonological accident that the Italian words *amore* 'love', *cuore* 'heart', and *dolore* 'pain' happen to rhyme.[15] But this phonological accident was certainly a boon to Petrarch and the poetic tradition which he inspired. The sharing of phonological content in rhyming words is able to set up associations at the semantic level, which are then reinforced through the use of the rhyming words, in close proximity to each other, in the prominent end-positions of the lines of poetry. Equally, a poet can highlight the clash between phonological commonality and semantic distance. Witness T. S. Eliot's exploitation of the rhythmical and segmental equivalences in *Michelangelo* and the banal *come and go* in *The Waste Land: In the room, the women come and go / Talking of Michelangelo*.

5.4.1 Phonological effects in word order

One generally thinks of the phonological form of an utterance as being subservient to what a speaker wishes to say. To be sure, phonological constraints may influence the actual phonological shape that a word or morpheme might take in the stream of speech. But the fact that a speaker says what she does— the fact that she uses this word rather than that word, and that words are spoken in this configuration rather than some other—is, one might suppose, a product of the conceptualization that the speaker wishes to express.

While this may be true, in general terms, there is evidence that phonological considerations can actually influence what speakers say.

This can be illustrated with respect to the order in which things are said. Often, when two words are conjoined, one order is preferred over the other.

---

[14] In terms of syllable structure (Figure 5.1), assonance consists in the repetition, over successive syllables, of a syllable onset.

[15] For the purposes of Italian poetic structure, words are considered to rhyme if they share the same segmental content from their stressed syllable nucleus to the end of the word.

(10) *Preferred word order*   *Disfavoured word order*
     men and women   women and men
     ladies and gentlemen gentlemen and ladies
     up and down   down and up
     come and go   go and come
     bread and butter   butter and bread
     North and South   South and North
     East and West   West and East

There are also many cases where speakers do not have strong preferences either way. *Boys and girls* seems just as acceptable as *girls and boys*; for my part, I have no preference with regard to *eggs and bacon* vs. *bacon and eggs*. (Though I do prefer *ham and eggs* over *eggs and ham*.)

For some of these expressions semantic factors are certainly playing a role. The general idea seems to be: put the more important, the more salient element first. *Bread and butter* is basically bread which is garnished with butter, it is not butter with a bit of bread added to it. Another principle that has been suggested (Cooper and Ross 1975) is egocentrism: the first element approximates to the prototypical speaker, i.e. an adult male (!), or takes the perspective of the prototypical speaker. Hence *men and women, father and son, husband and wife, sons and daughters, parents and children, here and there, now and then, life and death*. There are some obvious counterexamples. We prefer *ladies and gentlemen* to *gentlemen and ladies, you and I* to *I and you*.

Nevertheless, in many cases where word order is fixed, a semantic explanation is difficult to come by. Consider the following:

(11) *Conventionalized word order*   *Unacceptable word order*
     tit for tat   *tat for tit
     wishy-washy   *washy-wishy
     hanky-panky   *panky-hanky
     willy-nilly   *nilly-willy
     dribs and drabs   *drabs and dribs
     spic and span   *span and spic

Semantic considerations cannot be playing a role here, since the component elements, such as *tat* and *spic*, do not have any meaning at all, identifiable outside of the expressions in which they occur.

Why then do we say *tit for tat*, not **tat for tit*? One reason could be that *tit for tat* simply 'sounds better' than *tat for tit*. The vowel sequence [. . .ɪ. . .] [. . .æ. . .] is more harmonious than the reverse. Some readers might even feel that phonological factors are playing a role in the conjoined expressions in (10). It is not just that *bread and butter* makes better sense, conceptually, than *butter and bread*. Doesn't the expression also sound better, both rhythmically and in terms of the succession of sounds?

In Chapter 2 I mentioned delight in form-focused activities as one facet of human cognition that shapes human language (pp. 14–15). Expressions which exhibit 'pure phonology' exemplify our inclination to play with patterns of sound, without regard to their semantic import. The phonological principles underlying preferred order also testify to the role of phonological organization as a motivating factor in the acceptability of an expression. In Chapter 17 I discuss another form-focused phenomenon, namely inflection classes. Inflection classes trigger agreement, that is, the choice of a particular phonological form of a morpheme over another phonological form. To the extent that inflection classes lack a semantic basis, agreement patterns are solely a matter of phonological patterning.

Study questions

1. Assemble some reasons why it is necessary to recognize the syllable as a unit of phonological description.

2. Examine the traditional metrical forms that are used in poetry in different languages. Which phonological aspects of the languages are being exploited by the poetic forms?

3. Language games. The autonomy of phonology is nowhere better exemplified than in the secret languages that children sometimes invent for themselves. These gibberish languages are based on systematic distortions of phonological units of the source language. Some children become remarkably fluent in gibberish and are able to manipulate 'on the fly' the phonological structures of the source language.

   Describe some secret languages that you, or your colleagues, are fluent in. Pay attention to the ways in which phonological units of the source language get distorted.

   If—as is likely—the syllable plays a crucial role in the gibberish languages you are examining, consider whether it might be possible to apply the evidence of gibberish to some problematic aspects of syllabification. Problematic areas include the placement of syllable boundaries (e.g. in words like *discussed* vs. *disgust*) and the number of syllables in words such as *socialism*.

4. Filled onsets in English. Collect some data on the incidence of glottal-stop insertion in English. If you have access to non-rhotic accents of English, supplement the glottal-stop data with data on the incidence of 'r'-insertion.

   It is important, for this task, that you analyse recorded utterances and not rely on speakers' intuitions. The implementation of onset-filling strategies probably lies below the threshold of conscious awareness, so it is not a good idea to rely on what English speakers think they might say. Pay attention, not only to the occasions on which the glottal stop is used, but also to the occasions on which the glottal stop could have been used but was not. You might start by highlighting on a transcript all the words which commence in a vowel. Then, while carefully listening to the recording, mark those which were spoken with a glottal stop.

Do you detect any patterns in the incidence of glottal-stop insertion? What factors might be influencing the patterns you discern?

5. Preferred word order. Design (and, if resources permit, carry out) an experiment to test the hypothesis that phonological factors may influence preferred order in conjoined expressions. In order to demonstrate the role of phonological factors, you will need to eliminate, or control, other factors (especially semantic ones) that plausibly also influence word order. You might, for example, control for semantic factors by considering the conjunction of (same-sex) names, e.g. *Paul and Peter* vs. *Peter and Paul*. You might eliminate semantic factors altogether by using nonsense words. In this way, you could systematically investigate whether certain sequences of vowels or consonants are preferred, also whether there are preferred rhythmical patterns.

6. The word in Zulu. A phonological requirement in Zulu is that a word must consist minimally of two syllables. Mostly, this requirement is automatically fulfilled, since nearly all verbal and nominal stems are at least bi-syllabic. The bi-syllabic verb stems can easily be used as imperatives: *thanda!* 'love', *shaya!* 'strike'. There are, however, a few verb stems which are monosyllabic, such as *dla* 'eat', *thi* 'say'. When these verbs are used as imperatives, it is necessary to insert a supporting vowel, in order to guarantee the bi-syllabic structure: *idla!*, *ithi!*

For most Zulu verbs, the passive is formed by replacing the final vowel with the suffix -*wa*, e.g. *thanda* 'love', *thandwa* 'be loved', *shaya* 'strike', *shaywa* 'be struck'. How can one account for the following passives?

dla 'eat', *dliwa* 'be eaten'

thi 'say', *thiwa* 'be said'

On the basis of the following examples, what general principle underlies verb reduplication in Zulu? (The Zulu syllable has the structure CV. Orthographic *nd* represents a single complex segment, the pre-nasalized stop [ⁿd], while orthographic *dl* represents the voiced lateral fricative [ɮ].)

hamba 'walk'	*hambahamba* 'walk about a little'
ndiza 'fly'	*ndizandiza* 'fly a little'
gijima 'run'	*gijigijima* 'run for a bit'
mamatheka 'smile'	*mamamamatheka* 'smile a little'
akha 'build'	*akhayakha* 'build a little'
enza 'do'	*enzayenza* 'do a little'
dla 'eat'	*dlayidla* 'eat a little'
fa 'die'	*fayifa* 'feel unwell'

(Data from Doke 1981)

7. Syllabification in Zulu. The following examples illustrate different ways in which a phonological requirement in Zulu is satisfied. What is the requirement? How is it satisfied? The column on the left lines up the constituent morphemes in an utterance; the column on the right shows the integrated expression.

bonke abantu 'all people'	› *bonkabantu*
u-akha 'he builds'	› *wakha*
ku endlini 'it (is) in the house'	› *kusendlini*
indoda na umfana '(the) man and (the) boy'	› *indoda nomfana*

Further reading

There are important discussions of phonology scattered throughout FCG1; see especially pp. 328–348 and pp. 388–401. The Cognitive Grammar approach underlies the dissertations of Rubba (1993) and Kumashiro (2000). (Some aspects of Rubba's dissertation are summarized in Langacker 1999: 135–42.) Otherwise, the Cognitive Grammar literature on phonological matters is rather sparse. See, however, Bybee (1994); Taylor (1995a: ch. 12); and Nathan (1986, 1989, 1994, 1996).

On phonological units, see Nespor and Vogel (1986). Jackendoff (1997) contains some insightful remarks on the 'autonomy' of phonological organization.

There is quite a large literature on fixed-order expressions. See Malkiel (1959), Bolinger (1962), Cooper and Ross (1975), Oakeshott-Taylor (1984), and Lambrecht (1984).

CHAPTER 6

Semantic structure in Cognitive Grammar

In the last chapter we saw that phonological structure has a certain autonomy *vis-à-vis* its role in the symbolization of conceptual structure. In this chapter I show that a comparable state of affairs holds with semantic structure. The meaning of a complex expression is not simply a function of the meanings of its parts and the manner in which they are combined. Typically, the meaning of the whole is more specific than, or even at variance with, the meaning contributed by the parts, and may contain elements that are not actually symbolized by any of the constituent units. There are good reasons, therefore, to assume a level of conceptual organization which modifies and enriches the semantic content supplied by the symbolic units which make up an expression.

Taken together, the evidence from phonology and semantics reinforces the position taken in section 3.4. To be sure, symbolic relations between phonological and semantic structures must occupy a central place in linguistic enquiry. At the same time, phonological structure and semantic structure are subject to their own principles of organization, and need not link up in a strict one-to-one fashion.

6.1 Compositionality

We can approach the subject matter of this chapter by considering the issue of compositionality. According to the compositionality principle, the meaning of a complex expression results from the meanings of its parts and the manner in which they are combined.

There is a sense in which compositionality is not just a hypothesis about semantic structure, it is a self-evident fact. Speakers have at their disposal only a finite number of conventionalized linguistic units. Drawing on these finite resources, speakers are continuously creating new expressions which symbolize mostly unique conceptualizations, and which hearers (usually) are able to interpret without too much difficulty. Since language users can not have memorized each and every expression that they say and hear, there has to exist some mechanism for building up complex expressions from a stored inventory of units. To deny compositionality, it would seem, is to deny the very possibility that speakers can creatively use their linguistic resources. Sweetser put it like this:

I do not know any linguists who see semantics as intrinsically non-compositional. . . . Linguists all agree, and so does the average lay person, that the reason *The cat stole the hat* means something different from *The cat ate the hat* is that *stole* and *ate* make different contributions to the interpretation of the whole, and that those contributions are systematically related to the usual conventional ranges of interpretations of *eat* and *steal* in other possible uses by English speakers. We may disagree about major related issues: for example, the extent to which idioms are processed compositionally (whether as well as, or instead of, being processed as units); the extent to which it is important to talk about meanings of syntactic constructions; the relationship between 'semantic' and 'pragmatic' components of a linguistically conveyed message; the relationship between linguistic interpretation and general reasoning processes of context-based inference; of the assessment of what proportion of everyday utterance-content is produced and processed by accessing already-made routines, as opposed to by brand-new composition of elements. But the basic fact of compositionality remains, and remains also for more apparently complicated cases than those involving cats, hats, and mats. (Sweetser 1999: 132–3)

While compositionality is a fact, there are, as Sweetser states, numerous points of controversy. She specifically mentions the status of idioms and syntactic constructions, the role of pragmatic interpretation, and the extent to which complex expressions are stored ready-made. These are topics that we will address elsewhere in this book. One topic she does not mention is whether compositionality is strict or only partial.

The main burden of this chapter is to argue against strict compositionality and for partial compositionality. The component units certainly contribute semantic content to a complex expression, but the complex expression itself is often subject to interpretation on the basis of conceptual knowledge that goes beyond what is actually symbolized in a complex expression.

First, I examine more closely the notion of strict compositionality, and why it is problematic.

6.1.1 Strict compositionality

In many semantic theories, especially formal theories, strict compositionality is taken to be a fundamental property of semantic structures.[1] The compositionality principle can be stated as follows:

(1) <u>Strict compositionality</u>: The meaning of a complex expression is fully determined by (a) the meanings of its component parts, in conjunction with (b) the way in which the parts are combined.

This can be broken down into the following more specific propositions:

(2) a. Each component of a complex expression has a fixed and determinate meaning within the language system.
   b. The manner in which simpler items combine to form complex expressions makes a fixed and determinate contribution to the meaning of a complex expression.
   c. The semantic properties of the parts of an expression are fully maintained in the complex expression.
   d. There is no 'surplus' meaning accruing to a complex expression that is not attributable to its parts and the manner of their combination.[2]

Each of these propositions is highly questionable.

Statement (2a) is inconsistent with the fact that word meanings are not, in general, fixed and unchanging, but tend to vary according to the context of their use.[3] When predicated of humans, mice, and horses, the verb *run* does not designate exactly the same manner of motion. I refer to this phenomenon as **semantic flexibility**. I touch on the topic in section 6.3 and take it up again in Chapter 22.

Semantic flexibility shades into **polysemy**. Most words in a language are polysemous to some degree, that is, they have a range of distinct, though related senses, with more frequently used words tending to be more polysemous than less frequent ones. Adherents of strict compositionality have sought to minimize the extent of polysemy in language. It is easy to see why. If a word w has n meanings, then, on strict compositionality, any expression containing w will be n-ways ambiguous, since we shall have to compute n

---

[1] A good introduction to compositionality, and its role in formal semantics, is ch. 1 of Cann (1993).

[2] Note that a strict interpretation of the symbolic thesis (cf. section 3.4.1) entails strict compositionality at the semantic level—the semantic structure of a complex expression would be fully derivable from the semantic structure of its component parts and from the schemas which sanction their combination.

[3] I therefore concur with Quine's (1987) observation (cf. p. 63) that meanings are not to be thought of as if they were specimens in a museum of ideas, each bearing its own label.

different interpretations of any expression containing w.[4] If there are two words, w_1 and w_2, which have n_1 and n_2 meanings respectively, any sentence containing w_1 and w_2 will have $n_1 \times n_2$ different meanings. As more and more polysemous words are included in a sentence, the number of compositional meanings increases exponentially. Since most words are polysemous to some degree, the compositionality principle will attribute massive ambiguity to even very short sentences. To be sure, many of the compositionally derived meanings will be incoherent or implausible and will need to be discarded.[5] Notice, though, that the discarding of the unwanted readings will be based on an assessment of conceptual plausibility. In the last analysis, strict compositionality is not able to do without a background of conceptual knowledge that is not actually symbolized in the words of the expression. The final reading of an expression is not solely a product of its parts, but emerges relative to what is presumed to be plausible or possible.[6]

Statement (2b) asserts that the syntagmatic combination of units makes a fixed and determinate contribution to semantic structure. This is problematic in the case of certain constructions which are generally acknowledged to be semantically **vague**. Consider noun compounds of the form $[N_1\ N_2]$. These, normally, designate a kind of $[N_2]$ which bears some kind of relation to $[N_1]$. The kind of relation is not explicitly encoded. How an $[N_1\ N_2]$ compound is interpreted in any given case depends crucially on conceptual knowledge pertaining to $[N_1]$ and $[N_2]$, and on the kinds of relation that can plausibly hold between them. A 'water pistol' is a kind of pistol which bears one kind of relation to water (it is a pistol that shoots out water), a 'water truck' invokes a different relation (a truck that transports water), a 'water tower' is a tower for storing water, 'water colours' are paints made from a water base, 'water skis' invoke a different kind of relation yet again (skis that can be used on water).

If noun compounds are semantically vague, other syntactic constructions are plausibly regarded as polysemous, in that a particular pattern of syntagmatic combination can make different semantic contributions. Consider the following:

(3) a. Your mother drives well.
     b. Your car drives well.

---

[4] I find it useful to make a terminological distinction between 'polysemy' and 'ambiguity'. Polysemy is a property of decontextualized linguistic items, ambiguity is a property of expressions.

[5] As an illustration, consider the word *ring*. The word has at least three conventionalized senses: a circular piece of jewellery; a sporting arena (as in *boxing ring*); and an illegal association (*smuggling ring*). If I 'show someone a ring', any of the three senses might be implicated; a choice must be made on the basis of what is plausible (given the context of the speech event). But if I 'buy someone a ring', the first interpretation will be most likely (though the second cannot be ruled out, in certain circumstances).

[6] One might, alternatively, argue that the more outlandish compositional meanings are never computed in the first place, due to a prior selection from among the readings of the polysemous constituents. Again, though, the prior selection must also take place relative to background conceptual knowledge, which goes beyond the scope of the compositionality principle.

Syntactically, these are exactly parallel. In both cases, a verb (*drive*) combines with a subject nominal (*your mother*, *your car*) and an adverbial (*well*). But the semantic role of the subject is different in the two cases. In (3a) the subject designates a person who drives, while in (3b) the subject designates a vehicle that is driven. (3a) attributes a skill to the driver, (3b) attributes a quality—drivability—to the vehicle. Constructional polysemy gives rise to the same issues as lexical polysemy. To interpret (3a) we appeal to one meaning of the intransitive construction, to interpret (3b) we appeal to another meaning. The choice is based on conceptual knowledge concerning cars, people, and driving. The final interpretation we come up with is not determined solely by the compositionality principle.

(2c) comes up against some well-known problems with respect to expressions like *fake gun*, *stone lion*, *imitation fur*. The point is that a fake gun is not actually a gun at all, neither is a stone lion 'really' a lion. In these cases the first component does not just add specifications to the second (as happens, for example, with *loaded gun*, *small lion*), it drastically alters its semantic character.

The fallacious character of (2d) will become apparent in section 6.2, when we consider the meaning of *the football under the table*.

6.1.2 Out of bounds to compositionality

It is widely recognized, even by promoters of strict compositionality, that certain phenomena are not subject to the principle. I have already mentioned the case of inherently vague constructions, such as noun compounds. Other exceptions to compositionality are idioms, figures of speech (especially metaphor), and expressions which are subject to pragmatic interpretations.

The existence of non-compositional expressions need not, in itself, threaten compositionality—provided that the exceptions can be clearly identified as such. As a matter of fact, it turns out that the exceptions do not form a clearly identifiable category. What we find is that a very large number of things in a language are idiomatic to some degree, many expressions are metaphorical to some degree, and most expressions are subject to some kind of pragmatic interpretation. If anything, it is strict compositionality that turns out to be the exceptional condition.

(i) Idioms. Idioms are sometimes defined in terms of their non-compositionality: an idiom is an expression whose meaning cannot be computed from the meanings that its parts have elsewhere in the language. Consider (4):

(4) a. Don't spill the beans!
     b. You're opening a can of worms.
     c. He kicked the bucket.

To be sure, these *could* be interpreted in terms of the meanings of their parts, in which case (4a) would count as an instruction to the hearer to keep a quantity of beans within the confines of a container. The idiomatic reading—

Compositionality in phonology?

In many places in this book I draw attention to parallels between phonological and semantic structure. It is interesting to enquire, therefore, whether the compositionality principle (which is normally taken to be a principle of semantics) could be applied to phonology. Rephrasing (1), we might define phonological compositionality as follows:

(i)   The phonological structure of a complex expression is fully determined by (a) the phonological structure of its component parts, in conjunction with (b) the way in which the parts are combined.

This breaks down as follows:

(ii)   a. Each component part of a complex expression has a fixed and determinate phonological structure within the language system.
   b. The manner in which simpler items combine to form complex expressions makes a fixed and determinate contribution to the phonological structure of a complex expression.
   c. The phonological properties of the parts of an expression are fully maintained in the complex expression.
   d. There is no 'surplus' phonological structure accruing to a complex expression that is not attributable to its parts and the manner of their combination.

I leave it to the reader to apply these principles to concrete examples, also to consider whether the principles really do apply to phonological structure. For starters, re-syllabification, as exhibited by [ðiːz] [ɑː] --→ [ði. zɑː], and linking phenomena, such as [ðɔ] [aɪ] › [ðɔ raɪ], conflict with (iia). Assimilations across word boundaries, of the kind [rɛd] [pɛn] --→ [rɛbˀ pɛn], conflict with (iic).

---

roughly: 'Don't reveal the confidential information to a third party'—cannot be computed from the semantic values that *spill* and *beans* have elsewhere in the language. *Spill the beans* is a multi-word unit with a special meaning, which needs to be specifically learned by the language user.

As mentioned, the existence of idioms need not, in itself, threaten strict compositionality—provided that the idioms can be clearly identified as such. The matter becomes problematic to the extent that it might not be possible to clearly separate out the idiomatic from the non-idiomatic. Consider, by way of an example, the expressions in (5):

(5)   a. They came in {one by one / ?ten by ten / *several by several}.
   b. He spent the inheritance {bit by bit / ?dollar by dollar / *banknote by banknote}.
   c. The country got poorer {year by year / ?decade by decade / *century by century}.

One by one, *bit by bit*, and *year by year* are not obviously idiomatic in the way in which *spill the beans* is idiomatic. In the first place, there are semantic and formal similarities across the expressions—they each express, albeit in different ways, the rate at which some process unfolds, and they all share the same structure, namely, [N by N], where [N] designates the unit in terms of which the unfolding of the process is measured. Second, the [N by N] construction is quite productive: *They came in two by two*, *Translate the text word by word*, *Check the figures column by column*. Moreover, *by* has a similar 'unitizing' sense elsewhere in the language: *Sell them by the dozen*. In spite of all this, a certain degree of idiomaticity does attach to the expressions in (5). It is not so much that *one by one*, *bit by bit*, *year by year* are idiomatic in themselves, rather it is the construction [N by N] that is idiomatic. Even though *by* has a unitizing sense in *sell them by the dozen*, neither the meaning, nor even the grammaticality of [N by N] can be derived from this fact. Moreover, the [N by N] construction is not fully productive. There is something odd about *several by several*, even though there is nothing conceptually odd about saying that people came in several at a time.[7]

The situation is not at all unusual. In fact, as I shall argue in Chapters 27 and 28, a very great deal in a language is idiomatic in the way in which the expressions in (5) are idiomatic. The idiomaticity is to be located, not so much in the properties of specific expressions (such as *kick the bucket*), but in constructional patterns whose form and meaning are not fully compositional and which may be productive to a greater or lesser extent.

(ii) Metaphor. The idiomatic nature of *spill the beans* rests on a metaphor—confidential information is construed, metaphorically, as beans inside a container, revealing the information is construed as spilling the beans from their container.

Metaphor is just one of many figures of speech. Others are hyperbole (or exaggeration), irony, and metonymy. These are exemplified in (6).

(6) a. I have a thousand and one things to do.
    b. A real genius he is!
    c. It's 2 a.m. and the city is asleep.

In each of these cases, the figurative meaning deviates substantially from the literal meaning. Example (6a) means, simply, that I have many things to do, not that I have precisely one thousand and one tasks to complete; example (6b) means the person referred to is anything but a genius; while example (6c) means that the inhabitants of the city, not the city itself, are asleep.

A popular approach to figurative language (represented, for example, by Searle 1993) claims that a figurative meaning emerges only after a hearer has computed the literal (compositional) meaning and found it to be inappropriate or nonsensical. There are reasons to doubt this approach. There is abundant

---

[7] Possibly, the [N by N] construction is subject to a phonological constraint; the construction seems to work best with short, monosyllabic nouns.

evidence (summarized in ch. 3 of Gibbs 1994) that hearers can access figurative meanings more quickly than literal meanings, suggesting that people do not have to first go through the literal meaning in order to arrive at the figurative meaning.

As with idioms, the boundary between literal and figurative is not always cleanly drawn. Lakoff and Johnson (1980) argue that much of our thought is intrinsically metaphorical, and that certain domains of experience, such as time, can only be conceptualized in metaphorical terms. The following exploit metaphorical construals of time.

(7) a. Christmas is approaching.
     b. Time passes.
     c. You're wasting my time.

Example (7a) is based on a metaphor which construes the present as station-ary and future events as moving towards the present, (7b) construes time itself as a moving object, while (7c) construes time as a valuable and limited resource. There are no obvious non-metaphorical versions of these sentences. It is as if future events 'really' come nearer to the present. If metaphorical construal is as pervasive in everyday thought and language as Lakoff and Johnson argue that it is, it will be difficult in principle to cleanly separate out the metaphorical from the non-metaphorical. And if the metaphorical is deemed to be out of bounds to strict compositionality, it will not be possible in principle to cleanly identify the scope of strict compositionality.

(iii) Pragmatic interpretation. It is widely acknowledged that what a speaker intends to convey by an utterance may not coincide with what the speaker actually says. Someone who says (8) appears to be doing no more than making a statement about the current atmospheric conditions. The utterance, however, can be interpreted in a number of ways. It could be taken as a request to the hearer to do something about the stuffy conditions, that they should open a window, turn down the heating, or some such thing. Or it might be offered as an explanation for why the speaker is feeling unwell and wishes to leave.

(8) It's stuffy in here!

Such examples suggest the need to recognize two levels of meaning:

(i)   the literal meaning of an expression, roughly: 'what the words say', and
(ii) the interpretation that an expression receives when uttered in a certain context, roughly: 'what the speaker (probably) means'.

In many current theories the two levels are handled in terms of a distinction between semantics and pragmatics. What the words say is the province of semantics (hence, semantics is taken to be essentially a matter of composi-tionality), what the speaker is likely to mean when uttering the words is the province of pragmatics.[8]

---

[8] I will not review the main themes and controversies of theories of pragmatics; for this, the reader is referred to the standard textbooks, e.g. Levinson (1983).

Sometimes, the response of an uncooperative (or not fully proficient) conversational partner can jolt us into an awareness of the discrepancy between the literal and the intended meaning. You ring a friend and a young child answers the telephone. You ask, 'Is your mother in?' and the child responds, 'Yes'. There follows an embarrassing pause. Then you realize that you must spell out your intention more explicitly: 'Well, ask her to come to the phone'. The child took the question at face value and answered accordingly. The misunderstanding arose because the child failed to grasp the (unexpressed) intention behind the question.

Although the grounds for distinguishing between the semantic and the pragmatic seem very compelling, I suggest that the distinction is in fact far from clean-cut. Consider again the two examples presented above. *It's stuffy in here* is a statement; the speaker asserts that *p* is the case. *Is your mother in?* is a polarity question; the speaker asks for a specification of the polarity of a proposition: Is it, or is it not, the case that *p*?

Yet people do not, in general, go around making assertions, or asking questions, out of the blue. You would not say, out of the blue, *The Earth turns on its axis*; nor would you enquire, out of the blue, *Does the Earth turn on its axis?* Assertions and questions have to be relevant to the context in which they are uttered. They have to integrate with the ongoing discourse, with the shared knowledge of the conversational partners, and with the presumed concerns of a conversational partner. A major contribution of pragmatics theory has been to focus on precisely these issues. The 'pragmatic' interpretations of *It's stuffy in here* emerge in the context of their relevance to the context of utterance.

However, relevance to ongoing context is a factor in the interpretation of *any* assertion or *any* question that a person might utter, irrespective of whether the utterance should turn out to have a 'pragmatic' value wildly different from its 'semantic' value. A full specification of the conceptualization symbolized by an expression will need to incorporate these various aspects.

To the extent that we focus only on utterances, pragmatics is fully subsumed into a semantic characterization. The distinction between pragmatics and semantics only becomes relevant when we consider decontextualized expressions, where the 'pragmatic', context-specific aspects of meaning are filtered out, so to speak, leaving a shared core of conventionalized 'semantic' content.

Pragmatic aspects, though, are not always filtered out completely. Many expressions, by dint of their repeated use in certain kinds of situation, have acquired conventionalized pragmatic values. This is the case, I think, with the polarity question *Is X in?*, uttered at the beginning of a telephone call. The pragmatic value is part and parcel of the conventionalized meaning, so much so that it would probably be inappropriate for a speaker to begin a telephone conversation with a 'literal' statement of her intentions. *Is X in?*, or *Is X there?*, are the normal things to say.

Quite a number of polarity questions have taken on conventionalized pragmatic values. Example (9a) is the conventionalized way of asking for

Sentences and utterances

The traditional distinction between semantics and pragmatics rests on the distinction between sentence and utterance. Any semantic theory which makes the semantics/pragmatics distinction, not unsurprisingly, puts great store on the sentence/utterance distinction. A sentence is a decontextualized object, whose meaning (ideally) can be computed compositionally, without reference to the contexts in which a speaker might legitimately use the sentence. On this approach, an utterance is a context-dependent use of a sentence, whose interpretation emerges only with respect to the specifics of the usage event.

Cognitive Grammar views the distinction differently. The prime focus is on usage events (cf. p. 27); pragmatic (i.e. context-dependent) aspects are therefore integral to a full description of the semantic value of an expression (FCG1: 425–6). Sentences are abstractions over usage events, which filter out the context-specific particulars of the utterances. The distinction between sentence and utterance concerns the degree of abstractness, or schematicity, with which the linguistic expression is characterized. In brief, a sentence is schematic for utterances of the sentence, the utterances are instances of the sentence.

information, not at all a request concerning the hearer's ability. Examples (9b) and (9c) are conventionalized ways of making a request, while (9d) and (9e) are conventionalized responses to a surprising or unexpected piece of information.

(9) a. Could you tell me . . .
  b. Would you mind if . . .
  c. Why don't you . . .
  d. Would you believe it!
  e. Is that a fact!

6.2 'The football under the table'

In the previous section I reviewed a number of phenomena which, because of their ubiquity in language, cast doubt, not only on the centrality of strict compositionality in linguistic semantics, but also on the very viability of the compositionality principle. Nevertheless, the reader may still feel that there is a substantial core of expressions which are free from the contaminating effects of idiomaticity and the other phenomena. There is, after all, something intuitively appealing about compositionality; and, as mentioned earlier, given the creativity of language, one might well feel that semantics has to be compositional.

In this section I try to dispel this notion by looking in some detail at an expression which would seem to be as good a candidate as any for strict compositionality. If compositionality should fail here, then the principle is likely to fail in many other cases as well.

Consider the expression in (10). (The example, and my discussion of it, is based on FCG1: 279–82.)

(10) the football under the table

This expression is not at all idiomatic (at least, it is not idiomatic in the way that *spill the beans* is idiomatic), nor metaphorical, nor subject, in any obvious way, to pragmatic interpretations which are grossly at variance with its literal meaning. Moreover, polysemy (whether lexical or constructional) does not seem to enter into the picture. The expression, quite simply, designates a football which is located at a place which is under the table. Nothing, it seems, could be more straightforward.

Yet even this most banal of expressions turns out, on close examination, to have meanings that go beyond what is actually encoded.

We would almost certainly visualize 'the football under the table' something along the lines of Figure 6.1.[9] The first thing to note is that there are quite a few details in the Figure which are *not* encoded in the linguistic expression. The table is standing in its canonical orientation, with its legs on a level floor. The football is located on the floor, within an area circumscribed by the table's legs. An important aspect of the conceptualization, then, is the floor, on which the table is standing and on which the football is resting. However, there is no mention in (10) of a floor.

Although Figure 6.1 depicts what is probably the normal interpretation of *the football under the table*, there are many other configurations of football and table that would meet the description. Imagine that your garage is filled chock-a-block with old furniture and other kinds of junk. The table is over-turned and the football is squashed underneath it, as in Figure 6.2. If you let your imagination run wild, you could come up with some quite bizarre situations in which a football could be accurately (and literally) described as being 'under the table'. Suppose a helicopter is hovering overhead and that a table is

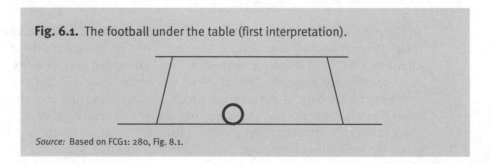

Fig. 6.1. The football under the table (first interpretation).

Source: Based on FCG1: 280, Fig. 8.1.

[9] In accordance with a convention introduced in Chapter 10, the entity that the expression designates, or profiles, is depicted in bold.

suspended by one of its legs from the helicopter, and that the football is in turn suspended from the table (Fig. 6.3). We see that it is hardly possible to visualize a football being under a table, in and of itself, divorced from more specific conceptualizations. The linguistic expression provides only the scaffolding, as it were, on which these interpretations are erected. In view of this, we might want to claim that the linguistic expression is simply vague, and that the interpretations emerge as contextually conditioned enrichments of the (compositionally derived) semantic content of the expression.

There is more to it than this, however. Strictly speaking, it is actually not the case that (10) is underspecified *vis-à-vis* Figure 6.1, nor is Figure 6.1 simply an

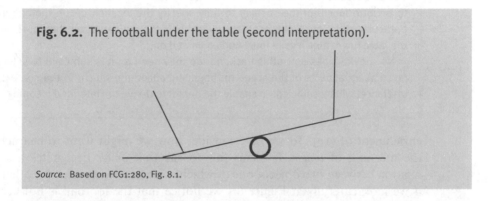

Fig. 6.2. The football under the table (second interpretation).

Source: Based on FCG1:280, Fig. 8.1.

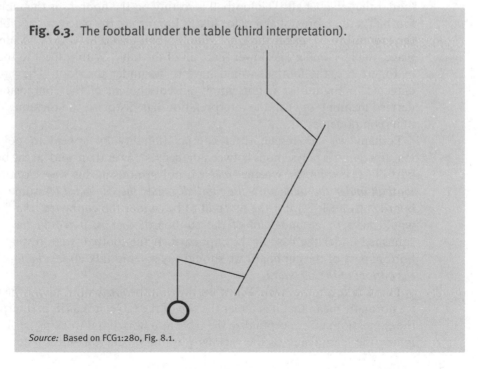

Fig. 6.3. The football under the table (third interpretation).

Source: Based on FCG1:280, Fig. 8.1.

The speaker's perspective

I have considered (10) from the point of view of how a hearer might interpret the expression. It is important, also, to consider the perspective of the speaker. A speaker, in uttering (10), wishes to refer to a specific football, and gives the hearer some clues as to where he may locate it. Suppose she wishes to refer to a football in the location depicted in Figure 6.1. Does she linguistically encode every facet of Figure 6.1, so as to rule out the other configurations? She could, perhaps, refer to *the football located on the floor, within an area circumscribed by the legs of a table standing in its canonical orientation, with its legs on a level floor*. Not only would this be a bizarre thing to do, there is ultimately no end to the detail that would need to be introduced for the speaker to fully specify the location of the football in a particular situation. Is the floor exactly level? Is there a carpet on the floor? Does the table have three legs or four? And so on and on.

No speaker goes down this track, nor do they need to. It is sufficient to select a few, salient aspects of the scene for linguistic encoding, which, in the context of utterance, will be sufficient to enable the hearer to derive the intended meaning.

---

enrichment of (10). To see this, consider how we might want to characterize the meaning of *under*. It seems fair to say that *under* designates a spatial relation between two objects, one of which is located lower than the other. But if we look carefully at Figure 6.1 we notice that the football is not actually 'under the table' at all. The football is resting on the floor, as is the table. The football is therefore not at a place that is lower than the place of the table. For the football to be 'under the table', the football would have to be located at a place which is 'under', i.e. lower than, all of the table. With respect to the table in Figure 6.1, the football would have to be under the floor. The situation depicted in Figure 6.1 is not simply an enrichment of the compositionally derived meaning of (10), the interpretation has distorted the meaning of one of its components.

Perhaps we can rescue strict compositionality by appeal to polysemy. Perhaps *under* is polysemous between the senses 'lower than' and 'at the bottom part of'. It is doubtful whether *under* is polysemous in this way. Contrast *the football under the table* with *the football under the cupboard* (Assume a cupboard without legs.) For the football to be 'under the cupboard' the football would have to be under all of the cupboard; that is, it would have to be squashed under the base of the cupboard. If the football were resting in the bottom part of the cupboard we should say so, and talk about *the football at the bottom of the cupboard*.

Let us take another tack. When we say that the football is 'under the table', we normally mean that it is under the top of the table; it is as if, in interpreting the expression, we conceptualize the table as a horizontal working surface and ignore the legs. Think of the various ways in which you would interpret *the chewing gum under the table*. The chewing gum could be stuck to the underside of the table top, in which case, again, the table legs get ignored. Alternatively, the chewing gum could be squashed under one of the legs.

Perhaps, then, *table* is polysemous. On the one hand, the word could designate a table as a whole, top, legs, and all. This sense of *table* would be implicated in Figure 6.3, where the football is indeed under all of the table. On a second sense, the word designates only a table top, without the legs. This sense would be implicated in Figure 6.1. By appealing to this second sense of *table*, we could say that the situation in Figure 6.1 fully matches the compositional meaning of (10).

Again, however, the polysemy approach fails. It just isn't true that *table* has, as one of its conventionalized meanings, 'table top'. Suppose I go to a joiner and ask him to make me a table, and the joiner delivers me a wooden board. I would certainly have reason to complain. And the joiner would not be able to defend himself by saying that he had misunderstood what I meant by my instruction—he had taken *table* to mean 'table top', whereas I had taken *table* to mean 'table top plus legs'. Clearly, *table* does not have, as one of its meanings, 'table top (without the legs)'. Even in Figure 6.1—which depicts a situation which the supposed polysemy of *table* is able to explain—the table does have legs.

The upshot is that even such a banal expression as *the football under the table* has a meaning which is not strictly compositional. To be sure, the meanings of *football*, *under*, and *table* contribute to the composite meaning. But the composite meaning goes beyond, and is partially at variance with, what can be worked out solely on the basis of the meanings of the component words.

6.3 Accommodation and active zones

The football and table example is symptomatic of a very general phenomenon. When conceptual structures are combined, often each has to 'accommodate' to the other, in such a way that they can participate coherently in the more complex conceptualization.

An analogy from phonology will be helpful. Consider the sounds [s, ʃ, iː, uː], as you would articulate them in isolation. Probably, you will articulate [ʃ] and [uː] with prominent lip rounding, whereas [s] and [iː] will have lip spreading. Predictably, [ʃuː] will have lip rounding throughout, whereas [siː] will have lip spreading throughout.

But now consider [ʃiː] and [suː]. The lip rounding, characteristic of [ʃ] and [uː], will be reduced, while [s] and [iː] might have some moderate rounding. Each sound has accommodated to its neighbour.

The phenomenon is well known to phoneticians and is called 'coarticulation'. Although each of the segments in a complex phonological structure may be associated with a characteristic articulatory posture, the complex structure

---

I wish she would *vs.* I wish you would

Remarkably, these two sentences, if spoken fairly quickly, may be indistinguishable, due to coarticulation effects of lip rounding and vowel fronting.

The contrasting words *she* and *you* occur between segments, namely the [ʃ] of *wish* and the [w] of *would*, which tend to be rounded. Rounding spreads into the [iː] of *she* and the [j] of *you*. Also, as the tongue moves from the front position of the vowel in *wish* to the back position of the vowel in *would*, the intervening words (*she, you*) are likely to be spoken with a centralized vowel, which effectively neutralizes the contrast between them.

---

does not consist of the aligning of a series of distinct postures. Some aspects of one sound may be anticipated in a preceding sound and may carry over to the articulation of the following sound. In the stream of speech, the ideal postures associated with the component sounds may not actually be attained at all.

We observe a similar kind of accommodation between semantic units. Langacker (FCG1: 76) cites the verb *run*. Although *run*, we might say, designates a rapid kind of motion on the part of a legged creature, the manner in which humans run is different from the manner in which horses run, which is again different from the manner in which cows, mice, or jaguars run. The process designated by the verb accommodates to the creature of which it is predicated. Or take the verb *eat*. Schematically, the verb designates the ingestion of solid food. But the actual process of a person eating a steak is different from how a person eats an ice-cream, which is different yet again from how a dog eats a bone, or a snake eats a bird.

Often, when entities participate in a situation, only some facets of the participating entities are implicated. Consider the expression in (11):

(11) John kicked the table.

The sentence describes an event involving two participants, John and the table. While we might say that John is the Agent (the one who does the kicking) and that the table is the Patient (the entity that gets kicked), it is evident that not all of John is equally involved in the kicking event, neither is every part of the table likely to be kicked. Probably, only one of John's feet made contact with the table, and only one part of the table (a leg, perhaps) was affected. The example illustrates what Langacker has called the 'active zone' phenomenon.

(12) Active zone. If an entity A participates in a situation, often certain parts of A are more intimately involved in the situation than others. These constitute the active zone of A.

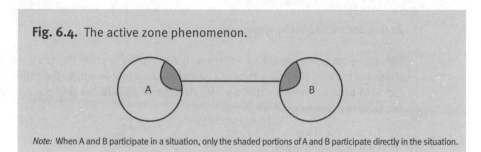

Fig. 6.4. The active zone phenomenon.

Note: When A and B participate in a situation, only the shaded portions of A and B participate directly in the situation.

The active zone phenomenon (see Figure 6.4) is ubiquitous.[10] Here are some more examples:

(**13**) a. I had my car serviced.
      b. I had my car washed and waxed.
      c. My car got scratched (in the accident).

(**14**) a. We had a picnic under the tree.
      b. We buried the box under the tree.
      c. The tunnel passes under the tree.

In (13), different facets of the car are involved in each of the three examples. In example (13a) only the mechanical parts of the car were serviced, in (13b) only the exterior metallic surface was washed and waxed, while (13c) would be true even if only a tiny portion of the exterior bodywork was scratched. Turning to (14), we note that *under the tree* designates a different kind of location in each of the three sentences. The different interpretations emerge because different facets of the tree participate in the 'under'-relation, as determined by the pragmatic plausibility of the designated situations.

The different interpretations of *under the tree* would be problematic for strict compositionality. We could hardly account for the differences by claiming that *tree* is polysemous between the readings (a) branches and foliage, (b) branches, foliage, and trunk, and (c) all of the tree, branches, trunk, roots, and all—and that each of the interpretations in (13) selects just one of these three meanings for combination with *under*. The active zone phenomenon is at the root of the problems that strict compositionality runs into with *the football under the table*. In certain uses of *table*, the table top is the active zone, which participates most directly in the complex configuration.

---

[10] As a matter of fact, it is actually quite difficult to cite an example in which the active zone phenomenon is entirely absent. *The Earth moves round the Sun* may be a possible example. (All parts of the Earth simultaneously move around all parts of the Sun.)

Active zones and metonymy

The active zone phenomenon has far-reaching ramifications. In the examples discussed in the text, the active zone is a part of the designated entity. The active zone can also extend to entities that are closely associated with the designated entity. Consider the following:

(i)   I heard the piano.
(ii)   I am in the phone book.

Strictly speaking, only sounds can be heard, not objects. What is conveyed by (i) is that I heard, not the piano as such, but a sound coming from the piano. The second example does not mean that I, as a physical being, am enclosed within the covers of the phone book, but that some attribute of me, namely, my name and telephone number (more precisely: a written representation of my name and telephone number) are printed on a page of the phone book.

Traditionally, these examples would be described as instances of metonymy: a word which, in its basic sense, refers to an entity *e*, is used to refer to an entity closely associated with *e*, within a given conceptual domain.

6.4 Mental spaces again: The case of the indefinite and definite articles

I already touched on mental spaces in Chapter 4 with respect to the sentence in (15).

(15) The girl with green eyes has blue eyes.

This example perfectly illustrates the topic of this chapter: the meaning of a complex expression can go beyond the meaning that is contributed by its parts. In terms of its compositional meaning, example (15) expresses a contradiction. Yet we can easily make sense of the sentence by assuming two mental spaces, one occupied by a girl with green eyes, the other by a girl with blue eyes, and a correspondence relation between the girls and the eyes (though not of the colour of the eyes) in the two spaces. Neither the mental spaces, nor the correspondence relations between the spaces, are overtly encoded in the linguistic expression. These aspects of the interpretation are beyond the scope of strict compositionality.

In this section I examine a couple more examples of the mental space phenomenon and the role of mental spaces in the interpretation of expressions.

6.4.1 Indefinites

The first example has to do with different interpretations of an indefinite noun phrase. Consider the expression in (16).

(16) Ursula wants to marry a millionaire.

This sentence has two distinct interpretations.

(i)   There exists a specific millionaire and Ursula wants to marry him. Ursula can identify the millionaire (she knows who it is that she wishes to marry). The speaker, however, may not be able to identify the millionaire, and certainly presumes that the hearer is not able to do so. This is the **indefinite specific** interpretation.

(ii)   Ursula has not yet found her millionaire (and may never do so). She merely has the desire to marry someone (whoever it might be) who is a millionaire. This is the **indefinite non-specific** interpretation.

These interpretations may be distinguished by the manner in which the millionaire is referred to in subsequent discourse. On the specific interpretation, the millionaire can be referred to as *he* or *him*, on the non-specific interpretation, the millionaire can be referred to as *one*.[11]

(**17**) a. Ursula wants to marry a millionaire. She met him at the Casino.
        b. Ursula wants to marry a millionaire. She hopes to meet one at the Casino.

One way to handle the difference would be to claim that the indefinite article *a* is polysemous between a specific and a non-specific reading. On this account, it is the polysemy of the indefinite article that gives rise to the ambiguity of the indefinite noun phrase.

But if the indefinite article is really polysemous, in the manner suggested, we shall have to say that every noun phrase introduced by *a* is potentially ambiguous. But this is not the case. The following is not at all ambiguous between a specific and a non-specific reading; example (18) can only mean that there was a specific millionaire and that Ursula married him.

(**18**) Ursula married a millionaire.

The non-specific reading only emerges under certain conditions. First, there has to be a secondary mental space—a mental space of a person's desires, hopes, or fantasies, for example—which is distinct from a base space. The designated entity exists in the secondary space but lacks a counterpart in the base space. An indefinite noun phrase merely designates an entity in *some* mental space. The ambiguity of example (16) is a consequence of mental space construction, it does not result from the polysemy of any of the participating semantic units.

6.4.2 Definites

The next example concerns different interpretations of a definite noun phrase introduced by *the*. Consider the expression in (19):

---

[11] Even on the non-specific reading, however, it is possible to refer to the millionaire by *he*. In the following example, the second sentence continues to refer to an entity in the hypothetical mental space.

(i) Ursula wants to marry a millionaire. But he's got to be a Catholic.

(**19**) Twenty years ago, the major of this city was a Communist.

This sentence has at least two distinct (and potentially incompatible) interpretations:

(i) The person who is now the mayor was, twenty years ago, a member of the Communist Party. (This person may not now be a member of the Communist Party and may not have been the mayor twenty years ago).

(ii) The person who, twenty years ago, was the mayor, was at that time a member of the Communist Party. (This person may not now be the mayor and may no longer be a member of the Communist Party. In fact, the person may no longer be alive.)

It would be hard to account for the different readings of example (19) in terms of the polysemy of any particular word. (Structural ambiguity is not an option, either.) It would be bizarre to say that a definite noun phrase, such as *the mayor*, is ambiguous between the readings 'the person who is now the mayor' and 'the person who used to the mayor'. The expression *the mayor* designates, quite simply, a person identifiable as 'the mayor', no more no less. The referent, however, has to be located in a mental space. The different interpretations come about because of the possibility of setting up two mental spaces, one representing the present situation, one representing the situation of twenty years ago. Each space is inhabited by various entities and relations between those entities. The entities and the relations in the one space may or may not have counterparts in the other space, and different interpretations come about because of different sets of correspondences.

There is a further reading of (19), according to which *the mayor of this city* does not refer to an individual at all, but to a role. Imagine that, twenty years ago, there was regulation which stipulated that whoever was mayor had to be a member of the Communist Party. Example (19) would be a true statement, even though the office of mayor might have been vacant twenty years ago. The role/value ambiguity, as we might call it, shows up elsewhere.

(**20**) The Pope lives in the Vatican.

Example (20) has the readings: 'The person who is now the Pope lives in the Vatican' and 'Whoever occupies the role of Pope lives in the Vatican'. On the second reading, the sentence could be true even though, at the time it is uttered, there might not actually be a Pope.

As with the other ambiguities discussed in this section, it would be an error to attribute the role/value ambiguity to the polysemy of any of the constituent parts of an expression. The ambiguity only arises in circumstances in which it is conceptually coherent to distinguish between a role and the individuals who can occupy the role. Again, we can appeal to mental space construction. The role interpretation emerges through the setting up of a mental space of roles.

It is a mental space of the world as constructed, for example, by bureaucrats and legislators.

These examples show how semantic structures, just like phonological structures, can take on a life of their own, over and above the concepts that are directly symbolized by a linguistic expression. To be sure, a complex expression is built up out of more elementary symbolic units. But the phonological and semantic representations of a complex expression cannot be taken to be a simple lining up of the sound patterns and concepts of the component words.

'Pure semantics'

We saw in the last chapter (section 5.4) that there can be utterances which are 'pure phonology', lacking any conceptual significance. Does an analogous situation hold with respect to conceptual structure? Can there be 'pure conceptualizations', which lack phonological expression?

There obviously can. We have all had the experience of knowing what we want to say (i.e. of entertaining a conceptualization) but being unable to find the right linguistic expression to symbolize it. Moreover, we can have concepts (understood as principles of categorization) which are independent of linguistic symbolization. I can have the concept of what a friend's face looks like, and what his voice sounds like, such that I can recognize that person when I see him or hear him. But there are no linguistic expressions which symbolize these visual and auditory concepts.

6.5 Why (strict) compositionality fails

Langacker has drawn attention to the necessity for some kind of compositional process:

It is worth pausing to consider why composite predications are necessary in the first place. The reason, quite obviously, is that linguistic convention cannot provide a fixed, unitary expression for every conceivable situation that a speaker might wish to describe. Instead it furnishes a limited inventory of fixed expressions, which are generally appropriate for coding only certain aspects of complex conceptualizations, together with a set of conventional patterns for combining these as needed. More often than not the speaker wishes to symbolize a coherent conceived situation that is relatively complex and for which no fixed expression is available. For purposes of linguistic coding, then, he is forced to dissociate his integrated conception into separate but overlapping 'chunks' for which conventional symbols are provided, and to invoke a number of compositional patterns sufficient to specify at least approximately the nature of their intended integration. (FCG1: 278)

It is almost a design feature of human languages that they allow the construction of semantically complex expressions out of simpler units. Without this facility, a language would be little more than a finite list of fixed messages, each linking an established sound pattern with a particularized meaning.

But while compositionality is a fact, strict compositionality fails, for two principal reasons.

(i) The conventionalized resources of a language (lexical, phrasal, and constructional) are abstractions over usage events. Their semantic content encapsulates common features of their many uses, filtering out, so to speak, the specifics of individual events. Even when a ready-made expression is applied to a situation, the specifics need to be filled in again.

(ii) When semantic units come together in a complex expression they need to accommodate to each other, their values shifting in order to be able to participate in the complex structure as applied to the intended conceptualization. A special case of accommodation is the active zone phenomenon—the fact that when an entity participates in a situation, typically some parts of the entity might be more immediately and intimately involved in the situation than others.

Overspanning the above considerations is the embeddedness of linguistic meanings within broader conceptual structures. Semantic structures do not exist as stable, free-floating, disembodied objects. All concepts are understood relative to a context. This is just as true of individual lexical concepts, such as [TABLE], as it is of complex concepts, such as [UNDER THE TABLE]. Crucial to the conceptualization of [TABLE] is knowledge of what tables are for, where they are usually found, how humans interact with them, their normal, or canonical position, and so on. Thus it can come about that a place 'under the table' gets interpreted as a place which is both 'under the table top' and 'on the floor'—even though these two aspects are not explicitly encoded.

Study questions

1. Losing money. The following sentences contain the identical expression *I lost £1,000*.

   (i) a. I lost £1,000 in the street. (My wallet containing the bank notes fell out of my pocket.)
   b. I lost £1,000 on the Stock Exchange. (I made a bad investment.)

   In both cases, I end up £1,000 the poorer. From this point of view, *I lost £1,000* has the same meaning in both sentences. Yet the actual *process* of losing the money, whether on the street or on the Stock Exchange, is different. Note that the two situations give rise to different entailments.

   (ii) a. If I lose £1,000 in the street (because my wallet containing the bank notes falls out of my pocket), there is a chance that I might *find* my £1,000 again.

b. If I lose £1,000 on the Stock Exchange (because of a bad investment), there is the possibility that I might *recover* my £1,000 (by making another, more successful investment), but there is no possibility that I might *find* my £1,000 again.

How might one explain these different entailments? Is the verb *lose* polysemous? Is the expression *£1,000* polysemous? Does *find* have one, or more than one meaning? What conditions have to be met for it to be appropriate for me to say that I 'found' £1,000? And what conditions would have to be met for me to be able to say that I found my £1,000 'again'?

2. Leaving the University. The following has two distinct interpretations.

(i) Mike left the University a short time ago.

(If you find it difficult to get the two interpretations, try replacing *a short time ago*, first, with *ten minutes ago*, and then with *ten years ago*.) Which words, if any, in this sentence can reasonably be regarded as polysemous? What inferences can you draw about Mike and his relationship to the University on the two interpretations?

3. Full of beer. Consider the ways in which the following sentences are interpreted:

(i) The bottle is full of beer.

(ii) The container is full of beer.

(iii) The fridge is full of beer.

Is the manner in which the beer 'fills' the bottle in (i) analogous to the manner in which the beer 'fills' the fridge in (iii)? What kind of container do you imagine in (ii)? How could one account for these effects?

4. In. In its spatial uses, *in* designates a relation of containment. The following seems to hold:

(i) If *a* is in *b*, *a* occupies a place that is contained within the place that is occupied by *b*.

While this characterization may be generally true, the manner of containment is conceptualized differently, according to the nature of the container and the contained. How is the containment relation conceptualized in the following?

(ii) the water in the vase
the crack in the vase
the flowers in the vase
the umbrella in my hand
the car in the street
the money in my hand
the diamond in the ring
the light bulb in the socket

Sometimes, more than one conceptualization is available:

(iii) the cigarette in my mouth
the splinter in my hand
ten children (standing) in a circle

Given the characterization in (i), the following should hold. (Technically, *in* expresses a **transitive relation**.)

(iv) if *a* is in *b*, and *b* is in *c*, then *a* is in *c*.

Does (iv) apply to the following?

(v) The money is in my briefcase.
My briefcase is in my car.
Therefore, the money is in my car.

(vi) The documents are in my car.
My car is in the car park.
Therefore, the documents are in the car park.

(vii) The flowers are in the vase.
The vase is in my hand.
Therefore, the flowers are in my hand.

5. **Near the house.** In a recent publication, Chomsky (2000: 35–6) drew attention to some (for him) curious aspects of the word *house*. If you *paint the house brown*, you (typically) paint only the exterior shell of the house. (Not all parts of the exterior, though; you wouldn't paint the window panes brown, for example.) If you *see the house*, you see its exterior; you are not able (according to Chomsky) to 'see the house' if you are sitting inside it. *House*, in these examples, therefore designates the exterior walls of a building.

Suppose, now, that two people, Irene and Olga, are each located three metres from the exterior wall of a house. Irene is inside the house, three metres from the wall; Olga is outside the house, three metres from the wall. We could say that Olga is 'near the house', but we could not say the same of Irene. How can we explain this, given that *house* is able to designate the exterior walls of a building?

Another question raised by Chomsky's observations is the following: What do you do if you *clean the house*? Is the expression open to different interpretations? Consider what a house-painter might mean, if he has to 'clean the house' before painting it. Which facets of a house are involved if we say that the house is *a mess*?

6. **Ambiguous sentences.** It is often assumed that the ambiguity of a sentence can be traced to a single source, i.e. the polysemy of a lexical item or to alternative syntactic structures. Consider the following 'textbook' examples of ambiguity:

(i)   I saw a man with a telescope.

(ii) She can't bear children.

(iii) Flying planes can be dangerous.

(iv) Time flies like an arrow.

The ambiguity of (i) results from two constituency structures: *with a tele-scope* can modify *man*, or it can modify *saw the man*. These two structures, however, go hand in hand with two different senses of *with*. What are they?

Identify the sources of the ambiguities in (ii) to (iv). Pay attention to both syntactic and lexical ambiguities. (Note that (iv) has at least three readings, a 'normal' reading, alongside two bizarre readings.)

7. **The young man's murderer.** The following sentence has two different readings.

> (i) The young man's murderer is a psychopath.

The two readings can be roughly paraphrased as follows. Note that on the second reading, sentence (i) could be a true statement even though the identity of the murderer is not known.

> (i′) 'This person, who murdered the young man, is a psychopath.'
>
> (i″) 'Whoever it was that murdered the young man, that person has got to be a psychopath.'

There are some affinities between the ambiguity of (i) and the role/value ambiguity of (19) and (20). Explain what they are. Can the ambiguity be traced back to the polysemy—lexical or structural—of any single item, or items, in (i)?

Under what conditions does this kind of ambiguity arise? Do the following display the role/value ambiguity?

> (ii) The people next door have noisy parties every night.
>
> (iii) The mayor {opened / always opens / will open} the flower show.
>
> (iv) The President was elected for life.
>
> (v) My computer crashes.

8. **Same.** Imagine a woman who says, on seeing another woman:

> (i) She's wearing the same dress as I'm wearing.

This does not mean that the two women are enclosed, like Siamese twins, within one article of clothing. It means that they are wearing dresses made to the same design. This interpretation still holds even with intensification of *same*, e.g. *the very same dress*, *exactly the same dress*. Likewise, (ii) does not necessarily impute theft to the other woman (although it could).

> (ii) She's wearing my dress!

These special readings might be accounted for by postulating a mental space of 'designs'. However, we do not always get the 'design' reading. Consider the following:

> (iii) My husband and I both drive the same car.
>
> (iv) My parents live in the same house as I live in.
>
> (v) They live in the same {street / city} as I live in.

(iv) would almost certainly be interpreted to mean that my parents and I share the same place of residence. It would be difficult to get the interpretation that they live in a house designed on identical architectural principles as mine. On the other hand, (iii) seems to favour the 'design' interpretation — we each drive a car of the same make.

Construct other examples with *same* (and supplement your intuitions with corpus data on this word). What are the factors which facilitate (and hinder) the creation of a 'design space'?

Further reading

For Langacker's critique of compositionality, see FCG1: 452–66. For active zones, see Langacker (1984). Cruse (2000*b*, ch. 4) contains a characterization of compositionality, and reviews its limits. Gibbs (1994, ch. 1) argues against the possibility of 'literal' meaning. Fauconnier (1994) is a rich source of examples in which the semantic interpretation is underdetermined by the words on the page. Jackendoff (1997, ch. 3) gives several examples suggesting that semantic interpretations are underdetermined by the words and syntax. (He calls the phenomenon 'enriched interpretation').

There is a vast literature on 'pragmatic' interpretations, i.e. on the manner in which supposedly compositionally derived meaning is elaborated relative to the context of the speech act. See Levinson (1983), and Sperber and Wilson (1986).

Part 2
Basic Concepts

The précis of Cognitive Grammar in Chapter 2 emphasized the minimalist assumptions of the theory. Only three kinds of entity are postulated – phonological structures, semantic structures, and symbolic relations between phonological and semantic structures. The seven chapters of Part 2 address the 'mechanics' of Cognitive Grammar – how a theory which makes such sparse assumptions is able to address the complexities of human languages.

Chapters 7, 8, and 9 discuss the 'vertical' relations (that is, the relations of instance to schema) that can hold between semantic units, phonological units, and symbolic units. Chapters 10 and 11 introduce the concepts of profile and base, and apply these to a characterization of the major word classes. Chapters 12 and 13 address the mechanisms whereby smaller units combine into larger configurations.

CHAPTER 7

Schema and instance

A language may be characterized as a structured inventory of linguistic units. The linguistic units comprise phonological units, semantic units, and symbolic units. The inventory is not only very large, it is also structured, in that units are interrelated in complex and intricate ways.

In this and the next two chapters, I focus on one kind of relation that can exist between linguistic units. This is the 'vertical' relation that holds between a more schematically characterized unit and more fully specified units that count as instances of the schema. The schema-instance relation applies equally to phonological, semantic, and symbolic units. In this chapter I introduce the relation with reference to semantic units.

7.1 Schema and instance

Conceptualizations may differ according to the richness of detail with which they are specified.

Compare, for example, the semantic units [DOG] and [ANIMAL]. It is evident that [ANIMAL] is a more general concept than [DOG] and is specified in less detail. As a consequence, there are going to be many more things that can be categorized as an animal than can be categorized as a dog. A similar state of affairs holds for verbal concepts. The concept symbolized by the verb *do* is much more general than the concept symbolized by *marinate*. The richly specified [MARINATE] can be applied only to a restricted range of activities, of a very specific kind, whereas the more general concept [DO] can be applied to a very much broader range of activities.

The concepts [DOG] and [ANIMAL] not only differ with respect to their detail, they bear a special relation to each other—a dog *is* an animal. There are many other entities that bear this relation to [ANIMAL], such as [CAT], [COW], [HORSE], etc. The relation is represented in Figure 7.1.

The more general unit is commonly referred to as the **superordinate**, the lower units as its **hyponyms**. A characteristic of hyponyms is that they are incompatible; if something is a dog, it cannot at the same time be a cat, and vice versa. There is a good discussion of this kind of semantic relation in Cruse (1986: 88–92, 136–56).

I will not use the term 'hyponym', for the reason that it is restricted to semantic relations. As we shall see in due course, the kind of relation that exists between [ANIMAL] and [DOG] shows up also between phonological and between symbolic units. Instead, following Langacker's practice, I shall refer to the relation exemplified in Figure 7.1 as the relation of a **schema** to its **instances**. The schema is specified in relatively general terms; the instances flesh out the schema by adding additional specifications. Different instances flesh out the schema in different and contrasting ways. I propose, then, to generalize the relation in Figure 7.1 to the one depicted in Figure 7.2. The slots in Figure 7.2 could be filled in with semantic units of many diverse kinds. The schematic item could be [COLOUR], the instances being the specific colours [RED], [GREEN], [BLUE], etc. The upper term could be the process [COOK], the lower terms the different manners of cooking, such as [ROAST], [BOIL], [FRY], [BAKE].

The salient properties of Figure 7.2 can be summarized as follows:

- Unit [A] is **schematic** for [B] and [C]; [B] and [C] **instantiate**, or **elaborate** [A]. An instance **inherits** the specifications of the schema, but fleshes out the schema in more detail. Different instances flesh out the schema in contrasting ways. Alternatively, we can say that the schema **abstracts** what is common to its instances.

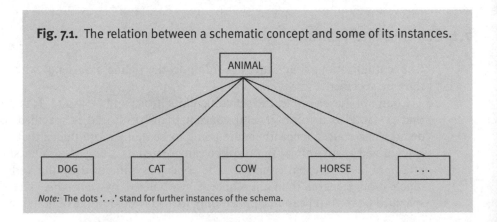

Fig. 7.1. The relation between a schematic concept and some of its instances.

Note: The dots '. . .' stand for further instances of the schema.

Tests for hyponymy

Cruse (1986: 88–92) proposes a number of tests for identifying the relation of hyponymy. One of these involves the semantic relation of **unilateral entailment**. *A* unilaterally entails *B* if *B* is true whenever *A* is true. The entailment relation works in only one direction—it is not the case that *A* is true whenever *B* is true. *B* is a hyponym of *A* if the following entailments hold:

> *This is a B* unilaterally entails *This is an A.*
> *This is not an A* unilaterally entails *This is not a B.*

With reference to the contents of Figure 7.1:

> *This is a dog* unilaterally entails *This is an animal.*
> *This is not an animal* unilaterally entails *This is not a dog.*

Cruse (p. 91) observes that items related by hyponymy are likely to occur in other environments, including the following:

> *dogs and other animals* (*dog* is a hyponym of *animal*)
> *There's no flower more beautiful than a rose* (*rose* is a hyponym of *flower*)
> *He likes all fruit except bananas*
> *She reads books all day—mostly novels*

- The instances are related by **similarity**; [B] and [C] are similar, precisely in respect to the fact that they both inherit the specifications of the schema [A]. Schema [A] encapsulates the way in which the instances are perceived to be similar.
- The solid lines indicate a relationship of instantiation; the broken line indicates the similarity between the instances. The solid lines have arrows pointing in both directions. This indicates that the relation can in principle go either way—from the schema to the instances, and from the instance to

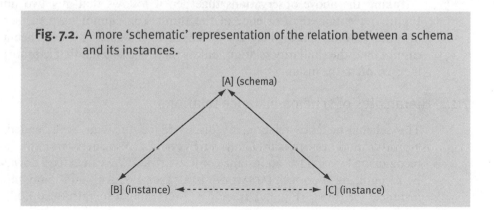

Fig. 7.2. A more 'schematic' representation of the relation between a schema and its instances.

the schema. The broken line has arrows pointing to both [B] and [C]; this indicates that the similarity relation may also go in both ways.

The triangle in Figure 7.2, and the relations it depicts, play a very important role in Cognitive Grammar. I would like to draw attention to some further aspects.

Figure 7.2 shows two instances of schema [A]. A schema typically has very many instances. In some cases, the number of instances may be to all intents and purposes open-ended; consider the number of instances of the concept [ANIMAL]. But I would argue that for the schema-instance relation to hold at all, **there has to be a minimum of two instances**. Unless there are at least two units that count as instances of [A], there is no basis for abstracting the commonality that constitutes the content of the schema.

What would it mean for a schema to have only one instance? Suppose everything in the universe were the same shade of blue. (More precisely: Suppose our visual apparatus were such that everything in the universe were perceived as being the same shade of blue.) Would we have the concepts [BLUE] and [COLOUR], with [BLUE] being an instance of [COLOUR]? We would presumably have the concept of the colour that everything is. But if there were no colours that contrasted with this colour, there would be no basis for abstracting the commonality of different colours, and for recognizing a schematic concept [COLOUR]. Neither would there be any basis for stating in what way the concept [BLUE] elaborated the concept [COLOUR]. In a monochromatic universe, there would simply be no basis for distinguishing the concepts [BLUE] and [COLOUR].

Consider now the similarity relation between [B] and [C]. Similarity resides in the fact that the specifications of [B] only partially coincide with the specifications of [C]. The units are similar precisely in respect to their shared content, and the shared content is captured in a schema of which [B] and [C] are instances. The very fact that a person recognizes two entities as similar, a cat and a dog, for example, is tantamount to the recognition of a schema which abstracts what is common to them.

Taking the above observations together, it follows that any two units in Figure 7.2 entails the existence of the third. You cannot have the schema-instance relation unless there are at least two instances of the schema; you cannot have the similarity relation, unless there is a schema that captures what is common to the instances.

7.1.1 Hierarchies of schema-instance relations

The schema-instance relation, as discussed so far, can be extended both 'upwards' and 'downwards'. Consider Figure 7.1. We can extend upwards, by recognizing [ANIMAL] as an instance of [CREATURE]. We can extend downwards by recognizing [POODLE], [ALSATIAN], [SCOTTISH TERRIER], and many more, as instances of [DOG] (Fig. 7.3 (p. 128)). We could also introduce additional

Schema and instance: Some non-linguistic examples

The notions of schema and instance apply not only to relations between linguistic units but also to aspects of non-linguistic cognition. The visual image of a person seen at a distance, or in poor visibility, is schematic for the image of a person seen close up, or in good lighting. The structure of a sonnet, or a classical symphony, is schematic for an individual sonnet, or symphony, which fleshes out the schema in particular ways. Algebraic expressions are schemas, which are instantiated when the variables receive numerical values. $x^2 = y$ is schematic for an infinite number of expressions, such as $2^2 = 4$, $3^2 = 9$.

Two notes on usage

1. I use the word 'schematic' in two distinct, though closely related senses. In describing Figure 7.2, I stated that unit [A] is schematic for unit [B]. This is a relational use of the term; a unit is schematic in relation to other units which are its instances.

Alternatively, we may say that a given unit is schematic, *tout court*. This is a non-relational use of the word. A schematic unit is one which is specified in very general terms. [ANIMAL], [THING], and [DO] could be described, without further modification, as 'schematic'.

2. It is important to be on one's guard for two different uses of the term 'abstract'. On the one hand we might say that a schema abstracts what is common to its instances; here, 'abstract' refers to the elimination of the particulars associated with the instances. In this sense, 'abstract' contrasts with 'specific'.

A second use contrasts 'abstract' with 'concrete'. 'Concrete' applies to entities that exist in the domain of three-dimensional space; 'abstract' refers to entities that exist in other domains. Concrete entities have weight and spatial extension, and, mostly, can be touched and manipulated. Abstract entities include mental phenomena, concepts of time, institutions, and so on. It is also legitimate to talk about concrete vs. abstract uses of verbs and prepositions, according to whether these words express relations between concrete or abstract entities. We could say that *the money in the box* exemplifies a concrete use of *in*, whereas *a week in my life* exemplifies an abstract use of the word.

The abstractness of a concept in this second sense is independent of its schematicity, i.e. its 'abstractness' in the first sense. While [ANIMAL] is schematic for [DOG], both concepts are concrete. On the other hand, both [EMOTION] and [ADORATION] are abstract, irrespective of the fact that [ADORATION] is specified in more detail than the more schematic concept [EMOTION].

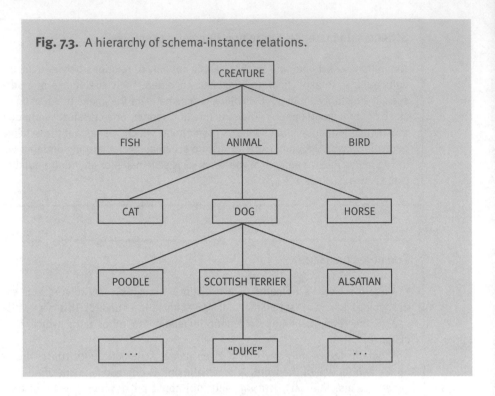

Fig. 7.3. A hierarchy of schema-instance relations.

intervening levels. The relation between [ANIMAL] and [DOG] could be expanded to incorporate the intervening concept [MAMMAL]. Between [MAMMAL] and [DOG] we could introduce the concept [CANIS], which is schematic for dogs and wolves, [CANIS FAMILIARIS] and [CANIS LUPUS].

There is a limit to how far upwards, and how far downwards, we can extend the hierarchy. The upper limit will be a concept which is schematic for everything. What about the lower limit? As concepts get specified in ever more detail they are applicable to fewer and fewer entities. Ultimately we arrive at concepts of individual entities. Once we get to the concept of my Scottish Terrier 'Duke' (now, regrettably, deceased), there is nothing for which this concept can be schematic.

Hierarchies of schema-instance relations, of the kind depicted in Figure 7.3, are often referred to as taxonomies. A **taxonomy** is a system for classifying things.

A well-known example of a taxonomy is the Linnaean classification of plants and animals. Figure 7.4 (p. 129) shows a Linnaean classifications of animals. Not all of the intervening levels are equally salient. In fact, many of the levels proposed in a scientific taxonomy will be virtually unknown to the lay speaker, while others, even if they are known to a speaker, will be invoked relatively infrequently. I address the topic of relative salience below.

Fig. 7.4. A partial taxonomy of animals.

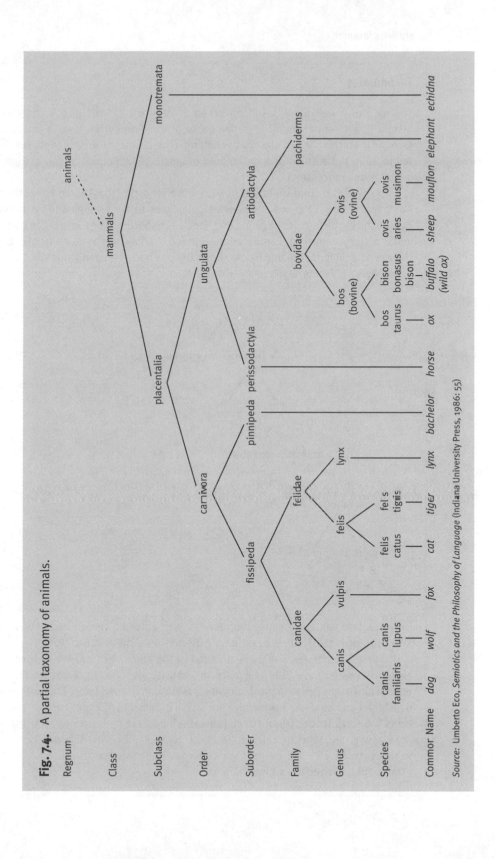

Source: Umberto Eco, *Semiotics and the Philosophy of Language* (Indiana University Press, 1986: 55)

Taxonomies

The idea of a taxonomy based on schema-instance relations has a venerable history in Western thought. It is the basis of the **Porphyrian tree**, a universal taxonomy which aimed to classify everything. (The taxonomy was, though, restricted to 'things', i.e. to entities designated in language by nominals, and excluded relations and processes.)

Porphyry was a third-century scholar, whose *Isagoge* (1975) is an exegesis of Aristotle's notions of **genus** and **species** (analogous to our schema and instance). By recognizing hierarchies of genus and species (a species of one genus can be the genus of further species), Porphyry endeavoured to show how a taxonomy of everything can be built up. The tree below shows the position of the individual 'Socrates' in Porphyry's universal taxonomy.

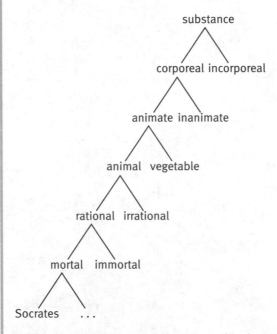

Universal taxonomies were also proposed in the eighteenth century as the basis of artificial languages. There is a fascinating discussion of these in Eco (1995).

Universal taxonomies, like those pursued by the scholastics and the eighteenth-century scholars, have little relevance in linguistic description. What we find in natural languages is not so much a neat classification of everything, but quite well-developed and compact taxonomies for specific domains of experience. The concepts [VEHICLE], [TOOL], [FURNITURE], [BUILDING], [ARTICLE OF CLOTHING], [EMOTION], [FOODSTUFF] are schematic for clusters of concepts, i.e. for different kinds of vehicles, tools, etc. The overarching concepts [VEHICLE], [EMOTION], etc., define what is often referred to as a **lexical field**.

7.1.2 The basic level

Taxonomies, like that in Figure 7.3, are based on the recursive application of the schema-instance relation. Given the principles which structure the taxonomy, it is apparent that any entity that can be appropriately named by a term in a taxonomy can be appropriately named by any of the higher terms. A dog can be appropriately called a 'dog', but also an 'animal', or a 'creature'. With respect to the Porphyrian tree in the Box, Socrates could be called a 'mortal substance', a 'rational substance', an 'animate substance', or, quite simply, a 'substance'. Each of these designations is equally valid. However, the different designations provide a different perspective on the entity. To call a dog a Scottish Terrier is to categorize him at a relatively low level of schematicity, drawing attention to the special characteristics that distinguish this breed of dog from the others; to call him an animal is to overlook his 'dogginess' and to categorize him at a more general, schematic level.

The level at which things are named obviously varies according to a person's interests and purposes. It generally turns out, however, that there is one level in a taxonomy which is particularly salient. This is the **basic level**—the level at which things are called unless there are good reasons to do otherwise. If asked what those things are in the field, you would probably respond that they are 'cows', not that they are 'animals', 'creatures', or 'Jerseys'—even though these latter responses would be equally true. In Figure 7.5, the salience of the basic level is represented by the thickness of the outline of the enclosing box.

What is it that confers salience on one particular level in a taxonomy? The question was addressed by Rosch (1975) and by Rosch and Mervis (1975). Rosch presented subjects with category names, at different levels in a

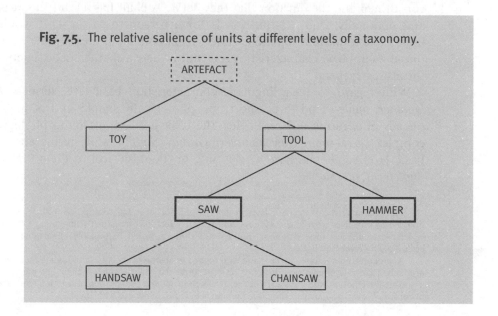

Fig. 7.5. The relative salience of units at different levels of a taxonomy.

taxonomy, and asked them to list the characteristic features of the categories. It turned out that units at the basic level were characterized by a relatively large number of features; also, basic-level terms tended not to share features among themselves. In contrast, units below a basic-level term shared attributes amongst themselves and with the basic level, while units above the basic level exhibited comparatively few nameable attributes at all. Units at the basic level are therefore maximally contrastive, and maximally informative. To call something by a name below the basic level adds relatively little information *vis-à-vis* naming it at the basic level or naming it by other subordinate terms. Units above the basic level are generally so schematic that they are applicable to a very wide range of entities. To call something by a name above the basic level actually tells you very little about the entity in question.

Because of their schematicity, it is difficult, if not impossible, to form a mental image of concepts above the basic level. We can easily form a mental image of a car, a dog, a cow, a hammer, a chair, or an apple. (We would have no problem in following an instruction to draw a picture of a car, or of a dog, for example.) These are basic-level concepts. We cannot, however, form a mental image of a piece of furniture that is schematic for all the different instances of this concept (chair, table, bed . . .). If asked to draw a picture of a piece of furniture, the best we could do would be to draw a picture of a particular kind of furniture, such as a chair. The same goes for other schematic concepts such as vehicle, animal, tool, and fruit. In fact, one way of characterizing the basic level is to say that it is the highest level in a taxonomy at which one is able to form a mental image of a concept.[1]

A related characteristic is that entities categorized at the basic level (or at a lower level) can often be described in terms of the parts of which they are constituted and the function that they serve. A chair has a seat, legs, a back, and optionally arms. Its function is for a person to sit on it. It would be impossible to make comparable statements about furniture. A piece of furniture does not have characteristic parts, nor is there a characteristic function of furniture in general.[2]

With regard to their linguistic characteristics, basic-level terms—*chair, hammer, apple*—tend to be short, morphologically simple, and of high frequency of occurrence. Terms below the basic level are often morphologically complex (*deck-chair, claw hammer, Granny Smith*), while terms above the basic level sometimes have a scientific, or 'bookish' feel to them (*mammal, implement, artefact*).

---

[1] This characteristic of the basic level probably holds for 'abstract' concepts as well. We can easily imagine to ourselves what anger, sadness, and jealousy feel like, perhaps by imagining situations in which we would feel these emotions. But I don't think it would be possible to imagine what 'an emotion' *tout court* feels like.

[2] Analogous observations can be made with regard to abstract concepts. Although 'anger' (which is arguably a basic-level emotion) does not have parts in the way in which a chair has parts, we can associate the emotion with a scenario of events which includes a provocation, a reaction, and attempts at control. We can also imagine the characteristic behaviour associated with anger.

7.1.3 Cross-cutting hierarchies

A semantic unit can often participate in more than one schema-instance relation. To be sure, [DOG] is an instance of [MAMMAL], which in turn is an instance of [ANIMAL]. But [DOG] may also be an instance of [PET]. This is not an intermediate category located between [MAMMAL] and [DOG]—you can have pets that are not mammals, such as pet fish, pet birds, pet snakes, and even an electronic pet tamaguchi; equally, not all dogs are pets. [PET] is a 'functional' category, having to do with how people interact with entities, and is independent of a zoologist's categorization. The schema-instance relation between [PET] and [DOG] cross-cuts the relation between [MAMMAL] and [DOG] (Figure 7.6).

Cross-cutting the Linnaean classification of plants and animals are other functional categories, such as [PEST], [VERMIN], [WEED], [GAME]. The category [WEED], for example, does not coincide with any of the biological categories; a weed is any plant that grows where a gardener or farmer doesn't want it to grow. What counts as a weed is not fixed, either; one person's weed is another person's cultivar.

Even if we consider tightly circumscribed lexical fields, we often find that different taxonomies are possible. Consider the four concepts [MAN], [WOMAN], [BOY], [GIRL]. While all these are instances of [HUMAN BEING], we can order them in two ways with respect to an intermediate level. We can make an initial distinction between [MALE] and [FEMALE], or between [ADULT] and [CHILD] (Fig. 7.7 (p. 134)).

Different taxonomic arrangements can be invoked in different contexts. If you say of a new-born infant that *It's a boy!*, [BOY] is being contrasted with [GIRL], both being instances of [CHILD]. You are invoking the taxonomy in the lower half of Figure 7.7. If, however, you remark that the army recruits are *only boys*, you are likely to be contrasting [BOY] with [MAN], both being instances of [MALE HUMAN BEING]. Here, you are invoking the upper taxonomy in Figure 7.7. In yet other cases, [BOY] will be an instance, quite simply, of [HUMAN BEING], with both age and gender being irrelevant.[3]

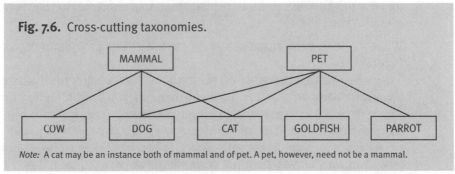

Fig. 7.6. Cross-cutting taxonomies.

Note: A cat may be an instance both of mammal and of pet. A pet, however, need not be a mammal.

---

[3] Complicating the matter further is the fact that *man* can have more than one meaning. The word could designate an adult male human, as depicted in Figure 7.7, or could be used in the sense of 'human being', in contrast to non-humans (a usage which is under increasing attack from proponents of non-sexist language).

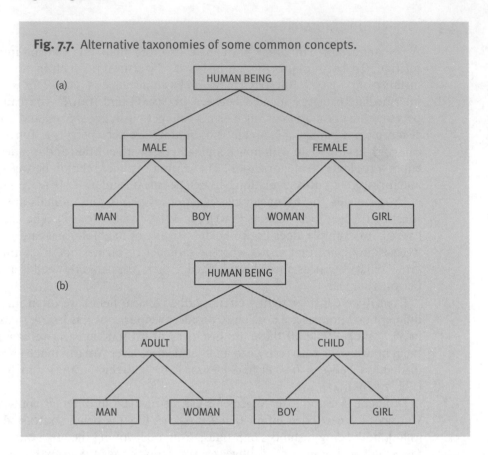

Fig. 7.7. Alternative taxonomies of some common concepts.

The possibility of alternative categorizations is nicely illustrated by the following story fragment:

During the night, looking out of the window of her home in the countryside, a wife tells her husband: Honey, there is a man on the lawn near the fence! Now, suppose the husband controls the situation and answers: No, honey, it's not a man. . . . (Eco 1984: 79)

What was it that the husband saw on the lawn? The problem is represented in Figure 7.8 (p. 135).

By asserting that the entity on the lawn was 'not a man', the husband sets up a contrast between [MAN] and some other entity, within a limited taxonomy. The task of the interpreter is to categorize [MAN] as an instance of a schema [A], and then to speculate on the identity of [C], a concept which is an instance of [A] and which contrasts with [MAN]. If [MAN] is taken to be an instance of [ADULT HUMAN BEING], then [C] takes the value [WOMAN]; if [A] is taken to be [MALE HUMAN BEING], then [C] is filled in with [BOY]. But [MAN] can be an instance of a large number of schematic units, each of which sets [MAN] in contrast with different kinds of entities. The thing on the lawn could have been

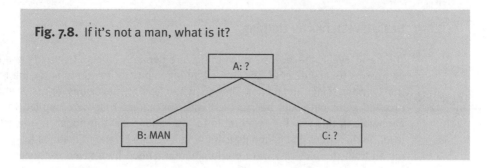

Fig. 7.8. If it's not a man, what is it?

a ghost, in which case [A] is schematic for human beings, corporeal or incorporeal. It could have been an alien, in which case [A] is schematic for creatures, terrestrial or extra-terrestrial. It could have been a giant teddy bear, in which case [A] would be schematic for anything with a vaguely animal-like shape. It could have been a boa-constrictor, in which case [A] is a schema for anything dangerous. The little story is potentially so scary, because the hearer is able to conjure up a number of different, and sometimes ad hoc schemas, each of which makes possible a range of values of [C].

7.1.4 Badly behaved taxonomies

A well-behaved taxonomy is one in which each schema is elaborated by a set of contrasting instances; each of the instances in turn is elaborated by a set of contrasting instances, and so on, down to individuals. Conversely, each schema is itself an instance of a higher schema, up to a maximally schematic entity. As we have noted, within the taxonomy, one level will be privileged; this is the basic level.

Often, however, semantic units do not pan out like this. Consider [CUP] and [MUG]. Both, we may agree, are instances of a schematic unit, which we might designate as [DRINKING VESSEL]. This unit is not particularly salient; witness the fact that it has to be called by a complex linguistic expression, an expression, moreover, that we would not use very frequently. You would hardly go into a department store and ask where the drinking vessels are to be found.

What, though, of the relation between [CUP] and [MUG]? Are they on the same taxonomic level, or is one schematic for the other? Are they basic-level concepts? If [CUP] and [MUG] are on the same level they will be incompatibles; that is to say, a cup cannot be a mug, and a mug cannot be a cup—which seems not to be true. An alternative would be to say that a mug is a kind of cup, or that a cup is a kind of mug. Neither of these seems quite right, either (though, to be sure, different speakers might have different intuitions).

Consider the situation depicted in Figure 7.9(a) (p. 137). The situation would be appropriate for a society in which tea drinking and coffee drinking are established social rituals, each associated with different kinds of drinking vessels. In this society, teacups and coffee cups would be salient and

Basic-level terms for clothing

The basic level is the level at which things are normally named. Geeraerts and his co-workers (Geeraerts *et al.* 1994) used an ingenious technique to study the relation between things and names. They searched fashion magazines for cases where pictured garments could be matched with the names that were applied to the garments. In this way they were able to 'operationalize' the notion of the basic level. To the extent that garments exhibiting a certain cluster of features (as determined from the pictures) were predominantly named by a given expression (as determined from the picture captions), that expression could be accorded basic-level status. Furthermore, the relative 'basicness' of a term could be quantified by calculating the number of actual uses of a term as a percentage of the number of potential uses (that is, the number of times a word was used of garments of a certain type as a percentage of the total number of times those garments were named).

Basic-level status turned out to be a matter of degree, rather than clear-cut. Here are some of the findings pertaining to names for trouser-like and shirt-like garments in Dutch (cf. Geeraerts 2000: 90).

Expression	Actual uses as a percentage of potential uses
legging / leggings / caleçon	45.50
short / shorts	45.61
broek 'trousers'	46.47
Bermudas [shorts]	50.88
jeans / jeansbroek / spijkerbroek	81.66
overhemdblouse	12.74
hemd	22.31
shirt	29.06
topje 'top'	29.62
overhemd	31.45
blouse / bloeze / bloes	61.52
T-shirt	70.61

Although jeans, shorts, leggings, and Bermudas [shorts] are kinds of trousers ('two-legged garments covering the lower part of the body'), jeans are likely to be referred to as such almost twice as often as the other kinds of items.

contrasting instances of a basic-level concept [CUP]. Mugs would be fairly non-salient and rather marginal instance of the category. A mug is not dedicated to the consumption of any particular kind of beverage, and it is not associated with ritualized occasions.

Imagine, however, that with changing lifestyles, people congregate less and less frequently for formal tea drinking and coffee drinking; they read the newspaper with a mug of tea by their side, they work with a mug of coffee on their writing desks. With changing lifestyles, [MUG] acquires increased salience,

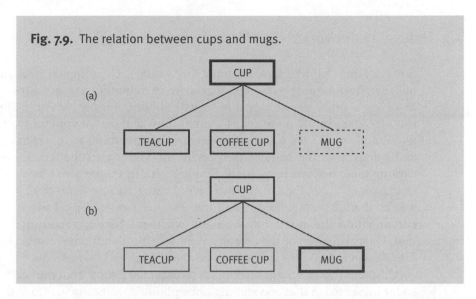

Fig. 7.9. The relation between cups and mugs.

it becomes almost the standard drinking vessel, and begins to acquire basic-level status. (For example, you would refer to the drinking vessel as a *mug*, not as a *cup*.) The salience of [MUG], however, does not completely deprive [CUP] of its basic-level status. The development is illustrated in Figure 7.9(b). I have used the thickness of the boxes surrounding the concepts to give an impressionistic rendering of their degree of salience. The Figure shows how basic-level status can attach to concepts at different levels in a taxonomic hierarchy.

Geeraerts *et al.* (1994) discovered a similar situation with respect to [TROUSERS] and [JEANS] (see the Box). As the name for a kind of garment, which covers the lower half of the body and which divides to accommodate each leg, *trousers* is no doubt a basic-level term (at least, for speakers of British and British-based English), and contrasts with terms such as *shirt*, *jacket*, *socks*, etc. We should expect *jeans* to count as a sub-category of *trousers*. However, jeans have now acquired such salience as a kind of garment in their own right that the term is acquiring basic-level status. For example, if you go into a clothing store and say you want to buy trousers, you would not expect to be shown to the jeans section.

The uncertain relation between *jeans* and *trousers* is illustrated by the following examples (from Cruse 2000*b*: 183).

(1) a. A: Haven't you got any trousers to wear?
       B: Yes, I've got my new jeans.
    b. A: Are you going to wear your jeans?
       B: No, I think I'll wear my trousers.

(1a) suggests that [JEANS] is an instance of more schematic [TROUSERS]. In (1b), [JEANS] and [TROUSERS] are being contrasted, suggesting that they are on the same taxonomic level.

7.2 Polysemy networks

So far in this chapter I have assumed that words such as *animal*, *dog*, etc., are associated with a single concept. This is to oversimplify matters. Most words associate a single phonological form with more than one meaning. *Dog*, for example, can denote a species of animal, in which case it contrasts with *cat*, *horse*, and so on. *Dog* can also be used in contrast to *bitch*, in which case the word designates the male of the species, in contrast to the female. We can capture these two meanings in the familiar way. In Figure 7.10 I have used the thickness of the outline of the box to indicate that one sense of *dog* is more salient than the other. If you ask me, *Do you have a dog?*, I would almost certainly take the question to be about whether I have a certain kind of animal. Only if the sex of the creature were specifically at issue (*Is it a dog or a bitch?*), would I take the question to be about whether I owned a male dog.

Although Figure 7.10 has a familiar structure, it differs from the taxonomies so far presented in that one and the same phonological form is associated with two different semantic units. I have distinguished these by means of superscripts: [DOG'] and [DOG"]. This situation, far from being unusual, is in fact extremely common. Consider again the example of *tree*.

Why is a family tree so called? The expression suggests that English speakers have perceived some similarity between 'trees' (of the botanical kind) and 'family trees' (of the genealogical kind). It is not that a family tree is a kind of (botanical) tree, in the same way in which an oak tree is a kind of tree. A family tree is a different kind of thing than a tree growing in the yard. Yet there is a similarity between the (botanical) tree-schema and the family tree. Both have a branching structure. With a botanical tree, you start from the trunk,

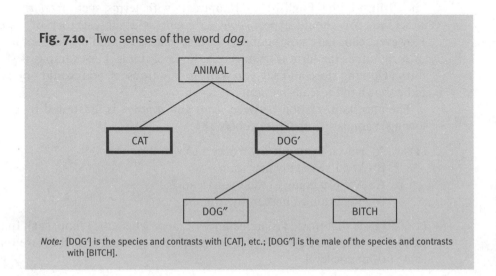

Fig. 7.10. Two senses of the word *dog*.

Note: [DOG'] is the species and contrasts with [CAT], etc.; [DOG"] is the male of the species and contrasts with [BITCH].

proceed upwards, the trunk branches, each branch (if you follow it), also branches, and so on. Likewise, with a genealogical tree, you start with EGO, proceed upwards to the parents, then to their parents, branching out sideways to the siblings of the parents, and so on. There are, to be sure, significant differences between the structures of botanical and genealogical trees. Nothing in the genealogical tree corresponds to the roots and leaves of the botanical tree, and nothing in the botanical tree corresponds to marriage relations in the genealogical tree. And whereas the structure of a botanical tree is determinate, with a genealogical tree you can proceed upwards and outwards as far as the historical records permit. Nevertheless, the similarities are sufficient for a speaker to extend the tree-concept to the structure of a genealogy.

The semantic extension is made possible by the perception of similarity between the two concepts. We can indicate the direction of the extension by means of a broken arrow: ⸱⸱⸱>. Recognizing a similarity between (botanical) trees and family trees is tantamount to the recognition of a concept that is schematic for both kinds. We can therefore propose a schema that abstracts what is common to both. I have sketched this in Figure 7.11. [TREE′] corresponds to the meaning of *tree* as applied to large plants, [TREE″] is the meaning of *tree* that is schematic for both plants and genealogies. (Further instances of [TREE″] might include the linguist's syntactic trees, as well as Porphyrian trees.) The overarching schema [TREE″] is much less salient than schema [TREE′]. Degrees of salience are represented by the thickness of the outlines of the surrounding boxes.

Figure 7.11 illustrates how the two relations in the categorization triangle— the relation of schema and instance, and the relation of similarity between instances—can apply 'recursively' even with respect to the meanings of a single lexical item. As a consequence, the semantic pole of a lexical item is constituted, not by a single concept, but by a network of related concepts.

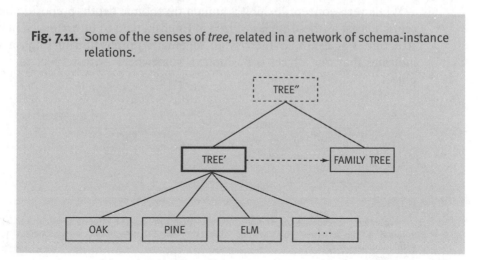

Fig. 7.11. Some of the senses of *tree*, related in a network of schema-instance relations.

7.3 Non-nominal concepts

Nearly all the examples discussed in this chapter have dealt with relations between nominal concepts, i.e. concepts designated by nouns. It is natural to ask whether the schema-instance relation is also valid for the meanings of verbs, prepositions, and other kinds of words.

With respect to verbs, this is certainly the case. [GO] is schematic for a large number of motion concepts, such as [WALK], [RUN], [DRIVE], while [KILL] is schematic for [MURDER], [ASSASSINATE], [EXECUTE], [SLAUGHTER], and other concepts which specify the manner of killing. And [DO] is maximally schematic for all activity concepts.

Nevertheless, verb meanings do not, in general, exhibit the taxonomic depth of many nominal concepts. Evidence is presented in Anglin (1986: 92). When adults were asked to give definitions of basic-level nouns, they often mentioned superordinates, and occasionally several of them. When asked to define *dog*, people would say that it's a 'mammal', a 'pet', an 'animal', a 'living thing'. When asked to define verbal concepts, people mentioned a superordinate less often, and when they did, they mentioned only a highly schematic verbal concept, such as 'mental process' (for *think*), 'physical activity' (for *jump*), 'feeling' (for *like*) (Anglin 1986: 91). Concepts intermediate between the highly schematic [MENTAL PROCESS] and [THINK] were not elicited.[4]

Anglin also asked children for word definitions. When defining noun-concepts, children appealed to superordinates less frequently than adults, and almost never mentioned superordinates when defining verbs. These results suggest, not only that the schema-instance relation plays a lesser role in our understanding of verb-meanings, but also that multi-level taxonomies, like those in Figure 7.3, are constructed gradually in the course of acquisition, from the basic level upwards.

While verb-concepts exhibit a limited taxonomic depth, prepositional concepts, at least as these are lexicalized in English, tend to be organized in a 'flat' structure. For example, there is no schematic preposition in English which indicates that one object is positioned 'somewhere' with respect to another object.

---

[4] Note that the responses of Anglin's subjects—that 'running' is a kind of 'physical activity'—have nominalized the activities. This could be taken as evidence that taxonomies are associated primarily with nominal concepts.

Study questions

1. On the basis of clear-cut examples of the schema-instance relation, such as the relation between [ANIMAL], [CAT], and [DOG], devise a set of tests for diagnosing the relation between a schema [A] and its instances [B] and [C]. Here are some examples of test sentences.

   B is a (kind of) A

   *A is a (kind of) B

   *B is a (kind of) C

   If it's B, it must be A

   If it's A, it may be (but need not be) B

   If it's B, it can't be C

   ?It's not a B, it's an A.

   Having satisfied yourself of the validity of your tests on a range of clear-cut examples of the relation, apply the tests to some not-so-clear data, for example:

   cup, mug, beaker, pot

   trousers, jeans, pants, shorts

   wife/husband, partner, girl-friend/boy-friend, friend

   house, home, cottage, bungalow, apartment, mansion, hovel, tent, hut, caravan, (my) place, residence

   red, scarlet, pink, crimson, maroon

   Because the words in these sets may not constitute clear-cut examples of the schema-instance relation, and may not lend themselves to an organization in a well-behaved taxonomy, speakers are likely to have fluctuating intuitions on your test sentences. It will be important to test your data on a sample of speakers.

2. The tests devised for (1) were applied to nominal concepts. How could these tests be modified so that they can be applied to relations between verbs and between prepositions? (Refer to note 4 to this chapter. If you are searching for a verb which is schematic for *(to) think*, it may not be legitimate to construct sentences of the kind *Thinking is a kind of mental activity*. This test sentence makes use of the nominalized form *thinking*, and shows, if anything, that the nominal concept [THINKING] is an instance of the nominal concept [MENTAL ACTIVITY], not that the verbal concept [THINK] is an instance of a more schematic verbal concept.)

   Are there prepositions that stand in a schema-instance relation? Consider the following:

   in–inside of

   on–on top of

over–above

under–underneath–below

3. Some words in a language have meanings that are highly schematic. Examples, in English, include *(to) do, thing, creature, stuff*. What other words in English could be regarded as semantically highly schematic? List some of the most highly schematic words in the languages with which you are familiar.

4. Select a semantic field for investigation, e.g. emotions, clothing, meteorological conditions.

   Design experiments for eliciting concepts within the domain. For emotions, for example, you might ask several subjects to give as many names for emotions as they can, within a set time period (say, two minutes). This procedure will provide you with a set of emotion names.

   Evaluate the results with a view to ascertaining whether any emotions are more salient than the others. Are there certain emotions that all, or nearly all, subjects include in their lists? Is there a tendency for certain emotions to be named earlier in the list? Which of the terms are candidates for basic-level status? Can some of the emotion names you have elicited be organized in schema-instance relations? Check whether the relative frequency of the emotion terms you have elicited correlates with their frequency of occurrence in the language. (You can obtain frequency data from Thorndike and Lorge 1944 or from Johansson and Hofland 1989).

   If you have access to subjects with different native languages, do the experiment in two or more languages. Are there similarities and differences between the languages?

   Prototype approaches to emotion terms are pursued in Fehr and Russel (1984) and Shaver *et al.* (1987).

Further reading

A good introduction to some of the topics dealt with in this chapter is ch. 2, 'What's in a Word: Lexicology', of Dirven and Verspoor (1998). For the schema-instance relation, see FCG1: 369–86. For basic-level terms, see Rosch (1975, 1978), Taylor (1995a: chs. 3 and 4), Ungerer and Schmid (1996: chs. 1 and 2). For an early statement of the issue, see Brown (1958a). Strongly recommended is the Geeraerts *et al.* (1994) study of clothing terms.

The semantic relation of hyponymy is dealt with in Cruse (1986); see especially section 4.4 (pp. 88–92) and ch. 6 (pp. 136–56). Cruse (1994) updated his views in light of the development of prototype theory. A more summary treatment is found in Cruse (2000b: 179–88).

The proper application of the term 'taxonomy' is controversial. See Wierzbicka (1994) and ch. 12 of Wierzbicka (1996). It should be noted that Cruse (1986) understands 'taxonomy' more narrowly than I have done in this chapter.

CHAPTER 8

Schema and instance in phonology

In Chapter 7 I examined the schema-instance relation that can hold between semantic units. In this chapter I turn to phonological units, focusing mainly on segments rather than larger phonological units such as syllables. (These are discussed in Chapter 13.) We will find that much of what was said in Chapter 7 about relations between semantic units carries over, with little modification, to relations between phonological units.

I should point out that this chapter presupposes some knowledge of basic phonological concepts; it is not meant as an introduction to phonology. Its purpose is to show how familiar notions in phonology can be represented in a straightforward and insightful manner using the apparatus and concepts of Cognitive Grammar.

8.1 Segments and the schema-instance relation

Consider again the 'categorization triangle' of Chapter 7, reproduced here as Figure 8.1. In Chapter 7 I drew attention to three salient aspects of the triangle: (i) the schema [A] abstracts what is common to its instances; (ii) the instances [B] and [C] elaborate the schema in contrasting ways; (iii) the instances are perceived to be similar to each other, precisely with respect to the content of the schema.

In Chapter 7 we discussed situations in which [A], [B], and [C] were occupied by semantic units. We can also fill out the Figure with phonological units.

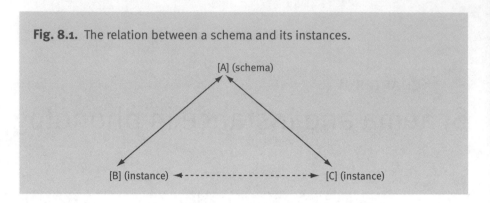

Fig. 8.1. The relation between a schema and its instances.

For example, schema [A] could be [VOWEL], the instances could include [iː], [ɑː], and [uː]. The schematic unit [VOWEL] may be characterized as a speech sound that is articulated with minimal constriction of the vocal tract and which can serve as the nucleus of a syllable. This specification is shared by sounds such as [iː], [ɑː], and [uː]. These sounds are similar in that they share the vowel specification; at the same time it is this perceived similarity that allows the emergence of the vowel schema. Each of [iː], [ɑː], and [uː] elaborates the schema in different and contrasting ways. Thus, [iː] is articulated with unrounded lips and with the tongue bunched up towards the palatal region, [ɑː] is articulated with lowered tongue and jaw, while [uː] is articulated with lip rounding and with the tongue pulled back towards the velar region.

It will be apparent that the relation between the phonological schema and its instances is exactly comparable to the relation between a schematic seman-tic unit, such as [ANIMAL], and its instances, such as [DOG], [CAT], and [COW].

Another example of the schema-instance relation in phonology concerns the relation between a phoneme and its allophones—the phoneme is schematic for its allophones, the allophones are instances of the phoneme. The aspirated [pʰ] in *pie* [pʰaɪ], the unaspirated [p] in *spy* [spaɪ], and the unreleased [pˀ] in *apt* [æpˀ·t], are actually quite different, both acoustically and in their articulation. The articulation of [p] in syllable onset position, as in *pay* [pʰeɪ], also differs significantly from its articulation in coda position, as in *ape* [ɛɪp]. Nevertheless, English speakers conceptualize these different sounds as instances of the voiceless bilabial stop /p/.[1] The relation is represented in Figure 8.2.

The allophones, as represented in Figure 8.2, do not yet correspond to the actual segments that occur in an utterance. Whereas [pʰ] represents an aspir-ated allophone, the precise duration and intensity of the aspiration remains unspecified. The allophone is schematic for its actual realization in an act of

---

[1] Where the distinction is relevant, I follow the traditional practice of writing phonemes between slashes // and allophones between square brackets [ ]. Otherwise, I place phonological representations between square brackets.

Fig. 8.2. The phoneme /p/ is schematic for its allophones; the allophones are instances of the phoneme.

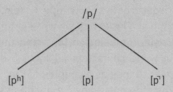

speech. The very lowest level in the phonological taxonomy is occupied by the segments that occur in an utterance.

A hearer encounters only the lowest-level instances. Acquiring the sound system of language involves the abstraction of schemas over the instances.[2] When listening to a language in which we are already proficient, we categorize the heard sounds in terms of the learned phonological schemas. Mostly, this proceeds smoothly, and proficient speakers are scarcely aware of the extent of acoustic and articulatory variation in the sounds of their language. 'Deviant' pronunciations that one might encounter—pronunciations by someone who is drunk, who has had their front teeth removed, or is speaking with a mouth full of food—may still be understandable, provided that the pronunciations can be assimilated to already existing schemas. An unfamiliar regional accent can sometimes cause difficulties, at least initially. Usually, though, speakers are able to quickly extend their phonological categories so as to incorporate the new variants into their existing phonological schemas.

8.1.1 A taxonomy of phonological segments

As with semantic units, we are able to arrange phonological segments in a taxonomy—a phonological Porphyrian tree, so to speak. A fragment of such a taxonomy is shown in Figure 8.3 (p. 146). At the top of the taxonomy stands the maximally schematic [SEGMENT]. A little lower are the major categories of vowel and consonant. These may be characterized with respect to the degree of constriction of the vocal tract and the role of the segments within the syllable. Further down are units that correspond to the traditional phonemes. Lower down (not shown in Figure 8.3) are the allophones; at the very bottom of the taxonomy stand the actual segments that occur in an utterance.

8.1.2 Alternative taxonomies and 'natural classes'

As we attempt to fill in the details of Figure 8.3, we quickly run into the problem posed by alternative taxonomies. The oral stops [p, t, k, b, d, g], for

---

[2] For the emergence of vowel categories in two different languages (English and Swedish), see Kuhl (1994), especially pp. 108–39.

Phonemes and graphemes

There is an interesting analogy between the phoneme-allophone distinction in phonology and aspects of the our writing system.

The actual shape of a letter that we write or print depends on many factors, such as handwriting style, the selected font, and the distinction between 'small' and 'capital'. The following characters all have a different shape. Nevertheless, we regard the different shapes as examples of the 'same' entity, i.e. the 'first letter of the alphabet'. The different shapes correspond to allophones (we might call them 'allographs'), the schematic entity of which they are instances corresponds to the phoneme (the 'grapheme').

A A *A* 𝒜 *a* a ɑ a

Note that the 'first letter of the alphabet', considered as a schematic entity, is not something that can be written down as such. What we write down are instances of the grapheme. The grapheme is an abstract entity. Similarly, a phoneme as such cannot be articulated. What is articulated, in an utterance, are instances of phonemes.

example, can be ordered in two ways (Fig. 8.4 (p. 147)). One possibility is to distinguish [p, t, k] from [b, d, g] in terms of voicing. Another possibility is to group the sounds in terms of a common place of articulation.

We encountered a similar situation when considering the concepts [MAN], [WOMAN], [BOY], [GIRL]. These fall under a more schematic concept [HUMAN BEING] but can be arranged in different ways according to the choice of inter-

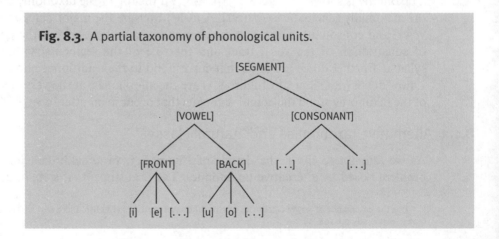

Fig. 8.3. A partial taxonomy of phonological units.

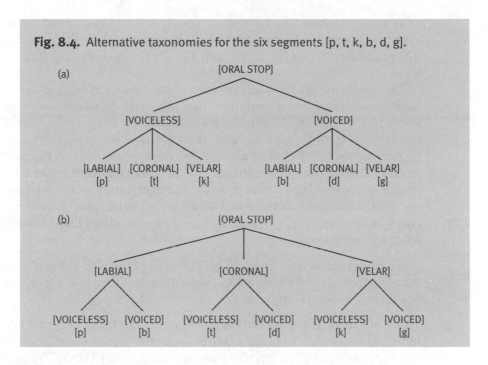

Fig. 8.4. Alternative taxonomies for the six segments [p, t, k, b, d, g].

mediate schemas (see Fig. 7.7). As with the semantics example, each of the phonological taxonomies is appropriate in different circumstances. The existence of aspirated allophones in *pie* [pʰaɪ], *tie* [tʰaɪ], and *key* [kʰiː] motivates the voiceless stop schema; the voiceless stops are similar precisely because they each have an aspirated allophone. On the other hand, classification by place of articulation is needed to account for place assimilations. Both [k] and [g] trigger the velar nasal in (1), while [p] and [b] both trigger the bilabial nasal; the voicing contrast between [k] and [g], and [p] and [b], is irrelevant in these cases.

(1) unconscious   [ʌŋ k. . .]
    ungovernable   [ʌŋ g. . .]
    unbelievable   [ʌm b. . .]
    unpopular   [ʌm p. . .]

Sets of sounds which behave in similar ways are often referred to as **natural classes**. In Cognitive Grammar, a natural class is simply a group of sounds which count as instances of a more abstract schema. The schema is proposed in order to capture the similarities between the relevant sounds. The above examples show that it is necessary to recognize a natural class in English which comprises [p, t, k]. Other facts of English require us to recognize [p, b], [t, d], and [k, g] as natural classes.

Other natural classes which are relevant to the phonological structure of English include:

(i) Long vs. short vowels. English vowels fall into two broad classes, the long vowels and the short vowels.[3] The long vowels include [iː, ɑː, uː, ɔː, ɜː], as well as the diphthongs [ɛɪ, aɪ, əʊ, aʊ]. The short vowels include [ɪ, ɛ, æ, ɒ, ʊ, ʌ, ə].

The two classes are necessary in order to account for syllable structure. The short vowels share the property that they can occur in stressed monosyllabic words only if they are followed by a consonant; the long vowels do not have this restriction. Whereas [biː], [suː], [kɑː] are possible (and, indeed, actual) English words, [bɪ], [sʊ], [kæ] are not. We can capture facts of this nature in terms of schemas for syllable structure which make reference to the schematic units [LONG VOWEL] and [SHORT VOWEL]. The distribution of the velar nasal [ŋ] also makes reference to the vowel schemas; the velar nasal may only occur after a short vowel: [fɪŋ] is a possible (though non-existing) English word, [fiːŋ] is not a possible word.

(ii) High vs. non-high vowels. This distinction is needed in order to explain the occurrence of 'r'-linking in non-rhotic dialects of English (see section 5.3). The linking 'r' occurs only after a non-high vowel.

(iii) Sibilants. If a noun ends in one of [s, z, ʃ, ʒ, tʃ, dʒ], its plural takes the suffix [əz] rather than [s] or [z]. Likewise, if a verb ends in one of these sounds it inflects in third person singular with [əz] rather than [s] or [z]. We can bring these six sounds together under the schema [SIBILANT].

(iv) Obstruents. Syllable codas in English exhibit some interesting patterns of voicing assimilation. In example (2a), the coda consonants agree in voicing. It is not possible for an English syllable to terminate in [pd, pz, gt, vt] and the like. In (2b), we note that the coda consonants do not have to agree in voicing. We can have words terminating in either [nz] or [ns], [lf] or [lv], [nd] or [nt].

(2) a. apt, lapse, act, axe, adze, lift, lived, fetched, judged, etc.
     b. lens, once; shelve, shelf; send, sent; hinge, inch; limp; sink, etc.

The sounds that agree in voicing comprise stops, fricatives, and affricates. (As it happens, these sounds come in voiced-voiceless pairs in English.) We can bring these sounds together under the schematic segment [OBSTRUENT]. The relevant generalization can be captured by means of a syllable schema which specifies that obstruents in coda position must agree in voicing. No such requirement holds if the first of the coda consonants is not an obstruent.

While there are, in principle, many possibilities for filling in the intermediate levels of a phonological taxonomy between the maximally schematic [SEG-MENT] and the fully specified allophones, certain intermediate categories, such as [VOWEL] and [CONSONANT], are universally valid and crucially involved in characterizing syllable structure in the world's languages. Decisions concern-

---

[3] While it is true that the 'long' vowels tend to be physically longer than the 'short' vowels, the distinction is not based on physical duration, but on the different distributions of the vowels.

ing other intermediate-level schemas will largely depend on the phonological organization of a specific language. The category [SIBILANT] is very likely a peculiarity of English. While it is always possible, in principle, to classify the vowels of any language by means of the cross-cutting schemas [HIGH], [LOW]; [FRONT], [BACK]; [ROUNDED], [UNROUNDED], these categories may be more salient in the phonological organization of some languages than in others. In Turkish, with its extensive system of vowel harmony, the above categories are more salient than they are in English, for example.

There is again an analogy with semantic units, in that different languages might fill out intermediate levels in a semantic taxonomy in different ways, and accord different degrees of salience to the intermediate categories. Probably, in most languages, the distinctions between animate and inanimate, and, among the animates, between human and non-human, are systematically exploited. But other distinctions, such as gender distinctions, may be more important in some cases than in others. The concept [COUSIN], in English, is indifferent to gender—in order to indicate the gender of a cousin one has to resort to phrasal means: *male cousin, female cousin.* German, on the other hand, differentiates *Vetter* 'male cousin' and *Kusine* 'female cousin', but lacks a common term schematic for both concepts.

8.1.3 A basic level in phonology?

In discussing semantic units I drew attention to the notion of the basic level. In a semantic taxonomy, the basic level is the level at which people tend to name things (in the absence of specific reasons to the contrary). The basic level in phonology would be the level in the phonological taxonomy at which speakers tend to conceptualize phonological structures. Is there a basic level in a taxonomy of phonological segments?

Clearly there is—it is the level of the traditional phoneme (or 'speech sound', in lay parlance).[4] Alphabetic writing systems are based on the salience of this level. To master an alphabetic writing system a person must realize that *cat, act,* and *tack* contain the 'same sounds' arranged in different sequences. Most people manage this task, without much difficulty, and at a fairly young age.[5]

Units below and above the phoneme tend not to be very salient. Most speakers are largely unaware of the extent of allophonic variation in their language. The 'h'-sound in *hat* is conceptualized as being the same as the

---

[4] It might be objected that the syllable is a more salient unit than the phoneme; many writing systems, such as Japanese, are in fact syllable based. The syllable, however, is a different kind of unit than the phoneme. Syllables have segments as their constituents. The relation between syllable and phoneme is not a schema-instance relation, but the relation of a whole to a part.

[5] It has been claimed (Mattingly 1972) that residual levels of illiteracy—even in societies with well-developed systems of primary and secondary education—could be due to the fact that a minority of children fail to become aware of the phoneme level of phonological organization. Sampson (1985: 163) makes a similar point.

'h'-sound in *heat*, even though, both acoustically and in their articulation, the sounds are rather different. Unsurprisingly, alphabetic writing systems rarely represent sub-phonemic variants by distinct symbols. Units that are higher in the taxonomy than the phoneme—categories such as [OBSTRUENT], for example—also tend to lack salience. Even linguistics students often have difficulty in grasping the content of such categories.

Why should the phoneme level be so salient? Again, we can draw an analogy with the basic level in a semantic taxonomy. Basic-level categories tend to maximize *informativity* (see p. 132). It is maximally informative to describe the initial sound of *pie* as a voiceless bilabial stop, i.e. as /p/, thereby differentiating the sound from /b/ and /t/. It is, after all, the choice of /p/ that differentiates *pie* from *buy* and *tie*. (This is the import of the traditional 'minimal pair' test.) To describe the sound at a lower level in the taxonomy, that is, to specify it as aspirated bilabial stop, thereby differentiating it from an unaspirated bilabial stop, adds little further information. Conversely, to describe the sound in terms of a higher category, e.g. as a stop, or as an obstruent, is even less informative.

There is another analogy with semantic categories. The basic level in semantics is the highest level in the taxonomy at which a person can form a mental image of a category (p. 132). The same goes for the phonemic level. A speaker can conceptualize, or bring to mind, an image of the /p/-phoneme in terms of its sound and its articulatory parameters, but can hardly conceptualize a schematic stop, even less, a schematic obstruent. We can even draw an analogy between the ease with which people can describe basic-level objects, such as a chair, or a hammer, in terms of their parts, and the way in which phonemes lend themselves to a description in terms of features, such as place and manner of articulation.

8.1.4 Badly behaved taxonomies

In discussing semantic units I drew attention to the fact that a taxonomy can be 'badly behaved'.

A well-behaved taxonomy has a characteristic 'branching' structure. If we ignore the unit at the very top and those at the very bottom of the taxonomy, we see that each unit is an instance of a higher unit and is itself schematic for lower units. Moreover, a particular level in the taxonomy will have special status as the cognitively salient basic level. We saw, with respect to clothing terminology and other semantic domains, that semantic units do not always pattern like this. Recall the trousers-jeans example (in Chapter 7), in which one unit, [JEANS], would seem to have basic-level status, but is at the same time an instance of a more schematic category, [TROUSERS], which itself is a candidate for a basic-level unit, and which contrasts with other presumably basic-level concepts, such as [SHIRT], [JACKET], [SOCKS], etc.

Badly behaved taxonomies in phonology lie behind some of the problems that have been associated with traditional phoneme theory.

Traditional phonemic analysis rests on the assumption of a well-behaved taxonomy of segments, with the following characteristics:

- in a given language, there is a fairly small, fixed set of phoneme categories;
- the phoneme categories are contrastive, as demonstrated by the minimal pair test;
- each phoneme is schematic for a set of allophones; the allophones may be associated with distinctive environments, as demonstrated by the criterion of complementary distribution;
- each allophone is an instance of one, and only one, phoneme.

An utterance can be represented by a (broad) phonemic transcription, consisting of a sequence of phonemes, and by a narrow phonetic transcription, consisting of a sequence of allophones, such that each allophone stands in a one-to-one relation to the phoneme of which it is an instance (Fig. 8.5 (p. 152)). According to traditional phonemic theory, the relationship between the two levels is constrained by what are sometimes called the 'bi-uniqueness condition' and the 'linearity condition' (Lass 1984: 27). The former stipulates a one-to-one relation of phoneme to allophone, the latter requires that the sequence of allophones corresponds to the sequence of the phonemes which they instantiate.

Let us look at a couple of cases where these assumptions are problematic.

(i) Nasal consonants in English. There are good reasons to recognize /m/, /n/, and /ŋ/ as phonemes of English; witness the contrast between *sum*, *sun*, and *sung*. A problem, however, arises with respect to the negative prefixes, *in-* and *un-*.

The nasal in these prefixes is typically subject to place assimilation to a following obstruent, as in examples (3a) and (3b). If the following sound is not an obstruent, no assimilation takes place and the negative prefix appears with [n].

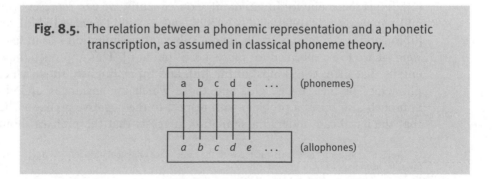

Fig. 8.5. The relation between a phonemic representation and a phonetic transcription, as assumed in classical phoneme theory.

(3) a. un[ŋ]conscious, un[ɱ]forgettable,[6] un[m]believable
     b. in[ŋ]conceivable, in[ɱ]voluntary, im[m]possible
     c. un[n]likely, un[n]available, in[n]human, in[n]appropriate

The words in example (3c) suggest that the prefixes are 'basically' [ʌn] and [ɪn], whereby a following obstruent may cause [n] to take on a different place of articulation. In some cases, assimilation causes [n] to be replaced by a sound that elsewhere in the language would count as a different phoneme, namely [ŋ] or [m]. In other circumstances, [n] assimilates to [ɱ], a sound that is not a phoneme of English. Presumably, in this case, [ɱ] would have to be regarded as an allophone of /n/.

Consider, now, such words as *comfort* [kʌɱfət] and *symphony* [sɪɱfəniː], which also contain [ɱ]. The place of articulation of [ɱ] is determined by the following [f]—but what is [ɱ] an allophone of? The spelling suggests /m/, but the sound could just as reasonably be regarded as an allophone of /n/. Or consider a word such as *sink* [sɪŋk], where place assimilation also takes place—there is no *[sɪmk] or *[sɪnk]. On standard phoneme theory, the [ŋ] of *sink* would be assigned straightforwardly to the /ŋ/ phoneme, not to /n/ (as suggested by the spelling). Although [ŋ] and [ɱ] are products of the very same phenomenon of place assimilation, the two sounds are accorded a different analysis.

These examples are problematic for bi-uniqueness (and hence for the idea of a well-behaved taxonomy of phonetic segments), in two respects:

- one and the same process (place assimilation) can sometimes determine the occurrence of one phoneme rather than another, in other circumstances it determines the occurrence of an allophone of a phoneme;
- there are circumstances where it is not clear to which phoneme a phonetic segment is to be assigned.

One way of handling such data could be to maintain that an assimilated nasal—i.e. a nasal whose place of articulation is determined by the place of articulation of a following obstruent—is actually an instance of a unit that is more schematic than any of the nasal phonemes. We can represent this unit as [N]. [N] is schematic for [n, m, ŋ, ɱ]. Consequently, we can represent *comfort* and *symphony* as [kʌNfət] and [sɪNfəniː], *sink* as [sɪNk], *lend* as [lɛNd], *limp* as [lɪNp], and so on. Nasals which are not subject to assimilation—as in *sum, sun, sung*—have to be specified for place, i.e. as [m, n, ŋ]. This approach, however, entails that there two 'kinds' of [n], [m], and [ŋ] in English, those which are phonemes in their own right, and those which are instances of [N]. The approach also raises a problem with respect to the negative prefixes. The fact that the nasal can undergo assimilation suggests that the prefixes should be

---

[6] [ɱ] is a labio-dental nasal, articulated with the same place of articulation as [f] and [v], i.e. with the lower lip in contact with the upper teeth.

represented as [ʌN] and [ɪN]. At the same time, the fact that the unassimilated nasal appears as [n], as in example (3c), suggests that the nasal needs to be represented as [n]. It looks as if the negative prefixes are associated with two representations, one with [N], the other with [n]. In order to avoid this conclusion, we might suppose that [n] is the default value of [N]—in cases where [N] fails to be specified for place through assimilation, the sound is articulated as alveolar.

The situation is represented in Figure 8.6. The sounds [m, n, ŋ] are positioned on the phoneme level. Each of the sounds can be an instance of the schematic nasal [N]. The heavy line linking [N] and [n] represents [n] as the default instantiation of [N]; the default, i.e. [n], has also been printed in bold. The labio-dental [ɱ] can be an instance, either of the phonemes [m] or [n], or, alternatively, of [N]. Observe that in the latter case, the traditional level of the phoneme has been bypassed.

Although problematic for phonemic analysis, situations like the one described do not, I think, justify a rejection of the phoneme notion. Phonemes *are* relevant to phonological analysis, and are psychologically real to speakers of a language. The phoneme concept, however, rests on the assumption of a perfectly well-behaved taxonomy of segments. As in semantic analysis, the assumption may not be borne out in all circumstances.

(ii) The PIN–KIN vowels in South African English. The second example has to do with 'marginal' phonemes.

I begin with an observation about my own speech, where I regularly make a small difference in the pronunciation of *eight* and *ate*. (I refer here to the diphthongal pronunciation of *ate*, not to the pronunciation with the short vowel of *pet*.) The difference is that the diphthong in *eight* begins slightly higher than the diphthong in *ate*. The difference, though small, is quite clear to me; also, fellow English speakers, whom I have tested on this, can hear the difference. Since *eight* and *ate* constitute a minimal pair, two distinct phonemes, say, /eɪ/ and /ɛɪ/, would need to be recognized. The snag is, this difference is relevant only to these two words. I make no comparable difference between, say, *gate* and *gait*, *wait* and *weight*. In all these words, I use the open version of the diphthong. The problem will be apparent. What to do with the close

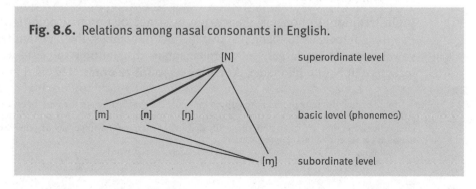

Fig. 8.6. Relations among nasal consonants in English.

version of the diphthong in *eight*? It would be grossly extravagant to increase the phoneme inventory of my variety of English in order to account for the pronunciation of just one word.[7] South African English provides a more complex example of a marginal phoneme.

Southern hemisphere Englishes are remarkable for the ways in which the front vowels have developed *vis-à-vis* the British standard. In Australian English, the PIN-vowel[8] is considerably raised *vis-à-vis* the British pronunciation, approaching almost [i], whereas in New Zealand English the vowel has centralized to schwa [ə]. New Zealanders stereotype Australians as people who want to 'leave in Seedney' and who have 'relationsheeps' with each other, while Australians stereotype New Zealanders as people whose staple diet is 'fush and chups'.

South African English is interesting in that the British English PIN-vowel splits into two quite distinct variants, one raised (as in Australian), the other centralized (as in New Zealand). The raised variant [ï] is virtually obligatory when the vowel is adjacent to a velar consonant; we can refer to this variant as the KIN-vowel. The raised variant also tends to occur word-initially and after [h], the centralized variant [ɨ] being used elsewhere:

(4) Raised [ï]   Centralized [ɨ]
     kin   pin
     sing   sin
     inn   bin
     hit   bit

So far so good. It looks as if we can recognize, in South African English, the /ï/ phoneme, which has two allophones, [ï] and [ɨ], whose distribution is determined by context.

Unfortunately, the two variants, [ï] and [ɨ], do not distribute exactly like this. Many speakers (not all) distinguish the words *finish* and *Finnish*, using centralized [ɨ] in the former, raised [ï] in the latter. Often, the choice between the two vowels appears to be lexically determined, with considerable variation in the speech community. For some speakers, the personal name *Lynn* might have the raised vowel; some speakers would systematically distinguish *hymn* and *him*, and so on (Taylor 1991).

On traditional phoneme theory, the existence of minimal pairs (*finish* vs. *Finnish*) compels us to recognize two distinct phonemes; the fact that the two vowel qualities are largely in complementary distribution suggests we need recognize only one phoneme. A further aspect is relevant. This is that it may

---

[7] Since writing this paragraph I have noticed that I use the close version of the diphthong also in the interjection *Eh?*, which thereby contrasts with the name of the letter 'A'. It is a characteristic of interjections that they are often phonologically deviant, or marginal, in some way or other. See study question 5 at the end of this chapter.

[8] Following Wells (1982), I name the vowels by reference to key words.

actually be incorrect to postulate two distinct sounds in the first place. Lass and Wright (1985) observed that the vowels in an individual's speech can occupy a continuum ranging between [ï] and [ɨ].

The example underlines the fact that speakers learn, first and foremost, the pronunciation of individual lexical items. In most cases, the phonological structure of lexical items can be represented in terms of units corresponding to the traditional category of phoneme. We need to bear in mind, however, that phonemic analysis is an idealization, which rests on the assumption of a perfectly well-behaved taxonomy of phonological segments—an assumption which may not always match the facts. The South African English example shows that speakers may sometimes operate with phonological representations that are more specific than the phonemic level.

As a matter of fact, the example of the English nasals suggests a similar conclusion. Again, it is reasonable to assume that speakers learn, first and foremost, the specific pronunciations of individual words. *Comfort* is learned with [ɱ], *sink* is learned with [ŋ], and the negative prefixes with the range of values that they have in different words. The higher units in Figure 8.6—the phoneme categories as well as the schematic nasal [N], together with phono-logical schemas for assimilation—emerge as generalizations over particular facts. Not all the data, however, are consistent with the generalizations, either at the phoneme level, or at a more schematic level. The possibility of schematic representations does not therefore eliminate the need for information on the specific pronunciations of individual lexical items.

8.2 More on phonological schemas

So far, in this and the preceding chapter, I have presented schema-instance relations as 'two-dimensional' objects, with an 'up-down' structure. This is an oversimplification. For example, the manner in which a schema is elaborated in its instances, or the kind of similarity relation between the instances, can itself become the basis for further schema-instance relations. In this way, we get schemas for patterns of instantiation and for patterns of extension. Networks of schema-instance relations thus become multidimensional objects. Phonology provides a simple illustration of this phenomenon.

The /p/ phoneme in English has, as a prominent allophone, the aspirated stop [pʰ]. The allophone occurs in onset position of stressed syllables whereas the unaspirated allophone [p] occurs after syllable-initial [s]. We can represent this state of affairs in the familiar way. A comparable situation holds for /t/ and /k/. These sounds also have, as instances, aspirated allophones, which occur in onset position of stressed syllables, and unaspirated allophones, which occur after [s].

We could represent these facts by three separate schema-instance relations, which show aspirated [pʰ], [tʰ], and [kʰ] and unaspirated [p], [t], and [k] as instances of /p/, /t/, and /k/, respectively. There is an obvious similarity between the three cases. This justifies the abstraction of a schema for the pattern of instantiation from phoneme to allophone. The new schema relates a schematic voiceless stop with its allophone-types and thereby captures the similarities across the three phonemes, factoring out the specifics of the individual cases.

Since we are here dealing with multidimensional schema-instance relations it is difficult to represent the relations in visual form. Figure 8.7 is a crude (and partial) attempt.

Parallels between /p, t, k/

Contrary to the import of Figure 8.7, the parallels between /p, t, k/ are not strict.

In many English accents, the aspiration associated with syllable-initial [tʰ] is so vigorous that the aspirated allophone could be more accurately represented as [tˢ], rather than [tʰ]; the sound is almost an affricate. The aspirated allophones of /p/ and /k/ rarely correspond to the affricates [pᶲ] or [kˣ].

With respect to /k/, the place of articulation of the allophones can vary quite considerably, depending on the identity of a following vowel. In *key* the consonant is palatal [c], whereas in *coo* it is velar [k]. Comparable effects are not observed with /p/ and /t/.

So, while Figure 8.7 remains generally valid, a particular instance of the voiceless stop schema may display properties that are not fully accounted for by the schema.

Patterns of assimilation require a similar account. Consider the following:

(1) good boy   [gʊd bɔɪ]   or   [gʊb bɔɪ]
     good girl   [gʊd gɜːl]   or   [gʊg gɜːl]
     state building [stɛɪt bɪldɪŋ] or   [stɛɪp bɪldɪŋ]
     ten people   [tɛn piːpl]   or   [tɛm piːpl]

On the one hand, we could propose a set of schemas, each of which would capture the particular facts of each of the above cases, and which would specify the phonological shape that a word may take when it occurs in a certain phonological environment. But the similarities between the cases are so compelling that we need a further schema which captures the commonality of the individual cases. The overarching schema specifies that certain word-final consonants may take on the place of articulation of a following word-initial consonant.

Not all word-final consonants are equally likely to undergo place assimilation. Assimilation is much more likely to affect word-final [t, d, n] than word-final [p, b, m, k, g, ŋ]. *Big boy* would probably not come out as [bɪb bɔɪ], while *lap dog* and *long book* would almost certainly not assimilate to [læt dɒg] and [lɒm bʊk]. The segments which are liable to undergo assimilation are often

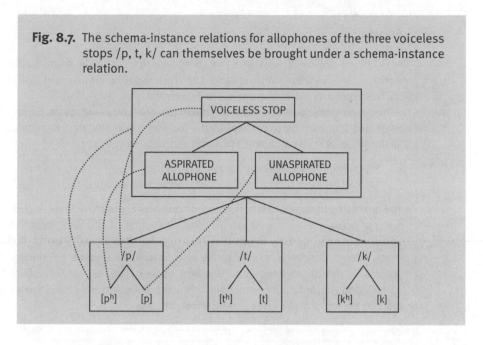

Fig. 8.7. The schema-instance relations for allophones of the three voiceless stops /p, t, k/ can themselves be brought under a schema-instance relation.

referred to as **coronals**; these are consonants that are articulated with the blade of the tongue, in contrast to labials (whose articulation involves one or both of the lips) and the velars (which involve the back of the tongue). It is as if coronals, being produced in the middle of the mouth, where the tongue is in its natural resting place, are able to wander forwards and backwards, as it were, whereas the place of articulation of labials and velars is relatively fixed.

These examples have illustrated schema-instance relations that are orthogonal, as it were, to specific phonological phenomena. Comparable situations are easy to find with respect to semantic units. Consider the semantic pole of the word *rabbit*. The concept [RABBIT] (the animal), exemplified in (6a), can be extended to [RABBIT MEAT], as in (6b).

(6) a. I {shot / killed / cooked} the rabbit.
    b. I don't like rabbit; I've never eaten rabbit; I don't fancy rabbit.

(7) They were feeding chickens with chicken.

Exactly the same semantic extension is available with *lamb, chicken, duck, tuna*, and several more. Both senses of *chicken* are illustrated in example (7).

The rabbit example illustrates a semantic extension from [RABBIT] to [RABBIT MEAT]; likewise with [CHICKEN] and the other examples. Given the similarity between these examples, we could propose a schema for the semantic extension from the name of an animal, fish, or bird to its edible flesh. The schema, to be sure, is not fully productive; it doesn't work with [HEN], [COW], or [PIG]. Still, the schema readily sanctions new instances. Although we might never

Ambiguities

Assimilation can sometimes give rise to ambiguities. Compare *a late cruise* and *a lake cruise*. Given the likelihood that *late cruse* might be pronounced [lɛɪk kruːz], the two expressions could be phonetically identical.

This raises the question how assimilations are processed by a hearer. You might find it interesting to perform a little experiment on this. Recite the following sentences, and ask your listeners to report exactly what you said.

(i)   In the evening, we decided to go on a [lɛɪk kruːz].
(ii) After an exhausting day's sight-seeing, we relaxed on a [lɛɪk kruːz].

You might find that your listeners report having heard *late cruse*, even though you had not actually pronounced *late* as [lɛɪt]. The point of the experiment is that assimilations are not only things that speakers do when they put words together in the stream of speech, assimilations also have to be undone by hearers. The process is not as mysterious as it might appear. Just as speakers introduce assimilations in conformity with phonological schemas, hearers categorize a heard utterance in terms of the same phonological schemas.

The direction of assimilation

An interesting fact about place of articulation assimilations is that they tend to be retrogressive, i.e. a segment is more liable to influence a preceding sound than a following sound. Whereas *good boy* is liable to come out as [gʊb bɔɪ], *big dog* will certainly not be pronounced as [bɪg gɒg]. Ohala (1990) argued that the prevalence of backward assimilation has a natural explanation in acoustics and perception. The acoustic cues for the place of articulation of a consonant, especially a stop consonant, are much more reliable in a CV sequence than in a VC sequence.

You can test this out by articulating the syllables [abˀ], [adˀ], [agˀ] without releasing the stops (and without letting your listeners watch your mouth!) and seeing if listeners can identify the place of articulation of the final consonant. The error rate will probably be quite high. Contrast the results with their performance when you dictate the syllables [ba], [da], and [ga]. Here, the error rate should be vanishingly small.

In a sequence VC_1C_2V, especially where C_1 and C_2 are stops, the place of articulation of C_1 is not likely to be accurately perceived, whereas the place of C_2 will be reliably identified. Since the place of articulation of C_1 can carry little linguistic information, this segment is especially likely to undergo assimilation, with minimal effects on overall intelligibility.

have encountered the usage, we can be fairly confident that *ostrich* and *emu* can be used to refer, not only to the birds, but also to the meat. Moreover, the semantic extension [ANIMAL] --→ [ANIMAL MEAT] goes hand in hand with a shift from count noun to mass noun status. The relation between *rabbit* as a count noun (*He shot a rabbit*) and *rabbit* as a mass noun (*He ate some rabbit*) can equally be brought under a schema relating count nouns (with certain semantic properties) and mass nouns (with certain semantic properties).

8.3 Features

This is a good place to discuss the role of features in the characterization of both semantic and phonological units. Consider once again the triangle in Figure 8.1. It is easy to 'translate' the relations depicted in the Figure into a featural description. We could characterize the schematic unit [A] in terms of a feature {A}. Instances of [A] could be characterized in terms of the inherited feature {A} with, in addition, the contrasting features {B} or {C}. Thus, the semantic unit [DOG] would be defined as the conjunction of the features {ANIMAL} and {CANINE}, [CAT] as a conjunction of the features {ANIMAL} and {FELINE}. With respect to phonological units, the vowel [i] could be defined as the conjunction of {VOWEL}, {HIGH}, {FRONT}; it would contrast with [u], defined as the conjunction of {VOWEL}, {HIGH}, {BACK}.

From one perspective, an analysis of semantic and phonological units in terms of features is simply a notational variant of their analysis in terms of taxonomies of schemas and instances. To this extent, a featural analysis is unproblematic in Cognitive Grammar. However, a featural analysis can be misleading, in that it can suggest that the features have some special ontological status, that is, that the features somehow 'come first', and that semantic and phonological units are built up through the combination of the features. Such a view is quite contrary to the spirit of the triangle in Figure 8.1. It is not at all being proposed that the [i]-vowel 'consists of', or is 'made up from', the components {VOWEL}, {HIGH}, {FRONT}, that the concept [DOG] emerges by adding the feature {CANINE} to the feature {ANIMAL}, or that the concept [BOY] is made up from the components {HUMAN}, {MALE}, and {NON-ADULT}. Rather, a unit, whatever its level of schematicity, emerges through a speaker's familiarity with instances. A person acquires the concept [DOG] through exposure to instances of [DOG]. The more schematic concept [ANIMAL] emerges through exposure of a range of different kinds of animals, and as a consequence of a person's recognition these different kinds have something in common. The same goes for phonological units. A speaker encounters a range of expressions which contain an [i]-like vowel. A speaker extracts the phoneme schema through recognizing the acoustic, articulatory, and functional similarity of these instances. A schema, as Langacker (FCG1: 371) has emphasized, is an 'integrated structure'. It is a concept on its own, it is not put together from its features.

In Cognitive Grammar, a 'feature' is simply a parameter of similarity that speakers recognize across a range of instances. Features, therefore, have the status of schematic entities, which emerge through encounters with instances. The practice, widespread in contemporary phonological theory, of classifying sounds in terms of a universal set of features is therefore quite alien to Cognitive Grammar. This is not to deny that certain features, such as {VOCALIC} in the case of phonology, or {HUMAN} in the case of semantics, might turn up in language after language. But the features—phonological or semantic—to which the analyst refers are construed as schemas that emerge from speakers' encounters with usage events in a specific language. Features have no special status as the building blocks of complex units, neither can they be regarded as universal primitives, given in advance, from which each language makes its selection.

8.3.1 Acquisition

The way in which we understand features leads to radically different predictions for language acquisition. If we regard features as components of complex entities, a taxonomy—as a matter of logical necessity—has to be acquired 'top-down'. First, it is necessary to acquire the most general feature, the one that defines the most schematic category, then differentiating features are acquired, which split the category into sub-categories. In contrast, on the Cognitive Grammar view, a taxonomy is acquired 'bottom-up'. A speaker first becomes acquainted with instances, then abstracts the commonality between the instances, and so on.

Consider how a child language-learner might acquire the concept [DOG]. On the featural approach, the child must first acquire the most general feature, say, {ANIMAL}, then differentiate the animal-concept through the addition of contrasting features, such as {CANINE}, {FELINE}. This approach predicts that a child's earliest words will have highly schematic meanings. On a usage-based approach, a child first becomes acquainted with individual dogs, then abstracts the schema [DOG], and subsequently the schema [ANIMAL]. This approach predicts that a child's earliest words will be restricted to the particularities of encountered instances and that abstraction will occur only later.

No one, to my knowledge, has proposed a full-fledged model of language acquisition based exclusively on the feature theory—although Clark (1973) did certainly appeal to some aspects of a feature analysis, observing that children do initially overextend words like *dog*, using the word in the schematic sense of 'animal'. Clark has since revised her analysis (1993). Indeed, there is abundant evidence that, contrary to the predictions of feature theory, young children are actually not very good at making abstractions (Barrett 1995). Evidence from child language tends strongly to support category acquisition as a bottom-up process.

Study questions

1. What is the justification for proposing that /p, t, k/ in English constitute a natural class?

   In spite of the similarities amongst the three voiceless stops, /t/ has certain properties that are not shared with /p/ and /k/. One such property was mentioned in the chapter, namely, the possibility that /t/ in syllable onset position may be affricated (in certain dialects). Are there any other special properties of /t/?

   Consider the possibility that /t/, in certain environments (and in certain dialects), may be glottalized, that is, it may be pronounced as [ʔt]; it may be flapped; or (in some dialects) may be articulated as [ɹ] (as in *I've gotta* [gɒɹə] *go*). Are there circumstances in which /t/ becomes voiced? Is the sequence [tj], as in *tune* [tjuːn], associated with special properties, not shared with [pj] and [kj]?

2. Why should the major division within a syllable occur between Onset and Rhyme, rather than, say, between a unit consisting of Onset + Nucleus and a unit comprising only the Coda? (Hint: If the Rhyme were not recognized as a component of a syllable, how could the distribution of long and short vowels in English be described? Are there any other phenomena which need to make reference to either the Rhyme or the Onset, for their description?)

3. Natural classes. Segments constitute a natural class to the extent that they are similar, that is, they can be brought under a schematic characterization.

   (i) Assemble some arguments in support of the claim that [j] and [w] in English constitute a natural class. In what respects are the sounds similar? You might consider such aspects as the way the sounds are articulated, their distribution in syllable onsets, and their occurrence as linking elements.

   (ii) Some varieties of English have a distinction between [w] and [ʍ]. For the speakers of these varieties, *witch* and *which*, *wear* and *where*, constitute minimal pairs.

   [w] is a voiced labio-velar glide; we might regard [ʍ] as its voiceless counterpart. This characterization is not quite accurate, since in order for the voiceless sound to be audible, it needs to be articulated with greater airflow, thereby causing the sound to be a noisy fricative. Whereas [w] can be described as an approximant, [ʍ] is better characterized as a voiceless fricative.

   Often, [ʍ] is represented, phonemically, as /hw/ (as in Ladefoged 1975). What could be the justification for this analysis?

   (iii) Given that [w] and [j] are similar in many respects, one might wonder whether there is a voiceless fricative which stands in the same relation to [j] as [ʍ] stands to [w]. Let us call this segment [@]. What is [@]?

   Note that the contrast between [w] and [ʍ] is made only in certain accents of English, e.g. in parts of Scotland and New Zealand. Even there, the contrast is being lost in the speech of younger speakers. Given this situation, and the similarities between [w] and [j], one might expect to find that the contrast between [j] and [@] is in the process of being lost. Is there any evidence for this? (Hint: Consider pronunciations of words such as *you* and *hue*. Some speakers pronounce *human* as [ju:mən].

4. Study question 3 suggested that sounds which belong to a natural class are liable to undergo similar processes of change over time.

Find arguments which suggest that [l] and [r] in English form a natural class. Again, you might look at the articulation of the sounds and their distribution within the syllable, across different accents of English.

Given that standard British and British-based accents of English have 'lost' post-vocalic 'r', one might expect that these accents should also be losing, or have already lost, post-vocalic 'l'. Is this in fact the case?

5. Most languages have words that are often described as 'interjections' or 'ideophones'. These items are not easily assigned to any of the traditional lexical classes, such as 'noun', 'verb', 'adjective', and so on. Typically, they symbolize kinds of sounds or manners of motion, they express speaker attitudes, or convey inter-speaker relations.

Interjections and ideophones are not only syntactically odd, they are often also phonologically deviant. That is to say, they fail to conform to the dominant phonological schemas of a language. Examples from English include:

(i) [pst], often spelled *psst!*, a surreptitious attention-getting expression. The word's syllable structure is highly deviant, in that the nucleus is constituted by a voiceless fricative [s].

(ii) *Whoosh!* [wu:ʃ], which indicates a sudden, rapid movement, often accompanied by a hissing sound. The word is unusual because of its syllable rhyme [u:ʃ]. While there are plenty of words, in English, which contain the rhymes [ʊʃ] and [ʌʃ], no others contain [u:ʃ]. Possibly, [u:ʃ] does not occur in English because of a constraint against adjacent lip-rounded segments in a syllable rhyme; both [u:] and [ʃ] are articulated with significant lip rounding. A similar prohibition applies in syllable onsets. There are, for example, no words commencing in sequences of labial segments, e.g. [bw] or [pw], and only foreign borrowings commence in [ʃw].

(iii) *Oink!* [ɔɪŋk], which represents that sound that pigs make. The word is odd because the velar nasal [ŋ] occurs following a long vowel (more specifically, a diphthong), something that is in general not possible in English. There is another respect in which the word is deviant. Generally, if a syllable rhyme contains more than three segments, the additional segments, beyond the third, must be coronal. While [sɛɪnt] is an acceptable English syllable, *[sɛɪmp] is not.

Compile a list of 'interjections', in English and other languages. Do the interjections conform to established segmental and syllable schemas of the languages? In what ways (if any) are they deviant?

Further reading

This chapter presupposes familiarity with basic notions of phonetics and phonology. Good introductions are Ladefoged (1975), Katamba (1989), and Roca and Johnson (1999). See the Suggestions for Further readings in Chapter 5 for Cognitive Grammar approaches to phonology.

CHAPTER 9

Schema and instance in symbolic units

We have seen how the schema-instance relation applies both to semantic and to phonological units. In this chapter I turn to symbolic units, i.e. associations between phonological and semantic structures. These, too, can stand in the schema-instance relation. A symbolic unit can be an instance of a more schematically characterized symbolic unit, and can itself be schematic for a range of more fully specified symbolic units.

Schema-instance relations between symbolic units are crucial to the viability of Cognitive Grammar. I have emphasized in several places already that Cognitive Grammar does not recognize a distinct level of syntactic organization. This does not mean that the existence of syntactic categories such as noun, verb, clause, subject, and the like, is being denied. Cognitive Grammar certainly makes reference to these and similar entities, just like most other linguistic theories. However, these categories are not regarded as elements of an autonomous syntactic level of organization, but are themselves taken to be symbolic units—symbolic units with a highly schematic content, to be sure, but symbolic units nonetheless.

In this chapter I focus mainly on word classes, with some incidental remarks on syntactic constructions.

9.1 Words and word classes

The word *tree* is a symbolic unit, which associates a phonological structure [tri:] with a semantic structure [TREE]. Both the phonological and the semantic sides of the unit can participate in schema-instance relations:

- The concept [TREE] is schematic for such concepts as [OAK], [PINE], [WILLOW], and, indeed, for a conceptualization of a specific tree. At the same time, [TREE] is an instance of more schematic concepts, such as [PLANT], [LIVING THING], and even [THING].
- On the phonological side, [tri:] is an instance of [SYLLABLE], and is itself schematic for various ways of pronouncing the syllable, such as [t̺ri:], [tʰɹəi], and so on.

But what about the symbolic unit itself? Could this be an instance of a more schematic symbolic unit? And could it serve as a schema for more fully specified units?

Let us take the second question first. A language user encounters the word *tree* in specific contexts of use. Each usage event associates a phonological and a semantic structure. On different occasions, and in different contexts, both the pronunciation and the concept will vary somewhat. No two pronunciations are exactly the same, while the conceptualization will vary according to the particularities of the designated entity. By noting what is common to the different uses of the word, a language user abstracts a schematic tree-concept, and, associated with this, a schematic phonological representation. It is this decontextualized unit that is at issue when we talk about 'the word *tree*', and it is this unit which gets listed, with its pronunciation and meaning, in our dictionaries.

If the decontextualized word is schematic for the word as used on specific occasions, is the decontextualized word itself an instance of some even more schematic unit? What is the word *tree* an instance of?

My phrasing of the question suggests a possible answer. *Tree*, considered as an established association of sound and meaning, is a word, more specifically, a noun. Just as, in Chapter 8, we proposed a taxonomy of phonological segments, and in Chapter 7 a taxonomy of semantic units, so also we can entertain a taxonomy of words and word classes. A fragment of such a taxonomy is shown in Figure 9.1 (p. 166).

At the top of the taxonomy stands the maximally schematic [WORD]. This unit has, as its instances, the different kinds of words—roughly, the traditional parts of speech, such as [NOUN], [VERB], [ADJECTIVE]. *Tree* is an instance of [NOUN]. At the very bottom of the taxonomy (not shown in Figure 9.1) stand the word-instances that occur in specific usage events. Pending a more contentful characterization, I have represented the semantic and phonological content of [WORD] and the word classes by means of ". . ." / [. . .].

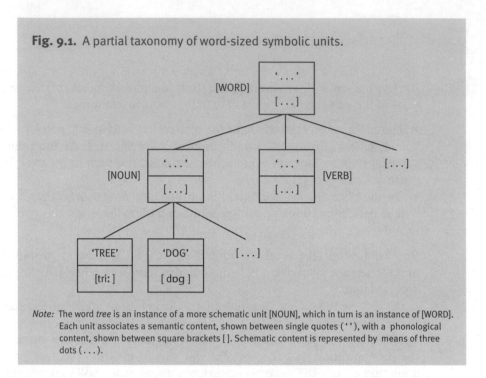

Fig. 9.1. A partial taxonomy of word-sized symbolic units.

Note: The word *tree* is an instance of a more schematic unit [NOUN], which in turn is an instance of [WORD]. Each unit associates a semantic content, shown between single quotes ('), with a phonological content, shown between square brackets [ ]. Schematic content is represented by means of three dots (...).

It is important to be clear about what exactly is entailed by Figure 9.1. The Figure is not simply a fragment of a (more or less) traditional taxonomy of word classes, it is a **taxonomy of symbolic units**. If we say that the symbolic unit *tree* is an instance of [NOUN], we are committed to the proposition that [NOUN], too, is a symbolic unit. As such, it associates a phonological structure with a semantic structure. [NOUN], in turn, is an instance of [WORD]. Again, [WORD] has the status of a symbolic unit, which likewise associates a phonological and a semantic structure.

Several things follow. First, [NOUN], [VERB], and the other word classes will need to be characterized in terms of their phonological and semantic poles and the symbolic relation between them. To assign a word to a particular word class—to say of a word that it is a noun, verb, or whatever—is to claim that the word instantiates the schematically characterized word class. It is not an option to regard the word classes as purely syntactic constructs, nor is membership in word classes a matter of arbitrary stipulation.

At first blush, this may not look like a very promising way to handle these most basic of linguistic notions. Any proposal to characterize 'noun' and 'verb' in terms of their semantic and phonological content would appear to conflict with one of the best-established principles of modern linguistics. The principle is that words are assigned to word classes on the basis of their syntactic and morphological behaviour, i.e. their distribution within larger configurations, not according to their meaning, even less, their phonology.

On the standard view of the matter, we determine that *earthquake* is a noun because it behaves like a noun. It can take a determiner, it can pluralize, it can be modified by adjectives and relative clauses, and, when suitably 'grounded'[1] (e.g. by a determiner), it can function as the subject or direct object of a verb. All these are typical distributional properties of nouns, and it is on this basis that we conclude that *earthquake* is a noun. We do not arrive at this conclusion by contemplating the word's meaning, even less its phonology.

In a sense, the standard view of word classes is unobjectionable. Imagine that the word class of *earthquake* was in dispute. We would attempt to settle the issue by reference to the word's distribution, not by reference to its meaning (or its phonology). We would not, for example, argue that since *earthquake* designates something that happens, the word has to be a verb. How, then, can we possibly defend a symbolic view of word classes, and claim that the word classes *are* characterized in terms of their semantics and phonology?

The question, as just posed, rests on a false premise. The error lies in assuming that distributional criteria and the symbolic approach are mutually exclusive possibilities. In promoting a symbolic view of word classes I am not at all denying the usefulness of distributional criteria. Conversely, to acknowledge the usefulness of distributional criteria does not undermine the symbolic approach.

Consider more closely what we mean by an item's distribution. Essentially, we are referring to the ways in which an item enters into syntagmatic relations with other items. As I shall argue in Chapter 12, the possibility of combining items derives rather directly from the semantic (and phonological) properties of the items in question. The fact that *book*, *on*, and *the table* combine in the way they do to form the expression *book on the table* is not a 'purely syntactic' phenomenon, it is motivated by semantic (and phonological) aspects of the component words.[2]

The fact that a number of words share similar combinatorial possibilities (i.e. they share a similar distribution) allows the emergence of word classes; a word class is simply a set of words which, because of their similar semantic/phonological properties, behave in a similar way *vis-à-vis* other symbolic units. At the same time, recurring patterns of combination can themselves achieve the status of symbolic units; they constitute a language's **constructional schemas**, which specify, among other things, the kinds of items that make up a composite expression and the order in which they occur.

The interplay of distributional and symbolic aspects of word classes is

---

[1] On the 'grounding' of nominals, see Chapter 18.

[2] Reference to phonological aspects may strike the reader as unusual. But since an important aspect of syntagmatic combination is the order in which the component units are arranged, and since constituent order is a matter of the order in which the components are spoken, word order turns out to be a matter of phonological representation.

nicely illustrated by the way we approach unknown words. Take the first lines of Lewis Carroll's *Jabberwocky*:

> 'Twas brillig, and the slithy toves
> Did gyre and gimble in the wabe

Distributional criteria establish that *gyre* and *gimble* are verbs. We do not come to this conclusion on the basis of the meaning of the words. *Gyre* and *gimble* are nonsense words, made up by Lewis Carroll, and which do not have conventionalized meanings in the language. Yet, once we have determined their status as verbs, we do have some vague idea of what the words could mean, for example, that they designate states or processes which persist over time. The semantic content that we attribute to the words derives from our recognition of their status as verbs. We are, in fact, allowing the words to inherit the schematic meaning of the word class of which they are instances.[3]

In the following section I take a critical look at the standard view, according to which distributional facts are all there is to word classes. I argue that a 'blind' application of distributional criteria in fact raises some serious methodological and conceptual problems, which put into question the viability of purely distributional criteria. Then, in section 9.3, I demonstrate the validity of the symbolic approach on the example of the highest unit in Figure 9.1, namely [WORD]. In the final sections, I address the semantic and phonological characterization of the word classes.

9.2 Distributional criteria for word classes

It is widely accepted that the major word classes can be associated with proto-typical semantic values. Nouns designate objects, verbs designate processes (and states), adjectives designate properties (of objects), while prepositions designate relations (especially spatial relations) between objects.

These correlations between word classes and semantic categories are far from perfect. Nouns can denote entities of many semantic types in addition to objects: abstract notions (*belief*), events (*earthquake*), states (*depression*), qualities (*strength*), and amounts (*kilogram*). The matter seems especially problematic in that the semantic category 'event' might be supposed to be the prerogative of the verb class, while qualities might be regarded as the speciality of the adjective class. Yet nouns can readily designate both events and qualities.

The possibility of a semantic definition of the noun category is rendered especially elusive by the phenomenon of **nominalization**. Practically any verbal expressions, and most adjectival expressions, can be converted into a nominal expression. Verbal *destroy the city* nominalizes to *destruction of the*

---

[3] The syntactic environment of the nonsense words provides further clues to their semantic content. *Gyre* and *gimble* are used intransitively, and hence inherit the schematic semantic content of [INTRANSITIVE VERB], i.e. the verbs designate a state or process which involves only one salient participant.

city, adjectival *fond of cheese* nominalizes to *fondness for cheese*. Alongside lexicalized nominalizations such as *destruction* and *fondness* there is the very general process of nominalizing a clause by means of *-ing*. *The farmer shot the rabbit* nominalizes to *the farmer's shooting of the rabbit*. To make matters worse, nominalization is cross-linguistically extremely widespread—much more widespread than the marking of nouns for number, or the marking of verbs for tense. Nominalization cannot be dismissed as a marginal, exceptional, or even an infrequent phenomenon.

Especially during the heyday of Bloomfieldian structuralism, linguists were scathing of conceptual definitions of word classes. It was argued that the only reliable criteria for defining parts of speech were distributional. Introductory texts of the time stressed that words are assigned to a word class solely on the basis of their occurring in similar syntactic frames; semantic considerations are irrelevant. Palmer (1971) is representative of this approach:

the definition [of noun as a word for naming something] is completely vacuous as we can see if we ask how on the basis of this definition can we find the nouns in *He suffered terribly* and *His suffering was terrible*? Is there any sense in which the last sentence has reference to things in a way in which the first does not? For these sentences are identical in meaning. Of course, we can say that 'suffering' is a noun and that in this sentence it refers to a thing, the act of suffering being 'treated' as a thing, but this is arguing back to front. (Palmer 1971: 39)

Palmer continues:

How can we possibly identify 'thing'? There is an easy answer. We do so by using an article or such words as *his*, *this*, in front of the words—*the fire, the suffering, the place*—and by making them the subject of the sentence. But that is to say that we identify 'things' by looking for the grammatical characteristics of nouns. In other words, 'things' are identified by being referred to by nouns. (Palmer 1971: 39)

To be sure, the procedure recommended by Palmer is the one that all practising linguists (including Cognitive Linguists) adopt. Nevertheless, there are a number of conceptual problems lurking behind the notion of distribution and its role in the determination of word classes.

Consider the category of verbs. One criterion for the categorization of a word as a verb (at least in English and other languages which have tense inflections) is the ability of the word to inflect for tense.[4] The fact that *suffer* has a past tense form, *suffered*, demonstrates that *suffer* is a verb. Notice, however, that this argument rests on the prior understanding of what 'tense inflection' is. Tense inflection is not simply a matter of time reference. *His present suffering* and *his past suffering* refer, respectively, to suffering that occurs now and to suffering that occurred in the past. But this fact does not entitle us to say that *suffering*, in these expressions, is a verb. It is not enough

---

[4] The criterion of tense inflection fails to apply to the so-called modal verbs. This is one of the distributional criteria that are typically used for identifying this sub-category of verbs.

The universality of word classes?

A corollary of a strictly distributional approach is that word classes have to be defined anew for each language under investigation; it is illegitimate to carry over word classes that are viable for one language to other languages. To quote from an introductory textbook:

[T]he number and nature of the word classes of a language must be worked out as the analysis proceeds, not assumed in advance, nor settled by reference to the grammatical class of the nearest translation equivalent of a word in English, Latin, or some other language. . . . The definition of a class, and its membership, can only arise from the criteria used to establish it in the first place. (Robins 1964: 228)

If the criteria for word class membership are language specific (which is neces-sarily the case with purely distributional criteria) it will not be possible to make generalizations over the word classes of different languages. A strict application of distributional criteria leads, inevitably, to a position of radical relativism (see p. 55).

Nevertheless, linguists do speak (and always have spoken) of nouns and verbs, adjectives and prepositions, from a cross-linguistic perspective. The basis for cross-language comparisons is ultimately semantic in nature. We recognize noun and verb as universal categories because of the universality of their (schematic) semantic content.

---

that an expression contains a reference to present or to past time. In order for a word to be identified as a verb it is necessary that time reference is achieved through tense inflection, not through modification by an adjective. But 'tense inflection'—the criterion for identification as a verb—is a quintessentially verbal category, whose characterization presupposes the very notion 'verb' that the criterion is meant to identify. As a means for defining the word classes, distributional criteria turn out to be ultimately circular. The circle can only be broken, I submit, by recognizing the semantic basis for word class definitions.

Consider, as another example, Palmer's observation that a characteristic of nouns is that they can combine with articles and that the resultant phrases can function as the subject of a clause. These criteria presuppose that we already have an understanding of 'clause', and of what it means for a noun phrase to function as 'subject of a clause'. On a purely distributional approach, 'clause' and 'clausal subject' will need to be defined in terms of the arrangement of their parts, one of which is . . . the noun. Again, distributional criteria turn out to be irreducibly circular.

Distributional criteria, as usually understood and practised by linguists, cannot then be regarded as the sole or final means for discovering and defining the lexical categories of a language; the criteria already presuppose a sophisticated (and, ultimately, semantic) understanding of lexical and syntactic categories.[5]

A further aspect is the question of 'granularity'; distributional criteria can be 'fine-grained' or 'coarse-grained'. If we apply the most fine-grained criteria, we should probably discover that each word's distribution is unique. *Dog* does not distribute exactly like *cat*, and *go* does not distribute exactly like *come*. As a consequence, we should have to assign each word to a word class with a membership of one. (As a matter of fact, some words probably do need to be regarded as *sui generis* in terms of their distribution and do need to be assigned to one-member categories.) In order for the major categories to emerge, we shall have to disregard numerous word-specific characteristics. This is tantamount to saying that the characteristic distribution of a word class is schematic for the range of distributions of its members. In fact, some of the traditionally recognized categories—especially 'preposition', 'adverb', and 'adjective'—turn out to be highly heterogeneous collections of items, with widely different patterns of distribution.

9.3 [WORD] as a symbolic unit

In this section I argue that the unit at the apex of Figure 9.1, namely [WORD], is susceptible to a characterization in symbolic-unit terms. The example will demonstrate, I hope, the general viability of the symbolic approach.

The sceptical reader might doubt the viability of an enterprise which aims to characterize [WORD] in terms of phonological and semantic aspects and the symbolic relation between them. In any language there are tens of thousands of words; how can we possibly bring them all under a common schema? It is unlikely that we can say anything substantial about the segmental content of the phonological pole. In principle, a word could have any phonological content whatsoever. The most we can say, perhaps, is that a word has *some* phonological content. The same goes for the semantic pole; a word can mean just about anything at all. But to claim that a word associates some phonological content with some semantic content is almost totally vacuous. It means that any phonological content, in association with any semantic content, constitutes a word. The schema places virtually no constraints on what might instantiate it, and offers no basis for ascertaining, in any particular case, where a particular association of meaning and sound constitutes a word or not.

Far from being an impossible task, a characterization of [WORD] in phonological and semantic terms is actually very compelling, and it succeeds rather well in capturing the intuitive notion of what words actually are.

We should note, at the outset, that the notion of 'word' is not without its problems. First, there is the ambiguity of the term itself. Do we say that *walk*,

---

[5] The application of distributional criteria also presupposes the prior analysis of a linguistic expression into its constituent elements. Analysability is addressed in Chapter 15.

walks, *walked*, and *walking* are four different words, or four different forms of one and the same word? The distinction here is between **word form** and **lexeme**; the lexeme 'walk' appears in four different inflected forms. Given the 'bottom-up', usage orientation of Cognitive Grammar, we will want to give priority to the word forms. Word forms are the entities that language users encounter. As I will show in section 16.3, there is evidence that speakers do store word forms (at least, frequently occurring word forms) as separate linguistic entities.

A second ambiguity concerns the distinction between **word type** and **word token**. The ambiguity shows up whenever we ask how many words there are in a text. Do we count the individual word forms or the number of different word forms (or the number of different lexemes)? In Cognitive Grammar terms, the word tokens are instances of the word types. Word types are the decontextualized items that are abstracted from their instances, the word tokens are contextualized instances of the word types.

There are, in addition, some problems in determining whether a particular sound-meaning relation should be considered a word (whether word-form or lexeme) or not, and whether a particular form consists of one or of more than one word.

Consider the distinction between so-called **content words** and **function words**.[6] Function words—these include the common prepositions, the determiners *a* and *the*, forms of the verbs *be* and *have*, and suchlike—tend to be short and are generally unstressed. When unstressed, they need to attach themselves to an adjacent (and usually stressed) word. In such circumstances, we might be inclined to count the combination of host-plus-clitic as a single word. This option is especially likely to present itself in cases where the function word undergoes phonological reduction, or 'coalesces' with its host. While we may agree that *he is*, when spoken [ˈhiː ˈʔɪz], contains two words, it is less obvious that *he's* [hiːz] is two words. We should be even less inclined to regard *ain't* (a substandard form which corresponds to 'is not', 'are not', 'has not', and several others) as two words. And if *aren't* is to be regarded as two words, the question arises what these two are in the interrogative *Aren't I?*

Compounds raise issues of a different kind. *Greenhouse* 'place for raising plants' would be listed as a single word in a dictionary, even though its parts—*green* and *house*—are also words. Although compounds are standardly made up of words (and are themselves words), it sometimes happens that the modifying element of a compound is a multi-word phrase; consider *a [couldn't-care-less] attitude*, or *a [wait-and-see] approach*. We should certainly hesitate to say that the bracketed expressions are single words, even less, that the compounds as a whole are single words. Things also become less clear when we consider that compounding is a recursive process; a compound can

---

[6] My use of these well-established terms should not be taken to imply that function words lack semantic content. The difference between 'content' and 'function' words essentially has to do with the schematicity of the symbolized content. See section 17.1.2.

be incorporated into a larger compound. We should probably be reluctant to assert that the compound *greenhouse manufacturer* (even less, *greenhouse manufacturer association*) is a single word. Also rendering the matter less than clear-cut is the fact that 'compound' might not be a well-defined category, anyway. Are *gold watch*, *stone wall*, *public school* multi-word phrases, or single word compounds? Probably, the question does not have a clear-cut answer.

We need not be unduly disturbed by the fact that what counts as a word may not be a clear-cut matter. If it is difficult to circumscribe precisely what counts as a word, it is also difficult to draw a clear line around what entities count as 'books', or, for that matter, 'phonemes'. In fact, most elements of linguistic structure (just like most aspects of our non-linguistic environment) resist clear-cut categorization. Importantly, the existence of these problematic cases does not invalidate 'word' as a linguistic category. Our strategy will be to characterize words on the basis of what are intuitively clear examples (or relatively clear examples), pointing out the problematic or ambiguous cases as we go along.

In Figure 9.1, the unit [WORD] is given a maximally schematic representation. Our task, here, is to give more substance to this characterization, so that it accords with our intuitive notion of what counts as a word.

To begin, we may note that for certain languages it may indeed be possible to make some general statements concerning what can constitute a word, for example, that a word must contain a minimum number of syllables (see Study question 6 of Chapter 5 for the case of Zulu). Even for English, such a possibility cannot be entirely dismissed. Content words, at least, must contain at least one stressed ('strong') syllable. Moreover, as noted in section 5.2.1, there is a marked tendency for polysyllabic words to commence with a stressed syllable.

We must do better than this, however. While (content) words may tend to coincide with the phonological foot, we certainly cannot identify words in terms of the phonological foot. Still keeping to phonological considerations, I propose that words can be characterized in terms of their phonological stability, their phonological integrity, and what I will call their phonological promiscuity.

(i) Words are <u>phonologically stable</u> in the sense that, whatever their segmental content, they tend to preserve this content, unchanged, in all of their uses. To be sure, some words are conventionally associated with alternative pronunciations, even within the speech of one and the same speaker; a well-known example is *economics*, pronounced [ɪkənɒmɪks] or [ɛkənɒmɪks]. There will also be variations in a word's phonology due to assimilations and other processes. *Red*, in *red pen*, can emerge either as [rɛd] or as [rɛbˀ]. It could not, however, emerge as [pɪŋk]; phonologically, this form is so far removed from [rɛd] that we should say that we are dealing with another word. Likewise, when a three-year-old child sometimes says *went* and sometimes says *goed*, we should probably say that the child is using two different words, not two forms of the same word, since the two forms are phonologically so different.[7]

(ii) Words have <u>phonological integrity</u> in that, whatever the segmental content, the content cannot be broken up by intervening material, nor can the different parts appear in a different sequence. Again, there are marginal and problematic cases. A well-known example concerns the 'separable prefixes' in the Germanic languages. Compare German *ankommen* '(to) arrive' and *anzukommen* '(in order) to arrive', and *(sie) kommen an* '(they) arrive'.[8]

The criterion of phonological integrity distinguishes multi-word phrases from compounds. As a phrase, *green house* 'house that is green' can be broken up by intervening material: *a green and dilapidated house*. The compound *greenhouse* cannot be broken up—at least, not if we wish to preserve the conventional semantic value of *greenhouse* 'place for raising plants'.

(iii) <u>Phonological promiscuity</u> refers to the fact that while the internal structure of a word remains stable and integral, there are typically very few requirements on the phonological properties of the units to which it is adjacent. While *red* may tend to occur before a noun or after the copula, these tendencies are easily flouted; in principle, a word can occur adjacent to just about anything. Moreover, if we allow that the phonological material either preceding or following a word can be silence (or a hesitation pause), we arrive at Bloomfield's well-known definition of a word as 'a minimum free form' (Bloomfield 1933: 178).

This aspect distinguishes words from bound morphemes; a bound morpheme has to occur adjacent to items of a certain kind. While *-ness* has the properties of phonological integrity and stability, the morpheme has to attach to a host of a certain kind, namely, an adjective (and not every adjective is an equally good candidate). Many affixes, moreover, place very strict conditions on the phonological aspects of the stems to which they can attach.

Summing up, then, we can say that [WORD], at its phonological pole, consists of a (relatively) stable and integral phonological structure, which is free to combine with virtually any phonological elements (including silence).

The phonological structure, so identified, is associated with a semantic structure. The semantic structure also possesses a certain stability and coherence. But just as the phonological shape of a word can vary somewhat, depending on its phonological environment, so too its meaning can adjust in order to accommodate to a larger conceptualization (the phenomenon of 'semantic flexibility': section 6.1.1). Moreover, it is readily accepted that a

---

[7] Bybee and Slobin (1982: 277) report that a child, when asked to produce the past tense of *go*, responded that you can't say *goed*, 'you have to use the word went', suggesting that the child was aware that *went* was a special word which replaced the expected word form.

[8] A well-known problem for the thesis of phonological integrity is 'expletive insertion' (McCarthy 1982, Jackendoff 1997: 119): *manu – fuckin'– facturer*. Note that expletive insertion only occurs within a word which consists, minimally, of two feet. It is as if a two-foot word splits into two foot-sized words.

word can have a range of related meanings, in which case the word is said to be polysemous (e.g. *ring*, in *wedding ring*, *ear ring*, *boxing ring*, and *smugglers ring*). But if the meanings are very disparate, we should probably say that the different meanings attach to different words which happen to share the same phonological form (a phenomenon known as homonymy). *Bank* and *ball* are often-cited examples of homonymy. The border line between polysemy and homonymy is not clearly drawn, however. Do we recognize a single word *board* in *board of directors*, *bed and board*, and *wooden board*, or two (or even three) different words?

With respect to compounds, the conventionalization of the meaning clearly plays a role in determining whether a compound counts as one word or more than one. *Greenhouse*, as mentioned, probably counts as a single word, in view of its fixed, conventionalized meaning. (The impossibility of inserting material into the compound—**a green-dilapidated-house*—is probably also a reflection of the item's conventionalized status.) *Greenhouse manufacturer* lacks this degree of conventionalization and would probably be regarded as a combination of two words. It is also worth noting that the possibility of incorporating phrases into compounds (*a couldn't-care-less attitude*) depends on the conventionalization of the incorporated phrasal unit (*couldn't care less*).

The approach sketched out here, I think, captures quite well the intuitive notion of what a word is, and also predicts where uncertainties will arise. There are, however, some interesting consequences. For example, forms such as *run*, *runs*, and *running* would need to be regarded as different words. Likewise, a rigidly fixed expression, such as *How do you do?* would emerge as a word, not as a phrase. If this expression is to preserve its conventionalized value (namely, as a greeting ritual) it cannot be changed, even minimally. It is not possible to change the tense (**He asked me, how did I do?*), nor to insert material into the expression (**How do you all do?*—intended as a response to being introduced to a group of people).

9.4 Semantic criteria for word classes

A symbolic view of word classes requires that these are characterized in terms of their semantics (as well as their phonology).

For reasons mentioned earlier in this chapter, many linguists have been sceptical of a semantic approach to word classes. This, after all, motivated the structuralists' insistence that word classes be defined solely on distributional criteria. At the same time, there are striking correlations between word classes and semantic categories. While it is obviously false to say that nouns, as a class, designate concrete objects, we should certainly expect a concrete object to be named by a noun.

Jackendoff's position on this issue is instructive. Jackendoff (1983: 13) proposed that linguistic theorizing should be subject to what he called the 'Grammatical Constraint'. According to this, 'one should prefer a semantic theory that explains otherwise arbitrary generalizations about the syntax and the lexicon':

Under the reasonable hypothesis that language serves the purpose of transmitting information, it would be perverse not to take as a working assumption that language is a relatively efficient and accurate encoding of the information it conveys.... [W]hat appears to be an irregular relationship between syntax and semantics may turn out merely to be a bad theory of one or the other. (Jackendoff 1983: 14)

According to Jackendoff, then, one should attempt to explain formal properties of a language in semantic terms (a programme which Cognitive Grammar would endorse). Ideally, 'formal' (i.e. syntactic) properties of a language will be explained by reference to semantics. As likely as not, what appear to be purely syntactic properties—properties not subject to a semantic explanation—might be such because of an inadequate semantic (or syntactic) analysis. Having stated this position, Jackendoff immediately points to two cases where syntax and semantics fail to match up; one concerns the grammatical relation of clausal subject, the other the lexical category of noun. The noun category, he claims, 'cannot be identified with any coherent semantic category' (p. 14); 'the relationship between syntactic and ontological categories is not one-to-one' (p. 68). With respect to the Grammatical Constraint, Jackendoff claims that the point of the Constraint is 'only to attempt to minimize the differences of syntactic and semantic structure, not to expect to eliminate them altogether' (p. 14).

It is the absence of a one-to-one relation between syntactic and semantic categories that leads Jackendoff to opt for a three-level representation of linguistic structure, comprising phonological, semantic, and syntactic aspects. Words, for example, are represented by their phonological form and their semantic content, and also by a stipulation of their lexical category. Cognitive Grammar, in contrast, recognizes only two levels—the phonological and the semantic. The lexical category to which a word belongs has to be derivable from these two levels, and the symbolic relation between them.

Jackendoff's approach highlights the high stakes involved in recognizing lexical categories as symbolic units. The issue strikes at the heart of the viability of the Cognitive Grammar view of language as a symbolic system. If the major word classes cannot be characterized as symbolic units, we will be forced to accept a syntactic level of representation, thus undercutting the grounding assumption of Cognitive Grammar, i.e. the Symbolic Thesis.

As the earlier quotation from Palmer shows, it is easy to be critical of a conceptual definition of word classes. More recently, however, a number of linguists have begun to take seriously the idea that word classes might be semantically based, and have looked to the possibility of universal characterizations of the word classes.

I review three approaches. The first, by Givón, is seriously flawed. The second, by Croft, is more promising and leads into Langacker's account of the word classes.

9.4.1 Givón and the prototype approach

Givón (1984) has pointed out that the referents of nouns and verbs tend to differ with respect to their time stability. His generalizations are meant to have universal, cross-linguistic relevance.

> Experiences—or phenomenological clusters—which stay relatively **stable** over time, i.e. those which over repeated scans appear to be roughly 'the same', tend to be lexicalized in human languages as **nouns**. The most prototypical nouns are those denoting **concrete, physical, compact** entities made out of durable, solid matter, such as 'rock', 'tree', 'dog', 'person' etc. . . .
> At the other extreme of the lexical-phenomenological scale, one finds experiential clusters denoting **rapid changes** in the state of the universe. These are prototypically *events* or *actions*, and languages tend to lexicalize them as verbs. . . .
> [T]he class 'adjective' is a bit problematic. In languages such as English, which has this class . . . adjectives occupy the middle of the time-stability scale. They may overlap with the *least* time-stable nouns, such as 'youth', 'adult', 'child', 'divorcee', 'infant'. Most commonly they embrace at least the time-stable physical properties such as size, shape, color, texture, smell or taste. Finally, they may overlap, at the other end of the scale, with the *most* time-stable adjectives/verbs, such as those expressed in English by the following adjectives: 'sad', 'angry', 'hot', 'cold', 'happy', 'ill' etc. (Givón 1984: 51–2; author's emphasis)

It is certainly true that one should expect names of time-stable entities, such as rocks and trees, to be nouns; nevertheless, time stability is a very poor correlate of word classes, little better, it would seem, than the traditional notional definition that Palmer had criticized. *Flash* can be a noun, *exist* is a verb, and *dead* (which is about as time stable as one can get) is an adjective. It is also clear that Givón himself had problems with his claim that adjectives fall midway between time-stable noun-concepts and transient verb-concepts.

In fairness, it should be noted that Givón's point is that time stability characterizes the 'core', 'prototypical' members of the classes. Around these 'core' exemplars we can imagine a penumbra of not-so-typical examples: nouns like *flash*, verbs like *remain*, and adjectives like *dead* and *instantaneous*. The problem here is that degree of semantic prototypicality fails to be reflected in distributional criteria. If, from the point of view of the time-stability criterion, *flash* and *explosion* are rather untypical nouns, from the point of view of their distribution they are not at all untypical. With respect to its syntactic behaviour, *explosion* is every bit as good a noun as *rock*.

The conclusion must be that attempts to characterize the word classes in terms of the properties of their referents is bound to fail. We need to move the discussion to another level. A functional approach to the categories is one option.

9.4.2 Croft and the functional approach

Croft (1991) proposes three basic functions that a language must fulfil if it is to serve as a means of symbolizing conceptualizations. These are reference, predication, and modification.

- reference. This has to do with 'get[ting] the hearer to identify an entity as what is being talked about' (Croft 1991: 52). This characterization of reference makes no mention of the semantic type of the referent. The 'entity' being talked about could be a material object, a fact, a situation, a quality, or whatever;
- predication. This has to do with 'what the speaker intends to *say about* what he is talking about (the referent)';
- modification. This, Croft explains, is an 'accessory function to reference and predication'. It 'helps fix the identity of what one is talking about (reference) by narrowing the description'.[9]

Corresponding to these three functions are three basic ontological kinds: objects, properties, and actions. These are distinguished by the properties of valence, stativity, persistence, and gradability.

- valence. This has to do with the 'inherent relationality' of a concept (p. 62);
- stativity. This concerns the 'presence or absence of change over time' (cf. Givón's 'time stability');
- persistence. This has to do with 'how long the state of affairs persists', i.e. whether the state of affairs is (relatively) persistent or (relatively) transitory;
- gradability. This is a matter of the 'extent to which the concept can be manifested in degrees' (p. 65).

Putting these together, we get the characterization of major ontological kinds shown in Table 9.1.

The next step is to correlate the ontological kinds with a functional approach to the lexical categories. This is illustrated in Table 9.2.

The left-to-right diagonal of Table 9.2 gives the prototypical values of nouns, adjectives, and verbs, as well as the prototypical ways of symbolizing objects, properties, and actions. These prototypical values match up with the functions of reference, modification, and predication, respectively. Nominal, adjectival, and verbal expressions can, however, be 'coerced' into serving a non-prototypical function. The coercion typically involves some kind of morphological and/or syntactic marking. When properties and actions become 'the entity that is being talked about' the adjectival and verbal expressions need to be nominalized (*fondness for cheese*, *the farmer's shooting of the rabbit*). When adjectival and nominal expressions are used predicatively, they need to be 'converted' into verbal expressions; typically, this is achieved

---

[9] In Chapter 18 I use the term 'specification' to cover Croft's functional notion of modification.

Table 9.1 Properties of the major ontological kinds

	Objects	Properties	Actions
Valency	0	1	≤1
Stativity	state	state	process
Persistence	persistent	persistent	transitory
Gradability	nongradable	gradable	nongradable

Source: Based on Croft (1991: 65).

Table 9.2 The functions of the major ontological kinds

	Reference	Modification	Predication
Objects	**vehicle**	vehicular of/in/etc. the vehicle	be a vehicle
Properties	whiteness	**white**	be white
Actions	destruction	destroying destroyed	**destroy**

Note: The left-to-right diagonal exemplifies the prototypical values.
Source: Based on Croft (1991: 53).

by the use of the verb *(to) be*: *be white*, *be a vehicle*. Various syntactic and morphological means are available for converting verbal and nominal expressions into adjectivals, including participle formation (for verbal expressions) and prepositional phrases (for nominal expressions).

9.4.3 Langacker and the conceptual approach

Langacker, not surprisingly, has also proposed conceptual definitions of the major word categories. A full understanding of his account must await our subsequent treatment of profiling and of conceptual autonomy vs. dependence (Chapters 10 and 11). Simplifying Langacker's account, however, we can say that a noun designates a conceptually autonomous 'thing', whereas a verb designates a 'process', i.e. the existence, through time, of a relation, whether this be stable and unchanging or inherently dynamic. [THING] and [PROCESS] are proposed as the schematic meanings of the two word classes. The other word classes designate atemporal relations.

Langacker emphasizes that the noun/verb distinction has to do with the manner in which a situation is conceptualized, it does not reside in any 'objective' properties of the situation. It may well be true—to take up Palmer's example—that *He suffered terribly* and *His suffering was terrible* both describe the same situation. It may be disputed, however, that the two expressions are identical in meaning (as Palmer asserted), since the expressions construe the

---

Skinner on word classes

B. F. Skinner, the behaviourist psychologist, is the linguist's bogeyman. Ever since Chomsky (1959) rubbished his theory that language can be reduced to a matter of stimulus-response associations, his name has been anathema in linguistic circles. Nevertheless, Skinner is still worth a read. (He had some quite insightful remarks on metaphor.) Also, the conceptual import of word classes was not lost on Skinner:

We tend to make nouns of adjectives and verbs and must then find a place for the things the nouns are said to represent. We say that a rope is strong, and before long we are speaking of its strength. We call a particular kind of strength tensile, and then explain that the rope is strong because it possesses tensile strength. The mistake is less obvious but more troublesome when matters are more complex. . . .

When a person has been subjected to mildly punishing consequences in walking on a slippery surface, he may walk in a manner we describe as cautious. It is then easy to say that he walks with caution or that he shows caution. There is no harm in this until we begin to say that he walks carefully because of his caution. (Skinner 1993 [1974]: 177–8)

Although one might not feel happy with the moralizing tone of this passage, Skinner's general point is a valid one—the very act of nominalizing an adjective compels us to construe the property as a 'thing'. The lexical category 'noun' imposes a distinctive 'nominal' construal. We can refer to the property as if it were a conceptually autonomous entity, the property can itself have properties, it can participate in processes, and it can be cited as a cause.

---

situation in different ways. The first construes the situation in terms of the process 'suffer'. The process unfolds over a period of time in the past and involves, as participant, the person designated by the subject nominal. The second construes the process as a thing—the verb has been nominalized by means of the *-ing* suffix—consequently, the temporal aspect of the process has been backgrounded. The 'thing' is then characterized by means of a predicate adjective.

9.5 A phonological characterization of noun and verb (in English)?

One might be inclined to dismiss out of hand the idea that the word classes can be characterized in terms of their phonological structure. After all, practically any phonological form could in principle function as a noun (or as a verb, or adjective). We can, of course, state that nouns, verbs, etc. have *some* phonological content; this much is entailed by representing the phonological content of these units as [. . .] in Figure 9.1. But this characterization verges on the vacuous, and provides no means for distinguishing nouns from verbs, or verbs from adjectives.

As a matter of fact, even for a language such as English, it turns out that different word classes—nouns and verbs, in particular—*can* be associated with characteristic phonological content. To be sure, it is not possible to *predict* word class from phonology—the associations are more in the nature of statistical tendencies than full regularities. However, the correlations have been shown to influence the performance of English speakers in experimental situations, suggesting that knowledge of the correlations needs to be incorporated into a psychologically real account of speakers' language knowledge.

(i) <u>Length</u>. On average, nouns in English are longer than verbs. If a word has, say, four syllables, there's a better than even chance that it will be a noun, not a verb. Table 9.3 is based on data reported in Berg (2000), and gives the average length of (uninflected) nouns and verbs in the 18-million word CELEX[10] corpus of English.

One might suppose that this difference in length could be a consequence of the fact that English is particularly rich in resources for deriving nouns from words of other classes. Suffixes such as *-ment*, *-ity*, *-ation*, and *-er* are used to form nouns that are of necessity longer than their bases. Verb-forming affixes are not so numerous. Nevertheless, data for monomorphemic nouns and verbs show the same tendency. If anything, the ratio of noun length to verb length is slightly higher.

Not only is there a reliable statistical difference between noun length and verb length, English speakers (including children) have been shown to exploit this fact in experimental situations.

In an experiment reported in Cassidy and Kelly (1991), adults heard a list of nonsense words of one, two, and three syllables in length and were required to use these words in sentences of their own making. Mostly, the syntactic form of the sentences the subjects produced indicated the part of speech to which the nonsense words had been assigned. There was an overall bias towards using the nonsense words as nouns. (This is not surprising. Nouns are more numerous than verbs, and noun-tokens outnumber verb-tokens in a text.

Table 9.3 Average length (in syllables) of nouns and verbs in the 18-million word CELEX corpus

	Nouns	Verbs	Ratio
All tokens	2.80	2.21	1.27 : 1
Monomorphemic tokens	1.90	1.49	1.28 : 1

Source: After Berg (2000).

---

[10] The corpus was compiled by the Centre for Lexical Information at Nijmegen in the Netherlands. For further information, see **http://morph.ldc.upenn.edu/Catalog/LDC96L14.html**.

Consequently, for any new word that one encounters, the chances are that it will be a noun, not a verb.) However, the bias towards using the words as nouns increased as the length of the word increased. Remarkably, even four-year-old children were sensitive to length. The children saw a video-taped scene and were required to match a nonsense word to the scene. The scenes were constructed in such a way that there were two main candidates for being named by the new word, either a participant in the scene or the action that was performed. Cassidy and Kelly found that the shorter the word, the more likely it was to be used to refer to the action rather than to the participant.

(ii) <u>Stress location</u>. If a word of two syllables has initial stress, the chances are that it will be a noun, not a verb. A general tendency towards the earlier stress location in nouns was confirmed by an analysis of textual data reported in Kelly (1992). This difference in stress pattern is systematically exploited in quite a few noun/verb contrasts.

(1) a pérvert   to pervért
    an ábstract   to abstráct
    an óbject   to objéct
    a súbject   to subjéct
    etc.

Data from the CELEX corpus show that this pattern generalizes to all bisyllabic nouns and verbs (Table 9.4). Curiously, though, this difference disappears with longer words.

(iii) <u>Final obstruent voicing</u>. The chances that a word is a verb are increased if the word ends in a final voiced, as opposed to a final voiceless obstruent.

This correlation between final obstruent voicing and word class is well entrenched in the English lexicon. It shows up if we compare examples such as those in List (2) on page 183.

Table 9.4 Stress pattern of all disyllabic and trisyllabic nouns and verbs in the CELEX corpus

	Nouns	Verbs
Bisyllabic words		
Stress on first syllable	10,150 (94.1%)	1,544 (58.9%)
Stress on second syllable	631 (5.9%)	1,077 (41.1%)
Trisyllabic words		
Stress on first syllable	5,124 (71.6%)	869 (71.3%)
Stress on second syllable	2,033 (28.4%)	348 (28.5%)
Stress on third syllable	3 (0.0%)	2 (0.2%)

Source: After Berg (2000).

(2) <u>Verbs</u> (with final voiced obstruent)   <u>Nouns</u> (final voiceless obstruent)

grieve	grief
glaze	glass
advise	advice
bathe	bath
house [haʊz]	house [haʊs]
live	life
conceive	concept
give	gift

As always, there are exceptions. Whereas *grieve* is a verb, the phonologically similar *sleaze* [sliːz] is a noun, while *grease* [griːs] functions as both noun and verb (though some speakers do make a contrast between the noun [griːs] and the verb [griːz], in accordance with the general pattern.) Corpus data, however, confirm the general pattern (Table 9.5 (p. 184)).

(iv) <u>stressed vowels</u>. A somewhat unexpected correlation concerns the frontedness of a stressed vowel and word class. Sereno and Jongman (1990) and Sereno (1994) found that the stressed syllables in verbs tend to have front vowels, and stressed syllables in nouns tend to have non-front vowels. (The

---

Stress patterns for nouns and verbs

Kelly and Bock (1988) suggest that the different preferred stress patterns for nouns and verbs in English is a consequence of a general preference, in the stream of speech, for an alternation of strong and weak syllables.

  If we suppose that a typical environment for a noun is following an unstressed determiner, there will be some pressure for a noun to have initial stress; in this way, the preferred alternation of weak and strong syllables is guaranteed. Sentence (i) has a 'better' rhythm than (ii).

(i)   The wóman stáyed behínd.
(ii) The políce stáyed behínd.

Similarly, if we assume that a typical environment of a verb is before an unstressed determiner, there will some pressure for the verb to have final stress, again, in order to ensure the preferred rhythm. Sentence (iii) is rhythmically better than (iv).

(iii) The mán dislíked the píll.
(iv) The mán swállowed the píll.

Berg (2000) extended Kelly and Bock's thesis to adjectives. He found that adjectives, on the whole, have the stress pattern that is characteristic of nouns, and he accounted for this in terms of the rhythmic contexts in which adjectives typically occur.

Table 9.5 Number of nouns and verbs in the COBUILD corpus which terminate in a voiced or voiceless obstruent

	Final voiceless obstruent	Final voiced obstruent	Ratio
Nouns	5,429	1,598	3.4 : 1
Verb	2,370	1,112	2.1 : 1

Source: After Berg (1993).

relation only holds, however, for high-frequency words.) Experiments with nonsense words showed that English speakers were sensitive to the correlation.

Combining all of the above tendencies allows us to characterize a phonological prototype for nouns and verbs.

- The prototypical noun may be (though need not be) quite long, stress will fall early in the word, the stressed vowel will be non-front, and the final consonant (if an obstruent) will be voiceless.
- The prototypical verb will be relatively short, it will have final stress, the stressed vowel is front, and the final consonant (if an obstruent) will be voiced.

The above characterizations incorporate tendencies rather than absolute properties. It would not be possible therefore to equate these characterizations with the phonological pole of [NOUN] and [VERB]. An alternative approach is to incorporate these characterizations into a phonological network (Fig. 9.2). Between the maximally schematic [. . .] and the fully specified phonology of individual nouns and verbs we can propose a number of intervening sub-

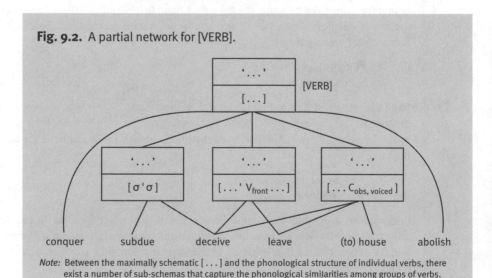

Fig. 9.2. A partial network for [VERB].

Note: Between the maximally schematic [. . .] and the phonological structure of individual verbs, there exist a number of sub-schemas that capture the phonological similarities among groups of verbs.

schemas which abstract preferred stress patterns, the features of the stressed vowels, and the features of a final consonant.

Study questions

1. **Inferring meaning from distribution.** Lewis Carroll's *Jabberwocky* is perhaps the most famous piece of nonsense verse written in English. Study the poem (or other examples of nonsense verse) with a view to understanding how a reader can infer the meanings of the nonsense words on the basis of their syntactic environment (and perhaps also the phonological form of the nonsense words).

2. **Compounds.** Do you have difficulties deciding how to write compound words in English? Are they written with or without a word space, with or without a hyphen?

    Compile a database (or should it be *data base*, or *data-base*?) of compounds from various sources (academic texts, newspaper articles, novels, etc.). Check out the recommendations in different dictionaries. Do you discern any patterns in the use of the word space and the hyphen? Assess the degree of variability in the usages you have assembled. Design a test to elicit written forms of compounds from subjects.

Further reading

On the semantic basis of word classes, see Langacker (1987b), Croft (1991, esp. chs. 2 and 3), and Wierzbicka (1988). On words, see Taylor (1995a: ch. 10).

CHAPTER 10

Meaning: Profile, base, and domain

Meaning is a difficult topic to address in a systematic way. In the recent past, many linguists considered semantics to be simply too hard to handle at all and directed their attention to more tractable topics in syntax and phonology. As a consequence, a good deal of linguistics, both in the Bloomfieldian and the Chomskyan traditions, has simply ignored semantics. However, if we take the idea of language as a symbolic system at all seriously, semantic representations are going to have to play a central role. In fact, it is probably fair to say that one of the major achievements of Cognitive Grammar to date has been in the area of semantic analysis, and in elucidating the semantic motivation of syntactic and morphological structure.

This chapter introduces some basic notions involved in the study of meaning. I begin, however, with some general observations on the ways in which this topic can be approached.

10.1 Approaches to the study of meaning

We can distinguish three general approaches to the study of meaning:

(i) The language-world approach. Meaning is studied as the relationship between linguistic expressions and states of affairs in the world.

(ii) The language-internal approach. Meaning is studied in terms of relations between expressions within a language.

(iii) The conceptualist approach. The meaning of an expression is equated with a conceptualization in the mind of a language user.

Let us consider these in turn.

10.1.1 The language-world approach

The language-world approach considers the kinds of situations to which a linguistic expression can be applied. Suppose we are interested in the meanings of *cup* and *mug* (and in the difference in meaning between the two words). It is evident that the meanings of the two words are rather closely tied up with the kinds of things in the world that can be appropriately called cups and mugs, and that knowing the meanings involves being able to apply the words appropriately to the things.

We can distinguish two perspectives, according to the direction of the relation between language and the world:

- the **semasiological**[1] perspective goes from language to the world, and asks: 'For this expression, what kinds of situations can be appropriately designated by it?'
- the **onomasiological**[2] perspective goes from the world to language, and asks: 'For this state of affairs, what range of linguistic expressions can appropriately describe it?'

With respect to the cups and the mugs, the semasiological perspective might involve asking English-speaking consultants to point to items that could appropriately be named by each of the two words. Taking the onomasiological perspective, we could present our consultants with an array of objects (comprising, obviously, things that we suspect might count as cups and mugs), and ask them what they would call them.

It would certainly be a good starting point, if you were trying to explicate the meanings of, say, *cup* and *mug*, to consider the kinds of things in the world to which the words may be applied. Or suppose you were studying the prepositions *over* and *above*, and were interested in the differences between the prepositions as well as the extent of overlap between them. A natural starting point, again, would be to consider which spatial configurations can be appropriately named by the two prepositions. I dare say that every linguist, when investigating the meanings of expressions (at least, the meanings of 'concrete' expressions) will invite judgements as to what the expressions can potentially refer to.

---

[1] From Greek *seīmasia* 'meaning', 'signification'.
[2] From Greek *onoma* 'name'. 'Onomasiological' is being used here in a slightly non-traditional sense. Traditionally, *onomastics* is the study of proper names (especially place names), while *onomasiology* is often used to refer to the study of semantic relations between words within a semantic field.

Onomasiology and semasiology

Some semantic domains are better suited to the language-world approach than others. We can point to an object and ask people what they would call it; equally, we can ask people to pick out objects that could be named by a 'concrete' word. We could not apply this methodology to abstract entities, such as emotions or beliefs. We could hardly ask a person to pick out, from an array of mental phenomena, those that count as 'beliefs', as opposed to 'thoughts' or 'knowledge', nor could we point to an emotional state and ask people what they would call it.

One semantic field that lends itself particularly well to the onomasiological and semasiological perspectives is colour. We might begin by presenting consultants with a series of colour samples and asking them to name the colours. This is the onomasiological perspective (from world to language) which serves to elicit the range of words that a person habitually uses to name colours. Subsequently, we might present subjects with a colour chart, on which colours are arranged according to hue and brightness, and ask subjects to indicate which of the colours could be named by each of the colour words they had volunteered in the first part of the investigation. This is the semasiological perspective (from language to world).

Both perspectives were systematically employed by MacLaury in his investigations of colour terminology in a wide range of languages. His results are especially interesting to the extent that the two perspectives do not always mirror each other. The fact that colour word *w* can be applied to colour sample *c* does not entail that colour sample *c* will be named by colour word *w*. MacLaury (1987) gives a brief overview of the methodology and discusses some of his findings; for more advanced accounts, see MacLaury (1995*a*, 1995*b*). For a brief summary see Taylor (1995*a*: 263–4).

The onomasiological and semasiological perspectives were ingeniously employed by Geeraerts *et al.* (1994) in their study of clothing terminology, already referred to in Ch. 1, p. 136. The data collected in the course of the research made it possible to enquire, for a given clothing term, the properties of the garments to which the term was applied; conversely, it was possible to enquire, for garments with a certain set of properties, which names were typically given to the garments.

Geeraerts relates the two perspectives to the notions of **prototype** and **basic-level**. A basic-level term is one that is habitually applied to an entity of a certain kind; basic-level terms can be characterized in terms of **onomasiological salience**. The prototype is the entity to which an expression is typically applied; prototypes can be characterized in terms of **semasiological salience**.

This said, there are several reasons why an approach which focuses exclusively on the relation between linguistic expressions and states of affairs in the world is inadequate:

(i) A first, and obvious limitation is that the approach is applicable only to expressions which designate 'concrete' entities. We would not get very far if we tried to explicate the meanings of *soul* and *spirit* by asking our language consultants to point to entities that could be named by these words.

(ii) As was pointed out in section 4.5, it is an error to suppose that linguistic expressions refer directly to the world at all; rather, linguistic expressions refer to entities in a mental space. The mental space may be taken to be veridical, in which case an expression's referent may be assumed to really exist in the world. Equally, the mental space could be hypothetical, imagined, or fictional. Presumably, Martians exist only in fictional mental spaces. We would not get very far by trying to explicate the meaning of *Martian* by linking up the word with things that exist in the world (or even with things that exist on Mars).

(iii) Even if we restrict ourselves to expressions for which potential referents can be identified, the language-world approach offers a less than complete account of meaning. There is more to the meaning of an expression than the relation between the expression and its referents. To know the word *carburettor* involves more than simply being able to identify the carburettor under the bonnet of a car. At the very least, we would expect knowledge of the word to include some notion of the role of a carburettor within the functioning of an internal combustion engine; indeed, it is precisely this knowledge which enables a person to identify the carburettor in the first place. The approach also fails in the case of expressions which involve the speaker's assessment of a situation. The words *stingy* and *thrifty* have to do not only with how a person handles their expenditures but also with how a speaker assesses the behaviour. And to return to our earlier example of cups and mugs, whether something is to be called a cup or mug might depend on factors that are extrinsic to the object as such, for example, the situations in which it might be used, the kinds of substances with which it might be filled, and even the price one paid for it.

(iv) It is often the case that one and the same state of affairs can be linguistically encoded in different ways. The sentences in (1) are truth-conditionally equivalent; if one of the sentences truly applies to a situation, then so will each of the others.

(1) a. Someone stole her diamonds from the Princess.
    b. Someone robbed the Princess of her diamonds.
    c. Her diamonds were stolen from the Princess.
    d. The Princess was robbed of her diamonds.

The sentences differ with respect to how they construe the described situation. Construal is a matter of how a situation is conceptualized, it cannot be reduced to the observable features of a situation. Matching the situation to the expressions is not likely to reveal the semantic difference between active and passive sentences, nor the difference between the verbs *rob* and *steal*.

In spite of the above critical remarks, I do not wish to deny the value of both the onomasiological and the semasiological approaches in semantic studies. Matching up expressions with states of affairs in the world—for those expressions for which the procedure is applicable—is a valid technique of semantic enquiry. But language-world relations cannot be the whole story. Even if we can establish that a given expression regularly matches up with a certain kind of situation, this is at best *symptomatic* of the expression's meaning, language-world relations are not to be equated with the meaning. The meaning, I would claim, is to be identified with the conceptualization symbolized by the expression. It is in virtue of the conceptualization that the expression can be used to refer to entities in the world.

10.1.2 The language-internal approach

A second approach to the study of meaning focuses on the relations between linguistic expressions within a language. Again, we can distinguish two ways of implementing this approach:

- we can focus on **paradigmatic relations**, that is to say, on the relations between different expressions;
- we can focus on **syntagmatic relations**, that is to say, on the relations between items which co-occur within an expression.

Paradigmatic relations include relations such as synonymy, hyponymy, opposites (of various kinds), and entailment. Perhaps the most fundamental of these is entailment. *A* entails *B*, if *B* is true whenever *A* is true. The sentences in example (2) illustrate the relation. If it is the case that the terrorists assassinated the President, then it has to be the case that the President died.

(2) The terrorists assassinated the President.
         entails
     The President died.

Entailment is fundamental because it underlies other paradigmatic relations. For example, it may be invoked to define synonymy: two expressions are synonymous (they have the same meaning) if each entails the other. As we saw in Chapter 7 (p. 125), we can appeal to entailment in order to define the relation between a superordinate term and its hyponyms. Entailment is also relevant for distinguishing different kinds of opposites. Complementary opposites—(3) are such that *A* entails *not-B*, while *B* entails *not-A*:

(3) a. The cat is alive.
             entails
         The cat is not dead.
     b. The cat is dead.
             entails
         The cat is not alive.

Gradable opposites, such as *tall* and *short*, are more complex:

(4) a. John is taller than Mary.
        <u>entails</u>
        Mary is shorter than John.
    b. John is taller than Mary.
        <u>does not entail</u>
        John is tall.
    c. Mary is shorter than John.
        <u>does not entail</u>
        Mary is short.

Converses, such as *husband* and *wife*, *buy* and *sell*, exhibit a slightly different pattern:

(5) a. Fred is Martha's husband.
        <u>entails</u>
        Martha is Fred's wife.
    b. Jim sold the car to Agatha.
        <u>entails</u>
        Agatha bought the car from Jim.

A different implementation of the language-internal approach focuses on a word's **collocations**, that is, on the kinds of words that a word typically occurs together with, or in the neighbourhood of. It is evident that (*to*) *bark* collocates with (typically occurs in the vicinity of) *dog*, but not at all with *cat*. One aspect of *heavy* is that it collocates with *drinker* and *smoker* (*heavy drinker*, *heavy smoker*), but not with *eater* or *spender* (**heavy eater*, **heavy spender*). Studies of collocations based on the analysis of large text corpora often throw up interesting and unexpected tendencies. Stubbs (1995) found that *cause* (both noun and verb) tends to be used of unpleasant events; we would talk of 'the cause of the problem' rather than 'the cause of my happiness'.

Linguists who have been sceptical of conceptualist semantics have sometimes opted to analyse meaning solely in terms of language-internal relations. John Lyons (see section 4.1) was one such:

Acceptance of the structuralist approach in semantics has the advantage that it enables the linguist to avoid commitment on the controversial question of the philosophical and psychological status of 'concepts' or 'ideas'. As far as the empirical investigation of the structure of a language is concerned, *the sense of a lexical item may be defined to be, not only dependent upon, but identical with, the set of relations which hold between the item in question and other items in the same lexical system*. (Lyons 1968: 443; emphasis added)

Cruse (1986) took a similar line:[3]

---

[3] Subsequently, Cruse (1992: 289) moderated his views: 'It is not sufficient, in my opinion, to treat word meaning exclusively in terms of relations between lexical items.'

It is taken as axiomatic in this book that every aspect of the meaning of a word is reflected in a characteristic pattern of semantic normality (and abnormality) in grammatically appropriate contexts. That which is not mirrored in this way is not, for us, a question of meaning; and, conversely, every difference in the semantic normality profile between two items betokens a difference in meaning. (Cruse 1986: 15–16)

It is interesting to note that several introductory linguistics textbooks treat word meaning largely in such terms. This is just as true of the well-established textbook by Fromkin and Rodman (first published 1974, and still going strong), as it is of the very recent introduction by Radford *et al.* (1999).

To be sure, every linguist, when pursuing a semantic investigation, will collect information about collocations and will elicit judgements about entailments, antonyms, and other meaning relations. There can be no doubt as to the value of investigating meaning from the perspective of language-internal relations. Indeed, in a very important sense, one aspect of knowing a word is to know how that word is used in relation to other words.

The language-internal approach becomes problematic, however, if meaning is *equated* with sets of relations between linguistic expressions. On this approach, the semantic structure of a language becomes a vast calculus of language-internal relations, which makes no contact at all with the way speakers conceptualize the world. The question then becomes, how does a language learner *bootstrap*[4] the conceptual content of linguistic expressions? Observation of the semantic relations between *dead* and *alive*, between *tall* and *short*, between *buy* and *sell*, actually tells us very little about the conceptual content of these words. Once again, language-internal relations must be regarded as *symptomatic* of meaning, not as meaning itself.

10.1.3 The conceptualist approach

I argued in Chapter 4 for the viability of a conceptualist approach to semantics. It is time, now, to begin to fill in the details and to see how such an approach can work. In this chapter, I focus on three basic notions in the Cognitive Grammar analysis of meaning: profile, base, and domain.

10.2 Profile and base

The notions of profile and base can best be introduced by way of an example. Consider the word *hypotenuse*. How can we characterize the semantic unit symbolized by this word? What *is* a hypotenuse? A minimal definition might go as follows: A hypotenuse is the longest side of a right-angled triangle, the side that is opposite the right angle.[5]

---

[4] How, in other words, does the learner gain a toe-hold into the conceptual system?
[5] The hypotenuse example has been used by Langacker (1988*b*: 59) and Fillmore (1985).

There are two components to this definition. First, there is the notion of a right-angled triangle. Second, one of the sides of the triangle is called the hypotenuse. A person who did not know what a right-angled triangle is could not know what a hypotenuse is. An understanding of what a hypotenuse is rests on a prior understanding of what a right-angled triangle is.

So, what *is* a hypotenuse? In a sense, a hypotenuse is nothing more than a straight line. The straight line is what the word **profiles**, or designates. The straight line, however, is one which functions as one side of a right-angled triangle. The right-angled triangle constitutes the **base**. The triangle itself is not profiled; the profile picks out one facet of the base and renders it particularly prominent. The distinction is represented in Figure 10.1. The expression's profile is represented by bold.

There is a simple linguistic test for identifying the profile in contrast to the base. Although the notion of the triangle is crucial to an understanding of *hypotenuse*, any statement about a hypotenuse is a statement about the profile—it is about the hypotenuse *qua* straight line, it is not about any aspect of the base.

(6) a. The hypotenuse is 3 cm long.
     b. *The hypotenuse is right-angled.
     c. *The hypotenuse has three sides.
     d. *The hypotenuse has an area of 10 cm².

How can we characterize the concept [HYPOTENUSE]? Earlier (in section 3.1.2), I proposed a preliminary definition of a concept as a principle of categorization—to have a concept is to be able to recognize instances. Now, it is clear that the concept [HYPOTENUSE] cannot be equated with the word's profile; the profile, as we have seen, is nothing more than a straight line. (As a matter of fact, we should have to say that the expressions *hypotenuse* and *straight line* profile exactly the same entity.) Although a hypotenuse *is* a

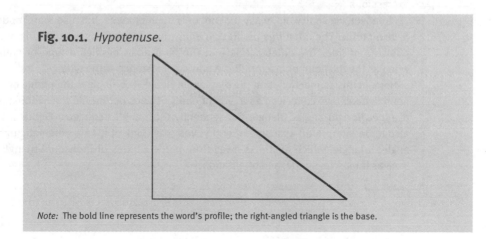

Fig. 10.1. *Hypotenuse.*

Note: The bold line represents the word's profile; the right-angled triangle is the base.

straight line, the expressions *hypotenuse* and *straight line* are not synonymous. Rather, the concept consists in knowledge of the profile against the appropriate base:

Perceived intuitively, the profile (in the words of Susan Lindner) 'stands out in bas-relief' against the base. The semantic value of an expression resides in neither the base nor the profile alone, but in their combination; it derives from the designation of a specific entity identified and characterized by its position within a larger configuration. (FCG1: 183)

Profile and referent

The profile of an expression is not to be equated with the expression's referent.

The term 'referring expression' is well established in the semantics literature. The term is traditionally used of noun phrases which designate an entity that exists in the real or an imaginary world. If I ask the question, 'Do you see that tree there growing in the yard?', in a situation in which there is indeed a tree in the yard, and I am enquiring whether you see that tree or not, there is a sense in which I am using the expression *that tree there growing in the yard* to refer to the tree; the tree is the expression's referent, and the noun phrase is a referring expression.

I have already emphasized (section 4.5.1) that even a referring expression does not actually refer to a thing in the world but to a thing as conceptualized by a language user and which inhabits, not the real world, but a mental space. With this proviso in mind, there is, I dare say, no great harm in claiming that the referent of the noun phrase *that tree there growing in the yard*, when uttered in appropriate circumstances, corresponds to the expression's profile.

But the notion of profile is much broader in scope. Expressions other than referring noun phrases have a profile. (In fact, it is axiomatic in Cognitive Grammar that *all* linguistic expressions profile something or other.) A clause profiles a situation or event, a verb profiles a process, a preposition profiles a kind of relation. Clauses, verbs, and prepositions would not normally be considered to be 'referring expressions'.

Moreover, we shall want to say that not only noun phrases, but also 'bare' nouns have a profile. The noun *tree* profiles an entity, just as much as the referring noun phrase *that tree*. The difference is that the bare noun profiles a type of entity, whereas the full noun phrase profiles a particular instance of the type.

Note, in this connection, that the diagram in Figure 10.1 displays the profile of the noun *hypotenuse*, conceived as a type of entity, it does *not* profile *the* hypotenuse of a *specific* right-angled triangle. Consequently, the triangle depicted in Figure 10.1 is also to be interpreted as a type of entity; you may think of it as a schematic right-angled triangle, which abstracts away from particularities of individual triangles, such as their size, shape, and orientation.

10.3 Domains

It is useful to make a distinction between the base against which an entity is profiled and the domain, or domains, against which concepts take shape. The **base** of an expression is the conceptual content that is inherently, intrinsically, and obligatorily invoked by the expression. A **domain** is a more generalized 'background' knowledge configuration against which conceptualization is achieved. To be sure, the distinction between base and domain is not always clear-cut. Essentially, the distinction has to do with how intrinsic the broader conceptualization is to the semantic unit, how immediately relevant it is, and to what extent aspects of the broader conceptualization are specifically elaborated.

A couple of examples will clarify the distinction. The notion of a right-angled triangle is intrinsic to the concept [HYPOTENUSE], in the sense that a hypotenuse cannot be conceptualized without reference to a right-angled triangle. There exists, however, a whole cluster of concepts, including [HYPOTENUSE], [TRIANGLE], [RIGHT-ANGLE], and even [STRAIGHT LINE], which can only be understood against general notions of planar geometry and of geometrical figures; these in turn rest on even more general conceptualizations of space. Planar geometry, or, more generally still, space, constitutes the **domain** against which triangles and their properties are conceptualized.

Take, as another example, the concept [FATHER]. The word *father* profiles an adult male human. (I ignore the use of the word to refer to a Catholic priest.) Any statement about a father is a statement about the father *qua* male human adult (the content of the profile). The word invokes, as its base, the notion of a relation between a profiled individual and one or more individuals who count as the father's offspring. If there are no offspring, a person cannot be called a father; a father is necessarily a father *of* someone. However, the very notion of the father-child relation—the conceptual content of the base—rests on more general notions of kinship and genealogy, and, more generally still, in notions of gender and procreation. The idea of a kinship network constitutes the domain against which a whole cluster of concepts are characterized: [FATHER], [SON], [AUNT], [COUSIN], etc.

For another example, consider the concept [THUMB-NAIL]. *Thumb nail* profiles an entity that is part of a thumb; the conception of a thumb constitutes the base against which [THUMB-NAIL] is profiled. A thumb, in turn, is conceptualized as one of five fingers[6] that protrude from a hand. The conception of a hand, with its fingers, constitutes the base against which [THUMB] is profiled. [HAND], in turn, is understood against the conception of an arm,

---

[6] Actually, *finger* is a bit more complicated. On the one hand, we can use the word to designate each of the five protuberances on a hand. Alternatively, we can distinguish between the thumb and the remaining four fingers.

while [ARM] is understood against the conception of a human body. Here we witness a kind of Russian doll situation, in which the base of one term is conceptualized against the base of another term, and so on. The concept of a thumb is the base specifically invoked to conceptualize a thumb-nail, while the human body is the domain against which a host of body-part terms are conceptualized.

10.3.1 Multiple domains

A domain may be defined as any knowledge configuration which provides the context for the conceptualization of a semantic unit.

More often than not, a semantic unit needs to be conceptualized against more than one domain. Moreover, it would be an error to suppose that domains constitute strictly separated configurations of knowledge; typically,

---

Of *and* have

The distinction between base and domain, though not always clear-cut, does have linguistic repercussions. One of the functions of the preposition *of* is to profile an intrinsic relation between entities. Since the base is intrinsic to a concept, it is not surprising that *of* can often be used to refer to the relation between a profiled entity and an entity in the base. On the other hand, the relation between a profiled entity and a domain is a more distant relation, and *of* is often inappropriate in such circumstances.

Thus, *the hypotenuse of the triangle* is a perfectly acceptable expression; *of* establishes the relation between the hypotenuse and an entity that is intrinsic in its base. *The triangle of two-dimensional space*, on the other hand, is decidedly odd. Likewise, it would be normal to speak of *the thumb of my left hand*, but very odd to speak of *the thumb of my left arm*.

The verb *have* often invokes an intrinsic relation. *The triangle has a hypotenuse* is acceptable, whereas *Geometry has triangles* is very peculiar. It is as if the conceptual link between 'hypotenuse' and 'triangle' is much closer than the conceptual link between 'triangle' and 'geometry'. For similar reasons, *A hand has five fingers* (or—see footnote 6—*four fingers and thumb*) is normal; we would not, however, say *An arm has five fingers*. An arm is invoked only at a distance, so to speak, in the conceptualization of a thumb. We need to be cautious, however, in applying the *have* test. The possibility of saying *I have a broken thumbnail*, or even *I have a missing thumbnail*, does not entitle us to say that the concept of a person is the base against which a thumbnail is conceptualized.

Finally, the very expressions *thumbnail* and *fingernail* show that noun compounding is sensitive to the profile-base distinction. The compounds take, as their first element, the base against which the nail is profiled. We do not speak of **hand-nail*, or **arm-nail*, even though, strictly speaking, the nails are a part of a hand and an arm.

domains overlap and interact in numerous and complex ways. Consider again the concept [FATHER]. I stated that the concept is understood against the domain of a kinship network. While this aspect certainly captures an important facet of the concept, other domains are involved as well. For example, a father is a physical being, with weight and dimensions; he is a living thing, who was born, grew up, ages, and will die; he has a characteristic role within a family unit, and is expected to display a certain behaviour towards other members of the unit; and so on. Physical object, living thing, and family unit each constitutes a domain against which [FATHER] is conceptualized. If we examine any one of these domains, we typically find that it relates with other domains. The notion of kinship, for example, rests on notions of gender, procreation, and family units; gender, in turn, is the domain against which a father is characterized as male.

Langacker (FCGI: 147) has used the term **matrix** to refer to the set of domains which provide the context for the full understanding of a semantic unit. In Figure 10.2, the three domains d′, d″, d‴ constitute the domain matrix against which the profile-base relation is conceptualized. With respect to [FATHER], the profile P is identified with 'adult male human'; the base B might be the relation between the profiled entity and a child/children; while 'kinship', 'family unit', and 'living thing' might constitute three partially overlapping domains against which profiling takes place.

From the above remarks, it is evident that Cognitive Grammar takes an essentially encyclopaedic view of meaning. Ultimately, even the meaning of

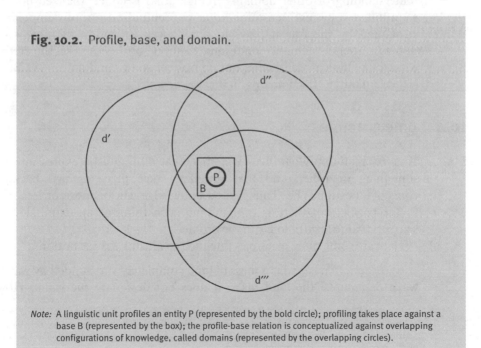

Fig. 10.2. Profile, base, and domain.

Note: A linguistic unit profiles an entity P (represented by the bold circle); profiling takes place against a base B (represented by the box); the profile-base relation is conceptualized against overlapping configurations of knowledge, called domains (represented by the overlapping circles).

common, everyday terms is supported by a vast network of interrelated knowledge. I take up this aspect again in Chapter 22, where I examine more closely its ramifications.

10.3.2 'It's domains all the way down'

Domains vary in terms of their internal complexity. The notion of a kinship network (the domain against which a host of kinship words are understood) is quite complex, and is itself understood in terms of such notions as gender, procreation, and the sharing of rights and responsibilities within a family unit. The question arises, whether there might be some domains which are 'basic', in the sense that they cannot be understood against other domains. Langacker (FCG1: 148–9) has proposed, as candidates for basic domains, such notions as space, time, pitch, weight, temperature, colour, taste, and smell. The claim is that the phenomenological experience of temperature, time, pitch, and so on, are qualitatively unique; they cannot be 'reduced' to any other domains.

It would be an error, however, to understand basic domains as conceptual primitives, on whose back more complex concepts emerge. In the first place, even the basic domains may be understood metaphorically in terms of other domains. Time can be conceptualized metaphorically in terms of space, while pitch and temperature can be thought of in terms of 'high' and 'low'. More-over, even though the phenomenological experience of the basic domains may be irreducible, the domains are structured by the role they play in the understanding of other domains. Temperature is conceptualized not just as a primitive physical sensation, our conceptualization of temperature is structured by the role it plays in our conceptualization of more complex domains, such as climatic conditions, the cycle of the seasons, the clothes we wear, our physical well-being, our emotional states, and so on. As Barsalou (1992: 40) put it, 'It's domains all the way down'.

10.4 Some examples

It is axiomatic, in Cognitive Grammar, that all linguistic expressions profile something or other, and that profiling takes place against background conceptualizations. The background knowledge can be more or less intrinsic to the profile, but there is probably no such thing as an expression whose semantic value resides solely in the profile.

Here are some more examples intended to illustrate these notions:

(i) Island. An island is a mass of land completely surrounded by water. The word designates[7] the land mass, it does not designate the water. However,

---

[7] As technical terms in Cognitive Grammar, the verbs *designate* and *profile* are roughly equivalent— at least, with respect to what they profile! The verbs do differ slightly with respect to their base. *Profile* focuses more on the contrast between highlighted and backgrounded entities; *designate* focuses more on the process of picking out an entity.

Austin on cricket

The philosopher John Austin is well known to linguists for his ground-breaking work on speech acts. In addition to his book *How to do Things with Words* (1980), Austin also wrote many shorter pieces which address problems in linguistic semantics, and his observations often prefigure some important themes in Cognitive Linguistics.

Consider the following passage from his essay 'The meaning of a word':

Take the sense in which I talk of a cricket bat and a cricket ball and a cricket umpire. The reason that all are called by the same name is perhaps that each has its part—its *own special part*—to play in the activity called cricketing: it is no good to say that *cricket* means 'used in cricket': for we cannot explain what we mean by 'cricket' *except* by explaining the special parts played in cricketing by the bat, ball, etc. (Austin, 1979: 73; author's emphasis)

Here, Austin is claiming that you can only understand what a cricket bat, cricket ball, and cricket umpire are against the knowledge of the rules and activities that make up 'cricketing'; in turn, cricketing cannot be understood independently of the role played by the bat, ball, and umpire. In our terms, cricket is the domain against which *cricket bat*, *cricket ball*, and *cricket umpire* are understood. Each term picks out and profiles an entity that plays a part in the complex activity. At the same time, the domain of cricketing is constituted by the very entities that can only be understood in terms of the domain. The domain does not exist independently of the entities that are profiled against it.

the notion of the surrounding water is intrinsic to the concept; if there were no surrounding water, there would be no island. While the notion of the surrounding water is in the base of the semantic unit [ISLAND], the profile-base relation itself presupposes the broader domain of the Earth's geophysical features.

There is probably more to the semantic structure of [ISLAND] than this. A piece of land surrounded by a moat would probably not be called an island. It would also be odd to talk about North and South America, taken together, as an island, or claim that the Panama Canal separates the island of North America from the island of South America. The actual size of the land mass (and perhaps even its shape), as well as the extent of the surrounding water, are further facets of the word's meaning.

(ii) Peninsula. The profile of *peninsula* is very similar to that of *island*. The difference is that the land mass profiled by *peninsula* is attached, by a narrow land strip, to some larger land mass. Neither the surrounding water, nor the larger land mass, are profiled by *peninsula*; nevertheless, these are intrinsic to the very concept [PENINSULA].

(iii) Saturday. The word profiles a 24-hour period, i.e. a 'day', against the

> ### Searle and 'the Background'
>
> John Searle is another philosopher who is well known to linguists for his work on speech acts (Searle 1969). A recurring topic in Searle's work has been the fundamental role of background knowledge in the understanding of even the most prosaic of expressions (e.g. Searle 1979). Take a statement that 'The cat is on the mat'. It seems like a straightforward matter to ascertain whether this statement might be true of a given situation — we need only look and see whether there is indeed a cat on the mat. But would we be so confident if cat and mat were floating around in outer space? Probably not — for in the absence of a gravitational field there would be no basis for determining whether the cat was *on* the mat, *under* it, *against* it, or whatever. Whereas *on* profiles a relation of contact and support between two entities, one of which is typically located higher than the other, the relation is conceptualized against the domain of a gravitational field, which provides the context for the very notions of support and verticality. The gravitational field and its effects are part of what Searle calls 'the Background'. Searle has emphasized the 'non-propositional' nature of the Background, as well as the fact that the Background cannot be 'reduced' to a set of simple concepts. In our terms, the Background is constituted by a network of unprofiled knowledge and beliefs which form the context for any conceptualization.
>
> Here is another and more recent of Searle's illustrations of the Background:
>
> To have one belief or desire, I have to have a whole Network of other beliefs and desires. Thus, for example, if I now want to eat a good meal at a local restaurant, I have to have a large number of other beliefs and desires, such as the beliefs that there are restaurants in the vicinity, restaurants are the sort of establishment where meals are served, meals are the sort of thing that can be bought and eaten inside restaurants at certain times of the day for certain amounts of money, and so — more or less indefinitely — on. (Searle 1992: 176)

base of the seven-day week. The concept presupposes a rich network of domain-based knowledge, including:

- the practice of designating the day-night cycle as a 'day', which is conventionally taken to begin at a point ('midnight') which is mid-way between successive high points of the sun;
- the convention of grouping days, as characterized above, into a seven-unit cycle, the idea of the seven-day cycle going back, ultimately, to the Biblical creation story;
- the convention of naming the component units of the cycle;
- the idea that different units of the cycle may be suitable for different kinds of activities, such as work, recreation, or devotion.

Ultimately, the domain matrix against which *Saturday* profiles a 24-hour period reaches into many aspects of our culture: astronomy, history, religion, work, time-measuring devices, recreational practices. The word nicely illustrates the encyclopaedic nature of linguistic meaning.

(iv) Vacation. This is another word which has to be understood against a rich background of cultural knowledge. As a preliminary to attempting a definition of the word, you might consider (a) the criteria by which you would evaluate a vacation as good or bad; (b) the frequency and the duration of a person's vacations; (c) the criteria by which certain destinations are considered to be suitable for a vacation; (d) the kinds of things that people typically do, or want to do, on a vacation; (e) the way people typically behave on a vacation; (f) the reasons why (some) people consider it necessary to take a vacation; (g) whether the taking of vacations is a universal practice, or whether it is limited to certain historical periods and certain cultural conditions. Answers to these questions are likely to activate numerous facets of the domain-based knowledge against which the concept [VACATION] is understood.

(v) Anger. Although this word designates an internal state, we understand anger not just as an internal state. Anger is a reaction to some offence—if a person is angry, there must have been some previous provocation (or the person believes there has been a provocation). Anger is manifested by characteristic behaviour—angry persons display exaggerated bodily movements, they raise their voices, they do unpredictable things. Moreover, a person in a state of anger may be expected to act in the future in certain ways—they may seek revenge, they may bear a permanent grudge. What this means, is that anger, as an internal state, is understood against a typical 'scenario', comprising initial provocation, anger, and retribution. The scenario is the base against which the emotion is conceptualized.

The anger scenario and its role in the conceptualization of the emotion have been studied by Kövecses (1986, 1990). Austin also drew attention to the scenario. He (1979: 109) remarked that anger should not be identified with the feeling alone; rather, it is made up of 'a whole pattern of events, including occasion, symptoms, feeling and manifestation, and possibly other factors besides'. There would be little point in asking what anger itself really is, divorced from these aspects.

10.5 Designation and connotation

The distinction between an expression's profile and the base or domain against which profiling takes place is able to accommodate the traditional notions of designation and connotation.

It is traditional to recognize two components of a word's meaning: one component (its 'designation') is responsible for what a word refers to, the other (its 'connotation') for usage aspects of the word, such as whether the word is formal or vulgar, whether its use implies an attitude of contempt or approval, whether the word is typical of a particular regional dialect, and suchlike. Also included under connotation are various 'associations' that a word might have.

Crystal, in his dictionary of linguistic terms (1980: 82), suggests in the entry for 'connotation' that *December* might have connotations of 'bad weather', 'dark evenings', 'parties', and 'Christmas'.

On the view presented here, all these aspects are handled straightforwardly in terms of domains against which an entity is profiled. Metalinguistic awareness of degrees of formality, dialectal diversity, and sociolinguistic variation are all candidates for conceptual domains against which profiling takes place, as are the various 'associations' of a word. We should also bear in mind that different speakers may understand a concept against slightly different configurations of domain-based knowledge. Not everybody associates December with dark evenings (some people live in the Southern hemisphere) or with parties, nor, for that matter, with Christmas (not all English speakers are Christians).

On the Cognitive Grammar view, 'connotation' is not a distinct (and secondary) level of meaning, but is fully incorporated into the semantic structure of a word. Moreover, discussion of connotation in terms of domains can often lead to greater insight. Compare the words *bachelor* and *spinster*. These words profile, respectively, an unmarried adult male and an unmarried adult female. *Spinster*, however, is a decidedly derogatory term; it implies that the woman is unmarried because no man wants her. *Bachelor*, on the other hand, tends to have a more favourable connotation; the man has remained unmarried because he has chosen to do so.

These connotations are not just arbitrary facts of usage, but fall out from the domain-based knowledge against which *bachelor* and *spinster* are understood (Taylor 1995a: 95–7). First, it has to be noted that the notions of 'adulthood' and 'unmarried' (and perhaps even 'male' and 'female') are themselves complex concepts which need to be understood against the appropriate domain matrixes. Moreover, concerning *bachelor*, it is not the case that any adult unmarried male can be appropriately called a bachelor. We would not call the Pope a bachelor, nor an unmarried man in an established relationship, whether the relationship be a heterosexual or a homosexual one. What is involved, in characterizing a bachelor as unmarried, is a somewhat idealized, and perhaps even outdated view of marriage practices, in particular, the idea that people above a certain age are expected to be married, that men and women can pass the marriageable age without marrying but that they do so for different reasons—a man, because he chooses to, a woman, because no man wants to marry her. Lakoff (1987) refers in this connection to an 'Idealized Cognitive Model', or ICM, of marriage. Given the ICM, the 'connotations' of *bachelor* and *spinster* fall out naturally from the broader matrix against which these words are understood. (The question why the Pope is not called a bachelor is also easily answered: the Pope simply is not covered by the idealized model.)

Frames, scripts, scenarios, and ICMs

In this chapter I have used the term 'domain' to refer, very generally, to background knowledge necessary for the understanding of semantic units. In principle, a domain may be any knowledge configuration, ranging from 'basic' notions of time, space, colour, and temperature, to complex and rather specific knowledge, such as the rules of cricket. Equally, a domain may consist in knowledge of typical scenarios, cultural conventions, and metalinguistic notions of dialectal and stylistic variation.

Other writers have used a variety of terms to refer to domains, or to particular kinds of domains. For Fillmore (1985), a 'frame' is a rather tightly organized configuration, such as the notion of a 'commercial transaction', which provides the background for the characterization of terms such as *buy*, *sell*, *price*, *cost*, etc. Workers in artificial intelligence (e.g. Schank and Abelson 1977) often refer to typical, or expected sequences of events as 'scripts'; the restaurant script, for example, provides the context for understanding such activities as ordering the meal and paying for it. Many writers have used 'scenario' in this sense (G. Palmer 1996: 75). Lakoff (1987) introduced the term 'Idealized Cognitive Model' (ICM), which focuses on configurations of conventionalized knowledge.

While some terminological distinction may well be justified—it is often convenient, for example, to talk of expected event sequences as 'scenarios', thereby focusing on the dynamic aspects of the conventionalized knowledge—I shall in general use the word 'domain' as a cover-term for any aspect of (unprofiled) knowledge against which profiling takes place.

Study questions

1. What do the following words profile? What is the base against which profiling takes place? What are the broader domains against which the words are understood? Assume that the words are nouns. For some of the words, you might try to represent the concepts diagrammatically, in the manner of Figure 10.1, drawing the profiles in bold.

lid	drawer
gap	portrait
hole	patch
spot	edge
corner	tear (as in a torn piece of cloth)
crack	flash (of light)
arc (of a circle)	orphan

2. It could be argued that *on land* and *on the ground* profile exactly the same kind of location. The expressions differ, however, in how the location is

conceptualized (Fillmore 1979). Explain what the difference is. (It may be useful to consider what the expressions might contrast with. If something is not 'on the ground', where might it be? If it is not 'on land', where might it be?)

3. Domain-based knowledge often contributes to the coherence of an utterance. Compare:

(i)   I left the restaurant without paying the bill.

(ii) ? I left the cinema without paying the bill.

   (i) is easily interpreted, since the mention of a restaurant activates the scenario associated with restaurants, one component of which is that the customer, having eaten, is presented with the bill and is expected to pay it. Notice that the definite noun phrase *the bill* refers specifically to the bill that features in the scenario. (ii) is odd because paying a bill plays no role in the cinema scenario.

   Consider the following pairs of sentences. You will probably find that those in (iii) are relatively easy to make sense of, those in (iv) less so. Explain the difference in terms of the scenarios that are necessary for understanding the sentence pairs, and the ease with which these scenarios are activated by specific words or phrases.

(iii) I'm sorry I'm late. I couldn't find my car keys.
     I'm afraid the beer is warm. There was a power failure.

(iv) I'm sorry I'm late. There was a power failure.
     I'm afraid the beer is warm. I couldn't find my car keys.

4. I mentioned colour and clothing as two conceptual domains that lend themselves particularly well to both the onomasiological and semasiological perspectives. Another domain is that of spatial relations.

   Design (and, resources permitting, carry out) an experiment to investigate spatial concepts such as [IN], [ON], [ABOVE], [OVER], etc. from both the onomasiological and semasiological perspectives.

Further reading

On domains and profiling, see Langacker (FCG1: ch. 4), Taylor (1995a: ch. 5), Croft (1993), Croft and Clausner (1999). On domains, scripts, and scenarios, see Ungerer and Schmid (1996), esp. chs. 4 and 5. For the semasiological vs. onomasiological perspectives, see Geeraerts *et al.* (1994). For a concise account, see Geeraerts (2000).

CHAPTER 11

Nominal and relational profiles

In the last chapter I introduced the notions of profile, base, and domain, and illustrated them on a number of examples. The examples all involved nouns: *hypotenuse*, *father*, *thumb*, etc. Nouns, by definition, have a nominal profile—they profile 'things'. Other kinds of words have a different kind of profile—they profile relations.

In this chapter I focus on items with relational profiles. These include the verbs, prepositions, adjectives, and adverbs. We shall see how these major word classes can be characterized in general terms by reference to the nature of their profile.

11.1 Relational profiles

Consider the phrases in (1):

(1) a. the picture above the sofa
    b. the sofa below the picture

The nominals *the picture* and *the sofa* both profile a thing. The prepositions *above* and *below* profile a relation between the things in the domain of vertical space.

The two expressions in (1) could be used to talk about exactly the same situation. The expressions differ in that they construe the situation differently. The difference, essentially, has to do with the relevant prominence of the two nominal entities. In any relation, one of the related entities is singled out as the primary focus of attention. In (1a), it is the picture that is being located *vis-à-vis* the sofa, in (1b) it is the sofa that is being located *vis-à-vis* the picture. We shall say, adopting Langacker's terminology, that in (1a) the picture is the **trajector**, or **tr**, of the relation, while the sofa is the **landmark**, or **lm**. The tr is the more prominent entity within the conceptualization of a relation, it is the primary focus of attention, whereas the landmark entity has secondary focus.[1]

A relational profile, as exemplified by *above* in *the picture above the sofa*, is represented schematically in Figure 11.1 (p. 207). This Figure employs a number of Langacker's pictographic conventions. These are:

- a thing is represented by a circle;
- a relation is represented by a line joining the related entities;
- profiled entities are represented in bold;
- the surrounding rectangle represents the conceptual domain of the relational profile. In the case of example (1), the conceptual domain is the conception of three-dimensional space.

One important aspect of Figure 11.1 needs to be addressed. Note that the relational profile includes not only the relation as such, but also the entities that are related. (The two circles in Fig. 11.1 are in bold, as well as the line joining them.) This means, in the case of the preposition *above*, that the word designates not only the vertical relation as such, but also the entities that participate in the relation.

How can this be? Surely, in example (1a), it is the nominals *the picture* and *the sofa* that designate the tr and the lm of the relation. How can we claim that the tr and lm are already part of the profile of the preposition *above*?

The answer is that the tr and lm entities are present **schematically** within the preposition's profile. Usually, a conceptualization in which both tr and lm are schematic will be scarcely viable by itself. Normally, the preposition will need to co-occur with expressions which give conceptual substance to the tr and lm. In *the picture above the sofa*, the two nominals serve this purpose. The picture and the sofa count as **instances** of the preposition's schematic tr and lm.

There are two kinds of evidence which support the view that both the tr and the lm are included within a relational profile:

(i) Although both tr and lm may be schematic within a relational profile, it is not normally the case that they are completely lacking in conceptual

---

[1] The distinction between trajector and landmark exemplifies the more general cognitive phenomenon of figure-ground organization (see above, p. 10). The relation that was introduced in the last chapter, between profile and base, can also be regarded as a manifestation of figure-ground organization.

Fig. 11.1. A relational profile.

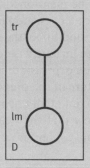

Note: The two circles stand for the trajector (tr) and the landmark (lm) of the relation, the line joining the circles stands for the relation between the tr and the lm. The surrounding box represents the domain (D) against which the relation is conceptualized. The profiled elements are in bold.

content. The preposition *above* (in its spatial sense) imposes restrictions on the kinds of entities that can serve as its tr and lm; both, for example, must be concrete spatial entities. It would be incoherent to speak of **the picture above the enmity* or **the enmity above the time*. The standard way of dealing with facts of this nature is in terms of 'selectional restrictions': *above* selects, as its complement and as its 'subject', nominals of a certain semantic type. Cognitive Grammar handles these facts by claiming that *above* already contains, within its profile, a schematic specification of its tr and lm as spatially bounded entities. Nominals which do not designate entities of the appropriate kind are not eligible to elaborate the schematic tr and lm.[2]

Other prepositions contain, within their profile, schematic notions of the kinds of entities that can figure as tr and lm. The preposition *in* requires that its lm be construable as a container (*in the box*, *in the square*, *in the sentence*, but not **in the dot*, **in the flash*, **in the point*). *Inside* requires that its lm have an internal region (*inside the square* vs. **inside the straight line*). *Throughout* schematically specifies its lm as a three-dimensional entity (*throughout the room* vs. **throughout the floor*).

Verbs, as we shall see later in this chapter, also profile relations, and most verbs impose quite tight restrictions on the kinds of items that can function as their lms (i.e., as their direct objects). The profile of *drink* specifies its lm schematically as a liquid; *kill* requires its lm to be a living thing; *assassinate* further specifies the lm as a person prominent in political life. Many verbs schematically specify their tr (i.e., their subject) as human: *admire* and *assassinate*, for example.

---

[2] Suppose we encounter an expression of the form *the X above the Y*, where *X* and *Y* are unfamiliar nouns. The semantics of the preposition will allow us to infer certain aspects of the semantics of the unknown nouns; it is not the case that the nouns could mean anything at all. The inferences come from the schematic content of the preposition's tr and lm.

(ii) Although it is often necessary to elaborate the tr and lm of a relational profile by use of overt expressions, there are circumstances in which an overt tr or lm does not need to be mentioned. In example (2a) the lm of *above* is not stated. Its conceptual content is supplied by the situational context. Probably, the lm would be understood to be 'the Earth's surface', 'where we now are', or some such. Although the lm entity is not specified lexically, it is still part of the semantic structure of the expression, and therefore needs to be incorporated into the semantic structure of the preposition. The other examples in (2) show that the phenomenon is not at all uncommon, with some prepositions at least. B's responses in (3) show that the tr also need not be overtly mentioned. In these cases, its conceptual content is derived from preceding discourse.

(2) a. the sky above
     b. Is the boss in?
     c. Your mother is out.
     d. Their house is quite near.

(3) a. A: Where do they live?
         B: Near the church.
     b. A: Where was the picture hanging?
         B: Above the sofa.

It is quite common for verbs, also, to tolerate omission of overt subjects and objects, and this again must be taken as evidence that the tr and lm are already present, if only schematically, in the semantic structure of the verbs. The lm of *eat* is schematically characterized as 'food'. This characterization is sufficiently contentful to render (4a) easily interpretable.

(4) a. I haven't eaten for two days.
     b. The strangers left.
     c. Eat this!
     d. Leave!

Leave profiles the movement of its tr out of a lm entity; in *Joe left the office* both tr and lm are overtly mentioned. In example (4b), the identity of the lm entity is able to be identified contextually. In an imperative (4c), the tr would be identified as the addressee. Finally, in (4d), we see a relational item being used without explicit mention of either tr or lm. We shall still want to say, however, that the verb in (4d) profiles the movement of a tr with respect to a lm.

11.2 Relational nouns

The preposition *above* profiles a relation. What about the profile of *the picture above the sofa*? This expression does not designate a relation, it designates a thing, namely, the picture. We can confirm this by applying the test introduced in section 10.2. Any statement that we make about *the picture above the sofa* is a statement about the picture, it is not about the sofa, or about the relation between the picture and the sofa.

(5) a. The picture above the sofa is a cheap print.
    b. *The picture above the sofa is a two-seater.

Using the conventions already available to us, we can represent *the picture above the sofa* as in Figure 11.2.[3] The profiled entity—the picture—is represented in bold; the relation between the picture and sofa, as well as the sofa, are unprofiled, and are relegated to the base of the expression

Interestingly, a word such as *father* has a semantic structure very similar to that shown in Figure 11.2. *Father* designates an adult male. The profiled entity participates in an unprofiled relation to an offspring. Neither the father-of relation, nor the offspring, are in the word's profile (Fig. 11.3 (p. 210)).

Father is a **relational noun**. Although the word is a noun (it profiles a thing), the profiled entity participates in an unprofiled relation to another entity. Relational nouns are quite numerous. In addition to kinship terms (*mother, niece, ancestor, husband*, etc.), relational nouns include:

• nouns which construe a human being in terms of a social or professional relation: *friend, enemy, neighbour, colleague, boss, rival*. If a person is designated as a 'friend', there must be some other person(s) to whom the designated person stands in a 'friend-of' relation. Both the relation as such and the lm of the relation are unprofiled;
• nouns which designate an entity which exists only as a part of a larger entity: *top, side, inside, edge, corner*. If something is designated as the 'top', there has to be some entity of which it is the top;

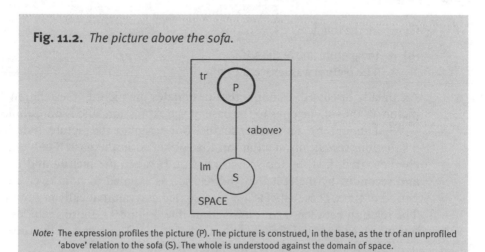

Fig. 11.2. *The picture above the sofa.*

Note: The expression profiles the picture (P). The picture is construed, in the base, as the tr of an unprofiled 'above' relation to the sofa (S). The whole is understood against the domain of space.

---

[3] I ignore the role of the definite determiners in the semantic structure of *the picture above the sofa*. The semantic contribution of determiners is addressed in Chapter 18.

Fig. 11.3. A relational noun.

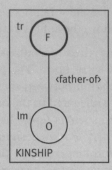

Note: The profile of *father* (F) bears an unprofiled 'father-of' relation to unprofiled offspring (O). The whole is understood against the domain of kinship.

- nouns which designate a representation of something: *statue*, *photograph*, *biography*, *story*, *description*. A statue is necessarily a statue *of* someone, otherwise we should probably call it a sculpture, not a statue.

Another important category of relational nouns is those derived from verbs. Agentive nouns, for example, are typically derived from a verb through suffixation of *-er*. *Singer*, *dancer*, *reader*, *murderer*, *robber*, *killer* all construe the profiled individual as the tr of an unprofiled activity.

11.3 Temporal profiles

Compare the following expressions:

(6) a. the picture above the sofa
    b. The picture was above the sofa.

As already discussed, example (6a) designates the picture; the relation of the picture to the sofa belongs to the base of the expression, and is not profiled.

What about (6b)? This sentence does not designate the picture, it designates a situation, specifically, a situation that obtained in the past. The situation is characterized, first, by the spatial relation between the picture and the sofa, and secondly, by the fact that the relation is claimed to hold over a certain period of time. These aspects are represented diagrammatically in Figure 11.4. The relation between tr and lm is in profile. Figure 11.4 also includes a time line which extends indefinitely in both directions. A segment of the time line is in profile; the tr-lm relation is valid over this time segment.

The picture was above the sofa profiles a **temporal relation**: the relation holds over a span of time that is part of the expression's profile. The relation is also **stative**, that is, it is construed as holding, unchanged, throughout the duration

Fig. 11.4. A simple temporal relation.

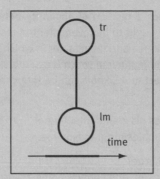

Note: The profile includes a time segment, of unspecified duration, over which the relation holds.

of the profiled time segment. These aspects are contributed by the verb *be*.[4] As a matter of fact, Figure 11.4, as it stands, could be taken as an adequate representation of the meaning of *be*, at least in many of its uses.[5] The nominals *the picture* and *the sofa* in (6b), as well as the preposition *above*, serve to give conceptual substance to the schematic components of *be*'s profile.

Quite a number of verbs profile a stative relation (7):

(7) a. Joe resembles his grandfather.
     b. Joe hates his grandfather.
     c. The picture hangs above the sofa.
     d. The lamp stands in the corner.
     e. Luxembourg lies between France, Belgium, and Germany.

Although these verbs—*resemble, hate, hang, stand, lie*—differ with respect to the content of the profiled relation, they each elaborate, in different ways, the profile of a stative temporal relation presented diagrammatically in Figure 11.4. This is tantamount to claiming that *be* is schematic for the class of stative verbs. On the one hand, then, Figure 11.4 can be taken as a representation of the semantic structure of *be*; at the same time, it can be taken as a schematic representation of any stative verb.

Many verbs do not profile a static relation, but a dynamic event, which involves a change in the relation between tr and lm over time. Consider the verb *leave*.

---

[4] I ignore here the role of tense. Because of the past tense, (6b) would normally be interpreted to mean that the relation between the picture and the sofa held over a span of time previous to the time of utterance. I address the contribution of tense in Chapter 20.

[5] A notable exception is the use of *be* in passive clauses. *This watch was stolen* could have a stative reading ('This was a stolen watch'); on this interpretation, the clause would not be considered to be passive, and *be* does indeed profile a stative relation. Alternatively, the clause could have a 'processual' reading: 'This watch was stolen (at the airport)'. Here, *be* does not profile a stative relation. For the treatment of passives in Cognitive Grammar, see Langacker (1982).

Joe resembles his grandfather

Resemble profiles a relation of similarity between two entities. Logically speaking, the relation ought to be reversible: If *A* resembles *B*, then *B* must resemble *A*. Moreover, the degree and the manner in which *A* resembles *B* ought to be identical to the degree and manner in which *B* resembles *A*. Yet it is not always the case that subject and object of *resemble* can be interchanged. For example, (a) is decidedly better than (b):

(a) Joe resembles his grandfather Daniel.
(b) ?Daniel resembles his grandson Joe.

Why should this be?
In any comparison, one entity is being assessed for its degree of similarity to the other. The entity that is being assessed is the tr, and this entity functions as the subject of the verb. The term of comparison constitutes a 'fixed point', as it were, against which the other entity is being assessed, and it naturally functions as the lm. (Resemblance, therefore, is not a purely logical relation; speaker construal is also important.) Sentence (b) is odd, because it would be strange to take the grandson as the fixed point of reference against which the grandfather is assessed. The grandson is growing and developing, whereas the grandfather's features are likely to be fixed and stable.

(**8**) Joe left the office.

Sentence (8) profiles a situation is which Joe is initially in the office; then he exits from the office, during which time he occupies a series of locations *vis-à-vis* the office; finally, he ends up in a place which is out of the office. If Joe was not initially in the office, or if he did not end up out of the office, we could not say that he left the office. In using the verb *leave* we track, as it were, the successive locations of the moving tr *vis-à-vis* the static lm. The verb profiles a **complex temporal relation**. The profile is complex in that it consists, not in a single tr-lm configuration, but in a series of relations which are tracked, as it were, through time. Moreover, the time segment over which the complex relation unfolds is in the verb's profile. Figure 11.5 attempts to represent the changing relation between the tr and the lm.

Consider, now, the expression in (9).

(**9**) Joe has left the office.

To simplify matters, I will ignore the precise contribution of the verb *have* to this expression.[6] What does (9) designate? Essentially, it designates a situation

---

[6] Since it ignores the semantic contribution of perfective *have*, Figure 11.6 is not a fully adequate account of English *Joe has left the office*. The Figure could, however, serve as a fair representation of Italian *Joe è uscito dall'ufficio* (literally: 'Joe is departed from the office'). The past participle *uscito* 'departed' profiles the final state of the tr, while the verb *è* 'is' contributes to the temporal profile.

Fig. 11.5. A complex temporal relation: *Joe left the office*.

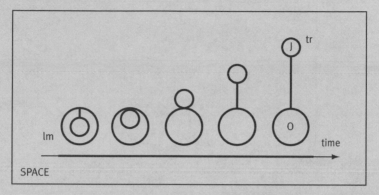

Note: The verb *leave* profiles the change over time in the relation between its tr, Joe (J), and its lm, the office (O). Initially, the tr is in the lm; the tr moves along a path, at the end of which the tr is out of the lm.

in which Joe is not in the office. Joe's not being in the office is, however, the result of Joe's having left the office. We can represent this situation by making an adjustment to the profile of Figure 11.5. The adjustment—see Figure 11.6 (p. 214)—consists in restricting the profile to the end-point of the tr's path. The previous movement of the tr is still part of the base of the expression. If Joe had not already been in the office, there would be no basis for describing his not being in the office as a situation of Joe's having left the office; we should say, quite simply, that Joe was not in the office, or that he was outside of the office.

---

go to vs. return to

Joe went to the office and *Joe returned to the office* profile exactly the same event, an event, namely, in which Joe is initially 'not in the office', he moves along a path such that he ends up 'in the office'. The expressions differ, in that *return* presupposes that the tr was at the office at some previous point in time and that he had left it. Joe's previously leaving the office is intrinsic to the conceptualization of *return*; it is part of the verb's base, even though it is not profiled.

11.4 More on trajectors and landmarks

So far, I have assumed that a relational profile involves two entities, the tr and lm; moreover, the tr and lm have in all cases been things, that is to say, they have had nominal profiles. We need to modify each of these assumptions.

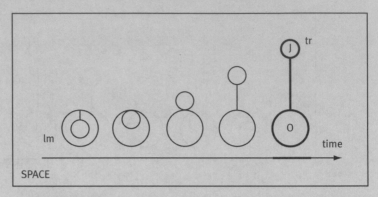

Fig. 11.6. The end-point of a complex relation is profiled.

Note: The situation of Joe (J) being out of the office (O) holds over the profiled time segment. The profiled situation presupposes Joe's previous movement out of the office, an aspect which is not in profile.

11.4.1 Multiple landmarks

For a number of relational items we need to recognize more than one lm. Of the two lms, one (the **primary landmark**) is more prominent than the other (the **secondary landmark**). Compare the verbs *steal* and *rob*. These verbs are understood against the same conceptual base. There is, namely, an event in which a person illegally takes a thing away from its rightful owner. There are three participants in the event: the person who takes the thing, the thing taken, and the rightful owner. The two verbs differ in how they construe the relative salience of the landmark entities. Compare:

(10) a. The thieves robbed the Princess of her diamonds.
      b. The thieves stole the diamonds from the Princess.

rob focuses on the relation between the thieves (the tr) and the Princess (the primary lm). The act of robbing primarily affects the Princess. The prepositional phrase *of her diamonds* specifies the way in which the Princess was affected by the act. It is significant that the secondary lm (the diamonds) need not be mentioned: *They robbed the Princess* is a perfectly coherent statement. *Steal*, on the other hand, focuses specifically on the relation between the thieves (the tr) and the diamonds (the primary lm); the sentence tells us specifically what happened to the diamonds. The Princess is now the secondary lm. Again, the secondary lm may be omitted: *They stole the diamonds* is a perfectly coherent statement.

Syntactically speaking, *rob* and *steal* differ with respect to the nominal that they select as their direct object. The subject of the verbs can be identified with the tr of the designated process. The direct object can be characterized as the landmark. In case there is more than one landmark, the direct object corresponds to the primary landmark.

Intransitive verbs

While some verbs take two lms, there are verbs which do not seem to have a lm at all. This is the case with intransitive verbs:

(a) The horse jumped.
(b) The Earth shook.
(c) The boy is growing up.
(d) Joe died.

Jump, *shake*, *grow up*, and *die* designate events in which there is only one par-ticipant. (The examples differ, therefore, from intransitive sentences of the kind *Joe left*, or *I haven't eaten today*. These inherently involve a relation between two entities; the lm, however, is not explicitly elaborated.) The sole participant is designated by the subject nominal and counts as the tr. Although there is no lm nominal, it is still appropriate to refer to these intransitive verbs as relational items. They profile a relation between the tr and an activity or change-of-state in which the tr participates.

Another verb which invokes primary and secondary lms is *give*. Any act of giving inherently involves three entities: the giver, the thing given, and the recipient. In sentence (11a), the recipient is the primary lm; the sentence tells us in what way the recipient was affected by the act. Sentence (11b) focuses on what happened to the thing. Interestingly, if these sentences are made passive, it is the direct object (the primary lm) that comes to function as the subject of the passive sentence (*The child was given a present* vs. *A present was given to the child*).

(11) a. They gave the child a present.
      b. They gave a present to the child.

11.4.2 Relations as trs and lms

In the examples discussed so far, both the tr and the lm of a relation have been things, designated by nominals. It is also possible for the tr and/or the lm of a relation to be itself a relation. Compare:

(12) a. the meal before the match
      b. We had a meal before the match.
      c. We had a meal before we watched the match.

In (a), *before* profiles a relation of temporal succession between two entities, both of which are designated by nominals. Parallel to our analysis of *the picture above the sofa*, we can say that (12a) profiles the meal, not the match, nor the relation between the meal and the match.

Sentence (12b) is substantially the same except that the tr of the 'before' relation is not a thing but is itself a relation (more precisely, the temporal relation designated by the clause *we had a meal*). The expression profiles the event of our having a meal, and characterizes it as one which occurred 'before the match'.

In (12c) *before* once again profiles a relation of temporal succession. But now the lm is also a relation (more precisely, the temporal relation designated by the clause *we watched the match*). As in (12b), the sentence profiles the event of our having a meal, and construes it in relation to a subsequent event.

Traditionally, *before* in (12a) and (12b) would be described as a preposition while *before* in (12c) would be described as a conjunction. The preposition and the conjunction are similar in that each designates a relation of temporal succession; they differ in that the preposition takes a nominal lm, the conjunction a relational (more specifically, a clausal) lm.

11.5 More on relations

We have so far encountered the following kinds of relations:

- temporal relations. These are relations whose profile includes a span of time over which the relation holds. Verbs designate temporal relations;
- atemporal relations. These are relations whose profile does not include a span of time over which the relation holds. Prepositions (*above*, *in*, *before*) and conjunctions designate atemporal relations;
- simple relations. These are relations whose profile consists of a single configuration. *Above*, *below*, *be*, and *be above* designate simple relations;
- complex relations. These are relations whose profile consists of multiple configurations. *Leave* (as in *Joe left the office*) designates a complex relation.

Let us examine these kinds of relations in more detail.

11.5.1 Temporal and atemporal profiles

The reader may be surprised to see *before* listed as an example of a word designating an atemporal relation. Doesn't *before* intrinsically involve a reference to time, and shouldn't this word, whether 'preposition' or 'conjunction', be described as designating a temporal relation?

Time is certainly an important facet of the semantic structure of *before*, just as space is an important facet of the semantic structure of *above*. As shown in Figure 11.2, space is the conceptual domain against which the 'above' relation is profiled. Similarly, time is the conceptual domain for the profiling of the 'before' relation. However, neither of the prepositions (*above* or *before*) profiles the existence, or persistence, of the relation at a point in time or through a span of time. This aspect would need to come from a verb. Thus, the difference between (13a) and (13b) exactly parallels the difference between (6a) and (6b).

(**13**) a. the meal before the match
  b. The meal was before the match.

(**6**) a. the picture above the sofa
  b. The picture was above the sofa.

In a sense, (13a) designates a 'timeless' relation; although the relation is profiled against the conceptual domain of time, the relation is not instantiated at any point or period of time. It is for this reason that it is appropriate to refer to prepositions and conjunctions as profiling atemporal relations. The profiling of temporal relations, where the time at which, or over which, the relations hold, is the special property of verbs.

11.5.2 Simple vs. complex relations

A simple relation is construed as a single configuration. A complex relation is one which profiles multiple relations. A characteristic of a 'dynamic' verb, such as *leave*, is that it designates a series of relations; first, the tr is in the lm, then the tr moves, through a series of locations, to a place which is out of the lm. Stative verbs, such as *be, resemble, stand, lie*, characteristically designate a single relation, which is, however, construed as holding, unchanged, over the profiled time segment.

Above, in *the picture above the sofa*, designates a simple relation. Even if there were several pictures above the sofa, or several pictures above several sofas, we should still want to say that *the pictures above sofa(s)* designates a simple relation; the pictures, considered as a group, bear the simple relation to the sofa(s).

Rather more complicated are prepositions such as *around, across, over* (in some of its uses), *all over, through, throughout*, and *along*. These require that their tr is either a spatially extended entity which can assume the appropriate configuration *vis-à-vis* the lm, or a multiplex entity whose various components can take on a characteristic disposition *vis-à-vis* the lm. We can speak, for example, of *a fence around the garden*, in which case the fence 'wraps itself', so to speak, around the lm, or of *trees around the garden*, where the set of trees encircles the lm (Fig. 11.7 (p. 218)). We cannot speak of **a tree around the garden*, since a tree lacks the required spatial configuration. Similarly, for something to be *all over* a lm entity, the tr has to be spatially dispersed (*water all over the floor*) or a multiplex entity whose various components are distributed so as to 'cover' the lm in the appropriate way (*soldiers posted all over the city*).

The prepositions under discussion generally allow two further uses (see Fig. 11.8 (p. 219)). First, a moving tr occupies a series of locations which collectively make up the appropriate configuration *vis-à-vis* the lm. In example (14a) the path of my walking is made up of a series of locations which, collectively, make up the spatial configuration describable by *across the field*. When I walk 'across the field' it is my successive locations *vis-à-vis* the field

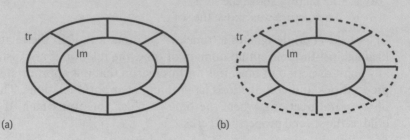

Fig. 11.7. A complex atemporal relation (*around*) in two of its uses.

(a)   (b)

Note: In (a), the tr is a spatially extended entity whose constituent parts bear a set of relations to the lm. In (b), the tr is a multiplex entity, whose various components bear a set of relations to the lm.

which collectively make up the 'across' relation. The relation designated by *across* is therefore complex, since it is made up of a multiplicity of locations. It is also an atemporal relation; although the idea of me walking across the field invokes temporal succession, progress through time is profiled by the verb, not by the preposition as such.

(14) a. I walked across the field.
      b. He lives across the field.

In (14b), *across the field* designates a simple relation, namely, the place where a person lives. The place is, however, construed as the end-point of an imaginary (and unprofiled) path whose disposition corresponds to the complex relation 'across the field'. It is as if, in order to locate the person's place of residence, one has to trace a path which extends 'across the field' from some unspecified starting point. Depending on the circumstances in which (14b) is used, the starting point of the imaginary path could be the place at which the sentence is uttered, the speaker's place of residence, or any other contextually salient location. The starting point could be linguistically encoded, as in *They live across the field from us*.

Among the prepositions that designate complex relations are *into* and *towards*. *Into* inherently profiles a series of locations which collectively make up a path which terminates in the interior of the lm entity, while the path profiled by *towards* stops short of the lm entity. Although these items invoke the notion of motion along a directed path, their profiles must still be regarded as atemporal. A temporal profile needs to be contributed by a finite verb, as in *I walked into the garden, We drove towards the sea*.

Again, it may strike the reader as strange to deny a temporal profile to words, like *into*, which inherently invoke the notion of movement along a path. Consider, however, the following expressions.

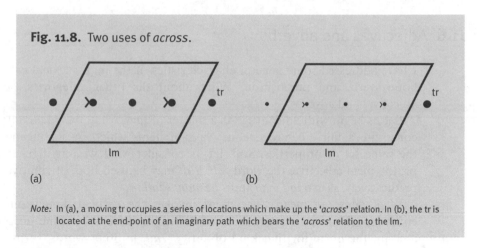

Fig. 11.8. Two uses of *across*.

(a)

(b)

Note: In (a), a moving tr occupies a series of locations which make up the '*across*' relation. In (b), the tr is located at the end-point of an imaginary path which bears the '*across*' relation to the lm.

(15) a. the gate in the garden
b. the gate into the garden
c. The gate leads into the garden.

Both (a) and (b) designate the gate. Though (15a) is unproblematic, as it designates the gate as one which is located at a place 'in the garden', (15b) is more difficult. It designates a gate, such that, if a person were to go through the gate, moving from a location which is 'not in the garden', they would end up at a place 'in the garden'. *Into* brings in the notion of a potential path through the gate and into the garden. The path, if it were followed, necessarily occurs over time. However, the path is not in profile, neither does the expression profile movement of a tr along the path. Sentence (15b) is quintessentially atemporal. In contrast, (15c) has a temporal profile. Note, however, that (15c) does not profile movement as such through time. The sentence designates a stative relation, characterized in terms of the potential path.[7]

The contrasts studied in this section—simple vs. complex, temporal vs. atemporal—are independent of each other. The four possible combinations are associated with different kinds of expressions.

- simple temporal relations (profiled by stative verbs);
- complex temporal relations (profiled by dynamic verbs);
- simple atemporal relations (profiled by 'simple' prepositions);
- complex atemporal relations (profiled by prepositions which require a multiplex or extended tr).

[7] Observe that *the gate into the garden* and *the gate out of the garden* could designate exactly the same entity, just as *The gate leads into the garden* and *The gate leads out of the garden* designate exactly the same stative relation. The differences reside in the direction of the potential path.

11.6 Adjectives and adverbs

I have addressed some general characteristics of the major lexical categories noun, verb, and preposition. What about the other categories, such as adjectives and adverbs?

Let us begin with adjectives. As a matter of fact, what are called adjectives constitute a fairly heterogeneous class of items which by no means share the same set of properties. Still, let us consider what we might regard as a prototypical adjective, the word *tall*. *Tall* may be used both attributively and predicatively, as in *a tall man* and *The man is tall*.

What does *tall* mean? The word invokes the vertical dimension of an entity; specifically, an entity is tall if its height exceeds by some unspecified amount the norm for that kind of entity. *Tall*, in other words, turns out to be a relational item: it profiles the relation between its tr (the entity that is claimed to be tall) and a region in excess of some norm, with respect to the vertical dimension (Fig. 11.9). *A tall man* and *The man is tall* differ in the usual way; the former has a nominal profile—it profiles the man, not the tallness of the man—while the latter profiles a stative temporal relation.

Although *tall* turns out to be a relational item, its lm is not stated in a separate expression, distinct from the adjective; its lm is incorporated, as it were, in the semantic structure of the word. In this respect, adjectives are exactly like intransitive verbs. The lm of an intransitive verb, such as *grow up*,

Fig. 11.9. The semantic structure of *tall*.

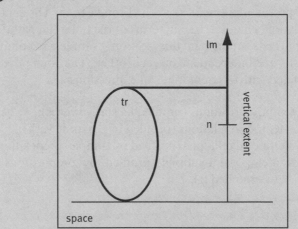

Note: The word *tall* profiles the relation between its tr (an entity that is a candidate for 'being tall') and its lm. The lm is a conception of the vertical extent of an entity. An entity counts as 'tall' if its vertical extent exceeds a norm (n).

is the notion of a change-in-state which is part and parcel of the semantic structure of the verb.

Adverbs differ from adjectives with respect to the nature of the tr. Compare:

(16) a. an intelligent pupil
     b. The pupil answered the question intelligently.

Intelligent and *intelligently* both profile a relation between a tr and a region in excess of a norm with respect to 'intelligence'. The words differ, in that the adjective takes a nominal as its tr, the adverb takes a relation (here, a temporal relation) as its tr.

11.7 Characterizing the word classes

By applying the notions already introduced it is possible to propose a very coarse-grained classification of the major lexical categories (Fig. 11.10).

All words designate an entity. (Note that 'entity' is a technical term of Cognitive Grammar and refers to anything that can be conceptualized or conceived of, whether this be a thing, a relation, a state of affairs, an event, or whatever.)

We can make a first distinction between words which profile things (nouns) and those which profile relations. Relational profiles divide into temporal profiles (characteristic of verbs) and atemporal profiles. The latter

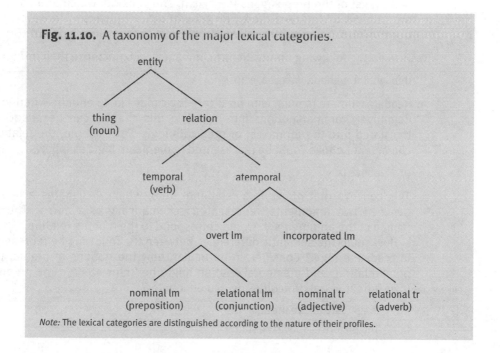

Fig. 11.10. A taxonomy of the major lexical categories.

Note: The lexical categories are distinguished according to the nature of their profiles.

are distinguished according to the properties of their tr and lm. The lms of prepositions and conjunctions are overt, at least potentially so; the lms, that is, can be explicitly elaborated by distinct expressions. The word classes differ in that the lm of a preposition is a thing, while the lm of a conjunction is a temporal relation. Adjectives and adverbs take an overt tr, nominal in the case of an adjective, relational in the case of an adverb. The two classes share the property that their lm is incorporated within the semantic structure of the adjective/adverb, and may not be elaborated in a distinct expression.

Study questions

1. Prepositions with 'sublexical' lms. It could be argued that *in* designates exactly the same relation in (i) and (ii). The difference has to do with whether the lm of the relation is overtly elaborated or whether its conceptual content is supplied contextually.

   (i)   The boss is in the office.

   (ii)   The boss is in.

   Not all prepositions allow their lm to be sublexical:

   (iii)   Joe walked into the room.

   (iv)   *Joe walked into.

   Make a list of the prepositions in English, and consider which of these tolerate 'sublexical' lms. Are there any general characteristics of those propositions which tolerate sublexical lms, in contrast to those which do not?

2. How do the following prepositions schematically characterize their lm?

   through, throughout, past, via, across

3. Readers who are familiar with predicate logic may like to enquire whether the Cognitive Grammar notions introduced in this chapter can be adequately translated into the formalism of predicate logic. For example, the relational character of *above* could be represented in predicate logic as follows:

   (i)   above (x, y)

   This conveys that *above* is a relational item, which designates a relation between two arguments, represented schematically as *x* and *y*. The first named of the arguments, *x*, would correspond to the tr of the relation.

   How could the semantic differences between the following be represented in predicate logic? Consider, in particular, how the notions of profile, temporal relation, and atemporal relation might be 'translated' in the predicate logic format. What difficulties do you encounter?

   (ii)   the picture above the sofa

   (iii)   The picture is above the sofa.

4. Trajector and landmark. The choice of an entity as tr is a consequence of a speaker's decision to construe that entity as the most prominent entity within a relational profile. Sometimes, either entity within a relation can be construed as the tr; sometimes, one construal is more viable than the other. What factors influence the choice of tr in the following?

(i)   My bicycle is near the church.
        ??The church is near my bicycle.

(ii)   Two plus two equals four.
        ??Four equals two plus two.

(iii)   The road follows the river.
        ??The river follows the road.

(iv)   The dictionary is on the table.
        ??The table is under the dictionary.

(v)   We are approaching Christmas.
        ?Christmas is approaching us.

5. In this chapter we compared the semantic structure of (i) and (ii).

(i)   the picture above the sofa

(ii)   The picture is above sofa.

What about (iii)?

(iii)   the picture being above the sofa

Consider the use of this expression in the following:

(iv)   Does [the picture being above the sofa] disturb you?

(v)   What's wrong with [the picture being above the sofa]?

What does (iii) profile?

6. Simple vs. complex atemporal relations. Describe the semantic structure of the prepositional phrases in the following. You may find it helpful to represent the semantic structure pictographically, incorporating the conventions introduced in this chapter.

(i)   His house is on the hill.
        His house is over the hill.

(ii)   The pantry is at the back of the house.
        The pantry is through the kitchen.

(iii)   The post-office is by the police station.
        The post-office is past the police station.

(iv)   I walked (around) in the city centre.
        I walked into the city centre.

(v)   I worked until 2 am.
        I worked until late into the night.

(vi)   We have a cottage deep in the forest.
        We have a cottage deep into the forest.

(vii)   We got onto an interesting topic.
        We are now onto an interesting topic.

Further reading

See Langacker (FCG1: chs. 5 and 6) on things and relations, also Taylor (1996: ch. 4). There is an extensive literature on prepositions. See especially Talmy (1983), Hawkins (1984), Dirven (1989a), Herskovits (1986), and Taylor (1993).

CHAPTER 12

Syntagmatic relations: Combining semantic units

In earlier chapters, especially Chapters 7–9, I focused on the 'vertical' relations between linguistic units, that is, the relations between a more abstractly characterized schema and its more fully characterized instances. In this and the next chapter I turn to 'horizontal' relations between units, that is to say, the syntagmatic combination of simpler units into larger, internally more complex units. (On 'vertical' vs. 'horizontal' relations, refer to the précis of Cognitive Grammar in section 2.1.1.)

Because symbolic units associate a phonological and a semantic representation, syntagmatic combination actually takes place on two levels, the semantic and the phonological. In this chapter I focus on the combination of semantic units. We shall see in the next chapter that the basic mechanism of syntagmatic combination—the establishment of 'valence relations'—is identical for both conceptual and phonological combination.

12.1 Autonomy and dependence

Units—whether these be phonological or semantic—differ with respect to their disposition to combine with other units. This 'disposition to combine' is a function of the degree of **autonomy** vs. **dependence** of a unit. Autonomy can

> **A terminological note**
>
> The term 'dependent', as used in Cognitive Grammar, has a different value from its use in other grammatical theories, for example, in so-called Dependency Grammars or in Richard Hudson's Word Grammar (Hudson 1990). Items that are termed 'dependents' in these theories tend to equate with the relatively 'autonomous' units of Cognitive Grammar.

be defined in terms of whether the unit can stand by itself, independent of any further conceptualizations. Dependence is the converse. A unit is dependent to the extent that it presupposes some other unit(s). Typically, a dependent unit will need to combine with other units, in order for a relatively autonomous structure to be created.

An autonomous semantic unit would be a concept that one can entertain, in and of itself, without the need to appeal to anything outside the concept itself. A dependent semantic unit would be a concept that necessarily makes reference to other conceptual structures. Given the embeddedness of concepts in encyclopaedic, domain-based knowledge (Chapter 10), there is probably no such thing as a fully autonomous semantic unit. Nevertheless, there are clear differences between semantic units with respect to their relative autonomy vs. dependence.

To begin, we can draw a very broad distinction between nominal concepts (those designated by nouns) and relational concepts, designated by prepositions (*on*, *above*, etc.), adjectives (*tall*, *intelligent*), adverbs (*intelligently*, *quickly*), as well as by verbs (*be*, *leave*, *give*, *put*). Nominal concepts are relatively autonomous, whereas relational concepts display a high degree of conceptual dependence. The dependence of relational concepts follows automatically from the Cognitive Grammar analysis of these items. The concept [ABOVE] consists in a relation (usually, a spatial relation) between a located object (the tr) and a reference object (the lm). One can scarcely conceptualize an 'above' relation, in and of itself, unless the tr and lm entities are given conceptual substance. Prepositions, adjectives, adverbs, and the verbs will typically need to occur in a context which lessens, as it were, their conceptual dependence. Consider the verb *put*. The concept [PUT] inherently involves the movement of a lm to a location or position. Unless this facet of [PUT] is given overt linguistic expression, a 'put' kind of event can scarcely be conceptualized. As a consequence, (1a–1c) are incoherent.[1]

---

[1] Notice that the unacceptability of (1a–1c) cannot be 'rescued' by aspects of the context of situation. Making a gesture towards the intended goal location, and/or towards the intended lm entity, is insufficient to render these sentences acceptable.

(1) a. *Put!
    b. *Put your clothes!
    c. *Put in the cupboard!
    d. Put your clothes in the cupboard!

Although nouns, in comparison to relational units, display a relatively high degree of semantic autonomy, some differences can be noted. Compare the concepts [TREE] and [UNCLE]. The word *uncle* designates a male human. The male human is conceptualized as participating in a kinship relation to at least one other person, the nephew(s) and/or niece(s). Neither the kinship relation, nor the nephew(s)/nieces(s), are profiled by the word. Nevertheless, these notions are intrinsic to the meaning of *uncle*; remove the idea of the kinship relation, and the very concept [UNCLE] dissipates and becomes indistinguishable from [MALE HUMAN]. The concept [UNCLE] is therefore conceptually dependent, in that the concept necessarily invokes at least one other person and the relation of that person to the profiled person. In contrast, concepts such as [TREE], [TABLE], [HOUSE] display a rather high degree of conceptual autonomy. It is true that the concept [TREE] might make background reference to the earth which contains the tree's roots, to the air in which the tree's branches are located, to the size of the tree relative to the height of humans, and to many other things besides. Still, these aspects are relatively extrinsic to the concept; the concept is coherent, without our having to make reference to the earth, air, and the tree's size, in a way that the concept [UNCLE] is not at all coherent if we remove the idea of the nephew(s)/niece(s).

The difference shows up in the ways in which the words *tree* and *uncle* are used. For a conceptually dependent unit, it is often necessary to embed the unit in a context which ensures that the notions schematically present in its semantic structure can be elaborated. Compare:

(2) a. A tree blew over in the storm.
    b. There's a tree growing in the yard.

(3) a. ?An uncle entered the room.
    b. ?There's an uncle waiting in the lobby.

The sentences in (2) would be perfectly intelligible, even if uttered 'out of the blue', with no special contextual support. Without further context, those in (3) are odd. This is because the sentences, as they stand, introduce a conceptually dependent unit, but give no clue as how the unit should be conceptualized. One is inclined to ask: 'Whose uncle?', 'Why is the person referred to as "an uncle"?' The following are much more acceptable, even if uttered out of the blue:

(4) a. An uncle of mine entered the room.
    b. I have an uncle in Australia.

Here, there is reference, within the sentences themselves, to the unprofiled lm in the semantic structure of [UNCLE]. In (4a), the lm entity is introduced by way of an '*of*' phrase, in (4b) the entity functions as the subject of *have*. Both contexts are adequate to enable the unprofiled lm of [UNCLE] to be identified.

Argument structure and subcategorization frames

In some linguistic theories, the ungrammaticality of (1a–1c) would be accounted for in terms of argument structure and subcategorization frame. A verb's subcategorization frame states the syntactic environment in which a verb must occur; thus, *put* must occur in the frame [_____ NP PP]. This is a syntactic fact about the verb. A verb's argument structure states the semantic roles of the obligatory participants; with *put*, these are the entity that is moved (often called the Theme), and the place to which the Theme is moved (i.e., the Goal). These are semantic facts about the verb. Syntax and semantics are related through the 'linking' of syntactic elements with semantic roles. With *put*, the direct object NP is linked to the Theme role, while the PP is linked to the Goal role. These aspects of *put* can be expressed as follows:

put   [_____ NP$_{Theme}$ PP$_{Goal}$]

For any use of *put* to be grammatical, the verb must co-occur with a Theme-NP and a Goal-PP.

In Cognitive Grammar, the semantic and syntactic aspects are given a unitary treatment, and follow from the conceptual dependence of the semantic unit [PUT]. The distinction between syntactic and semantic facts about the verb becomes redundant.

12.2 Conceptual combination

I now turn to the mechanisms whereby semantic units combine with each other. I illustrate on the example of *the book on the table*.

Take, first, the preposition *on*. *On* designates a relation between a tr and a lm. Like most words—especially words of high frequency—*on* is polysemous, that is, it has a range of related senses. Let us focus, however, on the use of the preposition to designate a spatial relation. Simplifying somewhat, we can say that the relation is one of support and contact. The lm must be a supporting surface whereas the tr is an object that is in contact with the lm in such a way that, were it not for the lm, the tr would fall downwards.[2] In other words, the preposition already contains, in its semantic structure, a schematic characterization of its tr and, especially, its lm. At the same time, it is scarcely possible to conceptualize an 'on' relation without giving the tr and lm more conceptual content. [ON] is conceptually dependent, in ways in which [BOOK] and [TABLE] are not.

---

[2] Spatial *on* is actually more complex than this, as shown by such uses as *the fly on the ceiling, the writing on the wall, the picture on the wall, the ring on my finger*.

[ON] enters into a syntagmatic relation with other conceptual units to the extent that the other units serve to **elaborate**, or give additional conceptual substance to the entities schematically present in its semantic structure. The schematic tr and lm within the semantic structure of [ON] constitute **elaboration sites**, that are 'open', as it were, to conceptual elaboration by more contentful expressions. These aspects determine a unit's **valence**:

> Valence: The valence of a unit X states the combinatorial possibilities of the unit. Typically, valence will be determined by the schematic entities in the semantic structure of X which are available for elaboration by other units.[3]

Units combine through the establishment of a **valence relation**:

> Valence relation: Two units, X and Y, enter a valence relation, if some element in the structure of X is construed as identical with some element in the structure of Y and can be unified with it.

Figure 12.1 (p. 230) displays the assembly of the complex concept [THE BOOK ON THE TABLE]. (Note that I ignore the contribution of the definite articles, both in the Figure and in the commentary on it.)

Let us go through Figure 12.1 step by step, beginning with the representation of [ON] in the lower left box.

The preposition *on* designates a (stative atemporal) relation between a schematic tr and a schematic lm. The nominal *the table* designates a thing. [ON] combines with [THE TABLE] in that [THE TABLE] is able to elaborate the lm of [ON], i.e. [THE TABLE] gives a fuller specification of the semantic content of the lm. The dotted line linking the lm of [ON] and the profile of [THE TABLE] symbolizes the identity, and unification, of the two entities. In virtue of this, [ON] and [THE TABLE] contract a valence relation.

The result of the combination—the complex concept [ON THE TABLE]—is still relational in character. The complex concept has **inherited** the relational profile of [ON]; the profile of [ON THE TABLE] is determined by the profile of one of its parts, namely, [ON]. In Langacker's terminology, [ON] is the **profile determinant** of [ON THE TABLE]. The profile determinant is represented, in the lower segment of Figure 12.1, by the heavy box around it.

The profile determinant corresponds rather closely with the traditional notion of **head**. In many grammatical theories, the head of a phrase is defined as that constituent which determines the syntactic category of the phrase; *on the table* is relational, because its head, *on*, is relational. It follows that the relation designated by *on the table* counts as an instance of the relation designated by *on*. The profile of *on* is schematic for the profile of *on the table*.

---

[3] The notion of 'valence' is based on a metaphor from chemistry: the valence (or valency) of an atom is the number of hydrogen atoms with which the atom can combine. The Cognitive Grammar notion of valence has some affinities with the notions of subcategorization frame and argument structure. Valence, however, is not seen as a distinctly syntactic phenomenon, nor indeed as a purely semantic (and non-syntactic) phenomenon.

Fig. 12.1. The assembly of [THE BOOK ON THE TABLE].

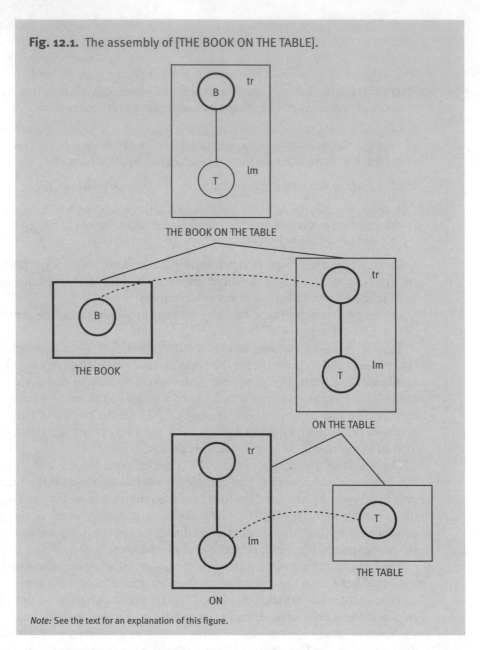

THE BOOK ON THE TABLE

THE BOOK

ON THE TABLE

THE TABLE

ON

Note: See the text for an explanation of this figure.

Both *on* and *on the table* designate exactly the same relation, albeit with differing degrees of specificity.

Head. In an expression XY, X is the head, if the profile of X is schematic for the profile of XY.

Alternatively: The head, and the expression which it heads, designate the same entity, albeit with differing degrees of specificity.

If *on* is the head, what is *the table*? Traditionally, this would be called the **complement** of *on*. We can define complement as follows:

> Complement. In an expression XY, which is headed by X, Y is the complement of X if Y elaborates a substructure in the semantic structure of X.
>
> Alternatively: The complement elaborates (gives additional conceptual substance to) an entity already present, schematically, in the semantic structure of the head.
>
> Typically, X (the head) will be conceptually the more dependent entity, Y (the complement) will be the more autonomous entity.

Let us turn next to the combination of [THE BOOK] with [ON THE TABLE]. Again, [THE TABLE] elaborates a schematic entity in the semantic structure of [ON THE TABLE], namely, the tr. The resultant complex expression, however, no longer profiles a relation, but a thing, namely, the book. *The book on the table* designates the book, specifically, a book which is in a certain spatial location *vis-à-vis* the table. In this case, *the book* is the profile determinant, alias the head of the phrase, and *on the table* is a **modifier**.

> Modifier. In an expression XY, which is headed by X, Y is the modifier of X if X elaborates a substructure in the semantic structure of Y.
>
> Alternatively: The modifier provides additional—and optional—conceptual substance to the head.
>
> Typically, the head will be conceptually the more autonomous, the modifier the more dependent entity.

Complements and modifiers may be distinguished by another characteristic, namely, by whether they are profiled or not. Within a head-modifier structure, the modifier is not profiled, whereas within a head-complement structure the complement is profiled. The profile of [ON THE TABLE] includes the complement [THE TABLE]; the profile of [THE BOOK ON THE TABLE] does not include the modifier [ON THE TABLE].

12.2.1 Constituent order

In representing the assembly of [THE BOOK ON THE TABLE] in Figure 12.1, I showed the complement to the right of its prepositional head and the modifier to the right of its nominal head, thereby suggesting that the complement follows the head, also that the modifier follows its head. Strictly speaking, these aspects are not part of semantic structure per se; where the head, modifier, and complement are placed on the page in Figure 12.1 is purely a matter of expository convenience. Rather, constituent order is determined by phonological structure. A full account of the expression *the book on the table* would need to show the combination of the phonological poles of the symbolic units which make up the complex expression. It is at the phonological pole that the temporal precedence of *on* with respect to *the table* would be specified; semantic structure itself is inherently unspecified for constituent order.

> ### Joe left the office
>
> The expression *Joe left the office* is assembled out of its parts in much the same way as *the book on the table* — with, however, a significant difference.
>
> *Leave*, like *on*, profiles a relation. The relational concept [LEAVE] can combine with [THE OFFICE] to the extent that [THE OFFICE] elaborates the schematic lm in the verb's semantic structure. (I ignore here, not only the role of the determiner in the nominal, but also the tense of the verb.) [LEAVE THE OFFICE] inherits the profile of [LEAVE], that is to say, *leave the office*, like *leave*, profiles a (complex temporal) relation.
>
> [LEAVE THE OFFICE] combines with [JOE] to the extent that [JOE] can elaborate the schematic tr in the semantic structure of [LEAVE THE OFFICE]. But notice that the resultant expression again inherits the relational profile of [LEAVE THE OFFICE]. The clause *Joe left the office* is headed by *left*; the clause designates an event of leaving, it does not designate Joe.
>
> Both the subject and the direct object of the verb turn out, therefore, to be complements. Subject and object are distinguished by the fact that the subject functions as the tr of the temporal relation, the direct object as its lm.

The reader may find it strange that constituent order is treated as an aspect of phonology. But if you think about it for a moment, constituent order has to be an aspect of phonology. What is constituent order, if not the order in which you *say* the constituents?

12.2.2 Constructional schemas

The assembly of [THE BOOK ON THE TABLE] has countless parallels in English: [THE CAT ON THE MAT], [THE PICTURE ABOVE THE SOFA], [THE EGGS IN THE BASKET], [THE DUST UNDER THE BED]. Each of these complex semantic structures is assembled out of its constituent parts in exactly the same way as [THE BOOK ON THE TABLE]. At the phonological pole, too, the complex expressions are exactly parallel, in that the expressions share the same constituent order.

Abstracting what is common to these, and countless other examples, we obtain a **constructional schema** for the assembly of this kind of expression. In the case in point, the constructional schema specifies the properties (semantic and phonological) of prepositional phrases with the structure $[_{PP} [P] [NP]]$, and noun-modifier expressions with the structure $[_N[N] [_{PP}P\ NP]]$.

Constructional schemas capture generalizations over specific expressions. Syntax, in Cognitive Grammar, reduces essentially to a knowledge of constructional schemas. For example, we can propose a constructional schema that abstracts what is common to verb phrases of the kind *leave the office*, *drive the car*, *push the cart*, and countless more. We could go further, and propose a constructional schema that covers both prepositional phrases of the type [$_{PP}$ [P] [NP]] and verb phrases with the structure [$_{VP}$ [V] [NP]]. What these have in common is that, at the semantic level, they are headed by a relational unit whose schematic lm is elaborated by a nominal expression and which therefore functions as the complement of the head. Phonologically, the schemas specify that the complement follows the head. It is generally the case, in English, that a complement follows its head; English is predominantly[4] a head-first language. By proposing a generalized head-complement schema, Cognitive Grammar can easily capture the phrase-structure generalizations of X-bar theory. For a head-final language, such as Japanese, the head-complement schema would specify that the complement precedes the head.

Constructional schemas have two principal functions. First, constructional schemas have a sanctioning function. They allow expressions which are constructed in conformity with the schemas to be rapidly and reliably categorized and interpreted (and to be judged as fully acceptable in the language). Secondly, the schemas have an enabling function. They facilitate the rapid and effortless creation of an indefinite number of new expressions, in conformity with the specifications of the schema.

12.2.3 Constituency

Figure 12.1 shows the assembly of [THE BOOK ON THE TABLE] as taking place in two stages: first, [ON] combines with [THE TABLE], then [ON THE TABLE] combines with [THE BOOK]. The order in which the elements combine corresponds to the traditional notion of **constituency**. The constituent structure of the expression can be visualized as in Figure 12.2.

Other constituencies can, however, be imagined. For example, in the first stage, [THE BOOK] could combine with [ON], in the second stage, [THE BOOK ON] combines with [THE TABLE]. Alternatively, the complex expression could be formed in a single process, with [THE BOOK] and [THE TABLE] simultaneously

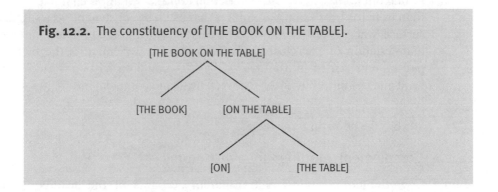

Fig. 12.2. The constituency of [THE BOOK ON THE TABLE].

[THE BOOK ON THE TABLE]

[THE BOOK]   [ON THE TABLE]

[ON]   [THE TABLE]

---

[4] Though not exclusively. For example, *notwithstanding* can both precede and follow its complement: *notwithstanding my protestations, my protestations notwithstanding*.

> ### The constituency of *Joe left the office*
>
> Most syntactic theories would analyse the sentence in the heading above into a subject nominal and a Verb Phrase: [Joe] [left the office]. This analysis is justified by virtue of the 'closeness' of the relation between the verb and its direct object. The verb, for example, imposes quite severe restrictions on the semantic character of its direct object—the verb, in other words, already specifies its lm as a schematic container. In contrast, the verb's tr is specified simply as an entity capable of motion.
>
> As noted in the Box on p. 232, both the subject and the object nominal of a verb have the status of a complement. We should therefore expect the alternative constituency—[Joe left] [the office]—to be viable. There are circumstances in which this latter analysis will need to be invoked:
>
> (a) Joe left, but everyone else entered, the office.
>
> See Langacker (FCG1: 316–21) for further discussion of variable constituency.

elaborating the tr and lm of [ON]. From one point of view, nothing much hinges on which of these alternatives we opt for. What matters is the interpretation that users of a language accord to a complex expression, and this, very often, has little to do with the manner in which the complex expression can be assembled. Having said this, there are certainly some grounds for preferring the constituency shown in Figure 12.2. Foremost among these is the fact that head and complement stand in a 'closer' semantic relation to each other than head and modifier. Recall that in a head-complement construction the complement is part of the expression's profile; the complement is 'intrinsic' to the profile. In a head-modifier construction the modifier is not part of the profile; the modifier is in a sense an optional extra. Moreover, a relational profile often imposes tighter restrictions on the semantic character of its lm than its tr. [ON], for example, requires that its lm be construable as a supporting surface, whereas restrictions on the character of the tr are much looser. One manifestation of the 'closeness' of head and complement is the fact that a pause—represented in example (5) by '#'—could easily be inserted between head and modifier, but hardly between head and complement:

(5) a. the book # on the table
     b. *the book on # the table

12.2.4 Complement/modifier not a dichotomy

Cognitive Grammar offers transparent accounts of the head-complement and the head-modifier relations. These syntactic relations play a fundamental role in most grammatical theories. In contrast with other theories, however, Cognitive Grammar does not take the head-complement and the head-modifier relations to be mutually exclusive. It is quite possible for an expression to exhibit facets of both relations. Consider (6):

(6) father of twins

On the one hand, this expression is exactly analogous to *book on the table*. [FATHER] elaborates the schematic tr in the semantic structure of [OF TWINS]. *Of twins* is therefore a modifier of *father*. On the other hand, *father*, unlike *book*, is an intrinsically relational noun; a father has to be the father *of* someone, whereas a book does not have to be a book in a certain location. To this extent, [OF TWINS] elaborates a schematic relation present in the semantic structure of [FATHER] and for this reason takes on features of a complement. We shall have to say that *of twins* exhibits features of both a modifier and a complement of *father*.

This situation is far from unusual, and would be problematic only in a grammatical theory that stipulates a unique syntactic analysis for each (non-ambiguous) expression. In Cognitive Grammar, we can simply say that the complex expression simultaneously satisfies the requirements of two different constructional schemas, the head-modifier schema and the head-complement schema.

12.3 Apposition

The foregoing analysis of [THE BOOK ON THE TABLE] enabled us to exemplify, and to define, three key grammatical notions: head, complement, and modifier. The question arises whether the head-complement and the head-modifier relations are themselves sufficient to describe all cases of conceptual combination. In fact, we need to recognize a third syntagmatic relation, that of **apposition**.

> Apposition. In an expression XY, X and Y are in apposition if X and Y each designate one and the same entity.

Apposition is a grammatical relation that is largely ignored in recent syntactic theory. (If you search the subject index of many recent introductions to syntax, you will probably draw a blank.) Nevertheless, the notion was well recognized in older grammatical theories, in school grammars of Latin, for example.

In an appositional relation, each component designates one and the same entity, but does so in different ways (or with different degrees of specificity). They combine to form a more elaborate conception of the entity. Some examples are shown in example (7). In (7a), one and the same person is characterized, first as 'my neighbour', and also as 'the butcher'. The person is construed, first, in terms of a relation to the speaker, second, in terms of their profession. The two designations combine to form a more complex designation of the person, namely, of the person *both* as a neighbour *and* as a butcher (Fig. 12.3). In (7b), a point in time is characterized, not only as coinciding with the moment of speaking, but also in terms of conventional clock-time. In (7e), a location is specified in two alternative ways, *down there* and *on the ground*; in combination, a more precise designation is achieved. In (7f), (7g), and (7h) the speaker attempts to explain, elaborate, or rephrase an expression already introduced, thereby rendering it more specific.

(7) a. my neighbour, the butcher
    b. now, at midnight
    c. Tomorrow, Tuesday
    d. We the people
    e. down there on the ground
    f. We were amazed, stunned, by the event.
    g. He ran—absolutely raced—up the hill.
    h. They sent him to Coventry, refused to speak to him.

Do appositional expressions have a head? The head is that constituent which contributes its profile to the profile of the complex expression. In an appositional relation, the complex structure, and each of the component structures, all profile one and the same entity. It is as if an appositional relation has two heads. This is represented in Figure 12.3 by the heavy boxes surrounding each of the constituent expressions; each constituent contributes its profile to the complex expression.

Nevertheless, it is generally the case that one of the two elements in

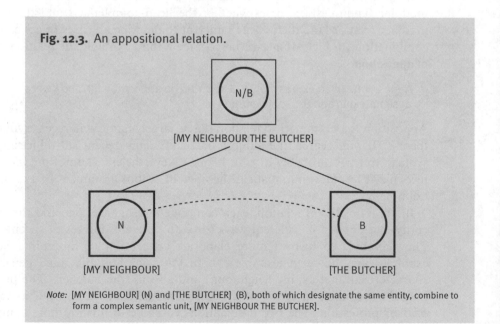

Fig. 12.3. An appositional relation.

[MY NEIGHBOUR THE BUTCHER]

[MY NEIGHBOUR]   [THE BUTCHER]

Note: [MY NEIGHBOUR] (N) and [THE BUTCHER] (B), both of which designate the same entity, combine to form a complex semantic unit, [MY NEIGHBOUR THE BUTCHER].

apposition does take precedence over the other. (The order of the constituents is also relevant here.) Compare:

(8) a. You the butcher are . . .
     b. *You the butcher is . . .
     c. *The butcher, you, is. . . .

Verb agreement in (a) and (b) suggests that the profiled individual is construed, primarily, as the addressee, not as the butcher. [THE BUTCHER] would have to be regarded as a modifier of [YOU], in that it gives additional conceptual substance to the first element. Symptomatic of this asymmetry is the fact that the two elements within the appositional relation are not easily reversible (8c).[5]

We conclude that *you the butcher* exhibits features of both apposition and modification.[6] The conclusion is not at all problematic. Just as relations of modifier and complement are not mutually exclusive, neither are relations of apposition and modification. The following combine elements of apposition and complementation:

(9) a. [The fact] [that the Earth is flat] must be obvious to everyone.
     b. [The question] [why they did that] is still unanswered.

A fact is necessarily a fact *that* something is the case. *That the Earth is flat* elaborates a notion that is schematically present in the semantic structure of *fact*. *That the Earth is flat* can therefore be regarded as the complement of *fact*. At the same time, *the fact* and *that the Earth is flat* are both nominals—both designate the same entity (i.e. the same 'fact'), and either can stand as the subject of a sentence:

(10) a. [The fact] must be obvious to everyone.
      b. [That the Earth is flat] must be obvious to everyone.

Appositional relations are sometimes found in nominal compounds:

(11) girl-friend; student-teacher; woman doctor; child prodigy; poet-painter

A person's girl-friend is both a friend and a girl. Here, it is the second element that takes on head properties, the first element being a modifier; a girl-friend is a kind of friend, not a kind of girl. If the compound is pluralized, the plural morpheme attaches only to the second element, not to the first, or to both:

---

[5] Several of the expressions in (7) are, of course, reversible, with, however, subtle semantic effects. A statement about 'my neighbour the butcher' would be primarily a statement about my neighbour, in contrast to a statement about 'the butcher my neighbour', which would be primarily about the butcher.

[6] Acuña-Fariña (1999)—from whom some of the examples in (7) are taken—finds symptoms of modification in many instances of apposition. However, since he attributes distinct, and incompatible, phrase structures to apposition and modification, he is forced to choose between one or the other analyses. Examples of sentences which, he claims, lack modification, and which are therefore 'pure' apposition, include (7g) and (7h).

girl-friends, *girls-friends, *girls-friend. (On the other hand, *women doctors* 'doctors who are women' is possible, alongside *woman doctors*.) Symptomatic of the asymmetry is the only limited possibility of reversing the two elements within a compound. Even when reversal is possible (*poet-painter* vs. *painter-poet*), there is a subtle difference in the salience of the two component entities.

12.3.1 Appositional 'of'

Some syntactic phenomena need to be understood specifically in terms of the apposition relation. For example, one of the semantic values of *of* is to join elements in apposition:

(12)   the crime of shoplifting
　　　 the Island of Madeira
　　　 the State of California
　　　 a feeling of despair
　　　 the thought of going there alone
　　　 the question of where to go
　　　 the fact of his absence

In *the crime of shoplifting*, one and the same entity is characterized, first, as a crime, and secondly, as shoplifting. The first element, *crime*, has a rather schematic profile, the second, *shoplifting*, is more fully specified. By virtue of the appositional relation, 'the crime' is elaborated as 'shoplifting', while 'shoplifting' is categorized as 'a crime'.

A similar situation holds in the following. In each case the first constituent is a so-called epithet; the epithet has a highly schematic profile, with speaker attitude towards the profiled entity very prominent in the base. The second constituent elaborates the epithet's profile.

(13)   a beast of a problem
　　　 an angel of a girl
　　　 that bastard of a man

Not only *of*, but also, in some cases, *as to* can serve to link elements in apposition. Again, the second constituent elaborates the schematic profile of the first.

(14)   [the question] [what to do]
　　　 [the question] of [what to do]
　　　 [the question] as to [what to do]

12.4 Parataxis

In this chapter I have discussed three mechanisms for combining simpler semantic units into more complex structures: complementation, modification, and apposition.

Do all expressions have a head?

The relations of modification, complementation, and apposition have this in common: they each entail that a complex expression has a head (in the case of apposition, there may be two heads). Expressions with a head are often called 'endocentric'. Some syntactic theories propose the endocentric constraint—all complex expressions must have a head. Headless ('exocentric') expressions do, however, exist. A classic example is noun compounds of the kind *pick-pocket*. A pick-pocket is not a kind of pocket, nor does it designate the process of picking a pocket, it designates a person who habitually picks pockets. The profile of the complex expression is not inherited from the profile of either of its constituents.

It can happen that speakers use none of these combinatorial devices, and simply line up linguistic expressions, one after the other, with no conceptual (or phonological) integration. The phenomenon is known as **parataxis**. Clauses, and, especially, sentences within a larger text can be lined up in this way.

(15) a. I came, I saw, I conquered.
     b. Your proposal, people are bound to have reservations.

The speaker in (15a) could have chosen to overtly mark the relations between these clauses, by means of linking elements such as *then*, and *finally*. Without these overt linking elements, the relations between the clauses in (15a) have to be inferred by the hearer. Parataxis is also evident in (15b). There is no overt link between *your proposal* and the clause that follows it; the nominal simply sets the context within which the clause is to be understood.

Study questions

1. Head, complement, modifier

   (a) Check out the definitions and explanations of these concepts in some of the standard textbooks on syntax. A good place to start is ch. 4 of Radford's *Introduction to Transformational Grammar* (1988). A more sophisticated account may be found in Borsley's *Syntactic Theory* (1999); this book compares ways of formalizing the head-complement relation in different syntactic theories.

   Apply the Cognitive Grammar account of head, complement, and modifier to some of the examples discussed by these authors. To what extent is the Cognitive Grammar account of these notions compatible with those of other theories?

   (b) It is often claimed that complements need to stand adjacent to their heads, whereas modifiers can be displaced. The following are from Radford (1988):

       (i) the student [of physics] [with long hair]
       (ii) *the student [with long hair] [of physics]

The unacceptability of (ii) would be due to the fact that *with long hair* is a modifier, which cannot intervene between the head (*student*) and its complement (*of physics*). Discuss this analysis in Cognitive Grammar terms.

What about the following? Both seem equally acceptable. What is the status of the two phrases *about physics* and *on the table*?

(iii) a book [about physics] [on the table]

(iv) a book [on the table] [about physics]

2. *Of* as a profiler of an intrinsic relation. One of the functions of *of* is to profile an intrinsic relation between a head and a complement. In *a student of physics*, the relation is intrinsic in that a student is necessarily a student of something; the subject studied is in the (unprofiled) base of the semantic structure of *student*.

How would you account for the acceptability of the phrases in (i) in contrast to the relative unacceptability of the phrases in (ii)?

(i) <u>acceptable</u>:
the story of her life
a biography of Stalin
a photograph of me at age 5
the author of the book
a portrait of Churchill

(ii) <u>more or less unacceptable</u>:
a novel of her life ('a novel which describes her life')
the novelist of the book ('the novelist who wrote the book')
a butcher of beef ('a butcher who processes and deals in beef')
a grocer of vegetables
a car of me ('a car that belongs to me')
a pupil of physics ('a pupil who studies physics')
a schoolgirl of mathematics ('a schoolgirl who studies mathematics')
the artist of the portrait ('the artist who painted the portrait')
the carpenter of the cupboard ('the carpenter who made the cupboard')

What about the following? To my mind, they are all unacceptable (though intuitions might vary slightly from example to example).

(iii) <u>unacceptable</u>:
the car designer of the Ferrari
the physics student of thermodynamics
the linguistics professor of syntax
the opera composer of *Aida*
the clothes designer of the outfit
Sam's father of Louise (= Sam's father is the father of Louise)

3. Profile shift. Generally, a linguistic expression has a more or less constant profile, irrespective of the contexts in which it is used. However, the nature of an expression's profile sometimes can change, depending on the context. Compare:

(i) the book [under the bed]

(ii) Take the book from [under the bed]

(iii) the chair [by the fire]

(iv) [By the fire] is nice and warm.

(v) Is [by the fire] nice and warm?

The bracketed phrases in (i) and (iii) have relational profiles, as discussed in this chapter. How would you characterize the profiles in (ii) and (iv)? For many speakers, (v) is fully acceptable. What does this suggest about the profile of *by the fire*?

4. Elaboration. Although relational concepts are, almost by definition, conceptually dependent, there are considerable differences with respect to the need to elaborate schematic entities that are present in their semantic structure. Three different cases are addressed below.

(a) Direct object omission. Compare:

(i)   I have eaten.

(ii)   *I have devoured.

(iii) *I have ingested.

(iv)   *I have consumed.

The verbs *eat*, *devour*, *ingest*, and *consume* profile similar processes; all inherently involve a lm entity (the food that is eaten, devoured, etc.). Yet *eat* can be used without overt elaboration of the lm, the others cannot.

Fillmore (1986) cites several examples of this phenomenon. The verbs in the left column readily allow the omission of their complements, the semantically rather similar verbs in the second column do not.

She promised	*She pledged, vowed, guaranteed
I tried	*I attempted
Her mother insisted	*Her mother required/demanded

Cases such as these are often cited as evidence for the autonomy of syntax *vis-à-vis* semantics. Why? How would you propose to counter the arguments?

(b) Make a list of verbs which designate caused motion, that is, verbs which designate an event in which an agent causes an entity to move from one place, along a path, to another place. Your list will include *put, move, push, pull, send*, and several more.

Consider the syntactic properties of these verbs. Is the elaboration of the lm (the thing that is caused to move) obligatory or optional? Is the expression of Source (where the thing is moved from), Path, and Goal optional, obligatory, or even prohibited? The most schematic of the caused motion verbs is probably *put*. Does *put* stand out from the others in any ways?

(c) Relational nouns, too, differ with respect to the need for the unprofiled lm in their semantic structure to be explicitly elaborated. Prepare a list of relational nouns. Possible examples include *father, ancestor, top, edge, corner, side, writer, dancer*.

Collect examples of how these words are used. (You might pull out at random some citations from a corpus.)

Is there a tendency for some of these words always to co-occur with an overt mention of the unprofiled lm in their semantic structure? Do you observe a tendency for some of these words to be used with a possessive, or with the definite determiner *the*? What could be the significance of this?

Further reading

Dependence and valence relations are discussed in Langacker (FCG1: ch. 8). Apposition is briefly mentioned in Langacker (FCG2: 149), also in Taylor (1996: 96–7). There are good discussion of apposition in Matthews (1981) and in Acuña-Fariña (1999).

Examples similar to *the book on the table* have been discussed in many places in the Cognitive Grammar literature. See, for example, Langacker (1990: 25–7).

CHAPTER 13

Syntagmatic relations in phonology

Given the bipolar nature of symbolic units, the combination of symbolic units into more complex units has to proceed simultaneously on the semantic and phonological levels.

In Chapter 12 we looked at how semantic units combine to form more complex units. In this chapter, I examine combination at the phonological level. We shall find that many of the principles of semantic combination are relevant to phonological combination. Notions such as dependence vs. autonomy, valence, valence relation, constructional schema, and even head and modifier, can be easily and insightfully applied to the phonological domain.

13.1 Phonological autonomy and phonological dependence

I began Chapter 12 by discussing the notions of autonomy and dependence with reference to semantic units. These notions are also applicable to phonological units. Just as an autonomous semantic unit is one that can be conceptualized by itself, without the need to invoke other semantic units, so an autonomous phonological unit is one which can be articulated by itself, without the support of other phonological units. A phonologically dependent unit is one whose articulation requires the support of other phonological units and which therefore cannot stand alone.

Phonological autonomy and phonological dependence do not stand in an either/or relation, but rather form a continuum (as was the case in semantics). Consonants, on the whole, are more dependent than vowels, in that consonants generally require the support of a vowel, whereas vowels, in general, can be articulated as single-segment utterances. Consider, for example, the oral stops, such as [p] and [b]. It is simply not possible to articulate these consonants without the support of another segment, typically a vowel. Try to say [b] by itself, and inevitably you have a 'ghost' vowel, probably schwa-like. Glides, such as [j] and [w], which are produced by a rapid movement of the articulators, either from, or more commonly towards a vowel articulation, are also dependent. It is impossible in principle to articulate a [j] or a [w] without a supporting vowel. On the other hand, consonants which consist of a prolonged steady-state, such as the fricatives and nasals, can easily be articulated in isolation; their articulation can even be lengthened so as to endure for a full period of breath exhalation. In fact, such sounds can have a marginal status within a linguistic system. In English, a prolonged [ʃ:::] can be used as a request for silence, while a prolonged [m:::], depending on the pitch contour it is associated with, can signal agreement, surprise, or simply the hearer's continued attentiveness.

There are some obvious correlations between the phonological autonomy of a segment and its sonority. In general, the more sonorous segments (such as the vowels) are likely to be phonologically more autonomous, while less sonorous segments (such as the stops) are likely to be phonologically dependent. The correlation, however, is far from perfect. The glides [j, w] are quite high on the sonority hierarchy but are phonologically dependent.

We should also bear in mind that the autonomy/dependence of a segment not only has to do with its inherent (phonetic) properties, it also is a function of the phonological system of a particular language. From a purely phonetic (language-independent) perspective, we should say that vowels are autonomous. However, as noted in section 5.3, most English speakers find it difficult to articulate a vowel without the support of an initial consonant, the default being the glottal stop [ʔ]. Strictly speaking, not even the vowels are phonologically autonomous in most accents of English. A similar state of affairs probably holds for other Germanic languages—not, however, for Romance languages. French speakers have no difficulty in articulating a vowel without the support of an onset consonant.

The vowels of English differ among themselves with respect to their relative autonomy. The English vowels can be divided into two broad classes (section 8.1.2), the so-called short vowels and the long vowels. When stressed, the short vowels only occur in closed syllables, that is, the vowels must be followed by a consonant in syllable-coda position. An isolated utterance of the vowels [æ, ɛ, ɪ, ɒ, ʊ, ʌ, ə]—even if the vowels are preceded by a glottal onset—is phonologically deviant in English. In comparison, the long vowels, which can occur in open syllables, show a higher degree of phonological autonomy.

The phonological dependence of stop consonants

The phonological dependence of a stop consonant follows as a matter of course from the way in which a stop is articulated. The following is a schematic illustration of the different stages of a stop articulation.

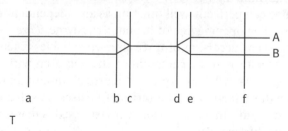

A and B represent the articulators involved in producing the stop—upper and lower lip in the case of a bilabial, tongue blade and alveolar ridge in the case of alveolars, the vocal folds in the case of the glottal stop. The arrow represents the passage of time. The stop consists in bringing the two articulators together, in time segment b–c, from a previous state in which the articulators were separated (time segment a–b). The closure is held for a short period (segment c–d), typically around 100 msecs. Thereafter the articulators move apart (d–e), and there then follows a segment in which the articulators are no longer in contact (e–f).

The distinctive articulatory posture associated with a stop resides in complete closure of the vocal tract. Unless there is activity at the glottis during time segment c–d, closure is associated with a period of silence. Paradoxical as it might seem, the essential (one might even say, the defining) component of a stop consonant— the component which makes the segment a stop, and not, say, a fricative—is silence. And silence is the same, whatever the stop's place of articulation. While a 100-msec. period of a silence might be a reliable acoustic cue for the presence of a stop consonant, cues to place of articulation can only be found in the closing and release gestures. However, the trajectory of the articulators during closure and release depends, not only on the place of articulation of the stop, but also on the identity of the segments adjacent to the stop. The trajectories associated with [idi] are not the same as those associated with [udu] and [ada].

Several things follow. First, in order to count as a speech sound at all, a stop has to occur in association with another segment. If I simply keep my lips closed I cannot be said to be articulating a bilabial stop. For lip closure to count as a consonant, there has to be a preceding or a following segment in which the lips are not closed. Secondly, as argued many years ago in a classic paper by Liberman *et al.* (1967), the acoustic cues for the identification of a stop vary according to the identity of the adjacent sounds. There are no invariant acoustic cues for, say, [d] in contrast to [g]. This follows from the fact that there is no unique articulatory trajectory associated with [d] or with [g]. The trajectory has to involve movement of the articulators from, or towards, an adjacent segment.

We can also apply the notions of autonomy and dependence to syllables. Take the contrast between stressed and unstressed syllables. On the one hand, we could argue that stress is a relational notion. A stressed syllable is such only in contrast to an unstressed syllable, while a syllable can only be described as unstressed if there is a stressed syllable with which it contrasts. Nevertheless, there is clearly an asymmetry between stressed and unstressed syllables. A single stressed syllable can perfectly well function as an independent utterance, as in *Yes, No, Please*. The opening line of the nursery rhyme, *Three blind mice*, could well be spoken as a succession of three stressed syllables (each of which constitutes a foot), which would be perceived as stressed even without a contrast with intervening weak syllables. An isolated articulation of an unstressed syllable, however, or the articulation of a series of unstressed syllables, would be phonologically deviant. In comparison with stressed syllables, a weak syllable is phonologically dependent.

Again, there are language-specific constraints. English readily tolerates a one-syllable foot (i.e. a strong without an associated weak), which may even function as a full utterance. In many languages (disregarding marginal cases of interjections, ideophones, and perhaps words signalling assent or dissent), an utterance has to be at least bisyllabic.

13.2 Valence relations in phonology

In the last chapter I illustrated the combination of semantic units of the example of [THE BOOK ON THE TABLE]. In order to bring out the parallels between semantic and phonological organization, let us consider the phonological combination of the units [b] and [ɑː] into the syllable [bɑː].

The consonant [b] is phonologically dependent, in that the sound needs to attach itself to a neighbouring sound. One possibility is that it attaches to a following vowel and thereby functions as a syllable onset. Since any of the English vowels are candidates for combination, we can represent the situation as follows:

(1)

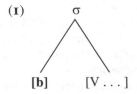

In example (1), [V] is a schematic vowel, [...] represents an optional coda, and σ is a syllable. The bold character represents the phonological unit under consideration, non-bold represents the context necessary for the articulation of the unit. There is an obvious (and intended) affinity with the profile-base relation introduced in connection with word meaning. The bold segment [b]

'designates' the consonant, but the consonant has to be 'conceptualized' against a larger phonological unit, i.e. a syllable.

Alternative pictographic representations of (1) can be entertained. Langacker (FCG1: 330) has used the device of concentric ovals, as in example (2a). A more compact, but perhaps less graphic way of representing the facts in (1), is shown in (2b).

(**2**) a.

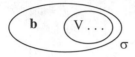

  b. [[**b**] [V . . .]]_σ

We now turn to the vowel. The vowel [ɑː], though relatively autonomous, requires a syllable onset. Again, there are no specific requirements as to the identity of the onset; any consonant can occupy the position. This aspect of the vowel can be represented as follows:

(**3**)   σ

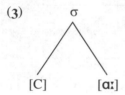

  [C]   [ɑː]

The two elements, [b] and [ɑː], are able to combine in that the schematic vowel present in the phonological structure of |b| can be construed as identical to the 'profile' of the phonological structure of [ɑː]; likewise, the schematic onset in the structure of [ɑː] can be unified with the profile of [b]. The two segments can therefore enter a valence relation, as shown in Figure 13.1. By the usual convention, the dotted lines in the Figure signify the correspondence relations between elements in the respective phonological structures.

A substantially similar account could be given for the assembly of any CV syllable. In fact, we could generalize from the representation of [b] in example (1) to a representation of any consonant—(4a). Similarly, we could generalize from the representation of [ɑː] in example (3) to a representation of any vowel as in example (4b).

(**4**) a. [[**C**] [V . . .]]_σ
      b. [[C] [V . . .]]_σ

The combination of these units, in the manner depicted in Figure 13.1, amounts to a constructional schema for a [CV] syllable.

A full description of the phonology of a language would comprise a large number of representations of the kind that have been illustrated. The combinatorial properties of a given segment, or class of segments, are stated in

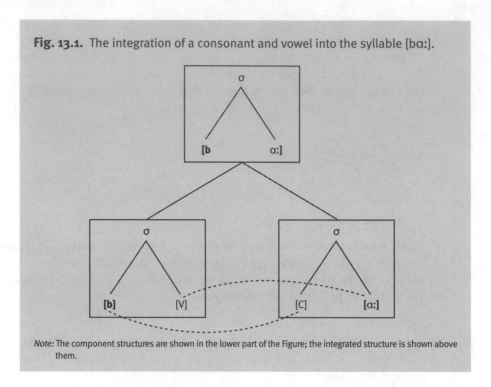

Fig. 13.1. The integration of a consonant and vowel into the syllable [bɑː].

Note: The component structures are shown in the lower part of the Figure; the integrated structure is shown above them.

terms of the segment's 'valence', in the manner of examples (1) and (3), while patterns of combination are stated in constructional schemas, in the manner of Figure 13.1. Both kinds of representation may be structured in the familiar schema-instance relations.

Let us consider a couple of examples:

(i) The aspirated stops [pʰ, tʰ, kʰ] share the property that they occur only in onset position before a stressed vowel. The special distribution of [pʰ] can therefore be represented as in example (5), where the subscript 'σs' characterizes the syllable as 'strong' (i.e. stressed).

(5) [[**pʰ**] [V . . .]]$_{\sigma s}$

Parallel representations are indicated for [tʰ] and [kʰ]. The similarity between these allows the formation of schema which states the valence of a segment that is schematic for [pʰ, tʰ, kʰ]. The relation is illustrated in Figure 13.2.

It will be observed that the schematic representation in Figure 13.2 is itself an instance of the more general representation of an onset consonant, namely [[**C**] [V . . .]]$_{\sigma}$ (4a). Likewise, the combination of an aspirated voiceless stop with a vowel within a stressed syllable allows the emergence of a constructional schema for a specific kind of syllable. On the basis of these examples, we see how statements of the phonotactic constraints of a language (that is, statements of the combinatorial possibilities of segments within larger

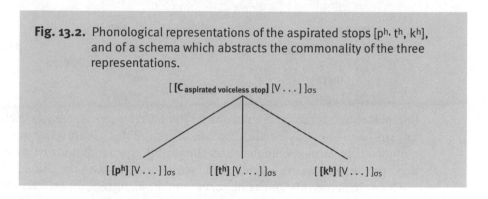

Fig. 13.2. Phonological representations of the aspirated stops [pʰ, tʰ, kʰ], and of a schema which abstracts the commonality of the three representations.

units, such as the syllable) are able to be organized in a network of schema-instance relations.

(ii) The short vowels of English. The distinctive distribution of the short vowels concerns the properties of the syllable rhyme in which they occur. Within a stressed syllable, the short vowel has to be followed by at least one consonant in coda position. This aspect is represented in (6a). A more 'compact' representation in shown in (6b).

(6) a.

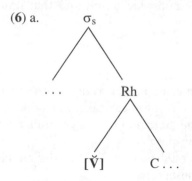

b. $[[[\breve{V}] C \dots]_{rhyme}]_{\sigma s}$

(iii) The representation in (1) does not exhaust the distributional possibilities of [b]. The consonant can occur not only as syllable onset (*bad*) but also as syllable coda (*tab*), as part of a stop + liquid onset cluster (*brat*, *blob*), and as part of a liquid + stop coda cluster (*bulb*). The consonant can also occur with [j], but only in the structure [bjuː . . .].

The possibility of [b] occurring as a syllable coda is represented in example (7a). The stop + liquid onset clusters [br] and [bl] can be represented separately, as in (7b) and (7c); these can also be brought under a more schematic representation (7d), in which 'L' is a liquid; that is, a segment schematic for [l] and [r].

(7) a. [. . . **[b]**]$_\sigma$
   b. [[**[b]** r] [V . . .]]$_\sigma$
   c. [[**[b]** l] [V . . .]]$_\sigma$
   d. [[**[b]** L] [V . . .]]$_\sigma$
   e. [. . . [l **[b]**]]$_\sigma$
   f. [[**[b]** j] uː . . .]$_\sigma$

In a non-rhotic accent, the coda cluster [lb] must be represented as such (7e); since [rb] is an impossible coda, there are no grounds for a more schematic representation [Lb]. Concerning the onset cluster [bj], this again must be stated in a very specific way; the cluster only occurs in association with the vowel [uː] (7f).

There are numerous similarities between the valences of [b] and the valences of 'similar' sounds, such as the voiced stops [d, g], the voiceless bilabial stop [p], and indeed the class of stops in general. These similarities allow the emergence of the appropriate schemas. Nevertheless, each of the six stops exhibits a distribution which is slightly different from that of all the others. For example, [t, d, k, g] can occur in onset clusters with both [juː] and [w] (*tune, dune, cue, gules*; *twin, dwindle, queen, Gwen*), whereas the clusters [bw] and [pw] are not attested. Whereas the codas [mp, nd, nt, ŋk] are possible, [b] and [g] are excluded from occurring in a nasal + stop coda. Facts such as these raise the question of how to represent 'negative' facts about an item's distribution, for example, the fact that [bw] is an impossible onset, and that [mb] is an impossible coda. I address the topic below.

13.2.1 Phonotactic restrictions

The astute reader may have noted that example (4a) is not quite accurate for English. The representation implies that a vowel can take, as its onset, any of the consonants of English. There is one exception to this generalization—the velar nasal [ŋ] may not occur in onset position.

One way of representing this fact would be to state the ungrammaticality of a syllable with the velar nasal as its onset (8).

(8) *[[ŋ] [V . . .]]$_\sigma$

Stipulations of ungrammaticality are problematic in a usage-based model such as Cognitive Grammar. A person's knowledge of their language is based on encounters with actually occurring expressions. Similarities across actually encountered expressions allow the extraction of schemas of varying degrees of abstraction. The schemas serve a dual function. On the one hand, they allow a speaker to categorize newly encountered expressions. They also allow a speaker to produce new expressions in accordance with the schemas. Within a usage-based model, therefore, there is no place for negative statements. To claim that a particular form is 'ungrammatical' is tantamount to saying that the form has never been encountered and that there is no schema which can sanction it. The grammar of a language comprises only 'positive statements' about what does occur, there is no need for 'negative statements' of what does not occur (cf. Langacker 1999: 120).

The 'positive statements' comprise schemas of varying levels of abstraction. The representation of [ɑː] in (1)—in particular, the claim that [ɑː] can take as its onset any of the consonants of English—is already highly schematic. It represents the commonalities that speakers have extracted on the basis of innumerable encounters with specific syllables. Alongside the general schema for a syllable-onset consonant, however, there exist more specific schemas concerning individual sounds (such as [pʰ]), classes of sounds (the aspirated stops), and so on. We need to postulate these low-level schemas if for no other reason than to capture the relative frequency of the different consonants in onset position. A quick glance through any English dictionary shows that the number of words commencing in 's' is many times greater than the number of words commencing in 'z'.[1] The schema for [s] in onset position, because it has been encountered more often, is more entrenched than the schema for [z] in onset position. More generally, voiceless obstruents are more frequent in onset position than voiced obstruents. Conspicuous by its absence among these lower-level schemas is a schema for syllables commencing in [ŋ]. This segment is unusual in other respects, too. It can occur in syllable coda position, but only after a short vowel. Even among the short vowels, its occurrence after [ʊ] is not attested and its occurrence after [ɛ] is rather rare. These peculiarities of [ŋ] suggest that the segment is indeed associated with very specific representations, which override more schematic representations.

There is a general principle to be drawn from these observations. Higher- and lower-level schemas serve different functions. High-level schemas represent broad generalizations. They provide a broad framework within which the facts of a language can be organized. The high level schemas, however, do not normally allow predictions to be made concerning exactly what is, and what is not, possible in a given language. This is the job of lower-level schemas. In the limiting case, the schemas are specific to individual forms. It is for this reason that schemas of varying degrees of generality need to coexist within the grammar. Langacker, in fact, suggests that the lower-level schemas may, on balance, carry a heavier burden than the high-level schemas.

Lower-level schemas, expressing regularities of only limited scope, may on balance be more essential to language structure than high-level schemas representing the broadest generalizations. A higher-level schema implicitly defines a large 'space' of potential instantiations. Often, however, instantiations cluster in certain regions of that space, leaving other regions sparsely inhabited or uninhabited altogether. An adequate description of linguistic convention must therefore provide the details of how the space has actually been colonized. Providing this information is

---

[1] The incidence of orthographic 's' and 'z' at the beginnings of words cannot, obviously, be equated with the incidence of the sounds [s] and [z] in syllable onset position. The orthographic facts, though, can reasonably be taken as symptomatic of the relative frequencies of the sounds in onset position.

an elaborate network of conventional units including both constructional sub-schemas at various levels and instantiating expressions with unit status. For many constructions, the essential distributional information is supplied by lower-level schemas and specific instantiations. (Langacker 1999: 118)

I return to the roles of higher- and lower-level schemas in Chapter 16, under the rubric of 'schema competition'.

'Head', 'complement', 'modifier', and 'apposition' in phonology?

To what extent are the terms 'head', 'complement', 'modifier', and 'apposition', which are so central in the study of semantic structures, relevant to phonological combination?

While I would not want to push the analogies too far, there is a sense in which one could say that a vowel 'heads' the syllable, in that a syllable has to contain a vowel (or a highly sonorous, vowel-like unit), and the syllable 'inherits' its essential nucleus from the vowel. If this is so, then the initial consonant would count as the modifier to the vowel. (The vowel, as head, elaborates a salient element within the phonological structure of the consonant.) On the other hand, in a closed syllable with a short vowel, the coda consonant would count as the complement. (The coda consonant elaborates an element in the phonological structure of the vowel.) Likewise, in a $[\sigma_s \; \sigma_w]$ foot, we should say that the strong syllable is the head, the weak syllable the modifier. The relation of apposition, however, would seem to have no obvious applications in phonology.

13.3 Phonological constructions: More on the filled-onset requirement

In this section I illustrate the role of phonological constructional schemas on a specific example. I return, for this purpose, to the filled-onset requirement, briefly introduced in section 5.3, and consider how the facts can be represented within a Cognitive Grammar approach. (The discussion to follow, like that in section 5.3, applies primarily to non-rhotic accents of English.)

According to the filled-onset requirement, every syllable in (most accents of) English has to have a filled onset. When it comes to pronouncing a word which commences in a vowel, four strategies are available for satisfying the filled-onset requirement: consonant sharing, glide insertion, r-insertion, and glottal-stop insertion.

Of the four onset-filling strategies, glottal-stop insertion has a rather special status. Whereas consonant sharing, glide insertion, and r-insertion are each restricted to a specific phonological environment, glottal-stop insertion can in principle occur before any vowel-commencing word, thereby overriding the other strategies. There is, moreover, considerable variation in this respect. The variation has a number of sources:

(i) Phonological. All other things being equal, glottal stop insertion is more likely before a stressed vowel than before an unstressed vowel.

(ii) Stylistic. Probably, in slow, careful, and clearly articulated speech, all English speakers will make increased use of glottal-stop insertion, especially before words commencing with a stressed syllable and before words which the speaker wishes to render particularly prominent. Conversely, rapid, informal speech may well be associated with a reduced incidence of glottal-stop insertion.

(iii) Dialectal. Among non-rhotic accents there is considerable variation with respect to the preference for glottal-stop insertion. South African English is characterized by a particularly high incidence of glottal-stop insertion, even in rapid, informal style, and even before unstressed syllables. Thus *Is it?*, for a South African, could well come out as ['ʔɪz ʔɪt]. South Africans might even insert a glottal stop before a stressed syllable within a word: *cre[ʔ]ation*, *ge[ʔ]ography*.[2] Speakers of New Zealand English, on the other hand, tend to favour r-insertion, whenever appropriate, even within a word; hence *withdrawal* [wɔθ.drɔː.rəl].[3]

(iv) Lexical. The preference for glottal-stop insertion over the other strategies may depend on the identity of one or the other of the juxtaposed words. Consider the traditional distinction between the so-called linking 'r' and the intrusive 'r' (p. 89). To the extent that speakers might avoid the intrusive 'r', the distinction essentially boils down to the fact that certain words whose pronunciation terminates in a non-high vowel are less likely to trigger r-insertion than others. The words, on the whole, are those whose orthographic form lacks a final 'r'.

The choice between r-insertion and glottal-stop insertion may also depend on the identity of the vowel-commencing word. I already mentioned (p. 90) the possible contrast between *for ever* and *for Ellen*. (I remind the reader that I presuppose a non-rhotic accent of English.) These are segmentally and rhythmically very similar. However, in my speech, the first is more likely to have an inserted 'r', the second a glottal-stop. Two factors may be relevant. The first is the relative frequency of the vowel-commencing word: it could be that less frequent words favour glottal-stop insertion. The second is the frequency of the word combination itself. *For ever* is a fixed, routinized, and rather frequent expression; *for Ellen* (at least, for

---

[2] Some South African speakers, especially those whose mother tongue is Afrikaans, have a further onset-filling strategy. This is the insertion of breathy-voiced [ɦ] before stressed vowels. I remember former South African President F. W. de Klerk, in his speeches, talking about 'the creation [kriːˈɦeiʃən] of a New South Africa'.

[3] Some of my New Zealand students report that they find it impossible to pronounce the word *withdrawal* without the inserted [r], so powerful is the filled-onset requirement!

speakers who are not acquainted with persons called Ellen, such as myself) is not.

(v) Syntactic. Another potential source of variation is the syntactic relation between the juxtaposed forms. It is possible that glottal-stop insertion might be preferred if there is a major syntactic break between the two words. On the other hand, r-insertion is certainly possible even between items which are not closely related syntactically. It can occur, even, between clauses:

(9) Where's the butter? (r)I can't find it anywhere.

Let us now turn to the question of how the four onset-filling strategies are to be represented. One option—the one traditionally adopted in phonological theory—is to describe the processes in terms of rules. The rules take as input the individual words as listed in the lexicon. The rules perform whatever operations are necessary in order to give, as output, the phonological form that is actually pronounced. The so-called linking 'r' might be handled by a rule of r-deletion—word-final [r] is assumed to be present in the 'underlying form' of a word but is deleted if the following word fails to begin with a vowel. On the other hand, the so-called intrusive 'r' requires a rule of r-insertion; an [r] is inserted between a vowel and a preceding non-high vowel. Other rules would account for glide insertion and consonant sharing.

Rules of this kind are problematic for a number of reasons. First, the postulation of different rules obscures the fact that the different strategies all serve a common purpose—they are implemented in order to satisfy, albeit in different ways, the filled-onset requirement. We need to focus, not only on the input and its transformation, but also on properties of the output, and on the strategies that guarantee an output with the appropriate properties.

Secondly, rules are not well adapted to accounting for variation. We might, to be sure, propose 'variable' rules, of the kind entertained by Labov (1972). A variable rule is one that has a certain probability of applying, as a function of dialect, the level of formality, and perhaps other factors. However, it is not so much the case that glottal-stop insertion is in itself variable, but that the strategy presents itself as an alternative to other strategies; if glottal-stop insertion fails to apply, one of the other strategies must apply, and vice versa. (The variability of one rule is therefore related to the variability of other rules.) Moreover, the variability of a rule would have to be sensitive to lexical factors that influence the rule's application. It would be necessary to mark individual lexical items, and perhaps routinized phrases, with respect to their probability of undergoing the various rules.

In any case, rules, whether variable or categorial, and the idiosyncratic marking of forms in the lexicon, are not available options in a Cognitive Grammar. What, then, might be a Cognitive Grammar account of the filled-onset strategies?

First, the filled-onset requirement itself can be stated as a very general schema for syllable structure. A syllable, in English, must conform to the following schema.

(10)

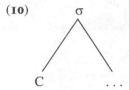

Any syllable which fails to accord with this schema will be phonologically ill-formed. In fact, for most English speakers, such a syllable will be simply unpronounceable.

The four onset-filling strategies can be captured by means of four constructional schemas. The shared-consonant option is represented in Figure 13.3. The items in the lower portion of the Figure represent the forms that are to be combined. Their relevant properties are that the first unit terminates in a consonant, the second commences in a vowel. The composite unit states the relevant aspects of the phonologically complex form. Note in particular that the second syllable conforms to the general syllable schema of example (10).

Figure 13.4 (p. 256) represents r-insertion.

Glide insertion collapses two separate phenomena—[j] insertion and [w] insertion. Figure 13.5 (p. 256) represents [j] insertion; [w] insertion could be handled in a similar way. The similarities between the two cases invite a schematic representation which captures the commonality between them. Thus, the word final vowel can be specified as [+HIGH] and [αFRONT] and the

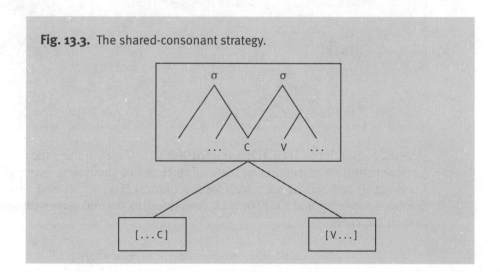

Fig. 13.3. The shared-consonant strategy.

Fig. 13.4. The strategy of [r] insertion.

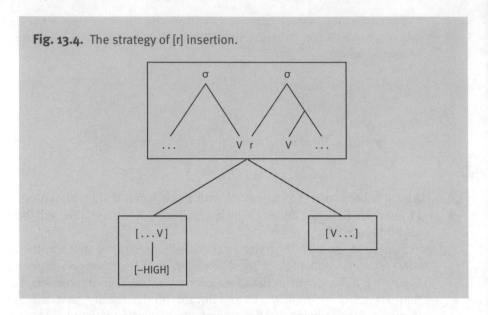

Fig. 13.5. The strategy of [j] insertion.

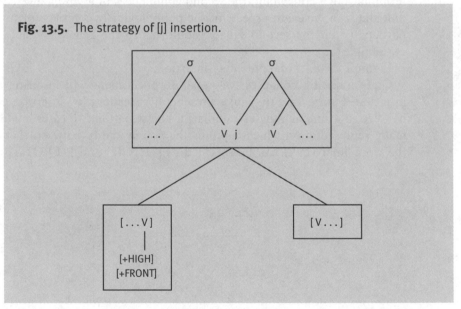

inserted consonant as [+GLIDE] and [αFRONT].[4] This captures the fact that [j, w] constitute a 'natural class' defined in terms of their both being glides. Likewise, [j] and high front vowels form a natural class with respect to their frontness, while [w] and the high back vowels form a natural class with respect to their backness.

---

[4] [α] is a variable which can take on either of the values [+] or [−].

Finally, glottal-stop insertion can be represented as in Figure 13.6.

Figure 13.6 makes no reference to the preceding context of the vowel-commencing word. The representation allows for the possibility that the schema for glottal-stop insertion can override each of the previously discussed schemas—it can 'get in first', so to speak, rendering the other strategies superfluous.

This means, concretely, that a vowel-commencing word occurring anywhere except utterance-initial position is potentially subject to two different schemas—glottal-stop insertion and one of the other three. The situation is a case of 'schema competition'—a phenomenon that is widespread throughout the grammar and which I discuss in more detail in Chapter 16. The crucial question becomes: if a linguistic unit falls under two (or more) different and conflicting schemas, which schema wins out? In the case of glottal-stop insertion vs. the other options, a number of factors (which are not mutually exclusive) are probably at work, among them the following:

(i) First, in the language system of an individual speaker, or in a community of speakers, the different constructional schemas may be differently 'weighted'. A schema would be more heavily weighted (it would be more 'entrenched') to the extent that speakers have encountered it relatively frequently; it would then be the preferred option whenever the schema is in competition with another schema. It would be plausible to assume, for example, that the glottal stop schema is very highly entrenched for speakers of South African English.

(ii) It is likely that certain high-frequency word combinations may be stored and accessed as such, complete with their linking consonants. High frequency phrases, such as *for example, for ever, or else, four o'clock*, are presumably stored and retrieved as ready-made forms (in my speech, complete with a linking 'r'). This is tantamount to claiming that specific expressions, such as

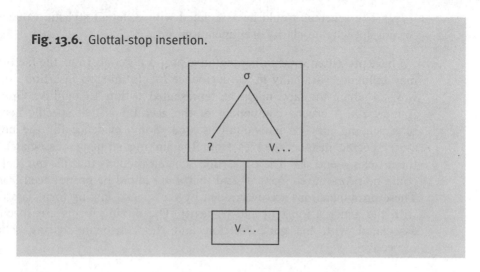

Fig. 13.6. Glottal-stop insertion.

for ever, are stored as fully specified instances of the r-insertion schema. Similarly, speakers of New Zealand English presumably store the word *withdrawal* as [wəθ.drɔː.rəl] rather than as [wəθ.drɔː.əl]. If [wəθ.drɔː.əl] were the stored form, we should have to assume that the r-insertion schema kicks in whenever the word is articulated—which seems rather counterintuitive, given that the word is always pronounced with the 'r'.

(iii) Likewise, certain words may be specifically associated with one or more of the schemas. Whereas *these are* could in principle come under two different schematic constructions, we could imagine that the form *these* is specifically associated with consonant sharing—*these* would be specifically listed as one of the instances of the consonant-terminating unit of Figure 13.3. On the other hand, the virtually obligatory insertion of the glottal stop in my pronunciations of *for Ellen, to Ellen, from Ellen*, and the like, could follow from the fact that my stored pronunciation of *Ellen* actually contains the glottal stop, viz. [ʔɛ.lən].

The contrast between the linking and the intrusive 'r' might also be understood in these terms. I suggested earlier (p. 89) that the distinction is largely an artefact of English orthography. The distinction may be relevant, though, to the extent that a speaker might habitually use the linking 'r' but tend to avoid the intrusive 'r'. This state of affairs suggests that the linking-r words are specifically listed under the r-insertion schema, whereas other words which terminate in a non-high vowel trigger the glottal stop schema. The words listed under the r-insertion schema consist in the main of those words whose orthography contains a final 'r', but it might also include some others. It is my impression that even speakers who habitually avoid the intrusive 'r'—they would be inclined not to use it in, say, *Ma and Pa, law and order, Asia and Africa*—would nevertheless insert an 'r' in *the idea of it*. In this case, *idea* will need to be listed amongst the 'r'-inserting words.

(iv) The schemas would be associated with different stylistic values, concerning speech rate, clarity of enunciation, etc.

I have presented some rather tentative proposals concerning the factors that may influence variability in the incidence of glottal-stop insertion, and the ways in which the facts might be represented within a Cognitive Grammar framework. A crucial component of the account is that specific instances of a schema may be individually stored. Some evidence for the need to store specific instances comes from the linking strategies associated with the articles *a* and *the*. The r-insertion schema predicts that *the ant* [ðə] [ænt] could be pronounced [ðərænt] and that *a ant* could be pronounced [ʔərænt]. These pronunciations are overridden by the special linking forms associated with the articles: [ðiːjænt] and [ʔənænt]. The linking forms are specifically associated with the glide-insertion and the consonant-sharing schemas, respectively.

13.3.1 French liaison

Superficially, so-called liaison in French operates much like r-insertion and other linking phenomena in English. In isolation, *les* 'the (pl.)' and *enfants* 'children' are pronounced [le] and [ãfã], respectively. In combination, *les enfants* 'the children' is pronounced [le zãfã]. A linking [z] intervenes between the vowel-terminating article and the vowel-commencing noun. It is as if the linking [z] provides an onset for the vowel-commencing word. No linking consonant intervenes before a consonant-commencing word, cf. *les gens* 'the people' [le ʒã].

There are, however, a number of differences between French liaison and linking in English.

(i) First, there exist several linking consonants in French. The choice of consonant varies according to the identity of the preceding word. In *les enfants*, the linking consonant is [z]. In *petit enfant* 'small child' [pti tãfã] the linking sound is [t]. While other liaising consonants, such as [p] and [n], do occur, most incidences of liaison in fact involve a linking [z] or [t]. Unlike in English—which also has different linking consonants, namely [r], [j], [w], and [ʔ]—the identity of the French consonants is not at all predictable from the phonological environment.

(ii) Liaison is highly sensitive to the syntactic–semantic relation between the adjacent words. It is virtually obligatory between determiner and noun (*les* [z] *enfants*) and between a numeral and a noun (*deux* [z] *enfants* 'two children'), it is optional between noun and adjective (*enfant* [t] *intelligent* 'intelligent child') but scarcely possible between a non-pronominal subject and a verb: *les enfants* [*z] *ont mangé* 'the children have eaten'.

Standard generative accounts of liaison propose 'underlying forms' of the articles, numerals, adjectives, etc. which contain the liaising consonant as a word-final segment. Thus, *les* would be represented underlyingly as [lez], *petit* as [ptit]. (The underlying forms, in fact, would be not too dissimilar from the standard orthographic forms.) Rules apply which delete the final consonant unless the following word commences in a vowel; special conditions restrict the occurrence of these rules to certain syntactic environments.

There are reasons to query this kind of approach, over and above our general scepticism for rules and their operations. In this connection we may note a third major difference between linking in English and French.

(iii) Whereas the linking phenomena in English are motivated by purely phonological considerations—ultimately, by the requirement that every syllable must have an onset—no such phonological motivation holds in French. There is, for example, no filled-onset requirement in French. Plenty of words begin with a vowel, and there is no requirement that vowel-commencing utterances be given a glottal onset. Combinations of vowels within and between words are also readily admitted. There is therefore no phonological schema requiring the insertion of liaising consonants between vowels. Neither are there any reasons why the liaising consonants should occur only before a vowel-commencing word, or, to put it another way, that liaising consonants should be 'deleted' before a consonant. It is not the case that consonants in syllable coda position are prohibited. There are numerous words whose pronunciation ends in a consonant: *petite* [ptit], *donc* [dɔ̃k], etc. There is nothing phonologically deviant about words terminating in [z] or [t], nor about clusters of consonants occurring between or within words.

Liaison would be a purely phonological phenomenon if it were the case that French were a strict CV language. If such were the case, some phonological strategy would have to kick in in order to avoid the adjacent vowels in *petit enfant* *[pti ɑ̃fɑ̃] and *les enfants* *[le ɑ̃fɑ̃]. This would be an argument for the insertion of a liaising consonant. Likewise—assuming a different underlying form of the article—there would have to be some strategy to avoid the occurrence of adjacent consonants in *les gens* *[lez ʒɑ̃]. This would be an argument for the deletion of word-final consonants. These kinds of approaches, however, are not applicable to French. Although CV might be a preferred syllable structure in French, there are abundant syllable types which counter this tendency. Consonant clusters are tolerated in onset and coda position, adjacent vowels are permitted, as well as syllables with empty onsets. Liaison cannot be motivated by phonological constraints on syllable structure.

What, then, would be an alternative account of French liaison?

Just as the English articles *a* and *the* are associated with distinct phonological forms, each appropriate to a certain phonological environment, so we might say that certain lexical items, such as the plural definite article *les*, or the adjective *petit*, are stored as two phonological forms, [le] and [lez], [pti] and [ptit]. The form [lez] is associated specifically with a schema [DET + PLURAL NOUN], where the plural noun commences with a vowel, whereas the form [ptit] would be associated with an [ADJ N] schema for (masculine) nouns commencing in a vowel.

Considering the form *les enfants* 'the children' [le zɑ̃fɑ̃] another possibility arises. As is well known, most nouns in French receive an orthographic 's' in their plural forms, which is, however, not manifested phonologically. Essentially, French nouns are not phonologically marked for plural—at least, they are not marked by the addition of a plural suffix. The form [le zɑ̃fɑ̃] suggests, however, that plural number may be marked on the noun by the presence of a prefixed [z]. Only nouns which, in the singular, commence in a vowel would be eligible for this kind of plural marking. Moreover, the prefixed form would only occur in association with the definite article (*les enfants*), possessive pronouns (*mes enfants* 'my children'), certain numerals (*deux enfants* 'two children'), the demonstrative *ces* (*ces enfants* 'these children'), and following adjectives (*petits enfants* 'small children'). The list of environments, in fact, is fairly exhaustive of the environments in which a plural noun is likely to occur.

Finally, it should be noted that in the case of high-frequency phrases, such as *c'est-à-dire* 'that is to say' [sɛ ta dir], these are plausibly stored as wholes, liaison and all. Perhaps, in the final analysis, French liaison and linking in English may not be so different after all.

Study questions

1. Study the distribution of [p, t, k, b, d, g] in English, paying attention to the possibilities of these consonants occurring in onset and coda clusters within word-sized units. To what extent is each of the consonants associated with a distinct distributional profile? Is it nevertheless possible to propose onset and coda schemas which capture broad commonalities amongst the consonants, or sets of the consonants? In light of your conclusions, evaluate the relative importance of lower-level and higher-level schemas for the distribution of the six consonants.

    You might extend the investigation to other sets of consonants (such as the fricatives) in English or another language.

2. It is common practice, in discussing an item's distribution, to distinguish between 'systemic gaps' and 'accidental gaps'. The fact that there are no words commencing in [ŋ] in English would seem to be a systemic gap — words commencing in the velar nasal are felt to be 'not English'. On the other hand, the absence of words terminating in [ʊŋ] may well be an accidental gap, a product, possibly, of the fact that both [ʊ] and [ŋ] are in themselves relatively infrequent in English.

    To what extent is the distinction between systemic and accidental gaps a valid one? Is the distinction a clear-cut one, or is it a matter of gradience? How might the distinction be represented in Cognitive Grammar?

3. Refer to Study question 4 of Chapter 5. Analyse your data on the incidence of glottal-stop insertion with respect to: (i) the phonological properties of the forms involved, (ii) the entrenchment of word collocations, (iii) the identity of the lexical items involved, (iv) the stylistic properties of the utterances, and any other factors that seem to be relevant.

    Overall, how variable is the phenomenon? Elaborate the approach sketched out in this chapter to account for the variability that you observe.

4. False liaison. A curious feature of French liaison is its occurrence in contexts which are not sanctioned by the presumed underlying forms of the items in question. The phenomenon is illustrated in (i).

(i)   les chefs d'état [z] africains 'the African heads of state'

The problem is that *chef d'état* 'head of state' forms its plural by pluralization of the head noun *chef*: *chefs d'état*. Phonologically, the singular and plural forms are identical: [ʃɛf deta]. The liaising consonant [z] suggests that the plural morpheme has attached—contrary to standard phrase-structure principles—to the final element of the complex nouns. It's as if, in English, one were to pluralize 'head of state' to 'head of states'.

How could the expression in (i)—which, incidentally, is regarded as substandard by speakers of French—be accounted for?

Consider also the following examples. The first two expressions conform to normative standards, the third exemplifies false liaison.

(ii)   c'est [t] à moi 'it's mine', lit. 'it's to me'

c'est pas [z] à moi 'it's not mine', lit. 'it's not to me'

c'est pas [t] à moi

The numeral *quatre* 'four' [katʁ] is sometimes associated with a liaising [z]—even though there is no 's' in the orthographic form; moreover, the insertion of a liaising consonant in (iii), rather than promoting a CV syllable structure, actually creates a complex consonant cluster [tʁz].

(iii)   quatre [z] enfants [katʁ zɑ̃fɑ̃]

What might motivate this example of false liaison?

Further examples of false liaison may be found in the recommended readings by Klausenburger and Bybee.

Further reading

The role of phonological constructional schemas is systematically pursued by V. Kumashiro (2000). Kumashiro first exemplifies the role of schemas on a range of English data, then applies the framework to some well-known problems in Japanese, Sanskrit, and German. There are also some brief, though valuable remarks in Langacker (1999: 128–31).

For French liaison, and various approaches to it, see Klausenburger (1984) and especially Bybee (2001). Swiggers (1985) is also of interest.

Part 3
Morphology

The chapters in Part 3 continue the discussion of internally complex units, with a focus on the internal structure of words.

Chapter 14 addresses aspects of morphologically complex words and the criteria that are relevant to morphological analysis. Chapter 15 pursues the discussion, arguing against what might be called the 'building block' model of morphology, and also addressing what might be regarded as the other side of analysability, namely, the productivity of morphological processes. Chapter 16 proposes an alternative to the view whereby morphologically complex forms are created by the application of 'rules' to a base form. Chapter 17 brings together a number of topics addressed in Parts 2 and 3, by applying these to a classification of symbolic units.

CHAPTER 14

Morphology

Morphology is the study of the internal structure of words. I approach the topic with a couple of very straightforward cases. The first example concerns a word whose analysis into its component morphemes is beyond dispute; the second example concerns a word which is clearly not analysable into component morphemes. In spite of their seeming simplicity, the examples will allow us to apply and refine some of the theoretical notions introduced so far, concerning, in particular, the function of schemas in linguistic analysis. Further aspects of word structure are addressed in Chapters 15 and 16.

Although the focus in this and the next two chapters is on the structure of words, it should be emphasized that morphology is not to be regarded as an encapsulated module of the grammar, distinct in principle from syntax. On the contrary, much of what we shall discover in the realm of morphology will be readily applicable to syntactic organization.

14.1 Morphemic analysis

Let us begin by considering the two words in (1):

(1) book; books

It is rather obvious that the two words are related. (Later in this chapter I suggest some reasons for this very clear intuition.) *Books* is internally complex, being composed of the base morpheme *book* and the plural affix -*s*.

When these morphemes are combined in the prescribed order, we get the plural form of *book*.

Each of the component morphemes is itself a symbolic unit; as such, they each associate a semantic and a phonological structure. *Book* associates the concept [BOOK] with the phonological form [bʊk]; the plural morpheme associates the concept of plurality [PLURAL] with the phonological form [s]. The complex form *books* associates the concept of a plurality of books with the phonological form [bʊks].

Let us first look at some of the characteristics of the component morphemes. I will do so with reference to some of the topics that have been introduced in previous chapters, namely autonomy vs. dependence, contentfulness vs. schematicity, and valence. To briefly rehearse these notions:

- the autonomy/dependence distinction has to do with whether a unit can be conceptualized in and of itself, without it being necessary to make reference to structures beyond the unit itself;
- the contentfulness/schematicity distinction has to do with the degree of detail with which the unit is specified;
- valence has to do with a unit's disposition to combine with other units. Taking up a distinction introduced in section 9.2, we can distinguish between units that are relatively **choosy** (that is, they combine only with units of a certain kind) and those that are **promiscuous** (they are able to combine with just about anything).

In considering these aspects it will be useful to pay separate attention to the phonological and the semantic aspects of the morphemes.

(i) First, the morpheme *book*. Both the phonological form [bʊk] and the conceptual unit [BOOK] display a high degree of autonomy; [bʊk] can be articulated as a phonologically fully acceptable one-syllable utterance, while it is possible to conceptualize [BOOK] without making necessary reference to anything outside of the concept itself.[1] Both the phonological and the semantic structures are specified in considerable detail. With respect to its valence, *book* is highly promiscuous. As a phonologically autonomous form, [bʊk] is free to occur, in the stream of speech, adjacent to just about anything. While there might be statistical preferences for certain combinations on the semantic level, these are not in the nature of absolute requirements or prohibitions.

(ii) The plural morpheme differs radically from *book* on each of the above dimensions. The phonological form [s] is highly dependent. While it

---

[1] The concept [BOOK] is not fully autonomous, of course. All concepts are profiled against conceptual domains (Ch. 10), consequently, there is probably no such thing as a fully autonomous concept. The concept [BOOK] might invoke the idea of an author, of readers, of a text in a given language, of its material properties (paper, pages, a typical size and weight), of commercial value, and so on. Nevertheless, such notions are not *intrinsic* to the concept [BOOK], in the same way, for example, as the notion of 'triangle' is intrinsic to the concept [HYPOTENUSE].

may be possible to articulate [s] by itself, an isolated [s] does not constitute a phonologically acceptable utterance in English. [s] has to attach to
something.

The plural morpheme is a little more difficult to characterize with respect to
its phonological contentfulness. Concerning the noun *books*, the phonological
shape of the plural morpheme is, of course, fully specified, namely as [s]. But
if we consider a broader range of plural nouns, the plural morpheme fails to
manifest itself in a constant manner. For the regular plurals, the morpheme
appears in one of three different shapes: [s], [z], and [əz]. To be sure, the three
shapes might be brought under a common schematic representation, say, as
an alveolar fricative [S], a segment unspecified for voicing, the selection of
one of the three fully specified forms being determined by the phonological
properties of the base. (More on this in Chapter 16). This is tantamount to
asserting that phonologically the plural morpheme as such is specified only
schematically. But in addition to the regulars there are quite a few nouns which
have irregular plural forms, in which the plural morpheme shows up in a
variety of shapes and guises (including zero, i.e. no overt manifestation at all,
as with *sheep*). If we take the irregulars into account, we shall have to say that
the phonological representation of the plural morpheme, abstracting away
from its particular instances, is highly schematic, so schematic, in fact, that it is
actually devoid of any specific content.

With respect to its semantic pole the plural morpheme is also highly
schematic. The morpheme merely designates a plurality of entities (all of the
same kind), but does not specify the kind of entities. The number of entities is
also left open; any number, greater than one, counts as a plural number.

The plural morpheme also has special valence properties. It is not just that
the morpheme has to attach to something, it has to attach to a host of a
certain kind, namely, a noun stem. The specific forms [s], [z], and [əz] are
even more choosy; [s] only attaches to nouns which terminate in a voiceless
segment, [z] only attaches to nouns which terminate in a voiced segment, while
[əz] is restricted to nouns which terminate in a sibilant, i.e. one of [s, z, ʃ, ʒ,
tʃ, dʒ].

In view of these facts, it turns out that [s] is inadequate as a phonological
representation of the plural morpheme as it appears in the word *books*. It
is not the case that each and every [s] in the language counts as a marker
of plurality. We want to say that [s] counts as a plural morpheme only when
two conditions are satisfied: (i) the segment is associated with the semantic
structure [PLURAL], and (ii) the segment attaches to a host of the appropriate
kind, whereby the 'appropriateness' of the host is determined both by its
phonological and by its conceptual aspects. The phonological representation
of plural [s] therefore needs to make reference to the item that the morpheme
can combine with: (2).

(2) [NOUN STEM] [PLURAL] / [. . . . C$_{voiceless}$] [s]

In (2), **bold** picks out the phonological form under consideration. The [s] must attach to a preceding item which terminates in a voiceless consonant. These two elements are associated with the semantic values shown to the left of the slash.

There is a general principle involved here:

(3) Units that are phonologically and/or conceptually dependent make reference, in their phonological and/or conceptual structure, to the kind(s) of item that are candidates for combination.

Summing up this part of the discussion, we see that on each of the parameters considered, the component morphemes of *books* turn out to be radically different. The stem morpheme *book* is:

- phonologically autonomous;
- conceptually autonomous;
- phonologically contentful;
- conceptually contentful;
- promiscuous with respect to the items it can occur adjacent to.

The plural affix, in contrast, is:

- phonologically dependent;
- conceptually dependent;
- phonologically schematic;
- conceptually schematic;
- very choosy with respect to the items it attaches to.

This marked asymmetry between stem and affix is rather typical. Affixes, generally, have the properties listed above and contrast significantly, in respect to the relevant parameters, with the stems with which they combine

14.1.1 Combining the morphemes

I now turn to the complex form *books* and the mechanism whereby the constituent morphemes come together. Combination takes place through the establishment of a valence relation (Chapter 12). Only three kinds of valence relation are posited in Cognitive Grammar: head-modifier, head-complement, and apposition. Which of these is applicable to the case in point?

Putting aside, for the time being, the possibility of an appositional relation, we need, first, to establish which of the component morphemes of *books* has the status of head. Then we need to clarify whether the non-head constituent is a modifier or a complement.

Most people, when asked to identify the head of a complex word such as *books*, are inclined to select the base noun, *book*. This response appears to be motivated by the belief that the head will be: (i) the conceptually more contentful, and (ii) the phonologically more autonomous element of an expression. *Book* can stand by itself as a semantically fully specified and phonologically autonomous utterance, whereas [s] fails on both these scores. Another consideration appears to be that the plural form is 'derived' from the base, hence the noun stem is a more 'essential', a more 'basic' component of the resultant form. Some grammatical theories, such as Phrase Structure Grammar (Borsley 1999), indeed adopt this analysis; both *book* and *books* are categorized as [NOUN], the latter, however, bears the distinguishing feature [+plural]. A similar account was proposed in Chomsky's *Aspects* (1965).

On the Cognitive Grammar approach, semantic contentfulness and phonological autonomy are not relevant to head status. The head is that constituent which lends its profile to the composite expression (section 12.2). *Books* profiles a plurality of entities of the kind 'book'. The word's semantic character—the fact that it designates a plural number of entities—is determined by the affix; it is the affix that makes *books* what it is, namely, a plural noun. We conclude that *books* is headed by the affix.

The valence relation between the two components is depicted in Figure 14.1. The affix itself profiles a plurality of entities. The kind of entity is not specified. When the plural morpheme combines with *book*, *book* elaborates the schematic entities in the profile of the affix. *Book* turns out to be the complement of the affix, in that it elaborates a substructure within the head.

Consider the alternative analysis, which has *books* headed by *book*. We should have to say that *books* and *book* designate one and the same entity, albeit with differing degrees of precision. The affix, presumably, would be a modifier, which adds conceptual substance to the head. What would this

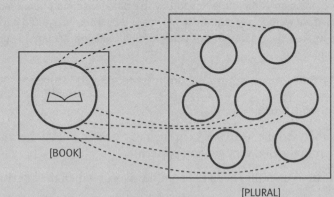

Fig. 14.1. The valence relation between the two component structures of *books*.

[BOOK]

[PLURAL]

Note: Book profiles an entity of the type 'book'; the plural morpheme profiles an unspecified plural number (seven are shown here) of entities, all of the same type, but the identity of which is not specified. The profiled entities are construed as instances of the type that is profiled by *book*. The plural morpheme is the profile determinant, in that the resulting complex expression inherits the profile of the affix and thereby denotes a plural number of books.

mean? It would be tantamount to claiming that *books* designates a kind of book, a 'plural book', presumably—which would be absurd.

Could the relation between [BOOK] and [PLURAL] be a relation of apposition? Apposition requires: (i) that the apposed elements designate the same entity, i.e. that their profiles coincide, and (ii) that the complex form designates the same entity as each of the component forms. Typically, in an appositional relation, each unit designates the same entity from different perspectives, or with differing degrees of detail. For reasons already mentioned, it would be difficult to maintain this analysis at face value. At the same time, there is a sense in which both the noun stem and the plural morpheme do share a common content. Both, for example, are nominal in character—they designate things, not relations.[2] At a very high level of schematicity, abstracting away from number, it could be claimed that their profiles do coincide. That plural nouns do have a whiff of apposition should not be too disturbing; as pointed out in section 12.3, the relations of modification, complementation, and apposition are not mutually exclusive.

Past-tense forms

What has been said about the plural form *books* can be applied, with little modification, to the past-tense form of a verb, e.g. *walked* [wɔːkt].

Just as *books* consists of *book* plus the plural morpheme, so *walked* consists of the base verb *walk* plus the past-tense morpheme. Semantically, the past-tense morpheme designates a situation that obtained in past time; the kind of situation, however, is not specified. The base morpheme *walk* designates a kind of activity, the time at which the activity is instantiated is not specified. The combined expression *walked* designates a past-time instance of the activity. The expression is therefore headed by the past-tense morpheme, not by the verb stem. If we were to say that *walked* is headed by *walk*, we should have to conclude that *walked* designates a particular kind of walking activity, a 'past walk', for example.

14.1.2 Affixes as heads

I have analysed the word *books* in such excruciating detail because the example is symptomatic of a very general pattern:

(4) Affixes (generally) head the complex words which they derive.

---

[2] It might seem strange to describe the plural morpheme as nominal in character. This characterization, however, falls out naturally from the Cognitive Grammar approach. Similarly, to take up the example discussed in the Box above, the past tense morpheme will need to be characterized as a verb, a highly schematic and somewhat unusual verb, to be sure, but a verb nonetheless, which profiles, schematically, the past-time occurrence of a situation.

Consider the agentive affix *-er*. This is the affix which occurs in words such as *walker*, *singer*, *murderer*, etc. These words are nouns, which designate a person who performs the activity designated by the base verb.[3] It is the affix that makes these words what they are, namely, nouns with this particular kind of meaning. Agentive nouns in *-er* are therefore headed by the affix. This is depicted in Figure 14.2.

We may rephrase (4) as follows:

(5) Affixes (generally) are schematic for the complex words which they derive.

Fig. 14.2. The assembly of an agentive *V-er* nominal.

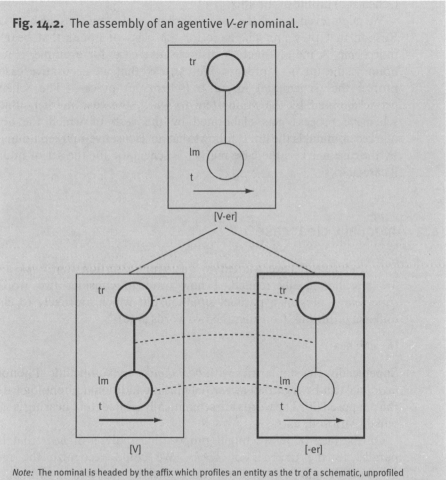

Note: The nominal is headed by the affix which profiles an entity as the tr of a schematic, unprofiled temporal process. The verb stem to which *-er* attaches provides conceptual content to the unprofiled process. The complex expression inherits the profile of the affix.

[3] There is more to the semantic content of agentive *V-er* nominals. A singer is not just a person who happens to sing (at some time or other); in order for a person to be called a singer it is necessary that they can be categorized in such terms, as with a professional singer. The suffix *-er* also has several values in addition to the one discussed here; consider such forms as *villager*, *geographer*, *cooker*, *quarter-pounder*, etc.

What do agentive nouns such as *singer, dancer, murderer, walker, speaker*, and many more, have in common? Phonologically, they all have the form [V-er] and semantically they all designate a person who Vs. These commonalities coincide exactly with the schematic content of the affix *-er*.

An analogous account can be given of many of the bound morphemes of English and other languages. The nominalizing affixes *-ness* and *-ity* derive nouns from adjectives. The derived nouns profile the quality that is salient in the semantic structure of the base adjectives. *Goodness* and *serenity* are nouns because of the affix. The words inherit their nominal character from the (schematic) profile of the affix.

We might even say of the case morphemes of languages such as Latin and Russian that they are schematic for the class of nouns that bear the case morpheme. A major function of accusative case, for example, is to mark a noun as the lm of a process. We can say that an accusative case marker profiles the (schematic) lm of a (schematic) process. The schematic lm gets elaborated by the noun stem to which the case marker attaches; the schematic process gets elaborated by the verb of which the accusative-marked nominal is the lm. It follows that an accusative-marked noun is headed by the case marker; the case marker is schematic for the set of nouns which it case-marks.

14.2 An equally clear case

Few readers will have wanted to query my assertion that *book* and *books* are morphologically related. I now want to consider two words which superficially present a parallel situation but which are likely to elicit quite different intuitions. Consider the two words in (6).

(**6**) ear; hear

Superficially, the similarities with *book/books* are compelling. Phonologically, *hear* [hiə] can be regarded as *ear* [iə] plus an additional phonological element, the pre-posed [h]. The words are semantically related, too; hearing is something you do with your ears.

On the face of it, we might propose an analysis of *hear* that is exactly parallel to the analysis of *books*. We could recognize the morpheme *h-* which designates, say, a schematic activity performed with X, where X appears as material following *h-*. *Hear* would be headed by *h-*, with *ear* as its complement.

This analysis is, of course, patently absurd. But why is it absurd?

Essentially, we reject the analysis because there are no other comparable examples in the English language. There are no other verbs beginning with *h-*, where the *h-* is detachable, so to speak, so that what is left over designates an entity used in the activity denoted by the *h*-word.[4] *Harass* is not something you do with an arras, and *heave* is not something you do with an eve. Neither can we create *h*-words from, say, *eye, ankle, elbow*, etc. There is no **hankle* or **helbow* (actions you perform with your ankle or elbow). However, the fact that the putative affix *h-* occurs nowhere else in the language is not in itself a reason to reject the bimorphemic analysis of *hear*.

Consider the word *cranberry*. There are no other words in English which begin with the morpheme *cran-*.[5] Yet we still want to analyze *cranberry* as *cran + berry*. In fact, the cranberry example has become a staple of morphological analysis; the expression 'cranberry morpheme' is standardly used to refer to a morpheme that is exemplified in only one word.

But while *cran-* occurs nowhere else in the language, *-berry* obviously does, and with a fairly constant semantic value, as in *strawberry, blackberry*, and several others. With respect to *hear* (= *h + ear*), not only are there no words in which an initial *h-* morpheme can be recognized, there are no words which we might want to analyse as AFFIX + *ear*, where the resultant complex word has something to do with one's ears. *Cheer, fear, peer, clear, near*, etc., have no semantic relation with *ear*.

Moreover, derivation by prefixation of a single consonant would go against the general pattern of word formation in English. In general, affixes attach to the ends of stems, in English, not to the beginnings. Derivational prefixes do exist, to be sure; examples include *un-, in-, dis-, pre-, ex-, over-, out-*, and a few more. There is even an example of a single-consonant prefix: consider *ever : never, either : neither, or : nor, one : none*,[6] and the now archaic *ay : nay, aught : naught*. Here, prefixed *n-* has the sense 'not', and modifies the meaning of the base accordingly. Numerically, however, these examples are by far eclipsed by the very large number of affixes which attach to the end of a base form.[7]

In brief, then, we reject the analysis of *hear* as *h + ear* because the analysis does not 'fit' into the system of English. In Cognitive Grammar terms, this boils down to the fact that **there is no schema which sanctions the analysis**. The relation between *ear* and *hear* turns out to be entirely accidental, and fortuitous.

The situation with the plural form *books* is vastly different. The analysis is supported by the fact that the vast majority of nouns, in English, form their plurals by addition of *-s* (or one of its variants). There are ample data, therefore, which allow the abstraction of the plural-forming schema. Not only

[4] The only counterexample to this claim that I can think of is *hedge*. The relation with *edge* is fairly tenuous, to be sure. (A hedge is something that goes round the edge of something.) You could hedge your garden by putting a hedge around its edge.

[5] At least, as Jackendoff (1997: 165) remarks, until cranapple juice was invented.

[6] *None* [nʌn] involves the replacement of the initial segment of *one* [wʌn] with [n], rather than the simple prefixation of [n]. Note also that while phonologically the relation between *once* and *nonce* parallels *one : once*, the semantic relation fails to hold (*nonce* ≠ 'not once').

[7] Phonological considerations also militate against the use of single-consonant prefixes. A prefix such as *n-* or *h-* will only be able to attach to a vowel-commencing base, a fact which would severely limit the prefix's productivity.

Prefixes in English

Prefixes, in English, differ from suffixed morphemes in that prefixation, in general, does not affect the semantic type of the base.

Happy and *unhappy* both profile a relation between a tr and an emotional state. Prefixation by *un-* does not change the adjectival status of *happy*. There are no grounds, therefore, to claim that *unhappy* is headed by the prefix. Rather, we should probably want to analyse the prefix as a modifier.

Verbal prefixes are more complex in their semantic effects. Compare *eat* and *overeat*. Both are verbs, and since overeating is a kind of eating, it might be supposed that the prefix modifies the base verb, rather in the manner of an adverb (such as *excessively*). Yet *eat* and *overeat* are not equivalent in their valence properties. You can *eat a meal* but you cannot **overeat a meal*. The prefix serves to render the base verb intransitive. To the extent that this property of *overeat* is determined by the prefix, the prefix must be regarded as the head of the complex verb which it derives.

The verbal prefix *out-*, in contrast, imposes a transitive profile on the verbs that it derives: you *outrun*, *outperform*, or *outmanoeuvre* a competitor. This aspect is contributed by the prefix, which again is reasonably regarded as the head of the words that it derives. It is even possible to create verbs from a noun base. You could say of a politician that they were able to *outBlair* Tony Blair. This further reinforces the analysis of *out-* as profiling a schematic transitive verb, which designates a schematic process of a certain kind.

this, but word formation in English, generally, consists in the addition of a bound affix to the end of a stem, with the affix functioning as the head of the complex form. The basic pattern of plural formation (namely, suffixation) is itself supported by a very general word formation schema.

From the two contrasting examples, we can derive the following principle:

(7) An expression can be analysed into component constituents to the extent that the analysis is sanctioned by a schema.[8]

In the next section I address some factors which allow these schemas to emerge.

14.3 Schema strength

We have considered two radically different, and equally clear-cut cases. With *books*, there is no question about the internal structure of the word; it is equally clear that *hear* cannot be analysed into component morphemes.

[8] The kinds of schema referred to in (7) are 'constructional schemas', of the kind discussed in section 12.2.2 in connection with the internal structure of phrases. The morphological constructional schemas encapsulate patterns for the internal structure of complex words.

Books is analysable because of a schema which sanctions the analysis; *hear* is not analysable because of the absence of an appropriate schema.

What about *never*? There are a few other English words (*neither, nor, none*) which appear to consist of a stem prefixed with the negative morpheme *n-*. These can certainly be brought under a constructional schema. I doubt, however, that the analysability of *never* is as evident to English speakers as the analysability of *books*. English speakers, I suspect, would not in general conceptualize *never* as being derived through prefixation from *ever*, in the way in which *books* is derived through suffixation from *book*.

Why should this be? Given the possibility of analysing *never* in terms of a schema, we should expect *never* to be no less analysable than *books*.

The reason, I suggest, is that the schema which sanctions the analysis of *never* is not very salient. It lacks salience because of the small number of instances that can be brought under the schema.

(8) Schemas vary in strength. A schema gains strength (it becomes 'established', or 'entrenched') in proportion to the number of instances which elaborate it. A schema which is elaborated by very many instances will tend to be highly entrenched; a schema which has only a small, fixed number of instances will tend to be weakly entrenched; in the limiting case, a schema with only one instance will not be entrenched at all.

Underlying the claims in (8) is the assumption that a linguistic unit— whether this be a schema or a fully specified linguistic expression—is strengthened ('entrenched') each time it is used. *Never* and *ever* are both rather frequent words in English, each with its own range of conventionalized uses. Repeated use strengthens the mental representation of these two words, but would tend not to strengthen the schema which analyses *never* as *n + ever*. The schema would only gain strength if there were a large number of different words which instantiated it.

The situation is sketched in Figure 14.3 (p. 276). The Figure shows the relative salience of a schema as a function of the number (and entrenchment) of its instances. Salience is represented by the heaviness of a surrounding box.

Schema 1 has a large number of instances. (For clarity of presentation I have shown only four.) Each use of a (different) instance strengthens the schema; the schema is, as it were, imminent in the use of the instances. The instances themselves, however, are not particularly salient. Plural formation in English (at least, 'regular' plural formation) exemplifies this situation. There are countless plural nouns in English; every use of a plural noun strengthens the plural-formation schema; the plural nouns themselves are probably not well entrenched (that is, they will tend not to be stored as fully-formed, composite expressions).[9] Schema 2 has only a small number of

---

[9] This statement needs to be understood in relative terms. Certain plural nouns, such as *stars*, due to their high frequency of use, probably are quite entrenched. Others, such as *suns*, which are rarely encountered, are probably not entrenched at all.

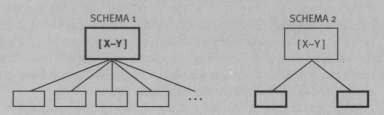

Fig. 14.3. The strength of a schema for combining units X and Y is related to the number and entrenchment of its instances.

Note: Schema 1 has very many instances and is strengthened each time one of the instances is employed. Schema 2 has few instances; usage is able to strengthen the instances, but is not likely to strengthen the schema.

instances. The instances themselves are highly entrenched. The entrenchment of the instances, however, does little to strengthen the schema. Words commencing in negative *n-* exemplify this situation. *Never*, *nor*, *neither*, *none* are all high-frequency words; they are entrenched as units, with their own specific semantic values, but their analysability is not particularly evident to the language user.[10] In the limiting case, a schema which has only one instance will not be strengthened at all; as suggested in section 7.1, for a schema to be recognized at all, there has to be a minimum of at least two instances.

At the close of the preceding section I proposed the following principle:

(7) An expression can be analysed into component constituents to the extent that the analysis is sanctioned by a schema.

In light of the above discussion, (7) can be made more precise:

(9) An expression can be analysed into component constituents in proportion to the strength of the schema which sanctions the analysis.

14.3.1 Type frequency and token frequency

The entrenchment of a linguistic form is a result of the frequency with which it is used. With respect to the entrenchment of a schema we need to be aware of the difference between type frequency and token frequency.

It may well be the case that *hear* and *ear* are both high-frequency items in English. Each occurrence ('token') of *hear* entails an occurrence of the initial *h-*. It follows, therefore, that the putative *h-* morpheme also has a high token frequency. In a sense, however, it is the 'same' *h-* that occurs in each of these

---

[10] Paradoxical as it might appear, the entrenchment of an instance tends not to entrench the schema which it instantiates. Compare *ever* : *never* and *ay* : *nay*. The fact that *ever* and *never* are high-frequency, hence highly entrenched units does little to render the internal structure of *never* more salient. On the other hand, the fact that *ay* and *nay* are low-frequency words probably does support the analysability of *nay*.

tokens. The putative morpheme may well have a high token frequency, but a very low type frequency. (In fact, the type frequency is one.)

With respect to the plural morpheme, it is not only the case that it occurs very often in English text, but it also attaches to very many different noun stems. The plural morpheme therefore not only has a very high token frequency, it also has a very high type frequency.

The case of the negative prefix *n-* falls between these two extremes. While the individual words *never*, *ever*, *nor*, *or*, etc. may well have a high token frequency, the negative morpheme *n-* has a rather low type frequency.

It is the type frequency of the instances which strengthen the schema. The fact that *ear* and *hear* are both high-frequency words merely entrenches each of these forms, it does nothing to entrench the putative relation between them. Moreover, the fact that there are no other forms related in this way precludes the emergence of a schema. As a result, speakers of English simply do not perceive a morphological relationship between these words. For the putative *h-* morpheme to be established, we would need to have several word types commencing with the putative affix.

The above discussion suggests the following revision of the principle stated in (8):

(10) A schema gains strength (it becomes 'established', or 'entrenched') in proportion to the type frequency of the instances which elaborate it.

With respect to the role of type vs. token frequency, we can state the following principles:

(11) a. High token frequency of an instance entrenches the instance and weakens (or at least, does not strengthen) the schema.
   b. High type frequency of the instances entrenches the schema and weakens (or at least does not strengthen) the instances.

Study questions

1. Relatedness of words. Do you judge the following pairs of words to be morphologically related? Consider the basis of your judgements. (Note that the point of this exercise is not to ascertain whether the word pairs are 'really' related. The point is that you should reflect on, and make explicit, the criteria which lead to a particular judgement.)

man	woman
man	manual
man	manufacture
Arab	arabesque
receive	deceive
contract	detract

disengage	discard
any	many
horizon	horizontal
grass	graze
(to) sit	(to) set
preside	president
bake	baker
drip	drop
obscene	obscenity
divine	divinity
sane	sanity
ten	teen (as in *thirteen*, *teenager*)
wend (one's way)	went
wife	housewife
well	wealth
cigar	cigarette
wind	window
state	station
(a) half	(to) halve
hand	handle
spark	sparkle
crack	crackle
wreak	wrought
draw	drawer (as in *cupboard drawer*)

2. Nouns in -*er*. The suffix -*er* has a wide range of semantic values, beyond those that are hinted at in footnote 3. Prepare a database of nouns ending in -*er*. You might, for example, do a corpus search using the wild card '*' to stand for any material preceding -*er*. Having eliminated those words which are not nouns (e.g. adjectives in -*er*), identify and characterize the different meanings of the suffix. A corpus-based search will also enable you to assess the relative frequencies of the different variants. (For the semantics of -*er*, see Panther and Thornburg, 2001.)

3. Verb prefixation. Compile a list of verbs that contain the prefixes *over*-, *out*-, *un*-, and *dis*-. (Be careful to select only *verbs* that are derived with the prefixes. While *unopened* exists as a participle which can be used adjectivally, there is no verb *(to) unopen*.) In case the prefixes appear to have more than one identifiable semantic value, group the verbs accordingly.

Ascertain, for each group, the semantic value of the prefix. How 'choosy' are the prefixes? (That is, do the prefixes combine only with stems with specific semantic and/or phonological properties?) Are there reasons for claiming that the verbs are headed by the prefixes?

4. Phonaesthemes. I mentioned in this chapter the absurdity of analysing *hear* as *h* + *ear*. *Hear* would normally be regarded as morphologically simple, without internal structure.

Nevertheless, it sometimes happens that words which, on conventional accounts, are morphologically simple, do allow some internal analysis.

Bloomfield (1933: 245) observed that words commencing in *fl-* tend to denote 'moving light', and that words ending in *-ump* tend to denote 'clumsiness'. The word-components are sometimes called 'phonaesthemes':

flash, flare, flame, flicker, flimmer

bump, clump, chump, dump, frump, hump, lump, stump, slump, thump

Could there be grounds for recognizing *fl-* and *-ump* as morphemes of English? Why? (Why not?) If you are inclined to answer with 'no', consider the fact that of the words that commence in *dr-*, a surprisingly large number have to do with water (or its absence). (There are obvious exceptions, such as *drama*, *draconian*, *drudgery*.) Here are some of them:

drip, drop, drench, dredge, drain, drizzle, draw (water from a well), drink, draft, drift, drunk, dry, drought

Consider now some words that end in *-oop*. There aren't many of them, but apart from *snoop* and *sloop* they all seem to involve circular or curved motion or shape.

hoop, scoop, loop, stoop, swoop, coop (= enclose)

Now consider *droop*. Remarkably, the meaning of this verb (as in *The flowers drooped*) can virtually be derived from the meanings of its parts: 'curvature resulting from absence of water'. It is as if the 'curved' meaning of *-oop* is modified by the 'absence of water' meaning of *dr-*.

This is not an isolated case; dozens of similar examples can be found in Rhodes and Lawler (1981) and Rhodes (1994). Study these examples with a view to exploring the 'sub-morphemic' structure of English words.

5. Idiosyncratic analyses. In this chapter I dismissed the analysis of *hear* as *h + ear*. Nevertheless, it might be unwise to rule out entirely the possibility that a speaker may make an idiosyncratic association between the two words.

Imagine the case of a foreign learner of English who confuses the verbs *hear* and *feel*. (The example is not so far-fetched. Quite a number of languages do not distinguish lexically between the different sense modalities. Italian *sentire*, for example, serves for auditory perception, tactile perception, and emotional 'feeling'.) The learner invents for himself the association between *hear* and *ear* as a memory aid for fixing the sense of *hear*. Or take the case of a person who confuses the spelling of the homophones *meet* and *meat*: *meat* is something that you *eat*. I myself still appeal to a mnemonic I learned in school for differentiating the spellings of *principle* (noun) and *principal* (adjective): The *adjective* is spelled with an *a*. And the fact that the director of a school is called the *principal* (not *principle*)? Another little mnemonic came to the rescue: *principal* ends in *pal*, *pal* designates a person, and the *principal* of a school is a person.

(a) Find out, by interviewing speakers, how widespread the use of these mnemonics is, among both native speakers and foreign learners. What kinds of problems do the mnemonics solve? What mechanisms do the mnemonics employ?

(b) Does the existence of mnemonic aids put into question standard morphological analyses, according to which *principal* and *pal*, for example, are not at all related? How could idiosyncratic relations be incorporated into Cognitive Grammar?

Further reading

Discussions of morphology are scattered throughout FCG1. A concise statement of some of the issues discussed in this and the following chapter is Langacker (1999: 131–42). For the stem-affix distinction, see Tuggy (1992). Notions of schema entrenchment, and the type vs. token frequency of instances, are an important component of Bybee's linguistic model. Bybee (1995) is essential reading. The idea of affixes as heads is not only found in Cognitive Grammar, it is quite well established in modern morphological theory (see Williams 1981).

CHAPTER 15

Analysability and productivity

The discussion in the last chapter was based on some relatively straight-forward examples. Words such as *books*, *singer*, and *never* can be exhaustively analysed into their component morphemes (even though, in the case of *never*, the analysis may not be particularly salient). Each of the component morphemes has an identifiable semantic and phonological content which it contributes to the meaning of the composite expression. The case of *hear* was equally clear-cut. The word, quite simply, is morphologically unanalysable. Very often, morphological analysis is less straightforward. In this chapter I consider some of the factors that render morphological analysis somewhat less clear-cut than in the case of *books* and somewhat more compelling than in the case of *hear*. I also address what may be regarded as the converse of analysability—the question of productivity.

15.1 Analysability

Morphologically complex words such as *books*, *singer*, and *never* share several characteristics. First, the words can be exhaustively analysed into their component morphemes. Once the two morphemes *sing* and *-er* have been identified in *singer*, there is no remaining residue which needs to be accounted for. Secondly, each of the component morphemes is associated with a fairly stable semantic and phonological structure which is preserved when they are combined.[1] It follows that the units identified on the phonological level, [sɪŋ] and [ə], match up, one to one, with units identified on the semantic level.

The building-block metaphor

Words such as *books*, *singer*, and *never* are suggestive of what Langacker has referred to as the 'building-block metaphor' of composition:

This all-pervasive metaphor portrays a composite structure as being assembled out of its component morphemes, which contribute all of its content in the form of discrete chunks. (FCG2: 186)

Langacker comments that while the metaphor might be 'helpful up to a point (and unavoidable for expository purposes)', it is 'far from adequate as a serious model for natural-language composition' (FCG2: 186).

The examples to be discussed in this chapter reveal the inadequacies of the metaphor. (Needless to say, the failure of the metaphor to apply to the examples merely shows the inadequacy of the metaphor, it does not put into question the viability of morphological analysis.) Morphological analysis is not so much a question of breaking up a complex form into its building-block components, it is a matter of whether a given form shares commonalities (phonological and/or semantic) with other forms in the language. Conversely, creating a complex form is not so much a question of putting together its component parts, but of creating a form in accordance with existing constructional schemas.

15.1.1 Phonological vs. semantic analysability

In the examples so far discussed, the analysis of a word into its component morphemes takes place in parallel at the phonological and the semantic levels. Sometimes, however, analysability at the phonological level does not match up with analysability at the semantic level, and vice versa.

Compare the words *books* and *men*. Semantically, the words combine the nominal concepts [BOOK] and [MAN] with the concept of plurality. On the phonological level, however, [mɛn] defies analysis into a noun stem and a plural morpheme. The same goes for a past-tense form such as *blew* [bluː], in contrast to a 'regular' past-tense form, such as *walked* [wɔːkt].

A similar situation holds for certain inflectional morphemes which are phonologically unanalysable but which symbolize a number of distinct semantic components. The ending -*o* in Italian *(io) parlo* 'I speak' symbolizes

---

[1] This is not to say that the conventionalized meaning of *singer* is fully derivable from the meanings of its parts and the manner of their combination. See note 3 of Chapter 14.

(i) first person, (ii) singular, (iii) present tense, and (iv) indicative (as opposed to subjunctive). These four semantic elements are 'fused' into a single, unanalysable phonological unit.

The examples illustrate conceptual analysability which fails to match up with analysability at the phonological level. What about the reverse situation, that is the phonological analysability which fails to match up with analysability on the semantic level? For an illustration of this state of affairs, consider the bisyllabic Latinate words (predominantly verbs) in English, such as *conceive, infer, translate, extend.*

Take the word *conceive.* There are quite a few words which commence in *con-* (*concur, confer, conflate, conduct, concise,* etc.), which suggests the possibility of identifying *con-* as a word-initial morpheme. Equally, there are a number of verbs which end in *-ceive* (*receive, deceive, perceive*), which would support the identification of the word-completing morpheme *-ceive.* Inspection of these and similar words suggests the existence of a number of word-initial and word-final units:

(1) a. <u>word-commencing units</u>   b. <u>word-completing units</u>

con-	-cur
de-	-ceive
ex-	-tend
ad-	-duct
re-	-port
pre-	-fer
per-	-spire
trans-	-late
in-	-flate
pro-	-cede

Not all possible combinations of initials and finals constitute existing English words, though quite a few of them do, as the reader can easily verify. On the phonological level, these words can be analysed as consisting of two morphemes. What is less clear is whether each of the word-fragments makes a distinct semantic contribution to the resulting expression. What might be the semantic value that *con-* contributes to *conceive, concur, conduct, conspire,* and *concede*? What is the semantic commonality of *conceive, perceive, receive,* and *deceive*? No doubt, a person with some knowledge of the Latin words from which the English word fragments ultimately derive, may be able to come up with an account for at least some of the English words.[2] Still, even with a knowledge of Latin roots, it is by no means obvious how one could recognize, in the meaning of *conceive,* the meanings of its components. And

---

[2] For example, *concur* (from *con* 'with' and *currere* 'run') can be assigned the etymological meaning 'run with'. Via a conceptual metaphor of the kind AGREEMENT IS PHYSICAL PROXIMITY, 'running with' someone can come to have the sense 'agreeing with'. For conceptual metaphor, see Chapter 24.

Latinate morphemes

One reason for recognizing the word-terminating fragments in (1b) as morphemes — apart from the fact that they occur in a number of different words — is that each item tends to be associated with specific derivational possibilities.

- Corresponding to verbs in *-fer* are nouns terminating in *-ference* (*infer*: *inference*, *defer*: *deference*, *confer*: *conference*, etc.). It will be noted that the nominalizing suffix causes word stress to fall on the word-initial syllable.
- Verbs terminating in *-cur* form nouns in *-currence* (*recur*: *recurrence*, *concur*: *concurrence*, *occur*: *occurrence*). Although these nouns, like those above, appear to be formed by the addition of *-ence* to the base verb, the addition of the suffix has no effect on the location of word stress.
- Verbs terminating in *-tend* form nouns in *-tension* or *-tention* (*extend*: *extension*, *intend*: *intention*, *contend*: *contention*);
- Verbs terminating in *-ceive* form nouns terminating in *-ception* (*deceive*: *deception*, *receive*: *reception*, *perceive*: *perception*, etc.). There is, though, no such unity when it comes to forming adjectives from this group of verbs. Some form adjectives in *-ceptual*, some in *-ceptive*, and at least one allows both possibilities (*conceptual*, *conceptive; *deceptual, *deceptive*; *receptual, *receptive*; *perceptual*, *perceptive*).

---

for a strictly monolingual English speaker, most of the words constructed from the word fragments in (1) will symbolize semantically unanalysable units. At best, the word fragments listed in (1) can be characterized as 'degenerate' morphemes, i.e. morphemes with a phonological content but lacking a semantic content.[3]

The three possibilities that we have considered are represented schematically in Figure 15.1. The 'standard' case is shown in (a), where phonological constituents match up, one to one, with semantic constituents. In (b), analysability at the phonological level fails to correspond with analysability at the semantic level; (c) shows a composite semantic unit paired with a phonologically unanalysable unit.

Interestingly, the three possibilities illustrated in Figure 15.1 are also applicable to syntax.

Case (a) applies routinely to syntactic phrases. The semantic units which comprise the complex expression *the book on the table* match up, one to one, with the phonological units which symbolize them.

Case (b), analysability at the phonological level which fails to match up with analysability at the semantic level, is, admittedly, somewhat infrequent.

---

[3] It would also be problematic to assign head status to either of the component morphemes.

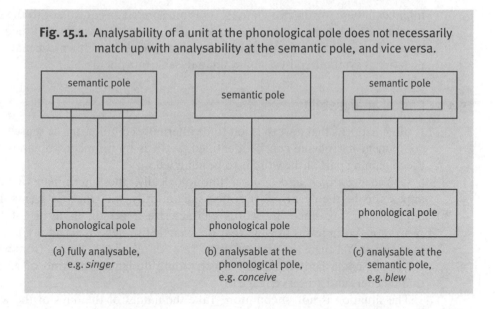

Fig. 15.1. Analysability of a unit at the phonological pole does not necessarily match up with analysability at the semantic pole, and vice versa.

(a) fully analysable, e.g. *singer*

(b) analysable at the phonological pole, e.g. *conceive*

(c) analysable at the semantic pole, e.g. *blew*

Consider, however, the expression *kick the bucket*, on its idiomatic reading. On the one hand, we can analyse the expression as a regular verb phrase, consisting of a transitive verb followed by its nominal direct object. The expression instantiates the very same constructional schema which sanctions innumerable phrases of the kind *open the door, write the letter, kill the chicken.* Semantically, however, the phrase does not designate a transitive process. There is no conceptual unit which can be identified as the designation of *bucket*, and no process which has this entity as its lm. The whole phrase is associated with the single semantic unit [DIE].[4]

For case (c), a phonologically simple expression which symbolizes a semantically complex unit, consider the meanings of *so* and *not* in the following:

(2) Would you like some coffee? If so, I'll make some, if not, I won't bother.

I suggest in Chapter 17 that *so* and *not*, as used in (2), have the status of 'proforms'. The category of 'pronoun' is a familiar one. A pronoun, such as *it*, is schematic for a definite noun phrase (with inanimate reference), and can be assigned an open-ended range of more specific semantic values. In (2), *so* is schematic for an affirmative clause, *not* is schematic for a negative clause; we

---

[4] The case of *kick the bucket* is unusual, even for an idiom. Many idioms are indeed analysable both phonologically and semantically, even though the component units may not have their standard semantic values. (This, after all, is what renders the expressions idiomatic.) If you *take the bull by the horns*, the 'bull' can be identified with a dangerous or difficult situation, 'the horns' with a central or intrinsic feature of the situation, which is tackled directly. See Chapter 27 for more on idioms.

might call these words 'pro-clauses'; *so* is interpreted as equivalent to the fully specified clause 'you would like some coffee', *not* is equivalent to a negative clause. In these cases, the complex content of the clause, either affirmative or negative, is symbolized by a single, unanalysable morpheme.

15.1.2 Partial analysability

It often happens that a word is felt to be internally complex, in the sense that a component morpheme can be identified, yet it is by no means obvious how the remaining part of the word is to be analysed.

Consider *butcher* and *grocer*. Phonologically, these terminate in what appears to be the agentive -*er* suffix; semantically, this analysis seems quite appropriate, too, since the words characterize a person in terms of their profession, i.e. in terms of what they do, exactly like *dancer*, *singer*, *writer*, and many more. Yet there are no base verbs *(to) butch* or *(to) groce* from which the nouns could be derived and which would designate the kind of activity that butchers and grocers engage in.

The situation is not uncommon. Take the names of the days of the week. These all end in -*day*, whose semantic value is fairly transparent. Yet, for most of the names, it is not at all obvious what to do with the remaining part. *Tues-*, in *Tuesday*, is in itself meaningless.

Or consider the forms *here* and *there*, and the now slightly archaic *hither* and *thither*, *hence* and *thence*. It looks as if we can associate the elements *h*- and *th*- with the meanings 'near the speaker' and 'far from the speaker'. But there is little to say about the meanings of the remaining fragments, -*ere* (which, incidentally, has different pronunciations in *here* and *there*), -*ither*, and -*ence*.

Consider, as another example, the names of the letters of the alphabet. Quite a number of these consist of a consonant (often, though not always, the typical 'phonetic' value of the letter) plus [iː], as with *B* [biː], *C* [siː], *D* [diː], *G* [dʒiː]. It is as if [iː] constitutes a morpheme, with the semantic value 'letter of the alphabet'. Speakers who call the last letter of the alphabet [ziː] rather than [zɛd] have extended this letter-naming schema to *Z*, which is indicative of the strength, and hence the productivity, of the schema. Questionable, though, is whether we should want to regard the onset consonant of the letter names also as a morpheme.

15.1.3 Unclear boundaries

It is not always clear where to draw the boundary between the component morphemes in a complex word. It follows, therefore, that it is not always clear what the constituent morphemes actually are.

The words in example (3) are unproblematic; these are adjectives derived by affixing -*ive* to the base verbs *act*, *effect*, *elect*, etc.

(3) active, effective, elective (surgery), adoptive (parent), dismissive (attitude), possessive (parents)

Slightly more difficult are the following:

(4) deceptive, receptive, consumptive, resumptive

We might want to recognize, on grounds of economy, the very same affix -*ive*. The adjective-forming affix could equally be identified as -*tive*, or even, in the case of *consumptive* and *resumptive*, as -*ptive*. The problem is caused by the fact that the base verbs—*deceive, receive, consume, resume*—have been considerably distorted in the derivational process, such that appeal to the verb gives little clue as to the most appropriate segmentation of the complex word.

Now consider (5):

(5) talkative, repetitive, additive, causative, figurative, punitive, laxative

Talkative is clearly derived from the base verb *talk*, parallel to the way in which *active* is derived from *act*. Yet in this case we should want to identify the suffix as bisyllabic -*ative*. The remaining examples raise the question whether the adjective-forming affix should be identified as -*ive*, -*tive*, or -*ative*/-*itive*. Some further complications arise. In the case of *causative* and *laxative*, we might argue that the derived forms are basically nouns, not adjectives, while in the case of *figurative* (and perhaps also *causative*), we might argue that the base form is a noun, rather than a verb.

Finally, there are words like those in (6), where the adjective-forming affix (whether -*ive*, -*tive*, or -*itive*) is again in evidence, but there appears to be no base from which the adjectives are derived. (A curious example is *restive*, whose meaning is at variance with the meaning of the presumed stem, i.e. *rest*.)

(6) passive, positive, genitive, primitive

Since there is no base from which *positive* is derived, there is no clue as to the identity of the adjective-forming morpheme (-*ive*, -*tive*, or -*itive*).

15.2 Coercion and bondedness

The internal structure of a word may be obscured by coercion effects. By **coercion** I refer to the phenomenon whereby a unit, when it combines with another unit, exerts an influence on its neighbour, causing it to change its specification.

Phonological coercion is illustrated by the words in (4), where the adjective-forming suffix -*(t)ive* has distorted the phonological shape of the base verbs.

Somewhat weaker coercion is observed in the plural form *houses* [haʊzəz], where the plural morpheme combines with a slightly distorted form of the noun stem [haʊs], namely [haʊz]. Interestingly, it is normally the affix which coerces the base, rather than vice versa. Recall from Chapter 14 that complex words are normally headed by the affix; it is the affix, not the base, which gives the word its semantic character. Coercion effects also demonstrate that the affix determines at least some of the phonological properties of the complex word.[5]

As is well known, the bound morphemes of English can be divided into two broad categories—those that coerce the stem to which they combine and those that do not. Among the latter are the suffixes *-less*, *-ness*, *-ly*, *-hood*, *-er*, and (barring isolated examples such as *houses* and *wives*), the plural morpheme, as well as prefixes such as *un-*, *dis-*, and *under-*. Non-coercing morphemes are illustrated in (6). Observe that as each morpheme is added to its base, the phonological structure of the base remains unchanged.

(6) friend, friendly, unfriendly, unfriendliness
    neighbour, neighbourhood, neighbourhoods

Coercive morphemes include *-ic*, *-tion*, *-(t)ive*, *-ian*. A particularity of adjective-forming *-ic*, for example, is that it requires that word stress falls on the immediately preceding syllable; the phonological shape of the base is adjusted accordingly.[6]

(7) démocrat:democrátic, phótograph:photográphic, réalist:realístic, póet:
    poétic

This aspect of *-ic* can be represented as follows.

(8) [. . .][ADJ]/[. . . 'σ] [ɪk]

The material to the right of the slash shows that the 'profiled' phonological element has to combine with an immediately preceding stressed syllable; the profiled morpheme contributes the semantic value 'adjective' to the composite expression.

As noted in the Box (p. 284), the suffixation of *-ence* to verbs terminating in *-fer* occasions a change in stress location (*prefér*:*préference*). However, when attached to verbs in *-cur*, no such coercion occurs (*recúr*:*recúrrence*).

As the above examples illustrate, change in stress location typically goes with a change in the phonetic qualities of the vowels of the stem; compare [prɪˈfɜː] and [ˈprɛfərəns]. Sometimes, the segmental content of the stem is also effected: *music* [ˈmjuːzɪk], *musician* [mjuːˈzɪʃən].

---

[5] With respect to 'regular' plural forms, where the shape of the morpheme—[s], [z], or [əz]—is determined by properties of the base, it could be argued that the affix is being coerced by the base.
[6] Note the contrast between the noun *arithmetic* and the adjective *arithmétic* (as in *arithmetic progression*).

When coercion occurs, it may be difficult to determine exactly where to place the boundary between the morphemes. The words in (4) illustrated the problem; is *deceptive* to be analysed as *decept + ive* or as *decep + tive*? *Musician* is even more problematic. Is the bound morpheme [ʃən] or [ən]? Is the base [mjuː'zɪ] or [mjuː'zɪʃ]? Here, the component morphemes have 'fused' into a tightly **bonded** structure.

Coercion effects may obscure the identity of the component morphemes. I have routinely found that speakers of English, when first asked about the relatedness of *horizon* and *horizontal*, *preside* and *president*, admit to not having noticed the connection previously. (Once apprised of the association, they readily concur that the forms are indeed related.) The similarity between the phonological forms [hə'raɪzən] and [hɒrɪ'zɒnt], and between [prɪ'zaɪd] and ['prɛzɪd], is clearly insufficient to suggest a morphological relationship to a significant number of English speakers.

Since coerced morphemes tend to lose their identity, bonded forms are liable to acquire idiosyncratic meanings, at variance with the composite meaning derived from their constituents. For example, *consumptive*, in the sense 'relating to tuberculosis', has only a very tenuous semantic relation to the verb *consume*. This should not be at all surprising. Since coercion has obscured the morphological relation between the verb and the adjective, the meaning of the derived form is free to drift away, as it were, from the meaning of the verb.[7]

15.3 Productivity

At this point one might well ask whether it matters for a speaker to be able to analyse a morphologically complex form. It could be argued that for a person to be able to use a word in accordance with the prevailing conventions of a language, it is necessary to learn only the conventions pertaining to the word in question. The relation of the word to other words in the language constitutes metalinguistic knowledge (that is, knowledge *about* the language, not knowledge *of* the language), which is strictly speaking irrelevant to a person's linguistic activity. It is beyond question that many speakers are able to use the words *horizontal* and *president* fully in accordance with the norms of the language, without being aware of their association with *horizon* and *preside*; it is not even necessary that they have the words *horizon* and *preside* in their lexicon. And if a person can use the words *butcher* and *grocer* appropriately, even though there are no verbs *to butch* and *to groce* from which these agentive nouns are derived, is it not also possible for a person to use the words *singer*

---

[7] I address the phenomenon of drift in the next chapter.

and *baker* appropriately, without awareness of the relation of these words to the base verbs?

I do not wish to underestimate the role of highly specific knowledge that makes up the grammar of a language. Certainly, speakers can, and probably do use complex forms without being aware of their internal structure. Nevertheless, there are two respects in which analysability may be relevant to a speaker's grammar.

First, the relatedness of forms will serve to structure the language's lexical resources. In addition to being associated with its own special semantic value, the word *singer* can be additionally 'filed' under: (i) 'sing', (ii) '-er', and (iii) the general schema for agentive nouns. The form *butcher* can obviously not be filed under a verb, but it can be filed under (ii) and (iii). These multiple links between words, between parts of words, and between words and schemas for words, plausibly enhance a speaker's ability to store and retrieve the lexical units of a language. A speaker does not have to learn tens of thousands of totally distinct phonological forms, each associated idiosyncratically with a meaning. Analysability introduces a degree of predictability (and hence, redundancy) into the language, thereby reducing storage requirements.

A second aspect concerns productivity. Productivity is the flipside of analysability. A word is analysable to the extent that it can be brought under a schema; the more salient a schema, the more readily a word can be analysed. Conversely, the more salient a schema, the more likely it is to be able to sanction new instances, created on the pattern of the schema. The fact that speakers are able to create new forms depends on their having recourse to schemas which sanction the new forms; the schemas, in turn, arise in virtue of the analysability of encountered instances.

The morphological devices of a language are liable to vary considerably with respect to their productivity.[8] Plural formation by suffixation of -*s* (or one of its variants) is highly productive in English; any noun (provided it has the appropriate semantics, i.e. if it designates a 'countable' entity) will have a plural form, and (unless the noun has an 'exceptional' plural) the plural form can be created through suffixation of -*s*. On the other hand, the derivation of 'negative' words through prefixation of *n*- is not at all productive. One cannot create new forms on the pattern of *or*:*nor*, *either*:*neither*. The number of negative words commencing in *n*- is essentially closed. Most morphological processes lie somewhere between these two extremes. Consider, for example, the productivity of adjectives in -*ive*, of verbs in *un*-, and of nouns in -*ance* and -*ness*.

---

[8] One reason for distinguishing between morphology (the internal structure of words) and syntax (the internal structure of phrases) is that syntactic schemas tend, on the whole, to be more uniformly productive than morphological schemas, which exhibit considerable variation in this regard. Even so, the distinction is not clear-cut. We shall see (Chapter 28) that syntactic schemas do vary in their productivity. As noted very early in this book, the distinction between morphology and syntax is best regarded as a cline, not an absolute.

A number of factors influence the productivity of a word-forming pattern.

(i) First, there is the salience of the schema which sanctions the new form. As argued in Chapter 14, schema salience is a function of the type frequency of its instances. All other things being equal, a schema which has a large number of different instances, none of which is itself particularly frequent, will be able to sanction new instances more readily than a schema with relatively few instances, each of which in itself may be quite frequent.

(ii) Secondly, the valence of a morpheme may severely restrict its usage potential. Every bound morpheme contains a specification of the kinds of items with which it can combine. Certain morphemes may be able to combine only with items with a very specific semantics; others may be restricted to occurring with items which have a very specific phonological structure.

For example, the morpheme *un-* can only attach to verbs which designate a 'reversible' process; moreover, the process is usually one that involves attachment, enclosure, or the 'bringing together' of entities: *unwrap, unfold, untie, unfasten, undo* (one's shoelaces), *unroll, unpack, unscrew,* but not **unopen, *unwrite, *uncook, *unsay,* or **unnail.* There is even the verb *unfurl* (a flag)— which exists in the absence of a corresponding verb *(to) furl.* The semantics of verb-deriving *un-* are such that the number of potential hosts is going to be rather limited, which necessarily restricts the number of verbs commencing in *un-.* Nevertheless, within the semantic boundaries set by the prefix, the prefix is quite productive. Essentially, any verb with the appropriate semantics can take the prefix. Thus, to cite some not so usual examples, I can *unclench* my fist, *ungrip* my toes, or *unplait* my hair.[9]

Concerning the phonological constraints imposed by a morphological process, consider plurals in [siːz], exemplified in *thesis* : *theses, hypothesis* : *hypotheses.* This way of forming plurals is restricted to nouns whose singular terminates in [sɪs]. Because of this restriction, plurals in [siːz] are bound to be rather few in number. Within the constraints set by the schema, however, plural formation in [siːz] is highly productive.

One fact that emerges from this discussion is that the productivity of a morphological device cannot be assessed simply by counting the number of derived forms. A morphological schema can be highly productive within the boundaries set by its phonological and semantic specifications, yet the number of actual forms sanctioned by the schema could be quite small.

(iii) Thirdly, it has to be recognized that quite a few bound morphemes idiosyncratically select their hosts. Consider the ways of forming abstract nouns from adjectives. There are quite a few possibilities in English. These

---

[9] Computer technology has given us the verbs *(to) undelete, (to) uninstall,* and *(to) unsubscribe.* These verbs are possible because of the 'reversibility' of the processes in question.

include *-ity* (*serene* : *serenity*), *-cy* (*proficient* : *proficiency*), *-ion* (*precise* : *precision*), *-th* (*long* : *length*), *-ance*/*-ence* (*abundant* : *abundance*). There is no phonological (or semantic) reason why we should say *abundance* rather than **abundity*, or *absurdity* rather than **absurdance* or even **absurdancy*; these are simply the established conventions of English. Each of the noun-forming suffixes selects a certain range of bases to which it attaches (or—which amount to the same thing—we could say that each base form selects its own affix).

There is, however, one noun-forming affix which is rather less choosy than those considered above, and which is rather freely available for the creation of nouns. This is *-ness*. Although not perhaps the standard form, one could easily speak of the *productiveness* (cf. *productivity*) of a process, the *preciseness* (cf. *precision*) of an operation, even the *deepness* (cf. *depth*) of a lake, or of one's sleep. Indeed, whenever a speaker is unable to retrieve the standard form (which, usually, involves some degree of phonological coercion and bondedness), a form in *-ness* can often be created 'on the fly'. This is the hallmark of productivity—the schema for nouns in *-ness* is available to sanction newly created forms. It may also be relevant that *-ness* has no coercive effect on the base to which it attaches; forms in *-ness* are therefore readily analysable, a fact which no doubt enhances the salience of the schema.

15.3.1 How to quantify productivity

Although a familiar and intuitively rather clear notion, there is a conceptual problem lurking behind the idea of productivity. The productivity of a particular word-forming device cannot be measured in terms of the number of established forms that conform to the pattern. Productivity, by definition, concerns the possibility of creating new forms—new for the individual speaker, and new for the language community. But if the forms are new (i.e., not already created), they cannot be listed and counted (since they do not as yet exist). One wants to speak, rather, of the number of potential forms. But how do we access the potential forms of a language?

The question receives a sophisticated treatment in an important paper by Baayen and Lieber (1991). Their approach rests on a statistical property of texts. In any text, the number of word tokens will exceed the number of word types. This is because certain words are bound to occur more than once. Even a very short text (say, a text of only 20 words in length) is likely to contain multiple instances of words like *the*, *a*, and *and*. As the length of a text increases, so also the number of word types will increase. The increase in word types, however, will not be proportional to the increase in the length of the text. If a text of 100,000 words contains n word types, doubling the size of the text will not result in a doubling of the number of word types. As the text (or corpus) increases in size, we will encounter more and more tokens of words that are already present, and fewer and fewer tokens of 'new' words. More-over, many of the new words will occur only once; these are the so-called *hapax legomena*.[10] The statistical properties of a large text (the relevant parameters being the number of word tokens, the number of word types, and the number of *hapax legomena*) enable predictions to be made concerning the properties of even larger texts, in particular, the number of 'new' words that are likely to be introduced.

The relevance of these considerations to the question of morphological productivity will be obvious. Suppose we are interested in the productivity of a bound morpheme. We take a large corpus and count: (i) the number of times the morpheme appears in the corpus (the token frequency of the morpheme); (ii) the number of different words which exhibit the morpheme (the type frequency of the morpheme); and (iii) the number of words con-taining the morpheme which occur only once in the corpus (the *hapax legom-ena*). The more productive a morpheme, the more types we will encounter relative to the number of tokens (each type will occur, on average, a small number of times) and the higher the number of hapaxes as a proportion of types. A non-productive morpheme will be characterized by a relatively high number of tokens of each type (each type will tend to occur very often) and by a virtual absence of hapaxes. As we increase the size of the corpus, the number of tokens of the morpheme will obviously increase. For a productive morpheme, the number of types will also increase, as will the number of hapaxes. For a non-productive morpheme, the number of types will increase hardly at all, and the number of new hapaxes will remain very low.

Table 15.1 (p. 294) shows some of the results of Baayen and Lieber's analyses. The noun-forming affixes are listed in terms of their declining productivity.

15.4 Hamburgers, cheeseburgers, and . . . burgers

I round off this chapter by commenting on the emergence of the morpheme *-burger*.

According to the OED, current at the beginning of the twentieth century was the expression *Hamburger steak*. This denoted a 'steak' (or something of the approximate size and shape of a real steak) but made out of minced beef. Initially, *Hamburger* was morphologically *Hamburg* + *er*. Hamburger steaks were associated with the city of Hamburg, just as Frankfurter sausages were associated with Frankfurt, and Londoners with London.

At a certain point, it would seem, speakers began to analyse the word as *ham* + *burger*. We can be confident of this because of the emergence of words like *cheeseburger*, *eggburger*, and even *burger*.

[10] The expression is Greek, from *hapax* 'once' and *legomenon* (pl. *legomena*) 'thing(s) said'.

Table 15.1 The relative productivity of noun-forming, adjective-forming, and verb-forming affixes

From verb bases	From adjective bases	From noun bases
(a) Noun-forming affixes		
-ee	-ness	-ian
-er	-ian	-ism
-ation	-ity	-al
-ment	-ism	
-al		
(b) Adjective-forming affixes		
-able	-ish	-ish
-ive	un-	-ous
	in-	-esque
(c) Verb-forming affixes		
re-	-ize	de-
be-	-ify	-ize
	en-	-ify
	be-	en-
		be-

Note: The affixes are listed according to their decreasing productivity.
Source: After Baayen and Lieber (1991).

The semantic motivation for the analysis (at the time when it was first made) is anything but obvious. First, *-burger* was not (yet) a meaningful morpheme. And while *ham* does mean something, its meaning is not strictly relevant to *hamburger*; hamburgers are not made of ham.

On the face of it, then, the recognition of a morpheme *-burger* in *Hamburger* is no less bizarre than identifying the morpheme *h-* in *hear*. When it was first made, the analysis of *hamburger* as *ham + burger* would appear to have been completely unmotivated, in that there could not have been a schema which sanctioned the analysis.

Or perhaps there was. I suggest that the schema was phonological in nature, rather than semantic. The second syllable in *Hamburger* contains the long vowel [ɜː]; being long, this vowel is likely to attract secondary stress: [ˈhæm ˌbɜːgə]. The word has the stress pattern appropriate for a compound noun: [ˈσ] [ˌσ σ]. The stress pattern is exhibited by compound nouns such as *dog-lover*, *man-hater*, *horse-breeding*, and countless more. Moreover, [ˈbɜːgə], with a strong-weak stress pattern, is able to constitute a foot. Given the tendency for polysyllabic English words to coincide with the foot (section 5.2.1), phonological aspects of *Hamburger* were able to trigger the emergence of *burger* as a bound morpheme, and even as an independent word.[11]

A comparable re-analysis of *Londoner* would not have been possible. The second syllable of *Londoner* ['lʌn.də.nə] contains the inherently unstressed vowel [ə]; *-doner* [dənə] could not have emerged as a morpheme, even less as a word.

Is the formation of words in *-burger* 'productive' in modern English? In a sense, it is. This does not mean that there are thousands of words (actual and potential) that terminate in *-burger*. The number of words in *-burger* is limited by the semantics of the resultant forms. Within these constraints, the fast-food industry has certainly displayed its linguistic creativity. New Zealanders are even able to enjoy 'kiwiburgers' (no, these are not made from the flesh of the flightless bird).

Study questions

1. Morphological analysis often assumes the building-block metaphor. According to the metaphor, complex words are assembled by placing the component morphemes side by side; conversely, complex words can be exhaustively cut up into their component parts. The metaphor works reasonably well in some cases, but fails in many others.

   Discuss the metaphor, and its general appropriateness in morphemic analysis.

2. Analysability of words. Wheeler and Schumsky (1980) presented speakers of English with a list of words and asked them to divide the words up into their component morphemes. The list included words whose component morphemes were fairly obvious (*advisable*, *faithfulness*), words where the morpheme boundaries did not seem so obvious (*cohesion*, *uproarious*, *nation*), words presumed to be morphologically simple (*radio*, *catalogue*), as well as some nonsense words (*flassion*, *dunctive*). They found that subjects brought three strategies to bear on the task: (i) identify a stem, and regard what is left over as an affix; (ii) identify an affix, and regard the remainder as a stem; and (iii) regard the word as an indivisible unit.

   One of the more curious findings of Wheeler and Schumsky was that more than half their subjects considered *baker* to be morphologically simple; neither the agentive suffix *-er*, nor the base verb *bake*, was identified as a part of the word. What might have been the reasons for the subjects' responses?

[11] Given that *burger* exists as an independent word, it could be argued that *cheeseburger* and the like are compound nouns, rather than morphologically complex words. A comparable situation holds for forms like *tableware*. To the extent that *ware* exists as an independent word, *tableware* might be analysed as a compound noun, rather than as a noun headed by the bound morpheme *-ware*. The examples suggest that the distinction between 'compounding' and 'derivation' is not a clear-cut one.

You might want to replicate Wheeler and Schumsky's experiment with your own set of test words, in English or another language.

3. *Alcoholic* is derived, by suffixation of *-ic*, from *alcohol*. In recent times, the word appears to have been re-analysed as *alco-holic*, as evidenced by such forms as *workaholic, chocaholic, technoholic, foodaholic, sexaholic*, and such like. On the gardening page of a local newspaper, I recently came across *hostaholic* 'a person keen on the cultivation of hostas'.

   (a) What could have initially motivated the re-analysis of *alcoholic*?

   (b) Investigate the spread of the suffix by doing a corpus search for creations in *-holic*. (This is easily done, on most electronic corpora, by searching for '*holic', where '*' is a 'wild card', standing for any combination of letters.)

   (c) Why are *chocaholic* and *foodaholic* acceptable creations, whereas **cookieholic* and **cookie-aholic* ('one who is addicted to eating cookies') are not?

   (d) Should the new morpheme be identified as *-holic*, or *-aholic*? If you opt for the former, how would you explain the presence of the 'a' in *workaholic*? Does the morpheme make phonological requirements on the host to which it attaches?

4. Reaganomics. The economic strategy of Ronald Reagan quickly became described as *Reagonomics*. (Do a corpus search to ascertain its usage.) Describe the process whereby this new formation could have come about.

   The free-market policies of the New Zealand politician, Roger Douglas, in the late 1980s, were dubbed 'Rogernomics'. Describe how this formation could have come about. Why was the word built up from the first name of the New Zealand politician, rather than from his surname (as was the case with Ronald Reagan)?

5. Kafkaesque. The morpheme *-esque* is attested in modern English in only a handful of words, prominent among which are *Kafkaesque* (which describes an irrational situation similar to those depicted by the novelist), *picturesque*, and perhaps *arabesque* and *grotesque*. (Recently, though, the form *Clinton-esque* has been in evidence.) Do a search on the electronic version of the OED for words in *-esque*. Could there be reason to claim that at an earlier period of English, formation of adjectives in *-esque* was rather more productive than it is today?

6. One sometimes comes across expressions like the following:

   That's a whole nother problem.

   It would appear that *another* (*an + other*) has been re-analysed as *a + nother*. What could have motivated the re-analysis?

   Do some corpus searches for occurrences of the form *nother*. The searches that I have conducted did not throw up much data. Why might this be?

   On the other hand, I have found that Internet searches may give a better indication of the incidence of the form. Try entering the collocation 'whole nother' on some of the Internet search engines. You may be surprised at the number of instances that are found.

Further reading

For the building-block metaphor, see FCG1: 452–66, and chs. 4 and 5 of Langacker (1999), esp. pp. 131–5. Morphological analysability is insightfully discussed in Gundersen (2001). A careful reading of Baayen and Lieber (1991) is strongly recommended.

CHAPTER 16

Schema competition

In this chapter I take up some further aspects of plural formation in English. There are, as everyone knows, different ways of forming plural nouns in English. The existence of different plural-forming devices raises a number of important questions. A single schema for plural formation will be inadequate—we will need a set of schemas, or sub-schemas, to cover the different cases. A speaker who wishes to produce a plural form cannot therefore appeal to *the* plural-forming schema; it will be necessary to select from a set of schemas that are, in a sense, in competition. In this chapter, I consider the factors that are relevant to this process.

The reader might feel that plural formation, in English, is pretty straightforward and lacking in inherent interest. The facts are, after all, well known and easy to state. But precisely because the facts are so uncontroversial, plural formation lends itself particularly well to illustrating some basic issues in grammatical theory.

16.1 Regular plurals

For the vast majority of English nouns there are three general patterns for the creation of the plurals:

(**1**) (i)   If the noun stem ends in a voiceless segment, the plural is formed by the addition of [s].
 (ii)   If the noun stem ends in voiced segment (including a vowel), the plural is formed by the addition of [z].
 (iii)   If the noun stem ends in one of [s, z, ʃ, ʒ, tʃ, dʒ], the plural is formed by the addition of [əz].

Although the facts are easy to state, there is a problem lurking in the distribution of the three forms. The problem is that (iii) constitutes a 'special case' vis-à-vis (i) and (ii). It is necessary for suffixation of [əz] to *override* suffixation of [s] and [z]. Otherwise, a noun like *dish* [dɪʃ], which satisfies the condition stated in (i), would be pluralized as *[dɪʃs].

How can we deal with this situation? Here are three possibilities:

(i) We write an algorithm for plural formation. An algorithm lays out a series of steps that need to be followed in order to get the desired output. In our case, the algorithm might consist of the three steps in (2). Note that the 'special case' *has* to be dealt with before the more general cases. If the special case were left to last, nouns ending in a sibilant would be supplied with [s] or [z].

(**2**) (i)   Does the noun end in one of [s, z, ʃ, ʒ, tʃ, dʒ]? If so, add [əz]. If not, go to (ii).
 (ii)   Does the noun end in a voiced segment? If so, add [z]. If not, go to (iii).
 (iii)   Add [s].

It would not be difficult, even for a novice, to write a computer program (in BASIC, for example) which would implement the algorithm and which would be guaranteed always to give the correct output. But even though the algorithm is guaranteed to work, there are several things about it that are problematic.

First, the ordering of the two general cases—those that add [s] and [z]—is arbitrary. Rules (ii′) and (iii′)—which reverse the application of the general cases—would give exactly the same output as (ii) and (iii).

(**2′**) (ii′) Does the noun end in a voiceless segment? If so, add [s]. If not, go to (iii′);
 (iii′) Add [z].

The ordering of the six sibilants in (2i) is also arbitrary. In fact, step (i), as formulated, collapses six separate procedures, whereby the noun stem is checked for each of the six sibilants, one by one.

A second aspect is that the three rules are themselves arbitrary. Why should [s] rather than [z] be added to stems that happen to terminate in a voiceless segment? Why should [əz] be added just in case a stem ends in one of [s, z, ʃ, ʒ, tʃ, dʒ]? This aspect could be addressed by appeal to natural classes defined over features such as {VOICED} and {SIBILANT}. Still, there is nothing in the format of the algorithm that requires reference to natural classes. Any process, even one that is highly 'unnatural', could be stated in an algorithm.

A more serious problem is the following. On the assumption that a linguistic description is a hypothesis of the contents of a speaker's mind (the 'cognitive assumption', section 1.3), the algorithm makes some curious predictions. For example, whenever a person wishes to produce the plural form of, say, *book*, they must first check whether the noun ends in one of the sibilant consonants. Not only is this counterintuitive, it predicts that plurals in [s] and [z] require more time to produce than plurals in [əz]. The special case turns out to be easier to process than the more general cases.

(ii) Another approach would be to postulate a single 'underlying form' of the plural morpheme—say, [z]—and then to derive the three 'surface' forms by the ordered application of rules. Two rules are needed: a rule of schwa epenthesis, which inserts [ə] between a sibilant and [z], and a voicing assimilation rule, which converts [z] to [s] after a voiceless segment.

(3) Underlying form: [dɒg] [z]   [kæt] [z]   [tʃɜːtʃ] [z]
   (i) Schwa insertion   [tʃɜːtʃ] [əz]
   (ii) Voice assimilation   [kæt] [s]
   Output: [dɒgz]   [kæts]   [tʃɜːtʃəz]

The rules have to apply in the given order. If the order were reversed, the plural of *church* would come out as [tʃɜːtʃəs].

A certain arbitrariness also attaches to this account. Plural formation would work equally well if the underlying form of the plural morpheme was taken to be [s] rather than [z], or indeed if it was taken to be [S], an alveolar fricative unspecified for voicing. (These alternative representations would require slightly different rules, as the reader can easily check.)

Needless to say, algorithms and ordered rules go counter to the basic assumptions of Cognitive Grammar. Let us now consider a third approach.

(iii) The choice between plurals in [s] and in [z] is determined by a constraint of voice assimilation, while the insertion of epenthetic [ə] follows from a prohibition against adjacent sibilants.

This last approach is clearly on the right track. It does not entail arbitrary rule ordering or counterintuitive processing steps. Let us consider how it might be implemented in Cognitive Grammar.

16.1.1 Three plural schemas

We can capture the three general cases by proposing three sub-schemas for the regular plurals, one for each of the affixes. The sub-schemas can be brought under an even more general 'superschema' (Figure 16.1). Each sub-schema specifies the phonological form of the plural affix and the relevant phono-

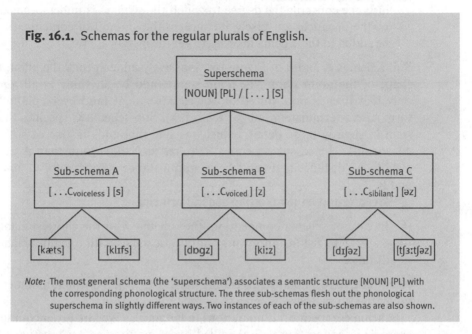

Fig. 16.1. Schemas for the regular plurals of English.

Note: The most general schema (the 'superschema') associates a semantic structure [NOUN] [PL] with the corresponding phonological structure. The three sub-schemas flesh out the phonological superschema in slightly different ways. Two instances of each of the sub-schemas are also shown.

logical characteristics of the noun stem to which it attaches. Not shown in Figure 16.1 is the fact that the content of each of the sub-schemas can be brought under other phonological schemas. Sub-schemas A and B are special cases of a voice assimilation schema, while C instantiates a schema which requires adjacent sibilants at the end of a word to be split up by an intervening [ə].[1]

The important question now is, how do we capture the fact that sub-schema C of Figure 16.1 'overrides' A and B? The problem is this: Any item that satisfies the conditions of C simultaneously satisfies either A or B. Noun stems such as *dish* [dɪʃ] or *judge* [dʒʌdʒ] give rise to **schema competition**. The stems satisfy the requirements of two competing schemas, schema C, and one of A and B.

(4) <u>Schema competition</u>. Schema competition occurs when two or more incompatible schemas are candidates for the categorization of a linguistic unit.

One factor influencing schema choice is the **elaborative distance** between schema and instance.

---

[1] Epenthetic [ə] also breaks up adjacent coronal stops in past tense formations *melted, coded,* etc. Schwa is inserted (sometimes optionally, sometimes obligatorily) between other pairs of word final consonants, as in *oven* [ʌvən], *often* [ɒfən], *mutton* [mʌtən], *little* [lɪtəl], *prism* [prɪzəm], *rhythm* [rɪðəm], and even *film* [fɪləm], though not in *kiln* *[kɪlən], *strength* *[strɛŋəθ], or *filth* *[fɪləθ]. The phenomenon of schwa insertion is therefore by no means limited to plural formation.

(5) <u>Elaborative distance</u>. The elaborative distance between a schema and an instance concerns the degree to which the schema is underspecified *vis-à-vis* the instance; conversely, it concerns the amount of content that has to be added to the schema in order to get the instance.

Sub-schemas A and B of Figure 16.1 massively underspecify the phonological shape of the noun stem. The noun stem could be anything at all, provided only that it ends in a voiced or voiceless segment (and every phonological form *has* to terminate in one or the other). Sub-schema C specifies the noun stem in slightly more detail, namely, as one that ends in one of six specific consonants. Hence, sub-schema C requires less 'filling out' than A or B; the elaborative distance between schema and instance is shorter for C than for A and B.

We can propose the following general principle:

(6) In case of schema competition, the schema with the shortest elaborative distance to the instance wins out over schemas with a greater elaborative distance.

According to (6), noun stems ending in [s, z, ʃ, ʒ, tʃ, dʒ] will automatically fall under the 'special case' schema C.

Schema competition is ubiquitous in language. (We already encountered an example in connection with the filled-onset requirement; see section 13.3.) It exists whenever a speaker is confronted with a choice between alternative forms. The noun designating the quality of being abundant could be *abundance*, *abundity*, or *abundancy* (section 15.3). All three forms are consistent with a noun-forming schema. Yet only the first is acceptable.

The question of schema competition arises in particular in connection with 'irregular' forms, that is, forms which are 'exceptions' to major patterns. It is to the irregular plurals that we now turn.

16.2 The irregulars

Alongside plural formation in [s], [z], or [əz], there exist a number of irregular plurals. In this section, I consider how these can be incorporated in the model that has been developed so far.

Although regularity and irregularity are familiar concepts, they are not without problems. We should certainly say, for example, that the plural form *books* is regular, since it is sanctioned by a very general schema. The form *theses* [θiːsiːz] (the plural of *thesis*) is not covered by this schema and to this extent it is irregular. At the same time, plurals such as *theses*, *hypotheses*, *bases* (plural of *basis*) can themselves be brought under a schema, as we shall discuss below. The schema for 'Greek' plurals in *-ses* is not as broad in its application as the schemas of Figure 16.1, since it applies to only a handful of nouns, but it captures a generalization nonetheless. In terms of the Greek-plural schema, *theses* is fully regular. (Take, for example, a word such as *osmosis*. If you should ever have occasion to use this word in the plural, chances are that you would create the form *osmoses* [ɒsməʊsiːz] rather than *osmosises* [ɒsməʊsɪsəz].) Regularity and irregularity, therefore, are not simple notions, but reflect the generality vs. specificity of the sanctioning schema. In the limiting case, a form will be *sui generis*. *Men* is the only example in English of a noun whose plural is marked by the replacement of a stem vowel by [ɛ]. It would be regarded as an irregular form *par excellence*.

One might expect that the existence of irregular forms would make a language more complicated. A language whose plural forms could all be brought under a single schema would, one might suppose, be 'simpler' than one in

---

German plurals: Regular and irregular forms

In German, there are eight ways of forming plurals:

1. The singular stem is unchanged: das Leben ~ die Leben 'life'
2. The stem undergoes vowel umlaut: die Mutter ~ die Mütter 'mother'
3. Suffixation of -*e*:   der Hund ~ die Hunde 'dog'
4. Suffixation of -*e* plus vowel umlaut: die Kuh ~ die Kühe 'cow'
5. Suffixation of -*(e)r*:   das Kind ~ die Kinder 'child'
6. Suffixation of -*(e)r* plus vowel umlaut: der Wald ~ die Wälder 'forest'
7. Suffixation of -*(e)n*:   die Straße ~ die Straßen 'street'
8. Suffixation of -*s*:   das Auto ~ die Autos 'car'

While various sub-regularities and statistical tendencies can be identified, depending on the gender of a noun and its phonological properties, it is a brute fact about German—and one which every foreign learner of the language knows only too well—that German plurals just have to be learned. It is significant, for example, that German dictionaries, including those intended for use by native speakers, give, for each head noun, its plural form. This procedure would be unthinkable in an English dictionary. The distinction, so clear-cut in English, between 'regular' and 'irregular' plurals, simply does not apply in German. In a sense, all German plurals are (more or less) irregular.

The situation has parallels in other languages. In Norwegian, there is a broad distinction, as in English, between a minority of 'strong' verbs, which form their past tense by a change in the form of the stem, and the remaining 'weak' verbs, which add a suffix. The 200 or so strong verbs are the 'irregulars'. Unlike in English, however, the weak verbs divide into two classes, those that form the past tense by suffixation of -*et* or -*a*, (where the choice of one over the other is determined by sociolinguistic or stylistic factors), and those that take the suffixes -*te* or -*de*. Since membership in the two weak classes is not fully predictable, even the weak verbs are irregular, to a degree. (See Endresen and Simonsen 2001 for more discussion.)

which there are several competing schemas, of differing degrees of generality, and removed from their instances by different elaborative distances. Paradoxically, however, native speakers of a language are not usually troubled by such matters. As a native speaker of English I do not feel that forms such as *men* and *theses* in any way complicate the language, nor do I experience any desire to 'regularize' these words. In fact, the very existence of irregularities shows that generation after generation of speakers have happily coped with these forms. Linguistic theory must reflect this fact. Irregularities have to be handled as natural aspects of a language, not as excrescences which needlessly complicate the grammar.

In this section, I consider how the irregular plurals of English can be represented, using the descriptive apparatus so far developed.

First, let us summarize the facts. The irregular plurals fall into a number of distinct groups:

(i)   A few words are unchanged in the plural form: *sheep, series, species, aircraft, grapefruit.*

(ii) A handful form their plural by changing the vowel: *man ~ men, woman ~ women,*[2] *mouse ~ mice, foot ~ feet, goose ~ geese.*

(iii) A few form their plural in *-en.* Two of these have a vowel change as well: *ox ~ oxen, child ~ children, brother ~ brethren.*

(iv) The plural affix [z] is sometimes associated with voicing of the stem-final fricative: *house* [haʊs] ~ *houses* [haʊzəz], *wife* [waɪf] ~ *wives* [waɪvz], *path* [pɑ:θ] ~ *paths* [pɑ:ðz] (for some speakers), etc.

(v)   Greek-sounding words ending in [sɪs] have plurals in [si:z]: *thesis* [θi:sɪs] ~ *theses* [θi:si:z], *hypothesis ~ hypotheses, antithesis ~ antitheses.*

(vi) Miscellaneous foreign plurals: *datum ~ data, phenomenon ~ phenomena, corpus ~ corpora, stigma ~ stigmata,* etc.

The possibility of establishing subgroups of irregulars suggests the existence of specific sub-schemas. Consider case (v)—nouns of (often) Greek origin which end in (unstressed) *-sis* [sɪs]. There are a fair number of these, and their common properties can be represented on the lines of Figure 16.2.

Figure 16.2 is headed by a very general plural schema. The schema merely associates the appropriate semantics [NOUN] [PL] with some phonological material. (Observe that the superschema in Figure 16.1 would in fact be an instance of this grand superschema.) The sub-schema associates the conceptual structure [NOUN] [PL] with the phonological form [... 'σ ... si:z]. This states that a 'Greek' plural terminates in [si:z] and that the preceding phonological material contains a stressed syllable. The plural forms *theses* and *hypotheses* instantiate the sub-schema. Observe that it is not possible to

---

[2] In varieties of English in which [ɪ] is centralized to schwa, e.g. South African and New Zealand English, the plural *women* becomes virtually identical in pronunciation with the singular *woman*.

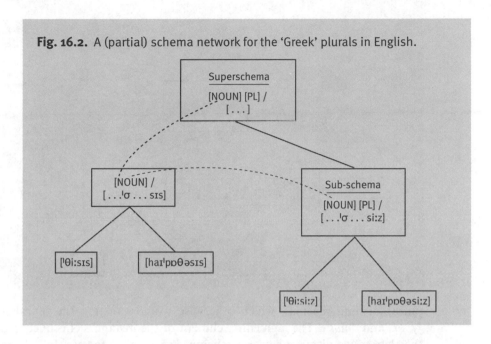

Fig. 16.2. A (partial) schema network for the 'Greek' plurals in English.

identify a segment, or segments, which uniquely symbolizes [PL]. The relation of the plurals to the singulars is captured by a relation between the semantic unit [NOUN] in the superschema and the schema for 'Greek' singulars, shown to the left. The schema specifies the noun, phonologically, as [. . . 'σ . . . sɪs]. Two instances of the schema (*thesis, hypothesis*) are shown.

The schemas for the Greek nouns already contain quite specific information about the phonological shape of both the singulars and the plurals. The elaborative distance between the schemas and their instances is therefore relatively short. Nouns which satisfy the schemas will tend automatically to be categorized by them, thereby pre-empting the application of the more general schemas in Figure 16.1. Concretely: if a speaker is looking to form the plural of a noun ending in unstressed [sɪs], the sub-schema in Figure 16.2 will immediately offer itself as the appropriate plural-forming pattern, thereby overriding the more general pattern of suffixation in [əz].

What about one-off plurals, like *foot ~ feet*? No other nouns form their plural in exactly this way, though a couple do undergo a change in vowel quality, and one of these (*goose*) has a plural in [iː]. Even so, it is clear that the items in question will have to be separately listed. The situation is sketched in Figure 16.3 (p. 306). The plural forms *feet, men*, and a few others may be brought under a schema which sanctions plural formation by means of a vowel change; the schema, however, does not specify the vowel. Because of the small number of instances, the schema for vowel-changing plurals has low entrenchment. The instances, on the other hand, will be highly entrenched. This fact causes the instances to pre-empt the application of more general

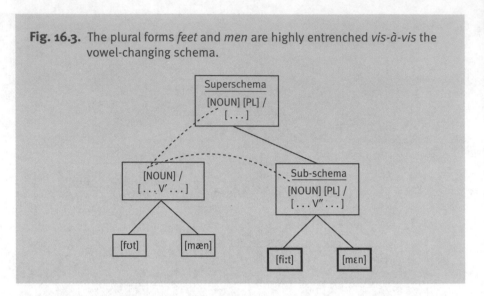

Fig. 16.3. The plural forms *feet* and *men* are highly entrenched *vis-à-vis* the vowel-changing schema.

plural-forming schemas, which otherwise would sanction the plural forms **foots* and **mans*. The high entrenchment of the instances effectively reduces the elaborative distance between schema and instance to zero. In a sense, the entrenched instances *are* the schemas for the forms *feet* and *men*.

Somewhat more problematic are the voice-changing plurals *wives*, *leaves*, *houses*, and *paths*. There is certainly a generalization to be captured here. Voicing affects only stem-final fricatives, mostly [f], and the preceding vowel in all cases is long. (There is no voicing change with *cliff*, *puff*, *stuff*, etc.) The problem is that not every noun that ends in [f, s, θ]—and none to my knowledge that ends in [ʃ]—undergoes the voicing change. Whereas *leaf* pluralizes to *leaves*, *reef* and *beef* do not undergo voicing. Some aspects of the situation are sketched in Figure 16.4.[3] The sub-schema captures the commonalities amongst a set of voice-changing plurals. At the same time, the forms which are covered by the schema also need to be individually listed. The instances are individually highly entrenched, more so, perhaps, than the schema which captures their commonality.

Since not every noun which terminates in [f] forms its plural in [vz], the situation depicted in Figure 16.4 is inherently unstable. We can imagine two kinds of change which might set in. On the one hand, the schema possesses a certain degree of entrenchment by virtue of the number of different plural forms which instantiate it (*leaves*, *knives*, *loaves*, *halves*, and several more). It is conceivable, therefore, that the schema could attract new instances, provided they match its specifications. This, however, seems not to be happening. (I cannot imagine English speakers wanting to pluralize *coral reef* to *coral reeves*.) We have to suppose that plural formation in [vz] is kept alive solely by

---

[3] A more comprehensive diagram would include sub-schemas for voice-changing plurals in [ðz] and [zəz], and which would be brought under a more general voice-changing schema.

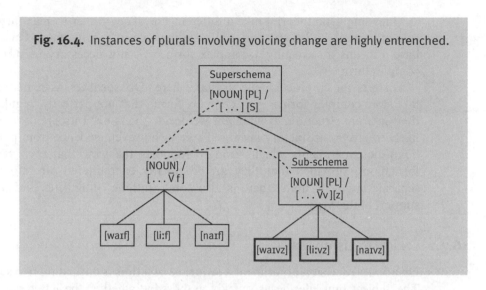

Fig. 16.4. Instances of plurals involving voicing change are highly entrenched.

the entrenchment of the instances, not by the entrenchment of the schema. However, not all the instances are equally entrenched. Low-frequency plurals, such as *rooves* and *hooves*, will be less entrenched than the higher-frequency items *leaves* and *knives*, and may tend to drift away from the schema towards 'regular' plural formation. Indeed, there does seem to be considerable variation here, with many speakers preferring *roofs* to *rooves*.

16.3 Rules and lists

Schemas emerge from acquaintance with the instances and are strengthened in proportion to the number of different instances. An entrenched and salient schema is readily available, both for the analysis of existing forms and for the creation of new forms. What would normally be called the 'rule' for plural formation is captured by the plural schemas.

In the case of frequently occurring plural forms, even 'regular' forms, such as *books*, it is likely that a speaker has stored these forms 'ready-made', and does not need to create them anew on each occasion of their use. At the same time, every use of a plural form (even a ready-made one) will reinforce the schema. In the case of rare words (and, obviously, in the case of newly invented, or newly learned words), the plural forms will need to be created. They are created in accordance with a schema—by analogy, as it were, with existing forms.

Cognitive Grammar therefore predicts that instances and schemas will generally co-exist and mutually support each other. Knowledge of the instances allows the schema to emerge, while the schema captures commonalities among the instances.

Many linguistic theories take a different line. They prefer to maximize the role of general statements and minimize the role of specific facts. Once you have a means for creating a complex form, it is not necessary to store the complex form.

There is an empirical issue at stake here. Do speakers as a matter of fact store complex forms, even complex forms that are perfectly 'regular' in their internal structure? How might we decide the issue? Introspection is unlikely to give a satisfactory answer. There is, however, evidence from psycholinguistic experiments which strongly supports the view that even regular formations, provided that they are frequently encountered, are stored as separate linguistic units; there is also some (indirect) linguistic evidence in support of this view.

16.3.1 Lexical decision tasks

On a lexical decision experiment a sequence of letters is flashed on to a screen. The subject must decide as quickly as possible whether the letter sequence constitutes a word or not. About half the letter strings constitute valid words, which are randomly interspersed with non-words.

One factor which influences performance on a lexical decision task is the frequency of the presented word—letter strings that constitute high-frequency words are recognized as words more rapidly than low-frequency letter strings. This is not surprising. High-frequency words, by definition, are encountered more often, and are therefore more strongly entrenched. The more entrenched a linguistic unit, the more quickly it can be activated.

It is easy to see how a lexical decision experiment can be brought to bear on the topic being discussed here. Suppose a person has to decide whether B-O-O-K-S is a word or not. Is the response time influenced by the frequency of the word form 'books', or by the combined frequency of the word forms 'book' and 'books'? If words are stored in their base form only, we should expect that response time to the plural will be a function of the combined frequency. If plurals are stored separately, we should expect that the frequency of the plural will be the crucial factor.

The experiment was performed by Sereno and Jongman (1997). They compiled two lists of nouns. The words on the two lists matched each other in terms of the combined frequency of the singular and plural forms. The words on one list, however, occurred predominantly in the singular, whereas the words on the other list occurred about equally often in the singular and the plural (Figure 16.5). Examples of high-singular nouns included *island, river, kitchen, village*. Nouns with higher-frequency plurals included *statement, window, expense, error*.

Sereno and Jongman found that it was the frequency of the word forms as such (singular or plural) that influenced decision time, not the overall frequency of the noun stem. Singulars from group A were recognized more

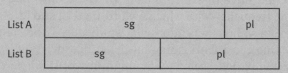

Fig. 16.5. Two groups of words tested in Sereno and Jongman (1997).

Note: Words in the two groups were matched for their combined singular and plural frequency; those in the first group, however, occurred predominantly in the singular, those in the second group were about equally split between singular and plural occurrences.

quickly than singulars from group B; plurals from group B were recognized more quickly than plurals from group A. They conclude:

the traditional rationale has been . . . that it is more efficient to derive morphologically complex items by rule, thus minimizing storage in memory for those derived forms. But it is also possible to look at the problem in terms of processing efficiency. One could argue that it is more efficient to store every piece of information separately, allowing direct access to all forms, without having to invoke the additional operation of a rule. The present series of experiments suggest that, at least for productive inflectional paradigms involving nouns in English, morphological processing is accomplished by individually representing all morphological variants . . . Storage limitations do not appear to be a critical factor. (Sereno and Jongman 1997: 434–5)

A similar conclusion was reached by Alegre and Gordon (1999) and by Baayen *et al.* (1997).

16.3.2 Past tenses in [t] and [d]

Bybee (2000) brings another kind of evidence to bear on the question of whether regular forms are separately stored. The evidence pertains, not to plural formation, but to an equally productive process in English—the formation of regular past tense verb forms through suffixation of *-d* (or one of its variants).

Walsh and Parker (1983) had found that the [s] at the end of monomorphemic words like *lapse* is slightly shorter than the segment at the end of words like *laps*, where the [s] constitutes a separate morpheme. Bybee refers to an unpublished dissertation by Losiewicz (1992), who showed that the same situation holds with final [t, d]; thus, 'morphemic' [d] in *swayed* is slightly longer than the [d] in *suede*. Durational differences were also found within instances of morphemic [d]—the past tense morpheme in high-frequency past tenses (such as *called* and *needed*) was shorter than the morpheme in low-frequency past tenses (such as *mauled* and *kneaded*). It would seem, then, that the high-frequency past tenses were being processed rather like the monomorphemic words, suggesting that, like monomorphemic words, they were being stored as preformed units.

A second piece of evidence cited by Bybee also pertains to [t, d] and concerns the frequency with which a word-final [t] and [d] is deleted. The deletion of these consonants was intensively studied by Labov (1972: 216–26) and Guy (1980). One consistent finding has been that deletion is more likely in monomorphemic words, such as *mist*, than in words where the final consonant is the past tense morpheme (as in *missed*). Bybee re-analysed the published data taking word frequency into account, and found that the deletion rate for high-frequency past tenses was higher than that for low-frequency past tenses, and more in line, in fact, with the deletion rate for non-morphemic [t, d]. Again, a reasonable conclusion is that high-frequency past tenses tend to be stored, and processed, as wholes.[4]

16.3.3 Drift

Indirect evidence for the storage of morphologically complex forms comes from the phenomenon of drift. When a complex form is constructed online from its constituents one should expect its meaning to be tightly constrained by the meanings of its constituents. However, if a complex form is stored as such it will become entrenched independently of its constituents, and will be liable to acquire idiosyncratic properties not sanctioned by its internal structure. It will be able to split off, as it were, from its base.

It is well known that derived forms do often drift away from their base forms and acquire specialized or idiosyncratic meanings. *Dirty* (Bybee 1985: 88, 90) has a range of uses that do not directly pertain to 'dirt', *terrific* is used with little reference to 'terror' or 'terrify', and *awesome*, especially in the speech of younger speakers, has lost all associations with 'awe'. The example of *consumptive* 'pertaining to tuberculosis' that was mentioned in the last chapter also illustrates the phenomenon.

In terms of its morphological structure, *dirty* is unremarkable. There are quite a few adjectives which are formed from nouns along the same pattern: *spicy*, *watery*, *oily*, *dusty*, *smelly*, *smoky*, etc. Not surprisingly, the adjective-forming schema is quite productive. Langacker (FCG1: 72) reports observing a child complain that he did not like a pie because it was 'too apricoty'. The child had created the form in response to his communicative intentions by application of the appropriate schema. But whereas *apricoty*—both for the child in question and probably for most adult speakers—is a novel, one-off creation, *dirty* is an established form. Symptomatic of this difference is the fact that *apricoty* refers directly to some characteristic of apricots (their flavour, probably), whereas *dirty* need not invoke associations with 'dirt'. It can be used in the sense '(mildly) obscene', 'pornographic', or even, simply, 'untidy'.

---

[4] R. Hudson (1997) has also re-analysed the [t, d] deletion data within the framework of Word Grammar, in terms of which are very compatible with the Cognitive Grammar approach.

The feet of the mountains?

We talk of the 'foot of a mountain', but what do we say if there are several mountains? The 'feet of the mountains' sounds odd, and to me, at least, invokes the image of mountains on the march. For me, *feet* specifically denotes those human or animal extremities which typically come in multiples of two. Similarly, many speakers baulk at 'computer mice'. For these speakers, *mice* specifically denotes the small creatures which scuttle across the floor.

The examples suggest that *feet* and *mice* are not simply the plural forms of *foot* and *mouse*, the words have acquired specialized meanings which are at variance with some uses of the corresponding singulars.

Since entrenched forms are liable to undergo drift, the existence of drift may be taken as evidence that a complex form has been individually stored. Significantly, examples of semantic drift can be observed even with regular plural forms. As the plural of *dish*, *dishes* can be used to refer to a plural number of entities of the kind 'dish'. Yet when you 'wash the dishes' you are probably not washing a plural number of 'dishes', you are washing plates, cups, knives, forks, in addition (possibly) to dishes. *Dishes* has acquired the idiosyncratic meaning 'collection of things that are used in preparing and eating a meal (and which will need to be washed afterwards)'. Similarly, *movies* can be used to refer to a plural number of entities of the kind 'movie', as when you ask whether a person has seen 'any good movies' recently. But when you 'go to the movies', *movies* refers to the kind of establishment where movies are shown.

The above examples concern semantic drift: a morphologically complex form, to the extent that it is entrenched independently of the base from which it derives, can acquire distinctive semantic nuances. Equally, a complex form can acquire distinctive phonological properties. (See, for example, the case study reported in Bybee and Scheibman, 1999.) The data cited in the preceding section can be seen as examples of just this phenomenon. The fact that a frequently encountered (and hence independently entrenched) past-tense form such as *needed* or *called* can acquire a phonological property of a monomorphemic word (namely, a reduction in the duration of the past tense marker) can be regarded as an instance of phonological drift.

16.4 Product-oriented rules

The evidence surveyed above suggests that speakers may well store complex forms ready-made, provided that the forms have been frequently encountered. This conclusion is at variance with the position of many grammatical theories, which seek to eliminate the storage of instances in favour of rule applications. Still, occasions are bound to arise in which a speaker will need to create a new form. The assumption, in most grammatical theories, is that speakers do this by applying rules to the simpler component elements. You create the plural form of a noun by applying a rule to the singular. The plural is created 'from' the singular, and morphological processes are often described as a way of 'getting from' a simpler form 'to' a more complex form.

Here I want to suggest that this process metaphor may not be appropriate. I begin by looking at an often cited study conducted many years ago by Jean Berko (Berko 1958).

16.4.1 The evidence of the wugs and the nizzes

Berko wanted to test children's knowledge of morphological rules. She did this by presenting the children with nonsense words and setting up situations which would elicit derived forms of the words. For example, the children see a picture of a bird-like creature called a 'wug'. Then they a see a picture of two of them and are prompted to refer to the creatures using the plural form, namely 'wugs'. Berko explained the rationale of the experiment as follows:

> If a child knows that the plural of *witch* is *witches* he may simply have memorized the plural form. If, however, he tells us that the plural of *gutch* is *gutches*, we have evidence that he actually knows, albeit unconsciously, one of those rules that the descriptive linguist, too, would set forth in his grammar. (Berko 1958: 150)

The experiment is often cited as evidence that even young children do know the rules and are able to apply them to the creation of new forms, and against the idea that complex forms are stored as wholes. In their recent textbook *Linguistics: An Introduction*, Radford *et al.* (1999) make just this point. The results of Berko's experiment go against the idea that speakers 'could simply have committed to memory' (p. 214) the plural forms; rather, the experiment shows that they 'do exhibit creative control of a variety of morphological processes' (p. 215). In another recent textbook, Berko herself (writing under the name of Gleason) repeated verbatim the above quotation from her 1958 article, and went on to draw an even more radical conclusion:

> In the linguistic view, language is an *autonomous* faculty, separate from intelligence, that infants are innately driven to acquire. The various subsystems of language are internalized as sets of algorithms or rules that allow the child to produce new utterances she has never heard before. For instance, a child of 3 or 4 years can produce the plural of a nonsense word *gutch*, which she has never heard before. (Gleason and Ratner 1998: 380)

The procedure of getting a speaker to perform a morphological operation on a nonsense form has been referred to as the wug-test (Pinker 1984: 187).

For Pinker, the fact that children 'pass the wug-test'[5] is evidence for the reality of symbol-manipulating rules. Such has been the influence of Berko's paper.

But let us go back to the original article of 1958. Remarkably, the article suggests conclusions that are at variance with those traditionally assumed.

There were 19 pre-schoolers, aged between four and five, and 61 first-graders, aged between five and a half and seven. The children were tested on a variety of morphological processes (past-tense formation of novel verbs, possessive forms of novel nouns, etc.). Results on plural formation are shown in Table 16.1

We see, first, that the children, even the youngest ones, were quite good on a real word—*glass*—that they would probably have encountered both in the singular and the plural. Their production of the correct plural might well have been due to their previous encounters with the word.

The nonsense words divide into two groups: *wug*, *lun*, *tor*, *heaf*, and *cra* (which more than half the children, even the youngest ones, got right), and the remaining four: *tass*, *gutch*, *kazh*, and *nizz*, which even the oldest ones got wrong about two-thirds of the time. It is therefore disingenuous, at best, for Berko to have intimated in the passage quoted above that young children's ability to form the plural of *gutch* indicates their mastery of a rule. Her

Table 16.1 Children's performance on the creation of novel plurals

Singular	'Correct' plural	Pre-schoolers N=19	First-graders N=61	Mean
glass	glasses	75	99	91
wug [wʌg]	wugs [wʌgz]	76	97	91
lun [lʌn]	luns [lʌnz]	68	92	86
tor [tɔr]	tors [tɔrz]	73	90	85
heaf [hiːf]	heafs [hiːfs]/[hiːvz]*	79	80	82**
cra [kraː]	cras [kraːz]	58	86	79
tass [tæs]	tasses [tæsəz]	28	39	36
gutch [gʌtʃ]	gutches [gʌtʃəz]	28	38	36
kazh [kæʒ]	kazhes [kæʒəz]	25	36	31
nizz [nɪz]	nizzes [nɪzəz]	14	33	28

* Both [hiːfs] and [hiːvz] were accepted as correct.
** These are the numbers cited in Berko (1958: 159, 161). There is obviously an error here; the mean of 79 and 80 cannot be 82! Calculations on other data in the table (which is compiled from Berko's Tables 2 and 3) suggest that some small errors have crept into the figures and/or the means cited for the two groups.
Note: The figures in the columns show the percentage of correct forms.
Source: Data derived from Berko (1958).

[5] Pinker (1999: 191) writes: 'when children are old enough to sit still in experiments, they pass the *wug*-test'. The importance that Pinker attaches to the test is indicated by the fact that 'wug-test' is included in the book's glossary (p. 296) and in the index, where there are more than a dozen references.

data show that only 28 per cent of the four- or five-year-olds were able to create the plural of *gutch*, and even the six- to seven-year-olds were not much better.

Ingram (1989: 440) interpreted Berko's data to mean that while children may have acquired the rules for plurals in [s] and [z] they had not yet acquired the rules for plurals in [əz]. This raises the question how the children handled the words which required a plural in [əz]. Did they attempt to apply the rules that they had learned, by wrongly attaching [s] or [z] to the more difficult items? This seems not to have been the case. Although Berko (1958) does not list all of the children's wrong responses, we are told that on the items *cra* and *lun* 'the child . . . answered . . . with silence: the wrong answers were invariably the unaltered form of the singular' (p. 162). Likewise with the forms *tass* and *nizz*:

Again, the wrong answers consisted in doing nothing to the word as given. It must be noted, however, that in these items, the children delivered the wrong form with a great deal of conviction: 62% of them said 'one *tass*, two *tass* as if there were no question that the plural of *tass* should and must be *tass*. (Berko 1958: 163)

Why should the children have been so insistent that *tass* remained unchanged in the plural? A plausible answer is that the word *tass* already 'looks'—or, more accurately, 'sounds'—plural; it ends in [s], which is a typical exponent of plurality. Berko herself put it like this:

the child's rule for the formation of the plural seems to be: 'a final sibilant makes a word plural'. (Berko 1958: 173)

This 'rule' can be interpreted in two ways. On the one hand, it could be an instruction to add a sibilant—specifically, [s] or [z]—to a noun stem. Alternatively, the rule describes the form of a plural noun. If a noun ends in a sibilant, the noun satisfies the rule description, and can therefore be regarded as a plural.

In fact, glancing over the items in Table 16.1, it is apparent that the error rate is roughly proportional to the degree of resemblance of the final segment to [s, z]. It appears that the children had acquired, not so much a rule for making plurals, but a schema of what a plural looks like. A plural noun is one which ends in [s] or [z], or in some consonant that sounds like [s] and [z].[6]

This suggests a somewhat different approach to morphological derivation. To use terms from Bybee (1995), rules for complex morphological forms may be product oriented rather than source oriented:

A source-oriented rule operates on an input form (the 'source'), and changes it in some specified way in order to get the output (the 'product').

---

[6] Solomon (1972) also reported that five- and six-year-olds had difficulty with [əz], observing that nonsense words ending in [θ, ð, f, v] tended to remain uninflected in the plural. She speculates that 'the children might be using a rule which reads (in sophisticated terms), "a fricative ending indicates plurality"' (Solomon 1972: 48).

A <u>product-oriented rule</u> states the characteristics of the output (the 'product'). The output may be created in accordance with a schema, or retrieved ready-made.

In terms of a product-oriented rule for the plurals, it is not so much a question of starting from a singular and doing something to it in order to create a plural; it is a question of producing (or retrieving) a form that conforms with the plural-schema.

The great wug hoax

Everybody has heard about the abundance of words that the Eskimos have for different kinds of snow.

Geoffrey Pullum's delightful essay 'The great Eskimo vocabulary hoax' (Pullum 1989) traces the myth back to some unsubstantiated remarks made by Benjamin Lee Whorf in his essay 'Science and Language' (in Whorf 1956). (Pullum surmises that Whorf got the Eskimo example from a passing remark in Boas 1911.) In his essay, Whorf claims that the different morphemes that the Eskimos have for 'snow' is testimony to the cultural salience of snow in the lives of these Arctic dwellers.

Somehow, the fact of the Eskimo snow words was taken up by popular culture. Subsequent writers inflated the number of snow words, often, it would seem, sucking numbers out of their thumbs, and always with the purpose of demonstrating the cultural relativity of vocabulary items. In point of fact, according to Pullum, the number of Inuit morphemes for 'snow' is not very different from the number of snow words in English.

Pullum makes the point that few writers who mention the abundance of snow words in Eskimo ever take the trouble to ascertain the facts, or even to go back to Whorf's (or to Boas's) original text. A similar situation, I think, has arisen with the wugs. The wug test continues to be cited as evidence that even young children are fully able to apply 'source-oriented' rules to input forms that they have never before encountered. A careful reading of Berko's 1958 article shows that this conclusion is not warranted. Even Berko herself, it seems, fell prey to the wug myth. Writing forty years later, she could state that a pre-school child 'can produce the plural of a nonsense word *gutch*, which she has never heard before' (Gleason and Ratner 1998: 380), even though her own research had shown that over 70 per cent of the four- and five-year-olds that she studied could *not* produce the plural form, and that those aged five and a half to seven did not perform much better.

16.4.2 The evidence from the past tense

Additional evidence for product-oriented rules comes from the English past tense.

There is a group of English verbs which are identical in present and past tense—*beat, put, set, cut, hit, spread*. Significantly, all of these end in [t] or, more rarely, [d]. These are the very sounds that are used to form the 'regular' past tenses.

Bybee and Slobin (1982), studying the acquisition of past-tense forms in English, found that pre-schoolers who are able to apply the regular suffixation rule ('add -*ed*') failed to apply it to verbs ending in -*d* or -*t*, even for verbs like *melt* and *pat* which take the regular suffix:

Our hypothesis is that the pre-schoolers, rather than functioning with a suffixation rule that requires that *t*/*d* be ADDED to the verb, are functioning with a schema . . . which says that if a verb ends in *t*/*d*, then it is an acceptable past tense. They are not concerned with the ADDITION of a marker, but rather with how the general shape of the word fits the pattern. Of course, they also show evidence of a suffixation process, but it is not strong enough to apply consistently to words that fit the schema. (Bybee and Slobin 1982: 271)

The similarity with Berko's results are striking. Berko's children failed to attach the regular plural ending just in those cases where the words terminated in [s] and [z] (or a similar sound).

The results from adult subjects were even more interesting. In order to induce errors with the adults, Bybee and Slobin put their 40 subjects under time pressure. About 80 per cent of the errors consisted in actual past-tense forms which failed to match the present tense forms that had been presented.

The errors can be divided into three groups (see Table 16.2). The largest group consisted in the subjects offering past-tense forms which displayed some phonological resemblance to the present tense and which were also semantically related. The second, smaller group consisted in past-tense forms which bore only a phonological resemblance to the present-tense form. The third and smallest group consisted in forms that phonologically resembled the present-tense verb, but were not in fact past tenses at all. Nevertheless, some of these forms did exhibit some phonological characteristics of past tenses. *Wed*, for example, which was offered as the past tense of *weed*, contains the rhyme [ɛd] which occurs in the past-tense forms *said*, *lead*, and *read*.

It is easy to see what was happening in these cases. When required, quickly, to come up with the past tense of a verb such as *(to) seat*, subjects retrieved a stored past-tense form (*sat*) that bore some semantic and phonological relation to the verb and which was indeed a past-tense form. If they had applied a 'rule' to the present-tense form they would surely have come up with the 'correct' form *seated*.

Further evidence of the strength of product-schemas comes from some subclasses of irregular past tenses. There is a small group of irregulars (7a) whose present tense contains a short [ɪ] vowel and whose past tense has short [æ]. The verbs also have past participles in [ʌ]. A further characteristic is that the verbs end in a nasal consonant, preferably [ŋ]. There is a somewhat larger

Table 16.2 Errors produced when
adults were required, under time
pressure, to give the past-tense forms
of English verbs

Present tense	Proffered past tense
Group A	
seat	sat (9)
set	sat (5)
lend	loaned (4)
raise	rose (4)
search	sought (4)
cite/sight	saw (1)
	sought (1)
crawl	crept (1)
Group B	
flow	flew (2)
lean	lent (2)
ride	rid (2)
shun	shone (1)
Group C	
glide	glow (1)
weed	wed (1)
wheel	weld (1)

Note: The number of error tokens is given in
parentheses.
Source: Data from Bybee and Slobin (1982).

group of verbs in (7b) which form their past tense in [ʌ] and which terminate in a velar nasal, a non-velar nasal, or a non-nasal velar.

(7) a. sing ~ sang   b. dig ~ dug
         ring ~ rang   stick ~ stuck
         drink ~ drank   hang ~ hung
         swim ~ swam   sneak ~ snuck
                                strike ~ struck
                                win ~ won

Observe that it would be difficult to capture the commonality of the verbs in (7b) in terms of a source-oriented schema, since the present tenses contain a variety of different vowels. What unifies the verbs in (b) is their past-tense forms.

Another group of verbs have [ɛ] in the past tense which corresponds, in the present, to either [ɛ] or [iː].

(8)   dwell ~ dwelt   smell ~ smelt
       bend ~ bent   feel ~ felt
       lend ~ lent   keep ~ kept
       sleep ~ slept   sweep ~ swept
       deal ~ dealt   dream ~ dreamt
       leave ~ left   cleave ~ cleft

Again, what unifies these verbs is their past-tense forms, not the properties of the present tenses. Observe that the past tenses all terminate in [t]. Mostly, the [t] has been 'added', in other cases the [t] 'replaces' the [d] of the present tense. Especially interesting in this regard are the last two examples, *leave ~ left* and *cleave ~ cleft*. These show a voicing change in the stem from [f] to [v]. This change can easily be explained on the assumption that the [v] assimilates to [t], in accordance with a past-tense schema (for the group of verbs in question) which requires a final [t] in association with the [ɛ] vowel.

16.5 Schema competition vs. dual processing

In a series of publications, culminating in Pinker (1999), Steven Pinker has argued for the existence of two distinct and independent cognitive mechanisms to handle 'regular' and 'irregular' forms. Regular forms, it is claimed, are handled by 'symbolic rules', that is, rules which manipulate symbols regardless of the symbols' semantic or phonological content. (For Pinker's use of the terms 'symbol' and 'symbolic', see the Box, p. 23.) Symbol-manipulating rules, it is claimed, constitute the very essence of a 'generative' grammar and lie behind a speaker's ability to produce an infinite number of new expressions. Irregular forms cannot be handled by symbolic rules (this, after all, is what makes them irregular) and have to be committed to memory one by one. Nevertheless, some patterns may be discernible amongst the irregulars, and these patterns may set up 'associative networks', whereby, for example, the association of present tense *shrink* with past participle *shrunk* reinforces, and is reinforced by, the association of present tense *string* with past participle *strung*; the association may even interfere with a form such as *bring*, causing a speaker to occasionally produce incorrect *brung*.

Regular and irregular inflection must be computed by two different systems. Regulars are computed by an implementation of a classic symbolic rule of grammar, which concatenates an affix with a variable that stands for the stem. Irregulars are memorized pairs of words, but the linkages between the pair members are stored in an associative memory structure . . . Thus, while *string* and *strung* are represented as separate, linked words, the mental representation of the pair overlaps in part with similar forms like *shrink* and *bring*, so the learning of *shrunk* is rendered easier given a constant number of learning trials, and analogies like *brung* occur with nonzero probability as the result of noise or decay in the parts of the representation that code the identity of the lexical entry. (Pinker and Prince 1991: 233)

It will be observed that Pinker's account of the irregulars bears certain affinities with the schema-competition model presented in this chapter. It is less clear, though, why it should be deemed necessary to handle the regulars by a different cognitive mechanism. In the model presented in this chapter, all forms, whether regular or irregular, are handled in the same way, namely, as forms sanctioned by a schema. Even if we disregard the fact that 'regularity' and 'irregularity' are probably not clear-cut notions anyway (see section 16.2), regular forms—whether these be plurals, past tenses, or whatever—are those forms which fall under more general schemas; the regulars are forms which fail to be categorized by more specific schemas, either because they fail to match the phonological specifications of the specific schemas, or because they are not specifically listed as instantiations of the specific schemas. Neither is it justified to draw a distinction between regulars and irregulars in terms of whether the forms have been committed to memory. As we have seen, there is evidence that even regular forms (at least, those with high frequency) may be stored as such, while sub-schemas for irregulars may display a limited productivity. A more parsimonious (and methodologically preferred) account would seek a unified treatment of both the regulars and the irregulars. As Langacker has observed, Pinker's insistence on proposing a dichotomous account of regular and irregular morphology 'inverts the usual scientific practice of seeking a unified account for seemingly diverse phenomena' (Langacker 1999: 143).

Wreaking havoc I

Put this sentence into the past tense:

(i)   He wreaks havoc wherever he goes.

Attempt this before turning to the box on the following page!

Wreaking havoc II

Many English speakers that I have tried this out on offer *wrought* as the past tense of *wreak*.

Wreak is a somewhat rare verb in English, restricted, in the main, to the collocations *wreak havoc* and *wreak vengeance*. The low overall frequency of the verb means that speakers will rarely have encountered the past-tense form; consequently, the past-tense form is unlikely to be entrenched in memory. In such a situation, one might expect subjects to apply the regular rule and to give the past tense as *wreaked*. As a matter of fact, *wreaked* is the 'correct' form; dictionaries do not list *wreak* as a strong verb. Moreover, *wreak* and *wrought* are etymologically unrelated. (Check out the forms in a good dictionary.) What, then, induces speakers to treat *wreak* as an irregular, strong verb, and to come up with the 'incorrect' form *wrought*?

Several factors may be relevant:

(i) First, there is the existence of the form *wrought*. Like *wreak*, this is also a somewhat rare word in English, by and large restricted to the collocation *wrought iron*. Since *wrought* is of low frequency, it will not be entrenched, and speakers may not be very confident about its accepted usage range. For reasons mentioned below, the word looks like a past tense (or a past participle—which it historically is), though there is no corresponding present tense form. (Actually, *wrought* is a past participle of an archaic form of *work*).

(ii) A number of verbs have past tenses in [ɔːt], irrespective of their present tense forms: *teach ~ taught, buy ~ bought, catch ~ caught, fight ~ fought*. In other words, [ɔːt] is quite strongly associated with past-tense forms.

(iii) There is a family resemblance between *wreak* and its putative past tense *wrought* and other strong verbs which have [iː] in the present: *seek ~ sought, teach ~ taught*, also *see ~ saw*. These form their past tenses with [ɔː].

All these factors 'conspire' towards making the already known form *wrought* a plausible candidate as the past tense of *wreak*.

Study questions

1. Devise and carry out an experiment in which subjects must rapidly produce the past-tense forms — or, alternatively, past participle forms — of a series of English verbs. (The effect is enhanced if some nonsense verbs are included.) The 'errors' on such an experiment can be quite startling. Analyse subjects' responses in terms of schemas for past tense formation.

2. I suggested in this chapter that the reason why some English verbs have past-tense forms that are identical to their present tenses is that the present-tense forms already end in a sound that is a typical marker of the past tense, namely [t] or [d]. In other words, the verbs already match a schema of what a past tense should sound like.

   Does a comparable situation hold with singulars and plurals? Is there a tendency for nouns which have irregular plurals — i.e. plurals formed in ways other than by suffixation of [s], [z], or [əz] — to be nouns which already end in [s], [z], or [əz]? Consider nouns which give rise to uncertainties. Ask subjects (under time pressure) to produce the plural of *octopus*, *rhinoceros*, *hippopotamus*, *excursus*, and *oasis*.

3. Processes. One sometimes hears the form ['prəusɛsiːz] as the plural of *process*. (The 'regular' form would be ['prəusɛsəz].) How do we account for this? One also hears the form ['spiːʃiː] intended as the singular of *species*. How can this be accounted for? What is the status of *faeces* (singular or plural)?

4. Consult some standard reference grammars of English in order to compile a list of nouns which undergo voice change in the plural (e.g. *leaf ~ leaves*, *roof ~ rooves*). Test some English speakers on their preferred usage. How much variation in usage is there among your subjects? How can your results be interpreted in terms of the schema-competition model?

Further reading

On salience and elaborative distance, see Tuggy (1993). For semantic drift, see Bybee (1985: 88–90). See Köpcke (1998) for a re-analysis of Berko's (1958) data on the acquisition of plural morphology.

There is a fairly extensive literature on the German plurals. A good starting point is Köpcke (1988). A major issue has been whether suffixation of -s, in spite of its low type frequency in the language, might not have the status of the 'regular' (or, at least, default) strategy of plural formation. See Clahsen *et al.* (1992) and Marcus *et al.* (1995). For a critical voice against the idea of -s as the 'regular' form, see Bybee (1995).

A topic not addressed in this chapter is connectionist implementations of the learning of regular and irregular morphology, and the affinities between this approach and the schema-competition model presented here.

Important landmarks in connectionist modelling are Rumelhart and McClelland's (1986) demonstration that a system, trained on pairings of present- and past-tense forms, exhibits a pattern of learning development not unlike that of children acquiring the past tense. More sophisticated models are described in Plunkett and Marchman (1993, 1996). For critiques of connectionism as a model of language knowledge, see the lengthy article by Pinker and Prince (1988).

A good overview of the issues (especially the symbolic vs. the associative network approach) may be found in Plunkett (1995) and in McLeod *et al.* (1998: 178–88). McLeod *et al.*'s book comes with software which allows the reader to run connectionist learning experiments, including the learning of the past tense.

CHAPTER 17

Kinds of symbolic units

This chapter recapitulates some of the concepts that have been introduced so far in this book. These concepts are applied to a discussion of symbolic units, and the parameters in terms of which different kinds of symbolic units may be characterized. The following parameters are considered:

(i) the extent to which the phonological and/or semantic poles of a symbol unit are rich in content or are schematic;

(ii) the extent to which the phonological and/or semantic poles are autonomous or dependent;

(iii) the valence of a unit, at both the semantic and phonological poles;

(iv) the degree to which a unit coerces, and is coerced by, a neighbouring unit;

(v) the degree of internal complexity of the unit;

(vi) the degree of entrenchment of the unit.

The procedure will enable us to characterize many well-established linguistic categories, such as 'bound morpheme', 'proform', 'function word', and so on. The chapter concludes with a discussion of agreement markers triggered by inflection classes. These are of interest to the extent that agreement markers seem, in many cases, to lack a semantic content, and may thus be considered to be potentially problematic in their status as symbolic units.

17.1 Contentful vs. schematic

The first parameter we consider has to do with whether a unit is richly specified or whether its content is schematic. The distinction can apply both to the phonological and to the semantic pole. We also need to bear in mind that schematicity vs. contentfulness is a matter of degree, it is not a clear-cut, either/or distinction. With this proviso in mind, we can make the following broad classifications:

(i)   a unit may be richly specified, at both the phonological and the semantic poles;

(ii)   a unit may be richly specified phonologically, while being semantically schematic;

(iii) a unit may be richly specified semantically, while being phonologically schematic;

(iv)   a unit may be schematic, both phonologically and semantically.

17.1.1 Phonologically contentful + semantically contentful

Most lexical words, such as *tree*, *house*, *run*, are richly specified, both semantically and phonologically. The same goes for phrasal and clausal expressions, whether these be ready-formed formulaic expressions or expressions that a speaker constructs online.

As noted, schematicity and contentfulness are a matter of degree. Even amongst lexical words there are differences in the degree to which semantic content is specified. [POODLE] is semantically more specified than [ANIMAL], [RUN] is more specified than [GO]. Certain lexical words, such as *thing*, *do*, and *something*, though fully specified phonologically, are in fact rather schematic in their semantic content. As a matter of fact, the semantic content of *something* is probably not too different from the schematic semantic content of [NOUN]. Whatever can be designated by a noun (with the exception of human entities), can also be designated by *something*.

17.1.2 Phonologically contentful + semantically schematic

In contrast to lexical words, most so-called function words, such as *the*, *a*, *of*, while phonologically fully specified, are semantically schematic.

A major use of the preposition *of*, for example, is to profile an inherent relation between two entities (see Study question 2, Chapter 12): *father of twins*, *victim of the crime*, *top of the cupboard*, *diagnosis of the patient*, *author*

of the novel. Each of these expressions invokes a different relation. The preposition itself, though, is not reasonably regarded as polysemous. It has a
unitary, albeit schematic value, which unifies with the more contentful relation
present in the semantic structure of the trajector noun.

The determiners *the* and *a* are likewise highly schematic in their semantic
content. *The*, for example, profiles a definite entity (that is, an entity identifiable to both speaker and hearer) whose conceptual content is supplied by
the noun with which the determiner combines. The indefinite determiner is
schematic for an entity that the speaker has singled out for attention, but the
identity of which is assumed to be unknown to the hearer. Determiners are
discussed in Chapter 18.

An important category of words which are semantically schematic is that of the
proforms. A proform is a 'substitute' for a semantically more elaborated
expression. Proforms are schematic for the range of expressions for which they
substitute.

The category 'pronoun' is a familiar one. There are quite a number of
pronouns in English which differ with respect to the range of more specific
concepts for which they are schematic. *It* designates an entity that is identifiable to both speaker and hearer (gendered entities, though, are excluded
from the schema). *It* is therefore schematic for a (singular) definite nominal.
He and *she* specify the schematic entity for gender. *One* is schematic for
indefinite nominals, while *someone* is schematic for indefinite person-referring
nominals. The interrogative pronouns *who?* and *what?* request specification of
an unknown entity. The proforms merely characterize the unknown entity as
human or non-human, respectively. *Which?*, on the other hand, presupposes
that the designated entity is one of a smallish group. Possessive pronouns
(*mine*, *hers*) are akin to the definite pronouns. Although indifferent to the
numerosity of the designated entity, they present it as one that bears a possessive relation to someone. *This* and *that* profile some entity that is taken to be
near, or not near, to the speaker. Interestingly, these words are schematic not
only for things, but also for locations, directions, manners, actions, extents,
and even non-linguistic noises. Consider the following uses of *this*:

(1) a. This is where I put it.
      b. This is the way he went.
      c. This is the way to do it.
      d. This is what he did.
      e. This is how big it was.
      f. He went like this [GESTURE].

In addition to the pronouns we can identify proforms which are schematic
for other kinds of semantic categories. *There*, in *Put it there!*, is schematic for
a range of more precisely characterized locations; it is kind of pro-
prepositional phrase. *Do* and *be* (in some of their uses) are candidates for the
status of pro-verbs. We have seen that one important function of *be* is to lend

a temporal profile to an otherwise atemporal relation (section 11.3). The word merely profiles the persistence, through time, of a relation, but lacks any specification of the kind of relation that is involved. *Be* could be described as the proform for a more fully specified stative relation. Likewise, *do*, in some of its uses, is schematic for any kind of event. In *Louise went to the museum and I did too*, *did* designates a schematic event which receives a more fully specified interpretation from the semantic content of the preceding clause.

We can even recognize pro-clauses. In the following, *so* is schematic for whatever situation is being entertained, while *not* is schematic for a negated clause. Again, the content of the pro-clauses is provided by the preceding context.

(2) Do you want some coffee? If so, I'll make some. If not, I won't bother.

Derivational and inflectional morphemes also fall under the rubric of phonologically specified but semantically schematic. The agentive suffix *-er*, in one of its uses, designates a person who performs some schematic activity; its schematic content is fleshed out when the affix attaches to a verb stem (section 14.1.2). The suffix *-ness* designates a quality, the identity of which is supplied by the adjectival stem with which *-ness* combines (*goodness*, *thoroughness*, etc.).

17.1.3 Phonologically schematic + semantically schematic

We turn next to symbolic units that are both semantically and phonologically schematic. Paradigm examples are lexical and grammatical categories, such as [NOUN], [VERB], [WORD], [MODIFIER], [HEAD], [COMPLEMENT], [CLAUSE], and many more. Constructional schemas, as discussed in section 12.2.2, fall into this category, too.

The characterization also applies, very often, to case categories, such as [NOMINATIVE], [ACCUSATIVE], [GENITIVE], in languages such as Latin or Russian. The semantic value of the cases is to profile an entity in terms of its semantic role within a larger configuration, usually a clause. The typical value of accusative case, for example, is to profile an entity as the primary lm of a verb, while the typical value of the genitive is to profile a thing as bearing a relation of some kind to another thing. Not only is the semantic value of the case categories highly schematic, in languages such as Latin or Russian the phonological shape of the case marker varies according to the inflectional class of the noun to which it attaches. It is not possible, therefore, to associate [ACCUSATIVE] or [GENITIVE] in these languages with any specific phonological form.

17.1.4 Phonologically schematic + semantically contentful

The fourth possibility is units that are semantically richly specified but phonologically schematic. It is difficult to find clear examples of this situation. For the designation of a specified semantic content it is necessary, it would

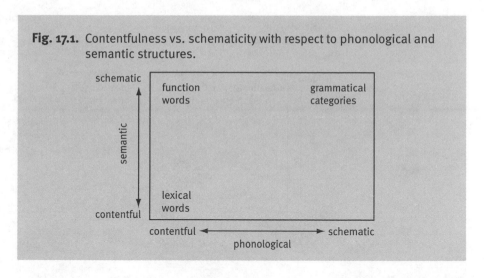

Fig. 17.1. Contentfulness vs. schematicity with respect to phonological and semantic structures.

seem, to use a specified phonological content. Perhaps some principle of iconicity is operative here. Alternatively, it might be argued that the very viability of a symbolic system rests on the requirement that richly specified concepts need to be designated by differentiated (and hence contentful) phonological forms.

The distinctions discussed above are represented in Figure 17.1 as regions in a two-dimensional space.

17.2 Dependence vs. autonomy

As with the distinction between schematicity and contentfulness, autonomy vs. dependence can be observed at both the phonological and the semantic pole of the symbolic unit. While bearing in mind once again that autonomy and dependence form a continuum rather than a dichotomy, we can envisage a number of possibilities. These are illustrated in Figure 17.2 (p. 328).

Content words are (generally) phonologically autonomous (see section 9.3). They can, however, vary in their degree of semantic autonomy/dependence. Names of whole physical objects (*tree*, *house*) are quite high in semantic autonomy; relational nouns (*uncle*), less so; verbs, prepositions, and adverbs are semantically dependent.

Bound morphemes, such as the plural morpheme in English and noun-forming morphemes such as *-er* or *-ity*, are phonologically dependent in that they need to attach to a phonological host. They are semantically dependent also, in that they require a host to provide semantic substance to the schematic entities present in their semantic structure.

Function words (articles, prepositions) also tend to be dependent, both phonologically and semantically. *The* and *of* are scarcely viable as independent

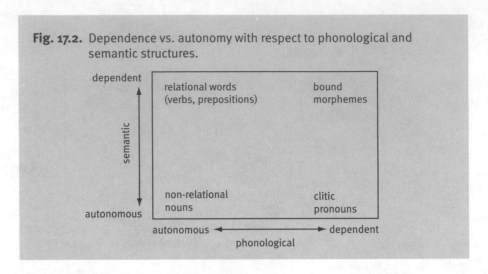

Fig. 17.2. Dependence vs. autonomy with respect to phonological and semantic structures.

phonological structures. Likewise, one can scarcely entertain the concepts [OF] and [THE] independently of a larger semantic configuration. Proforms, on the other hand, tend to be semantically autonomous, though they vary considerably in their phonological aspects. Demonstrative pronouns, such as *this* and *that*, are phonologically autonomous, whereas *it* tends towards phonological dependence.

Not infrequently, a concept can be designated by alternative forms which differ with respect to their phonological dependence. Consider the personal pronouns in French. These come in three forms. First, there is the distinction between the nominative and oblique forms (*je, tu, il,* vs. *me, te, le*). These are phonologically dependent, in that they need to attach to a verbal host (*Je le vois* 'I see him', *Il me voit* 'He sees me'). Phonologically autonomous forms of the pronouns also exist—*moi, toi, lui* (or even *celui-là* 'him there'). These are the forms that are used in the absence of a verbal host. It could even be argued (cf. Taylor 1996) that the possessive pronouns of English—*mine, yours, hers,* etc.—are phonologically autonomous forms which correspond to the phonologically dependent *my, your, her,* etc.

17.3 Valence (choosiness vs. promiscuity)

As explained in Chapter 12, the valence of a unit—its disposition to combine with other units—is closely tied up with its dependence. However, as noted in the preceding section, it is necessary to separate out phonological dependence from semantic dependence. French *je* and *moi* are distinguished with respect to their phonological dependence.

Here, I draw attention to a further aspect of a unit's disposition to combine, namely, the extent to which a unit is free to combine with virtually anything as opposed to the requirement that it combines only with units of a specified kind. I refer to this parameter as the choosiness vs. promiscuity of a unit (section 9.3). An example will illustrate the distinction.

Both the plural morpheme in English and the possessive morpheme can have the phonological form [s], as illustrated in (3).

(3) a. The cats are fighting.
     b. the cat's tail

Both instances of [s] are phonologically dependent (they have to attach to something). The morphemes differ, however, with respect to their choosiness. The combinatorial possibilities of plural [s] are more restricted than those of possessive [s]. The plural morpheme can attach only to nouns—specifically, to singular count nouns which do not have an irregular plural. The possessive morpheme, in contrast, attaches to the end of a noun phrase. The morpheme takes as its phonological host whatever item happens to stand at the end of a noun phrase. This could be a preposition, a verb, or a noun which does not in fact count as the 'possessor'.

(4) a. the people I was telling you about's new car
     b. the man I met's new car
     c. the people across the street's new car

The parameter of choosiness vs. promiscuity is crucial in differentiating the categories of word, affix, and clitic.

Words, as 'minimal free forms', are phonologically autonomous. They are also phonologically promiscuous, in the sense that a word can, in principle, combine in the stream of speech with just about any other word, or word class. There are few restrictions (and certainly no restrictions of a segmental nature) on the kind of words to which a word may be adjacent.

Affixes—of which plural [s] is an example—are phonologically dependent, and are extremely choosy with respect to what they attach to. An affix can attach *only* to items of a particular kind. The restrictions concern the semantic properties of the potential host as well as, in many cases, its phonological properties. Plural [s] attaches only to singular noun stems, more specifically, those which terminate in a voiceless segment. Often, the hosts to which an affix attaches is determined by convention. The situation characterizes the less productive affixes, such as noun-forming -*ity* or -*th* (section 15.3).

Clitics—of which possessive 's' is an example—share properties of both words and affixes. Like affixes, they are phonologically dependent. Like words, they are rather free with respect to which items they attach to. As we have seen, possessive [s] can in principle attach to practically anything.

17.4 Coerciveness and bondedness

The parameter of coerciveness and bondedness concerns the extent to which a unit, when it combines with another, exerts an influence on its neighbour, causing it to change its shape; the one unit 'coerces' its neighbour, forcing a change in its specification. When coercion occurs, the resultant complex form is liable to exhibit the property of bondedness—it becomes more difficult to segment the unit into its component parts.

Phonological coercion was discussed in section 15.2. When a noun stem and the plural morpheme combine, the phonological shape of the plural morpheme has to adjust to the phonological characteristics of the stem. A similar situation holds with the negative prefix *un-* ; the shape of the prefixes adjusts according to the phonological form of its host (section 8.2). Often, the bound morpheme coerces the phonological shape of the stem. In English, there are some derivational morphemes, such as *-ity*, which dramatically affect the phonological shape of the stem. When this kind of coercion occurs, the resultant form tends to lose its analysability. The component morphemes tend to coalesce into a highly bonded structure.

Coercion can also occur at the semantic level. Consider the case of the so-called phrasal verbs in English. You can 'look up' the chimney (in order to see what is there) and you can 'look up' a word in a dictionary (in order to learn about its meaning). In the former case, *look* and *up* preserve their usual meanings in the language. Neither word coerces the meaning of the other, and neither specifically selects the other. (You could, for instance, if you so wished, 'peer' or 'gaze' up the chimney, or, depending on your location, look 'down' or 'out of' the chimney.) In the second case, *look* and *up* coalesce to form a semantic unit in which the basic meaning of *up* has been coerced by a metaphorical meaning of *look*. In this expression, each word specifically selects the other. You cannot 'gaze up' a word in a dictionary, nor can you 'look down' a word in a dictionary. With coercion comes bondedness. Symptomatic of the bondedness of the expression is the fact that 'look up' functions as a single verbal unit in passive sentences. One could say that a word needs to be 'looked up', but it would be scarcely possible to say that a chimney has to be 'looked up'.

17.5 Internal complexity

In principle, internal complexity is a straightforward distinction. Monomorphemic units are (by definition) internally simple—they cannot be analysed into component units. Any expression which can be analysed into component units is (again, by definition) internally complex. Internally complex units comprise inflected and derived words such as *dogs* (which can be analysed into *dog* plus the plural morpheme) and *goodness* (which analyses into *good* plus the nominalizing morpheme *-ness*). Phrases (*book on the table*) and constructional schemas are also internally complex.

As discussed at length in Chapter 15, determining the internal structure of a unit is not always straightforward. First, there is the possibility that one pole of the symbolic unit (semantic or phonological) is internally complex, while the other pole (phonological or semantic, as the case may be) defies analysis. Secondly, analysability is itself a somewhat fuzzy notion. To what extent is *look up* (as when you look up a word in a dictionary) semantically analysable? Moreover, as expressions, by virtue of their frequent use, become entrenched, their internal structure may become less evident to speakers. The topic is addressed below.

17.6 Established vs. innovative

Whether expressions are established or innovative, again, looks like a fairly straightforward distinction. Idioms, formulas, and fixed expressions are established multi-word expressions which speakers have to learn as such. The greeting formula *How do you do?* is an established expression the form and meaning of which are fully determined. If a speaker did not know that this was the conventional thing to say on being introduced to someone, she would not be able to assemble the expression on the basis of more general principles in the language. Contrasting with formulaic expressions are innovative creations, which speakers construct online in order to symbolize situation-specific conceptualizations. It is well known that Chomskyan linguists have emphasized the 'creativity' of linguistic production—the essence of linguistic competence is that speakers are able to produce (and understand) an unlimited number of expressions which they have never before encountered.

The distinction between 'established' and 'creative' uses of language is certainly a valid one, in principle. However, it would be an error to restrict the set of established expressions to those that cannot be constructed from general principles. In section 16.3 I reviewed evidence that frequently occurring forms, even if they are internally complex, may be stored and accessed as units. As the internal structure of a unit fades from conscious awareness, a form is liable to undergo drift (both semantic and phonological), which further weakens the salience of its internal structure.

Many syntactically complex expressions—even those whose internal composition is quite unexceptional—have likewise achieved unit status. I would imagine that for most English speakers, the friendly warning *I wouldn't do that if I were you* is an established expression. It has been heard and used on many occasions, is stored as a unit, and does not need to be constructed online from its component parts. Yet the expression is perfectly 'regular' with respect to its internal structure and the meaning which it symbolizes. If we understand the category of 'established expressions' to include any complex expression which, through frequent use, has acquired unit status, then we shall have to admit that a very great deal of what speakers actually say consists of established chunks, and that knowing a language involves acquiring a huge number of such chunks.

According to the bottom-up orientation of Cognitive Grammar, constructional schemas, whether these pertain to the structure of words (i.e. morphological schemas) or phrases (syntactic schemas), emerge through familiarity with their instances. Once the schemas have emerged, instances can be created through application of the schemas. It is unlikely, however, that the emergence of a schema expunges a person's knowledge of instances which motivated the schema. Although an English speaker knows that nouns can be modified by a preceding adjective, the [ADJ N] schema can well coexist with knowledge of specific, frequently used collocations. Most English speakers, I would imagine, access *boiling water*, *mad dog*, *vicious crime*, *mashed potatoes*, and countless more, as preformed chunks.

17.7 Inflection classes and the problem of 'meaningless morphology'

In this section I address a phenomenon that is potentially problematic for the view that language is inherently symbolic. At issue are phonological forms the use of which does not appear to be motivated by semantic considerations. We can best introduce the issue by way of an example.

Why do we say, in Italian, *la casa* 'the house' but *il giardino* 'the garden'; or, in German, *das Haus* but *der Garten*? What governs the choice between the phonologically distinct forms *il* and *la*, *das* and *der*, of the definite determiner? The answer, of course, has to do with the 'gender' of the nouns in question. Italian *casa* 'house' is a noun of feminine gender, *giardino* 'garden' is a noun of masculine gender. (In German, the corresponding nouns are neuter and masculine, respectively.) It is a rule of Italian that the definite article has to 'agree' with the noun in gender. Hence, a singular masculine noun takes the definite article *il*, and a singular feminine noun takes the definite article *la*. The expressions **il casa* and **la giardino* are horribly ungrammatical. The ungrammaticality is not semantic in nature. It is not that the semantic unit [HOUSE] is in some way incompatible with the meaning of *il*. Rather, it has to do with a formal requirement of gender agreement.

Noun gender is an example of a more general phenomenon, that of inflection classes. We need to set up inflection classes whenever words of a particular lexical category, such as nouns or verbs (the 'controller'), select distinct phonological forms of items with which they combine (the 'target'). Symptomatic of inflection classes, therefore, are situations in which a semantic unit can be symbolized by a range of phonological forms, the choice between them being determined by some property of the controller.

Inflection classes, so defined, comprise traditional categories of noun genders, noun declensions, and verb conjugations. Verbs of different declensions select phonologically different forms for person, number, tense, and aspect inflections; nouns of different genders select phonologically different forms of articles and adjectives, and are associated with phonologically different proforms. Even English has inflection classes (though they are not traditionally regarded as such). The distinction between weak verbs (those which form their past tenses in -*ed*) and strong verbs (which form their past tenses in other ways) is a distinction between two inflection classes. (Actually, we should need to divide the strong verbs into a number of smaller inflection classes, some of which would have only one member, according to the particular way in which they form the past tense.) English nouns also form inflection classes with respect to how they form their plurals. One might even say that verbs form different inflection classes according to the nominalizing suffixes that they take. As noted in section 15.1.1, verbs terminating in -*fer*, -*tend*, and -*ceive* take different suffixes when abstract nouns are formed from the verbs.

Membership in an inflection class is not determined, primarily, by semantic considerations.[1] To be sure, in the gender languages of Indo-European, it is generally the case that noun gender does correspond to biological gender, at least with respect to nouns which designate humans or animals whose biological sex is of interest to humans. Paradigms such as the following suggest that one can recognize the morphemes -*o* and -*a* which designate entities as (schematic) males and females, respectively.

(5) il ragazzo 'the boy   la ragazza 'the girl
     il figlio 'the son'   la figlia 'the daughter'
     un tedesco 'a German man'   una tedesca 'a German woman'

In accordance with general principles, the affixes would be regarded as the head of the nouns, the stem (*ragazz*-, etc.) being the modifier. Concerning the definite articles, we would say that *il* designates a schematic (definite) entity of (biologically) male gender, whose semantic structure is fleshed out by the establishment of a valence relation with a noun which designates a kind of entity of (biologically) male gender.

With respect to the vast majority of nouns in the language which designate inanimate entities, the semantics-based approach fails. There is no way that gardens can be regarded as 'masculine' entities, houses as 'feminine' entities. We shall need to say that the gender-designating morphemes -*o* and -*a* establish two categories of nouns, namely [NOUN$_{MASC}$] and [NOUN$_{FEM}$]. At the

---

[1] Although gender in the Indo-European languages does not, on the whole, correlate with semantic categories, Corbett (1991) cites a number of languages in which noun classes are semantically determined. There is also a lively debate in Bantu linguistics over the semantic origins of the noun classes, and whether these are still operative in the modern languages (G. Palmer 1996: 126–41).

phonological pole, these are associated with [. . . o] and [. . . a], while the semantic representation (since the semantic import of the gender categories is nil) is in both cases [THING].[2] Likewise, for the adjectives, determiners, and pronouns, we need to recognize both masculine and feminine forms. Agreement patterns are captured by the content of the base of these forms, which specifies that the forms are eligible to enter a valence relation only with items of the same gender class.

While the facts of gender (and, more generally, of inflection classes) and of agreement patterns can be represented within a Cognitive Grammar framework (for a fuller discussion, see FCG2: 180–9), the very existence of inflection classes is somewhat puzzling, since they contribute little to the symbolization of conceptual structure. English, for example, which lacks noun gender, is thereby not one whit less efficient as a symbolic system than languages which do have gender systems. On the contrary, elaborate inflection class systems might seem to be dysfunctional, in that they place a heavy burden on a speaker's memory. But while inflection classes certainly present the adult foreign language learner with severe problems, they are a fact of many languages, and speakers of these languages show no sign of wanting to give them up. It would even seem that speakers take delight in the formal complexity of their language. For my part, therefore, I am inclined to see the complexities of inflection classes, and the sometimes elaborate systems of agreement patterns with which they are associated, as manifestations of humans' delight in what I called (p. 14) form-focused activities. To the extent that they lack a symbolic-conceptual content, agreement patterns are a further example of 'pure phonology' (section 5.4).

17.7.1 Noun gender in German

My claim that noun gender lacks a symbolic function (at least with respect to inanimate nouns) should not be taken to imply that noun gender is utterly arbitrary and unmotivated.

Consider the case of noun gender in German (Köpcke and Zubin, 1983, 1984). As is well known, nouns in German are assigned to one of three genders, masculine, feminine, and neuter. The gender of a noun controls the forms of the article, as well as the endings on adjectives. Noun gender is also a factor in plural formation.

For nouns denoting humans, grammatical gender correlates in the main with biological gender. The same goes for nouns denoting animals whose biological sex is relevant to humans, such as farm animals and household pets. (Even so, there are some well-known exceptions: *das Mädchen* 'girl' is neuter,

---

[2] Minor schemas for masculine and feminine nouns will also be needed, in order to capture the fact that gender, in Italian, is not always predictable from the final vowel. Nouns terminating, in the singular, in -*e* can belong to either gender, while some nouns in -*a* are masculine.

as is *das Kind* 'child'.) For the remaining nouns—the vast majority—gender assignment has nothing to do with biological sex. This is not to say that German gender is arbitrary. Köpcke and Zubin claim that the gender of a noun is motivated by a number of factors, morphological, phonological, and semantic.

(i) Morphological. For morphologically complex nouns, gender is determined by the gender of the final constituent. *Stadt* 'city' is feminine, *Theater* 'theatre' is neuter, *Stadttheater* 'city theatre' is also neuter. This fact should not be at all surprising. The final constituent is reasonably regarded as the head of the complex noun, and it is only to be expected that the head should contribute its gender to the complex form. Nominalizing suffixes also determine the gender of the nouns they derive. (Again, the suffixes are plausibly regarded as the head of the derived nouns.) Nouns derived by the suffixes *-heit*, *-keit*, and *-ung* are feminine, those derived by *-ling* and *-er* are masculine, diminutives derived by *-chen* and *-lein* are neuter.

(6) heizen '(to) heat'   die Heizung 'heating'
     schön 'beautiful'   die Schönheit 'beauty'
     wünschbar 'desirable'   die Wünschbarkeit 'desirability'
     früh 'early'   der Frühling 'spring'
     die Frau 'woman'   das Fräulein 'young (unmarried) woman'
     die Katze 'cat'   das Kätzchen 'kitten'

While the internal structure of the nouns in (6) is fairly transparent, this is less so in the case of many foreign borrowings (7).

(7) a. die Audienz, Kompetenz, Konkurrenz, Korrespondenz, Potenz, Tendenz, etc.
     b. die Bilanz, Performanz, Substanz, Toleranz, etc.
     c. die Aktion, Derivation, Korrelation, etc.

Even in the donor languages (French in the case of the more established items, English for the more recent ones), the corresponding words may not be fully analysable. Whereas English *performance* is clearly derived from *perform* through suffixation of *-ance*, there is no stem from which *substance* can be derived; once the nominalizing suffix *-ance* has been recognized, the residue *subst-* has no unit status in the language. The situation is likely to be more prevalent in German, in that the base form, if there is one, may not have been borrowed into the language.

Be that as it may, the suffixes in (7) all confer feminine gender. (It is possible that this aspect may itself have been borrowed from French, where the suffixes *-ence*, *-ance*, and *-ation* are all associated with feminine gender.) It is conceivable, even, that some speakers may not identify *-anz*, *-enz*, and *-ation* as morphemes at all, yet still associate nouns ending in these sounds with feminine gender. We should have to say, in this case, that certain phoneme sequences in a noun have come to be associated with a certain gender, irrespective of whether these phoneme sequences can be analysed as fully-fledged morphemes. This leads us to the second major factor that influences gender, the phonological structure of nouns.

(ii) Phonological. Köpcke and Zubin discovered that certain sound combinations tend to be associated with certain genders. The correlations they discovered are trends—exceptions exist, and sometimes a word may be subject to conflicting trends. Among the trends that they discovered are:

- nouns commencing in *kn-* are (with one exception) masculine: *der Knall* 'explosion', *der Knick* 'fold', *der Knödel* 'dumpling', etc. The exception is the neuter noun *das Knie* 'knee'.
- nouns ending in -NC, i.e. in a nasal plus consonant, tend to be masculine: *der Wind* 'wind', *der Hund* 'dog', *der Zimt* 'cinnamon', *der Wunsch* 'wish'. There are some exceptions, e.g. *das Amt* 'office', *die Hand* 'hand'.
- nouns ending in a fricative plus 't' tend to be feminine: *die Furcht* 'fear', *die Sicht* 'visibility', *die Angst* 'fear', *die Luft* 'air', *die Schrift* 'writing', *die Zukunft* 'future'. There are quite a few exceptions: *der Geist* 'spirit', *der Dunst* 'steam', *der Saft* 'juice', etc.

The psychological reality of these and other phonological principles was confirmed in an experiment in which subjects had to assign gender to nonsense monosyllabic words (Köpcke and Zubin 1983). If gender assignment were truly arbitrary, one would expect subjects to have responded randomly. In fact, about 70 per cent of the responses confirmed the gender assignments that had been predicted on purely phonological grounds.

(iii) Semantic. A particularly interesting finding concerns the correlation between gender and the schematicity of a word's meaning. Words with a rather general, or schematic meaning, tend to be neuter (8), superordinate terms also tend to be neuter (9), while names of basic-level entities tend to be either masculine or feminine (or, more rarely, neuter).

(8) General terms

das Material 'material'	das Gerät 'piece of machinery'
das Objekt 'object'	das Stück 'piece'
das Ding 'thing'	das Zeug 'stuff'
das Glied 'part, member'	das Teil 'part'

(9) Superordinate terms

das Obst 'fruit'	das Gemüse 'vegetables'
das Tier 'animal'	das Wild 'game animal'
das Vieh 'cattle'	das Metall 'metal'
das Instrument 'musical instrument'	das Lebensmittel 'foodstuff'

(10) Basic-level terms

(a) names of fruits	(b) names of musical instruments
der Apfel 'apple'	der Flügel 'grand piano'
der Pfirsich 'peach'	die Violine, die Geige 'violin'
die Birne 'pear'	die Bratsche 'viola'
die Pflaume 'plum'	die Klarinette 'clarinet'
die Traube 'grape'	die Orgel 'organ'
die Banane 'banana'	das Cello 'cello'
die Aprikose 'apricot'	das Saxophon 'saxophone'

There are also some minor conceptual categories: Beer names (*Alt*, *Pilsener*, etc.) are neuter, like the word *Bier* itself, while the names of other alcoholic drinks (*Wein*, *Schnaps*, *Gin*, *Sekt* 'champagne-like wine', are masculine).

It would be tempting, on the basis of these examples, to propose that the three genders do not constitute an even three-way contrast. Rather, at the basic level of categorization, the principal contrast is between masculine and feminine. Neuter is applied to concepts above the basic level, at which the masculine-feminine contrast is neutralized, as it were. Analogously, with respect to humans, masculine and feminine serve to differentiate individuals with respect to (biological) gender, whereas neuter serves to neutralize the gender distinction (e.g. *das Kind* 'child', *das Baby* 'baby'). Against this, it has to be emphasized that the semantic patterns identified by Köpcke and Zubin are tendencies, not absolutes. Moreover, the semantics-based account falls foul of the morphology. In terms of the agreement patterns which they trigger, masculine tends to go with neuter, and both contrast with feminine. With respect to the forms of the definite article, for example, masculine and neuter contrast only in nominative and accusative singular; elsewhere, the two genders trigger identical agreements. Feminine contrasts with both masculine and neuter, not only in nominative and accusative singular, but in genitive and dative singular as well.

In spite of the probabilistic nature of the patterns that they discerned, Köpcke and Zubin (1983: 168) claim that around 90 per cent of the 1,466 one-syllable words listed in the Duden dictionary can be assigned the correct gender through the interplay of phonological and semantic tendencies. The relatively small number of exceptions are mostly high-frequency words, such as *die Hand* (an exception to the generalization that words ending in NC tend to be masculine) and *das Knie* 'knee' (the sole exception to the masculine status of nouns beginning in *kn-*), whose 'irregularity' is maintained by their high degree of entrenchment within the language.

Although noun gender has only a limited symbolic role (namely, in designating differences in biological gender, in cases where this is relevant) the obligatory gender assignment of each and every noun in German cannot be regarded as purely arbitrary and lacking in any kind of motivation. Patterns of similarity (phonological and semantic) across nouns of the same gender

The function of inflection classes

I have argued that inflection classes (generally) lack symbolic significance. Do they nevertheless have other functions, which render them useful to speakers of a language?

Concerning gender classes, it is commonly asserted that this phenomenon aids referent tracking. Imagine a discourse about two entities, A and B. Suppose further that A and B are named by nouns of different genders and that the two genders are associated with distinct pronominal forms. In this situation, it will be easy to refer, unambiguously, to each of the two entities by means of the appropriate pronouns. Köpcke and Zubin (1984: 43) cite the following German example. Note the ambiguity of the English gloss.

(i)   Der Krug fiel in die Schale, aber *sie* zerbrach nicht.
       'The jug fell into the bowl, but it (= the bowl) didn't break.'
(ii)   Der Krug fiel in die Schale, aber *er* zerbrach nicht.
       'The jug fell into the bowl, but it (= the jug) didn't break.'

This argument is not very persuasive. Whether or not the discourse protagonists are named by nouns of different genders is a matter of chance. While in (i) and (ii) the nouns are of different genders, we can imagine situations in which this is not the case. If we should happen to be talking about a cup falling into a bowl, the choice of pronoun would not disambiguate the two readings (*Tasse* 'cup' and *Schale* 'bowl' are both feminine).

Speakers cannot therefore rely solely on gender differences to keep track of entities in a discourse; they need to have other resources at hand, just in case the discourse entities are designated by nouns of the same gender. (It also has to be admitted that in actual practice considerable ambiguity may be tolerated.) If such referent-tracking resources exist anyway (which they clearly must), the discourse motivation for gender becomes superfluous.

Gender systems also create some specific problems for their users. For example, when two nouns of different genders are coordinated, which gender functions as the controller? Then there is the problem of which gender to use when the speaker is ignorant of the identity of the referent. English speakers will be familiar with the problem—when referring to a person of unknown sex, do you use *he* or *she*? Likewise in a gender language. If demonstrative pronouns show gender agreement, which pronoun do you use if you do not know the identity of something, as when you ask 'What's that?'

All in all, one might well ask whether gender systems are worth the effort. All the more remarkable, then, is the fact that gender systems are so well established in so many of the world's languages.

can certainly be recognized. These 'schemas' for the different genders probably assist speakers to organize their mental grammars, thereby facilitating the memorization of noun genders; the schemas play a more active role when speakers are required (whether on an experimental task or in real life) to assign a gender to a newly encountered form. At the same time, gender *is* arbitrary, in the sense that the gender of a noun is fixed by the conventions of the language. A speaker is not able to exploit the correlation between, for example, neuter gender and superordinate terms, and masculine vs. feminine genders for basic-level terms, to symbolize the fact that for *her*, a word has superordinate status. An apple cultivator is not able to construe *Apfel* (by convention, masculine) as neuter, in order to convey that for her, [APPLE] is no longer a basic-level concept, but a superordinate.

Study questions

1. Define the notions 'word', 'phrase', 'affix', 'clitic', 'stem', 'bound morpheme', using the concepts presented in this chapter.

2. How would the underlined items in the following be described in terms of the parameters introduced in this chapter?

   table<u>ware</u>, foot<u>wear</u>, cheese<u>burger</u>, <u>butcher</u>, <u>wealth</u>, <u>prosperity</u>, <u>Euro</u>sceptic, <u>anti</u>-communist, <u>bio</u>-technology, by <u>dint</u> of, under the <u>auspices</u> of, an <u>ex</u>-girlfriend

3. Negative prefixes in English. English has a number of prefixes with a negative meaning, including *un-*, *in-*, and *non-*:

   Unbelievable, undeniable, unenviable, unfortunate
   Incredible, inaction, innocuous, inoperative,
   Nonsense, non-native, non-aggression treaty, non-compliance

   Investigate the ways in which the prefixes differ, referring to the parameters discussed in this chapter. (Hints: To what extent does the base form 'coerce' the phonological shape of the prefix? What kinds of items do the prefixes attach to? How choosy are the prefixes? How productive are they?)

4. The chapters on morphology (Chapters 14–16) had no discussion of the difference between inflection and derivation. In schematic terms, how would you characterize the difference between an inflectional and a derivational affix, and between an inflected and a derived form? To what extent is the distinction a useful one to make?

5. Reduplication. Reduplication consists in the repetition of part or all of a base morpheme. In Malay and Indonesian, reduplication of a base noun is a way of designating plurality:

   negeri 'country'   negeri-negeri 'countries'
   buku 'book'   buku-buku 'books'

What kind of morpheme is reduplication? Suggest (schematic) representations of the phonological and semantic structures of a reduplicated noun.

Malay and Indonesian also have a derivational process of 'partial reduplication'. Partial reduplication is a means for deriving nouns which bear some semantic relation to the base (Sneddon 1996: 21); especially in Malay, the process has been invoked by language planners for filling lexical gaps in the language.

tikus 'mouse'	tətikus 'computer mouse'
tangga 'stair'	tətangga 'neighbour'
cair 'watery'	cəcair 'liquid'
cekik 'strangle'	cəcekik 'noose'
laki 'husband'	ləlaki 'man'
langit 'sky'	ləlangit 'palate (of mouth)'
luhur 'noble'	ləluhur 'ancestor'

Suggest a schematic representation of nouns exhibiting partial reduplication.

Further reading

See Tuggy (1992) on the gradience of bound vs. free morphemes, Corbett (1991) on gender, and Carstairs-McCarthy (1992) on inflection classes.

Part 4
Nouns, Verbs, and Clauses

'Noun', 'verb', and 'clause' are fundamental categories in all languages and are central topics in all grammatical theories.

In terms of their profiles, nouns and verbs are maximally differentiated (section 11.7). A noun profiles a thing, i.e. a relatively autonomous configuration in conceptual space, while a verb profiles a temporal relation, or process, i.e. a relation as it evolves through conceived time. A clause designates a temporal relation which has achieved a certain degree of conceptual autonomy through the elaboration of entities schematically present in the verb's semantic structure.

Both nominal and verbal concepts are subject to 'grounding', that is, instances of the concepts are 'located' with respect to the circumstances of the speech act. Grounding is the topic of Chapters 18 and 20. A second parallel concerns the status of the designated things and processes as 'bounded' vs. 'unbounded'. Applied to things, the bounded-unbounded distinction gives the categories of count and mass nouns, discussed in Chapter 19; applied to processes, it gives the categories of perfective and imperfective verbs (Chapter 20). The chapter on clauses (Chapter 21) discusses clauses from the point of view of the kinds of situation they designate, the roles and syntactic expression of participants in the situations, and the manner in which clauses can be combined.

Nouns and nominals

In this chapter I address the ways in which a nominal expression can be 'grounded'. That is, the ways in which the designated entity can be 'located' with respect to the speech act situation (the 'ground'). A discussion of grounding involves examining the role of determiners and quantifiers, and other aspects of the noun phrase.

18.1 Nouns and noun phrases (nominals)

It is traditional to make a distinction between the lexical category 'noun' and the syntactic category 'noun phrase'. *House* is a noun, *the house*, *an old house*, *those three houses*, *a house I used to live in* are noun phrases. The difference can be summarized as follows: **A noun designates a kind, or type of thing; a noun phrase designates an instance of the type**.

Compare *house* and *the house*. *House* designates a type of entity. There exist countless instances of the type, present and past, real and imaginary, actual and potential. The contribution of *the* in the noun phrase is to convey that out of the countless number of instances, just one has been selected for attention. *The* also conveys that the designated instance is one that both speaker and hearer are able to uniquely identify. There may be several reasons why the exemplar is uniquely identifiable—it could be one that both speaker and hearer have already been talking about, or it could be one that both speaker and hearer are standing near to, or inside. Alternatively, the speaker may provide information that guides the hearer towards unique identification, by means of a descriptive relative clause (*the house that I bought last week*), by the use of a possessive (*my house*), by the use of adjectives and other modifiers (*the big house on the hill*), possibly accompanied by a pointing gesture (*the big house over there*).

Noun phrases, or **nominals**, can exhibit considerable internal complexity. Typically they consist of a noun, together with optional modifiers and complements, in association with a determiner and/or quantifier. If we focus, not on the syntactic structure of a noun phrase, but on its conceptual organization, we can identify four components. These are:

- Specification.[1] A bare noun, such as *house*, designates a type. The type may be specified in greater detail, e.g. by the addition of adjectival modifiers. *Big house* also designates a type, a type which is, however, more specific than the type designated by *house*.
- Instantiation. This is the relation between the type (designated by the noun, together with its modifiers, if there are any) and its instances (which are candidates for being picked out by the noun phrase).
- Quantification. This has to do with the number, or quantity, of the designated instance.
- Grounding. This is the process whereby the speaker 'locates' the designated instance from the perspective of the speech event. Differences between definite and indefinite, specific and non-specific, are aspects of grounding.

These four aspects stand in a logical relation to each other. A type may be (optionally) specified; the specified type is instantiated; an instance of the specified type may be quantified; the quantified instance is grounded. A nominal, then, has a 'layered' conceptual structure, shown in (1). Specification is internal to instantiation; quantification is internal to grounding.

(1) (Grounding (Quantification (Instantiation (Specification (Type)))))

The analysis of noun phrases would be a relatively straightforward matter were it the case that the conceptual structure in (1) mapped directly into morphosyntactic structure. To be sure, certain correspondences can be noted. Specification is the distinctive function of modifiers and complements; determiners (*the, a, this, my*, etc.) are quintessential grounding devices; while quantifiers (*each, every, many, three*, etc.) explicitly encode notions of quantity or amount. Accordingly, some aspects of conceptual layering are often preserved in the syntax. In the expression *the three big houses* we can observe a direct correspondence between syntactic constituency and the relevant aspects of conceptual constituency.

---

[1] 'Specification', as used here, is not to be confused with the notion of 'Specifier' in X-bar theory.

(2) (the   (three   (big   (houses))))
    (Grounding (Quantification (Specification (Type))))

Full isomorphism between the conceptual and syntactic organization is upset by a number of factors. Instantiation, in English, is always subsumed by some other process,[2] while grounding may be effected by quantifiers as well as by determiners. The interaction of quantification with grounding and instantiation is especially complex. Consequently, the conceptual organization in (1) rarely, if ever, maps directly on to morphosyntactic structure. It is this aspect, above all, that renders the study of noun phrases especially complex and controversial.

An analysis of nominals also needs to take account of the traditional distinction between count and mass nouns. As is well known, certain quantifiers and determiners are able to occur only with nouns of a given class. I shall deal with the count–mass distinction in the next chapter. We will see there that the traditional two-way distinction is better analysed as a three-way distinction: singular count nouns, plural count nouns, and mass nouns. Closer analysis reveals further subcategories. I shall argue, moreover, that these distinctions have to do with the manner in which type-concepts are instantiated rather than being inherent properties of the type.

I first introduce the concepts of grounding, instantiation, and specification, as these are manifested in a definite noun phrase such as *the old house*. The role of determiners and quantifiers, and the interaction of grounding and quantification, are dealt with in a later section.

A note on terminology: Noun, nominal, and noun phrase

I began this chapter using the traditional terms 'noun' and 'noun phrase'. Langacker's usage departs somewhat from tradition. He uses 'noun' as a cover term for any expression that profiles a thing, irrespective of whether the expression designates a type or an instance. Langacker's noun category therefore comprises the traditional category of lexical nouns, as well as noun phrases, proper names, and pronouns. It also incorporates what in X-bar theories of syntax are known as N-bars. (These are discussed in section 18.2.4). Langacker's 'nominal' corresponds roughly to the traditional noun phrase, but also includes pronouns and proper names; technically, a nominal is a 'grounded noun'.

In order to avoid confusion, I use the term 'noun' in this book predominantly to refer to lexical items, speaking of a 'bare noun' in cases where misunderstandings might occur. (Langacker speaks of 'simple nouns'.) In cases where the full implication of 'nominal' might not be apparent, I use the traditional term 'noun phrase'.

---

[2] I shall argue in section 19.4.1 that classifiers in Mandarin have the specific function of instantiating a noun-type. In English, there is no linguistic form with this specific function.

18.2 Some basic concepts: Grounding, instantiation, and specification

In this section I introduce the concepts of grounding, instantiation, and specification.

18.2.1 Grounding

The term 'ground' refers to the context of the speech event. The ground comprises the participants in the event, its time and place, the situational context, previous discourse, shared knowledge of the speech-act participants, and such like.

Grounding is a process that 'locates' an entity with respect to the ground. To use Langacker's metaphor, grounding enables the speech-act participants to 'establish mental contact with' the designated entity (FCG2: 98). The grounding of a definite nominal (such as *the house*) is presented in diagram form in Figure 18.1. The grounded nominal designates an instance (represented by I). The instance is conceptualized against the appropriate domain (represented by the square box). The instance is one that has been identified by both the speaker, S, and the hearer, H. Both speaker and hearer are situated within the ground (represented by the ellipse on the left). The broken arrows pointing from S and H towards the instance represent the singling out, by S and H, of the instance for special attention.

Observe in Figure 18.1 that the instance is in bold. By the usual convention, this signifies that the instance is profiled. A grounded nominal designates the grounded instance, it does not designate any component of the ground or the grounding relation between speaker and hearer and the instance. All these aspects belong to the base of a grounded expression.

It may be helpful to think of grounding in terms of the traditional notion of reference; a speaker, in using a grounded nominal, is 'referring' to the

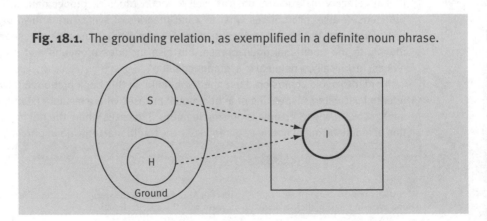

Fig. 18.1. The grounding relation, as exemplified in a definite noun phrase.

designated instance. It is important to bear in mind, however, that the referent of a grounded nominal is not some object out there in the external world, but an entity in a mental space. As noted in section 10.2, the mental space may purport to be a model of the external world, in which case there may be no harm in saying that the speaker is referring to a real-world entity. But we should also bear in mind that the referent could be an entity in a fictional or imaginary mental space, or even in a counterfactual mental space.

Shared gaze and the establishment of mental contact

If you are pet-owner you will probably have had the experience of trying to direct your pet's attention to, say, a plate of food located some distance from both you and the animal and out of the animal's line of sight. You look at the food, you point to it, but the animal seems not to realize what you mean by your gaze and your gesture. To get the animal to notice the food, you have to walk over to it.

Human infants, from the earliest months, do not behave like this. If we gaze at something the infant instinctively follows our line of sight, as if trying to identify the object of our gaze. 'Shared gaze' is plausibly the basis of the grounding relation — adult and child jointly focus attention ('establish mental contact with') a common referent. Locke (1995: 293) speculates that shared gaze 'may be one of the more important conceptual precursors to lexical acquisition'; this is because the object of an adult's gaze is more often than not the topic of her vocalization. Indeed, without this ability for infant and adult to coordinate their attention on specific features of the environment, it is difficult to imagine how the acquisition of a symbolic system such as language could ever get off the ground.

18.2.2 Instantiation

As it stands, Figure 18.1 is incomplete as a semantic representation of a grounded nominal, such as *the house*; the Figure depicts only the instance, it says nothing about the type to which the instance belongs. Figure 18.2 (p. 348) presents this latter aspect diagrammatically.

The format of Figure 18.2 should be familiar. In fact, it represents a special case of the schema-instance relation introduced in Chapter 7. Just as, in Figure 7.1, the concept [ANIMAL] is schematic for [DOG], [CAT], [HORSE], etc., so the type is schematic for instances of the type.

There is, however, an important qualification that we need to make. There is a sense in which [DOG], [CAT], [HORSE] are concepts of the same ontological kind as the more schematic concept [ANIMAL], that is, they are all 'types' of creature. In Figure 18.2 the instances are ontologically different from the type. Here we can appeal to the notion of domain. The concepts [DOG], [CAT], [HORSE], as well as [ANIMAL], occupy the abstract domain of types. A type,

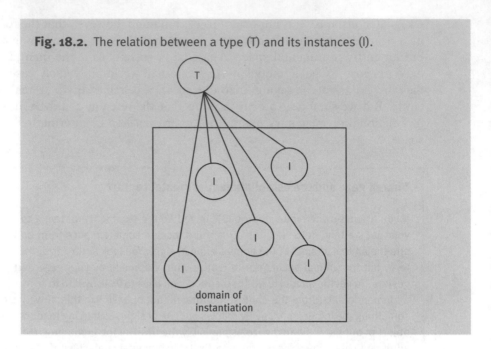

Fig. 18.2. The relation between a type (T) and its instances (I).

domain of
instantiation

however, is instantiated in its special **domain of instantiation**. The domain of instantiation of [HOUSE] is, normally, three-dimensional space.[3]

I have illustrated the notion of instantiation on the example of a singular count noun. Essentially the same analysis will apply to the instantiation of a mass noun and plural nouns. *The water* designates a uniquely identifiable instance of the type 'water', located in its domain of instantiation (probably, physical space). Similarly, *the houses* designates a uniquely identifiable set of entities of the type 'house'.

18.2.3 The semantic structure of a grounded nominal

Figure 18.1 represents a grounded instance but says nothing about the type to which the instance belongs. Figure 18.2 depicts the type–instance relation with no indication of the grounding relation. Because of their conceptual overlap, the two representations can be brought together in a valence relation; the instance profiled in Figure 18.1 can be unified with one of the instances depicted in Figure 18.2. In this way, we achieve a more complete representation of a grounded nominal (Fig. 18.3).

It follows from this account that the determiner is the head of a grounded

---

[3] The distinction being made here—between type and instance(s) of the type—is a subtle one, the more so since the distinction is not morphosyntactically marked. The matter is compounded by a folk theory of language (Radden and Kövecses 1999: 26), according to which words are names of things, not names of types of things. In terms of the folk theory, the word *cow* is the name of the animal, it is not the name of a type of animal.

Fig. 18.3. The semantic structure of a grounded nominal.

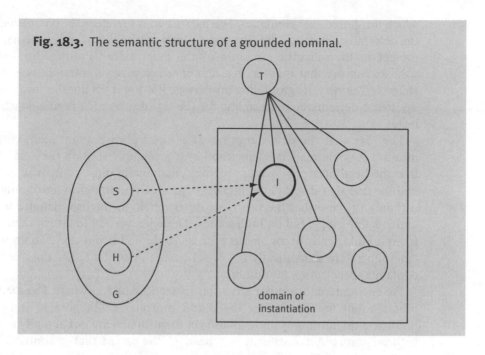

nominal. The bare noun designates the type. It is the contribution of the determiner to profile an instance of the type, identified from the ground. Since a grounded nominal designates an instance, not the type, the profile of the composite expression is inherited from the determiner, not from the bare noun. The determiner itself profiles a schematic instance, which receives semantic content from the type specification designated by the noun with

---

Domain ambiguities

Ambiguities can sometimes arise with respect to the domain of instantiation of a nominal. Consider the two readings of (i).

(i)   I don't like this jacket.

This jacket could designate a specific garment or a jacket design. In the first case, the domain of instantiation is physical space; on the second reading the domain of instantiation is what Langacker has called 'quality space' (FCG2: 18).

   The same ambiguity can occur with pronouns. The sales assistant who says (ii) is probably referring to articles of a certain design, whereas (iii) refers to a specific exemplar.

(ii)   I'm sorry, we don't stock it.
(iii) I'm sorry, we just sold it.

which the determiner combines. The bare noun is therefore the complement of the determiner, in that it fills in conceptual material that is only schematically present in the semantic structure of the determiner.[4] Putting this another way, we can say that it is the determiner which gives a nominal its semantic character, namely, its grounding properties. Putting it yet another way, we can say that a determiner is schematic for the set of grounded nominals which it heads.

The idea that the determiner heads a noun phrase might seem counter-intuitive to some readers.[5] This reaction is probably based on the assumption that the head of a phrase must be the semantically most contentful element and the one that displays the highest degree of phonological autonomy. It is certainly the case that the two basic determiners in English, definite *the* [ðə] and indefinite *a* [ə], fail on both scores. These items need to attach themselves to a phonologically autonomous unit, as in *the house, a house*. Moreover, the determiners are semantically highly schematic in content. *The* does not even contain a specification for number.

We encountered a similar situation in section 14.1.1, where I argued that plural nouns are headed by the plural morpheme. As pointed out there, phonological autonomy and semantic contentfulness are not actually relevant to head status. A constituent is a head to the extent that it contributes its profile to the profile of the complex expression. It was on these grounds that I argued that a plural noun is headed by the plural morpheme.

As a matter of fact, with respect to their phonological dependence, *the* and *a* may be somewhat untypical of determiners, even in English. Other determiners, such as *this, that,* and *these*, most of the quantifiers, such as *much, many, several,* and *some*, as well as the numerals, do possess a fair degree of phonological autonomy, in that they can occur without the support of a following noun.

(3) a. I don't want this.
     b. I bought three.
     c. I'd like some.

Here, *this, three,* and *some* function as grounded nominals. In (3a), *this* designates a uniquely identifiable instance located in the vicinity of the speaker. The type to which the instance belongs, however, is not stated, but must be inferred from the context. *This house* differs from *this* only in that the type to which the instance belongs has been elaborated.

---

[4] At the same time, a grounded nominal contains elements of apposition. Both the determiner and the noun profile things—both are nouns, on Langacker's definition of 'noun'. As remarked in section 12.3, syntagmatic relations, such as the relation of apposition and the head-complement relation, are not mutually exclusive.

[5] The layered structure in (2) might also encourage the view that it is the noun that heads a noun phrase; the formula suggests that a noun phrase is 'built up' around its innermost constituent, the noun. The point is, however, that as a noun phrase is progressively built up, the profile shifts from a type specification to a grounded instance.

In other languages, even the definite and indefinite determiners can be used on their own as schematic nominals. Consider the German determiners. In (4a), the determiner *den* can stand alone as a schematic definite nominal, while indefinite *einen* can stand as a schematic indefinite nominal.

(4) a. *Den Wein* mag ich nicht.   ~   *Den* mag ich nicht.
          'The wine I don't like.'   ~   'I don't like it.'
      b. Wir haben *einen Hund.*   ~   Wir haben *einen.*
          'We have a dog.'   ~   'We have one.'

The same goes for definite determiners in Spanish and Portuguese. The following examples are from Hewson (1991: 322). Note that the definite determiners *la* and *a* can be used as schematic (definite) nominals.

(5) a. La educación española, como *la* de la mayoría de los países europeos o americanos, no es perfecta.
      b. A educação portuguesa, como *a* da maioria dos paises europeus ou americanos, não é perfeita.
          'Spanish/Portuguese education, like that of the majority of European and American countries, is not perfect.'

I mentioned, a few paragraphs ago, the conceptual structure of a plural noun, such as *houses*. What of the internal structure of a plural definite, such as *the houses*? One approach would be to say that pluralization applies to the grounded singular. Pluralization, however, is a kind of quantification; as such it is 'internal' to grounding. A plural noun designates a plural number of instances; these are then grounded by the determiner.[6] Consequently, a grounded plural nominal has the internal structure shown in Figure 18.4.

18.2.4 Specification

Many syntactic theories recognize a category intermediate between the lexical category 'noun', symbolized by N, and the phrasal category 'noun phrase', symbolized by NP. In X-bar theories this intermediate category is called N-bar, or N'. N-bar consists of a noun together with its optional complements and modifiers, but lacks a determiner. The category is recursive, in that an N' can be part of a larger N'. The tree-diagram in (6) (over) illustrates.

---

[6] The suggestion that pluralization is internal to grounding (and that, consequently, it is not the grounded singular that is pluralized), is supported by those languages in which singular and plural nouns are marked by distinct affixes. The plural marker *-e* of Italian *case* 'houses' is not appended to the singular *casa* but rather 'replaces' the singular marker *-a*; both forms are derived from the type specification *cas-* (which, needless to say, is unspecified for number). A similar situation holds in the Bantu languages (cf. FCG2: 74–5). Zulu *abantu* 'people' is not derived from *umuntu* 'person', but from the type specification *-ntu*. English differs from these languages in that the type specification *house* is phonologically identical with the singular form.

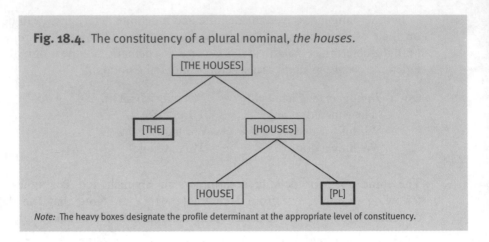

Fig. 18.4. The constituency of a plural nominal, *the houses.*

Note: The heavy boxes designate the profile determinant at the appropriate level of constituency.

(6)

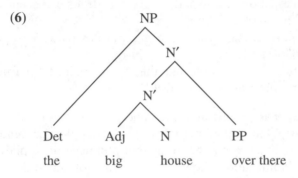

The adjective *big* and the prepositional phrase *over there* are both modifiers; they characterize the concept [HOUSE] in greater detail, by adding additional specifications to the concept.

The addition of modifiers does not in itself amount to the grounding of a noun. While specification may serve to narrow down the set of possible instances, grounding only occurs through the addition of a determiner or quantifier. Without such elements, the N-bar continues to designate a type. This is true even if the type is specified in such detail that there is only one conceivable instance. The expression *house that I now live in* still designates a type, not an instance.

The N-bar category corresponds to a type specification. Although a salient component structure of a grounded nominal, the assembly of a type specification is not a major issue in Cognitive Grammar. The tree diagram in (6) shows the constituency [[big house] over there], that is, *house* first combines with *big*, to form the more specific concept [BIG HOUSE], which subsequently combines with *over there*, to form the even more specific concept [BIG HOUSE OVER THERE]. But it would be equally possible to assemble the expression in the reverse order, or even in a single operation. The different constituencies do not materially affect the semantic structure of the complex expression.

18.3 Determiners and quantifiers

Determiners have the specific function of grounding a noun. Grounding can also be effected by the use of a quantifier. Determiners pick out the profiled instances, quantifiers characterize the profiled instances in terms of number or amount.

A comprehensive account of the determiners and quantifiers, even for a single language, would go far beyond the scope of this section. In the first place, any given language has a fair number of determiners and quantifiers. Each of these items will have its special semantic value which determines its usage range, including the possibility of its co-occurring with other determiners and/or quantifiers within a single nominal. At a very fine-grained level of analysis, each determiner and quantifier will probably turn out to have a distribution unique to itself. Moreover, comparison between related languages reveals considerable language-specificity in the use of the grounding devices. As every language student knows, the usage range of the definite determiner in French or Spanish does not exactly correspond to the usage range of *the* in English.

Rather than attempt a comprehensive overview, I restrict myself to some observations on the different kinds of grounding devices. I hope that these remarks will provide a scaffolding on which readers can construct a more elaborate account of the grounding devices in the languages in which they are interested.

18.3.1 Determiners

Determiners profile an instance of a type. A major distinction is between definite and indefinite determiners. Indefinite determiners, in turn, can be divided into specific indefinites and non-specific indefinites (Fig. 18.5).

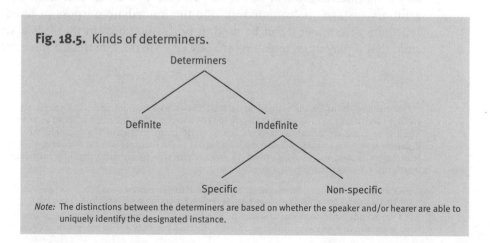

Fig. 18.5. Kinds of determiners.

Determiners

Definite   Indefinite

Specific   Non-specific

Note: The distinctions between the determiners are based on whether the speaker and/or hearer are able to uniquely identify the designated instance.

A **definite** determiner profiles an instance that the speaker has singled out for attention; the speaker also supposes that the hearer, too, can uniquely identify the instance. (The speaker may of course be mistaken in this supposition; on hearing (7a) a person could respond, 'Which house are you talking about?') The possibility of joint identification may be due to various factors. In (7a) it is likely that previous discourse between speaker and hearer has already established a unique referent for *the house*; in (7b) the context of situation limits the reference of *the fire* to one instance only; in (7c) the relative clause instructs the hearer how to locate the intended referent; in (7d) the speaker invites the hearer to set up a mental space which contains a uniquely identifiable instance.

(7) (a)   I bought the house after all.
     (b)   The fire's gone out.
     (c)   The man I was telling you about.
     (d)   The man I'm going to tell you about.

Among the definite determiners are the demonstratives *this* and *that*, *these* and *those*. Demonstratives are slightly more contentful than *the*, in that their profile already contains some notion of number (singular vs. plural); they also convey the proximity of the profiled instance to the speaker.[7]

Prenominal possessives (*John's car*, *my hat*) normally function as definite expressions.[8] *John's car* designates a specific instance, and simultaneously instructs the hearer how to uniquely identify the instance; it is, namely, a car that is identified with reference to a previously established entity, John. Normally, the expression would be interpreted as the car that belongs to John, though other interpretations (e.g. the car that John designed) are easily imaginable.

Indefinites have in common that the hearer is not expected to be able to uniquely identify the instance. In the case of a specific indefinite, the speaker has a specific instance in mind; in the case of non-specific indefinites, an arbitrary instance is 'conjured up' for the immediate purpose at hand. The indefinite determiner *a* can be used in both functions. In (8a) it is a specific child that is playing, whereas in (8b) any egg will do. Unstressed *some* and *any*

---

[7] 'Proximity' is to be understood in at least two senses: spatial proximity (physically near the speaker) and discourse proximity (a recently spoken about entity, or one that is about to be mentioned). The use of the demonstratives, however, is subject to many subtleties. For example, with respect to discourse structure, an entity about to be introduced (by the speaker) into the discourse will typically be referred to by *this*, whereas *that* tends to refer backwards to an entity recently introduced by an interlocutor. Compare:

   (i) This is the point I want to emphasize. (Speaker proceeds to elaborate the point.)
   (ii) That is the very point that I want to emphasize. (Speaker refers to a point made by someone else.)

[8] Prenominal possessives can also function as indefinites, especially when the possessor nominal is itself indefinite, as when you say that you need 'a doctor's prescription' to buy a certain drug.

also function as indefinite determiners; again, they can have either specific or non-specific reference.

(8) (a)   There was a child playing in the park.
    (b)   You need an egg for this recipe.

(9) (a)   There were some children playing in the park.
    (b)   You need some milk for this recipe.

As argued in section 6.4.1, we should not want to regard *a* and *some* as polysemous in respect of specificity. In (8) and (9) the non-specific readings emerge in the context of a mental space that is distinct from a base space and which is introduced by the verb *need*. The specific vs. non-specific distinction is therefore a function of the context in which the determiner is used; the determiner itself is neutral in this respect. In *I used an egg for this recipe, an egg* is specific.

Note that in the examples in (9), *some* is already taking on features of a quantifier; the idea is of a smallish number of children, or a smallish portion of milk. The examples show that the distinction between determiners and quantifiers is not an absolute one. Even *a* has a minimal quantifying function: it conveys the singular number of the profiled instance.

18.3.2 Quantifiers

Quantifiers include items such as *many, most, a few, several, one*, and the numerals. (The plural morpheme also has a quantifying function.) These items give some idea of the number, or quantity, of the profiled instance. In virtue of this function, quantifiers subsume instantiation; the very fact that a particular quantity is involved entails that the type has been instantiated. Quantifiers can also assume a grounding function. Again, the very fact that the speaker singles out an instance of a certain magnitude entails that the instance has become the focus of the speaker's conscious awareness. By default, quantifiers are indefinite. Their use does not presuppose that the hearer is able to identify the quantified instance. With some of the quantifiers, this aspect can be overridden by the additional use of a definite determiner.

Quantifiers comprise a fairly heterogeneous set of items. As with the determiners, however, we can make a broad two-way distinction, between the absolute and the relative quantifiers. A special sub-category of the latter comprises the so-called universal quantifiers.

Absolute quantifiers give an indication of the size or number of the designated instance. They do this without any presuppositions regarding the total number of possible instances. The absolute quantifiers are, in a sense, 'pure' quantifiers—they simply give a notion of quantity and nothing else. Canonical examples are the numerals (*one, three*, etc.), as well as somewhat vaguer expressions such as *a few, a little, much, many, several, numerous*, and unstressed *some*.

Quantifiers, by default, are indefinite. Appropriate contexts can cause either a specific or a non-specific reading to emerge. In (10a) it is asserted that three specific instances of the type 'man' entered the room; the hearer is not supposed to be able to uniquely identify them. By contrast, (10b) is non-specific; any three instances of the type will do.

(10)   a.   Three men entered the room.
     b.   We need three men for this job.

Though indefinite by default, the absolute quantifiers can be rendered definite through the use of a definite determiner. Thus (11a) merely profiles the number of instances and is indefinite; (11b) profiles three uniquely identifiable instances.

(11)   a.   Three men entered the building.
     b.   The three men entered the building.

Relative quantifiers give a notion of quantity but at the same time make implicit reference to a presupposed 'reference mass'. Compare *many people* and *most people*. *Many people* simply gives an idea of a large number, whereas *most* implies the majority with respect to a larger set. (Drawing on notions of profile and base introduced in Chapter 10, we can say that the concept of the reference mass belongs to the base against which the relative quantifiers profile a given quantity.) Relative quantifiers include *all*, *most*, and stressed *some*. For a reference mass of exactly two instances, *both* is used. *None* and *neither* might also be included here, though the former has the peculiar feature that it requires a partitive expression (see below): *none of the children*. Especially if they bear stress, relative quantifiers are liable to be understood contrastively. This is not too surprising, given the implicit reference, within the base, to a reference mass. A statement about *sóme children* might contrast with *móst children*, while *móst children* might contrast with *áll children* (i.e. 'most but not all').

The larger set, or reference mass, against which relative quantifiers are understood could be constituted by all possible instances of the type; contextual factors, however, may suggest a more restricted set. In (12a) the reference mass would probably not be identified with the set of all adult males (everywhere at all times). It would more likely be taken to comprise only men in domestic relationships, in Western or Westernized societies in the post-industrial era. In (12b) the set of households has been explicitly delimited by the modifying phrase *in this neighbourhood*. With respect to the type specification 'household in this neighbourhood', the sentence probably would be interpreted as an assertion about the majority of members of this maximally construed set.

(12)   a.   Most men help with the housework.
     b.   Most households in this neighbourhood own two cars.

A special subcategory of the relative quantifiers are the so-called **universal quantifiers**. These presuppose a reference mass consisting of all possible instances and their use can be interpreted, under appropriate circumstances, to entail a 'universal' statement about all instances. An example of this kind of universal statement is (13a). While *all* is the canonical universal quantifier, other quantifiers, such as *every*, can entail universal reference.

(13) a. All cats are carnivores.
      b. Every cat is a carnivore.

Although (13b) can be understood as making a universal assertion about cats, it does so in a very particular way. Note that the verb is in the singular form, as is the subject nominal. Although only one instance of the type is profiled, the import of *every* is to suggest that the same predication—'is a carnivore'—could be made of all conceivable instances of the type. The profiled instance is taken to be representative of the members of the maximum set of instances. Any property ascribed to the instance therefore applies to all members of the reference mass (Langacker 1999: 256).

Each is similar to *every* in this respect. *Each* also profiles a single instance which is taken to be representative of the members of a reference mass. A major difference is that *each* presupposes a reference mass that is quite restricted in extent, such that it would in principle be feasible for the members of the reference mass to be inspected, one by one, in order to ascertain the validity of the predication that is being made. For this reason, it would be odd to construe *Each cat is a carnivore* as a universal statement about cats; there is no way that all cats could be inspected, one by one, to ascertain their carnivorous habits. A more appropriate use of *each* is illustrated in (14). The sentence presupposes a smallish group of children—say, the children in a school, in a neighbourhood, in a large family—such that it might be possible to inspect each child and make the appropriate assertion.

(14) Each child was vaccinated.

The contrast between *each* and *every* nicely illustrates the role of the base against which an entity is profiled. *Each* and *every* are identical with respect to their profiles; both words profile an arbitrary instance of a type. They differ with respect to the size of the reference mass for which the instance is taken to be representative. The difference helps explain the different syntactic distributions of the two quantifiers. *Each* readily lends itself to use in a partitive: *each of the children*, where *the children* limits the reference mass to an identifiable set of children. *Every* is inappropriate with a partitive: **every of the children*.

18.3.3 Generics

There is another grammatical device which appears to function as a universal quantifier. This is illustrated in (15).

(15) a. Cats are carnivores.
     b. Dogs make good companions.
     c. Water boils at 100° Centigrade.

Here the subject nominals *cats*, *dogs*, and *water* lack both a determiner and a quantifier. In such cases it is common to speak of the nouns taking the 'zero determiner', ∅. (In fact, it might be more accurate to speak of a 'zero quantifier', since the 'bare' nouns serve to designate a quantity or amount.) Talk of a zero morpheme could be misleading, in that it suggests that there is a morpheme present in the expressions which has semantic content but no phonological expression. Phonologically 'invisible' entities such as this could be problematic in Cognitive Grammar. While it may be convenient to speak of nominals taking the 'zero determiner', this should be understood as a shorthand way of referring to nominals which lack a determiner.

Concerning the semantics of such nominals, one might be inclined to interpret the statements in (15) as universal statements about all instances of the types in question. On this account, we could say that the plural marker on *cats* designates a plural number of instances. When used without further quantification or grounding, the plural form comes to designate an unspecified number of instances, by default, all instances; the 'bare' plural therefore subsumes quantification, instantiation, and grounding. Likewise, we could say that the mass noun *water*, when used without further quantification or grounding, comes to designate the maximal extent of the designated substance.[9]

There are reasons to question such an account. If it were the case that (15a) refers to all instances of the type, then the existence of a toothless, vegetarian cat would necessarily render the sentence untrue. But this, I think, is not the case. Nor is (15c) rendered untrue by the fact that water can be 'superheated' to above 100°C without its boiling. And the existence of vicious dogs does not, of itself, render (15b) invalid. Compare, in this respect, expressions containing a zero-quantified noun as subject with expressions containing a noun quantified by *all*.

(16) a. Cats are carnivores.
     b. All cats are carnivores.

(17) a. Unicorns have one horn.
     b. All unicorns have one horn.

---

[9] This account entails that the word form *water* has two semantic values. As a bare noun, *water* is a type specification, the use of which in a nominal requires instantiation, quantification, and grounding. Exactly the same form can subsume these three elements—*water* can designate all conceivable instances of the type. In languages which lack definite and indefinite determiners equivalent to English *the* and *a*, such as Latin or Russian, this kind of polysemy is very widespread. With respect to Latin *Agricola videt puellam* 'the farmer sees the/a girl' (literally, 'farmer sees girl'), we need to say that the type specification *agricola* can also function as a grounded nominal, with no overt marking of grounding or instantiation.

I think it would be truc to say that (16b) *would* be rendered untrue by the existence of a vegetarian cat, whereas (16a) would not. *All* specifically invokes a reference mass which, by default, comprises the totality of instances. The contrast is even more striking in (17). Whereas (17a) can be taken to be a true statement about unicorns, (17b) is rather odd, at least when spoken of the 'real' world, in which unicorns do not exist. This is because (17b) tends to be interpreted as a statement about (really existing) instances, of which there are none. If this is so, what, then, is (17a) a statement about?

One answer is that it is a statement about the type, considered irrespective of its instantiation in the world. Irrespective of whether they exist or not, and (were they to exist) irrespective of any malformed, mutilated, or genetically mutated exemplars, the 'essence' of unicorns, as a type of creature, is that they have one horn. Likewise, irrespective of the properties of any particular cat, cats as a type have the property of being, by their nature, flesh-eaters.

Although this approach adequately captures the semantic properties of gcneric statements about cats and unicorns, it conflicts with the syntactic form of the expressions. *Cats* and *unicorns* in (16a) and (17a) are plural in form, and therefore designate a plurality of instances, not the type as such. The correct approach, I suggest, is to interpret generic statements as statements which pertain, not to the 'real' world, but to an idealized 'model' of the world—what Langacker (FCG2: 264) calls a 'structured world model'—in which things are constituted in a certain way and have certain predictable properties. If we take this approach, we will be able to claim that the plural nouns *cats* and *unicorns* do indeed refer to all possible instances of the type—but with the proviso that the domain of instantiation is not the real world, with its imperfections, aberrations, and abnormalities, but an idealized world in which things have a predictable structure. I take up the idea of the structured world model in Chapter 20, in connection with certain uses of the present tense.

18.3.4 Partitives

Nominals can receive an extra degree of layering through the use of a partitive construction. Compare the following:

(18) a. Three men entered the building.
     b. The three men entered the building.
     c. Three of the men entered the building.

We have already discussed the indefinite and definite nominals in (18a) and (18b). In (18c) we see an example of the partitive construction. A reference mass—*the men*—is asserted. The reference mass is definite. *Three* picks out three specific (but indefinite) instances from the mass. Since relative quantifiers, in their base, presuppose a reference mass, it is not surprising that they too should be highly compatible with the partitive construction (*most of the children*, etc.). The partitive construction serves to make explicit the unprofiled reference mass in the semantic structure of relative quantifiers.

The partitive construction has a number of variants and a wide range of uses. For some quantifying expressions, use of the construction is obligatory (19a). In other cases, where the totality of the reference mass is quantified, the use of *of* appears optional (19b). The apparent optionality reflects the conceptual equivalence of the expressions with and without *of*. A further and very important use of the construction is to designate certain characteristics of the instance, such as its shape, size, extent, or spatial configuration (19c). Here, the first noun is taking on characteristics of a classifier. These kinds of expressions easily slide into pure expressions of quantity; *a cup of flour* (19d) designates a certain quantity of flour, which need not have been measured out in a cup.

(**19**) a. dozens of people, millions of years, neither of my children, none of my friends
   b. both my children ~ both of my children
      all my friends ~ all of my friends
      half the people ~ half of the people
   c. a bunch of flowers, a glass of beer, a grain of rice, a cube of sugar
   d. a cup of flour, a bucket of water
   e. piles of money, heaps of people

Some partitive-like expressions have come to designate simply a large quantity (19e). In such cases, the partitive construal has largely faded. In (20), *a lot of* and *lots of*, though no doubt partitive in origin, are probably now felt to be quantifiers. This is shown by the fact that number agreement is with the quantified noun (*people, champagne*), not with the quantifying noun (*a lot, lots*). *A bunch (of)* and *heaps (of)* are similarly construed as quantifying expressions in (21).

(**20**) a. A lot of people {*is/are} expected at the reception.
   b. Lots of champagne {was/*were} consumed.

(**21**) a. A bunch of people {?was/were} standing on the corner.
   b. Heaps of money {has/*have} disappeared.

18.4 Ungrounded nouns

The major use of nouns is to designate instances; nouns, mostly, are grounded, in one way or another. However, there are circumstances in which nouns are not grounded. I consider two cases below.

18.4.1 Compounds

The first case concerns the use of a noun as a modifier in a compound. *Dog-breeder* designates a kind of person, namely, one that breeds creatures of the kind 'dog'. To speak of someone as a dog-breeder does not invoke the conception of any particular dog or any particular number of dogs. It invokes only the conception of the type. Significantly, *dog* cannot take any markings of grounding or quantification; **a dogs-breeder*, **a these-dogs breeder* are hopelessly ungrammatical. It may be possible, though, to specify the type in somewhat greater detail through modification of the noun: *a [small dog] breeder*, *a [guard dog] breeder*. The possibilities are limited in the main to conventionalized type-specifications. *A [brown dog] breeder*, I think, is hardly possible.

The status of the modifying noun as a type specification explains the (usual) absence of plural inflection within noun compounds. Even nouns such as *groceries* and *trousers*, which in their referential use obligatorily appear in plural form, lack the plural inflection in compounds: *a grocery store, a trouser factory*. Nevertheless, exceptions to this generalization are easily found:

(22) sports administrator, parks commissioner, telecommunications engineer

One factor which renders the plural nouns acceptable as modifiers could be the fact that the plural nouns have been subject to semantic drift and have acquired a semantic nuance that is lacking in the singular noun. *Telecommunication* (singular) designates the phenomenon of communication at a distance, whereas *telecommunications* (plural) designates the technology(ies) which render telecommunication possible. On the other hand, even though *dishes* has been subject to semantic drift (section 16.3.3), we still speak of a *dish washer*, not a **dishes washer*. Another factor may be the need to avoid ambiguities; compare *goods train* and *passenger train*; *good train* would hardly be feasible as the name of a train which carries goods. Even so, it has to be conceded that quite a lot of idiosyncrasy surrounds this topic. We speak, for example, of a *share trader*, but of an *equities trader*.

18.4.2 Predicate nouns

A second case of ungrounded nouns concerns the use of nouns in predicative expressions. Compare the following:

(23) a. John is the teacher.
     b. John is a teacher.

Although superficially parallel, these are conceptually very different. The first equates the person identified as 'John' with the person identified as 'the teacher'. (As in a relation of apposition—section 12.3—both nominals designate the same entity, but do so in different ways.) Both *John* and *the teacher* are grounded nominals, while *be* profiles the existence through time of a relation of identity between the profiled entities. Identificational expressions can often be reversed: *The teacher is John*. The choice of one order over the other concerns the selection of one of the nominals as the tr of the relation.

The second example (23b) demands a different account. The sentence does not equate the person 'John' with a person characterized as 'a teacher'. Consider the fact that the nominals in the expressions cannot easily be reversed. (To the extent that *A teacher is John* is acceptable, it is acceptable in the same way as *Ambitious were his plans* is acceptable; that is, in spite of its preverbal position, *a teacher* is not functioning as the subject, of tr, of the verb.) Rather, we want to say that *John is a teacher* predicates a property of the subject nominal—John has the property of 'being-a-teacher'. For this reason, it may be questioned whether *a teacher* in (23b)—despite the presence of the indefinite article—does in fact profile a grounded instance (though Langacker does take this line); if anything, *a teacher* is taking on adjective-like characteristics. In fact, Langacker (FCG2: 65–6) claims that predicate nouns have a relational profile, and that *be* profiles the existence over time of this relation. In (23b) the relation in question is John's 'being-a-teacher'; the properties of the arbitrary instance conjured up by *a teacher* are ascribed to John. Indirectly, this leads to the inference that John is a member of the class of 'teachers'.

The use of the indefinite article with predicate nouns is to some extent an idiosyncratic feature of English. In other languages, such as French and German, predicate nouns occur without the article: *Il est professeur* (French), *Er ist Lehrer* (German). Even in English, a bare noun can be used in cases where a unique role is ascribed to the subject referent (24a). The absence of the article may be motivated by the fact that unique positions (such as 'chairman of the committee') are inconsistent with the conjuring up of arbitrary instances.

(24) a. He is (the) chairman of the committee.
      b. He became King of England.
      c. She was elected vice-president.
      d. They made him headmaster of the school.
      e. As managing director, I propose . . .

We see from the above examples that predicate nouns are not restricted to expressions involving the verb *be*. *Become*, *be elected*, *be appointed*, etc., also serve to ascribe a property to a subject referent. In fact, predicate nouns do not even require the use of a verb at all:

(25) a. What! John, a teacher! I don't believe it.
      b. What! John, managing director! You've got to be joking.

These examples further demonstrate the affinity between predicate nouns and (predicate) adjectives. Structurally, *They made him headmaster* is exactly parallel to *They made him famous*. Both sentences can be roughly paraphrased as 'They brought it about that he exhibited property X'; in the one case, 'property X' is the property of 'being headmaster', in the other case, it is the property of 'being famous'.

Study questions

1. The following pairs of expressions contrast with respect to the presence vs. absence of the determiner. Explain the semantic contrast between them.

   go to church vs. go to the church
   go to prison vs. go to the prison
   be in hospital vs. be in the hospital

2. Bare nouns often appear in idiomatic expressions, especially when the nouns are conjoined or listed:

   She played *cat and mouse* with him.
   He fell for it, *hook, line, and sinker*.
   He sold it all, *lock, stock, and barrel*.
   They live *from hand to mouth*.
   You would think they were *father and son*.
   She is both *wife and mother*.
   He stands *head and shoulders* above the rest of us.

   Why do you think the nouns in these expressions lack any grounding elements, such as a determiner?

3. That. Traditionally, two values of *that* are distinguished—the word can be used as a determiner (*That car is mine*) and as a pronoun (*Whose is that?*). It could, however, be argued that the two *that*'s belong to the same category (more specifically, that they share an identical profile). Assess these two approaches.

4. Kind(s) of. There is considerable uncertainty in English with respect to number agreement in partitive expressions involving *kind(s) of*. We can speak about (i) *these kinds of problems*, (ii) *these kind of problems*, (iii) *these kinds of problem*—though (iv) **these kind of problem* seems to be excluded. Expression (ii) is particularly interesting, in that plural *these* fails to agree with singular *kind*.

   Do a corpus search to establish the incidence of the different usage patterns of *kind of* and *kinds of* within partitive expressions. (You might also want to consider the uses of *sort of* and *sorts of*.) What might motivate the different structures and their use?

5. Generics and universals. English has a palette of resources for making generic statements:

   (i)   Cats are carnivores.
         A cat is a carnivore.
         The cat is a carnivore.

   Although these sentences appear to be more or less equivalent, differences between the three patterns emerge when other properties are predicated of other kinds of entities.

(ii) Dinosaurs are extinct.
      *A dinosaur is extinct.
      The dinosaur is extinct.

(iii) Zebras have stripes.
      A zebra has stripes.
      ?The zebra has stripes.

(iv) Tigers are rare.
      *A tiger is rare.
      ?The tiger is rare.

(v)   Unicorns do not exist.
      *A unicorn does not exist.
      *The unicorn does not exist.

(vi) Right-angled triangles have a hypotenuse.
      A right-angled triangle has a hypotenuse.
      *The right-angled triangle has a hypotenuse. (unacceptable on a generic
      reading)

Paying attention to the syntactic form of the subject nominals (bare plural, indefinite singular with *a*, definite singular with *the*), analyse the different conceptualizations symbolized by the three constructions, with a view to how these might explain the above acceptability patterns.

In view of the acceptability judgements above, it would appear that the bare plural is the 'unmarked' means for making generic reference. Why should this be so? In what ways are the other devices special?

6. Nominal compounds (e.g. *dog-breeder*) have been an established feature of English for many centuries. As observed in this chapter, the modifying noun is ungrounded.

Ungrounded nouns can also be incorporated into compound verbs. In fact, this phenomenon, though comparatively rare, appears to be on the increase in present-day English. The following are some examples that I have recently encountered:

If your dog is looked after properly, he won't be prone to <u>attention-seek</u>.
Did he lie under oath? Did he <u>witness-tamper</u>?
We don't want to <u>price-regulate</u> the charges.
Please <u>name-label</u> your luggage.
The minor party in the coalition government needs to <u>product-differentiate</u> itself from its partner.
The player is thought to have <u>match-fixed</u>.
First you must <u>course-advise</u> the student.

(a) Suggest alternative wordings of these sentences which do not involve the incorporation of nouns into compound verbs. Sometimes it will be easy to come up with a rewording, in other cases less so.

(b) What do you think motivates the use of the compound verbs?

Further reading

On grounding, determiners, and quantifiers, see FCG2, Ch. 3. On predicate nouns, see FCG2: 64–71.

The thesis of 'determiners as heads' has been argued by Hewson (1991), as well as by Hudson (1984: 90–2, 1990: 268). For a counter view, see van Langendonck (1994). Recent developments within X-bar theory—especially following Abney (1987)—have also proposed that noun phrases (or, rather, what used to be called noun phrases in earlier versions of the theory) are headed by the determiner. Following these developments, nominals are referred to as 'determiner phrases' (DPs).

CHAPTER 19

Count nouns and mass nouns

In the last chapter I largely overlooked the conceptual (and grammatical) differences between count and mass nouns. While the notions of instantiation, quantification, and grounding are applicable to all nominals, their morpho-syntactic realization may be affected by the status of a noun as count or mass.

After examining the conceptual basis of the count-mass distinction, I argue, in this chapter, that a more sophisticated set of categories is required and also that the categories pertain to how a noun type is instantiated—they do not inhere in the type specification. I round off the chapter by considering the case of so-called numeral-classifier languages, which typically lack the morpho-syntactic distinctions (especially, singular vs. plural) characteristic of English.

19.1 Count nouns and mass nouns

The count-mass distinction is a prominent feature of English and many other languages (though by no means all). Perhaps the basic manifestation of the distinction concerns the possibility of a noun's occurring in the singular and/or plural form. Count nouns can occur in both singular and plural: *cat* ~ *cats*, *car* ~ *cars*, *symphony* ~ *symphonies*. Mass nouns are generally thought of as nouns which occur exclusively in the singular: *meat* ~ **meats*, *traffic* ~ **traffics*, *music* ~ **musics*. There exists, however, a smaller group of nouns which occur only in the plural: *clothes* ~ **clothe*, *oats* ~ **oat*, *groceries* ~ **grocery*. These share some of the conceptual and syntactic properties of the singular mass nouns. The appropriate generalization with respect to mass nouns, however, is not so much that mass nouns fail to pluralize, but that they **fail to exhibit the singular–plural contrast**.

The count-mass distinction is crucial to the analysis of English nominals, due to the fact that certain determiners and quantifiers are restricted to occurring only with certain kinds of noun. The following is a sample of some of these restrictions.

- The indefinite determiner *a* and quantifiers such as *one*, *another*, *each*, and *every* can only occur with singular count nouns: *a boy*, **a music*, *another car*, **another traffic*.
- Numerals (greater than *one*) are restricted to occurring with plural count nouns: *seven boys*, **seven clothes*, *three cars*, **three groceries*.
- Partitive expressions are appropriate with plural count nouns or with mass nouns (whether singular or plural) but not with singular count nouns: *a group of boys*, *a bottle of water*, *a bag of groceries*, **a crowd of boy*. A similar restriction applies to the quantifying expressions *a lot of* and *lots of*: *a lot of meat*, *lots of cars*, *a lot of clothes*, **lots of boy*.
- When used in a generic sense, only mass nouns and plural count nouns are able to occur without a determiner or quantifier: *Water is colourless*, *Groceries are expensive*, *Dogs make good companions*, **Dog makes a good companion*.

19.1.1 The conceptual basis

The conceptual basis of the count-mass distinction is fairly transparent; it has to do with the distinction between an individuated 'object' and an unindividuated 'substance'. An individuated object has its own internal structure and composition—split it up and it loses its identity. Dismantle a car and you have car parts, not a car any more. But if you divide up a quantity of meat you still have meat, and if you put two quantities of meat together you have, again, meat. If you put one car next to another car you have, not 'car', but 'two cars'.

The distinction between count and mass can be appropriately captured in terms of **internal homogeneity**. Flowing from this are the properties of **divisibility**, **replicability**, and **inherent boundedness**.

- A <u>substance</u> is internally homogeneous, hence any portion of the substance counts as a valid instance of it and a multiplication of instances also counts as an instance. To be sure, any instance will be bounded in its domain of instantiation. The water in a lake constitutes a bounded instance of 'water'. However, the boundary is not inherent to the concept [WATER].
- <u>Individuated objects</u> differ on all these properties. First, they lack internal homogeneity. A part does not count as an instance while an accumulation

of instances counts as just that: a multiplicity of instances. Moreover, individuated things are inherently bounded; the boundary does not simply define the extent of the instance, it legitimizes the categorization of the entity as an object of the appropriate kind. The boundary of a lake is inherent to the concept [LAKE].

The count-mass distinction, though explicated most easily on the example of concrete objects and physical substances, applies equally to entities in other domains. A symphony is an individuated thing which, in performance, is demarcated in the domain of time. A part of a symphony—say, the second movement—is not a symphony. Naturally enough, you can replicate the instance, in which case you have 'several symphonies'. Music, in contrast, is mass. Multiple instances of 'music' still count as 'music'.

Although well founded conceptually, there is an important respect in which the count-mass distinction is a matter of how speakers construe a thing. Take the issue of homogeneity. At the molecular level, water is not homogeneous, it consists of individuated objects, namely molecules. In the case of sand and gravel, the individual particles are easily visible, as are the objects that make up furniture and cutlery. Nevertheless, even with respect to furniture and cutlery, the criteria for a substance conceptualization apply. If you divide a quantity of furniture up into two portions, each portion is still 'furniture', if you put together several sets of furniture you still have 'furniture'.

The role of construal is apparent from the fact that a given entity can often be construed in alternate ways. We can speak about the 'houses' in the neighbourhood (focusing on the individuated things) or about the neighbourhood's 'housing' (focusing on the houses as a collective entity). We talk about the 'machines' in a factory or about the factory's 'machinery', about the 'pebbles' on a beach or about the 'shingle'. Moreover, one and the same noun can often be used as both count and mass. You can eat your stew with 'potato' or with 'potatoes'. In the first case, the stew is accompanied by 'potato-substance' (probably, potatoes in their mashed form). In the second case the stew is accompanied by 'potato-objects' (probably, roast or boiled potatoes). Given the possibility of construing an entity in alternate ways, it should not be too surprising that different languages should encode different conventionalized construals. In English, information, advice, evidence, research, and news are construed as mass; in German, the corresponding nouns (*Information, Hinweis, Beweis, Forschung, Nachricht*) have count-noun status. Unlike their English equivalents, the German nouns are compatible with the indefinite article (*eine Information*, etc.) and can occur in the plural (*Nachrichten*, etc.)

19.1.2 Developmental aspects

There is evidence that English-speaking children as young as two and under may be sensitive to the conceptual distinction between objects and substances.

At this age, the children have no productive command of the morphosyntactic correlates of the distinction. Consider the experiment reported in Soja *et al.* (1991).

The experimenter points to an object of a certain shape and constitution, such as a wooden pyramid, and tells the young child 'This is my blicket'. When shown a pyramid made of another substance, and pieces of wood not in the shape of pyramid, and asked which is the blicket, the children would point to the pyramid. The children interpret the unknown word *blicket* as the name of a rigid bounded object of a distinctive shape, whose material substance is a secondary feature. A blicket remains a blicket, even though it might be made of something else. However, when the unknown word was applied to a quantity of a malleable substance, such as Nivea cream, arranged in a certain shape, the children would apply the word to the substance, not to the shape in which the substance was arranged. Asked to pick out the blicket when presented with the same shape formed out of another malleable substance (such as hair-setting gel) and Nivea cream arranged in another shape, the children choose the Nivea cream. The form in which the substance appeared is a secondary characteristic. The blicket retains its identity as blicket, irrespective of the shape in which it is arranged.

The experiment suggests that the ontological distinction between objects (which have a characteristic and stable shape) and substances (which can be moulded into different shapes) is available to children prior to their command of the linguistic resources (use of determiners, etc.) that encode the distinction. Imai and Gentner (1997) present evidence that Japanese-speaking subjects are also sensitive to the object-substance distinction, even though the count-mass contrast is largely irrelevant to the morphosyntactic structure of the Japanese nominal. Objects and substances, therefore, are reasonably regarded as 'conceptual archetypes' (Langacker 1999: 9–10), which emerge on the back of innate cognitive abilities. Imai and Gentner did find, however, that older Japanese subjects were somewhat less sensitive to the distinction, tending to construe as substances what for English speakers (and the younger Japanese subjects) are objects. This development suggests that the conceptualizations conventionally encoded in Japanese (which does not exhibit what is arguably the hallmark of the count noun category, namely the distinctive marking of nouns as either singular or plural) had influenced the way the subjects conceptualized the entities used in the experiment.

English-speaking children very soon catch on to the correlation between the conceptual distinction and the distributional cues for it. In a well-known experiment, Roger Brown (1958*b*: 250–2) showed children aged between three and five a picture which involved (i) a salient kind of activity, performed on (ii) a mass-like substance, in (iii) a container of a characteristic shape. A nonsense word was introduced in three grammatical frames: the children were told that in the picture they could see (i) 'sibbing', (ii) 'some sib', or (iii) 'a sib'. They were then shown other pictures and asked to pick out the ones that showed 'sibbing', 'some more sib', or 'another sib'. About three-quarters of the responses of the 16 children correctly matched 'sibbing' to a similar kind of activity, 'some more sib' to a similar kind of substance, and 'another sib' to a similar kind of object. The experiment shows that the children are able to pick up on the distributional cues for the identification of (i) an unbounded process, encoded by -*ing*, (ii) a substance, encoded by quantifiers which are appropriate only with mass nouns, namely *some* and *some more*, and (iii) an object, as conveyed by the use of *a* and *another*, which are appropriate only with singular count nouns.

Gordon (1985) goes further, and claims to have shown that distributional cues outweigh the conceptual distinction between object and substance. He taught children aged three to five years nonsense words which were presented with the syntax of either mass or count nouns. The words were matched up with situations which supposedly would favour either a substance or an object interpretation. In one condition, the grammatical count-mass distinction correlated with the conceptual object-substance distinction; in the other condition the linguistic cues were in conflict with the conceptual distinction. Gordon found that the children overwhelmingly followed the linguistic cues, even when they were in conflict with the conceptual cues. He concluded that 'there is no support for the claim that children represent the count-mass distinction in terms of a distinction between objects and substances' (p. 236); rather, he claimed, the distinction is essentially distributional. According to Gordon, count nouns are identified as such, not because they designate individuated objects but because of a cluster of distributional facts. It is the fact that a noun is encountered with the determiner *a* that allows the language user to predict that the noun can be pluralized (conversely, the fact that a noun is encountered in both singular and plural allows the prediction that the singular can be used with *a*); what the noun designates is irrelevant.

We need to evaluate Gordon's conclusion with some caution. First, we need to emphasize that a purely distributional basis for grammatical categories is not ruled out in principle in Cognitive Grammar. In fact, distribution-based categories (such as inflection classes, see section 17.7) are by no means infrequent in the languages of the world. In many languages, for example, noun gender is largely a matter of agreement patterns between a noun and other items, such as determiners, adjectives, and pronouns, and is not based in properties (let alone, universally recognized properties) of the entities which the nouns designate. To be sure, it may be the case, in a gender language, that male and female persons will be designated (usually) by nouns of masculine and feminine gender, respectively. But the fact that Italian *giardino* 'garden' is of masculine gender, whereas *casa* 'house' is feminine, can in no way be derived from any properties of gardens or houses as such. The gender of these nouns is simply a matter of the agreement patterns which the nouns trigger. Having observed that *giardino* is used with one form of the definite article (*il*), and that *casa* is used with the other form (*la*), the language learner knows that *giardino* will co-occur with one form of an adjective (e.g. *piccolo* 'small') and that *casa* will co-occur with another form (*piccola*). Young children are known to be extraordinarily adept at picking up these patterns. Children may even pick up the distributional nature of grammatical gender before they learn the appropriate conditions for using gender-specific pronouns (*he* vs. *she*) with reference to male and female persons (Levy 1983).

Gordon's suggestion that the count-mass distinction is purely a matter of distribution cannot therefore be dismissed out of hand. However, a closer look at Gordon's experiment suggests that he may have downplayed the conceptual basis for the distinction. Consider the kinds of entities that supposedly favoured an object vs. a substance interpretation. For objects, Gordon used a jumble of unusual looking electrical components; for substances, he used portions of liquid in test tubes. Both entities, it seems to me, are inherently ambiguous with respect to the count-mass conceptualization. Suppose an adult English speaker were shown an array of strange-looking electrical gadgets. One could equally well refer to the entities as 'gadgets'—which I just did in the last sentence, focusing on the individual components of the set of entities—or as 'gadgetry', focusing on the collective. The test-tube samples were also inherently ambiguous, in that the substance—a coloured liquid—was presented in a discrete number of bounded instances. Suppose that an adult English speaker were presented with glasses filled with an unknown kind of liqueur. I suspect that one might be equally inclined to refer to instances, collectively, as 'liqueur', or, focusing on the bounded instances, as so many 'liqueurs'. It is therefore disingenuous of Gordon to suggest that in one of his experimental conditions linguistic cues for count vs. mass nouns correlated with the conceptual distinction between objects and substances, while in the other condition the formal and conceptual aspects were in conflict. Rather, the entities that were used were able to be construed in alternate ways. The distributional cues served to coerce one or the other of the potential construals.

Given the possibility of alternate construals—along with the fact that different construals might be conventionalized in different languages (recall the earlier example of *information* and its German equivalent)—it would be an error to claim that the status of a noun as count or mass is fully determined by the object- vs. substance-properties of the entities that the noun can designate. Equally erroneous is the claim that the count-mass distinction is purely a matter of morphosyntactic patterning. Rather, we need to recognize a dialectic relation between (language-independent) ontological categories and formal linguistic categories. On the one hand, how an entity is conceptualized can *motivate* a word's status as count or mass; conversely, the status of a noun in the language can *coerce* a certain conceptualization. The interplay of motivation and coercion will sometimes create tensions—how a person conceptualizes an entity may conflict with the conventionalized resources of a language. It is not surprising, therefore, that we encounter considerable fluidity in the linguistic data, with predominantly mass nouns sometimes being used as count, and vice versa, both of these deviations from the dominant pattern being due to the speaker's desire to encode special conceptualizations.

The situation contrasts sharply with the case of morphosyntactic categories that are based solely on distributional patterns, such as (in many cases) noun gender. A speaker of Italian is not free to manipulate the gender of *giardino* in order to convey distinct construals of 'garden', since noun gender is not motivated by any conceptual aspects. But a speaker of English *is* free to play around with the count or mass status of a noun in order to encode distinct construals of an entity.

19.2 Refining the count-mass distinction

To talk—as I have done so far in this chapter—about a two-way distinction between count nouns and mass nouns possibly oversimplifies, and even misrepresents the situation in a language such as English. In terms of patterns of distribution, we need to recognize at least three categories: (i) singular count nouns, such as *boy*, (ii) plural count nouns, such as *boys*, and (iii) mass nouns (which, for the time being, we can take to be invariably singular in form), such as *air*.

Table 19.1 shows the possibility of these nouns co-occurring with various determiners and quantifiers (including the so-called zero determiner). Of the nine criteria listed in the Table, only one—(5)—distinguishes count from mass as such. What we find is that one set of criteria—(6–9)—differentiates

Table 19.1 Co-occurrence possibilities of three kinds of noun with various determiners and quantifiers

	Singular count (*boy*)	Plural count (*boys*)	Mass (*air*)
1. ∅ __	−	+	+
2. a(nother) __	+	−	−
3. some (more) __	−	+	+
4. a lot of __	−	+	+
5. (not) much __	−	−	+
6. this __	+	−	+
7. these __	−	+	−
8. (not) many __	−	+	−
9. three __	−	+	−

singular nouns (whether count or mass) from plurals, whereas another set of criteria—(1–4)—aligns mass nouns with plural count. Two cross-cutting distinctions therefore emerge: singular vs. plural, and singular count vs. plural and mass.

From a conceptual point of view, these cross-cutting distinctions make perfect sense. Plural is reserved for cases where there are a number (greater than one) of individually identifiable objects; hence, plural count stands out from singular count and mass. Equally, there is a certain affinity between mass and plural. For example, plural entities exhibit the very same properties of internal homogeneity, divisibility, and replicability as masses. If you divide up a set of boys into smaller groups, each group is still 'boys'. Put together groups of boys, and you have . . . boys. (The mass-like characteristics of a plural vanish, though, once a specific number is designated. *Five boys* constitutes a bounded entity which lacks the property of internal homogeneity. If a group of five boys is divided into smaller groups, none of these will be an instance of 'five boys'.)

Though plurals and mass share the property of internal homogeneity, they differ according to the 'granularity' of the designated entities. As we zoom in on a mass, the particles which compose it become individually identifiable; the mass turns into a multiplex entity. Conversely, as we zoom out from a multiplex entity, the particles lose their individuality and the entity becomes a mass. Lakoff put it like this:

> The relationship between multiplex entities and masses is a natural visual relationship. Imagine a large herd of cows up close—close enough to pick out the individual cows. Now imagine yourself moving back until you can no longer pick out the individual cows. What you perceive is a mass. There is a point at which you cease making out the individuals and start perceiving a mass. It is this perceptual experience upon which the relationship between multiplex entities and masses rests. (Lakoff 1987: 428)

19.2.1 Finer distinctions

On closer examination, even the three-way classification presented above (singular count, plural count, and singular mass) turns out to be too crude, in that there are nouns which do not fit into any of the three categories.

Consider the noun *groceries*. The word bears the plural morpheme, it can take a plural determiner (e.g. *these*), and it triggers the plural form of a verb—(1a). The bare noun can also be used in a generic sense—(1b). We might be inclined, therefore, to consider *groceries* to be a perfectly normal plural noun—until we realize that the word lacks a corresponding singular—(1c). We cannot speak **a grocery*, **one grocery*, or **the grocery*.

(1) a. These groceries were expensive.
     b. Groceries are getting more expensive.

c. *This grocery was expensive.

d. We need {*three / ?several / ?numerous} groceries.

Not only this, but *groceries* fails to exhibit the full range of properties that are typical of a plural count noun (1d). Although we can speak of *a lot of groceries, a week's supply of groceries, some more groceries, not many groceries*, we cannot designate a precise number of groceries (**three groceries*), nor even a vaguely specified number (*?several groceries*).

As suggested at the beginning of this chapter, *groceries* can be classified as a plural mass noun. Its invariable plural form (traditional grammar gives the name 'plurale tantum' to a noun that is always plural) is motivated by the coarse granularity of the items that make up the mass. Groceries, namely, consists of different kinds of things (bread, tins of beans, etc.) that are easily individuated and which, considered in themselves, are readily distinguished. Its mass status is motivated by the fact that the individual components are not particularly prominent in the conceptualization—this, presumably, is the reason why we cannot enumerate *groceries* with words like *three*. The emphasis, rather, is on the fact that the different things all serve a common purpose (they are raw foodstuffs that we buy for the kitchen), they come from a common source (the supermarket), and they have typically been assembled in a particular place (the supermarket trolley, the shopping basket, or the car boot).[1] This last aspect, it seems to me, is particularly prominent. Once the items that make up 'my groceries' have been separated—some going into a cupboard, some going into the fridge, some going straight into the evening meal—it becomes less appropriate to refer to the items collectively as 'groceries'.

There are quite a few plural mass nouns which exhibit the above properties. Examples include *leftovers, remains, supplies, belongings, valuables, dishes* (as in *wash the dishes*), *clothes, bedclothes, contents,*[2] and (for many speakers), *goods*. Use of these words focuses attention on the common function—and usually also the common place—of items that, from one point of view, are easily individuated (cf. Wierzbicka 1985).

Conceptually (and grammatically) somewhat different are words such as *trousers, pants,* and *jeans,* as well as *scissors, glasses* ('spectacles'), and *bin-*

---

[1] There are clear affinities with singular count nouns such as *furniture* and *cutlery*. These also designate collections of things of different kinds (tables, chairs, etc., in the case of 'furniture', and knives and forks in the case of 'cutlery'), but which serve a common function (furniture makes our homes more comfortable to live in, cutlery is used for eating) and which usually are found assembled in a certain place (in the home or on the dining table). It is not surprising, therefore, that *furniture* translates into other languages as a plural mass noun (German *Möbel*, French *meubles*). Even in English it is possible (in estate agents' jargon at least) to refer to *movables* and *immovables*, but not, I think, to *a movable* or to *an immovable*.

[2] Observe that *contents* (as in *the contents of the book*) is not strictly speaking the plural of *content* (as in *the content of the book*). We cannot speak of the 'three contents' of the book, nor can we enquire 'how many contents' a book has. *Contents* and *content* need to be regarded as two distinct lexical items, the former being a plural mass noun, the latter a singular mass noun.

oculars. These words designate individuated objects. A common feature of the objects is their bipartite structure. Scissors consist (obligatorily) of two cutting blades, spectacles comprise two lenses, while the clothing terms designate garments which accommodate the two legs. It is remarkable that other items of clothing which also have a prominent bipartite structure are named by singular nouns (*pullover*, *bra*), as are items which actually consist of distinct parts (*suit*, *bikini*). The status of plural mass is restricted to those items which Wierzbicka (1991: 377) has called 'leg-dividers'.

There is undoubtedly a certain conflict between the plural status of words like *trousers* and the fact that the words designate individuated objects (albeit objects with a prominent bipartite structure). What do I say when I wish to buy an object of the kind 'trousers'? If I am in a pedantic frame of mind, I could say that I need to buy 'a pair of trousers'. *Trousers*, being a plural mass noun, cannot take the determiner *a*. It is necessary to 'unitize' the substance conceptualization imposed by the mass noun, the conventional unit, in this case, being 'pair'. Note the conflict between the conceptualization and the conventional linguistic resource. In speaking of 'a pair of trousers' I am not referring to two items, but to one. If I am in a less pedantic frame of mind, I would probably say that I need to buy 'some trousers'. The quantifier *some* is consistent with the plural status of *trousers*. This more concise usage, though, comes at a price. *Some trousers* fails to specify the number of garments that I wish to purchase; *some trousers* could designate any number of 'pairs of trousers'.

In view of these conflicts between conceptualization and grammatical status, it is remarkable that the mass noun status of *trousers*, and the other words cited above, has persisted over the centuries and has been so resistant to change.[3] The plural conceptualization is so entrenched that when pointing to a single 'pair of trousers', or 'pair of binoculars', a person would use a plural pronoun, not a singular. One would ask *How much are these?*, not *How much is this?*

Some plural mass nouns are restricted to occurring in specific syntactic environments. Consider *whereabouts* (as in *His whereabouts are unknown*). Since the word designates the place where a person or thing might be, it is not surprising that the word occurs principally with a possessive determiner (*his whereabouts*) or, less frequently, with *the* in association with a postnominal *of*-phrase (*the whereabouts of the fugitive*). Other uses (*his many whereabouts, some of his whereabouts, these whereabouts of his*) are scarcely imaginable. Or consider *workings*, as in *the workings of a watch*, *the workings of Parliament*, *the workings of the market economy*. *Workings* designates the internal mechanism of a machine or an institution; its plural form is motivated by the fact that the mechanism is viewed as complex, i.e. it has many parts, which interact in

---

[3] In sub-standard South African English, the form *a scissor* (= 'a pair of scissors') is sometimes heard.

intricate ways. The word is virtually restricted to occurring with *the*, optionally with an intervening adjective (*the mysterious workings of the stock market*). Partitive uses (*some of the workings*) hardly seem possible, neither is it easy to imagine the word being used in a generic sense, i.e. without a determiner or quantifier.[4]

Especially curious is *premises*. The word designates a building, part of a building, or group of buildings (and perhaps also the surrounding land) which is used for a certain purpose, typically trade, business, or manufacturing, or, less usually, habitation. Its plural form is probably motivated by the fact that the designated entity may consist of numerous parts (different rooms, work-shops, etc.). Like *workings* and *whereabouts*, *premises* is typically used with *the*: *live on the premises, conduct one's business from the premises, search the premises*. Not surprisingly, the word is also compatible with a possessive: *The police searched his premises*. Observe that in this and the previous examples, the number of distinct 'premises' is left unspecified. (We encountered a similar situation with *trousers*.) The ambiguity can be resolved by quantification of the noun: *He bought several premises, a number of premises, three new premises*. In this respect, *premises* distributes rather differently than other mass plurals, such as *trousers* and *groceries*. It is even possible to construe the word with a singular determiner: *He acquired a new premises*. *Premises* is therefore by no means a 'typical' mass plural; it has a distribution that very likely is unique to itself.

In fact, as we delve more deeply into the distributional properties of individual words, it becomes apparent that broad generalizations about the syntactic properties of plural mass nouns are inadequate for predicting a noun's acceptable range of uses. There are, to be sure, some general features that characterize the class—indeed, it is on the basis of these that we are able to propose 'plural mass noun' as a distinct subcategory. But at a sufficiently fine level of analysis, and taking into account a noun's pre-ferred distributional patterns, each word may well turn out to have a unique distribution.

It is worth noting, in this connection, that quite a few invariably plural nouns are restricted to occurring in fixed idiomatic expressions:

(2) ways and means; goods and chattels; bits and pieces; odds and ends; (the) ins and outs (of the matter); (the) ups and downs (of life); to all intents and purposes; under the auspices of; give oneself airs and graces

For a good many of these nouns, a statement of the idiomatic expressions in which they occur constitutes, to all intents and purposes, an exhaustive description of the words' distribution.

---

[4] A sample of expressions from the British National Corpus confirmed these observations. The only syntactic environment, apart from *the (ADJ) workings*, in which *workings* occurred was within a possessive expression: *its essential workings* (speaking of a guitar).

Plural mass nouns and semantic fields

A notable fact about plural mass nouns is that they tend to cluster in certain semantic domains. (We have already encountered the case of terms that designate leg-dividing clothing articles.) One such domain pertains to sums of money and, more generally, to possessions and things of value:

> wages, earnings, means (as in *a person of means*), expenses, resources, assets, effects, goods, goods and chattels, riches, savings, takings, proceeds, pickings, belongings, things (as in *my things*, i.e. 'my possessions')

Another group concerns parts of the body which have a complex internal structure:

> guts, innards, intestines, brains, bowels, genitals, testicles

Quite a few have to do with locations, including the names of geophysical phenomena:

> whereabouts, headquarters, grounds, premises, woods, wetlands, uplands, outskirts, surroundings, the Midlands, the Canterbury Plains, the great outdoors, (plumb) the depths, (scale) the heights, (live) out in the sticks

Names of mountains, islands, and countries are sometimes invariably plural (usually with the definite article *the*).

> the Alps, the Pyrenees, the Blue Mountains, the British Isles, the Seychelles, the Camorras, the West Indies, the Netherlands, the Low Countries, the States

---

19.3 Representing the count-mass distinction

It is common practice to speak of *cat, house*, and *car* as 'count nouns', and of *water, air*, and *sand* as 'mass nouns'. This practice—which I have also followed in this chapter—suggests that status as count or mass is an inherent property of a noun, and that 'count noun' and 'mass noun' can be regarded as subcategories of the more schematic category 'noun'.

Complicating this neat schema is the fact that many nouns can be used as either mass or count. Consider words like *beer, coffee*, and *water*. It seems reasonable to say that these nouns are 'basically' mass, in that they designate a kind of substance, but that they can also be used as count under special circumstances and with special meanings. *A beer* can mean either a standard portion of the substance (*order a beer*) or a variety of the substance (*an imported beer*). On these interpretations, *beer* can easily appear in the plural (*two beers, imported beers*).

In other cases we might want to say that a noun is 'basically' count but can be used as mass in special circumstances. Thus, *chicken* denotes the bird and is count (*There are chickens in the yard*). But as with the names of many animals, *chicken* can also be used to designate chicken meat, in which case it is mass (*I don't eat chicken*). Even nouns which at first blush might seem to resist a substance interpretation can sometimes be used as mass. One does not have to imagine someone 'eating cat' in order to construe *cat* as a mass noun—see the examples in (3)—while the mass use of *car* (again, a pretty good candidate, one might think, for an exclusively count noun) has become familiar from the advertising slogan *More car for your dollar!* In fact, it may not be too outrageous to suggest that just about any noun—some more readily than others, to be sure—can, under special circumstances, be used as either count or mass.

(3) a. After the accident, there was cat all over the road.
     b. There's a smell of cat in this room.

While there might be good conceptual reasons to claim that *cat* is 'basically' count and that *water* is 'basically' mass, with some nouns it is difficult to make a decision either way. Consider *lawn*, *ocean*, and *desert*. In what is perhaps their most typical uses, namely as definite singulars, the distinction between count and mass is not encoded. The following are consistent with either status:

(4) a. mow the lawn; sit on the lawn
     b. live by the ocean; hear the sound of the ocean
     c. drive into the desert; the desert is encroaching

In the following, the words are being used as count, as shown by their occurring with *a* and *another* and by the fact that they can pluralize.

(5) a. There's a lawn in front of the house; there's another lawn behind the house.
     b. From this viewpoint, you can see the two oceans.
     c. The Kalahari is one of the most arid deserts in the world.

They can also be used as mass:

(6) a. {There isn't much lawn / There's a lot of lawn} in front of the house. Lawn is available from the garden centre.
     b. We looked out onto a vast expanse of ocean. Most of the Earth's surface is covered with ocean.
     c. Whichever way you looked, there was nothing to see but desert. The country consists largely of desert.

Which of the two statuses should we regard as basic? The question, I think, has no clear answer. Either construal seems equally 'normal'. This ambivalence is plausibly related to the nouns' semantics. The words designate spatially extended (and potentially extendable) entities, whose boundaries may or may not be in profile, and which are characterized mainly in terms of their homogeneous internal structure. There are quite a few words in this category.

Examples from the meteorological domain include *fog, mist, frost, drizzle*, and *rain*.

Another word of ambivalent status is *education*. It is readily used as a mass noun: *They place a high value on education, Education is important for most communities*. The word can also take the indefinite determiner: *a good education*. Yet it is difficult to pluralize the word: ?*They received good educations*. (A search of the 100 million words of the British National Corpus threw up only 14 examples of plural *educations*.) As with some of the examples discussed earlier in this chapter, the case of *education* suggests that when we examine a word in any detail, it may turn out to exhibit a rather distinctive pattern of distribution, which cannot be captured by its categorization in terms of schematic categories such as 'count' and 'mass'.

Here I want to raise the question of the way in which nouns should be represented with respect to the count-mass distinction. As suggested, the traditional view would be that nouns are marked as either count or mass. *Chicken* belongs to the first category, *water* to the second. To explain the mass use of *chicken* and the count use of *water* we might propose some general processes of semantic extension. In Cognitive Grammar, these patterns would take the form of schemas which relate a count noun conceptualization to a corresponding mass noun conceptualization. Sub-schemas relate the count and mass conceptualizations for specific groups of nouns, e.g. animals and animal meat, beverages and portions of beverages (see Fig. 19.1 (p. 380)). The sub-schemas, in turn, are instantiated by the count-mass construals of specific lexical items.

Observe, however, that once we have a schema network for count and mass conceptualizations, it is no longer strictly necessary to classify nouns as 'inherently' count or mass. Nouns, as names of types of things, are unspecified for the count-mass distinction. The distinction only emerges when the types are instantiated. A noun will be used as count or mass to the extent that the conceptualization can be brought under the appropriate schema. This approach is particularly apt for words such as *lawn, desert, fog*, and *mist*, which are liable to be used as either count or mass. Words such as *cat* and *car*, on most occasions of their use, will fall under the object-schema, while *air, traffic*, and *music* will nearly always fall under the substance-schema. That *cat* is felt to be a quintessential count noun is due to the fact that the type 'cat' is typically instantiated as a bounded object. Nevertheless, as already suggested, it is probably fair to say that just about any noun, given the appropriate context, could be used as either count or mass, even though some of the conceptualizations might be highly unusual.

This approach, though no doubt unconventional, has two unexpected, but welcome, benefits. First, it strengthens the analogies between nouns and verbs. As we shall see in the next chapter, there are compelling reasons to claim that the process type designated by a bare verb is indifferent to the perfective-imperfective distinction; the distinction only emerges when verbs are specified

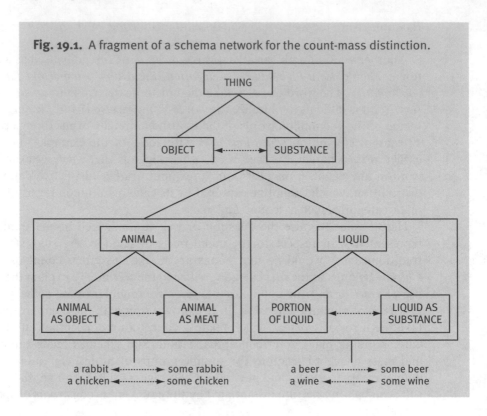

Fig. 19.1. A fragment of a schema network for the count-mass distinction.

and instantiated. Secondly, it brings a language like English (in which the count-mass distinction is well entrenched, principally through the existence of the singular-plural contrast) into line with languages whose nouns do not inflect for number (such as many Asian languages). Or, to put it less contentiously, what we might call the singular-plural languages (such as English) and the numeral-classifier languages (such as Chinese) turn out to be not as radically different as some scholars have suggested.

19.4 Numeral-classifier languages

The distinctions between singular and plural, between count nouns and mass nouns, are fundamental to nominal structure in English. Indeed, to speakers of English (and of similar languages), the distinctions seem not only natural but also conceptually necessary. Nevertheless, many languages do not make these distinctions. In Chinese (and many Asian languages), nouns do not inflect for number and it is not possible to quantify a noun through the simple addition of a numeral. In fact, nouns in Chinese distribute rather like mass nouns in English. This is true even of nouns like *shū* 'book', which, to an English speaker, looks like a pretty good candidate for a count noun prototype. In English, if we wish to refer to a bounded instance of a substance, it is necessary for the mass to be unitized (*a grain of sand, a piece of furniture*) or quantized *(a handful of sand, a litre of water)*. Similarly, in order to refer to a bounded instance of *shū* (that is, to 'a book', or to 'two books'), it is necessary to unitize the Chinese noun by means of a classifier. Once unitized, the noun can take a range of quantifying expressions, including numerals.

The affinities between nouns in the numeral-classifier languages and the mass nouns in English have been noted by Foley:

> There are many languages of the world in which all or the great bulk of nouns behave like the [English] mass noun *rice* and few or none like the [English] count noun *book*. . . . The semantics of these nouns in numeral classifier languages are like those of mass nouns in English; they refer to stuff, substances, or material without definite shape or a determinable unit in its own right. (Foley 1997: 231)

Foley goes on to draw conclusions about the manner in which speakers of numeral-classifier languages habitually conceptualize things:

> the ontology of speakers of numeral classifier languages may be systematically different from that of English speakers. Rather than an ontology which gives prominence to 'bodies', reflected in English and other European languages, theirs might be weighted towards substances. (p. 231)

Foley cites some evidence in support of this view. He refers, for example, to Imai and Gentner's (1997) study (mentioned above, p. 369) which showed that older Japanese-speaking subjects tended to be biased towards substance conceptualizations over object conceptualizations. It is worth emphasizing, however, that the absence of count nouns in Japanese did not totally suppress object conceptualizations. I will suggest below, in fact, that in terms of their conceptual structure, nominals in a numeral-classifier language may not differ significantly from those in singular-plural languages. A key element of the analysis is that a bare noun, in both kinds of language, designates a type which is inherently unspecified, both for number and for the count-mass distinction.

19.4.1 Chinese

Chinese is good example of a numeral-classifier language. The following examples illustrate the use of the bare noun *shū* 'book'.[5]

(7) a. shū   hěn guì
       book very expensive
       'Books are very expensive.'
    b. wǒ xǐhuān kàn shū.
       I   like   read book
       'I like to read books.'

---

[5] Some of the Chinese examples are from Langacker (FGC2: 164). I am grateful to Yuejin Feng for additional data.

  c. wǒ mǎi-le shū.
   I buy-PERF book
   'I bought a book / books / some books.'

The bare noun can be used in a generic sense (a) and in situations in which number is unspecified or irrelevant. Contra Foley, I do not think that these examples testify to a 'substance' conceptualization of 'book'. What seems to be involved is the notion of 'book' as a *type* of entity. Books—in English one is forced to used the bare plural—as a type have the property of being expensive (a); the speaker of (b) likes to read entities of the type 'book'; while (c) invokes some unspecified number of entities of the type.

  When it comes to specifying the number of books (one or more than one) a classifier has to be used. The classifier conventionally associated with *shū* is *běn*:

(8) a. wǒ kàn-le {yī-běn shū / sān-běn shū}.[6]
    I read-PERF {one-CLSF book / three-CLSF book}
    'I have read {a book / three books}.'
  b. wǒ kàn-le {zhè-běn shū / nà sān-běn shū}.
    I read-PERF {this-CLSF book / that three-CLSF book}
    'I have read {this book / those three books}.'

The expressions in (8a) are indefinite. If definiteness is to be conveyed, demonstratives are used, e.g. *zhè* 'this, these' or *nà* 'that, those' (8b). Again, these must co-occur with a classifier. It is not possible to combine a numeral or demonstrative 'directly' with a noun (*sān shū 'three book', *zhè shū 'this book').

  The numeral (or demonstrative) plus classifier can be used in a pronominal sense.

(9) a: nǐ mǎi-le dūoshǎo běn shū.
    you buy-PERF how many CLSF book
    'How many books did you buy?'
  b: wǒ mǎi-le sān-běn.
    I buy-PERF three-CLSF
    'I bought three.'

Similarly, speaking of books, *yī-běn* means 'one', *zhè sān-běn* means 'these three'. Pronominal uses of classifiers are also evident in the following:

(10) a. tā xǐe xiǎoshuō xǐe-le yī-běn yòu yī-běn.
    He write novel write-PERF one-CLSF and one-CLSF
    'He wrote novels, one after another.'
  b. tā xǐe rìjì xǐe-le hǎojǐ běn.
    He write diary write-PERF several CLSF
    'He kept a diary and wrote several volumes.'

---

[6] PERF glosses the marker of perfect aspect. CLSF stands for a classifier.

Structurally, the Chinese nominals look very different to English nominals. Nevertheless, the Chinese nominals can be easily explicated with respect to the conceptual schema that was proposed in Chapter 18, repeated here as in (11). In fact, the Chinese nominals arguably preserve the conceptual structure in (11) more transparently than their English equivalents.

(11) (Grounding (Quantification (Instantiation (Specification (Type)))))

A bare noun in Chinese designates a type of entity. The type is unspecified with respect to the object-substance distinction. The type is invoked in generic expressions and in situations in which quantity is irrelevant—(7). The type can be specified in greater detail, e.g. through the addition of modifiers (*yǔyánxúe de shū* 'book on linguistics'). The classifier serves to instantiate the type.[7] Classifier languages typically dispose of a range of classifiers, which focus on the properties of the instance (perceptual, functional, etc.). The instance may then be subject to quantification (e.g. by a numeral). By default, the instances are construed as indefinite. Definiteness needs to be explicitly encoded by a demonstrative; the demonstrative, therefore, counts as an explicit grounding device.

Consistent with this analysis is the fact that a Chinese nominal appears to be headed by the classifier. As noted, classifiers (together with an appropriate numeral and/or determiner) can be used pronominally. A classifier, then, is a schematic nominal—it designates an instance, the instance receives conceptual substance from the noun with which the classifier combines, and the classifier is schematic for the set of classifier-noun expressions.

Given the underlying conceptual commonality between English and Chinese nominals (or, more generally, between singular-plural and numeral-classifier languages), it may be unwise to insist, as Foley did, on the different ontologies of English- and Chinese-speakers. Although the ways in which a nominal is assembled in the two languages may differ in significant ways, the resultant composite structures are highly compatible.

19.4.2 Malay

Malay represents an interesting fusion of numeral-classifier and singular-plural types of languages.

As in Chinese, a bare noun in Malay can be used to designate a type, as in generic expressions—(12). A bare noun can also be used whenever the number of instances is irrelevant, or when number can be inferred from context and so does not need to be specified—(13).

---

[7] This seems to be the import of Goddard's (1998: 303) remark that 'classifiers . . . do not classify nouns but the referents of nouns—the actual things in the world which the speaker "picks out" to say something about on a particular occasion.'

(12) a. Orang kampung orang kaya.[8]
  man village   man rich
  'Villagers are rich people.'
  b. Anjing suka tulang. (Sneddon 1996: 17)
  dog like bone
  'Dogs like bones.'
(13) a. Ada burung di luar   tingkap.
  exist bird   at outside window
  '{There's a bird / There're some birds} outside the window.'
  b. Saya mahu kereta.
  I   want car.
  'I want a car.'
  c. Saya membeli   ikan di pasar.
  I   TRANS-buy fish at market[9]
  'I bought fish at the market.'

The number of *burung* 'bird' in (13a) is irrelevant. In (13b)—given pragmatic knowledge—*kereta* 'car' would probably be interpreted as singular, while *ikan* 'fish' in (13c) would most likely be taken as plural ('several fishes'). Note that the nominals in (13) are indefinite, and, in (b), perhaps even non-specific. In fact, the construction with *ada* 'there is', 'there are' is incompatible with definiteness; note the impossibility of (14), where definiteness has been conferred by the demonstrative *itu* 'that'.

(14) *Ada burung itu di luar   tingkap.
  Exist bird   that at outside window
  'There is that bird outside the window.'

As in Chinese, number can be expressed by a numeral in association with a classifier (15a, b). For reference to a single instance, the numeral *satu* 'one' typically amalgamates with the classifier to give a form which is analogous to the English indefinite determiner *a* (15c).

(15) a. Ada dua ekor   burung di luar   tingkap.
  exist two CLSF bird   at outside window
  'There are two birds outside the window.'
  b. Saya membeli   dua ekor   ikan di pasar.
  I   TRANS-buy two CLSF fish at market
  'I bought two fishes at the market.'
  c. Saya mahu sebuah   kereta.
  I   want a-CLSF car
  'I want a car.'

---

[8] I am grateful to Jhy Wee Sew for advice on the Malay data.
[9] TRANS refers to the verbal prefix *meN-*, which renders a verbal root transitive. Note that verbs in Malay are not marked for tense.

Malay differs from a 'pure' numeral-classifier language in that a bare noun *can* take a numeral; the classifier, in many cases, is optional (Mintz 1994: 298). Observe the following possibilities:

(16) a. Saya membeli   dua   ekor   ikan di   pasar.
          I   TRANS-buy two   CLSF fish at   market
      b. Saya membeli   dua   ikan   di   pasar.
      c. Saya membeli   ikan   dua   ekor di   pasar.[10]
          'I bought two fishes at the market.'

Likewise, the demonstratives *itu* 'that/those' and *inu* 'this/these' (which, like the Chinese demonstratives, confer definiteness) can be used together with a classifier, but (unlike in Chinese) need not be.

(17) a. Saya membeli   dua ekor   ikan itu.
          I   TRANS-buy two CLSF fish that
          'I bought those two fishes.'
      b. Saya mahu kereta itu.
          I   want car   that
          'I want that car.'

The fact that Malay disposes of a kind of plural morphology, namely reduplication, brings the language even closer to a singular-plural type language.

(18) a. Anak-anak Ali sudah   tidur.
          child-child Ali already sleep
          'Ali's children have gone to bed.'
      b. Pelajar-pelajar hari ini semakin   malas.
          student-student day this be increasingly lazy
          'Today's students are becoming more and more lazy.'

Not all nouns can be reduplicated. *Rumah* 'house', *buku* 'book', and *ikan* 'fish' are among those that can be reduplicated; *air* 'water', *nasi* 'rice', and *gula* 'sugar'[11] cannot be reduplicated. The basis for the contrast is, evidently, the object vs. substance conceptualization of the designated entities.[12]

Reduplicated nouns have some special properties. First, they cannot be associated with a numeral, whether a classifier is present or not—(19a) (Sneddon 1996: 128). This suggests that reduplicated nouns are conceptually mass. They can, however, be rendered definite by means of *ini/itu*—(19b).

---

[10] It is plausible to analyse *ikan dua ekor* in terms of an appositional relation between *ikan* 'fish' and *dua ekor* 'two instances (of fish)'.

[11] At least, *gula* cannot be reduplicated to refer to a large quantity, or several portions, of sugar. *Gula-gula* exists as a lexicalized form to mean 'sweets', 'candy'.

[12] The count-mass distinction also shows up in the compatibility of nouns with certain quantifiers, such as *tiaptiap* 'each' (only compatible with object conceptualizations) and *selurah* 'whole' (only compatible with substance conceptualizations): *tiaptiap rumah* 'each house', *tiaptiap nasi* 'each rice', *selurah negara* 'the whole country', *selurah wang* 'the whole money'.

(19) a. *tiga rumah-rumah; *tiga buah   rumah-rumah
      three house-house   three CLSF house-house
  b. Saya mahu kereta-kereta itu.
      I   want car-car   that
      'I want those cars.'
  c. *Anjing-anjing suka tulang-tulang. (cf. 12b)
      dog-dog   like bone-bone
      'Dogs like bones.'
  d. *Ada burung-burung di luar   tingkap
      exist bird-bird   at outside window
      'There are birds outside the window.'

Moreover, reduplicated nouns may not occur in generic statements—(19c) nor in existential expressions—(19d). These are environments in which a type specification is indicated.

In contrast to reduplicated nouns, a bare noun is unspecified for the singular-plural distinction. Given an appropriate context, a bare noun can in fact be interpreted as plural—(13). Since reduplication also designates plurality, the question arises, what motivates the use of an explicitly plural noun (i.e. a reduplicated noun) in contrast to a bare noun? Mintz (1994: 259), addressing the issue on the following example, suggests there is a conceptual distinction.

(20)   Pedagang dari seluruh dunia dating ke
     Trader   from whole   world come to
     {pelabuhan /pelabuhan-pelabuhan} Malaysia.
     {port   / port-port}   Malaysia
     'Traders from all over the world came to Malaysian ports.'

He comments:

What is important in the use of the nonreduplicated noun(s) is that the referent is considered unitary. . . . The Malaysian ports, no matter how many there might be, are seen as a single unit. In other words, in the context of this utterance, all ports are seen as one group.

These remarks are consistent with the view that the bare noun designates a type, which is indifferent to number. The reduplicated noun, in contrast, explicitly profiles a set of individuals:

the intention . . . would be to consider the ports of Malaysia not as a single unit but as a number of individual units. It is for this reason that reduplication is said to indicate individuality or variety and not plurality. (Mintz 1996: 260)

On the whole, however, there appears to be considerable variation in usage regarding the choice of reduplication (Mintz 1994: 260; Sneddon 1996: 17). Pragmatic factors may also be relevant. Sneddon (1996: 17) notes that reduplication tends to be preferred if a plural interpretation of the bare noun is not evident from the speech context.

Study questions

1. **Number agreement.** Normally, there is strict number agreement in English between a clausal subject and the verb: *The car is . . .* vs. *The cars are . . .* One could, however, argue that verb number (singular or plural) is selected independently of the number of the subject. With reference to the following, consider the factors that influence verb number. (You may wish to dispute some of my acceptability judgements. The question, then, becomes what is the motivation for *your* judgements.)

    (i)   His family {comes / come } from Ireland.
          His family {*is / are } all tall.

    (ii) The crowd {has / have } dispersed.
          A crowd { has / *have } assembled.

    (iii) The Army { has / have } trained him as an engineer.
          The Army { has / have } taken control.

    (iv) The United States { has / ?have } intervened.

    (v)   Five dollars { is / *are } too much to pay.

    (vi) The cabbage I planted {*has /have } all gone rotten. (Assume that several cabbage plants were planted.)

2. Here are some nouns which occur mostly, or only, in the plural form. (You might try to extend the list, by adding more words which occur only, or predominantly, in the plural).

    noodles, scissors, scales ('machine for weighing things'), stairs, bowels, guts, highlands, books ('accounts', as in *cook the books*), coffee-grounds, dregs, odds and ends, whereabouts, premises, barracks, headquarters, chives, the Alps

    Ascertain the distributional properties of these nouns. Do they trigger plural agreement on a verb? Which quantifiers and determiners can they occur with? Can the designated entities be enumerated, and if so, how? Can the words be used in partitive expressions of the kind *a kilo of X*? You may find it helpful to extract some data on these words from a corpus, e.g. the British National Corpus. You will probably find that if you apply a sufficiently large battery of tests, each of the words turns out to be pretty much unique.

    Having ascertained the distributional properties of the nouns, consider whether there might be a semantic motivation for the data. Consider such aspects as the internal consistency (homogeneity) of the designated entities, whether the nouns designate individuated objects, whether the entities consist of identifiable parts, whether the entities could be separated out into their parts, the typical extent of the entities (whether they occur in small amounts, whether they are spatially distributed, and such like), whether the entities are close-knit or dispersed, etc.

3. Using a corpus, ascertain the ways in which *data* is used, paying attention to number agreement and to count vs. mass construals. What motivates these different usages?

4. Also using a corpus, check out the usage of the singular-plural pairs *content ~ contents*, *interest ~ interests*, *brain ~ brains*, *account ~ accounts*. Could there be reasons to claim that the singular and plural forms have the status of separate lexical items?

5. I suggested in the text that words like *fog*, *mist*, *drizzle*, *lawn*, and *ocean* are ambivalent with respect to the count-mass distinction. Is this suggestion corroborated by corpus data?

Further reading

Discussions of number and the count-mass distinction are scattered throughout the first four chapters of FCG2. On number in English and other languages, see the detailed and enlightening analyses in Wierzbicka (1985, 1991). There is also a good discussion in Allan (1986). On numeral-classifier languages, see Foley (1997).

CHAPTER 20

Tense and aspect

In this chapter I turn to the second category of grounded expressions: finite clauses. Grounding, in a clause, is effected by tense inflection on the verb, alternatively (in English) by the modal auxiliaries. Whereas a grounded nominal designates an instance of a thing (identifiable from the perspective of the speech-act situation), a grounded clause designates an instance of a process.

Tense, in English, is closely bound up with aspect, and a study of these topics involves examining the distinction between perfective and imperfective processes. This distinction, like that between count and mass nouns, is based on the boundedness of the designated entity. Further parallels (and differences) between clauses and nominals will be noted as the discussion proceeds.

20.1 Tense and grounding

First, let us recapitulate the account of a grounded nominal. In (1), the bare noun *house* designates a type of entity, which is specified in greater detail by its adjectival and prepositional modifiers. The type specification 'big house over there' is instantiated, the instance is quantified, and it is explicitly grounded. *The three big houses over there* thus profiles three uniquely identifiable exemplars of the specified type.

(1) the three big houses over there

On the basis of these considerations, I proposed, in Chapter 18, that a nominal has the following layered structure:

(2) (Grounding (Quantification (Instantiation (Specification (Type))))))

With the above in mind, consider now the clausal expression in (3).

(3) Louise walked to the store.

This expression designates an event which took place at a time preceding the time of utterance. The event is a 'walking' kind of event, which involves a certain participant (Louise) and which proceeds along a certain path (to the store). A speaker, in uttering (3), designates an instance of this event type. By asserting that the instance took place at a previous time, the speaker is 'locating' the instance both in time and in reality. In this way, the event is grounded from the perspective of the speaker.

The layered structure proposed in (2) for nominals applies also to the finite clause. The innermost constituent in (2) is a type. In the clause, the type is given by the verb. The bare verb *walk* designates a type of process. The type is specified in greater detail by mention of the participant in the process—Louise—and the path along which the walking proceeds. It is not just any walking that is at issue, but walking specifically 'to the store', as performed by a particular person, namely, Louise.

The more fully specified process 'Louise walk to the store' is still a type specification which has an indefinite number of potential instantiations; these could be real or imaginary, past or future, actual or hypothetical, possible or implausible. As with types designated by nouns, the process type is subject to instantiation, quantification, and grounding. In (3), these are subsumed by the past-tense marking on the verb. In virtue of the past-tense marking, the clause 'locates' one specific instance of the process at a time preceding the moment of speaking.[1]

20.1.1 Specification

In the case of a grounded nominal (section 18.2.4), specification of a bare noun is usually optional. *The house* is conceptually autonomous; it is not strictly necessary to specify the type in greater detail in order for the expression to be conceptually coherent.

With verbs it is different. A bare verb, such as *walk*, profiles a process, but leaves unspecified the participants and the circumstances of the process. In

---

[1] I assume what is probably the normal, or default reading of (3), according to which the sentence profiles a single instance of the walking event. The sentence could also be interpreted as referring to Louise's regular habit: before she became incapacitated, Louise (always) walked to the store. On this reading, the sentence profiles an indefinite number of (past-time) instances. The number of profiled instances can be explicitly stated, namely by the use of 'quantifying' adverbials such as *once*, *every day*, *always*, etc.

order for the verbal concept [WALK] to achieve a minimal degree of conceptual autonomy, it is necessary, at the very least, for the tr of the process to be explicitly elaborated; usually, the place or path of the walking will also need to be explicitly stated.

I shall use the traditional term 'clause' to designate a verbal concept that has achieved conceptual autonomy through specification of its essential participants and circumstances. An **ungrounded clause** (i.e. a clause that lacks tense inflection) corresponds to the traditional category of non-finite clause. A **grounded clause** corresponds to the traditional category of finite clause.

As already mentioned in section 12.2.3, there are in principle different ways in which to assemble a clause from its constituents; these different assembly paths correspond to different constituencies. To the extent that different paths do not materially affect the resulting complex conceptualization, the path by which a complex expression is assembled is not a major issue in Cognitive Grammar. With respect to the overall conceptualization symbolized by the clause, it is largely immaterial whether the type specification in (3) has the constituent structure (a) or (b) of Figure 20.1.

Nevertheless, as remarked in Chapter 12, there might be reasons for attributing some special status to a structure intermediate between the bare verb and the fully specified clause, consisting of the verb with its complements

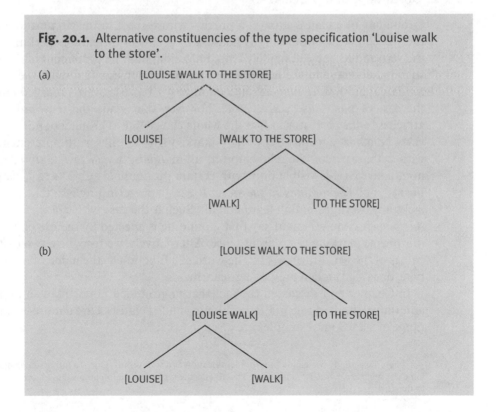

Fig. 20.1. Alternative constituencies of the type specification 'Louise walk to the store'.

(a)   [LOUISE WALK TO THE STORE]

           [LOUISE]   [WALK TO THE STORE]

                    [WALK]   [TO THE STORE]

(b)   [LOUISE WALK TO THE STORE]

            [LOUISE WALK]   [TO THE STORE]

           [LOUISE]   [WALK]

(and possibly modifiers) but excluding the subject (i.e. the tr of the process). This intermediate structure corresponds to the traditional category of verb phrase. If this intermediate category is recognized, the constituency in (a) would be preferred over that in (b).[2]

The category 'verb phrase' is justified to the extent that the relation between a verb and its tr is typically looser than between a verb and its other complements and even its modifiers. Generally, a verb imposes much tighter restrictions on its non-subject complement than on its subject. *Walk* schematically specifies its tr merely as a mobile legged creature, whereas the postverbal complement is inherently locative. *Drink* inherently specifies its lm as something 'drinkable', i.e. as a liquid that can be ingested; *write* requires that its lm be a linguistic text that is created through the writing process; *discover* entails a lm entity that, prior to its discovery, was unknown. These and many other verbs require of their tr merely that it designates an animate or human entity. A similar situation holds with atemporal relational items. A preposition such as *on* (in its spatial sense) schematically specifies its lm as a supporting surface; its tr could be just about anything at all (in the spatial domain). For this reason, it is in general legitimate to speak of a closer semantic 'bonding' between a relational item and its lm than between a relational item and its tr.

20.1.2 Grounding of a process

Grounding of a clause situates a process with respect to the circumstances of the speech event. Grounding is marked by a cluster of features pertaining to the verb and its subject, namely tense inflection, number agreement of the verb with its subject, and the nominative case of the subject. (I discuss the use of modals as grounding elements in section 20.3.) Tense is overtly marked only in the case of past-tense verbs. Note, however, that while the tense inflection attaches to the verb, it is in fact the whole clause that is grounded, not just the verb. Number agreement is overtly marked (by *-s*) only in the present tense with a third-person singular subject, as in *Louise walks to the store*, while nominative case is visible only with certain pronominal subjects (e.g. *they* vs. *them*), as in *They walked to the store*. It can happen (in English) that a clause lacks any overt grounding feature at all. Such is the case with *The men work in the factory*. Here we might say that grounding is effected by the use of a 'zero' morpheme marking the present tense. Alternatively, we recognize two distinct values of the word-form *work*. The word can function as the name of a process type, or as a grounded present-tense form.

In Chapter 19 I discussed the fact that ungrounded nouns play an important, though limited role in English. Ungrounded clauses have a more extensive range of uses. Some examples are given in (4):

---

[2] There are actually two candidates for identification as a verb phrase. One is a fully grounded clause minus its subject, e.g. *walked to the store*. The other is the type specification minus the subject, e.g. 'walk to the store'.

(4) a. I don't want [Louise to walk to the store].
    b. For [Louise to walk to the store] would be dangerous.
    c. I don't like the idea of [Louise walking to the store].
    d. What? [Louise walk to the store]! You must be joking.
    e. Did you see [Louise walk to the store]?

The bracketed phrases all invoke the same process type. In none of the sentences is the process 'located' with respect to the ground; what is involved, rather, is the 'idea' of the process, in one form or another. It will also be noted that the ungrounded clauses sometimes contain additional elements, namely *to* and *-ing*. I discuss the role of these elements in Chapter 26.

The examples nicely illustrate the role of number agreement in clause grounding. Consider (4d) and (4e). Although the verb has a singular third-person subject, the verb lacks the *-s* inflection. Moreover, if the subject nominal *Louise* were replaced by a pronoun, the pronoun would have to be in the objective case (*her*), not the nominative case (*she*): *What? Her walk to the store! You must be joking.*

20.1.3 Complex verb forms: 'be' and 'have'

Consider the bracketed expressions in (5).

(5) a. Louise [is walking] to the store.
    b. Louise [has walked] to the store.
    c. Louise [has been walking] to the store.

One approach to these complex verb forms might be to analyse exponents of progressive and perfective aspect (*be* and *have*) as modifiers of the bare verb. On this approach, 'be walking', 'have been walking', and the like, would count as elaborations of the process type 'walk'. This approach fails, on two counts.[3] First, it does not make sense, conceptually, to claim that 'be walking', and the others, are more fully specified processes of the type 'walk'. 'Be walking' profiles a different kind of process than the bare verb 'walk'. Secondly, the approach fails to take account of the morphosyntactic form of the complex expressions. In (5a), grounding is marked on the verb *be*, not on the verb form *walk*. Although much of the semantic content of *be walking* is contributed by the bare verb *walk*, what is grounded is a process designated by *be*, not a process designated by *walk*. In other words, we need to say that a complex verb form such as *be walking* is headed by the auxiliary *be*, not by the content verb, *walk*. Not surprisingly, the complex verb forms can appear in ungrounded clauses.

---

[3] We must also reject approaches which attribute to a verb the features [±PROGRESSIVE] and [±PERFECTIVE]. A progressive verb form, such as *be walking*, cannot reasonably be analysed as a bare verb supplemented by the feature [PROGRESSIVE]; if anything, it is the schematic notion of progressivity that is fleshed out by incorporation of the semantic content of the bare verb.

(6) a. What! [Louise be walking to the store]! You must be joking.
    b. I don't believe [Louise to have walked to the store].
    c. For [Louise to have been walking to the store] would have been dangerous.

These preliminary remarks have drawn attention to some parallels between nouns and verbs and the manner of their grounding. The grounding of clauses is, however, much more complex than the grounding of nominals. This is due in part to the complex interactions of tense and aspect. I address this topic below.

A note on terminology: 'verb', 'clause', and 'process'

As noted on p. 345, Langacker uses the term 'noun' to refer to any expression that profiles a thing. The term 'nominal' is restricted to a grounded noun—roughly equivalent to the traditional notion of noun phrase.

Similarly, Langacker proposes to use 'verb' to refer to any expression that profiles a process (i.e. a temporal relation: FCG1: 494). According to this usage, not only the lexical category of verbs, but also finite and non-finite clauses, as well as the traditional category of verb phrase, all count as verbs. This use of 'verb' is potentially very confusing and I do not adopt it. Rather, I shall use the term in its traditional sense, to refer to lexical items which profile a temporal relation. I also use the term 'clause' in its traditional sense, to refer to a fully specified process. A 'finite clause' is grounded, a 'non-finite clause' is ungrounded.

The term 'process' also requires some comment. Following Langacker's practice, I use the word as a cover term to refer to the profile of a temporal relation, whether this be a verb, verb phrase, or clause. 'Process' is therefore schematic for different kinds of temporal relations, such as 'state', 'event', 'activity', etc.

20.2 Tense and aspect

English has only two tenses, the so-called past tense and the present tense. (For ways of referring to future events, see Study question 6.)

The prototypical value of the past tense is to situate a process at a time before the moment of speaking. There are, however, other uses of the past tense for which a strictly past-time interpretation is not available. It is notable, for example, that fictional narratives—novels, stories, jokes—are usually told in the past tense; this is true even of science fiction stories, which purport to depict future events. In these cases, we can say that the past tense serves to locate a process in a fictional space, distinct from present reality. In certain constructions, exemplified in (7), the past tense can even denote a counter-

---

Tense inflection as the head of a finite clause

In Chapter 18 I argued that a grounded nominal is headed by the grounding element, i.e. by the determiner, or, in some cases, the quantifier, on the basis that it is the determiner (or quantifier) which gives the nominal its semantic character, namely, its grounding properties.

We can address a similar question with respect to a grounded clause, such as *Louise walked to the store*. What is the head of this expression? Which element in the sentence lends its profile to the sentence?

The sentence designates an event. With respect to an ungrounded clause, this property comes from the verb. An ungrounded clause is therefore headed by the verb. The semantic character of the grounded clause — the fact that it designates an event which is claimed to have taken place in the past — is contributed by the past-tense morpheme. It follows, therefore, that the finite clause is headed by the tense inflection. The tense inflection designates a grounded instance of schematic process; the clause inherits the profile of the tense inflection.

---

factual situation — that is, a situation which is presented as contrary to that obtaining at the time of speaking. A further use is as a 'pragmatic softener', as in (8). A person who utters (8a) is not locating his wanting in the past; he is trying to be less intrusive *vis-à-vis* the hearer. The speaker 'distances himself', so to speak, from the speech act that he is performing.

(7) a. If only I knew. (entails 'I do not know')
    b. I thought you were married. (entails 'you are not married')

(8) a. I wanted to ask you something.
    b. What was your name?

These examples suggest a more schematic characterization of the past tense; the past tense presents a situation as 'located distant from the ground', whether this be distance in time or distance in reality.

If the past tense conveys distance from the speech event, the present tense conveys proximity. In the limiting case, the profiled situation coincides exactly with the moment of speaking. An example of this coincidence is given by 'performative' expressions, which may be marked as such by the use of *hereby*:

(9) a. I promise I won't tell anybody.
    b. I hereby declare this meeting open.

The very utterance of (9a) constitutes the promise; the promising and the utterance of the promise are one and the same thing. Of necessity, the designated process coincides exactly with the time of utterance.

Other uses of the present tense might suggest a less rigorous interpretation of 'the present':

(10) a. She lives in an apartment overlooking the river.
     b. He smokes a packet a day.
     c. Oil floats on water.

Here, the designated situation holds over a period of time which includes the present. To assert (10a), is not just to state that she lives in the apartment at the moment of speaking, but that her residence in the apartment extends over a period of time, which began in the past, which obtains at the present, and which will (presumably) continue into the future. The example suggests that the notion of present time is flexible; it is as if 'the present' is able to expand from a strict interpretation ('the precise moment of speaking') so as to incorporate larger periods of time which include the present. Thus, (10b) refers to a person's long-term habit, while (10c) expresses an eternal truth, valid at all times, including, obviously, the present.

The suggestion that 'the present' is expandable would be consistent with the way in which *now* and *here* are used. *Now* can denote the precise time the word is spoken, as in a performative utterance: *I now declare the meeting open*. The word can also be used to designate periods of time, of greater or lesser duration, which include the present, often in contrast with other periods which exclude the present. The designated period of time can range from a quite brief period ('today') to more extended periods ('while I am on vacation', 'in the post-Cold War era', 'in the Christian era'). *Here* exhibits a similar flexibility. The word can designate the speaker's precise location ('exactly where I am now standing'), or can incorporate a surrounding area of greater or lesser extent: 'here in my house', 'here in London', 'here in Asia', 'here in the solar system'.

In many languages, the present tense seems to function in the manner suggested. Thus, in German, an enquiry into a person's present activity would be phrased in the present tense; the same tense is used in the answer.

(11) a. Was machst du gerade?
        'What do you do right now?'
     b. Ich schreibe einen Brief.
        'I write a letter.'

English is different, as is apparent from the unidiomatic nature of the glosses in (11). *What do you do now?* would normally be taken as an enquiry into a person's line of work, not about their activity at the moment the question is asked. In order to enquire into a present activity, the present progressive must be used: *What are you doing right now?* Likewise, *I write a letter* cannot mean that my letter-writing coincides with the moment of speaking. One has to say, rather, *I am writing a letter*, with the progressive aspect. In fact, *I write a letter now* might even be considered ungrammatical.

In order to elucidate these effects we need to consider the special semantic contribution of the progressive in interaction with a taxonomy of process types.

20.2.1 Perfective and imperfective processes

We can make a broad distinction between two kinds of processes, perfective and imperfective. A perfective process is temporally bounded—that is, its characterization makes reference to its beginning and end-point. An imperfective process is one whose characterization does not make reference to its beginning or end.

We can illustrate the difference by comparing 'write a novel' and 'write novels'. The first is perfective, in that the process terminates when the novel is finished. If the novel is not finished, the writing activity does not count as an instance of 'write a novel'. In contrast, 'write novels' is imperfective. While any instance of the process obviously does terminate at some point in time, the idea of a termination point is not inherent to the concept. In principle, the novel-writing activity can go on for as long or as short a time as one wishes.

There are some striking analogies between the perfective-imperfective distinction in verbs and the count-mass distinction in nouns. In fact, the very same criteria—homogeneity, divisibility, replicability, and boundedness—apply in both cases. Mass nouns designate substances. Substances are construed as internally homogeneous. Consequently, a substance is divisible (any portion is a valid instance) and extendable (instances can be amalgamated into a larger instance). While any instance of a substance is necessarily bounded, the boundary is not inherent to the concept. It is exactly the same with imperfective processes. These are construed as internally homogeneous, such that any segment counts as a valid instance and the temporal boundary can be indefinitely extended. Perfective processes, on the other hand, are analogous to individuated things; they have an internal structure and are inherently bounded. Just as a part of a house is not a house, so a part of the process 'write a novel' does not count as an instance of 'write a novel'. If the process is replicated, we end up with multiple instances of 'write a novel', not a temporally extended instance.

With nouns we saw that the distinction between count and mass was to some extent a matter of construal rather than of objective reality. With verbs, the role of construal is, if anything, even more important. On a strictly objectivist view, the world is in a constant state of flux; events do not present themselves to us neatly demarcated one from another. It is not, however, simply a question of a conceptualizer carving out discrete events from a constantly changing world. There is a sense in which the process 'write a novel' consists of myriads of episodes, of different natures, of different durations, distributed over a longish period, each of which is temporally bounded. The episodes that make up 'write a novel' are probably not too different, in character, from those that make up the imperfective process 'write novels'. Crucial for the perfective-imperfective distinction is that for a process to be viewed as perfective its temporal boundary has to be part of the profiled

Fig. 20.2. A schematic representation of (a) a perfective process and (b) an imperfective process.

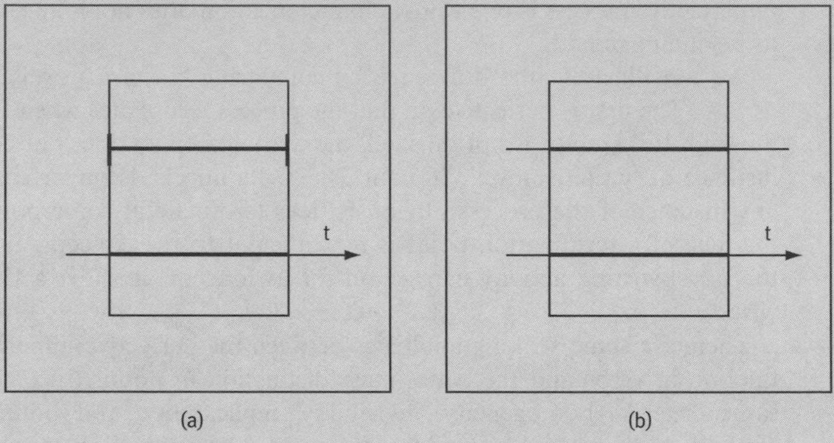

(a)   (b)

Note: The perfective process (including its beginning and its end) lies wholly within the profiled time segment. Only a segment of the imperfective process is in profile; in principle the process could extend beyond the confines of the profiled segment.

process. It is not enough that an instance of the process terminates at some point in time (all instances of a process have this property), the termination point has to feature as an integral component of the designated concept (Fig. 20.2).[4]

Moreover, it often makes little sense to ask whether the process designated by a bare verb, such as *write*, is perfective or imperfective. As a process type, the concept [WRITE] is simply indeterminate with respect to the distinction. At the very least, the process type needs to be specified in greater detail. (Are we dealing with the process 'write a novel', or with the process 'write novels'?) Even what looks like a good candidate for a perfective process ('write a novel') can sometimes be construed as imperfective. In fact, the perfective-imperfective distinction is only really applicable to a process that has been specified, instantiated, and grounded.

One manifestation of the perfective-imperfective distinction concerns the appropriateness of a temporal phrase. In (12a) the perfective process is fully contained within a specified time period designated by the 'in'-phrase. In (12b) the process is able to extend over a period of time designated by the 'for'-phrase.

---

[4] Note the analogies with nouns. *Lake* as a count noun designates a bounded thing. One might want to say that the internal structure of a lake is homogeneous—one part of a lake is just as watery as any other part. What makes *lake* a count noun is the fact that the boundary of the watery expanse is part of the word's profile.

(12) a. She wrote the novel {in six months / *for six months}.
    b. She wrote novels {for ten years / *in ten years}.

Another reflex of the distinction shows up in the use of the progressive aspect. In the present tense, we have the following situation:

(13) a. *She writes a novel.
      She's writing a novel.
    b. She writes novels.
      She's writing novels.
    c. She likes cheese.
      *She's liking cheese.

Perfectives (13a) are incompatible with the present simple. On the other hand, some imperfectives (13b) are compatible with both present simple and present progressive, whereas others—the so-called statives, as in (13c)—are compatible only with the simple present.

In order to explain these effects we need to make a digression and look at the meaning (and internal structure) of the progressive *be V-ing* construction.

20.2.2 The progressive

The English progressive has the form *be V-ing*. Let us consider, first, the *V-ing* component.

The *-ing* form of a verb has a number of semantic values. One value nominalizes the process and causes it to be construed as an unbounded thing. The nominalized form is often called the 'gerund'. The nominal character of the *-ing* forms in (14) is apparent from their syntactic environment. *Jogging* occurs as the complement of a preposition and is in paradigmatic contrast with other nominals (*I don't go in for that*, *I don't go in for this sport*). The nominal character of *complaining* is shown by the fact that it takes a possessor *your*, it is modified by an adjective, and the whole phrase *your constant complaining* functions as a clausal subject.

(14) a. I don't go in for jogging.
    b. Your constant complaining is getting on my nerves.

Practically any verb can be nominalized in this way. The *V-ing* forms generally function as mass nouns,[5] as shown by the fact that they do not pluralize, and they take only determiners that are appropriate for mass nouns.

A second value of the *V-ing* form retains the relational character of the verb. This form is often called the present participle. Its use is exemplified in

---

[5] There are some exceptions to this generalization. One can speak of the 'killings', the 'poisonings', or the 'kidnappings' that have occurred. We also need to distinguish gerunds (which nominalize a process as such) from result nouns, which designate an entity that results from the process. Result nouns, such as *building* (something which results from the building process) and *finding* (something which results from an investigation), are typically count nouns, and readily pluralize.

(15). Observe that the tr of the participle is understood to be identical with the subject of the main clause.

(**15**) a. While writing the novel, she needed to research the history of the family.
    b. Arriving early, he found the building deserted.

Although the participle designates a relation, it lacks a temporal profile. A participle cannot therefore be grounded. The participle does not inflect for tense, nor does it exhibit number agreement with its subject—there is no *she writinged*, *he arrivings*. To the extent that the process invoked by the participle is located in time, this property is contributed by the tense of the main clause (*needed, found*), not by the participle as such.

Since it designates an atemporal relation, the present participle is akin to both prepositions and adjectives (see section 11.7 for a characterization of major word classes). It is not surprising, therefore, that present participles can sometimes function as prepositions (*concerning, considering, regarding* are representative examples). Equally, participles can sometimes be used as attributive adjectives: *the sleeping child, the leaning tower, the ringing telephone*. Like adjectives and other items which designate an atemporal relation, the participle can enter a valence relation with *be*. As pointed out in section 11.3, the standard value of *be* is to profile the continuation over time of a stable relation. It follows that *be V-ing* designates the continuation over time of the relation profiled by the participle. Given that *be* is a stative verb, the beginning and end-point of the profiled relation is not at issue, that is to say, the profile of *be V-ing* is imperfective. The English progressive therefore has the overall effect of 'imperfectivizing' a process.

We are now in a position to explain the obligatory use of the progressive in (13a)—*she is writing a novel* vs. *she writes a novel*. English, it would seem, very strongly requires that a process designated by the present tense has to be fully instantiated at the moment of speaking. For perfective processes, this requirement will rarely be met. 'Write a novel' has a temporal extent which far exceeds the time segment of the utterance *She writes a novel*. Performatives constitute a special case—the utterance *is* the event and is therefore temporally extensive with it. For this reason, in a performative utterance, even a perfective process is compatible with the simple present.

Imperfective processes are internally homogeneous (or rather, are construed as being internally homogeneous); consequently, any portion of the process— even a very short one—will count as a valid instance. Since 'be writing a novel' is imperfective, it is possible for an instance of the process to be coextensive with the utterance *She is writing a novel*. For a perfective process to be compatible with present tense, the process must first be imperfectivized by the use of the progressive *be V-ing* construction.

20.2.3 Kinds of processes

Much of complexity in the use of tense and aspect in English derives from the fact that the categories of perfective and imperfective allow a number of subcategories. It must also be borne in mind that it is rarely the case that a verb, per se, is inherently perfective or imperfective. Different kinds of complements and modifiers can often coerce a perfective or an imperfective reading.

Let us consider, first, a more fine-grained taxonomy of process types (Fig. 20.3).

Inherently bounded processes ('perfectives') can be divided into punctual events and extended events. Punctual events are conceived of as occurring at a point in time and therefore lack temporal extension. Extended events are those that unfold, as it were, over time. We can think of these as internally complex, in that they typically consist of an imperfective process which 'culminates' in the termination. Examples of punctual events are given in (16); extended events are exemplified in (17).

(16) <u>Punctual events</u>: sneeze, cough, blink, die, arrive, finish the novel, begin the novel, reach the summit, etc.

(17) <u>Extended events</u>: travel from A to B, play a Mozart sonata, write a novel, build a house, walk to the store, etc.

As always, whether an event is punctual or extended is a matter of construal. Strictly speaking, a sneeze or a cough does take place over time. Symptomatic of their punctual construal is the fact that the predicates in (16) are compatible with a temporal phrase headed by *at* whereas those in (17) are not: *I arrived at*

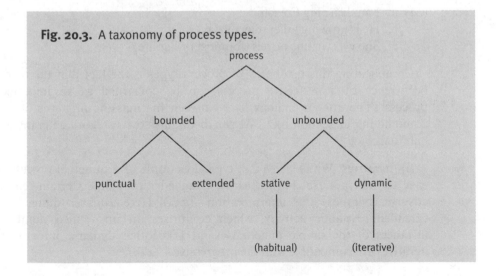

Fig. 20.3. A taxonomy of process types.

6 p.m., **He built a house at 6 p.m.* Extended events, in contrast, *take* time (*It took me half an hour to get to the office*), and occur *in* a period of time (*I got to the office in half an hour*).

A subcategory of extended events are those which involve a specific number of events (whether these in themselves be punctual or extended). Notice that in order for these complex events to be perfective the number of component events has to be specified precisely. 'Walk to the store three times' is perfective, 'walk to the store every Saturday' is imperfective.

(18) <u>Enumerated events</u>: cough twice, play three Mozart sonatas, walk to the store every day last week, etc.

Let us turn now to imperfectives. These can be divided into those that are traditionally called statives and those which are inherently dynamic; the latter I shall call activities. A **stative** process is one which actually involves little or no change: the situation simply goes on. Dynamic imperfectives (**activities**) are those where things happen, things get done, there is change, but there is no inherent end-point.

(19) <u>Statives</u>: be tall, know the answer, like cheese, etc.

(20) <u>Activities</u>: write novels, learn French, grow taller, work on a dissertation, etc.

Characteristic of statives is that they are generally incompatible with the progressive, irrespective of tense—(21). Dynamic imperfectives, i.e. activities, are compatible with the progressive, again irrespective of tense—(22).

(21) a. *He is being tall.
     b. *I am knowing all your secrets.
     c. *Are you liking cheese?

(22) a. I am learning French.
     b. He is growing taller (day by day).
     c. She was writing novels (for most of her life).

Complicating this taxonomy of process types is the fact that the repeated occurrence of a perfective process can be construed as an imperfective process. (There is an analogy here between the mass-noun status of plural count nouns; cf. section 19.2.) We can distinguish two categories, iteratives and habituals.

(i) **Iteratives**. While *cough* is a typical example of a punctual process, it is easy to interpret *He coughed* as 'he coughed repeatedly'. Certain temporal adverbials impose this interpretation—(23a). Here, *coughed* designates an extended, dynamic activity, which comprises an unspecified number of instances of the simple punctual event. Like other dynamic imperfectives, iteratives are compatible with the progressive—(23b).

(23) a. The child coughed all night.
     b. Listen, the child is coughing again.

In order to obtain the iterative reading, the number of iterations has to be left open, such that an end-point of the complex process is not inherent to the conceptualization. Note the increasing ungrammaticality of the following:

(24) a. The child is coughing.
     b. ?The child is coughing repeatedly.
     c. ??The child is coughing many times.
     d. *The child is coughing twice.

(ii) **Habituals**. Certain processes can easily be construed as habitual, as when a process occurs at more or less regular intervals over an unspecified period of time. Examples include 'read the newspaper every morning', 'have breakfast at 8', 'drive to work', 'smoke a packet a day'. Like iteratives, habituals are imperfective, but they differ from iteratives in that habituals take on the character of statives. While the processes that make up the habit, if considered individually, might involve dynamic change, the habit as such is static and unchanging. Consistent with their stative character, habituals are incompatible with the progressive:

(25) a. I have breakfast at 8. (habitual reading)
     b. *I'm having breakfast at 8. (Impossible on a habitual reading, in the sense 'This is my habit; I always have breakfast at 8.')

The matter becomes still more complex, however, in that habits, as such, can change over time. States, too, can change. Consider the following examples involving what appear to be classic examples of stative predicates, namely *cost*, *like*, and *be ADJ*.

(26) a. Vegetables are costing more and more these days.
     b. I'm liking this food {more and more / less and less}.
     c. Now you're being offensive!

Because the state undergoes change over time, the process takes on the character of a dynamic activity; as such, it can readily take the progressive. Likewise, a habit can manifest change over time, whence the possibility of using the progressive in (27).

(27) a. I'm now having breakfast at 8. (I used to have breakfast at a different time)
     b. He's smoking a packet a day!
     c. I'm driving to work less frequently these days.

Sometimes, the very use of the progressive can suggest that a state (or habit) is subject to change. Compare:

(28) a. Where do you live?
    b. Where are you living?

(29) a. How many do you smoke?
    b. How many are you smoking?

Both questions in (28) enquire about a person's address. The present simple in (28a) construes the situation as stative, whereas (28b) suggests that the person has recently changed their address (or has the habit of moving house).

These considerations suggest a more refined account of the progressive. The progressive, to be sure, requires that a process be construed as imperfective, such that any instance or portion of the process, irrespective of its duration, counts as a valid instance of it. But whereas the progressive profiles an instance, contained within the unprofiled base of the progressive is some notion that the state is of limited duration. The use of the progressive there-fore implies some notion of change—change towards the stative situation, and/or change away from it.

This is the reason, I suspect, why the progressive cannot be used with sta-tives. On the face of it, the situation is rather paradoxical. If the progressive can only be used with imperfectives, why is it not possible to use the progres-sive with quintessential examples of stative predicates, such as *be tall* and *know French*? It is sometimes said that the reason why *I am being tall, I am knowing French* are ungrammatical is that the progressive would be redundant; a pro-cess that is already inherently imperfective cannot be marked a second time as imperfective through the progressive. This explanation is far from convincing. While a speaker may sometimes expose herself to censure on stylistic grounds for redundantly conveying the same information twice, redundancy does not normally lead to ungrammaticality. The multiple marking of plurality (on the determiner, on the noun, and on the verb) in *Those houses are old* is obligatory and certainly does not lead to ungrammaticality. The reason, I suggest, why the progressive is unacceptable with truly stative situations is that the progres-sive and 'true' stativity are conceptually incompatible.

20.2.4 Present tense and the 'structured world model'

Let us reconsider the use of the simple present in examples such as the following.

(30) a. Oil floats on water.
    b. I drive to work.
    c. He smokes a packet a day.

The discussion so far will have cast doubt on my initial suggestion that the present tense is appropriate because the 'the present' is able to 'expand' so as to include stretches of time which include the precise moment of speaking. The sentences in (30) are acceptable in the present simple because the designated processes are fully instantiated at the moment of speaking. In terms of the taxonomy of process types presented above, this is because the processes are construed as stative, i.e. as imperfectives.

Note that (30a) is a generic statement about oil. The other sentences in (30), though not strictly speaking generics, raise the same kinds of problems that we noted with generics (cf. 18.3.3). Just as *Cats are carnivores* is not rendered untrue by the existence of a vegetarian cat, (30b) would still be a true statement even though there are occasions on which I do not drive to work.

I suggested in Chapter 18 that generic statements pertain, not to the 'real' world, but to an idealized model of the world in which things have certain predictable properties. Likewise, the examples in (30) pertain to a model of the world in which certain relations hold and certain events are predictable. They concern, not so much 'the way the world is', as 'the way the world is taken to be'. Langacker calls this the 'structured world model':

[According to the structured world model], the world is structured in a particular way, so that certain kinds of events are capable of occurring while others are impossible. Within the realm of possibility events differ in their status. Some are *incidental*, arising in ad hoc fashion from particular circumstances; though compatible with the structure of the world, they are not specifically anticipated or predicted in terms of it. On the other hand, certain events are direct manifestations of the world's structure—they are in some sense regular or predictable, and are thus expected to occur whenever the appropriate preconditions are satisfied. It is in reference to such occurrences that we speak of the *normal course of events*. (FCG2: 264).

Thus, in the normal course of events, I drive to work, and the smoker smokes a packet a day, even though incidental circumstances might cause variations to these routines.

We are still able to maintain that the examples in (30) designate imperfective, stative processes. The states, however, are claimed to hold, not in the real world, with all its aberrations, irregularities, and day-to-day contingencies, but in the 'structured world', which abstracts away from incidental circumstances.

20.3 Modals

So far in this chapter I have considered the grounding of a clause solely with respect to present vs. past tense of the verb. Prototypically, these 'locate' a situation in present time or past time. Another set of grounding elements, in English, are the modals: *can, must, might, should*, and several more.

The modals share a number of distinctive properties. For example, they do not inflect for past tense,[6] and with a third-person singular subject they do not take the characteristic -*s* inflection. These seemingly unrelated facts point to the status of modals as grounding elements. The modals do not take the characteristic exponents of grounding (tense inflection and subject-verb agreement) because the modals are themselves grounding elements. To put it another way: tense inflection and subject-verb agreement on the one hand, and the modals on the other, are in complementary distribution. If a clause is grounded by one of the devices, it may not be grounded by the other.

Semantically, the modals offer a special perspective on a situation. A speaker who states that *Louise walked to the store* is committed to the 'actuality' of the situation, whether in 'reality' or in a fictional space. Modals, in contrast, assess a situation with respect to its likelihood. A number of different modalities can be distinguished. The situation 'Louise walk to the store' may be assessed as probable (*Louise might walk to the store*), as impossible (*can't*), as desirable (*should*), as necessary (*must*), as possible (*can*), and so on.

These different modalities can often be understood in terms of some notion of force (for more discussion, see section 26.2). The force may be one which impinges on a participant or a state of affairs, rendering the situation necessary (*must*); the force may prevent a situation from being the case (*can't*); there may be an absence of force requiring or preventing a situation, hence, something is possible (though not necessary) (*can*). The 'strength' of the force, and hence also of the modality can vary. *Must* is a high-strength modal, *should* is low strength.

The traditional distinction between the 'root' (or 'deontic') uses of the modals, and their 'epistemic' uses, has to do with the source of the force. The **root** modals construe the force as emanating from the laws of the physical world, from the psychophysical world of intentions, desires, and plans, or from the psychosocial world of norms, laws, regulations, and moral values. In *You must do it this way*, the necessity may derive from the nature of the world, from a previous agreement, or from prevailing customs. In their **epistemic** uses, the force derives from logic, reasoning, and common sense. The necessity in *He must be there by now* is a 'logical' necessity; given what we know, we can infer with a high degree of certainty that 'he is now there'.

I will not, here, go into a detailed analysis of the modals from these perspectives. The modals constitute one of the most hotly contested aspects of modern English, and a detailed discussion is beyond the scope of this section. (See the suggestions for further reading at the end of the chapter for more detailed accounts.) Two points, however, need to be emphasized.

First, the English modals offer a perspective on a process assessed at the time of speaking. If the modality concerns a past-time situation, the modal as

---

[6] It might be objected that *could* is the past-tense form of *can*, *might* the past tense of *may*, *should* the past tense of *shall*, and so on. While it may be true that historically the one set of items were past-tense forms, in the modern language they do not function as such—that is, they do not locate a situation in past time, but rather offer a present-time perspective on a situation.

such does not appear in a past-tense form. *He might be joking* presents a speaker's present-time evaluation of the likelihood of a present situation; the force of logic suggests the possible conclusion that 'he is joking'. *He might have been joking* also presents a speaker's present-time evaluation, but of a past situation. The modal itself (*might*) remains the same.

Secondly, all the various kinds of modality can be expressed (some more idiomatically than others) without the use of the modal verbs. Probability, for example, can be conveyed by an adverbial, as in (31b), or by a clause, as in (31c). In (b) and (c), grounding is effected in the normal way, by a tense inflection.

(31) a. She may have walked to the store.
      b. She probably walked to the store.
      c. It was probably the case that she walked to the store.

In other languages, the various modalities are indeed expressed by means of 'normal' verbs which exhibit none of the peculiarities of the English models. French *pouvoir* 'be able to' and *devoir* 'have to' are normal verbs, which take the full range of tenses and inflections of other verbs in the language; the same goes for German *müssen* 'have to', *sollen* 'ought to', *dürfen*, 'be required to', and *können* 'be able to'. Not only this, but English *be able to, have to, be supposed to, be allowed to*—which express modalities of various kinds— are, from the point of view of their grounding by tense inflections, perfectly normal verbal expressions.

20.3.1 Subjectification

An enduring question, in the study of modality, concerns the process by which expressions which pertain to various degrees of likelihood in the physical world come to refer to the psychosocial world of norms and regulations, and to the epistemic world of reasoning and inference. Compare the following:

(32) a. I must leave now / I have to leave now / I've got to leave now.
      b. You must be joking / You have to be joking / You've got to be joking.

(33) a. You can't swim across the river—it's too wide.
      b. You can't swim across the river—it's not allowed.
      c. That answer can't be correct.

Example (32a) concerns physical, or psychophysical necessity. My leaving is rendered necessary because of the force of my will or because of the force of external agents or circumstances. In (32b), the necessity is a matter of a logical inference. Note that the very same meanings are associated with the modal *must* and with the 'normal' verbs *have (to)* and *have (got to)*. A similar meaning contrast shows up in (33). The impossibility may be physical or social (i.e. regulatory) in origin, or may have to do with logical inference.

Johnson (1987: ch. 3) and Sweetser (1990) see here the workings of conceptual metaphor. Force in the physical world is mapped on to the psycho-social world and on to the domain of reasoning. There is more to this process, however, than mapping from one domain to another. In order to see this, consider the following sentences.

(34) a. I am able to solve this problem.
     b. This problem is able to be solved.

Sentence (a) pertains to my mental abilities, whereas sentence (b) states a property of the problem. The examples are of interest in that not all speakers accept (34b). Those who reject the sentence restrict *be able to* to entities that are the locus of the ability, primarily to conscious agents. Since an abstract entity, such as a problem, does not possess the 'ability' to do anything, (34b) strikes these speakers as rather odd. Even for speakers who regard (34b) as fully acceptable, it still remains the case that the 'locus' of the ability lies, not with the subject of *be able to*, but elsewhere. It is not just a question of the 'ability' pertaining, in (a), to the domain of mental capacities, and, in (b), to the domain of logic.

Langacker discusses this phenomenon in terms of 'subjectification'. Subjectification is a process whereby some feature of a designated situation gradually drifts from the profile and comes to occupy the ground. The ability in (34b) is located in the ground and concerns the speaker's conception of the force of logic. The solvability of the problem is assessed from this perspective. As the locus of the ability comes to be located in the ground, the selectional restrictions between the verb and its subject become loosened. *Be able to* is no longer restricted to taking as its subject nominals, which designate entities that possess 'abilities'.[7]

As the example shows, subjectification can occur with 'normal' verbs (that is, with verbs which do not exhibit the special properties of the English modals). Although French *pouvoir* and *devoir* are 'normal' verbs (they have past-tense forms, for example), the verbs, like their English modal equivalents, exhibit subjectification. These considerations help explain some well-known differences between the English and French modals.

(35) a. Il a pu partir.
        'He was able to leave' *or* 'He could have left'
     b. Il aurait pu partir.
        'He would have been able to leave' *or* 'He could have left (but didn't)'

---

[7] Different judgements as to the acceptability of (34b) suggest that *be able to* is currently undergoing subjectification in modern English. (In contrast, the subjectification of *can*, *can't*, *must*, and the other modals, is a long-established fact of English.) In fact, I have noticed that my own usage has changed over the years towards greater tolerance and increased use of examples like (34b). *Be capable of* seems to be undergoing the same process, as suggested by the (perhaps marginal) possibility of *The problem is capable of being solved*. On the other hand, *have the ability to* has not (yet) undergone subjectification. *The problem has the ability to be solved* strikes me as unacceptable, due to the violation of the selectional restriction between the verbal expression and its subject.

    c. Il a dû partir.
      'He had to leave' *or* 'He must have left'
    d. Il aurait dû partir.
      'He would have had to leave' *or* 'He should have left'

On its first interpretation, (35a) locates potentiality in the past. The grounding of the past situation is achieved, in French, through a past form of *pouvoir* and, in English, through a past form of *be able to*. The situation is construed 'objectively'. The ability is located in the subject nominal and the subject's ability (in the past) is profiled by the (past form of the) verb.[8]

On the second interpretation, (35a) presents a present assessment of the potentiality of a past situation. The potentiality in this case is more likely to be epistemic; nothing prevents us (now) from drawing the inference that he left. This interpretation 'it is possible that he left' is subjective (in Langacker's sense) in that the possibility derives from the speaker's assessment of the likelihood of the situation, given certain processes of logical inference; these are aspects of the ground and are not explicitly profiled. It is here that we observe a major difference between the two languages. French *pouvoir* appears in a past-tense form, even though a past situation is not predicated of the verb's subject, whereas in English the post-modal complement is marked as past. In both French and English, there is a loosening of selectional restrictions between a verb and its subject, which we observed in the case of English *be able to*. The subject nominal of both *pouvoir* and *could* is not a person of whom ability as such is predicated.

Study questions

1. **Process types.** *Flash*, like *cough*, is a verb that can designate either a punctual event (*The light flashed once*) or an iterative activity (*The light flashed repeatedly*). The different construals of the process are 'coerced' by the adverbials.

    Explain the different ways in which the process is construed (punctual event, extended event, imperfective process, etc.) in the following.

The light flashed at 3 a.m.
The light flashed until dawn.
The light flashed until dawn every day.
The light flashed until dawn every day for a month.

---

[8] As a matter of fact, we can distinguish two variants of 'he was able to leave'. One interpretation pertains to 'physical' possibility, the other pertains to the absence of a regulatory prohibition. The former is fully 'objective'—the ability is located in the referent of the subject nominal. The latter is somewhat less objective, in that the ability derives from the absence of some (non-specified) prohibition.

The light flashed until dawn every day for a month in the 1950s.
The light flashed until dawn every day for months on end.

The light flashed once.
The light flashed once every evening.
The light flashed once every evening at 10 p.m.
The light flashed once every evening at 10 p.m. in January last year.
The light flashed once every evening at 10 p.m. for weeks on end.
The light flashed once every evening at 10 p.m. for weeks on end last year.

2. In the text I suggested that the phrases *in X* and *for X* (where *X* is an amount of time) can be used as a diagnostic of perfective and imperfective construals. Investigate the compatibility of the following items with expressions designating various process types:

since X, until X (where *X* is a point in time)
take X, spend X (where *X* is a period of time)
finish V-ing, stop V-ing.

Sample data:

(i)   She {has been writing novels / has written novels} since her childhood.
      She {has been writing the novel / *has written the novel} since her childhood.

(ii) She {was writing novels / wrote novels} until her death.
      She {was writing the novel / *She wrote the novel} until her death.

(iii) He took six months {to write the novel / *to write novels}.
      He spent ten years of his life {writing the novel / writing novels}.

(iv) She finished {writing the novel / *writing novels}.
      She stopped {writing the novel / writing novels}.

3. Explain the following entailments:

(i)   She was writing novels.
          <u>entails</u>
      She wrote novels.

(ii) She was writing the novel.
          <u>does not entail</u>
      She wrote the novel.

4. Can you imagine a context in which *The volcano was erupting twice* would be a grammatical sentence?

5. The reader will no doubt have been able to suggest counterexamples to some of the generalizations proposed in this chapter. For example, it was asserted that 'play a Mozart sonata' is an extended event, and that extended events are incompatible with *at*. Yet (i) is perfectly acceptable. Similarly, 'reach the summit' and 'arrive home' might be considered to be punctual events, and, as such, ought to be incompatible with the progressive. Yet (ii) and (iii) seem perfectly natural.

(i)   He played a Mozart sonata {at 6 p.m. / at the beginning of his recital}.

(ii) She is now reaching the summit.

(iii) The guests were arriving all morning.

Are these genuine counterexamples to the generalizations proposed, or can they be explained in terms of special construals of the processes in question?

6. Future events. English does not have a future tense as such. English exploits other resources for referring to future events. These include:

(i)   the present simple, used especially with scheduled events: *My plane leaves at noon tomorrow*;

(ii) the present progressive, typically used with planned events: *We are leaving for the coast tomorrow*;

(iii) *be going to*, typically used to express a person's intention or to predict a future event from observation of present circumstances: *They're going to meet me at the airport*; *Be careful, you're going to fall*;

(iv) certain modals, which can have a future orientation: *You must reply to him soon*;

(v)   *will*, perhaps the most 'neutral' way of referring to the future, suggestive of the 'normal course of events': *The building will be finished soon*.

To what extent are the particular semantic values of these resources derivable from their morphosyntactic form? Is there, for example, a reason why the present simple (i) should be preferred for scheduled events, while the present progressive (ii) is preferred for planned events?
     Does the use of the *will*-future in conjunction with the progressive have a special semantic value? Consider the following:

Will you be doing anything at the weekend?
We'll be going away for Easter.
We'll be seeing each other again some time, I dare say.

Try rephrasing these expressions with other future forms. What differences in meaning do you detect between the different wordings?

7. Tense in subordinate clauses. A curious feature of English is the avoidance of the *will*-future in certain subordinate clauses:

If you {come / *will come} to London, you must visit us.
When you {come / *will come} to London, you must visit us.
We will visit New Zealand after we {have visited / *will have visited} Australia.

What might be the reason for this restriction?

8. If you give a synopsis of the story-line of a play, an opera, or a novel, you would probably do so using the present simple. Newspaper headlines ('Vicar elopes with housekeeper') typically summarize a narrative in the present simple, whereas the body of the article narrates the events in the past tense. What could be the motivation for the 'synoptic' use of the present simple?

Further reading

For tense as a grounding relation, see FCG2: 240–81. For the progressive, see Langacker (1990, ch. 3). The taxonomy of process types goes back to Vendler (1967).

For modality, see Sweetser (1990, ch. 3), Johnson (1987, ch. 3), and FCG2: 269–81. For a more recent treatment by Langacker, see Langacker (1999, ch. 10). For a descriptive survey of the use of the English modals, see Dirven and Taylor (1994).

On subjectification, see Langacker (1990: ch. 12).

Clause structure

The clause is a fundamental unit in language, and clausal structure is a major topic of investigation in all recent linguistic theories.

Like a verb, a clause designates a process—that is, a relation tracked through time. Mostly, the relation designated by a plain verb is conceptually dependent. One can scarcely conceptualize the process of 'giving', or of 'putting', in and of itself; like most verbal notions, these presuppose various additional entities that participate in the processes. Specification of these entities results in a process that is conceptually autonomous. A clause may be defined as a linguistic structure that designates this kind of conceptually autonomous process, created through the elaboration of the participants in a temporal relation.

One facet of clause structure has already been discussed, namely grounding. In this chapter I look at the internal structure of the clause—its participants, the semantic role of the participants, and their syntactic expression, in relation to the kinds of situations that clauses designate. I conclude with some observations of the combination of clauses.

21.1 Types of situation

Clause structure can be characterized by a number of interrelated parameters. These include the number of participants in the designated process, the semantic role of the participants, and the manner in which the participants are expressed syntactically. I begin, however, with the more general question of the type of process which a clause may designate.

There is a sense in which every clause designates a unique kind of process. Nevertheless, it is useful to distinguish a number of schematic process types.

(i) Dynamic processes. A dynamic process is one in which something happens. We can distinguish two types. In one type, the world comes to be in a different state as a consequence of the process. Change-of-state processes are exemplified in (1). In (1a) the house ceases to exist as such, in (1b) the rabbit ends up dead, while in (1c) Peter ends up owning the book.

(1) a. The house collapsed.
     b. The farmer shot the rabbit.
     c. I gave Peter the book.

In a second type, there is energy input into a situation, but the process does not result in a change of state. After the telephone has creased ringing (2a), and after the light has flashed (2b), the world reverts to its previous state.

(2) a. The telephone rang.
     b. The light flashed.

(ii) Stative processes. Here, there is neither energy input nor change. A situation simply exists, or persists.

(3) a. The book is 200 pages long.
     b. The book is boring.
(4) a. The road follows the river.
     b. The picture hangs above the sofa.
(5) a. Your cat is the one that stole the liver.
     b. The photographer was Beryl.

Again, we can distinguish several sub-types. In example (3), certain properties are attributed to an entity, in (4) the disposition of one entity with respect to another is stated, while in (5) an entity is identified.

(iii) Cognitive processes. Mental and perceptual processes may also be described in terms of the dynamic vs. stative distinction. The examples in (6) refer to dynamic cognitive processes, those in (7) to stative cognitive processes. As we shall see, it is often useful to recognize cognitive processes as distinct from 'external' processes.

(6) a. I watched the film.
     b. The noise frightened me.

(7) a. I liked the film.
   b. I'm afraid of the dark.

   (iv) Complex processes. A clause can designate a complex process—that is, a process which is made up of two or more component processes:

(8) a. Jane returned the book to the library.
   b. They elected him president.
   c. I broke the vase.

Example (8a), for example, can be broken down into three component processes:

   (1) Jane does something with respect to the book.

   (2) The book changes its location.

   (3) The book ends up in a new location (in the library).

The three sub-components stand in a causal relation: (1) causes (2), and (3) is the result of (2). Clauses with a cognitive content may be complex in a similar way:

(9) a. His girlfriend taught Jim Spanish.
   b. I learned the poem by heart.

Example (9a) consists of a dynamic process on the part of the girlfriend which causes Jim to learn Spanish and which results in the state of Jim knowing Spanish.
   The analysis of complex processes in terms of component processes is justified in that it is sometimes possible to focus on just one component in contrast to the process in its totality. 'Breaking a vase' consists of two sub-processes—an activity *vis-à-vis* the vase and a change in state of the vase. Example (10a) could mean that I was on the point of doing something *vis-à-vis* the vase but didn't. It could also mean that I did do something to the vase but that this failed to result in the vase breaking.

(10) a. I almost broke the vase.
   b. They didn't elect Joe president.

Negation can also selectively focus on different sub-processes. Example (10b) could be interpreted to mean that nothing happened at all, or that there was an election process but that this did not result in the stative situation of Joe being president.

21.2 Number of participants

The number of participants in a clause is relevant to the traditional distinction between intransitive clauses (which have only one participant), transitive

clauses (with two participants), and ditransitive clauses (with three participants). Some examples:

(11) a. Joe sneezed; the telephone rang; the vase broke; the guests arrived.
      b. Joe dropped the vase; I rang my friend; he shot the rabbit.
      c. I gave the child a present; I told him my opinion; I faxed my col-
          leagues the report.

Determining the number of participants in a process is not always easy. It
is not, for example, simply a question of counting up the number of entities
that are mentioned within the clause. For example, the entities mentioned
within a clause are likely to differ with respect to how inherent they are to the
designated process. Some entities are likely to the essential to the conceptualization, others will have the status of optional, additional specifications.
We can reserve the term 'participants' for inherent entities, and use 'circumstances' to refer to the non-inherent entities.

Participants proper have the status of complements to the verb—they elaborate concepts that are inherently (though schematically) represented within
the semantic structure of the verb, while circumstances have the status of
optional modifiers (see section 12.2). Generally, statements of the time and
place at which a process occurs count as circumstances, as do statements of
manner, cause, and reason. The bracketed phrases in (12) would not therefore
be regarded as participants. The phrases can be omitted without loss of grammaticality and without change to the character of the designated processes.

(12) a. The guests arrived [in a taxi].
      b. He shot the rabbit [with a shotgun].
      c. He dropped the vase [from nervousness].
      d. I met with John [several times] [last week].

In the following we observe an entity construed alternately as a circumstance and as a participant:

(13) a. He suffocated.
      b. He suffocated in the heat.
      c. He suffocated from the heat.
      d. The heat suffocated him.

Example (13a) designates an intransitive event in which the sole participant
undergoes a change in state. It is possible to specify the setting in which the
event takes place (13b). The use of the preposition *from*, in (13c), however, construes 'the heat' not just as a setting, but as the source, or cause, of the suffocation.
This aspect is explicitly encoded in (13d). The heat is now a full-fledged participant in a transitive clause. Symptomatic of the participant status of *the heat* is the
fact that (13d) can be made passive: *He was suffocated by the heat.*

Examples like (13c) suggest that the distinction between participant and
circumstance may not always be easy to draw. I examine this topic below.

21.2.1 Participants and circumstances

Normally, participants need to be explicitly stated while circumstances can be omitted. Nevertheless, there are cases in which the statement of what looks like a circumstance appears to be obligatory. Conversely, there are cases in which what looks like a participant can be omitted.

Consider the verb *live*. The verb appears to designate a one-participant process. Yet a bald statement that 'he lived' is hardly acceptable (14a). Some kind of circumstance—whether of place, time, or manner—needs to be stated (14b). Alternatively, the verb might be construed with the direct object 'life' (14c).

(14) a. ?He lived.
　　 b. He lived {in the eighteenth century / in England / happily / in poverty / with his mother}.
　　 c. He lived a happy life.

Take, as another example, the process designated by *sell*. It is evident that if I sell something, I sell it to someone and for a certain price. Seller, buyer, merchandise, and price are essential to the process. One might conclude from this that *sell* designates an inherently four-participant process. It is possible, however, to omit mention of the buyer, of the price, or of both, suggesting that *sell* is better regarded as basically transitive, the buyer and the price counting as circumstances.

(15) a. I sold the vase to Bill for £100.
　　 b. I sold the vase to Bill.
　　 c. I sold the vase for £100.
　　 d. I sold the vase.
　　 e. I'll only sell when the price gets to £10.

However, under special contextual conditions, even the entity being sold need not be explicitly stated. Thus (15e) would be acceptable if the identity of the saleable entity (shares, for example) were manifest from the context.

21.2.2 Non-participant nominals

One tends to think of participants in a process as nominal entities designated by noun phrases. However, it is not always the case that a nominal (even if its presence in a clause is obligatory) designates a participant. The case of predicate nouns has already been discussed (section 18.4.2). The predicate noun 'a teacher' in (16a) does not designate an individual with which the subject referent is being identified; rather, the predicate noun is taking on adjective-like characteristics.

(16) a. John is a teacher.
　　 b. The book costs £50.

Similarly, (16b) predicates a property of the book, namely, the property of 'costing £50'. The sentence can be analysed as a one-participant stative expression, it does not express a relation between the entity identified as 'the book' and an entity identified as '£50'. Syntactically, the sentence is analogous to *The book is expensive*, where the property of the book is expressed by a predicative adjective. Symptomatic of the non-participant status of £50 is the fact that (16a) may not be made passive: **£50 is cost by this book*. Moreover, £50 may not be modified: **The book costs the £50 that I have.*[1]

In other cases, although more than one nominal is mentioned, it may not be clear how many distinct participants are involved. In (17a), the bursting process involves only the tyre, the car being the larger entity of which the tyre is a part. Although the car may be affected by the process—with respect to its drivability, for example—the car is not directly involved as a participant in the process. In (17b), the subject referent would only count as a participant if Jim wilfully inflicted the damage on himself. Otherwise, Jim is merely the 'location' of the intransitive process of his arm breaking.

(17) a. My car burst a tyre.
     b. Jim broke his arm (while skiing).
     c. He lived a happy life.

One may also question whether two distinct entities are involved in (17c). Although nominal in form, *a happy life* states the manner of his living, not the relation between the person who lived and the thing that was lived.

Reflexives sometimes give rise to the same problem. Although two participants (the observer and the image observed) seem to be involved in (18a), the distinction is less clear in (18b).

(18) a. I saw myself in the mirror.
     b. I cut myself (while shaving).
     c. Er hat sich verändert.
        'He has changed', lit. 'He has changed himself'.

In other languages, reflexives are even less amenable to a two-participant interpretation. The German example (18c) does not designate a process which the subject referent performs on himself, it designates a process of change which the subject referent undergoes with respect to his former appearance or nature.

A further problem is raised by examples such as the following.

(19) a. It's raining.
     b. It seems that we'll have to leave.
     c. It annoys me that I keep forgetting his name.
     d. There's someone at the door.

---

[1] It would, however, be possible to say *The book cost me my last £50*. This sentence does not predicate a stative property of the book, it designates an interaction between three participants.

It is sometimes claimed that *it* and *there* are 'dummy' nominals—noun phrases which occupy syntactic positions but which lack semantic content. In fact, these properties are sometimes cited as an argument for the autonomy of syntax over conceptual structure. I address the Cognitive Grammar analysis of these words later in this chapter.

21.2.3 Non-nominal participants

A participant need not only be a thing, it can also be a location, a manner, or a state. In (20a), *put* designates a three-participant process. Inherent to the process is the thing which changes location, the thing which causes the change in location, and the resulting location. A locative is essential to any expression involving *put*; even if the intended location is evident from the context, the locative may not be omitted. In this respect, *put* differs from other caused-motion predicates, such as *move* and *throw*. You can 'move the furniture', without it being necessary to specify where the furniture is to be moved to.

(20) a. The child put his things *(away).
     b. You look {tired / as if you've been up all night}.
     c. He lived recklessly.

(21) a. Do you remember [what happened]?
     b. [That you don't remember] disappoints me.
     c. You should watch [how I do it].

In (20b), *look*, in the sense 'have the appearance', also requires a non-nominal complement, while a statement of manner (or of some other kind of circumstance) is essential to the process designated by *live*. As the examples in (21) demonstrate, the participant in a clause can itself be a clause.

21.3 Participant roles and grammatical relations

In this section I address the semantic roles of participants and their syntactic expression in the clause. The topic is of interest in that the number of semantic roles is in principle open-ended, whereas the number of grammatical relations (subject, direct object, etc.) is quite limited. The question therefore arises how a participant with a certain semantic role is 'mapped' in to the syntax.

There is a sense in which each verb in a language associates with a distinct set of participant roles. At a fine-grained level of analysis, the role of subject and object is different in *I read the book, I wrote the book, I dropped the book, I liked the book*. Nevertheless, different roles can be brought together under more schematic characterizations. Among those commonly recognized are:

Agent (AG): typically an animate entity which instigates, or which provides the input energy to the process designated by the verb. Example: *John opened the door*.

Instrument (INSTR): typically an inanimate entity used by the Agent to affect the Patient. Example: *John opened the door with a key*.

Patient (or Undergoer) (PAT): this is an entity which is affected by the process designated by the verb. The entity may undergo a change in state, it may come to occupy a new location, it can change ownership, etc. Examples: *John opened the door*, *The child put her toys away*, *The building collapsed*.

Various locative roles such as Place, Source, Goal, and Path. Examples: *In the study* (PLACE) *I moved the books from the table* (SOURCE) *onto the bookshelf* (GOAL) . These roles can also be understood metaphorically, as in *I put my affairs* (PAT) *in order* (GOAL).

Experiencer (EXPER): An animate entity which is the locus of a cognitive activity or a cognitive state. Examples: *I know, I itch, I heard a noise*.

Stimulus (STIM): An entity which causes a cognitive activity or a cognitive state in the Experiencer. Examples: *I heard the noise*, *The noise startled me*.

Zero: This is the role of a participant which merely exists, or which exhibits a property, but which does not interact with another entity. Examples: *Alice is asleep*, *The book costs £50*, *The telephone rang*.

The above categories are not mutually exclusive, in that a nominal can sometimes exhibit features of more than one role. In *I watched the film*, the subject referent is both the Experiencer of the visual process and the Agent which consciously initiates it.

Finer distinctions are also possible.[2] Langacker (FCG2:285) distinguishes Mover and Patient—a Patient undergoes an internal change of state, a Mover changes location. It is also possible to 'lump' some roles together. Langacker groups together Patient, Experiencer, Mover, and Zero into the macro-role Theme. The four roles have in common that they are each able to define an autonomous one-participant process: *The ice melted* (PAT), *I itch* (EXPER), *The balloon rose* (MOVER), *She is tall* (ZERO). Contrasting with these 'thematic' roles are Agent and Instrument. Agent and Instrument are not able to occur in a conceptually autonomous one-participant process; there has to be a 'thematic' relation which is affected in some way by the action of the Agent or Instrument.

It is well known that participant roles do not match up, one to one, with grammatical relations. While an Agent is typically expressed by the subject of a clause (though in a passive sentence the Agent, if expressed, occurs in a '*by*' phrase), a nominal in subject position is able to bear any of the participant roles. This fact is sometimes cited as evidence for the autonomy of syntax.[3] In contrast, an important topic in Cognitive Grammar approaches has been the attempt to account for grammatical relations in conceptual terms.

---

[2] One might, for example, distinguish degrees of Agenthood. The subject nominal in *I watched the film* is rather less agentive than in *I scrutinized the box*.

[3] See Jackendoff's remarks (Jackendoff 1983: 14), cited in section 9.4.

21.3.1 The action chain model

Elaborating on early suggestions by Fillmore (1968), Langacker (FCG2 : 283) proposes to characterize the prototype of a dynamic situation in terms of the transfer of energy from an initiator (the Agent), through an intermediate entity (the Instrument), to the energy sink (the Patient):

(22) AG → INSTR → PAT

For example, a person (AG) uses a key (INSTR) to open a door (PAT). Different segments of the chain can be profiled. Here are some possibilities.

(23) a. John opened the door.
    b. John opened the door with the key.
    c. The key opened the door.
    d. The door opened.

We see that whenever the verb has both a subject and object, the subject is 'higher' on the action chain that the object. The Agent, if mentioned, functions as subject, otherwise the subject encodes the Instrument. If neither Agent nor Instrument is mentioned, the subject designates the Patient. Otherwise, the Patient functions as the object.

It is worth observing that the appearance of a participant in subject position (the position prototypically associated with an Agent) can often attribute agent-like properties to the subject. This aspect is made explicit in the following.

(24) a. The key easily opened the door.
    b. The key just won't open the door.
    c. The door refuses to open.

Example (24a) seems to suggest that the key didn't need to exert much effect to affect the Patient while (24b) suggests that the key is being stubborn. In both cases, the success or failure of the opening activity is attributed to some property of the subject referent. This aspect is quite explicit in (24c). It is as if the door (strictly speaking, a Patient) is behaving like an uncooperative Agent.

A configuration of participants can sometimes be construed in alternative ways:

(25) a. John opened the door with the key.
    b. John used the key {to open the door / for opening the door}.
(26) a. This key will open the door.
    b. The door will open with this key.

In (25a) the focus is on the interaction between Agent and Patient; the Instrument appears in a 'with'-phrase and has the status of an optional circumstance. In (25b) the key is construed as the Patient, the purpose of the Agent's manipulation of the Patient being expressed in an optional purpose clause.

The contrast in (26) is especially subtle. The first example profiles the inter-action between an energy source and a patient. The success of the operation is due to properties of the key. The second construes the opening of the door as a one-participant event, whose success is attributable to the properties of the door.

21.3.2 Cognitive processes

The action chain model applies prototypically to dynamic interactions involving the transfer of energy between participants. Cognitive processes lend themselves less well to this construal. The prototype of a cognitive process involves, not an Agent and a Patient, but a Stimulus and an Experiencer. Either the Stimulus or the Experiencer can often be attributed an Agent-like, or, alternatively, a Patient-like role.

The paired examples in (27) suggest an increasingly Agent-like role for the Experiencer. If you 'see' a movie, you merely register the visual impression; if you 'watch' a movie, you actively focus your attention on it.

(27) a. I saw the movie ~ I watched the movie.
  b. I know the answer ~ I worked out the answer
  c. I like that one ~ I decided on that one.

The following pairs show how a Zero participant—the music in (a), the behaviour in (b), the story in (c)—can take on the role of an Agent-like Stimulus.

(28) a. The music is boring ~ The music bores me.
  b. That behaviour is disgusting ~ That behaviour disgusts me.
  c. The story was interesting ~ The story interested me.

Through the attribution of Agent-like properties to either a Stimulus or an Experiencer a situation can sometimes be construed in alternative ways. In (29a) the Experiencer entertains a certain attitude towards the Stimulus, while in (29b) it is the Stimulus which takes on Agent-like properties and 'affects' the Experiencer; here, the Experiencer is a kind of Patient. Similar contrasts are shown in (30) and (31).

(29) a. I look forward to the event.
  b. The event excites me.

(30) a. I fear the consequences.
  b. The consequences frighten me.

(31) a. She likes him.
  b. He attracts her.

Given the possibility of construing cognitive processes in alternative ways, it is not surprising that different constructions have become conventionalized in different languages. In English, there is a tendency for the Experiencer to be encoded as the subject, suggestive, perhaps, of a conceptualization in which the Experiencer is 'in control' of his or her experience. A common strategy in some languages is to construe the Stimulus as subject and the Experiencer in the dative case (32).

(32) a. I like modern music.
    b. Mi piace la musica moderna. (Italian)

21.3.3 Circumstances as clausal subjects

A curious feature of English concerns the encoding of a circumstance as a clausal subject. Consider the following (from Dowty 2000):

(33) a. His face dripped with sweat.
    b. The wall crawled with roaches.
    c. The church echoed with the voices of the choristers.

The subject nominals in (33) designate the location at which the respective processes—sweat dripping, roaches crawling, voices echoing—take place. The processes, it will be noted, are intransitive. Although the sentences predicate a property of the subject, these are not strictly speaking participants in the processes.

These clauses exemplify what Langacker (FCG2: 346–7) refers to as the 'setting-subject construction'. The subject nominal specifies the setting within the confines of which the intransitive process takes place. Further examples are shown in (34) and (35). Whereas in (34) the subject referents may well be affected by the designated process (to this extent the subject nominals have Patient- or Experiencer-like properties), even this aspect is lacking in (35).

(34) a. My guitar broke a string.
    b. My car burst a type. (cf. (17a))
    c. I had my money stolen.

(35) a. The fifth day saw our departure.
    b. The hall has witnessed many historic events.

Symptomatic of the non-participant status of the subject referents is the fact that none of these clauses may be made passive: *A string was broken by my guitar, *Our departure was seen by the fifth day.

It is along these lines that we can account for 'dummy' there and it. Observe that if (36) were spoken with the appropriate prosody (THÉRE's the vase, on the table!), there would be little reason to doubt that there designates a specific location; the sentence could be analysed as a 'topicalized' version of The vase is THÉRE, on the table!

(36) There's a vase on the table.

If there is unstressed, it merely designates a more generalized, schematic location, which 'hosts' (FCG2: 352) the profiled situation. In this way, there comes to have a presentational, or existential function, introducing a referent into a discourse (*There was a woodcutter who had three daughters*), or proclaiming the existence of an entity (*There IS a God*).

It is amenable to a comparable analysis. As a pronoun, the word designates a schematic thing whose identity may be inferable from the context: *It* (= 'the thing we are looking at') *is red*. Alternatively, it refers to a situation: *It* (= 'the situation you have just described') *is possible*. In these 'referential' uses, *it* is replaceable by the deictic pronouns *this* and *that* (*This is red, That is possible*). The difference between these examples and (37a) is minimal. *It*, in (37a), does not designate an independently identifiable situation, the word designates a schematic situation which is elaborated only in the subsequent '*that*' clause. *It* and *that the earth is flat* are nominals in apposition—the schematic content of *it* is fleshed out in the following '*that*' clause.

(37) a. It's possible that the earth is flat.
     b. It's raining.

'Meteorological' *it* (37b), on the other hand, designates the climatic situation. To be sure, one cannot rephrase (37b) as 'The weather is raining'. On the other hand, one could certainly enquire, speaking of the climatic situation, 'What's it like outside?', 'What will it do this afternoon?'

These uses of *there* and *it* are somewhat marginal extensions of the basic 'referential' uses of the words. Considerable diversity across languages is to be expected in the treatment of 'schematic settings' and 'schematic situations'. For some discussion of examples in German and Dutch, see FCG2: 351–4. On meteorological expressions, Ruwet (1986) is especially informative.

21.4 Clause types

We can bring together the discussion so far by considering different clause types in English. A basic classification concerns the number of participants in the clause.

21.4.1 One-participant clauses (Intransitives)

An intransitive clause presents a situation as involving only one participant. As suggested earlier, the sole participant in an intransitive process will be a Patient or Mover, an Experiencer, or a Zero nominal.

It is traditional to distinguish two types of intransitives, which are sometimes referred to by the strange (and quite misleading) terms, 'unergative' and 'unaccusative'. Compare:

(38) a. The telephone rang; the child slept. ('unergatives')
     b. The guests departed; the building collapsed. ('unaccusatives')

In (a), the subject referent would be assigned the role of Zero, in that there is no interaction between the entity and other entities. After the telephone has ceased ringing, the world returns to its previous state. In (b), the subject referent is a Patient (or Mover). After the guests' departure, the world is in a different state—the guests, namely, are in a different location.

The distinction is important in a number of ways. First, it is relevant to the formation of the perfect tense in many European language. In German and the Romance languages, situations like (a) require, in the perfect tense, the equivalent of the verb 'have', those in (b), the equivalent of the verb 'be'. The use of 'be' focuses on the changed state of the Patient subject.

(39) a. Er hat geschlafen (German), Ha dormito (Italian) 'he has slept'.
      b. Er ist weggefahren, È partito 'He has (lit: is) departed'.

The distinction is relevant to English, also. Guests who have departed are 'departed guests', whereas a telephone which has rung may not be referred to as a 'rung telephone'. The motivation is similar. The participle characterizes an entity in terms of its resultant state, and is therefore compatible with a Mover or a Patient, but not with a Zero or an Agent.

Another reflex of the distinction in English concerns the use of the nominalizing suffixes -er and -ee. A major use of -er is to profile an entity as an Agent or Instrument; a *buyer* is one who buys something, an *opener* is a device one uses to open things. In contrast, -ee designates an affected entity, 'downstream' in the action chain: a *nominee* is one who has been nominated, an *amputee* is one who has undergone amputation, an *addressee* is one to whom a message is addressed.

Consider, now, the affix that would be chosen to designate the participant in an intransitive process. A person who runs is a 'runner', a person who talks is a 'talker', a 'sleeper' is one who sleeps, a 'good-looker' is a person who looks good. However, a prisoner who escapes is not an 'escaper'—he is an 'escapee'. A person who retires (from work) is a 'retiree', not a 'retirer'. We see that the -er affix applies to a Zero participant, whereas -ee applies to Patients and Movers.

To be sure, the use of -ee to derive Patient and Mover nominals is not fully productive. We would not, for example, refer to people who arrive as 'arrivees' (but neither would we call them as 'arrivers'), nor would we call people who depart 'departees'. Nevertheless, the distribution of -ee and -er as nominalizing affixes does correlate, by and large, with the distinction between, on the one hand, those participants which undergo a change of state or location, and which are 'downstream' in the action chain, from all the others.

21.4.2 Two-participant clauses (Transitives)

The prototype of a transitive clause involves the transfer of energy from an Agent (the subject) to a Patient (the object). Prototypical transitive clauses (*The farmer shot the rabbit*) have some well-known properties. One can enquire what the Agent did (*What did the farmer do?*), what the Agent did to the Patient (*What did the farmer do to the rabbit?*), and what happened to the Patient (*What happened to the rabbit?*). The prototypical transitive clause can also be made passive (*The rabbit was shot by the farmer*).

A remarkable fact about English is that the schema for a prototypical transitive clause [NP$_{Ag}$ V$_{trans}$ NP$_{Pat}$] has generalized so as to accommodate all manner of relations between entities. The following exhibit the syntax of a transitive clause, but fewer and fewer characteristics of a transitive interaction. For example, none of the clauses—except, possibly, the first and the last—can be made passive.

(40) a. I remember the event.
      b. My car burst a tyre.
      c. The road follows the river.
      d. Joe resembles his grandfather.
      e. The road crosses the railway line.

The examples also illustrate a point made earlier, namely, that a subject nominal can instantiate all manner of participant roles, in addition to its prototypical use to designate an Agent. What unifies the subject nominals is their status as the trajector of the designated processes. The subject designates the more prominent entity in the conceptualization. This aspect is particularly evident in the case of 'symmetrical' relations, like those exemplified in (d) and (e). If the road crosses the railway line, the railway line also crosses the road. The choice of one or the other of the clauses depends on which entity is singled out by the speaker for assessment.

21.4.3 Three-participant clauses (Double-object clauses)

Three-participant clauses have loomed large in recent theoretical discussions. Pinker (1989) devoted a whole book to the issue. The problem is the following. Certain verbs, which seem inherently to involve three participants, are compatible with two syntactic constructions.

(41) a. I'll mail you the report.
      b. I'll mail the report to you.

(42) a. I'll bake you a cake.
      b. I'll bake a cake for you.

Other verbs, with rather similar meanings, allow only one possibility:

(43) a. ? I'll donate the charity £50.
      b. I'll donate £50 to the charity.

(44) a. Do your old friend a favour.
      b. ? Do a favour to/for your old friend.

The different syntactic expressions in (41) and (42) reflect two different ways of construing the processes. In each case there are three participants. There is the Agent, there is a thing that undergoes change at the hands of the Agent, and there is a person (or institution) which benefits from the change. Characteristic of the (a) examples is that the Beneficiary is construed as the Patient of the interaction; accordingly, it appears immediately after the verb, as the verb's object. In (41a), for example, my action directly affects you, the Beneficiary, in that you come to receive the report. Symptomatic of its object (and Patient) status is the fact that if the (a) sentences are made passive, it is the Beneficiary that functions as the new subject, e.g. *You will be mailed the report*. In this construal, all three participants need to be mentioned. We are dealing with a genuine three-participant construction. Since a second post-verbal object is obligatory, the construction may be referred to as the double-object construction.

The (b) examples construe the situation differently. Here, the Patient is the thing that undergoes a change of state due to the action of the Agent. The Beneficiary appears 'downstream', in a prepositional phrase. Moreover, the prepositional phrase is often optional. *I'll mail the report*, without mention of the intended recipient, is fully acceptable. Predictably, if the (b) clauses are made passive, it is the post-verbal Patient that comes to serve as the subject: *The report will be mailed (to you)*. Strictly speaking, therefore, the (b) examples illustrate a two-participant interaction.

That different verbs behave differently with respect to the two constructions would be due to the incompatibility of a given verb with one or the other of the constructions. *Donate* focuses specifically on the giving of money, not on the benefiting of an institution. *Announce* specifically profiles the making public of some information, and only secondarily the informing of an audience. Hence you 'announce your decision to the delegates', you do not 'announce the delegates your decision'.

Verbs which appear only in the double-object construction are not so numerous. Examples include *envy* (*I envy you your success*), *refuse* (*They refused us entry*), and *forgive* (*Forgive us our sins*). Another group is made up of expressions of the kind *give (the door) a kick*, *give (someone) a kiss*, and the colloquial *Gimme a break!* In these latter examples, the second post-verbal nominal does not designate a true participant; the only true participants are the Agent and the Patient.

21.4.4 Motion events

Motion events have also been subject to quite intensive investigation, especially following Talmy's (1985) analysis. These are of interest, once again, because of the possibility of alternative construals.

Consider the following English sentence and its French equivalent (from Ungerer and Schmid 1996: 233–4).

(45) a. Blériot flew across the Channel.
b. Blériot traversa la Manche en avion.

The French clause construes the crossing of the Channel as a transitive event. If the manner of the crossing is specified, this is done in an (optional) modifying phrase. Such a construal is possible also in English (46a). The preferred construal in English, however, is to encode the manner of motion by means of the verb, and to specify the path by means of a prepositional phrase. Such a construal is not possible in French (46b). To the extent that (46b) is acceptable, it would mean that Blériot flew (around) at a place which was 'over the Channel'.

(46) a. Blériot crossed the Channel by plane.
b. *Blériot vola par-dessus la Manche.

The difference illustrated here shows up in innumerable other examples. English (and other Germanic languages) tends to conflate motion and manner of motion in the verb, while the path is expressed in a prepositional phrase. In French (and other Romance languages), the verb tends to designate the path of a tr *vis-à-vis* a lm, while the manner of motion has to be expressed in a modifying expression. In English, you 'creep out of the room', 'swim over the river', 'limp down the hill'. In the Romance languages, you 'exit the room creeping', 'cross the river swimming', and 'descend the hill limping'. Talmy makes the further claim that languages tend to behave either on the Germanic model or on the Romance model. Chinese, for example, construes motion events like English, and Japanese adheres to the Romance model.

21.5 Complementation

We have seen that a participant in a clause can be a thing and a location, but also a process. A clause which is 'embedded' inside another clause, and which functions as a participant within the containing clause, is commonly referred to as a 'complement clause', and the process by which one clause is embedded in another is called 'complementation'.

Complementation is a complex topic, largely because of the different syntactic forms that a complement can take. Complement clauses can differ with respect to whether the clause is grounded independently of the main clause, according to the form of the complement verb, or according to the presence of morphemes which introduce the clause.

21.5.1 Complementation structures

Here are the main complementation patterns in English:

(i) The complement clause appears as a plain infinitive (that is, an infinitive without *to*). The subject of the clause appears in the 'oblique' (i.e. non-nominative) form, symptomatic of the fact that the nominal also functions as the object of the main verb.

(47) a. I saw [them break into the house].
    b. They made [me sign the letter].

  (ii) The complement appears as a 'to'-infinitive. In (48) the subject is stated, in (49) it is not.

(48) a. I advise [you to wait a while].
    b. I want [you to go there yourself].

(49) a. I hope [to see you again soon].
    b. I want [to go there myself].

  (iii) The complement verb appears with -*ing*. In (50) the subject is not stated. If the subject is stated, it may appear either as an oblique or as a possessive (51).

(50) a. I avoided [meeting them].
    b. I propose [adjourning the meeting].

(51) a. I can't imagine [him saying that].
    b. We were talking about [your leaving early].

  (iv) The complement clause is grounded and may be introduced by *that*. Although *that* appears to be optional, there are distinct preferences. *That* is perhaps less likely to be omitted in (52b) than in (52a).

(52) a. I hope [(that) we will see each other again soon].
    b. I don't believe [(that) unicorns exist].

Embedded questions are introduced by the appropriate question words, or, in the case of an embedded yes/no question, by *whether* or *if*.

(53) a. I wonder [what we should do].
    b. I wonder [whether/if we should leave (or not)].

Question words can also introduce a non-grounded clause:

(54) a. I don't know [what to do].
    b. I'm wondering [whether to leave].

  (v) A somewhat minor pattern introduces a 'to'-infinitive with *for*.

(55) a. I would prefer [for you to do it like this].
    b. I would hate [for you to be late].

  (vi) Another minor pattern anticipates the content of the complement clause with *it*:

(56) a. I would hate [it] [for that to happen to you].
    b. I must insist on [it] [that you get here by the arranged time].

(vii) In addition to the above, there is the possibility of introducing a clause as the complement of a preposition. If the subject is stated, it may appear in either the oblique or the possessive form.

(57) a. I look forward to [meeting you].
     b. I insist on [(you/your) leaving immediately].

The above, I should emphasize, is only a summary review of the complementation patterns in English. A finer analysis would need to distinguish between, for example, oblique vs. possessive forms of the subject and between the use of *if* and *whether* in embedded questions. Also not considered here are the various options that exist when the embedded clause functions as the subject of the main clause.

It should also be pointed out that the above complementation patterns are to some extent specific to English. French, for example, does not associate infinitives with a morpheme equivalent to English *to*. Instead, there is the contrast between infinitives introduced by the prepositions *à* and *de*. French also has the option (which exists also, but very marginally, in English) of the embedded clause appearing in the subjunctive mood. Another complement construction that is well established in French consists in the appearance of the complement verb immediately after the main verb. Compare English *He makes the students laugh* with French *Il fait rire les étudiants*.[4]

21.5.2 Degree of integration of clauses

A further issue in the study of complementation concerns the distinction between complementation and other ways of combining clauses. At issue is the degree of integration between clauses. A number of possibilities can be distinguished. Needless to say, the distinctions form a continuum, rather than discrete categories.

(i) **Minimal integration**. Two clauses are simply juxtaposed, with no overt linking: *I came, I saw, I conquered*. By a general principle of iconicity (section 3.2.1), the clauses would normally be interpreted sequentially—the first mentioned was the first to occur.

(ii) **Coordination**. Each clause is fully grounded, and could in principle stand alone as an independent conceptualization. The clauses are linked ('coordinated') by means of words such as *and*, *but*, and *or*: *She prefers fish, and/but I prefer pasta*. A slightly higher degree of integration is possible if both clauses share the same subject: *I went up to him and asked the way*.

---

[4] The pattern is marginally represented in English by *He let go the rope*, in contrast to *He let the rope go*. Symptomatic of the marginal status of this construction in English is the fact that many English speakers prefer the variant *He let go of the rope*.

And

And may be regarded as the prototypical coordinator, which links clauses which are equivalent in status.

Nevertheless, there are some specialized uses of *and* in which the word suggests the subordination of one clause to the other. Consider the following:

Come one step closer and I'll shoot.
One more beer and I'm leaving.
Believe that, and you'll believe anything.

The first example has the force of a conditional: If you come one step closer, then I'll shoot. (Naturally enough, this example would be also interpreted as a warning.)

(iii) **Subordination**. Here, there are two clauses, but one is understood in terms of a relation (temporal, causal, etc.) to the other. Typical subordinators are *after*, *if*, *whenever*, *although*.

(iv) **Complementation** represents a closer integration of clauses, in that one clause functions as a participant in another.

(v) **The highest degree of integration** occurs when the two clauses fuse into a single clause. Certain so-called raising constructions exhibit this state of affairs. Consider *These cars are expensive to repair*. One could, no doubt, 'unpack' this sentence into two independent clauses, designating two different processes. On the one hand, there is the idea of someone repairing the cars, then there is the idea that this process is expensive. However, when we speak of the cars being expensive to repair, the two clausal conceptions have effectively fused into one. We characterize the cars as 'expensive' with respect to a certain process.

21.5.3 Strategies for analysis

It will be apparent from the above survey that clause combination is a complex matter. Given the language specificity of the complementation processes, it is not surprising that the issue looms large in pedagogically oriented language descriptions. Learners of English need to know that *manage* takes a 'to'-infinitive complement, not a *V-ing* complement (*I managed to finish*, **I managed finishing*), whereas *avoid* prefers a *V-ing* complement (*Avoid doing the housework*, **Avoid to do the housework*). Does the language student simply have to learn, by rote, which complementation patterns are associated with each verb in the language, or are there general guiding principles which account for the complementation patterns?

I will not, in this section, attempt to answer these questions, even less, to offer semantically-based explanations of the complementation patterns

---

One clause or two?

In English, *I must speak to him* would be taken to be a single clause, 'modulated' in terms of necessity by the modal verb *must*.

As argued by Achard (1998), the French equivalent *Je dois lui parler* is properly regarded as a case of complementation. The main verb, *dois*, is a 'full' verb, which is able to bear the full range of tense inflections, and *parler* is its infinitival complement. The clausal status of *parler* is suggested by the placement of the clitic pronoun *lui*. If the French sentence were a single clause, the pronoun would appear before the clausal verb: **Je lui dois parler*.

A second argument for the bi-clausal analysis concerns the choice of auxiliary verb in the perfect. *Partir* 'leave' forms the perfect tense with 'be', not 'have': *Je suis parti*, **J'ai parti*. *Je dois partir* 'I have to leave' forms its perfect with 'have', as determined by the main verb: *J'ai dû partir*, **Je suis dû partir*.

Interestingly, Italian wavers between the two possibilities. The perfect of *Devo partire* 'I have to leave' may be formed either with 'have' (suggesting a bi-clausal status) or with 'be' (suggesting a single-clause status). Likewise, a clitic pronoun (e.g. *gli* 'to him') can occur either before the first verb or before the infinitive:

Ho dovuto partire	or	Sono dovuto partire 'I have had to leave'
Devo parlargli	or	Gli devo parlare 'I must speak to him'

---

surveyed above. Instead, I focus on some of the strategies that might be used in approaching the issue.

(i) One strategy appeals to the notion of iconicity, specifically, to the idea that things that are close in conceptual space tend to be close in phonological space (that is, they tend to be spoken closer together).

Consider some cases of causation. Causation can differ with respect to its directness. One can 'directly' coerce a person into doing something or one can influence their behaviour indirectly, by means of verbal instructions, recommendations, or advice. It does seem that the directness of causation correlates on the whole with the distance between a main verb and the verb designating the desired behaviour:

(58) a. I {made / let} them work.
      b. I {got / persuaded / wanted / allowed} them to work.

The examples in (58a) suggest direct coercion (or, in the case of *let*, its complete absence), whereas those in (58b) suggest more indirect persuasion. Significantly, the more direct causation lacks the intervening morpheme *to* between the main and the subordinated clause.

Similar effects may be observed with perception verbs:

(59) a. I saw him leave.
      b. I saw that he left.

Example (59a) designates 'direct' perception; the person who left was observed to do so by the main clause subject. Moreover, the seeing and leaving occurred at the same time. In (59b), perception is more indirect, and may be based on the observed consequences of the person's having left rather than on the observation of the process as such. Moreover, the 'seeing' and the 'leaving' need not occur at the same time. *I see* (present tense) *that he left* (past tense) exploits this possibility.

Although iconicity effects are certainly to be observed, it has to be admitted that iconicity is a fairly blunt tool with which to explicate the complexities of English complementation patterns.

(ii) A second approach is to consider the possibility that certain complementation types might be associated with schematic meanings. The acceptability of a complementation pattern with a given verb would then be a consequence of the compatibility of the conceptualizations denoted by the main verb and the complementation pattern.

We might approach this matter by surveying all the verbs which take a certain kind of complement clause—a 'to'-infinitive, for example, or a *V-ing* form. We might ask whether the verbs in each set share any semantic features which might be compatible with a unitary value of the different complement types. A complementary strategy focuses on those verbs which are compatible with a number of different complement types and considers the semantic contrasts associated with the different complement types. (As a matter of fact, most verbs do allow a range of complementation patterns.) Sometimes, the semantic contrast can be quite striking (e.g. *I remember locking the door* vs. *I remembered to lock the door*), in other cases the contrast is more subtle (*It began to rain* vs. *It began raining*).

Applying these strategies to English, Taylor and Dirven (1991) suggested that the 'to'-infinitive tends to be associated with a specific instance of the process in question, often with a future orientation, whereas the *V-ing* form tends to be associated with a type specification. *I would like to go for a walk* expresses my desire to undertake (in the future) an instance of the activity, whereas *I like going for walks* expresses my liking, in general, for a kind of activity. *My doctor advised me to take more exercise* refers to a specific recommendation that I should follow; *Doctors advise taking more exercise* refers to a more generalized recommendation.

As stated, I will not here go into a full analysis of the semantics of the English complementation patterns. My intention was to sketch out a strategy for analysis that would be applicable to data in any language. Underlying this approach is the assumption that the different syntactic patterns do in fact correlate with semantic distinctions.

Study questions

1. Not mentioned in this chapter is a special category of one-participant clauses exemplified below:

    The book sold well.
    The book didn't sell.
    The car drives smoothly.
    The ice-cream scoops out easily.
    This poem doesn't translate.
    The food won't keep.
    The dirt brushes off easily.
    I don't photograph very well. (= I am not very photogenic)

    Here, the subject designates a Patient-like entity. Clauses of this type are often referred to as 'middles'. On the basis of these examples, list the syntactic and semantic properties of middle expressions.
    A long-standing problem with middles has been that not all verbs are equally likely to occur in the construction. The following are scarcely possible:

    *The book buys well.
    *This food doesn't eat. (= This food is inedible)
    *His name doesn't remember easily. (= It is difficult to remember his name)
    *The small print doesn't see very well.
    *Your essay doesn't understand at all.
    *The bowls put easily into the cupboard.

    The following, though perfectly acceptable, might nevertheless be regarded as somewhat untypical for the category of middles. In what way?

    This microphone doesn't record very well.
    That corner doesn't sell. (= Merchandise exhibited in that corner doesn't sell)
    This knife cuts well.

    (For discussions of middles from the Cognitive Linguistic perspective, see Van Oosten, 1986 and Yoshimura, to appear.)

2. It is well known that not all clauses with the structure [NP$_1$ V NP$_2$] have passive equivalents. The following clauses have passive equivalents:

    (i) The farmer shot the rabbit. ~ The rabbit was shot (by the farmer).
         Everyone admires you for your courage. ~ You are admired (by everyone) for your courage.
         We will contact you in due course. ~ You will be contacted (by us) in due course.
         The clown amused the children. ~ The children were amused by the clown.
         Everyone likes him. ~ He is liked by everyone.

    The following, however, do not have a passive counterpart:

    (ii) The book costs £50. ~ *£50 is cost (by the book).
         The accountant lived a happy life. ~ *A happy life was lived (by the accountant).

Joe resembles his grandfather. ~ *Grandfather is resembled by his grandsons.
The tent sleeps six people. ~ *Six people are slept by the tent.

Identify the properties of the active clauses which render the designated situations compatible with a passive construal. (You might find it useful to consider clauses which designate cognitive processes separately from the others.) Why are the clauses in (ii) incompatible with a passive construal?

The clauses in (iii) also have passive counterparts, even though these do not strictly speaking have the structure [NP₁ V NP₂]. Suggest some reasons why the passive construals are possible in (iii) but not in (iv).

(iii) We must go into this matter more deeply. ~ This matter must be gone into more deeply (by the researchers).
The police are looking for three suspects. ~ Three suspects are being looked for (by the police).
Everyone laughed at him. ~ He was laughed at by everyone.

(iv) The police went into the building. ~ *The building was gone into by the police.
We looked out of the window. ~ *The window was looked out of.
She smiled at the news. ~ *The news was smiled at.

3. Verbs of cognitive processes in English can be divided into two broad classes: those that take the Experiencer as their subject, and those that take the Stimulus as subject.

(i) Experiencer-subject verbs: *like, love, hate, detest, admire, esteem, enjoy, forget, remember, recall,* etc.
(ii) Stimulus-subject verbs: *sadden, scare, frighten, amuse, bore, astonish, surprise, terrify, thrill, fascinate,* etc.

There are a number of quasi-minimal pairs: *fear ~ frighten, like ~ please, forget ~ slip one's mind, think of ~ cross one's mind, get mad at ~ infuriate, get bored with ~ bore*. Notice that the stimulus-subject verbs are able to be predicated of an Experiencer if they are used in the passive: *be saddened, be scared*, etc. Sometimes, the passive versions allow other prepositions than *by*: *be amused by/at, be fascinated by/with*.

Examine the two groups with respect to the ways in which the cognitive processes are conceptualized. Are there differences with respect to the stative vs. dynamic distinction, or, in the case of dynamic situations, with respect to the perfective vs. imperfective distinction?

Cognitive processes are liable to be encoded in different ways in different languages. Compare the English expressions with their translation equivalents in, for example, Spanish or German, or indeed any other language with which you are familiar.

Further reading

Clause structure is addressed in chs. 7, 8, and 9 of FCG2 and in ch. 1 of Langacker (1999), while coordination and subordination are discussed in chs. 10 and 11 of FCG2. See also Croft (1991).

On the semantics of locative subjects, as in *The garden is swarming with bees*, see Dowty (2000). For the double-object construction, see Taylor (1997). For the encoding of motion events, see Talmy (1985). For an application of Talmy's theory, see Slobin (1996). For a refinement of Talmy's analysis of motion events in Spanish, see Aske (1989). There is a good overview of the issues in ch. 5 of Ungerer and Schmid (1996).

For complementation patterns in English, see Dirven and Radden (in press) and ch. 1 of Wierzbicka (1988). For French, see Achard (1998).

Part 5
More on Meaning

Part 5 addresses some further topics in the study of meaning. Chapter 22 takes up the notion of 'domain', which was introduced in Chapter 10. It will be shown that reference to domains is necessary in order to account for the ways in which simpler semantic units combine into larger configurations. We will also have reason to question the notion that words are associated with fixed, invariant chunks of meaning. Chapter 23 shows that the semantic (and also, the phonological) pole of a symbolic unit is typically represented, not by a single unit, but by a network of units related by similarity and by schema-instance relations.

Domains

A domain—the term was introduced in Chapter 10—may be defined as any knowledge configuration which provides the context for the conceptualization of a semantic unit. In this chapter I explore further the role of domains and domain-based knowledge in the semantic structure of words and complex expressions.

For most concepts, we need to make reference to more than one domain for their full characterization. The set of relevant domains constitutes the domain matrix against which a concept is characterized. Not all of the domains, however, have equal status. Some will be more central, more intrinsic to the concept than others. Moreover, it is not the case that each domain will be invoked on each occasion on which the word is used. One topic to be explored is the fact that different uses of a word may activate only certain facets of domain-based knowledge. A second topic concerns the role of domain-based knowledge in the interpretation of composite expressions. An important consequence of this approach is that word meanings turn out to be inherently flexible entities; meanings are constructed, or 'emerge', in specific contexts of use.

22.1 The domain matrix and encyclopaedic semantics

A domain may be defined as any knowledge configuration that is relevant to the characterization of meaning. Domains vary in complexity from 'basic' conceptions of colour, temperature, space, time, and so on, which cannot reasonably be reduced to other, simpler conceptions, to highly complex knowledge structures, such as the rules of a game, social practices, complex technologies, and typical event scenarios. Most semantic units need to be characterized against more than one domain. The set of domains is called the domain matrix.

Langacker illustrated the notion of domain matrix on the example of the word *banana*.

Most concepts require specifications in more than one domain for their characterization. The concept [BANANA], for example, includes in its matrix a specification for shape in the spatial (and/or visual) domain; a color configuration involving the coordination of color space with this domain; a location in the domain of taste/smell sensations; as well as numerous specifications pertaining to abstract domains, e.g. the knowledge that bananas are eaten, that they grow in bunches on trees, that they come from tropical areas, and so on. (FCG1: 154)

He goes on to ask:

Which of these specifications belong to the meaning of the lexical item *banana* and are therefore included in the grammar of English? Otherwise phrased, which of these specifications are linguistic (or semantic) in nature, and which are extra-linguistic (pragmatic)? Which constitute the predicate [BANANA], i.e. the semantic pole of the morpheme *banana*? (FCG1: 154)

As the reader might have anticipated, Langacker's answer is that all these specifications belong to the concept [BANANA]. A full characterization of the meaning of the word needs to make reference to these domains and to incorporate them into the semantic value of the expression. Such an approach commits us, inevitably, to an encyclopaedic conception of meaning.

The reason why we need to adopt an encyclopaedic approach is easily stated: We need to appeal to domain-based knowledge in order to account for how words are used. The very fact that we can talk of *a bunch of bananas* (as compared to the impossibility of talking about **sprigs of bananas*) rests on our knowledge of how bananas grow (and of what bunches look like). If we were to excise this knowledge from the meaning of *banana*, we should have to regard *bunch of bananas* as an arbitrary collocation—or else deny that the collocation is a linguistic fact. Neither option is satisfactory.

Still, some readers might feel a bit wary of an encyclopaedic approach. Surely, it might be objected, not everything that a person knows about an entity is linguistically (semantically) relevant? An encyclopaedic view certainly does not commit us to the view that each facet of what a person knows is equally central to the concept; some facets are clearly more intrinsic, others may be quite peripheral, while others yet again might be to all intents and purposes irrelevant. The shape, colour, and nutritional value of bananas are probably quite central to the concept and would need to be included in even a summary account of the word's meaning. The fact that people can slip on banana skins is probably rather peripheral, but still capable of being invoked in stereotyped notions of slapstick comedy. Or consider the role of bananas in the economies of small countries in Central America. This is not central to the banana concept, yet it is this knowledge (along with further, perhaps stereotyped notions of the political systems in these countries) that motivates the expression *banana republic*. On the other hand, the fact that your aunt doesn't like bananas is probably quite irrelevant to your understanding of the word. Even so, one can imagine circumstances in which even this fact might impact on your use of the word within a domestic context. Indeed, it is remarkable the extent to which incidental knowledge about an entity can sometimes have linguistic manifestations. It would be wrong, therefore, to exclude in principle the possibility that even highly contingent aspects of encyclopaedic knowledge could, in certain circumstances, impact on the way a word is used.

Encyclopaedic knowledge in semantic change and semantic extension

Perusal of any etymological dictionary will throw up numerous examples of words whose semantic development has been affected by circumstances which would have to be regarded as highly peripheral to a word's 'basic' meaning.

Consider the practice, among Roman Catholics, of counting off repetitions of a prayer on the beads of a rosary. On the face of it, the fact that prayers were so counted would seem to be pretty peripheral to an understanding of [PRAYER], and even more peripheral to the concept [BEAD]. Yet, as is well known, the prayer-counting practice motivated the semantic development of Middle English *bedes* from the sense 'prayers' to its current sense 'small decorative spheres on a string'. (The example is discussed in Langacker FCG1: 383–4; see also Ayto 1990: 56.)

Another example is *buff*. The word has a variety of uses in current English which are related by all sorts of odd circumstances. The word appears to have originated as a shortened form of *buffalo*. It came to refer to buffalo hide, then to other kinds of leather, then was used as a colour term to denote a dull yellowish-brown. According to Ayto (1990: 83), in the 1820s, volunteer firefighters in New York City wore buff-coloured uniforms, and came to be known as 'buffs'. The word can now be used to refer to any amateur and knowledgeable enthusiast, as in *opera buff*, *film buff*. The fact that a certain colour was characteristic of the uniforms of a certain group of people in a certain city at a certain time, must surely have been highly peripheral to the semantics of the colour word. Yet precisely this fact triggered a significant semantic extension of *buff*.

An encyclopaedic view of word meaning does not therefore commit us to the proposition that all facets of domain-based knowledge are equally central to a word's meaning. Equally, it is not being claimed that each facet is relevant to each use of a word. On the contrary, certain contexts can cause a particular domain to be highlighted, while others (even 'central' ones) might be backgrounded. I examine this phenomenon in the next section, on the example of the word *photograph*.

22.2 Semantic flexibility

The concept [PHOTOGRAPH] needs to be characterized against a number of different domains.

(i)   Central to the concept is the idea of a photograph as a representation of a visual scene.

(ii) Photographs are created through a certain technology, involving specialized equipment and processing, certain skills on the part of their users, and so on. The concept presupposes a technology domain.

(iii) Typically, a photograph exists as an image on paper. The image can exist in other formats, on a glass plate, for example, or even as an electronic document. Moreover, the same image can be replicated an indefinite number of times, in different formats.

(iv) The concept is closely tied up with sociocultural practices. People take photographs as mementoes of episodes in their life, some people make their living by taking photographs, a photograph of a person can be used as a means of identification, and so on.

With these points in mind, consider now some sentences with the word *photograph*.

(1) a. The photograph is torn.
     b. The photograph is out of focus.
     c. This is a photograph of me at age 10.
     d. This is not a very good photograph of you.
     e. This photograph has been re-touched.
     f. The photograph was awarded a prize.
     g. The photograph appeared on the front page of all the newspapers.
     h. I'll send you the photograph as an electronic attachment.

These different uses highlight different domains against which the concept is understood.

(i) (1a) draws on the notion of a photograph as a material object, characteristically as a piece of paper. It is the photograph qua piece of paper that is torn. In this usage, the technological and sociocultural domains are backgrounded.

(ii) (1b) activates the notion of a photograph as a visual image. The image has been created by a certain technology which, in this case, has been applied with less than optimal results.

(iii) (1c), (1d), and (1e) highlight the notion of a photograph as a (veridical) representation of a scene, thing, or person. (1c) brings in the idea that a photograph can be historical record of a person's earlier appearance; (1d) brings up the idea that the representation can be valued in terms of the quality of the representation; while (1e) introduces the idea that although photographs are supposed to be faithful representations, technologies are available for altering the image.

(iv) (1f) focuses on the aesthetic value of photographs—a photograph can display the artistic skill of its creator.

(v) (1g) and (1h) bring in further aspects of the image. The image can be replicated, and can be stored in a non-visual format.

The phenomenon illustrated on the word *photograph* is ubiquitous and has been studied for some time by psycholinguists. Consider the two uses of *television* in (2). Mention of the repairmen in (2a) activates the conception of a television as an intricate piece of machinery, while (2b) focuses on the appearance of a television and its place in a room layout.

(2) a. Televisions need expert repairmen.
     b. Televisions look nice in family rooms.

These sentences are taken from Anderson and Ortony (1975), an early attempt to verify experimentally the context-dependent conceptualization of word meanings. Anderson and Ortony used the technique of cued recall. Subjects are exposed to a list of unrelated sentences, which they are asked to memorize. Some time later, cue words are presented which may bear some semantic relation to the test sentences. The effectiveness of the cue as an aid to the recall of a test sentence is taken as a measure of the semantic closeness of the cue word to the subject's interpretation of the test sentence. On the assumption that different uses of a word will activate different facets of the word's semantic structure, we may anticipate that cue words pertaining to the high-lighted domain will be more effective than words pertaining to a non-highlighted domain. This is exactly what Anderson and Ortony found. Sentence (2a) was more reliably recalled when cued with the word *appliance*, while *furniture* was a better cue for the second sentence.

The phenomenon has come to be known as 'semantic flexibility' (see Barclay *et al.* 1974, Greenspan 1986, and references cited therein). Consider two more examples, involving the words *piano* and *tree* (from Greenspan 1986).

(3) a. The young man played the piano.
     b. The young man lifted the piano.
(4) a. In the late afternoon Henry chopped up the tree.
     b. After school the children played in the tree.

Example (3a) presents the piano as a musical instrument, while (3b) presents the piano as a heavy object. As one might expect, *heavy* serves as an effective cue for the recall of the second sentence, but not for the recall of the first sentence. This suggests that the properties of a piano qua physical object are activated in the understanding of (3b) but not in the understanding of (3a). However, Greenspan did find that *music* was equally effective as a recall cue for both of the sentences. We may infer from this that certain domains are central to a concept and are liable to be activated irrespective of context, while more peripheral domains are selectively activated. With respect to *piano*, status as a musical instrument is central, while heaviness is more peripheral. Similar effects showed up with the sentences in (4). *Wood* was effective as a cue for the recall of both sentences, while *climb* was effective only for the recall of (4b). The material composition of trees thus turns out to be more intrinsic to the concept than the activities that people can perform with respect to them.[1]

These findings, along with our observations on *photograph*, have important implications for the nature of word meanings. First, it is evident that word meanings cannot be regarded as fixed, invariant chunks of information. The conceptualizations associated with a word will tend to vary somewhat according to the contexts in which the word is used. The cited examples with *television*, *piano*, and *tree* point to the variable salience of the different domains against which the entities are profiled. In the case of *photograph*, different uses may even profile different entities. According to a test introduced in section 10.2, whatever is predicated of a nominal is predicated of the nominal's profile. In *The photograph is torn*—(1a), *is torn* is predicated of the photograph qua piece of paper, not of the photograph qua visual image. In *The photograph is out of focus*—(1b), *is out of focus* is predicated of the image, not of the paper. Nevertheless, it is easy to combine both conceptualizations without any sense of anomaly—(5).

(5) a. I tore up the photograph that was out of focus.
     b. The out-of-focus photograph is torn.

How, then, should we characterize the concept [PHOTOGRAPH]? With respect to [HYPOTENUSE], discussed earlier (section 10.2), I argued that the concept cannot be identified with the profile, but rather resides in a combination of profile and base. The case of [PHOTOGRAPH] is more complex. First, the background knowledge necessary to understand the concept is distributed over several domains, which may be selectively activated according to context, even to the extent of promoting different facets to the status of profile. This suggests that the photograph concept is not a clearly defined, static entity, but is one that emerges in specific contexts of use. In particular contexts, the

---

[1] Greenspan and other authors cited here do not frame their discussion in terms of domains. Greenspan (1986: 539) simply speaks of the 'properties' of an entity, pointing out that he uses this term in a broad sense to 'include concepts that are related to the structure and function of an object'. Strictly speaking, however, 'music' is not a 'property' of pianos; rather, the concept [PIANO] is understood against the domain of music, and of music-making.

concept is 'constructed' out of elements which reside in a rich network of encyclopaedic, domain-based knowledge.

This idea is already articulated in Anderson and Ortony's 1975 paper:

Our thesis is that sentence comprehension and memory involve constructing particularized and elaborated mental representations ... Specifically, we claim that the representation is generally more detailed than the words in the utterance might appear to entail; that the words only loosely constrain the representation; and that one's store of knowledge about the word and analysis of context are heavily implicated in sentence comprehension and memory. Two corollary notions are that only in a vague, abstract sense could words be said to have fixed meanings and that it is impossible that the sense of an utterance could consist solely of a concatenation of the dictionary readings of its individual words. (Anderson and Ortony 1975: 167–8)

It has been stated even more forcibly by another psychologist, Lawrence Barsalou:

Rather than being retrieved as static units from memory to represent categories, concepts originate in a highly flexible process that retrieves generic and episodic information from long-term memory to construct temporary concepts in working memory. (Barsalou: 1987: 101)

Geeraerts (1993: 259) has also remarked that it could be error to suppose that meanings are 'prepackaged chunks of information':

The tremendous flexibility that we observe in lexical semantics suggests a procedural (or perhaps 'processual') rather than a reified conception of meaning; instead of meanings as things, meaning as a process of sense creation would seem to become our primary focus of attention. (Geeraerts 1993: 260)

The view of word meanings as inherently flexible may strike some readers as a very radical proposal, and counter to intuition. After all—barring cases of metaphorical extension—the words *tree*, *piano*, and even *photograph* do appear to be associated with reasonably stable and invariant meanings.

This impression could be due to a number of factors. In the case of *photograph*, the close interconnections and interrelationships between different aspects of domain-based knowledge could give the subjective impression that we are dealing with a unitary, undifferentiated concept. This is probably the reason why the examples in (5) are not felt to be anomalous—the different uses of *photograph* are compatible in virtue of the common domain matrix against which they are conceptualized. In the case of *piano*, it may well be the case that most uses of the word will tend to activate a common core of domain-based knowledge, pertaining to the status of a piano as a musical instrument. As for a word like *tree*, we have already commented on variations in the word's profile due to active zone effects (section 6.3). Again, however, it is likely that most uses of the word will serve to highlight a recurring configuration of conceptual knowledge. The apparent stability of meanings could therefore be a consequence of the dominance (and salience) of particular types of usage. Nevertheless, as the above discussion has shown, a close examination reveals subtle variations in conceptualization, even in the case of very ordinary, and seemingly unproblematic words like *tree* and *photograph*.

22.2.1 Limits to flexibility?

Our discussion of semantic flexibility, of the selective activation of domain-based knowledge, and of 'emergent concepts', might give the impression that concepts are pretty amorphous kinds of things and that word use is pretty much unconstrained. This, of course, is not the case. Semantic flexibility has its limits. Certain conceptual construals are not at all possible.

I want to illustrate this on the nouns *tale*, *story*, *book*, and *novel*. These have much in common, in that they all designate similar kinds of entities that need to be characterized against similar domains. For example, they can all designate a fairly substantial, coherent, and self-contained linguistic text. The text can be characterized in terms of its length and inherent interest. Thus, a tale, story, book, or novel can be described as long, short, interesting, boring, exciting, and so on.

Differences emerge, however, when we refer to the creation or performance of the linguistic text.

(6) a. Tell me {a tale / a story / *a book / *a novel}.
    b. I wrote {?a tale / a story /a book / a novel}.

It looks as if *tale* is understood primarily as an oral event, *book* and *novel* are understood as written texts, while *story* allows both possibilities.

A tale being an oral composition, its essence lies in the actual linguistic utterances as much as in the symbolized content. The linguistic utterances can be repeated (7a), but not translated (7b).

(7) a. I repeated {the tale / the story / *the book / *the novel}.
    b. I translated {?the tale / the story / the book / the novel}.

Consider next the physical manifestation of the texts:

(8) a. I bought {*a tale / ?a story / a book / a novel} in the bookshop.
    b. It's an expensive {*tale / ?story / book / novel}.
    c. I'll order {?the tale / ?the story / the book / the novel} at the bookshop.

Tale and *story* do not readily denote the physical object that contains the text. This is confirmed by the following:

(9) a. That table is wobbly. You need to put something under one of its legs. This {*tale / *story / book / novel} will do the trick.
    b. It's a very thick {*tale / ?story / book / novel}.

It seems, then, that *tale* and *story* are understood primarily as linguistic artefacts (the former primarily oral). *Book*, naturally enough, is the physical object and only secondarily the content. The interesting one is *novel*. One would expect *novel*, as a literary form, to follow the same pattern as *story*, but it doesn't. The conceptualization of a novel as a book is particularly prominent.

Acceptability judgements

In considering these examples, readers may well find themselves 'adjusting' the form of the examples in order to render them more acceptable. For example, *I bought a story in the bookshop* seems to become slightly better if pluralized and made definite: *I bought the stories in the book*. (A newspaper can also, of course, 'buy a story'). The question now becomes, why this should be so.

Let us turn next to the information content of the texts. All four nouns readily accept a modifying phrase *about X*, where *X* designates the topic of the linguistic text.

(10) These are {tales / stories / novels / books} about her childhood.

When it denotes the subject matter of the text, *of*, however, goes only with *tale* and *story*, not with *book* and *novel*:

(11) These are {tales of her childhood / stories of her childhood / *books of her childhood / * ?novels of her childhood}.[2]

As noted elsewhere (section 17.1.2), one of the functions of *of* is to profile an inherent relation; thus, a prepositional phrase headed by *of* can function as a complement to an inherently relational noun. We can infer from (11) that *tale* and *story* are inherently relational; they designate linguistic representations *of* events, an aspect that appears to be lacking in *book* and *novel*. This difference shows up again in the following. *Improbable* assesses the plausibility of the represented situation, while *believe* designates an attitude towards the represented situation. The designated situation is quite prominent in *tale* and *story*, but not at all in *book* and *novel*.

(12) a. That's an improbable {tale / story / ?book / *novel}.
      b. I don't believe the {tale / story / book / *novel}.

The point is confirmed by the different ways in which a possessive is interpreted with the four nouns.

(13) This is {my tale / my story / my novel / my book}.

---

[2] The asterisked examples are acceptable if *of her childhood* is interpreted as 'from (i.e. written during) her childhood'.

My story could be a story that I composed or a story about me; *my novel* and *my book* could be a novel or book that I wrote or one that I bought. They could not, however, be a novel or book about me.

As a final twist, consider the possibility of referring to an electronic version of the texts designated by our four nouns. *E-book* is now almost an established term, *e-novel* perhaps less so. But *e-tale* and *e-story*, I think, are definitely out. Books and novels can exist in cyberspace, but tales and stories cannot.

The discussion suggests that each of the four nouns is understood against distinct, though partially overlapping, sets of domains. Also, the relative salience of the domains may differ from noun to noun. These factors place limits on semantic flexibility. They also circumscribe the linguistic contexts in which the words can be used. Another factor that may be relevant is notions about prototypical exemplars of the four categories. In terms of length, content, intended audience, and literary style and merit, the prototypical novel differs significantly from the prototypical story.

Nouns denoting linguistic objects

There are quite a few nouns in English which designate information-bearing linguistic objects. These include *narrative, narration, biography, autobiography, saga, legend, epic, poem, adventure, history, anecdote, fable, joke, report, text, letter, memorandum* . . .

Try out the proposed tests with these additional words denoting linguistic creations. Feel free to come up with additional test frames. Consider also the characteristics of prototypical instances of the respective categories.

22.3 Adjective-noun combinations

I have already drawn attention in several places (e.g. section 4.4) to the problems raised by adjective-noun combinations. I now want to examine adjective-noun expressions in light of the theory of domains and the selective activation of domains in semantic interpretation.

To begin, it will be useful to outline what a strictly compositional view of adjective-noun combination entails. Consider Quine's account of 'composite terms' (here: adjective-noun combinations). These are formed by

the joining of adjective to substantive in what grammarians call *attributive position*. 'Red' has attributive position in 'red house', as against its predicative position in 'Eliot House is red'. A composite general term thus formed is true of just the things of which the components are both true. (Quine 1960: 103)

A red house, then, is a house that is red. We identify 'red houses' as things that are (i) red, and (ii) houses. According to Quine, something is a 'red house'

Red houses

Even the seemingly unproblematic expression 'red house' fails to illustrate the point that Quine was endeavouring to make in his presentation of 'composite terms', namely, that an Adj-N expression is true of just the things of which the components are both true.

First, there is the problem of identifying the set of red things (or red substances) in the world. [RED] is a fuzzy concept, which shades imperceptibly into orange, purple, brown, and pink. Leaving this aspect aside (many words exhibit some degree of fuzziness with regard to the range of entities that they can designate), the colour typically denoted by *red* varies according to what it is that is being described. Compare *red wine*, *red hair*, *red eyes*, *red lettuce*, and *red fire-engine*. *Red hair* is probably orangey-brown, rather than red, and no one, I suspect, would fancy drinking a red wine that had the colour of blood.

More damaging for Quine's set-intersection theory is the fact that for a house to qualify as being red only certain parts of it have to be red, probably the exterior. But not all of the exterior. The window frames, the front door, the door knocker, the roof do not have to be red.

Even here, however, some flexibility is allowed. Even the expectation that the outside walls need to be red for the house to be a 'red house' can be overridden. Suppose you have been house-hunting. You've seen so many houses that it's difficult to recall them individually or to find expressions that uniquely identify them. But you do remember that one house you saw had a bathroom painted in a prominent bright red and that, on looking over the house, you remarked on this fact to your partner. Some time later, searching for an expression that would uniquely identify that house in contrast to all the others, you refer to it as 'the red house'.

if it lies in the intersection of things that are red and things that are houses (Fig. 22.1 (p. 450)).[3]

Mostly, this view of adjective-noun combinations just doesn't work. (As noted in the Box, it doesn't work even for *red house*.) An important reason for this is that most nouns and most adjectives have rather complex semantic structures. The complexity resides, not so much in the nature of the profile as in what is not profiled—the things, relations, or processes that constitute the background against which profiling takes place.

Thus it can come about that in an adjective-noun expression the adjective modifies, not the noun's profile, but some entity in the noun's base. Moreover, adjectives very often do not simply designate a property as such, which

---

[3] Quine wrote about red houses almost half a century ago. The idea of the compositionality of adjective-noun combinations is still alive and well, however. Thus, Fodor (1998) argues for the correctness of compositionality on the example of *brown cow*. The composite expression derives its meaning from the fact that the component terms 'contribute the properties that they express to determine what the descriptions that contain them specify'—'it's because "brown" means *brown* that it's the brown cow that "the brown cow" picks out'. (Fodor 1998: 99)

Fig. 22.1. The set of 'red houses' lies at the intersection of things that are red and things that are houses.

things that
are red

things that
are houses

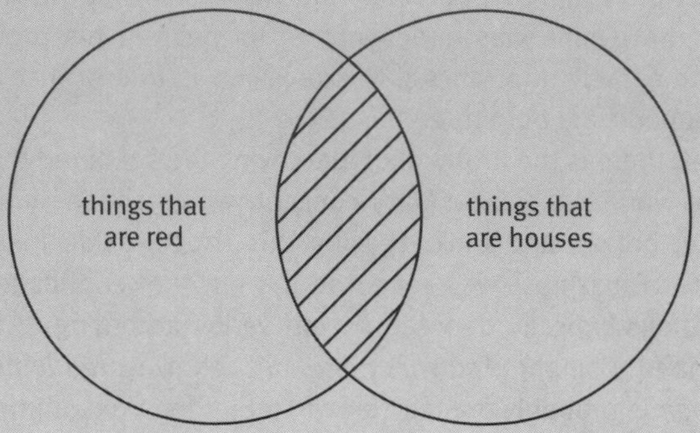

attaches 'directly', as it were, to an entity in the noun's semantic structure, but may evoke various kinds of relations and processes, as well as things which participate in these unprofiled relations and processes. Consequently, putting an adjective alongside a noun can trigger a complex interaction between the semantic structures of the two items.

Let us look at some examples, beginning with some relatively simple ones.

(i) Red pen. A red pen could be red on the outside or it could be one which writes in red. The former interpretation is relatively straightforward—at least, it is no more complex than Quine's example of the red house. The second interpretation is less straightforward, and comes about because pens are conceptualized, not just as physical objects, but as a kind of instrument that people use to perform certain activities; pens also have a certain internal structure which enables these activities to be performed. That pens are used to make marks is fairly intrinsic to the semantic structure of the word. *Red* comes to designate a property of the marks that the pen can (potentially) make.

(ii) Beautiful dancer. *Dancer* profiles a person who participates in a process. *Beautiful* can modify the profiled entity, i.e. the dancer qua person, or it can characterize the process that the person engages in. A beautiful dancer can be one who dances beautifully, rather than a person who is both a dancer and who is beautiful (as a person).

(iii) Small. Dimensional adjectives, such as *big*, *small*, *long*, *short*, etc., do not designate some invariant region on the respective dimensions. They have within their semantic structure some notion of a 'norm', which is set differently according to whatever it is that is described as 'big', 'small', etc. Thus, a small elephant is small for an elephant (but still, probably, big for an animal). Whereas *red pen* and *beautiful dancer* owe their interpretations to complexities in the semantic structure of the modified nouns, the interpretation of *small elephant* depends on some facet of the semantic structure of *small*.

(iv) Good. Somewhat more complex than dimensional adjectives are evaluative adjectives such as *good*. Goodness is not an absolute quality, but concerns an evaluation of an entity with respect to some purpose. The purpose has to be derived from the semantic structure of the noun. A 'good friend' is good as a friend—the evaluation takes place with respect to the friendship relation implicit in the semantic structure of the noun. Similarly, a 'good knife' is good for cutting—the cutting function is salient in the semantic structure of *knife*. Consider, however, an expression like *good mountain*. Mountains are not inherently associated with a function or purpose, so it is necessary to appeal to more peripheral domain-based knowledge about activities that people perform with respect to mountains. Here, different interpretations are possible. For a mountain climber, a 'good mountain' may be one thing, for a landscape artist it could be something very different. Should a person not be able to access the appropriate domain-based knowledge, *good mountain* will be uninterpretable and therefore rejected as semantically ill-formed.

(v) Fast. Strictly speaking, only processes can be described as fast, whereby the word designates the pace at which the process unfolds (relative to the norm for the process in question). The basic use of *fast* is therefore adverbial (*He ran fast*). In *fast runner*, it is not the runner qua person that is fast, but the person as s/he participates in the activity of running. The notion of the process—running—is in this case contained within the base of the agentive noun, *runner*. Likewise, a 'fast car' is a car that can be driven fast (that cars are entities that are driven is intrinsic to their conceptualization), while a 'fast road' is a road on which one can drive fast (roads are inherently entities along which people travel). In the case of 'fast food' we should say that *fast* modifies processes that are in the domains against which food is understood, namely its preparation, its delivery (in a restaurant), and its consumption.

(vi) Likely. Strictly speaking, only events have a likelihood of occurring. If a thing is described as likely (similar considerations apply to the description of a thing as *possible*, *probable*, *certain*, *impossible*, *unlikely*, etc.), the adjective has to modify some process in which the designated thing participates. A 'likely outcome' is an outcome whose occurrence—given a certain train of events—may be expected. The 'likely murderer' is a person who probably committed the murder. But what should we make of a 'likely person'? Since *person* does not intrinsically invoke a process, the expression, as it stands, is uninterpretable. We need some context which will suggest the participation of the person in a process. Thus we can speak about 'a likely person for the job'.

(vii) Old friend. This example also illustrates the interaction between the semantic structure of adjective and noun. *Old* is a dimensional term, which characterizes an entity as one that has endured, or existed, over a period of time in excess of some norm (determined for the kind of thing in question). Thus, an 'old building' is old for a building. But consider *old friend*. *Friend* is a relational noun (section 11.2) which profiles a person in terms of their participation in a relation. If *old* applies to the profile of *friend*, *old friend* designates an old person ('agèd friend'). *Old* is also able to characterize the friendship relation as one which has endured over a long period of time; thus, an 'old friend' is someone who has been a friend for a long time, without the person as such necessarily being old. (There is also a third interpretation of *old friend*, namely 'former friend'—an interpretation which is perhaps more forthcoming in *old colleague*, *old school-mate*. What is at stake here is the existence of a relation at some time previous to a reference time.)

(viii) Safe. Especially complex is the adjective *safe* (Sweetser 1999). *Safe* evokes, in its semantic structure, at least the following aspects:

- There is an entity that is of some value (to someone). If nothing of value is at stake, *safe* is simply not applicable to the situation.
- There is an event or situation that is a potential source of danger to the valued entity. If no potential danger exists, there would, again, be no reason to use the adjective *safe*.
- There is a desire to protect the valued entity from danger, hence, certain precautions can be taken to reduce its exposure to the danger; alternatively one might seek out a situation which does not present a danger. Even so, there is an implicit contrast to similar kinds of situations which *do* present danger.

For an entity to be described as 'safe', it is necessary, first, to be able to construct a scenario in which each of the above three components is present. It is also necessary for the entity to be able to slot into the scenario. There are three possibilities, corresponding to the three components of the scenario:

- A valued entity can be described as safe if it is not exposed to, or is protected from, danger. 'Safe money' is money that is protected from thieves, currency devaluations, stock market collapses, or suchlike. A house or a bridge could be described as safe if it is adequately protected against earthquake damage.
- An entity can be described as safe if it does not present a danger to a valued entity (though things of a similar type might well present a danger). A 'safe beach' is one which does not present a danger to bathers, a 'safe driver' is one who does not endanger his passengers or other road users, a 'safe surgical procedure' does not present a risk to a patient.
- An entity can be described as safe if it offers protection to the valued entity. Thus, on another reading, a 'safe house' could be a house that offers protection to political dissidents or battered women. If you keep your money in a 'safe place', the place is such that your money is not exposed to danger.

It will be observed that an expression of the form *safe N* can sometimes be interpreted in different ways, according to the role of the nominal entity in the scenario. A 'safe house' could be a house that offers protection (to a valued entity), or the house itself could be the valued entity, that is protected from danger.

A second point to note is that the actual linguistic expression *safe N* provides only the scaffolding, as it were, on which the 'protection from danger' scenario is erected. The elaboration of the scenario takes place in virtue of domain-based knowledge. Consider *safe beach* again. We know that beaches are valued as places where people can swim. (Actually, it is not the beach as such where people swim, but the contiguous margin of ocean—a striking case of the active zone phenomenon.) We also know that there are dangers inherent in swimming in the ocean—from violent waves, from strong drifts, even from sharks. On the basis of this kind of background knowledge we construct an interpretation of *safe beach*—it is one where the life of the swimmer is not threatened by any of the potential dangers. But none of this—to reiterate the point—is actually encoded in the linguistic expression. But unless this kind of background knowledge were available, the expression *safe beach* would have no coherent interpretation.

A final point concerns the meaning of the adjective *safe*. Given the three ways in which the adjective can combine with a noun, we could characterize the three variants of the adjective as 'not exposed to danger (said of a valued entity)', 'not presenting danger', and 'offering protection from danger'. One point that will have emerged from the above discussion is that the meaning of *safe* cannot be adequately captured by these paraphrases-cum-definitions. The word, in its different uses, evokes a complex scenario in which the modified noun also has a role to play. While it may be useful to distinguish a range of uses of *safe*, these different uses are based in the common scenario. To take up Geeraerts's image, one cannot regard the meaning of *safe* as a 'prepackaged chunk of information', which is simply attached to the noun which it modifies.

22.3.1 Possessives

Although not strictly examples of adjective-noun combination, it may be appropriate here to mention the ways in which prenominal possessives can be interpreted, especially in cases in which the 'possessed' noun is semantically complex.

In the prenominal construction, exemplified by *John's car*, a specific instance of 'car' is identified from the perspective of the 'possessor', i.e. John. The possessor names a 'reference point', which provides conceptual access to the possessed entity. Normally, access is achieved through invoking some kind of relation between possessor and possessed. By default, the relation is one of possession, in the strict sense of the word. Thus, *John's car* would normally be interpreted as the car that John owns. Other relations may also be invoked.

John's car could be the car that John designed, the one that he built, or even the one that he dreams of owning. In brief, the relation invoked by a possessive construction is one in which the two nominal entities—those designated by the possessor and the possessed nouns—can participate.

Relations that are implicit in the semantic structure of a possessed noun can affect the range of plausible interpretations of a possessive construction. Consider the possible interpretations of *my photograph*. This could be:

- a photograph that belongs to me (photograph qua physical object);
- a photograph that I took (photograph qua product of technology);
- a photograph that represents me (photograph qua representation).

The first interpretation invokes the default relation of possession. Here, the photograph is construed as a material object, which—like a car—can be owned by someone. The other interpretations rely specifically on aspects present in the semantic structure of the noun—a photograph is an entity that was created by someone, and a photograph is an entity that represents someone (or something). Interestingly, an '*of*' phrase—*a photograph of me*—invokes only the third interpretation. At stake here is the inherently relational character of *photograph* as the name of a representation *of* a scene.

22.3.2 Attributive vs. predicative uses

A curious fact about adjectives and the way they modify nominals is that very often predicative uses have a more limited range of meanings than the attributive uses.

Arguably, there is little difference between 'a red house' (attributive use) and 'a house that is red' (predicative use). Whenever we can say of a house that it 'is red', we can call it a 'red house', and vice versa (but see the Box, p. 449). Often this is not the case. We sometimes find that predicative uses are simply not possible. We can describe a person as an 'utter fool', but we cannot say that a fool 'is utter'. In other cases, the predicative use has a more restricted range of meanings than the attributive use. *Old friend* has a range of meanings, as discussed above. But to say of a friend that she 'is old' invokes only the age of the person; *My friend is old* could not mean that the person has been my friend for a long period of time. A similar situation obtains with possessives. *John's photograph* can have a range of interpretations, as already discussed. But to say of a photograph that it 'is John's' can only mean that the photograph is in his possession, it can not mean that the photograph depicts him.

These effects can be explained if we consider more closely the function of attributive and predicative adjectives. An attributive adjective modifies an ungrounded noun, thereby contributing to the specification of the type designated by the noun. The semantic structures of adjective and noun are able to interact in the manner we have discussed. In its predicative use, however, an adjective does not, strictly speaking, predicate a property of a (bare) noun; in association with a verb (*be*, *seem*, *appear*, *become*, etc.), an adjective predicates a property of the entity profiled by a fully grounded nominal. *My friend* profiles a person; 'is old' is predicated of the profile, hence it is the friend qua person that is old, not the (unprofiled) friendship relation. Similarly, *utter* modifies a substructure in the base of the noun *fool*, the adjective does not modify the profile of *fool*. *Fool*, like *friend*, merely profiles a person. *The fool is utter* is meaningless for the same reason that *The person is utter* is meaningless.

In section 9.4.2 I suggested, following Croft (1991), that the 'basic' function of adjectives is to contribute to a type specification (cf. section 18.2.4.). Their attributive use is therefore primary, their predicative use is secondary. Moreover, the predicative use of an adjective requires a verb—typically *be*—which lends a temporal profile to the relation profiled by the adjective (see section 11.3). The predication applies to the profile of a grounded nominal, it does not modify the type specification symbolized by the bare noun contained within a grounded nominal.

This account helps explain a frequently observed difference between attributive and predicative uses. This is that attributive adjectives tend to characterize a thing in terms of a stable, inherent property, whereas predicative adjectives tend to denote more temporary, circumstantial properties (Bolinger 1967). For example, a 'handy tool' is a tool that is inherently easy to manipulate, whereas a tool that 'is handy' is likely to be one that is momentarily within easy reach. Cruse (2000: 289) cites the following examples, observing that (14a)—which predicates a temporary property of the water—is more normal than (14b), whereas (15b), which characterized the water in terms of an inherent property, is more normal that (15a).

(14) a. Be careful, that water is hot.
     b. Be careful, that is hot water.

(15) a. Don't add too much detergent—our water is soft.
     b. Don't add too much detergent—we have soft water.

That attributive uses denote a fairly stable property results from the fact that the adjective serves to specify the type; the type is such that it exhibits the property in question. Predicative use concerns a property of the designated instance; as such, the property is liable to change.

22.4 Other approaches

In this section I want to mention briefly two approaches to word meaning that have some affinities with the domain-based approach presented in this chapter.

22.4.1 Wierzbicka and the dictionary vs. the encyclopaedia

Wierzbicka (1996) proposes semantic definitions that incorporate a great deal of circumstantial knowledge about an entity. Her definition of *mouse* (pp. 340–1) includes such facets as the typical colour of mice, the fact that mice are reputed to like cheese, that cats are disposed to catch them, and much else. The breadth of information in the definition is motivated by the existence of widely shared beliefs about mice, and, more importantly, by the fact that these beliefs find linguistic expression in all manner of collocations, sayings, and idiomatic expressions.

Wierzbicka's approach is highly compatible with the one advocated in this chapter. Essentially, her definitions summarize a pool of shared knowledge which may be selectively activated according to context. It comes as a surprise, therefore, to learn that in spite of the incorporation of so much 'encyclopaedic' knowledge into her definitions, Wierzbicka insists on the need for a strict division between linguistic-semantic knowledge and encyclopaedic knowledge. Many things that a person could know about mice, she argues, are not part of the linguistic meaning of the word. Knowledge about the breeding habits of mice, she claims, properly belongs in the encyclopaedia, not in the linguistic definition. Wierzbicka is probably correct to claim that this kind of knowledge is so peripheral to most people's understanding of *mouse* that it can easily be excluded from the definition. It is different, of course, with rabbits—the phrase 'breed like rabbits' shows that the breeding habits of rabbits would be part of the definition of *rabbit*. But suppose that a group of people, having observed their houses being infested by a rapidly increasing mouse-population, were to start using among themselves the expression 'breed like mice'. Langacker's approach, which conceives of the domain matrix as an essentially open-ended knowledge base, could easily accommodate this new usage. Wierzbicka, presumably, would have to propose a realignment of the boundary between the dictionary and the encyclopaedia, between specifically linguistic knowledge and non-linguistic knowledge.

I suspect that Wierzbicka's insistence on the strict distinction between linguistic and non-linguistic (encyclopaedic) knowledge is tied up with a number of theoretical commitments that underlie her approach. One of these is the belief that words have definitions, that definitions rigidly circumscribe the usage range of a word, and that definitions can be fully and explicitly stated. As suggested earlier in this chapter, there may be good reasons to question this 'hypostatization' of word meanings.

22.4.2 Pustejovsky and qualia structure

The computational linguist James Pustejovsky has also proposed to incorporate domain-based information into semantic representations. Consider the expression *John began a novel*. This can be interpreted in various ways, e.g. John began to write a novel, he began to read a novel, and several more. To explain these effects, Pustejovsky (1991, 1995) proposed that a semantic representation of *novel* needs to incorporate the noun's **qualia structure**. Qualia structures contain four kinds of argument structures, with variables specifying various kinds of roles:

- what the entity is made of (the *constitutive role*);
- factors pertaining to the entity's perceptual identification, such as size, shape, dimensionality (the *formal role*);
- the purpose or function of the entity (the *telic role*);
- knowledge about how the entity was created, or came about (the *agentive role*).

All this 'structures our basic knowledge about the object' (Pustejovsky 1991: 427). This knowledge is differentially activated by context. *Read a novel, write a novel, buy a novel, print a novel*, each activates a different component of the qualia structure, thereby 'coercing' a particular interpretation of the noun. *Read a novel* coerces the telic role inherent in the noun, *write a novel* coerces the agentive role, *burn a novel* actives the constitutive role, whereas *drop a novel* activates the formal role. One consequence of this approach is that *novel*, in spite of the different ways in which it can be interpreted, need not be assigned a range of semantic values. The different interpretations emerge through the interaction of a unitary semantic representation with a 'coercing' predicate.

A difference between Pustejovsky's theory and the one advocated here is that Pustejovsky's formalizations rather strictly circumscribe the kinds of domains against which word meanings are characterized. Moreover, the approach does not easily lend itself to representing degrees of 'intrinsicness' of various roles. The four qualia roles seem eminently suited to man-made artefacts, especially those that are characterized at the basic level. Things such as tables, hammers, and cars are constituted in a characteristic way, they can be recognized by their perceptual properties, they have a function, and they were created with some purpose in mind. The four roles are more or less equally balanced in terms of their relevance to the concepts in question. This is not the case, however, with superordinate concepts. Toys, tools, and weapons are characterized primarily in terms of the telic role. Irrespective of what a thing is made of, what it looks like, or how it was created or came about, as long as a child can play with it, a thing can be characterized as 'a toy'. The four roles are even less suited to many natural kind entities (what might be the telic role of hydrogen?) as well as to a range of abstract concepts (do phonemes have an agentive role?). Moreover, an expression's interpretation may invoke background knowledge that cannot easily be subsumed under any of the four roles. Consider the 'safe beach' example. That a beach might present danger to a bather is only tangentially related to the telic role. And what about a 'good mountain'? The possibility of interpreting this expression at all rests on the attribution of a telic role to a mountain—an entity can be described as 'good' only if it is good for some purpose. *Good mountain* is difficult to interpret (out of context) because mountains do not intrinsically have a purpose. The telic role has to be contextually constructed on the basis of encyclopaedic knowledge, it cannot reasonably be regarded as a fixed component of the word's semantic structure.

Study questions

1. Corner. What, exactly, *is* a corner? What kinds of entities have corners? What are the characteristic features of the corners of these entities? What are the locations designated by *in the corner*, *at the corner*, *on the corner*, *round the corner*?

    Can you think of contexts in which *above the corner*, *over the corner*, *under the corner*, *on top of the corner*, *through the corner*, *along the corner* would be meaningful? If not, why not? (For some brief but illuminating remarks on *corner*, see Fillmore 1997: 29.)

2. Adjective-noun combinations. Explain the ways in which the semantic structures of noun and adjective combine in the following expressions.

    a possible solution
    a possible textbook (for the course)
    a possible candidate (for the position)
    an impossible child (cf. *a possible child)
    an empty house
    an empty oil-drum

3. Fast vs. quick. Explain the semantic contribution of these adjectives in the following expressions. What is the difference between *quick* and *fast*? What renders some of these examples less than fully interpretable?

    a quick decision / ?a fast decision
    a quick description / ?a fast description
    ?a quick car / a fast car
    ?a quick road / a fast road
    ?a quick driver / a fast driver
    a quick meal / ?a fast meal
    a quick recipe / ?a fast recipe
    a quick cup of coffee / *a fast cup of coffee

4. Risk. Fillmore and Atkins (1992, 1994) drew attention to the following seemingly incompatible uses of the verb *risk*. Remarkably, both sentences could be used to describe much the same kind of situation.

    He risked his life (to save the children).
    He risked death (to save the children).

    Sketch out a scenario against which *risk* is understood. Consider such elements as the alternative courses of action available to a protagonist, the possible consequences of these actions, the goal of the protagonist, and things of value to the protagonist. Show how different uses of *risk* are able to activate different components of the scenario.

Is there is difference between 'taking a risk' and 'running a risk'? (Pull out some examples of these collocations from a corpus.) To what extent is the 'risk-scenario' relevant to your observations?

You may wish to extend your investigation to include words which are semantically related to *risk*, such as *peril*, *danger*, *dare*, *daring*, etc.

5. Fresh. Geeraerts (1993) associated Dutch *vers* 'fresh' with two distinct senses. The first has to do with the 'recency' of an entity (e.g. a foodstuff which has been recently bought, produced, harvested, etc.). The second has to do with 'optimality for human consumption' (as with 'fresh air'). Mostly, the two aspects are strongly correlated. Fresh bread is bread that has been recently baked, and, for this reason, is optimal for consumption. Geeraerts notes, however, that the two aspects can be dissociated. 'Fresh cigars' (*verse sigaren*), if recently produced, are not optimal for consumption, while it makes little sense to say that 'fresh air' (*verse lucht*) has been 'recently produced'.

Collect some characteristic uses of English *fresh*. (As always, supplement your intuitions with corpus data.) To what extent can the uses of the word be adequately described in terms of Geeraerts's analysis of the Dutch word? Might there be a case for claiming that 'fresh' is understood against a scenario, involving, for example, the changes that an entity or a situation might undergo in the course of time, whether through natural processes or through human intervention? How does the entity designated as 'fresh' fit into the scenario? Might Pustejovsky's 'agentive role' be relevant to the entity described as 'fresh'?

A further topic of investigation could be the extent to which the usage range of English *fresh* corresponds to that of Dutch *vers*, and, following on from this, a comparative analysis of the meanings of the words in the two languages.

6. Adjective order. When adjectives are stacked up in front of a noun they generally need to occur in a given order. Compare:

small ripe bananas	?ripe small bananas
big red bus	?red big bus
a slow, narrow, winding road	*a winding, narrow, slow road

What could lie behind these preferences? Consider the possibility that certain properties of an entity might be more 'intrinsic' to its specification than others. (In order to carry through this argument, it will be necessary to explicate the notion of 'intrinsicness'.)

7. Fakes. Expressions of the kind *fake gun* have received considerable discussion in the semantics literature. The problem is that a fake gun is not, strictly speaking, a gun. In what way does *fake* modify the semantic structure of *gun*?

There are quite a few modifying expressions which, like *fake*, cancel some typical property of a concept with which they combine. These include *false, counterfeit, bogus, phony, imitation, fraudulent, spurious, hypothetical, fictitious, pretend, would-be, so-called.* These contrast with *real, genuine, true, authentic, veritable, actual.*

Each of these words has a story to tell. What kinds of entities could be described with these words? What is the specific contribution of the adjectives? How do they differ?

Further reading

On domains, see Langacker (FCG1: ch. 4), Croft (1993), Croft and Clausner (1999).

Dillon (1977, ch. 4) is a good descriptive overview of the different kinds of adjective-noun expressions. The idea that adjective-noun combinations rarely, if ever, have a strictly compositional meaning (i.e., the meaning of the noun 'interacts' with the meaning of the adjective) is explored in Platts (1997: ch. 7). The example of *safe* is based on Sweetser (1999). *Old* is discussed in Taylor (1992).

For experimental evidence confirming the role of encyclopaedic knowledge in concept understanding, see Murphy (1988).

CHAPTER 23

Networks and complex categories

Early in this book I illustrated the symbolic thesis on the Saussurean example of *tree*; this is a symbolic unit which associates a phonological representation [triː] with a semantic representation |TREE|. It is rarely the case, however, that a symbolic unit has, at its conceptual pole, a single semantic representation. A phonological form tends to be associated with a cluster of more or less distinct though related senses. Equally, the phonological pole cannot be regarded as a unitary entity. Words, for example, have a range of different pronunciations, according to speech style, accent, and the phonological and morphological environment. A symbolic unit, therefore, is more accurately regarded, not as an association of a concept with a sound pattern, but as an association of a network of semantic representations with a network of phonological representations.

23.1 Meaning variation

On various occasions in this book we have seen that there are good reasons for claiming that words and other linguistic units do not normally have a fixed, determinate meaning which they contribute to the complex expressions in which they occur. Among the phenomena that we have encountered are the following:

(i) Accommodation (section 6.3). Just as the articulation of a phonetic segment adjusts to the articulation of an adjacent segment (a phenomenon known as 'coarticulation'), so a contributing semantic unit typically varies according to the units with which it combines. You eat a steak differently from how you eat an ice-cream, you cut the grass differently from how you cut a cake, cutting your finger is different from cutting your finger-nails, you paint the kitchen wall differently from how you paint a portrait.

(ii) The active zone phenomenon (section 6.3). Typically, only some facet of a profiled entity participates in a profiled relation. If you wash your car you do not wash all parts of the car, if you sharpen a knife you sharpen only the blade, if you work at the table only the table top constitutes the place of your working. We noted (p. 112) that the active zone need not be an actual part of the designated entity but may be something that is closely associated with it. (In such cases, it is common to speak of metonymy.) If you hear the piano, it is not strictly speaking the piano as such that you hear, but the sound that emanates from it. If I say that I am parked in the street, it is not strictly speaking me (i.e. my body) that is parked in the street, but my car.

(iii) Semantic flexibility (section 22.2). Most concepts are understood against a complex domain matrix. Typically, only some domains will be prominent in a given conceptualization. *Repair the television* construes the television as an intricate electronic device, *move the television* construes the television simply as an object with certain physical properties (weight, size, etc.). This phenomenon can sometimes cause a shift in the nature of the profile. *Torn photograph* designates the physical object, *out-of-focus photograph* refers to the image. *Move the television* involves the physical object, *write for television* refers to the broadcasting institution, *watch too much television* involves the televised content, *the invention of television* refers to the technology.

Each of the above examples (and countless more—the phenomena are truly ubiquitous) raises the question of how to represent the semantic structure of the words in question. Are the words to be assigned a unitary semantic value which is elaborated differently in different contexts? Do the words have a unitary value which is extended in different ways in different contexts? Are the different senses stored as distinct (though related) semantic units?

Consider a concrete example: how is the meaning of *eat*, as exemplified in *eat a steak* and *eat an ice-cream*, to be represented? We can imagine at least three possibilities. (Comparable accounts could be given for the other words introduced above, such as *(to) paint*, *(to) cut, car, television*, etc.)

(i) We propose a schematic meaning—say, 'ingest (solid) food through the mouth'. The specific images of how a person 'eats a steak' and 'eats an ice-cream' (cutting up the foodstuff, raising a cut-up portion to the mouth with a fork, inserting the portion into the mouth, chewing it, and then swallowing it vs. raising the foodstuff to the mouth and licking off a portion) are contextualized elaborations of the schematic meaning, which are not independently stored.

(ii) We propose as the semantic representation the 'standard', or 'prototypical' situation involving the consumption of solid foodstuffs which need to be cut up before being placed, piece by piece, into the mouth and then chewed and swallowed. The eating of ice-cream and of chocolate bars—which are consumed by being licked or nibbled at—has the status of a context-conditioned extension from the prototype. Bear in mind, however, that the very possibility of semantic extension entails a schema which abstracts the commonality of the prototype and the extension (section 7.1).

(iii) A third possibility is that *eat* is associated with distinct semantic representations according to the nature of the foodstuff being ingested; *eat'* refers to the eating of a steak, *eat''* to the eating of an ice-cream. The similarity between the different cases may be captured in a more schematic representation.

These three possibilities are sketched in Figure 23.1. Stored mental representations are represented in the diagram by boxes outlined by heavy, unbroken lines, extensions and abstractions over instances by dotted-lined boxes.

According to (a) and (b) of Figure 23.1, *eat* would be monosemous—that is, it would be associated with a single semantic representation; according to (c) the word would be polysemous. It will be apparent, however, that the distinction is not a clear-cut one. Even if we take the word to be monosemous, we still need to account for the different semantic values of the word in different contexts, while if we take the word to be polysemous we will need a unitary schematic meaning which captures the similarities between the related senses.[1]

For my part, therefore, I am inclined to see features of both monosemy and polysemy in a word's semantic structure. On the one hand, a speaker will

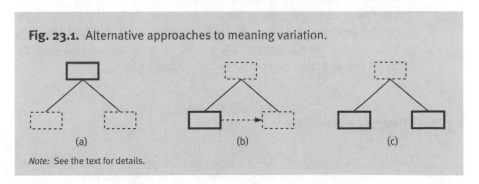

Fig. 23.1. Alternative approaches to meaning variation.

(a)   (b)   (c)

Note: See the text for details.

[1] In the case of words which are associated with a large number of different senses, linked by numerous and cross-cutting extension relations, there may not be a single overarching schema that covers all the different senses.

be familiar with a range of conventionalized uses of a word. These are likely to be associated with quite specific conceptualizations. At the same time, the conventionalized uses may be perceived as similar and may well be consistent with an overarching schema. New uses can be interpreted, and created, by extension from one of the conventionalized uses, often in conformity with the schema.[2] The monosemy-polysemy distinction is relevant to the extent that the unifying schema may be particularly salient (in which case we would speak of monosemy), alternatively, the particularized uses may be highly salient (in which case we would incline towards a polysemy analysis).

Let us consider another example in illustration of these remarks. The verb *cut* is associated with a number of specific semantic values: cutting the grass, cutting a cake, cutting a piece of string (in two), cutting your fingernails, cutting your finger, and so on. These variants are associated with rather specific 'images', having to do with the instrument that is typically used, the motor actions that are involved, and the purpose for which the activity is carried out. You cut the grass by manipulating a lawnmower in a certain way with the aim of shortening the grass and making it look neat; you cut a piece of string with a pair of scissors, which you handle very differently from a lawnmower, in order to get a piece of the desired length; you cut a cake with a knife in order to divide the cake up into manageable portions. There are some important differences between the uses. You cut a fingernail by removing a portion of the nail with the intention of making it shorter, but if you cut your finger you do not lop off a portion of your finger—you make an incision (probably by accident) in your finger.

All these different uses, I maintain, are represented (some more saliently than others, perhaps) as instances within the semantic structure of *cut*. This assertion is warranted because of the need to represent the particularized knowledge associated with the different uses. This does not exclude the possibility of a schematic representation which captures the commonality of the various uses. Indeed, the schema serves to structure the knowledge of the instances, bringing them together into a coherent network.

The approach suggested here has some interesting consequences. It might be unclear, in any given case, whether a word should be regarded as polysemous or monosemous. Moreover, it may be unclear just how many different meanings a polysemous word actually has.

23.2 Category extension

Let us now consider the mechanisms by which the semantic pole of a symbolic unit comes to be associated with a network of semantic units.

---

[2] For 'marginal' examples of *eat*, consider whether the verb would be appropriate with reference to soup and vitamin pills. Are these 'eaten'?

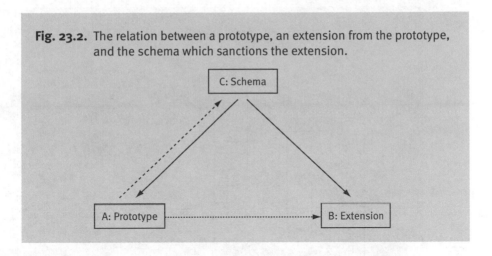

Fig. 23.2. The relation between a prototype, an extension from the prototype, and the schema which sanctions the extension.

Figure 23.2 is a slightly modified version of the categorization triangle introduced in Chapter 7. Imagine that the symbolic unit is initially associated with a single concept—the prototype [A], shown at the bottom left. A speaker entertains a conceptualization that is slightly at variance with the specifications of [A]. Assume that there is no standard way of designating this new concept in the language. The similarities with [A] are such, however, that the new conceptualization can be easily assimilated to it. This gives rise to a second semantic value, the extension [B]. At the same time, the recognition of the similarity between [A] and [B] triggers the formation of a schematic representation [C] that captures the commonality between the more specific units.

The process exemplified in the Figure can take place recursively on any of the three units. As more and more extensions are assimilated, and schemas of varying degrees of generality are abstracted, the semantic pole can come to be associated with a highly complex network structure, with many levels of schematicity and chains of extensions. Typically, the units within the network will differ with respect to their entrenchment, an aspect that can be represented diagrammatically by means of the heaviness of the surrounding boxes. A simple illustration was provided in Chapter 7 on the example of the different semantic values of the word *tree* (Fig. 7.11). Figure 23.3 is a more elaborated example, adapted from Tuggy (1988).

23.2.1 Polysemy and monosemy

This model provides a useful way to approach the question of whether a linguistic form is to be regarded as polysemous. At issue is the relative salience of the schema and the instances. If the prototype and the extension are more salient than the overarching schema, we should regard the form in question as polysemous. If the schema is more salient than its instances, we should regard

Fig. 23.3. Schematic hierarchy for *run*.

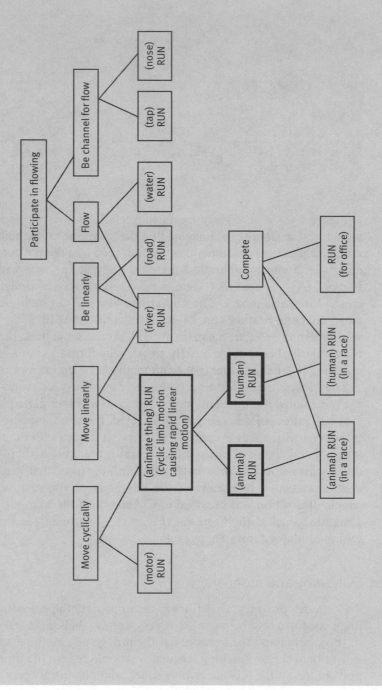

Source: Adapted from Tuggy (1988: 588). Reproduced with permission.

the form as vague with respect to the instances. Sometimes, context can increase the salience of either the instances or the schema, thereby making it difficult to decide whether the form is polysemous or not.

Let us consider examples of the three situations.

A clear case of polysemy is the word *tree*, as applied, first, to things that grow out of the ground, and, second, to genealogical networks. The two senses are strongly entrenched, and therefore salient. The unifying schema is not very salient, for several reasons. First, the commonality between the specific senses is rather tenuous, having to do, as suggested in Chapter 7, with the branching structure of both kinds of entity. Secondly, the instances are characterized against different conceptual domains (biological kinds vs. kinship networks)—a fact which also reduces the conceptual commonality between them. Third, the elaborative distance between the schema and the instances is rather large. A considerable amount of conceptual substance has to be added to the schema in order that the instances can be specified. Moreover, the manner in which the schema is elaborated is idiosyncratic to the instances—it is not the case that anything with a branching structure can be called a tree. Given its low salience, the schema will not normally be invoked when it comes to describing someone's genealogy as their family tree; the expression *family tree* is readily available as an established unit.

A clear case of monosemy is provided by *grandfather*. My grandfather could be my father's father or my mother's father. The two interpretations are subsumed under the more schematic meaning 'father of a parent'. In this case, the elaborative distance between the schema and its instances is rather short. Moreover, there are in principle only two ways in which the schema could be elaborated, the instances are not characterized by 'idiosyncratic' features, and the instances pertain to the same conceptual domain of kinship relations. Consequently, the grandfather schema is highly salient, whereas the difference between two kinds of grandfather is not at all salient.[3]

The two cases described above enable us to understand the operation of the some of the well-known 'tests' for polysemy vs. vagueness (Geeraerts 1993). One such test involves the possibility of asserting of an entity that it 'is p' and at the same time that it 'is not p'. Paradoxical assertions of this kind are possible just in case the focus is on the contrasting instances, not on the overarching schema. Thus, I could assert of an oak that it 'is a tree' (of the biological kind) and that it 'is not a tree' (of a genealogical kind). I could not, however, assert that Jack 'is my grandfather' (that is, the father of my mother) but that he 'is not my grandfather' (that is, the

---

[3] The non-salience of the two readings of *grandfather* is perhaps reinforced by the fact that other kinship terms which invoke a relation via one or the other of a person's parents do not specify which of the parents is implicated; consider *aunt*, *uncle*, *cousin*, *nephew*, *niece*. Other languages (and other cultures) put great emphasis on this aspect.

father of my father). *Grandfather* invokes the schema, not the contrasting instances.

Another test concerns certain syntactic constructions which require that a word has a constant semantic value. One instance of the test concerns the use of anaphoric *so*.

(1) a. Jack is my grandfather and so is Jim.
    b. This is a picture of a tree and so is that.
    c. Jack and Jim are both grandfathers.
    d. We were all drawing pictures of trees.

Example (1a) is acceptable if Jack is my maternal grandfather and Jim is my paternal grandfather. The normality of this sentence suggests that *grandfather* is understood at the level of the schema, not at the level of the contrasting (and therefore incompatible) instances. Similarly, example (1b) is acceptable if both the pictures depict trees of the biological kind or if both depict trees of the genealogical kind, but not if one of the pictures depicts an oak and the other a family tree; at best, the 'crossed interpretation' would be perceived as facetious or as a pun. This suggests that *tree* is understood at the level of the instances, rather than at the level of the schema which neutralizes the differences between the instances. Other variants of the test involve predicating a word of coordinated entities (c) or of a plural number of entities (d).

While *grandfather* and *tree* are clear examples of monosemy and polysemy, respectively, many cases are not so easy to classify. An example is the English verb *paint*. (The following remarks are based on the discussion in Tuggy 1993.) The word can be used of various kinds of activity—you can paint a portrait, you can paint the kitchen, you can paint white stripes on the road, you can paint your fingernails. It is easy to bring these different uses under a single schematic representation. Painting involves putting a coloured substance ('paint') on to a surface. But various subcategories can be identified. For example, we can make a broad distinction between 'artistic painting' and 'utilitarian painting'. These are performed for different purposes, they require different kinds of skills, and are evaluated by different criteria. Moreover, in the case of artistic painting, the direct object of the verb ('portrait', 'landscape', etc.) designates the entity that is created through the activity, whereas in the case of utilitarian painting the direct object typically designates the entity whose surface becomes covered with paint. These conceptual differences no doubt reinforce the salience of the two kinds of painting. Accordingly, the 'so' test suggests that *paint* is polysemous. Example (2a) is at best facetious if I have been painting white lines on the road and Jane has been painting a portrait in oils. Likewise, (2b) suggests that Jane and I are both engaged in artistic painting (we are both creating a representation of the house) or in utilitarian painting (we are putting paint on the house). The distinctness of the two senses is exploited in (c).

(2) a. I have been painting, and so has Jane.
     b. I am painting the house, and so is Jane.
     c. Little Johnny is painting grandfather's portrait—all green!
     d. When I'm painting, I try to put the colour on evenly, and so does Jane.

While these examples suggest that *paint* is polysemous, we can imagine contexts which focus specifically on the commonality of both artistic and utilitarian painting. An example is (2d). This sentence can easily support a crossed interpretation, suggesting that *paint* is monosemous.

23.3 Issues in polysemy

Polysemy is a problematic notion for a number of reasons. As with many technical terms, there are, first of all, issues of definition and of demarcation. These concern the distinction between polysemy and homonymy, and between polysemy and monosemy (or 'vagueness').

Another issue is the following. One might imagine that the existence of extensive polysemy would severely undermine the communicative efficiency of language. Yet speakers of a language do not, on the whole, perceive polysemy to be a problem. Speakers are also very adept at resolving the ambiguities that polysemy engenders. Polysemy does, however, pose severe problems in computer applications, such as automatic translation. The problems encountered in computational linguistics, and the proposed solutions, have interesting implications for linguistic theory.

23.3.1 Polysemy, homonymy, and monosemy

The distinction between polysemy and homonymy is usually drawn in terms of whether the different meanings associated with phonological form are related (as in polysemy) or whether they are unrelated (in which case we should speak of homonymy). In the case of homonymy it could be argued that we are dealing, strictly speaking, with two different words which happen to share the same phonological form.

The relatedness of meanings, however, is a gradable phenomenon, and perceptions of relatedness are likely to differ from speaker to speaker. Historically, the two meanings of *port*—'harbour' and 'fortified wine'—are related; port wine is associated with the Portuguese city of Porto, whose name, in Portuguese, means 'port' (i.e. 'harbour'). A person with some philological education may be aware of the relatedness, others may not. Perception of the meaning relation, however, probably has little bearing on how a person uses the word *port*. All that is required is that a speaker recognizes the two distinct meanings and is familiar with the usage ranges associated with the them.

In Cognitive Grammar terms, meaning relatedness is a question of the salience of a unifying schema and of the elaborative distance between the schema and the instances. In the limiting case, the unifying schema will be so lacking in conceptual substance that it scarcely serves to relate the specific meanings at all. The two meanings of *ball*—'spherical object' and 'social event'—can be united only at a very high level of abstraction. Probably, the best we could do would be to propose the unifying schema 'thing' (in the technical sense in which this word is used in Cognitive Grammar). Similar remarks apply to *bank* 'financial institution' vs. 'side of a river'. The elaborative distance between 'thing' and the two particularized meanings is very large indeed. To all intents and purposes, the schema is non-existent—which is tantamount to saying that the two meanings of *ball* and of *bank* are not perceived to be related at all. *Ball* and *bank* are classic examples of homonymy. Nevertheless, even in these cases, it may be possible to construct contexts which serve to create a temporary and more contentful schema. The following example is from Deane (1988: 345).

(3) Financial banks resemble those that you find by rivers; they control, respectively, the flow of money and of water.

The salience of the instances may obscure the salience of a unifying schema. I dare say that many English speakers may not perceive a relation between *over* in *Come over here*, in *Turn over the page*, and in *water all over the floor*. The particularized uses are so entrenched, and are associated with conceptualizations of such specificity, that a unifying schema may be irrelevant to a person's ability to use the word correctly. All that is required of a speaker is that she is familiar with the particularized uses.

A second demarcation problem concerns the distinction between polysemy and vagueness, which we addressed in previous sections. Much has been written on this distinction, and the ways in which it can be diagnosed. In light of our earlier discussion, it is not surprising that a clear-cut distinction is often difficult to make.

23.3.2 Polysemy and communicative efficiency

One might expect that the existence of widespread polysemy would be a troublesome feature of a language. The association of a single phonological form with a range of semantic values would, one might suppose, hinder the process of language comprehension and thereby threaten the semiotic efficiency of a language. A language without polysemy would assuredly bring enormous benefits to its users. No expression would ever be ambiguous, and this, one might think, would greatly enhance communicative efficiency. Anttila (1989: 181) asserted that 'a maximally efficient system avoids polysemy', while Geeraerts (1997: 105) suggests that 'natural languages aspire towards a one-to-one relationship between lexical forms and meanings' (the 'isomorphic principle'). It is significant that many linguists have sought to limit the role of polysemy in linguistic semantics, if not to eliminate it altogether.[4]

Yet polysemy is endemic to natural languages, as a detailed analysis of just about any word will confirm. All the same, language users rarely experience polysemy as a problem or a hindrance to effective communication. Speakers, it seems, are able to tolerate a multiplicity of meanings, especially with high-frequency words. Indeed, as a general rule of thumb, we can say that the more frequent a form is, the more polysemous it is likely to be. Polysemy, far from being dysfunctional, would seem to be an essential aspect of natural languages. It is worthwhile considering why this should be so.

Imagine a language with a strict one-to-one relation between forms and meanings, where each concept is designated by a unique phonological form and each phonological form symbolizes a different concept. A language like this would be a static system—the only concepts that could be symbolized are those that are already codified. However, many of the conceptualizations that we wish to symbolize are probably unique. These need to be categorized in terms of already available resources. If a new experience is repeated often enough (and if the phonological form used to designate it becomes the established means of referring to it), the phonological form will have become polysemous; it is associated both with its 'established' meaning and with the new experience. Polysemy, then, is testimony to the ways in which speakers categorize (or have categorized) their ever-changing environment and their conceptualizations of it. A language without polysemy would be usable only in a world without variation and innovation, in which speakers need never respond to new experiences or symbolize new conceptualizations. In brief, polysemy is conceptually necessary in an evolving semiotic system that can accommodate the dynamic aspects of conceptual structure.

There is an intriguing comparison to made here with synonymy. In polysemy, a single phonological form is associated with a range of distinct meanings. In synonymy, a single meaning is symbolized by distinct phonological forms. While polysemy, one might imagine, could threaten the communicative efficiency of language, synonymy would be an extravagant luxury. Yet while extensive polysemy is tolerated, synonymy tends to be avoided. To be sure, *near*-synonyms—words with similar, though not identical meanings—are legion (think of *big/large*, *small/little*, *tall/high*, *road/street*, *engine/motor*, and many more). Yet it is difficult to find pairs of words which have *exactly* the same semantic value. (A possible candidate might be *sofa* and *couch*). In cases of potential synonymy, 'corrective' mechanisms come into play—one of the words may fall into disuse, or the words become associated

---

[4] Wunderlich (1993) claims that polysemy is merely an effect of 'conceptual' elaboration of unitary (i.e. monosemous) 'semantic' representations. For Coseriu (1977), polysemes are a matter of usage 'norms', distinct from the unitary values that constitute the language 'system'. See also Kirsner (1993). Essentially, these linguists have sought to minimize the import of polysemy by treating it as something outside the language system proper.

with different nuances, possibly of a stylistic or sociocultural nature. Occasionally, polysemy is also subject to corrective mechanisms. (The use of *gay* to refer to homosexuality has effectively suppressed the earlier meaning 'joyous, carefree'.) Yet such mechanisms, it would seem, are last resorts, which apply only when the ambiguities become too onerous to handle. There are certainly no grounds for proposing a general 'polysemy-avoidance' principle.

23.3.3 Polysemy in natural language processing

While unproblematic for ordinary language users (the extent of polysemy probably goes unnoticed, for most speakers, most of the time), polysemy has turned out to be a major problem in automatic text processing, whether this be automatic translation, parsing, or data extraction. The problem was identified long ago by Bar-Hillel (1960) with reference to the sentence *The box is in the pen*. To properly understand this sentence we need to select the sense 'enclosure (typically for animals or for playing children)' of *pen*, not the 'writing implement' sense. In contrast, to understand *The pen is in the box* we need to select the 'writing implement' sense.

The standard approach to polysemy in natural language processing has been to break down the problem into two sub-tasks (cf. Ravin and Leacock 2000: 24–5). The first is to determine, for each word in the language, the different senses it is associated with. The second task is that of sense-selection, or disambiguation. Given that a word has *n* different senses, we need a procedure for selecting just that sense that is appropriate to the context in which the word is used. Both of these aspects have turned out to be fraught with difficulties.

One might suppose that the first issue—listing the distinct senses of a lexical item—could be easily handled, given a sufficiently elaborate and sophisticated semantic analysis. It might even be argued that the work has already been done, namely by the lexicographers, and has been incorporated into the larger dictionaries of the better studied languages. Published dictionaries, however, are notoriously inconsistent when it comes to identifying word senses (see Study question 1). It would be unfair to blame this state of affairs on the lack of linguistic sophistication of the dictionary-makers. Lexicography is one of the most developed of the applied linguistic disciplines. Even practitioners of Cognitive Linguistics do not always agree when it comes to identifying the senses of a word. The continuing discussion of *over* is a case in point (see the next section).

In fact, the question of how many senses a word has may be badly put, in that the question rests on a false presupposition. The question presupposes that a word is indeed associated with a fixed number of discrete senses. If meanings are not clearly identifiable entities (and we have seen in the earlier sections of this chapter and elsewhere in this book that there are good reasons to hold this view), it could be futile to try to enumerate the distinct senses of a word. At best, a dictionary can enumerate only some of the more salient semantic distinctions, and different lexicographers are liable to employ different criteria in their assessments. A 'complete' dictionary would be virtually coextensive with a person's full knowledge of their language. Published dictionaries are a compromise between this (unattainable) ideal and practical considerations.

The imperfections of polysemy analyses have not deterred computational linguists from attempting to devise algorithms for disambiguation and sense selection. The procedure has involved incorporating all manner of encyclopaedic knowledge into the characterizations of major sense distinctions and applying conceptual schemas to assess the plausibility of the different possible interpretations. Take Bar-Hillel's example of the *box in the pen*. Pens (on both the 'enclosure' and the 'writing implement' senses) will need to be characterized in terms of their likely size, as will boxes. On both senses, 'pens' can be construed as containers (we can have ink in pens, as well as boxes in pens). The interpretation of *box in the pen* depends on knowledge of the relative sizes of the boxes and pens, in their various senses.

Needless to say, such an approach requires a massive amount of encoding by the programmer. The programmer will need to enter, laboriously, for each word in the system's lexicon, the different senses and the associated encyclopaedic knowledge. Bar-Hillel's point was that the programmer will be unable to foresee all the possibly ambiguous contexts in which a word may occur. One never knows which bit of common-sense knowledge is going to be relevant to the next example of ambiguity that will turn up. Consequently, sense-disambiguation systems tend to be limited to restricted domains of discourse.

It is interesting to note that practitioners of natural language processing have attempted to by-pass the problems of sense listing and disambiguation by recourse to statistical aspects of word use.

A text about pens ('writing implements') is not likely to involve reference to pens ('enclosures for animals or for playing children'), and vice versa. Moreover, the one sense is likely to co-occur with words such as *ink*, *write*, and *paper*, whereas the other is likely to co-occur with words such as *children*, or the names of animals. The possibility thus arises that a word sense can be characterized in terms of a distinctive contextualization pattern, concerning the probability of the word in that sense occurring with certain other words, within a window of a given size (cf. Miller and Charles 1991; Schütze 2000). This approach entails (i) that words are similar in meaning to the extent that their contextualization patterns are similar, and (ii) that a word is polysemous to the extent that uses of the word cluster in different contextualization patterns.

Within the computational-statistical approach, the question whether different uses of a word exemplify one or more senses hinges on the degree of tolerance that is allowed when different contextualization patterns are assessed for their similarity. A high tolerance factor will lump different contextualization patterns together; a low tolerance factor will result in a proliferation of different senses. In fact, since most contexts of use will be unique, the number of different senses will be in principle open-ended. These conclusions are not incompatible with the Cognitive Grammar approach to sense identification. How many distinct senses we associate with a word depends on the extent to which we zoom in on the instances rather than the unifying schemas.

In an earlier chapter (Chapter 10, section 10.1.2) I briefly discussed the possibility that word meaning can be understood in terms of the linguistic environment in which a word is used. I rejected the idea that word meaning can be identified with the way a word is used in association with other words. Contextualization patterns are symptomatic of a word's meaning, they are not to be identified with its meaning. Nevertheless, bearing in mind the special constraints of natural language processing (these have to do with the impossibility, in principle, of providing a system with a truly encyclopaedic knowledge base), the computational-statistical approach turns out to be compatible in principle with the Cognitive Grammar approach to issues of word meaning and meaning disambiguation.

23.4 The case of 'over'

It seems fair to say that the popularity of Cognitive Linguistics in the 1980s and beyond was triggered by its treatment of polysemy. A major landmark was, and remains, Brugman's analysis of *over* (Brugman 1988 [1981]), and Lakoff's re-presentation of it in Lakoff (1987). (An equally impressive, though perhaps less well-known, study of polysemy was Lindner's 1981 account of the prepositions *up* and *out* in English; Lindner's dissertation is the background to the more recent discussion in Morgan 1997.)

The example of *over* was an especially good candidate for a polysemy study. Not only is the word itself highly polysemous, many of the different senses, especially those pertaining to the spatial domain, can be easily represented by means of little sketches. In fact, Brugman's methodology (and especially Lakoff's presentation of it) relied heavily on the possibility of representing the various senses in visual terms, a procedure which was able to portray graphically the similarities and differences between the various senses.

Rather than attempt to summarize Brugman's findings, I will only list some of the distinct senses (or clusters of senses) that emerge from her analysis.

(i) First, there is the 'traversing' sense, in which the tr goes across the lm. This sense—represented in Figure 23.4(a)—is exemplified in (4).

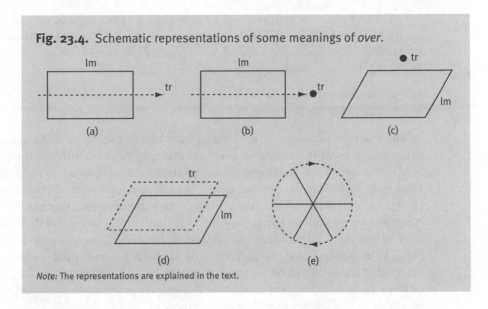

Fig. 23.4. Schematic representations of some meanings of *over*.

Note: The representations are explained in the text.

(4) a. She swam over the river.
    b. He walked over the bridge.
    c. They flew over the city.

(5) a. They live over the hill.
    b. Come over here.

A variant of this sense construes the location of a tr as the end-point of an imaginary path traversing a lm (5a); see Figure 23.4(b). A further extension, (5b), merely designates a place construed as the end-point of a path from a non-specified source which traverses a non-specified lm.

(ii) Secondly, there is the 'higher than' sense, see Figure 23.4(c), in which the tr is located higher than the lm (but still in proximity to it):

(6) a. They live over me.
    b. The lamp hangs over the table.

(iii) Next is the 'covering' sense, in which an extended tr covers the lm; see Figure 23.4(d). In (7), coverage is by means of a two-dimensional tr; in (8a), the tr traces a convoluted path which effectively 'covers' the lm, whereas in (8b) the components of a multiplex tr are distributed within the area of the lm.

(7) a. The tablecloth is over the table.
    b. I put my hands over my eyes.
    c. I pulled my hat down over my eyes.

(8) a. We drove all over the city.
    b. There were soldiers posted all over the hill.

(iv) There is also a 'reflexive' sense, in which an entity rotates, or is made to rotate; see Figure 23.4(e). Note that (9a) specifically invokes rotation around a horizontal axis; rotation around a vertical axis would be described by *(a)round: I turned round.*

(9) a. I turned over (in bed).
     b. Turn over the stone / page.

There are in addition various metaphorical extensions of these senses to other domains: *have power over someone* metaphorically construes the power relation in terms of the higher-than relation; *get over one's divorce* metaphorically construes the divorce as an obstacle that has to be traversed on the (metaphorical) path of life; *the lesson is over* metaphorically construes the state of completion as the end-point of a path. Not to be overlooked are uses of *over* as a derivational morpheme, as in *overeat, overdo, over-interpret.* Here, *over-* conveys that the activity is carried out beyond, or in excess of an acceptable limit. At issue in these examples is the metaphorical construal of amount in terms of verticality; the designated processes are carried out to an extent that is 'higher than' the expected norm.

The complexities of English *over* have spawned a veritable cottage industry of polysemy studies. (See the references in the Further readings to this chapter.) The issues raised by the preposition include:

(i) Are there any features which are common to all uses of *over*? The answer, probably, is 'no'. Consider the question of contact between tr and lm. The higher-than sense excludes this possibility. If there is contact between the lamp and the table, we should say that the lamp is *on* the table, not *over* it. But in the covering sense ('the tablecloth over the table') contact is certainly possible, if not expected. Similar remarks apply to the verticality of the tr with respect to the lm. This is a requirement in the higher-than sense, though it is relaxed in the covering sense, and is actually contradicted in *I pulled my hat down over my eyes, Her skirt comes down over her knees.* Another feature of many uses concerns the arc-like trajectory of the tr. In 'climb over the wall' this aspect is especially prominent, as it is in the reflexive uses ('turn over the page'). The idea of the curved configuration of the tr is also quite prominent in the image of a person *bending over*, of dogs *fighting over* a bone, or of people *squabbling over* money. On the other hand, this idea is absent in the covering sense ('all over the city'), and in some uses of the traversing sense, e.g. *fly over the city.*

(ii) How many distinct senses are there, actually? The issue is whether, given two uses of *over* which differ in some small way, the difference is to be attributed to the semantics of the preposition or to aspects of the context. Consider example (10):

(10) a. walk over the field
      b. fly over the city

In (a), there is contact between the tr and lm, in (b), there is not. Are these two distinct senses? Or is the notion of contact (or its absence) inferred from the semantics of the verbs *walk* and *fly*?

We might investigate this by trying out *over* with a verb which is indifferent to contact, such as *go*.

(11) a. To get to his house, you have to go over the field.
     b. To get to Poland, you have to go over Germany.
     c. *To get to Hamburg, you have to go over Bremen.

The results, I think, are inconclusive. Example (11a) is fine—but this is because the manner of my going is likely to be interpreted as 'walking'. Example (11b) is also fine—but only to the extent that the manner of travelling would be taken to be flying, rather than driving or walking. However, example (11c) is odd. *Over* cannot be used in the general sense of 'go past'. The concept would be better expressed by *via*, or *by way of*.

Alternatively, we might try out *over* with motion verbs which inherently require contact between the moving entity and the lm:

(12) a. climb over the fence
     b. ?walk over the fence
     c. *stroll over the fence

We see that it is not the case that any verb of motion is compatible with *over* in its traversal sense. Somehow, the inherent semantics of *over* in association with an obstacle-like lm is incompatible with the manner of motion of 'walking' and 'strolling'.

The examples suggest that the particular conceptualizations in example (10) cannot be regarded simply as contextually conditioned elaborations of a schematic traversal meaning of the preposition, which is indifferent to contact between tr and lm. The manner of motion, as well as the properties of the lm, are also relevant. It would seem that the examples in (10) do indeed represent distinct semantic values of the preposition.

(iii) How are the different senses related? How does it happen that a phonological form which designates traversal ('walk over the field') can come to designate covering ('the tablecloth over the table')? How is it possible that a form which designates a higher location ('lamp over the table') can at the same time designate a place identified from the perspective of the speaker ('over here', 'over there')?

The Brugman/Lakoff solution was to propose a radial network of senses. Chains of meaning extensions radiate outwards from a 'central' sense, whereby adjacent senses in the chain differ only minimally. Senses at the periphery of the network will differ significantly from each other, as well as from the central sense.

Thus, starting from the traversal sense (with contact between tr and lm), as in 'walk over the field', we can imagine, as an extension, that the tr follows a convoluted path, which effectively 'covers' much of the surface of the lm ('walk all over the field'). As a further extension, we can imagine a multiplex tr whose units are randomly distributed on the surface of the lm ('soldiers posted all over the hill'). From here, we can propose a two-dimensional tr which effectively covers the lm ('cloth over the table'). At the end of the chain we have arrived at a meaning that is quite different from (and inconsistent with) the meaning at the beginning. Another chain radiating out from the traversal sense involves, first, a focus on the end-point of a traversed path ('They are now over the hill'), then, a focus on the end-point of an imaginary path ('They live over the hill'), and finally, a location *tout court*, identified from the perspective of a speech act participant ('over here', 'over there').

(iv) How are the meanings and meaning relations represented mentally? While the radial model is able to structure the different senses in an elegant and coherent way, it by no means follows that speakers of a language mentally structure a polysemous word in such a way. It is unlikely, for example, that acquisition proceeds from the putative central sense, to which others are added as the network gradually extends. It is plausible that a child might initially acquire, independently of each other, the deictic use ('over here') and the covering use ('all over the floor'), and only subsequently the traversal and the higher-than senses, without ever coming to perceive the chaining relations between these different uses.

That certain uses of the preposition might have a relatively independent cognitive status is suggested by the fact that certain sub-senses have highly particularized values. Take the use of *all over* in connection with a convoluted or multiplex tr. First, we note the obligatory occurrence of *all* in the relevant expressions:

(13) a. There's water *(all) over the floor.
     b. There are soldiers posted *(all) over the hill.

While *all* appears to serve a quantifying function, it is not possible to employ other quantifying expressions. We cannot say that there's water 'half over' the floor. It would be odd, even, to say that there's water 'over part' of the floor. We should say, rather, that there's water 'all over a part of the floor'.

Another aspect is that *all over* does not just designate 'multiplex coverage', the coverage involves what Queller (2001) refers to as 'chaotic dispersal'. The examples in (14) differ significantly in their acceptability. Whereas the red squares are an aspect of the tablecloth's design, the red stains are not supposed to be there. The acceptable example focuses, not just on coverage, but on the random, uncontrolled, or undesired dispersal of the tr. As Queller notes, these nuances are not predictable from the position of the multiplex coverage sense within a radial model of the polysemy of *over*.

(14) a. The tablecloth has red stains all over it.
     b. ?The tablecloth has red squares all over it.

(15) a. He had guilt written all over his face.
     b. ?He had satisfaction written all over his face.

A similar contrast is apparent in example (15). The idea, in (a), is that a person's attempt to present a composed appearance was messed up by involuntary facial movements. A person's intended expression in (b) is not so compatible with *all over*. The idea of 'chaotic dispersal' sense is further exploited in some even more particularized, 'idiomatic' uses of *all over*.

(16) a. His research essay was all over the place.
     b. The driver was all over the road.
     c. When it comes to defining these terms, we're all over the map.

Example (16a) conveys that the research essay lacks focus, example (16b) that the driver did not have control over the vehicle, and example (16c) that the definitions fail to be unified by a commonly agreed upon content.

   The overall conclusion to this survey is not very different from my initial remarks on much simpler examples, such as the verbs *eat* and *cut*. To be able to use *over* appropriately, a speaker needs to have learned a large number (a *very* large number) of particularized uses. A speaker needs to have learned, not only the special 'chaotic dispersal' value of *all over*, but the even more specialized value of idiomatic constructions such as 'have [an unintended emotional display] written all over one's face', through to the still more specialized value of 'be all over the place [speaking of a student's essay or dissertation]'. Schemas which unify groups of senses may, or may not, play a role in structuring a person's overall representation of the word's meanings.[5] (In any case, considerable variation across individuals is to be expected in this regard.) In the last analysis, the radial model may be little more than a hypothesis concerning the plausible historical developments that resulted in the array of conventionalized uses in the modern language.

23.4.1 Women, fire, and dangerous things: The Dyirbal noun classes

Readers will no doubt be familiar with the strange title of Lakoff's 1987 book, *Women, Fire, and Dangerous Things*. An explanation of the title is hinted at right at the beginning (p. 5); for the full story, the reader has to wait until ch. 5 (pp. 92–104).

   The title alludes to the four noun classes in Dyirbal, a now almost extinct language of Queensland, Australia. Lakoff argued that membership in the

---

[5] One might suppose that the various 'tests' for polysemy vs. vagueness, mentioned in section 23.2.1, might be relevant to deciding the salience of the generalizing schemas. One problem with these tests, however, is that they can be applied only if the different senses of a word are associated with similar contextual frames. Since the various senses of a preposition, such as *over*, are typically associated with different and incompatible contexts, the tests are impossible to apply.

four noun classes was structured in radial networks. He proposed the following 'basic', or 'central' meanings of the noun classes:

- Class 1: human males
- Class 2: (human) females
- Class 3: non-flesh food
- Class 4: everything else

Membership in the categories is extended through various kinds of links and associations. Fire is assigned to Class 2 because fire is associated with the sun, and the sun, in Dyirbal mythology, is a female. Dangerous things, such as spears, are associated with fire because fire, too, is a dangerous thing. There is therefore a chaining relation: human female → female → sun → fire → dangerous things → spears. It is specifically not claimed that women, fire, and dangerous things belong to the same noun class because women are perceived to be 'fiery' or 'dangerous'. The association is indirect, achieved via the intervening links in the chain.

Lakoff's analysis has been challenged by Mylne (1995). Mylne points out that Lakoff's analysis assumes that the noun classes basically have to do with (biological) gender; in fact, Chasses 1, 2, and 4, in their basic senses, correspond remarkably with the semantic values of the pronouns *he*, *she*, and *it* of English. Mylne proposes a different organizing principle—one, he claims, which was highly salient in the culture of Dyirbal speakers, namely 'potency'. Accordingly, he (p. 387) assigns the following schematic meanings to the four classes:

- Class 4: Non-potent things which contribute to, or at least do not disturb, harmony of living.
- Class 3: Non-potent things which contribute specifically and importantly to harmony of living by serving as food.
- Class 1: Potent and ingenious beings and things which contribute to, or at least do not disturb, harmony of living.
- Class 2: All things which are set apart as being associated with the disruption of harmony of living (and which are consequently regarded as potent).

It is natural that fire and dangerous things should go into Class 2. But women? Mylne comments:

I hypothesize that it was . . . true in Dyirbal society that the opposition between the culturally based idealized cognitive models 'male' and 'female' was an asymmetric one, in which 'male' equated to 'normal/ordinary' and 'female' to 'other/extra-ordinary'. (This is not to suggest, of course, that the specific attributes associated with ordinariness and otherness were the same in Dyirbal society as they are in western society.) I hypothesize further that femaleness was not seen as a subcategory of trouble, but that both are manifestations of a subtle notion which might be described as 'the other, the extra-ordinary, that which is set apart as being associated

with the potential to disrupt harmony'. It is this notion, I suggest, which characterizes [Class 2]. (Mylne 1995: 392)

Mylne claims that his account succeeds in explaining some gender assignments that Lakoff handled only with difficulty. Take the harmless bandicoot,
which goes into Class 2. For Lakoff (p. 101), this is an 'exceptional animal'.
For Mylne, the issue is simple: being easy to catch, bandicoots were reserved
as food for the old folk. They constituted a kind of 'old age pension scheme'
(p. 394), and were taboo for young, healthy, active persons.

The example of the Dyirbal noun classes is instructive, because it illustrates
the potential danger of overinterpreting linguistic facts, attributing to users of
a language categorizations imposed by the analyst but which the users may not
share. (As far as I know, Mylne may be just as guilty of this as Lakoff.) Eco,
having reviewed Lakoff's analysis of the Dyirbal noun, comes to a similar
conclusion. He expresses his misgivings regarding

investigations in which classifications familiar to the experimenter but not shared by
the subjects are presumed, or in which the experimenter vainly struggles to deduce
classifications where the subjects do not classify at all and merely follow grammatical
automatisms. (Eco 2000: 201)

23.5 Phonological networks

Polysemy is commonly thought of as the association of multiple meanings
with a single phonological form. This characterization is misleading. Just as a
symbolic unit is rarely associated with a fixed, invariant value at its semantic
pole, so, too, we typically find a range of values at the phonological pole.

There are some well-known examples of this phenomenon:

(18) economics   [ɛkənɒmɪks] or [ɪkənɒmɪks]
     either   [aɪðə] or [iːðə]
     yogurt   [jɒgət] or [jəʊgət]
     privacy   [praɪvəsiː] or [prɪvəsiː]
     tomato   [təmɑːtəʊ] or [təmɛɪtəʊ]
     ate   [ɛɪt] or [ɛt]

In none of these examples would we want to say that we are dealing with
homonymy, i.e. distinct phonological forms that happen to be associated with
the same concept (or cluster of concepts). Although for a given speaker one or
the other of the two forms might be more entrenched, most speakers, I should
imagine, are familiar with both, and associate them with the same semantic
values.[6]

Sometimes, different phonological forms are associated with different

---

[6] For a more complex example, see Langacker's discussion of the pronunciation variants he associates with *route* (FCG1: 398).

phonological environments. A case in point is the indefinite article, which can appear as [ə], [æ], [ɛɪ], [ən], or [æn], depending on the degree of stress and the identity of a following sound. Many function words take on different values according to whether they are stressed or unstressed. *To*, for example, has the values [tuː], [tʊ], and [tə]. Even among so-called content words, there is often considerable variation in the pronunciation of unstressed vowels. The vowel in the first syllable of *proceed* can take on a range of values between the full diphthong [əʊ] and a somewhat indistinct and rapidly articulated schwa. If we consider finer phonetic details, we should probably need to associate every word in the language with a range of pronunciations. Pronunciations of *tree* differ according to the precise quality of the vowel and the degree to which the initial cluster is affricated; *upper* will sometimes be pronounced with bilabial closure [ʌpə], sometimes without complete closure [ʌɸə], to cite just two examples at random.

The pronunciation variants mentioned above are not likely to be equally salient to speakers of English. This could well be a consequence of the salience of the phoneme as a basic-level phonological category (section 8.1.3). Sub-phonemic differences are likely to be eclipsed by the salience of the phonemes which are schematic for them. Consequently, English speakers will not normally think of words such as *tree* and *upper* as having different pronunciations. (The situation, in fact, is comparable to that depicted in Figure 23.1(a), in which the schema is more salient than its instances.) In contrast, the alternative pronunciations [aɪðə] and [iːðə] *are* likely to be salient. This is not only because the difference can be represented at the phonemic level, but also because there is no salient unit which is schematic for [aɪ] and [iː]. (This situation is comparable to that depicted in Figure 23.1(c), in which the instances are more salient than the schema.)

In some cases, the different pronunciations clearly need to be separately listed in the grammar. Such is the case with forms of the indefinite article with [n] vs. those without [n]; there is no general schema in English which sanctions the insertion of [n]. In other cases, the pronunciation variants may indeed fall under more general phonological schemas; this would be the case with degrees of vowel reduction in the unstressed syllable in *proceed* and the sub-phonemic differences in the pronunciations of *tree* and *upper*. The question arises whether these variants are also stored as distinct phonological representations of the units in question. I suggest that in many cases they are.

Some evidence that speakers do in fact store even minute phonetic details has already been presented. Recall the case of the front vowels in South African English (section 8.1.4). If it were the case that the raised and the centralized variants of the [ɪ] vowel were in complementary distribution in this accent, one could, perhaps, make out a case that the vowel has a unitary representation, its variants being predictable from context. As noted in Chapter 8, however, the two variants are not quite in complementary distribution. For any given word, speakers have learned which of the two variants has to be used, or even, for some words, that both variants are possible. Moreover, it might be inaccurate, at a very fine level of phonetic detail, to speak of only two variants. It is likely that speakers store the words along with very detailed specifications of their phonetic properties.

Storage of even minute phonetic detail is suggested by another consideration. Speakers of a language are remarkably good at detecting minor variations in accent, often as a marker of regional provenance. This ability would be inexplicable if linguistic forms were associated only with schematic phonological representations, which abstract away from phonetic detail.

Bybee (1994) cites another phenomenon which points to the same conclusion. In words bearing stress on the third last syllable, and in which the penultimate syllable contains a schwa followed by either [l] or [r], there is a tendency for the schwa to be elided. The [l] or the [r] may take on the function of a syllable nucleus, thus preserving the overall number of syllables in the word, or the word may effectively lose a syllable. The occurrence of these processes depends on the frequency of the word. A frequent word such as *every* is almost invariably bisyllabic. Relatively rare words such *mammary* and *artillery* retain the syllable with the schwa vowel. Words of intermediate frequency, such as *memory*, *celery*, *family*, and *summary*, are variable. The schwa may be present or absent, and, if absent, may alternate with a syllabic [l] or [r]. These facts, according to Bybee, show

that the degree to which a schwa is present is associated with a particular word or lexical unit; it is not phonetically or morphologically predictable . . . The difference in the pronunciation of *memory* and *mammary* is something that must be learned about these individual words. It is, however, something that follows directly from the input and is learned as the word is learned. If *mammary* is always heard with three syllables but *memory* is heard sometimes with two and a half and sometimes with two, that is the way these words are stored. Just as detail about the meaning and co-occurrence patterns of words is acquired and stored with the word, details about its phonetic representation are also acquired and stored. (Bybee 1994: 293)

Study questions

1. Polysemy networks. Imagine that you are a lexicographer and you have been assigned the task of writing entries for the following verbs: *crawl*, *creep*, *leave*, *open*, *settle*, and *turn*. Access examples of each word from a corpus. How many distinct senses can you identify? On what basis do you assign two uses to the same or to different senses? How are these senses related? How would you construct dictionary entries for the words? (On *crawl*, see Fillmore and Atkins 2000.)

   Check out the words in several dictionaries. How consistent are the dictionaries with respect to the number of senses they assign to each word, and the way in which these senses are characterized? Do not restrict yourself only to monolingual dictionaries; also check out some bilingual dictionaries for the senses which they differentiate.

2. Having studied various approaches to the preposition *over* (see Further readings), investigate some other of the English prepositions, such as *above*, *across*, and *(a)round*.

How does *above* differ from *over*? Can the preposition *around* in all cases be substituted by the preposition *round*? Are there contexts in which *round* is preferred? In what ways do *around* and *round* differ?

Further reading

There is a vast literature on polysemy and related topics. A good overview of recent approaches is Ravin and Leacock (2000). On meaning variation, see Cruse (2000b: ch. 6). On the distinction between polysemy and monosemy ('vagueness'), see Geeraerts (1993), Tuggy (1993), and Taylor (1995a). Networks are discussed in FCG1, ch. 10.

Brugman's analysis of *over* continues to attract attention. See Vandeloise (1990), Deane (1993), Dewell (1994), Kreitzer (1997), Tyler and Evans (2001a), and Queller (2001). See also Geeraerts (1992) on the Dutch preposition *over*, and Taylor (1988) on Italian *su*, *sopra*, and *al di sopra* in comparison and contrast to English *on* and *over*.

On the issue of the psychological reality of network analyses, see Sandra and Rice (1995), Croft (1998), Sandra (1998), and Tuggy (1999).

Part 6
Approaches to Metaphor

The study of metaphorical expressions has played a central role in the development of Cognitive Linguistics.

Chapter 24 presents the 'Lakovian' theory of metaphor, according to which the existence of 'conceptual metaphors' makes possible the construal of a more abstract domain in terms of more concrete experience; the chapter also raises some problematic aspects of the Lakovian theory. Chapter 25 addresses some uses of the verb *go* which, on the Lakovian theory, would be analysed as instances of metaphor, but which have been analysed in a quite different way by both Jackendoff and Langacker. Both of these scholars analyse spatial and non-spatial *go* as instances of a more abstract concept. Chapter 26 reviews some further approaches, which likewise put the emphasis on schematic concepts, rather than on mappings from the concrete to the abstract. The chapter concludes with a brief outline of Fauconnier and Turner's theory of conceptual blending, a theory which is able to reconcile aspects of the Lakovian and other approaches.

Metaphor: The Lakovian approach

In this chapter I offer a presentation and a critical appraisal of Lakoff's approach to metaphor.

Probably the one publication which has done more than any other to popularize the Cognitive Linguistics movement was Lakoff and Johnson's short and very readable book, *Metaphors We Live By* (1980). Lakoff and Johnson made three principal claims. First, metaphor is ubiquitous in ordinary language—it cannot be dismissed as a mere figure of rhetoric, confined to certain literary genres. Secondly, the metaphors of ordinary language display a high degree of coherence and systematicity. Thirdly, metaphor is not just a manner of speaking, it is a mode of thought; the concepts that metaphorical expressions designate are themselves structured in terms of metaphor.

Metaphors We Live By was the first of a series of books and articles, by Lakoff and others, which proclaimed the centrality of metaphor in language and thought. Lakoff's *Women, Fire and Dangerous Things* (1987) addressed the broader philosophical framework of the approach, while Lakoff and Johnson's *Philosophy in the Flesh* (1999) aims to put metaphor at the very centre of cognitive science.

A person whose familiarity with Cognitive Linguistics is limited to the reading of works by Lakoff and his circle could well come away with the impression that Cognitive Linguistics *is* the study of metaphor. Nevertheless, others within the Cognitive Linguistics movement lay much less emphasis on metaphor. One finds only sporadic references to metaphor in the writings of Langacker and Talmy, while some, such as Wierzbicka, have been openly critical of the Lakovian approach (as I will call it). It also has to be borne in mind that the Lakovian approach is undergoing revision, especially in the context of the theory of conceptual blending, itself a development of Fauconnier's notion of mental spaces. Conceptual blending is discussed in Chapter 26.

24.1 Lakoff and conceptual metaphors

The essence of the Lakovian approach[1] to metaphor is easily stated: metaphor involves a mapping[2] relation between two domains (more precisely, between elements in two domains). The **source domain** corresponds to the traditional notion of the metaphor vehicle, while the **target domain** is equivalent to the traditional metaphor tenor.

Consider some of the metaphorical expressions cited in Chapter 1:

(1) a. We started out from these premises.
    b. We came to these conclusions.

The source domain has a traveller who, in (1a), moves away from a place, and in (1b) arrives at a place. The target domain is reasoning. The traveller maps on to the thinker, the starting place maps on to the premises, the destination maps on to the conclusion, while motion by the traveller maps on to the reasoning process:

Source domain (travelling)		Target domain (rational thought)
traveller	*corresponds to*	thinker
departure point		premises
arrival point		conclusion
motion		reasoning

The upshot is that reasoning is spoken of as though it were a journey. Expressions that are 'basically' understood against the domain of spatial locations and motion are used to talk about a different domain, involving ideas and reasoning.

It is easy to come up with expressions which map some further aspects of travelling on to further aspects of reasoning (cf. Lakoff and Johnson 1999: 236–7):

(2) a. We have arrived at the crucial point in the argument.
    b. Where are you in the discussion?
    c. Where are you going with this?

---

[1] In speaking of the 'Lakovian approach', I do not wish to suppress the contributions of other scholars closely associated with Lakoff, in particular Johnson and Turner. I refer to the approach as 'Lakovian' in recognition of Lakoff's role as an active synthesizer and promoter.

[2] 'Mapping' is used here in the mathematical sense of 'a correspondence between two sets that assigns to each element in the first a counterpart in the second' (Fauconnier 1997: 1).

    d. I see where you are coming from.

    e. Let's move on to the next point.

    f. Harry kept going off on flights of fancy.

    g. You're wandering from the topic.

    h. Don't stray too far away from the topic.

(3) a. I'm stuck!

    b. I can't go any further along this line of reasoning.

(4) a. Slow down, you're going too fast for me.

    b. I can't keep up with you.

    c. Can you go over that again for me?

The examples in (2) show that the places the traveller passes on the journey to the destination correspond to 'points' in a rational argument. To proceed from one place to the next is to go from one 'point' in the argument to the next, while to wander from the path is to digress from the 'line' of argument. The examples in (3) introduce another aspect—the traveller can get stuck. This maps on to the thinker who cannot progress further in the reasoning process. The examples in (4) introduce a second participant into the scenario—the companion who follows the traveller. The traveller guiding another person along the path corresponds, in the target domain, to the thinker who explains the argument to a hearer; to follow the traveller is to 'follow' the thinker's account of the argument. Example (4c) introduces yet another variation; to repeat a part of an argument (so that someone else can understand it better) is to guide a person along a path another time.

Source domain (travelling)		Target domain (rational thought)
path	*corresponds to*	argument
places on a path		points in an argument
straying from the path		straying from the argument
following a traveller		understanding a person explaining an argument
going over (part of) the path again		repeating (part of) the argument

    Given the extent and, above all, the coherence of the mappings between the two domains, it is evident that the essence of a metaphorical expression resides, not so much in the metaphorical value of any single component element, such as the particular value of *start out* in (1a) or *go over* in (4c), but in more general correspondences between the two domains. Lakoff and Johnson (1980) capture these cross-domain correspondences by means of **conceptual metaphors**.

    Some of the conceptual metaphors which underlie the expressions in (1)–(4) can be stated as follows. By convention, conceptual metaphors are written in small capitals and take the form X IS Y, where X is (an element of) the target domain and Y is (an element of) the source domain.

(5) A LINE OF THOUGHT IS A PATH
     A PREMISE IS A STARTING POINT
     A CONCLUSION IS A DESTINATION
     REASONING IS TRAVELLING ALONG A PATH
     STRAYING FROM THE TOPIC IS STRAYING FROM A PATH
     COMMUNICATING IS GUIDING (ALONG A PATH)
     UNDERSTANDING IS FOLLOWING (ALONG A PATH)
     RETHINKING IS GOING OVER THE PATH AGAIN

Underlying these conceptual metaphors are even more general metaphors (Lakoff and Johnson 1999: 236–7):

(6) IDEAS ARE LOCATIONS
     THINKING IS MOVING
     THE MIND IS A BODY

The conduit metaphor

One of the most frequently cited studies of conceptual metaphor is Reddy (1993 [1979]). Reddy identified a cluster of conceptual metaphors that motivate much of our talk about verbal communication:

i.   Ideas and thoughts are objects.
ii. Words and sentences are containers for these objects.
iii. Communication consists in finding the right word-container for an idea-object, sending this filled container along a conduit or through space to the hearer, who must then take the idea-object out of the word-container.

Collectively, these are known as the 'conduit metaphor'. The metaphor shows up in countless everyday expressions: *Empty words*, *Put one's ideas into words*, *Your ideas came across very clearly*, *I didn't get very much out of the lecture*. For his part, Reddy stressed the pernicious effects of the conduit metaphor on our conceptualization of verbal communication. The view that words and sentences have fixed meanings (a view that we have rejected — section 22.2) may be seen as one of the entailments of the metaphor.

   Alongside the conduit metaphor, there exist other minor metaphors of communication, which arguably give a better 'handle' on the real nature of the process. For example, understanding may be construed as 'following' a speaker or a text (*I can't follow you*, *I can't follow what you're saying*). Alternatively, the meaning of a text is something that a hearer 'constructs' (*I couldn't make anything out of what they were saying*). Both these metaphors attribute a more active role to the hearer than the mere unpacking of the containers that are words and sentences.

   For some reflections on the impact of these metaphors on language pedagogy, see Taylor (1987).

In *Metaphors We Live By*, a large number of conceptual metaphors were identified and exemplified. Further work in this tradition—by Lakoff and his circle, and by others—has identified many more.

A remarkable aspect of conceptual metaphors concerns the general direction of the mapping relation. Overwhelmingly, the source domain is concrete, and can be experienced or perceived 'directly', while the target domain is more abstract or concerns 'subjective' experience.

> Source domains: motion, location, containment (in/out), distance, size, orientation (up/down), perception (especially: seeing and sight), brightness, weight, temperature, etc.

> Target domains: time, life, thinking, reasoning, communication, the mind, emotions, intentions, causation, morality, love, marriage, society, economics, politics, etc.

Given the ubiquity of metaphor, and the general direction of the mapping relation, Lakoff and Johnson (1980, and especially 1999) draw the far-reaching conclusion that abstract domains cannot be conceptualized in their own terms, as it were, but must always be accessed through metaphor. Metaphor, therefore, is not just a way of speaking, it is intrinsic to abstract thought. For my part, I am somewhat sceptical of this claim. The first point below concerns the conceptual basis of the Lakovian theory; the next two are methodological in nature; while the fourth raises questions about the adequacy of the domain-mapping theory as a general theory of metaphor.

(i) In order for a target domain to be subject to mapping from a source domain, there has to be some prior conceptualization of the target domain. We need to know, at the very least, which elements of the source domain can map into which elements of the target domain, and this presupposes that the target domain already has some initial 'pre-metaphorical' structure. This is not to deny that metaphor can enrich the target domain and our conceptualization of it, and even influence the way we behave with respect to it. Still, it is implausible that it is metaphor that *creates* our conceptions of reasoning, time, morality, and so on.

Grady (1997a) has suggested that the initial motivation for metaphorical mapping may not, in fact, be the need to understand a target domain, but the need to symbolize our conceptualizations of it in a way that can be apprehended by others. Statements pertaining to concrete domains (such as the location or motion of one object with respect to another) can be easily verified by other observers. Inter-subjective agreement on the meanings of 'concrete' terms—spatial terms, in particular—is therefore relatively easy to establish. It is more difficult to establish consensus with respect to abstract domains. Indeed, concerning a person's mental or emotional states, 'objective' confirmation across individuals is in principle impossible. By talking about the abstract in terms of the concrete, we create the illusion of objectivity, and thereby facilitate communication about the abstract:

Perhaps, because we do not have access to each other's minds, when we attempt to externalize information about our internal states through language, humans have resorted to talking about such internal states in terms of experiences which are verifiable, inter-subjective and so consistent across individuals. The issue may not be that the internal experience is less direct or less fully experienced than the sensorimotor experience for the experiencer/speaker but that the speaker's internal experience is less direct for the listener. (Tyler and Evans 2001b: 77)

(ii) The fact that a given expression is used of more than one domain does not entail that one use is a metaphorical extension of the other. It could be the case that both are instances of a more schematic meaning, neutral between the domains in question. In fact, in order for the mapping relation between source and target domain to be possible at all, there has to be a perceived similarity between the two domains.

(iii) The metaphorical nature of an expression can fade over time and with repeated use. An expression which might in the past have been perceived as metaphorical becomes, over time, the normal, conventionalized way of talking. For highly conventionalized expressions, it is implausible to maintain that the entity designated by the expression is being conceptualized in terms of metaphorical mapping.

(iv) There are certain metaphorical expressions which appear problematic for the domain mapping theory. Consider (7), from Gibbs (1994: 217):

(7) That surgeon is a butcher.

Here, we might say that aspects of the butchering domain are mapped on to the surgical domain. The surgeon corresponds to the butcher, the surgeon's scalpel to the butcher's knife, the anesthetized patient to the animal carcass. But it is less clear what the conceptual metaphor might be that sanctions the metaphorical mappings. The domain-mapping theory also fails to explain why it is that (7) is interpreted to mean that the surgeon is incompetent. Butchers are not normally incompetent, any more than surgeons, or any other group of workers for that matter. This aspect, therefore, cannot derive from the source domain.

In spite of these reservations *vis-à-vis* the Lakovian theory, the fact remains that many of the metaphors that lie behind common everyday expressions (even if these may not be perceived as metaphorical) display some striking coherences and systematicities. Appeal to conceptual metaphor, therefore, can have considerable explanatory power, especially when it comes to explicating and motivating the usage range of many elements in a language. It is especially fruitful in studies of polysemy and idiomaticity, and readily lends itself to applications in second-language pedagogy.[3]

[3] See, for example, Dirven (1989a) and Radden (1989).

24.2 Conceptual metaphors as schemas

The relation between a conceptual metaphor, such as A CONCLUSION IS A DES-
TINATION, and specific metaphorical expressions, such as *We arrived at the
conclusion*, *Where are you heading with that argument?*, is easily handled in
Cognitive Grammar. The relation is the familiar one between a schema and
its instances. A conceptual metaphor is schematic for the metaphorical
expressions which instantiate it. The expressions *Christmas is approaching*,
The holidays are not far away are instances of the conceptual metaphor
FUTURE EVENTS MOVE TOWARDS US. The conceptual metaphor captures what is
common to the metaphorical mappings of the specific expressions.

Given the status of conceptual metaphors as schemas, much of what has
been said in earlier chapters about the schema-instance relation can be
brought to bear on conceptual metaphors.

For example, schemas can stand in a taxonomic relation; a schema can have,
as its instances, lower-level schemas; conversely, a schema can be an instance
of a higher-level schema. The conceptual metaphor A CONCLUSION IS A DESTINA-
TION is itself an instance of a more schematic metaphor, IDEAS ARE LOCATIONS.
Relations between conceptual metaphors, and between a conceptual metaphor
and its instantiation in specific expressions, are illustrated in Figure 24.1.

High-level schemas capture commonalities across a large range of examples.
Because of their generality, the elaborative distance between a high-level
schema and particular usage events is large; in order to be instantiated in
an actual linguistic expression, a high-level schema needs to be filled out with
a great deal of additional substance. Consequently, high-level schemas are
generally not very useful when it comes to accounting for the full range of
fully specified instances. Given the conceptual metaphor IDEAS ARE LOCATIONS,
a person would be hard pressed to predict just which expressions will be
conventional in a given language and which will not.

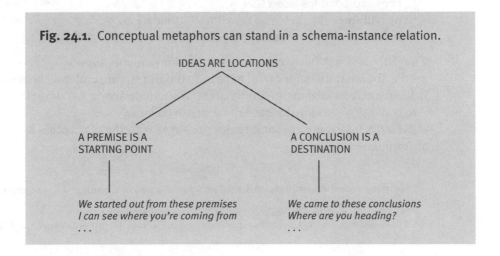

Fig. 24.1. Conceptual metaphors can stand in a schema-instance relation.

IDEAS ARE LOCATIONS

A PREMISE IS A
STARTING POINT

A CONCLUSION IS A
DESTINATION

*We started out from these premises
I can see where you're coming from
. . .*

*We came to these conclusions
Where are you heading?
. . .*

Low-level schemas are applicable to a smaller range of data. They capture low-level generalizations and the elaborative distance between the schema and its fully specified instances is shorter. Since low-level schemas are closer to fully specified instances, they have greater predictive power. Given the metaphor A CONCLUSION IS A DESTINATION, a person is more likely to be able to predict just which metaphorical expressions will be acceptable in a language.

24.2.1 Getting the schemas right

Even a cursory glance at the metaphor literature, especially the works of Lakoff and of Lakoff and Johnson, reveals a veritable proliferation of conceptual metaphors. The proliferation (and the different wordings) of the metaphors can partly be put down to the fact that metaphors are being formulated at different levels of schematicity, according to the descriptive tasks in hand. However, the taxonomic relations between the metaphors are not always spelled out clearly. A further aspect is that the formulation of the metaphors often does not seem to be quite right.[4]

We can illustrate with reference to one of the conceptual metaphors proposed by Lakoff and Johnson (1980):

(8) THEORIES (AND ARGUMENTS) ARE BUILDINGS[5]

Lakoff and Johnson (1980: 46) cite the following as instantiations of the metaphor:

(9) Is that the foundation of your theory?
    The theory needs more support.
    The argument is shaky.
    We need to buttress the theory with solid arguments.
    The theory will stand or fall on the strength of that argument.
    The argument collapsed.
    They exploded his latest theory.
    We will show the theory to be without foundation.
    So far we have put together only the framework of the theory.

The mappings are fairly obvious. Facts and arguments support a theory, just as the foundations support a building. Buildings can collapse because of inadequate foundations; so can theories. You can destroy a building (i.e. cause it to collapse); you can also cause a theory to collapse.

Nevertheless, there are some major problems with the conceptual metaphor as formulated in (8):[6]

---

[4] For some critical observations on Lakoff and Johnson's metaphor IDEAS ARE ORGANISMS, see Goddard (1998: 84, 363).

[5] Note that *argument* here has the sense 'rational argument', not 'dispute'.

[6] The inclusion of 'and arguments' in parentheses in (8) raises some further problems, which I do not address.

(i) Not every component of the building-domain maps on to theories. Buildings have rooms and windows; they have a front entrance, perhaps also an attic, a mezzanine, and a fire escape; they may have a heating and an air-conditioning system. These aspects do not readily (if at all) map on to theories. The examples in (10)—from Clausner and Croft (1997: 257)—are simply bizarre. Nevertheless, with a bit of ingenuity, even plumbing and gargoyles can be incorporated into a metaphor. The examples in (11) are from Lakoff and Johnson (1980: 53).

(**10**) a. Is that the *basement* of your theory?
　　　 b. That line of reasoning has no *plumbing*.
　　　 c. The theory has a *broken pipe*.
　　　 d. the *attic* of the theory

(**11**) a. Complex theories usually have problems with the plumbing.
　　　 b. He prefers massive Gothic theories covered with gargoyles.

Another point is worth noting. Given the emphasis in the Lakovian theory on experiential aspects of the source domain, and the role of experiential aspects in the structuring of the target domain, it is curious that the *function* of buildings (as places for shelter and habitation, or for the storage of goods) does not map at all on to the target domain.

(ii) Those aspects from the building domain that *can* be mapped on to a theory can usually be mapped on to other domains as well, such as economics, politics, society, and interpersonal relations.

(**12**) a. Agriculture remains the *cornerstone* of the country's economy.
　　　 b. The dollar *collapsed*.
　　　 c. Terrorism undermines the *foundations* of civilized society.
　　　 d. the *Architect* of the Revolution
　　　 e. Their love is *founded* on mutual respect.

(iii) There are aspects of the target domain that have no correspondences in the building domain. Such is the case with the progression, in a line of argument, from premise to conclusion, via points. These aspects would be handled by the traveller metaphor, not by the building metaphor.

Independently of each other, it would seem, Grady (1997*b*) and Clausner and Croft (1997) noted these failures of the THEORIES ARE BUILDINGS metaphor and came up with different solutions.

Grady (1997*b*) identifies two component metaphors of the THEORIES ARE BUILDINGS metaphor, both at a high level of schematicity:

(**13**) ORGANIZATION IS PHYSICAL STRUCTURE
　　　 PERSISTING IS REMAINING ERECT

Each of these metaphors is applicable to more domains than theories and arguments: *the foundations of the economy* exemplifies the first, *his reputation*

> **The 'Invariance Hypothesis'**
>
> Lakoff and Johnson (1980: 52–3) recognized that not all aspects of the building domain map on to the theory domain. They appealed to a contrast between the 'used' parts of the conceptual metaphor and the 'unused' parts. Foundations and cornerstones are used parts, staircases and gargoyles are unused parts. Lakoff and Johnson allowed the possibility that unused parts might be activated in special contexts, for special rhetorical effect.
>
> Subsequently, Lakoff (1990) attempted to offer a more principled constraint on metaphorical mapping. The Invariance Hypothesis stipulates that 'what is mapped [from the source domain to the target domain] preserves image-schematic structure, though not all image-schematic structure need be mapped' (p. 72).
>
> Brugman (1990) gives a critical appraisal of the Invariance Hypothesis, noting, among other things, that Lakoff neglected to spell out, in a non-circular way, what precisely is meant by 'image-schematic properties'.

still stands exemplifies the second. According to Grady, the THEORIES ARE BUILDINGS metaphor arises through 'unification' (p. 275) of the two metaphors. (Actually, it might be more appropriate to speak of their *intersection*.) The THEORIES ARE BUILDINGS metaphor involves, as its source, only those 'physical structures' that are 'erect'. Although the intersection of 'physical structures' and 'erect things' certainly includes 'buildings', it does not, however, uniquely identify buildings in contrast to other kinds of erect physical structures (such as power pylons). It is also not clear how the unification/intersection of 'organization' and 'things that persist' serves to identify the target domain of arguments and theories. Grady's approach conspicuously fails to address the second of the problematic aspects mentioned above.

Clausner and Croft (1997) take a different tack, and conclude that the conceptual metaphor THEORIES AND ARGUMENTS ARE BUILDINGS has been stated at too high a level of schematicity.

Noting, like Grady, that only certain parts of a building are relevant to the metaphorical mapping, they propose that the source domain should be more appropriately characterized as 'the structural integrity of a building' (this captures more or less the intersection of the source domains in Grady's account). Equally, not every aspect of a theory or rational argument is construed in terms of the source domain. For example, the stages of an argument are better handled by the journey metaphor. What is involved, they argue, is how convincing an argument is. Hence, Clausner and Croft (p. 260) propose that the metaphor be more appropriately formulated as follows.

(14) THE CONVINCINGNESS OF AN ARGUMENT IS THE STRUCTURAL INTEGRITY OF A
       BUILDING

Metaphor conflict

It is usually the case that a given domain can be structured in terms of mapping relations from a variety of source domains.

The discussion so far in this chapter has already illustrated this phenomenon. Rational arguments can be understood in terms of both a journey and a building's structural integrity. Interestingly, when the two metaphors are combined within a single expression, the result is sometimes slightly comic:

(i)   Where are you heading with that argument that you have constructed?

To me, this invokes the bizarre image of a traveller proceeding to a destination dragging a large building along. (The name for this inappropriate 'yoking' of incompatible elements is **zeugma**.)

The existence of alternative metaphorical construals of a target domain can be taken as evidence that the target domain has a conceptual integrity independent of its metaphorical construals. It is not the case that our concept of rational argument is the creation of metaphorical mappings. If this were so, we should have to say that we have several different, and incompatible concepts of rational argument.

As a matter of fact, even this formulation is not fully adequate. For example, I can *demolish* an argument. This is not because the argument is unconvincing, but because of its faulty logic. The following, therefore, might be an even better formulation.

(15) THE VALIDITY OF AN ARGUMENT IS THE STRUCTURAL INTEGRITY OF A
      BUILDING

As mentioned, Clausner and Croft criticize the formulation in (8)— THEORIES (AND ARGUMENTS) ARE BUILDINGS—because, they claim, the metaphor has been stated at too high a level of schematicity. They propose (14) as a lower-level formulation. However, it is not the case that (8) is schematic for (14). It looks as if the formulation in (8) is simply wrong.

24.2.2 Metaphor productivity

As extensively discussed in Chapters 15 and 16, a schema is productive to the extent that it is entrenched. A schema becomes entrenched through being instantiated by a large number of different instances (i.e. through the type frequency of the instances). A conceptual metaphor becomes entrenched to the extent that it is elaborated by a range of differently worded expressions. The metaphor will be productive to the extent that speakers will be able to create a large (and open-ended) set of expressions which instantiate the metaphor. The conceptual metaphors discussed so far in this chapter are productive in just this sense.

Not all conceptual metaphors are equally productive. Consider some metaphors of time. Time is predominantly construed in terms of motion. On one metaphor, future events 'come towards' us, they 'pass' us, and then 'recede into the past'. On another metaphor, we 'go' into the future (Lakoff and Johnson 1980: 41–5). Both metaphors are highly productive, each having a very large number of instances.

There is also a more minor metaphor, which construes time as a cycle:

(16) a. Spring came round again.
      b. the daily round
      c. the cycle of the seasons
      d. the growth cycle

The metaphor has some limited productivity, in that some lexical variation is permitted: *Monday comes round again, The holidays are coming round.* We can *watch the seasons go round*, and we can talk about *a life cycle*, or *a developmental cycle*. Generally, though, instances of the metaphor need to preserve roughly the syntactic structure of the examples in (16). The following are scarcely possible:

(17) a. *The building renovations went round till spring. ('lasted until spring')
      b. *We live our lives round the years.
      c. *The seasons go round.
      d. *Spring comes round and round.
      e. *Wait until the week has gone round. ('wait until this time next week')

For examples of non-productive metaphors, consider the following:

(18) a. let the cat out of the bag
      b. spill the beans

We can readily appreciate the metaphorical nature of these. Confidential information is construed as the contents in a container, and revealing the information is releasing the contents. Nevertheless, the expressions in (18) are lexically fixed.[7] You cannot *let the bird out of the cage, the chickens out of the coop*, or *the rat out of the sack* (at least, not in the metaphorical sense of revealing confidential information).[8] Neither can you *spill the peas* or *empty the coals*. It would be odd, even, to advise someone to *keep the cat in the bag*.

These are one-off, 'idiomatic' metaphors, with minimal type frequency and minimal productivity. As Clausner and Croft (1997: 271) aptly observe, they are analogous to highly irregular morphological forms, such as the past-tense

---

[7] Some limited syntactic variation is possible: *The cat is out of the bag, Don't let the cat out of the bag.*

[8] You can, to be sure, *let the genie out of the bottle*—but this has a quite different interpretation, namely 'let loose ideas whose effects cannot be foreseen'.

form *went*. This way of forming the past tense is totally unproductive, because of its minimal type frequency. (Given a new verb *jo*, we should not form the past tense as *yent*.)

24.2.3 Conventionalized metaphors

Lakoff and Johnson's *Metaphors We Live By*—and much subsequent work that the book inspired—focused on the conventionalized metaphors that are ubiquitous in ordinary, everyday language.[9]

A conventionalized metaphor may be characterized as one that speakers are able to use without awareness of its metaphorical nature—without, that is, actively construing a target domain in terms of the source domain. I daresay that when we speak of someone 'coming to' a conclusion, we are not actively construing the reasoning process in terms of a journey. *Come to a conclusion* is a ready-made phrase, with a ready-made semantics, whose proper use does not require a mapping from a source domain. Even so, it is not difficult to raise a person's awareness of the metaphorical nature of a good deal of ordinary language. With suitable probing, speakers readily appreciate the traveller metaphor in (1)–(4) and many of the other conceptual metaphors that have been discussed within the Lakovian approach.[10]

The conventionalization of a metaphor—and the possibility of (re-) activating awareness of the metaphorical mappings—has analogues elsewhere in language. Consider the case of a morphologically complex expression which, by dint of frequent usage, is stored and accessed as an integrated unit. Speakers are able to make appropriate use of the expression without having to be aware of its internal structure. Yet, with suitable prompting, the internal structure can be made apparent. An example of just this phenomenon was mentioned earlier, p. 295. A linguistically aware speaker (such as a student of linguistics) will surely recognize the presence of the agentive morpheme *-er* in the word *baker*; a baker is one who bakes. Yet Wheeler and Schumsky (1980) found that over half the subjects in their investigation took the word to be morphologically simple. These speakers, it would seem, had simply learned the phonological form [bɛɪkə] as the name of a certain kind of profession (or retail outlet). No doubt, if such speakers were suitably prompted, they would easily see that *baker* is morphologically complex, on a par with *singer* and *walker*. But this insight into the structure of the word is not a prerequisite to being able to use the word appropriately. Analogously, a conventionalized metaphor is one which can be used, in full conformity with the conventions of the language, without a speaker needing to actively construe the target domain in terms of the source domain.

---

[9] This is not to say that 'literary' metaphors have been ignored; see Further readings.

[10] Possibly, one reason for the success of *Metaphors We Live By* has been the fact that the book so readily triggers a feeling of discovery: 'Yes, of course all these everyday expressions are metaphorical. It's so obvious! Why didn't I notice that before?'

Conventionalization

We 'dial' telephone numbers, even though telephones with dials are now largely a thing of the past.

We can be confident that not so long ago there was a transparent semantic relation between the noun *dial* (designating the numbered circular disc found on telephone receivers) and the verb. The verb designated a process in which the noun entity played a crucial role. (The process of creating verbs from nouns is very common: *pocket* the money, *butter* the toast, *hand* over the money, also, of course, *telephone* a friend.) But as the technology changed, the language did not. *Dial a number* became, and has remained, the conventionalized expression for talking about delivering an instruction to a telephone network. No doubt, future generations of English speakers will still be using the verb *dial* with this meaning, but without any awareness of the word's origin.

What kinds of evidence can we bring to bear in order to find out whether the source domain is indeed relevant to how an expression is understood?

One approach is to ask speakers directly. Gibbs and O'Brien (1990) probed subjects on how they understood various metaphorical idioms, such as *spill the beans*. Subjects were asked to describe the mental images they associated with the expression, and also responded to questions concerning, for example, the likely size of the container from which the beans had been spilled. Subjects' responses were remarkably detailed and consistent. For example, the container was said to be roughly the size of a person's head—suggesting that that is where the (metaphorical) beans (i.e. the confidential information) had been kept. Gibbs and O'Brien found that 'literal' expressions, such as *reveal the information*, failed to elicit mental images of similar richness and specificity.

Spill the beans is a strikingly picturesque idiom. Nowhere in the language, outside of this idiom, is *beans* used in the sense 'confidential information'. (This is another way of saying that the metaphor is unproductive.) Moreover, the 'conceptual distance' (Traugott 1985: 23) between information and legumes probably forces an imagistic construal. The expression wears its metaphorical nature on its sleeve, so to speak. For this reason, one-off metaphors like this are probably untypical of the vast range of ordinary-language metaphors that have been studied within the Lakovian tradition.

A second approach is to consider the linguistic evidence itself. If we find that a metaphorical expression has undergone semantic drift (section 16.3.3)—that is, the expression has acquired nuances that are not predictable from the source domain, or which may even be in conflict with the logic of the source domain—we can infer that the appropriate use of the expression does not depend on activation of the source domain; in fact, appeal to the source domain could be counterproductive, as it could highlight the mismatch between the two domains. Conversely, if we find that a metaphor can be creatively elaborated, by bringing in various aspects from the source domain, we can be confident that the source domain is active in the expression's use.

For an example where the source domain is probably inert, consider the expression *look forward to (an event)*. The expression exploits the very general spatialization of time metaphor—the future lies ahead, in front of us, it is 'visible' to us, and we look 'forward' towards it. Nevertheless, the expression has nuances that are absent from the source domain. We look forward only to pleasant things, or to things that we anticipate will be pleasant. You cannot 'look forward' to events that you anticipate will be unpleasant, even though— in terms of the spatialization of time metaphor—you know that the events are out there, in front of you.[11]

Moreover, the form of the expression is rigidly fixed. The following variations are not possible:

(19) a. I'm looking {forward to / *towards / *at / *in the direction of} meeting you.
      b. *I'm looking directly forward to meeting you.
      c. *I'm looking {in front of me / ahead of me} to meeting you.
      d. * I glanced forward to the happy event.
      e. *Where are you looking forward to?

From this, we can conclude that *look forward to* is a conventionalized metaphor. Although its metaphorical basis can be detected, the expression does not actively construe the anticipation of pleasant events in terms of source domain.

Compare *look forward to* with some of the metaphorical expressions that are emerging in the domain of computer technology. An example is the virus metaphor. The computer virus is conceptualized in terms of (folk medical beliefs about) the biological micro-organism. The computer virus is invisible to the ordinary computer operator, it replicates itself, it infects your hard drive, it destroys your files. Your computer gets a virus through connections with other computers, or through the use of infected disks. You therefore need to be particularly vigilant when your computer is in contact with other computers. The virus has to be destroyed, you need to disinfect your machine, you need a program which acts as an antidote to the virus, in serious cases you call in the virus doctor. The exuberance of the new creations—a reflection, no doubt, of the fact that the source domain maps so well on to the target domain—suggests that our talk about computer viruses is being actively structured by our knowledge and beliefs about the biological organisms.

---

[11] The idea of pleasurable expectation is perhaps contributed by *forward*. The word implies movement towards a desired goal, hence, towards a good (or better) situation. Still, the exact value of *look forward to* is not simply the intersection of the spatialization of time metaphor and the idea of movement towards a goal.

Study questions

1. Take a random sample of 'ordinary' (i.e. non-literary) prose, in English or any other language, and identify the metaphorical expressions. What proportion (roughly) of the text is constituted by metaphorical expressions? Identify the source and target domains of the metaphorical expressions. Assess the metaphors in terms of their degree of conventionalization.

2. Technological innovations are often the site of metaphorical innovation, in two respects. First, aspects of the new technology need to have names; these are often metaphorical extensions of already existing terms. Secondly, as the technology becomes more familiar, the technology itself becomes the source domain for metaphor.

   The major technological innovation of the late twentieth century was the digital computer. We are probably on the threshold of the next technological revolution, in the domains of biology and genetics. Study the language associated with these domains from the two perspectives identified above. You might also look at technological innovations of previous ages, e.g. the automobile, the steam train, television and radio, printing, sea-faring, etc.

3. With the help of a good dictionary, check out the etymologies of Latinate words in English that are used in connection with communication, argumentation, and verbal interaction. Examples include: *retract* a statement, *proffer* a suggestion, *translate* a text, *concur* with a speaker, *announce* a decision, *renounce* a belief, *conclude* a discussion.

   Identify the conceptual metaphors lurking in the etymologies. Are the conceptual metaphors still operative in modern English?

   Traugott (1985: 21) observed that it is sometimes possible to 're-etymologize' a word by the simple device of inserting a hyphen between what once were component morphemes. She cites the examples *re-present*, *dis-close*, *re-search*. What is the effect of this device? Have you come across other examples?

4. Check out the words *tell*, *type*, and *tall* in an etymological dictionary; also study the use of these words in older forms of English (using the *Oxford English Dictionary* as a resource). Are the following uses of these words at all related?

   tell a story, tell the time, a bank teller
   type a letter, type of person
   a tall tree, a tall story, a tall order

5. Talking about time. The following expressions were heard on talk radio. Identify the conceptual metaphor(s) which motivated the expressions. How productive are the metaphors?

   We're coming up to the news.
   These commercial announcements will take us up to the news.
   I must stop now; I've got the news coming up.

We're almost on top of the news.
The news is almost on top of us.
We have a full news bulletin at the top of the hour.
We'll have a news summary at the bottom of the hour.
We'll continue this discussion on the other side of the news.
We're a few minutes out from the news.

6. Understanding the self. Study the following expressions with regard to the way(s) in which the self is conceptualized. (See Lakoff and Johnson 1999: ch. 13; Fauconnier 1997: 25–33.)

   (i)   If I were you, I'd shoot myself.
         If I were you, I'd shoot me.

   (ii) If I were you, what would I think of myself?
         If I were you, what would I think of me?

   (iii) I'm not myself today.
         I couldn't stop myself saying that.
         I have to ask myself, why am I doing this?
         I did it in spite of myself.
         Get in touch with yourself.
         Look at yourself!
         I can hardly recognize myself.

   (iv) I can't keep up with myself
         I can't catch up with myself.

7. The polysemy of *out*. A remarkable feature of English is the large number of what are generally called 'phrasal verbs'. These are combinations of a verb with one, sometimes more than one, preposition-like or adverb-like word. Typically, the verb and particle are both high-frequency items, and the combination has a conventionalized meaning. Consider the following examples with *out*.

The stars came out. / The stars went in.
The light went out. / The light came on.
The secret is out.
find out the answer / work out the solution
It turns out that . . .
write out / spell out / set out / lay out (the details)
give out the papers / hand out the copies / write out the solution
shout out, yell out, / *say out (the answer)
Speak out!
figure out / work out (the solution)
check out the situation
freak out / burst out (in tears)

Is it possible to identify the semantic contributions of *out* in these examples? How can the meanings of *out* be related to the 'basic' spatial meaning of the word? (See Lindner 1981; Morgan 1997).

Further reading

Lakoff and Johnson (1980) is obligatory reading. A précis of Lakoff's approach is Lakoff (1993). For applications of the Lakovian approach to the study of metaphors in literature, see Turner (1987, 1996) and Lakoff and Turner (1989). For philosophical implications, see Johnson (1987). For applications to politics and morality, see Lakoff (1996). For a grand synthesis, see Lakoff and Johnson (1999).

For a devastating critique of *Metaphors We Live By*, see Wierzbicka (1986). Another critique of the Lakovian approach is Jackendoff and Aaron (1991).

There are numerous studies focusing on specific conceptual metaphors, or clusters of metaphors that structure a given domain. See Reddy (1993 [1979]) on the conduit metaphor of communication, Jäkel (1995) on metaphors of the mind, and Kövecses (1986, 1990) on the metaphorical construal of emotions. Matsuki (1995), Taylor and Mbense (1998), and Mikołajczuk (1998) apply Kövecses's methodology to the study of anger in Japanese, Zulu, and Polish, respectively. Geeraerts and Grondelaers (1995) is an important critique of Kövecses's methodology. Dirven (1994) has ingeniously applied Lakoff and Johnson's methodology to another language, Afrikaans. For the virus metaphor, see Fauconnier (1997: ch. 1) and Rohrer (2000). For the role of conceptual metaphor in language change, see Sweetser (1990: ch. 2).

An invaluable collection of papers presenting different perspectives on metaphor is Ortony (1993 [1979]). Collected volumes on more recent Cognitive Linguistic approaches include Gibbs and Steen (1999) and Dirven and Pörings (2002).

CHAPTER 25

Jackendoff and Langacker on 'go'

In this and the next chapter I consider some alternative approaches to metaphor (perhaps I should say: some approaches to phenomena which are often regarded as matters of metaphor). These have put the emphasis, not on the construal of one domain in terms of another, but on cross-domain similarities, and on conceptual schemas that abstract what is common to different domains.

In this chapter I focus specifically on spatial and non-spatial uses of the verb *go*. Jackendoff and Langacker—whose approaches I consider—suggest that non-spatial uses of *go* may not involve metaphor at all. Jackendoff denies that similarities across domains are evidence for conceptual metaphor; he claims, rather, that the similarities reflect abstract conceptual structures that are subject to specification in different domains. While there are severe problems with Jackendoff's summary dismissal of metaphor, the idea of schematic, cross-domain similarities is prominent in Langacker's work. In his analysis of motion verbs, Langacker has focused, not on metaphorical mappings between domains, but on abstract conceptual structures which are schematic for different domains.

25.1 Jackendoff and the 'Thematic Relations Hypothesis'

Jackendoff's work holds a special interest for Cognitive Linguists. Although raised in the Chomskyan tradition, and a major contributor to it, Jackendoff has come to occupy a position that is at odds with the 'syntactocentrism' of mainstream Chomskyan linguistics, and which bears some affinities with the Cognitive Grammar view. On closer examination, however, major differences still remain. Jackendoff's treatment of what he calls 'thematic relations' is a case in point.

An important theme in Jackendoff's work has been some striking analogies between the ways in which different domains are structured (see especially Jackendoff 1983, chs. 9 and 10 and Jackendoff 1990, chs. 1 and 2). Consider the following:

(1)   a. I went from the hotel to the airport.
      b. The inheritance went from George to Philip.
      c. The light went from green to red.

These expressions designate events in three different domains: motion in space, transfer of ownership, and change of state. Yet the same verb, *go*, is used in all three sentences, in association with the same prepositions, *from* and *to*.

Examples like these are prime candidates for a Lakovian analysis. We might say that (1b) and (1c) illustrate that change of ownership and change of state are metaphorically construed in terms of an experientially more basic domain, change of location. Thus, in (1c), the light 'goes' from one metaphorical location (the state of being green) to another metaphorical location (the state of being red). The conceptual metaphors motivating the spatial construals are the following:

(2)   STATES ARE LOCATIONS
      A CHANGE OF STATE IS A CHANGE OF LOCATION

Jackendoff takes a different tack. He captures the similarities across the different kinds of situation by assigning them the very same conceptual structure. Essentially, this involves a function [GO] which maps a [THING] and a [PATH] into an [EVENT]. Jackendoff formalizes this as follows:

(3) $[_{Event}$ GO $([_{Thing}$ x$], [_{Path}$ y$])]$

As Pinker (1989: 177) aptly remarks, Jackendoff's formalism, with its strings of brackets, quickly becomes unreadable once the concepts become internally complex. An expansion of the [PATH] concept is more conveniently represented as in (4). Here, I follow Pinker's proposal and 'translate' Jackendoff's formulas into tree structures (shown opposite).

The three expressions in example (1) differ with respect to the 'semantic field'[1] in which the [GO] event is instantiated. Jackendoff marks the semantic

---

[1]   Jackendoff's 'semantic fields' (Jackendoff 1983: 188) correspond roughly to Cognitive Grammar's 'semantic domains'.

(4)

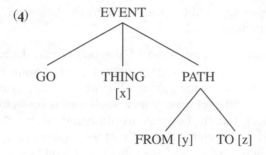

field by means of subscripts. Thus, the function [GO] appears, variously, as [GO$_{Spatial}$], [GO$_{Poss}$], and [GO$_{Ident}$].[2]

Jackendoff claims that a relatively small number of conceptual structures underlie all expressions of state and change, regardless of semantic field. The conceptual structures involve a small number of ontological kinds, such as [THING], [PLACE], [PATH], [EVENT], and [STATE], in association with a small number of functions, such as [BE], [GO], [STAY], and [CAUSE]. This is the essence of the Thematic Relations Hypothesis: 'all [EVENTS] and [STATES] in conceptual structure are organized according to a very limited set of principles' (Jackendoff 1983: 209).

Having discovered this common organization across different domains, Jackendoff considers its broader cognitive basis. One possibility is that it 'reveals widespread systems of metaphor in our language and thought'. Jackendoff dismisses this appeal to metaphor as 'facile':

I think it debases both the theory of thematic relations and the concept of metaphor, for, unlike metaphor, thematic relations are not used for artistic or picturesque effect. Rather, thematic structure is the only means available to organize a semantic field of events and states coherently—it is an indispensable element of everyday thought. Moreover, the most remarkable aspect of metaphor is its variety, the possibility of using practically any semantic field as a metaphor for another. By contrast, thematic relations disclose the same analogy over and over again: time is location, being possessed is a location, properties are locations, events are locations. That is, the theory of thematic relations claims not just that some fields are structured in terms of other fields, but that all fields have essentially the *same* structure. (Jackendoff 1983: 209).

Summing up, he states:

I am inclined to think of thematic structure not as spatial metaphor but as an abstract organization that can be applied with suitable specialization to any field. (Jackendoff 1983: 210)

---

[2] [GO$_{Ident}$] represents the 'identificational field', which has to do with categorization and the ascription of properties (Jackendoff 1983: 194).

Jackendoff, then, is proposing a radical alternative to the Lakovian theory of metaphor. What are we to make of it?

(i) First, it has to be admitted that some of the points that Jackendoff makes hardly count as knock-down arguments against the Lakovian theory. For example, Jackendoff associates metaphor with 'artistic or picturesque effect'. Since examples (1b) and (1c) clearly lack such effect, he would not regard them as metaphorical. Lakoff, however, would maintain that thought and conceptualization are so thoroughly imbued with metaphor that it is not at all surprising that the metaphors of everyday language should lack a picturesque effect. This is not to say that the conceptual metaphors that underlie everyday language cannot also be used for poetic effect. Lakoff and Turner (1989) showed that 'artistic' metaphors elaborate, in sometimes new and surprising ways, the very same conceptual metaphors that underlie everyday 'prosaic' language.

As a matter of fact, it probably is not true that thematic relations, as understood by Jackendoff, cannot be put to 'picturesque' use. Consider the following:

(5) a. The boy threw the ball over the wall.
   b. I put the kettle on the stove.

(6) a. The psychic will think your husband into a new galaxy.
   b. They prayed the boys home again.

The sentences in (5) are examples of what Goldberg (1995) calls the 'caused motion construction'. In (5a), the boy acts on the ball, in a way which causes the ball to change its location and to end up in a place that is 'over the wall'; in (5b), I cause the kettle to change its location, such that the kettle ends up in a place 'on the stove'. The skeletal[3] thematic structure of these sentences might be represented as follows:

(7)

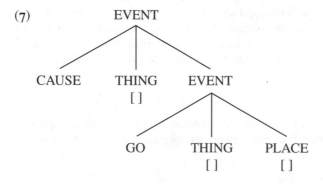

---

[3] The structure in (7) is 'skeletal' in that it ignores the manner in which the motion is caused. For a more detailed and differentiated account of the construction, see Goldberg (1995: ch. 7).

Whereas the examples in (5) are quite ordinary, prosaic expressions, those in (6)—which are adapted from Fauconnier (1997: 184)—do have a certain 'picturesque' quality to them. Notice that the same skeletal structure—(7) underlies these sentences. The [CAUSE] function, however, takes on a different character. In example (5), causation is a matter of direct physical interaction between entities, whereas in (6) we are dealing with 'psychic', or even 'super-natural' causation: a person's thoughts (6a), or prayers (6b), cause a person to change their location, without any direct interaction between the causer and the affected person. Moreover, in (6a), the change of location is presumably to an imagined, not to a real location. Whether one calls it metaphor or not, there is a sense in which the syntactic (and conceptual) schema underlying the expressions in example (5) has been creatively extended to non-typical examples of caused motion.

(ii) Jackendoff notes that all manner of different domains are structured in terms of the same, small number of recurring thematic relations, and suggests that speakers have little choice in this matter. Lakoff makes a similar point. The source domains of locations and spatial relations metaphorically structure a very large number of abstract domains, such as events, states, and change of state; and these latter, it is claimed, can only be understood via metaphor. The metaphor STATES ARE LOCATIONS is ubiquitous.

With respect to possession, however, Jackendoff probably exaggerates the role of location, whether this be understood as a source metaphor or as an abstract element of conceptual structure. To be sure, the notion of location, however it is analysed, is rendered quite prominent by the wording of (1b). It is also true that a person's possessions may often be located (literally) in the vicinity of their owner, sometimes on the person's body (*Watch out! He has a gun!*). On the whole, though, an understanding of possession in terms of location ('my possessions are located at me') would seem to be rather marginal, at least in English. The two most basic means for expressing possession in English are the prenominal possessive construction (*Joe's car*) and the verb *have* (*Joe has a car*). The prenominal construction has little to do with location; rather, as argued in Langacker (1993) and Taylor (1996), the possessor nominal designates a 'reference point entity', which provides conceptual access to the possessee. Langacker (FCG2: 212) proposes a similar analysis for *have*. The many uses of this verb (*The robber had a gun in his hand, Brygida has a new chainsaw, Sally has a dog, We have a lot of skunks around here*) share the property that the verb's tr serves as a reference point for identifying (or establishing mental contact with) the lm. Often, this relation may be overlaid by the notion of the tr's exertion of control over the lm (*He has them in his power*). This latter aspect may be a vestige of the verb's etymology: English *have* is cognate with Latin *capere* 'to grasp'. Although the etymology of *have* is surely lost to modern English speakers, it is interesting to observe the use, especially in British and British-based dialects, of *have got* as a possessive verb (*I've got a car*), where the relation between 'possessing' and 'obtaining' is quite transparent.[4] It is also worth noting that Lakovian analyses often count possession among the experientially more accessible experiential domains, in terms of which others are metaphorically construed, rather than as a domain which is itself metaphorically construed. Part–whole relations (*She has blue eyes*), kinship relations (*She has a daughter*), the relation of experiencer to experienced (*We had a good time*) have been analysed as metaphorizations of possession.[5]

Jackendoff's principal reasons for rejecting the metaphor analysis—the absence of 'picturesque' effects, and the inevitability and omnipresence of certain construals of abstract domains—turn out to be unconvincing. But there are other issues that arise from Jackendoff's approach:

(iii) In searching for cross-domain correspondences, we should not overlook the fact that there appears to exist a great deal of idiosyncrasy at the lexical level. It is true that *go* can be used to designate a change of state in non-spatial domains. Yet there are countless examples where *go* is inappropriate, even though its use might appear to fall under the purview of the conceptual metaphors in example (2) and the conceptual structure in (4). Whereas the examples in (8) are fine, those in (9) are not.

(8) Joe went {mad / crazy / berserk}.
　　Joe went from ecstatic to dejected (and back again) in the space of a few
　　　minutes.
　　The milk went sour.
　　The bread went stale.
　　The meringue went soggy.
　　His face went pale.
　　The lights went {out / (?) on}.
　　The phone went dead.

(9) *Joe went {sane / healthy / unhappy / dejected / ill / dead}.
　　*She went pregnant.
　　*The bread went baked.
　　*The toast went burnt.
　　*The meringue went crisp.
　　*The lights went from on to out (*and back again).
　　*The carpet went {stained / dirty / clean}.
　　*The patient went dead.

The verb *go* cannot be used productively to designate *any* change of state. With respect to the Lakovian theory, we might suppose that the conceptual

---

[4] As discussed extensively by Heine (1997*a*: ch. 5; 1997*b*), other languages exploit different construals of possession. Prominent in Bantu languages, for example, is the notion of possessions as accompaniments. Thus, possession is typically expressed in Zulu by the accompaniment morpheme *na* 'with': *Nginendodana* (= Ngi + na + indodana) 'I have a son', literally 'I with son'.

[5] See e.g. Nikiforidou (1991). For a critique, see Taylor (1996).

metaphors in (2) have been formulated at such a high level of schematicity that they fail to predict the range of possible instantiations (cf. section 24.2.1), and that they therefore need to be supplemented by lower-level metaphors, which do have greater predictive power. At any rate, we would need to look more closely at the specific properties of the English verb *go*, with a view to elucidating those aspects of its semantics that render its use acceptable in (8) but unacceptable in (9). It will be important, in this enterprise, to contrast *go* with other change-of-state verbs in English, such as *come*, *become*, and *turn*.

Turning to Jackendoff's theory: Is the theory of thematic relations threatened by the peculiarities of individual lexical items, such as *go*, *come*, and the others? Probably not.[6] This is because Jackendoff takes conceptual structure to be a level of organization that is independent of syntactic structure. Conceptual structure is an autonomous level of representation that 'interfaces' with an autonomous syntactic level of representation. There is therefore no requirement that elements of conceptual structure correspond directly to lexical or syntactic elements. The function [GO] is not to be equated with the lexical item *go*, and the conceptual structures in (4) and (7) are not supposed to be isomorphic with syntactic structures. In fact, Jackendoff's theory is easily able to tolerate massive discrepancies between an expression's syntactic and lexical form and the form of its supposed conceptual structure. For a case in point, consider the three conceptual structures in (10). Jackendoff (1983: 192) presents these as the conceptual structures of, respectively, *Beth owns the doll*, *Beth lost the doll*, and *Beth received the doll*.[7]

(10) a. $[_{\text{State}} \text{BE}_{\text{Poss}} ([\text{DOLL}], [_{\text{Place}} \text{AT}_{\text{Poss}} ([\text{BETH}])])]$

    b. $[_{\text{Event}} \text{GO}_{\text{Poss}} ([\text{DOLL}], [_{\text{Path}} \text{FROM}_{\text{Poss}} ([\text{BETH}])])]$

    c. $[_{\text{Event}} \text{GO}_{\text{Poss}} ([\text{DOLL}], [_{\text{Path}} \text{TO}_{\text{Poss}} ([\text{BETH}])])]$

Here we touch on a major divergence between Jackendoff's theory and the Cognitive Grammar approach. In Jackendoff's theory, the semantic and phonological levels are mediated by an independent level of syntax; Jackendoff does not postulate a direct symbolic relation between semantic structures and phonological structures. There is therefore no requirement that elements of conceptual structure correspond directly with the semantic pole of the words and morphemes of an expression.

(iv) Finally, an aspect of Jackendoff's methodology needs to be mentioned. Jackendoff postulates the [GO] function and applies it to all manner of change-of-state expressions, but nowhere does he attempt to explain what the

---

[6] Jackendoff (1990: 26) observes that a word such as *go* is 'quite particular about what fields it appears in'. However, as the examples in (8) and (9) show, it is not just a question of *go* being appropriate to certain fields and not to others; even within a given field we encounter some rather specific restrictions. Thus, for change of psychological state, *go* is restricted to occurring with *mad* (and its near synonyms). Moreover, some expressions have specialized semantic values. *The children went hungry* does not simply mean that the children began to feel hungry; the expression implies neglect, or poverty, on the part of the caregivers.

[7] See Casad (1995: 30–1) for a critique of Jackendoff's analysis of these sentences.

semantic content of this function might be. Neither does he explicate the relation between the abstract function [GO] and its domain-specific variants, such as [GO~Spatial~] and [GO~Poss~]. (For reasons mentioned above, we are not even entitled to equate [GO] with the meaning of the verb *go*.) The assumption appears to be that [GO], [CAUSE], [BE], [AT], and the rest of them, are conceptual primitives; as such, they are not in need of further explication.

25.2 Langacker and 'abstract motion'

The discussion in the preceding section was inconclusive. While certain theoretical assumptions of Jackendoff's approach—in particular, the postulation of an autonomous syntactic level—are incompatible with Cognitive Grammar, and while Jackendoff's specific arguments against the Lakovian theory of cross-domain mapping are less than convincing, we have not settled the more general question whether cross-domain similarities are to be explained in terms of metaphorical mapping from one domain (pre-eminently, space) to others, or in terms of conceptual structures that are in a sense domain-independent.

To readers who have become familiar with Cognitive Linguistics through the works of Lakoff and Johnson, it may come as a surprise to learn that metaphor features hardly at all in Langacker's theory. Langacker does not ignore the presence of metaphor in language: see, for example, FCG1: 93–4. But unlike Lakoff and Johnson, he does not see metaphor as the major principle structuring thought and language.[8] Metaphor, for Langacker, is mainly a matter of semantic extension, especially in the case of conventionalized metaphors, specifically, a semantic extension which involves a domain shift (FCG1: 379).

Given this approach, the focus shifts to the abstract conceptual structures that are schematic for domain-specific instantiations. Interestingly, Langacker's position on this matter is closer to Jackendoff's than to Lakoff's. Like Jackendoff, Langacker rejects the suggestion that change-of-state expressions are based on metaphor. Langacker, however, arrives at this view through a careful conceptual analysis of motion and change-of-state expressions. Whereas Jackendoff merely postulates abstract functions such as [GO], and asserts that these become specified when applied to different domains, Langacker is intent on giving explicit characterizations, both of the abstract structures, and of the way they become instantiated in different domains.

I illustrate Langacker's approach on the use of a motion verb, *go*, in a non-motion context:

(11) The milk went sour.

---

[8] Langacker's most extensive discussion of metaphor is in FCG2: 507–14. Here, the focus is not on metaphors *in* language, but metaphors *of* language. Consistent with the Lakoff and Johnson approach, Langacker believes that metaphors of language can profoundly influence linguists' conceptions of the object of study. He draws attention, for example, to the pernicious effects of the building block metaphor in morphology, syntax, and semantics (cf. section 15.1). At the same time, he believes that linguists should be capable of surmounting the potentially misleading entailments of conceptual metaphor.

When considering an expression like (11), Langacker (FCG1: 168) admits that one's first inclination is to appeal to spatial metaphor and to the 'intuitively natural' claim that (11) involves 'the spatial construal of [a] basically non-spatial domain'. This, certainly, would be Lakoff's position. Moreover, on the Lakovian theory, metaphor is *constitutive* of the conceptualization of the target domain (in this case, a change-of-state event).[9] On the Lakovian theory, it will not be possible to conceptualize the milk's change of state without appeal to the spatial metaphor. We should have to say—as Langacker (FCG1: 169) phrases it—that anyone uttering (11) necessarily conceives of the milk as 'transporting itself across a boundary into a spatially interpreted region of sourness, somewhat like a ball rolling out of bounds'. Put like this, the metaphorical construal does sound rather fantastical.

To what extent is the event described in (11) susceptible to a non-spatial conception? Can we conceive of milk becoming sour 'without construing it as moving from one spacelike region to another'? (FCG1: 169). Langacker believes that we can. Indeed, the wording I have just used (with the verb *become*, rather than *go*) has essentially removed the metaphorical flavour from the expression.[10]

But if (11) is not metaphorical in the way that the Lakovian theory would have it, there is still an important sense in which (11) exemplifies a semantic extension of *go* from the spatial to a non-spatial domain. It is not just an arbitrary fact about *go* that it can be used of both motion events (*I went to the airport*) and change of state events (*The milk went sour*); intuitively, we feel that the two uses are related. How can we account for this intuition?

Let us consider more carefully the conceptualization of spatial motion (FCG1: 172). Take the case of a moving entity m. At successive points in time, $t_1, t_2 \ldots t_n$, m occupies locations $l_1, l_2 \ldots l_n$. Using $[m/l_1]t_1$ to designate the location of m at t_1, the movement of m through space and time can be expressed as follows.

(12) $[m/l_1]t_1 > [m/l_2]t_2 > \ldots [m/l_n]t_n$

Let us now bring in a person who conceptualizes the motion of m. The conceptualizer C tracks the motion of m from l_1 to l_n. The conceptualization also occurs in time. Corresponding to each of the stages in (12) is an event in processing time T.

(13) $\begin{bmatrix} [m/l_1]t_1 \\ C \end{bmatrix}T_1 > \begin{bmatrix} [m/l_2]t_2 \\ C \end{bmatrix}T_2 > \ldots \begin{bmatrix} [m/l_n]t_n \\ C \end{bmatrix}T_n$

---

[9] Cf. Lakoff and Johnson (1999: 171): 'Metaphor is, in a sense, constitutive of all event-structure concepts'. Statements to the same effect are to be found scattered throughout the book.

[10] Although there is a morphological relation between the change-of-state verb *become* and the motion verb *come* (the two words in fact share a common ancestor), the relatedness exists only at the phonological level, not at the semantic level.

If a person observes the motion of m as it occurs, event time t (or, as Langacker calls it, **conceived time**) will coincide with **processing time** T (give or take a few milliseconds for the neurological transmission of the visual percept). But if a person recalls the motion, or imagines it, the two do not coincide, even though they are presumably coordinated, in the sense that both t_1 and T_1 precede t_2 and T_2, and so on. As we recall the trajectory of a thrown ball, the time taken to imagine the trajectory (in processing time, T) could well be more compressed than conceived time, t; moreover, processing time T is displaced *vis-à-vis* the conceived time of the event, t.

It is easy to see how the formula in (13) enables us to recognize the commonality between change of location and change of state. All we need do to capture a change of state is to give l a different value. Instead of m being in a series of locations, m is in a series of states, instantiated through conceived time. In the case of a light getting brighter, $l_1, l_2 \ldots l_n$ would represent differing degrees of luminosity; in the case of milk going sour, $l_1, l_2 \ldots l_n$ would represent differing degrees of freshness (or, conversely, sourness).

If we make this slight modification to (13), it is apparent that the formula becomes so general as to be applicable, not just to change of location, but to change of any kind. The upshot is that change of location is but a specific instance of change of state. We have effectively replaced the metaphor A CHANGE OF STATE IS A CHANGE OF LOCATION with a schematic notion of change which can be instantiated in different domains (location, luminosity, sourness, etc.), while the verb *go* emerges as a very general predicate which designates precisely this abstract concept (albeit subject to numerous idiosyncrasies, as mentioned earlier). We might still want to say that change of location is the perceptually and experientially most accessible and most salient manifestation of change, and that *go* prototypically, or basically designates spatial motion. This fact probably lies behind the intuition that non-spatial *go* represents an extension of spatial *go*. The experience of spatial motion provides the input prototype for the emergence of a more schematic notion, whose instantiations can be perceived as extensions from the prototype.

I next want to look at two further ramifications of Langacker's analysis of 'abstract motion'. In both cases, the distinctive uses of *go* derive, not from metaphorical extension of a basic motion sense, but from the abstract characterization of motion/change in (13).

25.2.1 'Stative' *go*

Consider the following uses of *go*.

(14) a. Highway 36 goes from Denver to Indianapolis. (Jackendoff 1983: 173)
    b. There's a fence going from one end of his property to the other.

Although *go* is basically a motion verb, no actual motion is involved in (14). The highway and the fence are elongated objects which remain in a steady-state location. Metaphor is not involved, either; the sentences in (14) designate spatial configurations, so it is not the case that spatial notions are being mapped on to a non-spatial domain. The problem is to account for the fact that a basically change-of-state verb can come to designate a steady-state situation.

Even though the examples in (14) designate a static situation, the idea of motion is not completely lacking. The motion, however, comes, not from the object of conceptualization (the highway, the fence), but from the manner in which it is conceptualized. It is as if the conceptualizer scans the highway from one end to the other, gradually building up a profile of its overall configuration.

In this connection, Langacker makes a distinction between **sequential scanning** and **summary scanning**. Sequential scanning is represented in example (13); the conceptualizer C tracks the changing state of m through processing time. In summary scanning, it is as if each new location of m is added to the previous location, thus building up a complex profile consisting of the simultaneous activation of its component states (Fig. 25.1). It is as if the road 'lengthens' at its leading edge, until the full conception of the road as an elongated object is built up. The examples in (14) designate the final configuration, but at the same time invoke the manner in which it was achieved. Note that the final configuration can be built up in alternative ways. The highway from Denver to Indianapolis is the very same entity as the highway from Indianapolis to Denver. What differs is the manner in which the conceptualizer, C, builds up the conception of the highway in processing time, T.

Langacker's notions of sequential and summary scanning have attracted criticism. Francis (2000: 100), for example, refers to sequential and summary

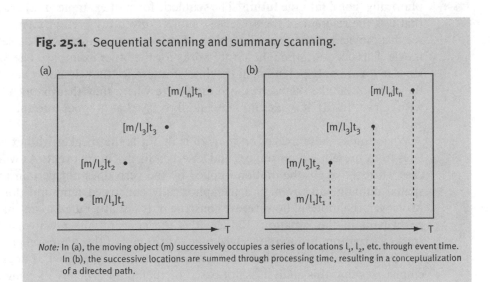

Fig. 25.1. Sequential scanning and summary scanning.

(a)

$[m/l_n]t_n$ •

$[m/l_3]t_3$ •

$[m/l_2]t_2$ •

• $[m/l_1]t_1$

→ T

(b)

$[m/l_n]t_n$ •

$[m/l_3]t_3$ •

$[m/l_2]t_2$ •

• m/l_1t_1

→ T

Note: In (a), the moving object (m) successively occupies a series of locations l_1, l_2, etc. through event time. In (b), the successive locations are summed through processing time, resulting in a conceptualization of a directed path.

scanning as 'highly esoteric concepts for which there could be no counter-examples'. I leave it to the reader to choose between Langacker's attempts to grapple with the conceptual structure of (14) and Jackendoff's treatment of the very same phenomenon. Jackendoff (1983: 173) simply proposes an extensional variant of the [GO] function, namely [GO$_{Ext}$]; unlike other [GO] functions, which map on to [EVENT], this one happens to map on to the ontological category [STATE]. Thus, the expressions in (14) are ascribed the following conceptual structure:

(15) [$_{State}$ GO$_{Ext}$ ([$_{Thing}$ x], [$_{Path}$ y])]

Jackendoff, it seems to me, has simply described the semantic extension of *go*, he has not explained the extension.

25.2.2 'Future' *go*

A further use of *go* is in expressions of future time:

(16) a. I'm going to see that movie tonight.
      b. Be careful, you're going to fall.
      c. Problems are going to arise.
      d. It's going to rain soon.

In considering these examples, one's first inclination, again, might be to appeal to metaphorical mapping, in this case, from the spatial to the temporal domain. Times are locations; the present 'goes' into the future; future events are locations that one 'goes' to.

   However, if one thinks carefully about this account, and follows through the mapping relations, a severe problem emerges. What, precisely, is it that metaphorically 'goes' into the future? The syntactic form of example (16a) suggests that it is the referent of the sentence's subject; given my present intention to see that movie, I metaphorically 'go' to a future situation in which I do see the movie. This account, though, hardly works for the other examples. The 'problems' in (c) are only potential; at the time of utterance they do not yet exist, so they cannot betake themselves into the future where they then happen. And with respect to (d), it makes no sense at all to say that 'it' goes into the future and rains.

   What unifies these uses of *be going to* is that it is the speaker who extrapolates from present circumstances and asserts a likely future event. As was the case with stative *go*, the motion implied by the verb does not pertain to the spatial domain, nor even to a metaphorically construed temporal domain. Moreover, the motion, however we construe it, is not attributed to any named participant in the situation. Rather, it is the conceptualizer who mentally tracks a situation through conceived time. At the end of this temporal path lies the event or situation whose future occurrence is predicted. Langacker emphasizes that this analysis is not based on metaphor. The use of *going to* in a future sense exemplifies, not metaphor, but the process of subjectification (section 20.3.1). The motion ascribed to the tr in an objectively construed motion event (as in *Louise goes to the store*) becomes an aspect of the ground from which a situation is conceptualized:

there is no transfer from the spatial to the temporal domain. . . . It is specifically *not* claimed that the subject of *be going to* is metaphorically construed as moving along a temporal path (analogous to a spatial path)—only the conceptualizer is claimed to move along a temporal path, mentally and subjectively. (Langacker 1999: 394)

Study questions

1. There is a long tradition in Western philosophy, going back to Plato, of presenting controversial issues in the form of an imaginary dialogue between opposing parties. For a modern example, see Geeraerts (1999).

   Write a dialogue between two linguists arguing over the question whether *Joe went mad* is an instance of metaphor or not.

2. In this chapter I cited some acceptable and some impossible uses of *go* as a change-of-state verb. Here are some more examples, which also bring in the contrast between *come* and *go*.

   The project {came / *went} to nothing.
   The project {went / *came} wrong.
   The whole office {came / went} down with flu.
   The lights went out, and then suddenly came on again.
   The soup {came / *went} to the boil.
   He {went / *came} insane.

   Find more examples of change-of-state uses of *come* and *go*. (In order not to complicate matters excessively, steer clear of idiomatic combinations of the verbs with prepositions and particles, such as *go on* 'continue', *come off* 'succeed'). You should be able easily to come (!) up with several dozen.

   (a) Try to account for the usage range of *come* and *go*. Can these be related in any way to the 'basic' spatial uses of the verbs? (This latter topic is actually quite complex; see Fillmore 1997 for a discussion of the 'basic' uses of the verbs.)

       In cases where both verbs are appropriate, is there still a difference in meaning? Is there a difference between *The temperature has gone down* and *The temperature has come down*?

   (b) *Bring* and *take* can be regarded as the causative counterparts of *go* and *come*. If you 'bring something to me' you 'cause it to come to me', if you 'take something away from me' you 'cause it to go away from me'. Corresponding to *The soup came to the boil* we can have a causative, *The cook brought the soup to the boil*. We cannot, however, say that the cook 'took the soup to the boil', for the same reason, presumably, that we cannot say that the soup 'went to the boil'.

Construct causative wordings of your sentences with *come* and *go*. Is there in general a correspondence between *go/take* and *come/bring*? Are there cases in which *bring/take* fail to correspond to *come/go*? How might these be accounted for?

(c) Another motion verb, *turn*, can also be used to designate a change of state: *The milk turned sour*, *He turned pale*. The verb can be used both as an intransitive and a causative: *The milk turned sour*, *The warm weather turned the milk sour*. In general, though, *turn* is more restricted in its change-of-state sense than *come* and *go*.

Collect examples of change-of-state *turn*. Does *turn* have a special value in contrast to *go/come*?

(d) The rather special values of the English motion verbs become evident when cross-language comparisons are made, e.g. between English *go* and French *aller*, German *gehen*, and Dutch *gaan*. Undertake a contrastive analysis between motions verbs in different languages.

3. *Be going to*. This way of referring to future events is associated with different semantic nuances. Sometimes, an expression is open to different interpretations. *She's going to have another baby* could mean (i) she is visibly pregnant, or (ii) she intends to have another child (though she may not yet be pregnant). These uses may be characterized as (i) a prediction based on what is presently observable, and (ii) a prediction based on the intention of the subject referent.

How are these two uses related? How do they derive, via subjectification, from the motion sense of *go*?

Further reading

For abstract motion, see Langacker (1986; FCG1: 166–82; 1999: ch. 10) and Talmy (1996). On the verbs *come* and *go*, see Fillmore's *Lectures on Deixis* (1997, esp. pp. 77–102) and Radden (1996).

CHAPTER 26

Alternatives to metaphor

In this chapter I consider some themes in Cognitive Linguistics which, independently of their inherent interest, offer alternative ways of approaching metaphor (or, rather, phenomena which the Lakovian theory takes to involve metaphor). The fact that a linguistic expression can be used of both an abstract and a concrete domain does not entail that the one is construed metaphorically in terms of the other. It is conceivable that both are structured in terms of a schematic conceptualization that abstracts what is common to the two domains. Langacker's theory of 'abstract motion', presented in the last chapter, is an example of how domain-specific conceptualizations may be derived from a more schematic understanding of change. Johnson's 'image schemas' and Talmy's 'imaging systems'—to be discussed in this chapter—can also be understood in this way. Also of significance to our topic is Fauconnier and Turner's theory of 'conceptual blending', a theory which incorporates aspects of both the domain-mapping and the cross-domain similarity approaches, and which, moreover, has applications outside the study of metaphor, and even outside the study of semantic structures.

26.1 Image schemas

A considerable amount of work in the Cognitive Linguistics tradition is quite compatible with the view that cross-domain similarities are due, not to metaphorical mapping from a concrete to an abstract domain, but to the instantiation of abstract structures in a range of more specific domains. In this section, I consider the case of 'image schemas'.

Mark Johnson, who appears to have invented the term, characterizes an image schema as 'a recurring, dynamic pattern of our perceptual interactions and motor programs that gives coherence to our experience' (Johnson 1987: xiv). A little later, he expands on this definition as follows:

human bodily movement, manipulation of objects, and perceptual interactions involve recurring patterns without which our experience would be chaotic and incomprehensible. I call these patterns 'image schemata', because they function primarily as abstract structures of images. (Johnson 1987: xix)

As the name suggests, image schemas are 'imagistic', that is, they are representations of kinetic and perceptual experiences. As such, they are 'non-propositional' (Johnson 1987: 29). At the same time they are 'schematic', that is, they are not restricted to any particular activity or perception. Johnson emphasizes the abstractness of image schemas *vis-à-vis* the richness of visual and kinetic images; image schemas lack 'the specificity of rich images or mental pictures', they are at a 'level of generality and abstractness above concrete, rich images' (p. 29). In virtue of their abstractness, or schematicity, it becomes possible for 'indefinitely many perceptions, images, and events' to be structured in analogous ways.

The above characterization of image schemas may strike the reader as irritatingly vague. Precisely because image schemas are, well, schematic, and also non-propositional, it is not surprising that it is difficult to define them in a concise and concrete manner. A common strategy has been to explain the notion by way of examples. Following this strategy, let us look at how Gibbs and Colston illustrate the image schema BALANCE. The following passage is based on the discussion of the BALANCE schema in Johnson (1987: 73–5).[1]

We can illustrate what is meant by the notion of image schema, and how its internal structure is projected onto new domain [*sic*: presumably, *domains* is meant, JRT] via metaphor, by considering the BALANCE schema. . . . The idea of balance is something that is learned 'with our bodies and not by grasping a set of rules' (Johnson 1987: 74). Balancing is such a pervasive part of our bodily experience that we are seldom aware of its presence in everyday life. We come to know the meaning of balance through the closely related experiences of bodily equilibrium or loss of equilibrium. For example, a baby stands, wobbles, and drops to the floor. It tries again and again, as it learns how to maintain a balanced erect posture. A young boy struggles to stay up on a two-wheeled bicycle as he learns to keep his balance while riding down the street. Each of us has experienced occasions when we have too much acid in our stomachs, when our hands get cold, our heads feel too hot, our bladders feel

[1] 'Based on' is too generous an expression. The quoted passage in fact is largely a collage of statements and examples taken from Johnson's discussion of the BALANCE schema in Johnson (1987: 73–5).

Image schemas

Johnson (1987: 126) gives the following selective list of image schemas. The list, he claims, contains 'most of the more important'. (By convention, the names of image schemas are written in small capitals.)

CONTAINER	BALANCE	COMPULSION
BLOCKAGE	COUNTERFORCE	RESTRAINT REMOVAL
ENABLEMENT	ATTRACTION	MASS–COUNT
PATH	LINK	CENTRE–PERIPHERY
CYCLE	NEAR–FAR	SCALE
PART–WHOLE	MERGING	SPLITTING
FULL–EMPTY	MATCHING	SUPERIMPOSITION
ITERATION	CONTACT	PROCESS
SURFACE	OBJECT	COLLECTION

The reader will note, in this list, some notions that have been introduced in other chapters of this book, such as the count–mass distinction, iteration, and notions of an object and a process.

distended, our sinuses become swollen, and our mouths feel dry. In these and numerous other ways we learn the meanings of lack of balance or equilibrium. We respond to imbalance and disequilibrium by warming our hands, giving moisture to our mouths, draining our bladders, and so forth until we feel balanced again. Our BALANCE image schema emerges, then, through our experiences of bodily equilibiums and disequilibriums and of maintaining our bodily systems and functions in states of equilibrium. We refer to these recurring bodily experiences as *image schemas* to emphasize means of structuring particular experiences schematically so that we can give order and connectedness to our perceptions and conceptions. (Gibbs and Colston 1995: 349–50)

According to this account, the notion of balance emerges, primarily, through our experience of maintaining an upright posture. The balancing experience involves a 'point or axis around which forces and weights must be distributed so that they counteract or balance off one another' (p. 350). The notion then gets extended to other domains, such as bodily systems, psychological states (*a balanced personality*), judgements (*a balanced opinion*), financial situations (*a balanced budget*), artistic composition, power relations (*a balance of power*), and several more. Thus, a *balanced opinion* is one which establishes an equilibrium between opposing views, 'weighing' one set of views against the other. In this way, the primarily kinetic notion of balance comes to structure a large number of abstract domains.

A question of interest is whether the construal of non-physical domains in terms of balance (as when we speak of a 'balanced judgement', a 'balanced personality', or a 'balanced diet') is a case of metaphorical mapping from the domain of kinetic experience, or whether it represents domain-specific elaborations of a schematic notion, neutral with respect to the domains in which it is elaborated. Gibbs and Colston fail to adequately distinguish the two possibilities:

The same image schema can be instantiated in many different kinds of domains because the internal structure of a single schema can be metaphorically understood. (p. 350)

A little later, referring to the many uses of the word *balance* in English, they state:

we use the same word for all these domains because they are structurally related by the same sort of underlying image schemas, and are metaphorically elaborated from them (p. 350).

Strictly speaking, Gibbs and Colston are guilty of a confusion of categories. The elaboration of a schema is *not* a process of metaphorical understanding. The fact that the concept [OAK TREE] elaborates the more schematic concept [TREE] does not mean that oak trees are metaphorically understood as trees. Metaphorical extension does, however, presuppose the recognition of similarities, or correspondences, between the source and the target domains. The similarities can themselves become the content of a more abstract representation that is schematic for both source and target. We can elucidate this situation in terms of the 'categorization triangle', introduced in Chapter 7. (See Fig. 26.1.)

The prototype constitutes the 'input' into the triangle. In the case of balance, the prototype is direct physical experience of maintaining an upright posture, as when walking, riding a bicycle, standing on one leg, standing upright while carrying a heavy weight in one hand, staying upright in a gusty wind, and so on. The similarities between these experiences allow the

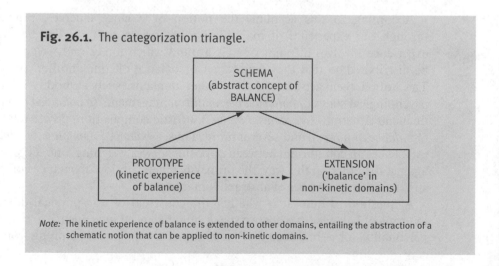

Fig. 26.1. The categorization triangle.

Note: The kinetic experience of balance is extended to other domains, entailing the abstraction of a schematic notion that can be applied to non-kinetic domains.

formation of a schematic representation, that unifies the different experiences as instances of the same concept. Then, as the notion of balance is extended (metaphorically) to non-physical domains, there simultaneously emerges an even more schematic representation, which in turn allows the concept to be applied to an ever greater variety of different domains. Assuming that the experiential source of the BALANCE schema remains salient, we can reconcile the status of image schemas as both schematic (i.e. domain independent) and experiential (based in bodily experience) concepts.

Importantly—and this is what I take to be the core of the image schema notion—certain structural properties of the image schema are preserved across all its domain-specific instantiations. BALANCE is not just (or not intrinsically) a matter of remaining upright, it involves the distribution of 'weights', or 'forces', around a central 'axis'—whereby the notions of 'weight', 'force', and 'axis' are themselves understood abstractly (or perhaps I should say, 'image-schematically'). We understand the notion of a balanced diet in such terms: certain kinds of foods are opposed to other kinds, and the consumption of the one kind has to be offset by the intake of the other kind. The kinetic experience of remaining upright is, I think, irrelevant in this case.[2]

26.2 Talmy and 'force dynamics'

A central theme in Talmy's work over the past decades has been the elucidation of general conceptual principles that structure many different domains. Talmy refers to these as 'imaging systems' (1983: 253). One such imaging system is responsible for the distinction between figure and ground. Although primarily a matter of selective attention in visual perception, the notions are readily extended to differences in conceptual salience generally. Indeed, the distinction—crucial in Cognitive Grammar—between trajector and land-mark is one manifestation of the figure–ground distinction. As will have been apparent from the discussion in Chapters 10 and 11, the tr-lm asymmetry is a highly schematic notion, not restricted to any specific domain; neither is it reasonably regarded as involving metaphor.

---

[2] Gibbs and Colston, in the passage cited above (pp. 520–1), as well as Johnson (1987: 75), illustrate the notion of the BALANCE image schema by reference to, among other things, our experience of a distended bladder. I do not think that the example is appropriate. It suggests (wrongly, I believe) that BALANCE has to do with feeling at ease, with the avoidance of extremes, and with the return to normalcy after an extreme has been experienced. But the essence of the BALANCE image schema surely resides in the notion of opposing weights or forces; metaphorically (image-schematically) speaking, more on this side has to be offset by more on that side. But what might counterpoise a distended bladder? A contracted bladder, presumably. This does not make sense. Phenomenologically, I experience a distended bladder as a desire to go and urinate; I have no idea what a contracted bladder might feel like, nor how this feeling would counterbalance the feeling of a distended bladder, such that I may arrive at a balanced situation in which my bladder is neither distended nor contracted.

Perhaps, in this case, we need to recognize two distinct image schemas, one of BALANCE, the other of BEING AT EASE.

One of Talmy's major achievements is to have identified, as a ubiquitous structuring principle in language and thought, the system of force dynamics (Talmy 1988). Before discussing the notion, let us first consider a problem that Jackendoff raised on the opening page of his *Semantics and Cognition* (1983). How can we explain the fact that one and the same verb, *keep*, can be used of so many different kinds of situation? Here are a few examples of the verb's use:

(1) a. I kept the book on the shelf.
    b. Keep off the grass!
    c I kept the book.
    d. He kept the crowd happy.
    e. I kept Bill working.
    f. Keep working!
    g. Let's keep the trip on Tuesday.

Jackendoff's approach appeals to functions such as [BE] and [STAY]. I have already commented on the problematic nature of Jackendoff's conceptual structures, and will say no more about his approach here.[3] Alternatively, we might consider an account in terms of metaphorical mapping. Once again, we can call on the ubiquitous STATES ARE LOCATIONS metaphor. The first two examples in (1) have to do with an entity remaining in a spatial location ('on the shelf', 'off the grass'). If we regard emotional states as (metaphorical) locations, we can easily see the metaphorical mapping that underlies (1d); the crowd is to remain in a (metaphorically construed) location.

(I leave it to the reader to work out the details of the metaphorical mappings in the other examples in (1). In pursuing this exercise, note, with respect to (e) and (f), that activities (such as 'working') might be construed as states/ locations, while (g) suggests a spatial construal of times. One also needs to pay attention to the syntactic form of the sentences. There is a syntactic parallelism between (a), (d), (e), and (g) on the one hand, and between (b) and (f) on the other. We should expect the two groups of sentences to differ systematically in their semantic structure, too. In terms of its syntactic structure, however, (c) differs from both sets.)

While an appeal to spatial metaphor certainly brings some order to the superficially rather diverse uses of *keep* in example (1), an important element is missing from such an account. Although (1a) has to do with the spatial location of the book, there is more to the sentence than just the book's location. To say that I 'kept the book on the shelf' suggests that I resisted an inclination to put the book somewhere else. In other words, the sentence contains a prominent force-dynamic component. In fact, a force-dynamic content

---

[3] The interested reader can refer to Jackendoff (1983); for a more elaborated account, which coerces Talmy's theory into a formalism of Jackendoff's invention, see Jackendoff (1990: 130–51).

is a unifying feature of all the uses of *keep* in (1), and it is arguably this aspect, as much as spatial metaphor, that motivates the diverse uses of the verb.

Force dynamics has to do with the way in which entities interact in dynamic situations. Minimally, two entities are involved, which Talmy (1988) refers to as the Agonist and the Antagonist.[4] Our focus goes mainly on the behaviour of the Agonist in relation to the Antagonist. (The Agonist is therefore the trajector of the relation between the entities.) The Agonist has a natural disposition towards either rest (or inaction) or motion (i.e. change). The Antagonist is able to exert a force on the Agonist. The force may overcome the natural disposition of the Agonist; alternatively, the Agonist resists the force of the Antagonist.

In the simplest case, Agonist and Antagonist are in a steady-state relationship. There are four basic possibilities, illustrated below:

(2) a. The ball kept rolling because of the wind blowing on it.
         (The wind overcomes the ball's natural disposition towards rest)
     b. The log kept lying on the incline because of the ridge there.
         (The ridge overcomes the log's natural disposition towards motion)
     c. The shed kept standing despite the wind blowing against it.
         (The wind fails to overcome the shed's disposition towards rest)
     d. The ball kept rolling despite the stiff grass.
         (The grass fails to overcome the ball's natural disposition towards motion)

More complex effects arise if (a) the Antagonist begins to impinge on the Agonist, (b) the Antagonist disengages from acting on the Agonist, or (c) the Antagonist fails to impinge on the Agonist. Representative examples are as follows:

(3) a. The ball's hitting it made the lamp topple from the table.
         (The ball comes to impinge on the lamp, overcoming its natural disposition towards rest)
     b. The plug's coming loose let the water flow from the tank.
         (The plug disengages from its blocking location)
     c. The fan's being broken let the smoke hang still in the chamber.
         (Because of its broken state, the fan is not able to exert a force on the smoke)

The above sentences are from Talmy. Their somewhat unusual expression reflects Talmy's attempt to represent the force dynamic relations in their purest form. In more idiomatic usage, the Antagonist may not be mentioned, its identity being inferred from the context (*The shed kept standing*). Alternatively, there may be mention of a human agent who brings about the

---

[4] The terms are taken from physiology. An agonist is a muscle whose action is opposed by another muscle, the antagonist.

force-dynamic interaction, a possibility which adds an extra layer of force-dynamic interaction, and which allows a variety of syntactic constructions (*I let the water out of the tank by loosening the plug*; *I loosened the plug so that the water could flow out*, and such like). Nevertheless, even from these few examples, we are able to appreciate that the meanings of quite a few lexical items, such as *make*, *let*, *keep*, and *despite*, are inextricably linked to force-dynamic concepts. Thus, *X lets Y VP* construes *X* as a more powerful Agonist which fails to engage the Antagonist; *X VP despite Y* construes *Y* as the Antagonist whose force fails to overcome the natural disposition of the Agonist *X*.

Further predicates with a force-dynamic content are the verbs *prevent*, *stop*, *force*, *enable*, *stay*, *remain*, *hold*, and *manage*, Thus, (4a) suggests that the Agonist (i.e. the speaker) exerted increasing force on the Antagonist (the door), until such time as the Antagonist's natural disposition towards rest was overcome. A similar force-dynamic interpretation applies to (4b), and is contributed by the adverbial *finally*.

(4) a. I managed to open the door.
     b. The door finally opened.

Especially interesting, in view of my introductory remarks to this section, is the verb *keep*. *Keep* indicates the continuation of a steady state, whether this be through the superior force of the Antagonist or of the Agonist. Compare the following:

(5) a. The ball rolled along the green.
     b. The ball kept rolling along the green.

In terms of the objective, observable properties of the situation which they describe, these two sentences are indistinguishable; if the one can be truthfully applied to a situation, so can the other. The sentences are not, however, synonymous; what distinguishes (5b) is its force-dynamic content. There are two ways in which this can be construed. The continued rolling of the ball could be due to the ongoing application of force from an unnamed Antagonist (such as the wind) which overcomes the ball's natural tendency towards rest. Alternatively, an unnamed Antagonist (such as the stiff grass) fails to counteract the inherent tendency of the ball towards motion.

It is easy to see how force-dynamic interactions apply to domains other than the physical. The following have to do with social or interpersonal interactions. In (6a) the Agonist opts not to counteract my natural inclination to leave, while in (6b) the Agonist does counteract my natural inclination not to wait.

(6) a. They let me leave early.
     b. They kept me waiting.

Force-dynamic interactions also apply to the 'divided self'. These involve a force-dynamic conflict between two aspects of a person's psyche.[5]

(7) a. I kept myself from responding in kind.
    b. He forced himself to respond.
    c. She responded in spite of her better judgement.

Not to be overlooked is the force-dynamic content of modal expressions of possibility and necessity, whether in the psychosocial domain (8) or the epistemic domain (9).

(8) a. I can't leave. (An unnamed Antagonist overcomes my disposition to leave)[6]
    b. I had to leave. (An unnamed Antagonist overcomes my disposition to stay)

(9) a. That can't be true. (The force of reason overcomes a fact's appearance of being true)
    b That has to be true. (The force of reason overcomes a fact's appearance of being false)

Although force-dynamic notions are most easily illustrated on examples of interactions between concrete entities, the notions readily generalize, as we have seen, to other domains, such as interpersonal relations, psychological processes, and modal expressions of necessity and possibility. I think it would be wrong to claim that these latter domains are understood by a metaphorical mapping from force-dynamic interactions of concrete objects. As with Johnson's image schemas, force-dynamic relations have to do with schematic patterns of interaction, which can be instantiated in many different domains.[7] In fact, force-dynamic interactions (notions of letting, making, keeping, preventing, and so on) could themselves be reasonably counted as image schemas.

Force-dynamic effects are ubiquitous in language; the above discussion has only scratched the tip of the iceberg. Even from this brief presentation, however, it should be clear that force-dynamic concepts offer themselves, if not as an alternative to the theory of metaphorical mapping, then as a valuable supplement to it, by putting the spotlight on conceptual notions that are not specific to any particular domain. To return to the example which introduced this section: the wide range of uses of the verb *keep* are better unified by an

---

[5] As Talmy (1988) observes, the Freudian concepts of the Id, Ego, and Superego lend themselves rather naturally to a force-dynamic interpretation of the divided self.

[6] The unnamed Antagonist can be anything from a person issuing a specific instruction, a legal proscription, moral or ethical considerations, or a physical impediment (such as a broken leg or a locked door).

[7] While Talmy (1988: 50) does mention the possibility of 'metaphorical extension' from 'physical force interaction' to the psychological and social domains, his general stance is that force dynamics constitutes a 'fundamental notional system' which structures conceptual material across a range of conceptual domains.

appeal to force dynamic concepts than in terms of metaphorical mapping from a spatial domain.

Force dynamics and naive physics

Where do force dynamic concepts come from?

Johnson (1987) argued that image schemas emerge from bodily experiences and perceptions. It is plausible that force-dynamic concepts have a similar origin, for example in our experience of things colliding into each other (and of ourselves colliding into things).

The source of force-dynamic conceptions may lie deeper than this. Talmy (1988) draws attention to some analogies between force-dynamic concepts and certain notions of 'naive physics' (pp. 91–4), the latter contrasting sharply with concepts of scientific physics. For example, the idea that objects have an 'inherent' tendency towards rest or motion makes no sense in a scientific theory of mechanics; a ball rolls, or fails to roll, through an interaction of many forces, it is not an inherent property of the ball. Moreover, we conceptualize force-dynamic interactions in terms of a figure–ground contrast; we focus on what happens to a 'privileged' entity, the Agonist. On a strictly scientific account of mechanics, there are no privileged entities.

26.3 Metaphors without mapping: Glucksberg and Keysar (1993)

In this panorama of alternative approaches to metaphor, I would like to mention the views of the psychologists Glucksberg and Keysar, and relate them to some central constructs of Cognitive Grammar.

John Searle asked: 'Why do we use expressions metaphorically instead of saying exactly and literally what we mean?' (1993: 83). Lakoff's answer would be that we have no choice but to speak metaphorically, since thought is intrinsically metaphorical. Glucksberg and Keysar (1993) argue that Searle misstated the problem. Even when speaking metaphorically, people *do* say exactly and literally what they mean.

This looks like a major paradox. If someone utters example (10) with reference to a person called Sam, surely they cannot literally mean that Sam is a pig. How can Glucksberg and Keysar claim that the sentence—on its 'metaphorical' reading—is 'literally' true?

(10) Sam is a pig.

Glucksberg and Keysar's position is indeed paradoxical on a theory of metaphor which involves mapping from a source to a target domain. Assuming such a theory with respect to (10), elements of a source domain ('animals', or 'animal characteristics') are mapped on to a target domain ('humans', or 'human characteristics'); the mapping relation might be brought under a more general conceptual metaphor PEOPLE ARE ANIMALS. On such a theory, (10) has to be false with respect to its source domain—Sam is not 'literally' a pig. He is a pig only if 'pig' is metaphorically mapped into the domain of humans.

Glucksberg and Keysar do not appeal to metaphorical mapping. Instead they claim that a metaphorically used word temporally sets up a superordinate category which has, among its instances, both the 'literal' and 'metaphorical' senses of the word. Thus, example (10) invites the hearer to create a category that is schematic for (real) pigs and dirty, greedy, and uncouth persons. The category is named by reference to its prototypical exemplar, namely, a pig. The assertion that Sam is a member of this category is then 'literally' true. The metaphorical flavour of the expression results from the fact that members of the category—pigs and persons—feature in different domains.

Take another set of examples:

(11) a. Mary's marriage became a jail.
    b. She's imprisoned in her marriage.
    c. By marrying Jim, Alice sentenced herself to a long prison term.

On the Lakovian theory, these are elaborations of the familiar STATES ARE LOCATIONS metaphor. A marriage is not 'literally' a jail; it is a jail only on the metaphorical reading. Glucksberg and Keysar, however, maintain that the sentences in (11) set up a category that comprises 'real' jails and (certain) marriages. This new category is schematic for 'any involuntary, unpleasant, confining, punishing, unrewarding situation' (p. 414); jails and (certain) marriages are instances of this category. Again, the superordinate category is referred to by naming its prototypical instance, namely, a jail. The assertion that a marriage 'became a jail' can be 'literally' true.

Not surprisingly, Lakoff (1993: 236) gives Glucksberg and Keysar's theory short shrift. Nevertheless, their theory meshes neatly with some fundamental constructs of Cognitive Grammar. Recall again the categorization triangle. The recognition of similarity between entities entails the abstraction of a schema which represents those aspects in terms of which the entities are perceived to be similar. The jail example is represented in such terms in Figure 26.2 (p. 530).

In the case of a novel metaphor, the superordinate category may be a one-off creation; the metaphorical expression invites the hearer to create such a category.[8] Many metaphors, though, are conventionalized. It is significant that the COBUILD dictionary lists two senses of *imprison*: one involves being locked up in a prison, the other has to do with 'a condition or situation that . . . restricts your freedom or restrains you in some other way'. The first sense

---

[8] The creation of *ad hoc* superordinate categories need not be problematic, and is by no means restricted to the understanding of metaphors. Barsalou (1983, 1987) has extensively studied people's ability to create and understand *ad hoc* categories, and to assign members to them. Among the categories that Barsalou investigated have been 'things to eat on a diet' and 'times to go on vacations'.

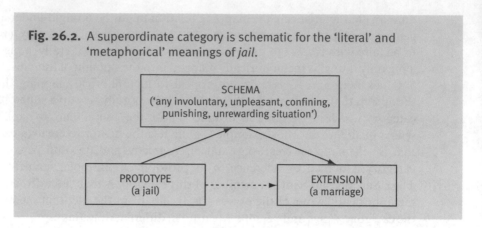

Fig. 26.2. A superordinate category is schematic for the 'literal' and 'metaphorical' meanings of *jail*.

is a particularized instance of the second, which might count as the superordinate category that is set up in order to accommodate both 'literal' and 'metaphorical' uses of the word.

26.4 Conceptual blending: Fauconnier and Turner (1998)

I have already referred in several places in this book to Fauconnier's theory of mental spaces. Recent developments of the theory offer yet another approach to metaphor. The theory of conceptual blending covers a wider range of data than metaphor narrowly construed. As a consequence, metaphor comes to be seen as an instance of a more general phenomenon, and loses the pre-eminent position that some linguists have ascribed to it.

Conceptual blending involves at least four mental spaces:

- at least two input spaces, I_1 and I_2;
- at least one generic space, G, which captures what is common to the input spaces, and which facilitates the establishment of correspondences between elements of the input spaces;
- a blended space, which incorporates selected elements from the input spaces.

The theory can be illustrated on the following examples. (The example, incidentally, does not involve metaphor; as stated, conceptual blending is not specifically a theory of metaphor.)

(12) In France, Bill Clinton wouldn't have been harmed by his relationship with Monika Lewinski.[9]

(Before proceeding, the reader may want to pause, and consider how he or she interprets example (12). Consider, in particular, what inferences can be

---

[9] The example is adapted from Fauconnier (1990), which dealt with Nixon and Watergate. I have updated the example for the benefit of readers for whom Nixon and Watergate are ancient history.

drawn from (12)—about the French, about the Americans, or indeed about anything else.)

Example (12) invites us to set up two mental spaces. One mental space, I_1, is populated by the 'reality' of recent US politics; there is the President, there is Lewinski, there is the President's relationship with Lewinski, there is the scandal, the denials, the attempt at impeachment, the revelation of all the sordid details in the press and on the internet. *In France* invites us to set up a second mental space, I_2, populated by entities which correspond to entities in I_1. We can do this because of the existence of a generic space, G, which is schematic for both I_1 and I_2. Probably, in this case, two generic spaces need to be postulated. The first (call it 'Western democracies') contains entities such as an elected Head of State, the media, public opinion, and so on. The second generic space ('personal relations') contains such entities as married, middle-aged men and their sexual encounters with younger females.

In order to interpret example (12) we need to construct a blend. The blend is hypothetical, as indicated by the presence of *would*. (Observe how the interpretation of (12) radically changes if *wouldn't have been* is replaced by *wasn't: In France, Bill Clinton wasn't harmed by his relationship with Monika Lewinski.*) The blend incorporates features of both of the input spaces, such as a hypothetical president of France who nevertheless exhibits some of the characteristics of the American president, a hypothetical lover, and so on. We then 'run' the blend, that is, we let the elements of the blend interact, and we can draw certain conclusions and inferences with respect to the input spaces. Schematically, blending can be represented in Figure 26.3 (p. 532).

Fauconnier makes the point that there are several ways of constructing the blend, hence, there are different ways of interpreting (12) and different inferences that can be drawn. Perhaps the most likely inference from (12) would be that the French public have a more relaxed and more tolerant attitude towards the sexual behaviour of public figures than the Americans (or, conversely, that the Americans are fixated on sexual matters.) But other inferences are equally possible. For example, one could interpret (12) to mean that the media in France refrain from discussing the private lives of politicians, or that the media are subject to censorship in such matters.

I have illustrated conceptual blending on a non-metaphorical example. With respect to metaphor, conceptual blending would work as follows:

- the input spaces are the source and the target domains;
- the generic space is a schematic conceptualization that captures cross-domain commonalities. Candidates for generic space concepts are image schemas, force-dynamic interactions, abstract motion, or the superordinate concepts envisaged by Glucksberg and Keyser;
- the blend consists of items selected from the input spaces.

An important aspect of the theory is that the blend can acquire a dynamism of its own, not predictable from either of the input spaces alone, nor from the

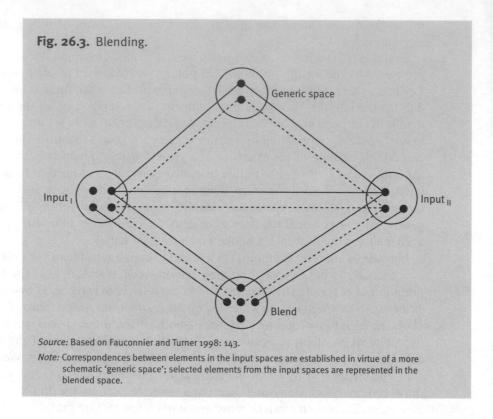

Fig. 26.3. Blending.

Source: Based on Fauconnier and Turner 1998: 143.

Note: Correspondences between elements in the input spaces are established in virtue of a more schematic 'generic space'; selected elements from the input spaces are represented in the blended space.

generic space. That a metaphorical blend can indeed take on characteristics of its own is easily illustrated. Consider again example (11b):

(11) b. She's imprisoned in her marriage.

On the blending theory, the generic space is 'any involuntary, unpleasant, confining, punishing, unrewarding situation'. The input spaces are a prison and a marriage. The blend—which determines our actual interpretation of (11b)—contains selected elements from the input domains, and acquires a logic that is not present in either. For example, if a woman is 'imprisoned in her marriage', she has the option of 'escaping' from her marriage. But the manner of her escaping (in the blend) is quite different from the manner of her escaping if she were (literally) a prisoner in a jail. Escaping from a (literal) prison will bring heavy penalties to the escapee and the prospect of an even lengthier imprisonment; to 'escape' from a marriage, all you have to do is remove yourself (physically) from the marital home and file for divorce.

Take, as another example, the problem raised in Chapter 24 in connection with the following expression.

(13) That surgeon is a butcher.

The problem, for the domain-mapping theory, is that the evaluation of the surgeon as incompetent—this is the way in which (13) would normally be understood—does not derive from the source domain; butchers are not normally incompetent. The evaluation derives, rather, from the incongruity of combining, in the blend, the kinds of things a surgeon does with the kinds of things a butcher does, while recognizing at the same time that both kinds of activities can be brought under a more schematic notion of 'cutting flesh with a sharp instrument'. A butcher's activities and a surgeon's activities constitute the input spaces, the commonality between the two domains is captured in a generic space, while the blend derives its properties by selectively incorporating aspects of the two input spaces.

As already mentioned, the theory of conceptual blending transcends the study of metaphor. It may, therefore, be applied to matters of syntax, morphology, and phonology. For a syntactic example, consider some data from the last chapter.

(14) a. The boy threw the ball over the wall.
    b. I put the kettle on the stove.

(15) a. The psychic will think your husband into a new galaxy.
    b. They prayed the boys home again

The sentences in (14) are fairly standard examples of the caused-motion construction. The somewhat picturesque quality of (15) results from the blending of the construction with the specific semantics of the designated situations. For a phonological example consider the case of a slip of the tongue: *Not in the sleast.* The input spaces are the competing forms *not in the least* and *not in the slightest.* The generic space is the semantic and morphophonological commonality between the two expressions. The blend consists of a selection of elements from the input spaces, sanctioned by the schema in the generic space. In fact, 'blend' is an established term in morphological theory and is used to refer to forms created by combining elements of input forms: *motel* (from 'motor' + 'hotel'), *brunch* (from 'breakfast' + 'lunch'), and *pulsar* (from 'pulsating' + 'star').

Study questions

1. Balance. Assemble a representative sample of the uses of *balance* and *balanced.* Study these uses with respect to the BALANCE image schema and the issues raised in section 26.1.

2. How are the following interpreted? How can the interpretations be explained?

> That surgeon is a butcher.
> That butcher is a surgeon.

3. How would you interpret the statement that 'Jane is married to a library'? How would you explain these interpretations in terms of Glucksberg and Keysar's theory?

4. Analyse the car-sticker slogan *My karma ran over my dogma* in terms of the theory of blending. Pay attention to phonological, syntactic, and semantic aspects. (The example is from Coulson and Oakley, 2000.)

5. Proverbs, and other kinds of pithy aphorisms, are good examples of expressions whose meaning is highly schematic and which are therefore able to be applied to a wide range of situations in different domains. Here are some well-known examples.

> Make hay while the sun shines.
> Kill two birds with one stone.
> Don't kill the goose that lays the golden egg.
> Don't look a gift horse in the mouth.

Are proverbs metaphorical? Lakoff and Turner (1989) and Lakoff (1993) claim that they are. They constitute 'generic-level metaphors', which present 'a very general schema characterizing an open-ended category of situations' (Lakoff 1993: 233).

Precisely for this very reason, it could be argued that proverbs should *not* be regarded as metaphors. There is no mapping from a source domain, neither is there semantic extension across domains. To be sure, *Make hay while the sun shines* invokes an agricultural scene, but I dare say that the expression would hardly ever be used 'literally', of a haymaking situation. The import of the proverb is that a person should take advantage of favourable circumstances while they last, and in this schematic sense it can be applied to all manner of situations

Consider the circumstances in which the other proverbs are typically used, with a view to deciding on their metaphorical character or otherwise.

6. Proverb fragments. Barlow (2000) presents the results of a extensive corpus search regarding the proverb *Make hay while the sun shines*. Remarkably, he found no instances of the proverb in its canonical (imperative) form, but he did find quite a range of examples in which parts of the proverb, especially the collocation *make hay*, were used. Here are some examples:

> X's plant hire business made hay while the rest of the construction industry suffered from a drought.
> If Tony Blair cannot make hay in such political sunshine, how will he fare when winter comes?
> Those companies with money to spend will continue to make hay.

Explain the special semantic values that have come to attach to the collocation *make hay*. Is metaphor involved? How might the theory of blending be relevant?

Replicate Barlow's study by looking at the incidence of other proverb fragments, such as *gift horse*, *golden egg*, *two birds*, and others.

Further reading

The standard text on image schemas is Johnson (1987). See also Lakoff (1987: 271–8). To my mind, one of the best implementations of the image schema notion is Cienki (1998) on STRAIGHT. For force dynamics, the basic reading is Talmy (1988). For an application of force-dynamic concepts to the domain of modality, see Sweetser (1990). On conceptual blending, see Fauconnier (1997) and Fauconnier and Turner (1996, 1998).

Part 7
Idioms and Constructions

The final two chapters address the interrelated topics of idioms (Chapter 28) and constructions (Chapter 29). The topics are interrelated in that both idioms and constructions can be regarded as symbolic units, which associate a phonological (or 'formal') representation with a semantic representation. Constructions, usually, are specified at a high level of schematicity and are able to sanction an open set of expressions. Nevertheless, a construction's usage range may not be fully predictable; constructions, in other words, display varying degrees of idiomaticity. Idioms generally need to be specified at a lower level of schematicity. In the limiting case, a fully specified phonological form is associated with a fixed, conventionalized meaning. It is rarely the case, however, that an idiom is unanalysable, whether in its formal or semantic aspects, which is tantamount to saying that even idioms can be brought under more general schemas.

The difference between idioms and constructions turns out to be a gradient distinction, having to do, essentially, with the schematicity at which a unit is specified. Pursuing the matter further, it can be argued that knowledge of (the syntax of) a language amounts to knowledge of a vast inventory of construction-idioms (or Idiom-constructions).

CHAPTER 27

Idioms, formulas, and fixed expressions

The topic of this chapter is the vast inventory of multi-word expressions—idioms, fixed expressions, formulaic phrases, familiar turns of phrase, frequent collocations, catchphrases, clichés, proverbs, witty sayings, literary quotations, song refrains—that are familiar to all competent users of a language. There is no standard term to refer to this class of linguistic expressions; the triad 'idioms, formulas, and fixed expressions' is intended merely as a convenient descriptive label. The chapter examines some general properties of these expressions, and their status within Cognitive Grammar.

27.1 Idioms in the grammar

Although their existence is universally recognized, idioms, formulas, and the like have enjoyed a somewhat marginal status in many linguistic theories. This is especially true of theories which accord a central place to the syntactic component and which make a clean distinction between the lexicon and the syntax. The lexicon lists the words of the language and states their individual properties—their pronunciation, their meaning, the lexical category to which they belong, together with any other idiosyncratic aspects that may be relevant (such as their membership in an inflection class). The syntax deals with the combination of words into larger units. Whereas the lexicon is the domain of individual facts, the syntax is regarded as the domain of the regular and the predictable. It is here, namely, where generalizations can be sought and rules can be formulated. Whereas speakers of a language manifestly have to learn the words of their language, they do not have to learn the sentences. The sentences can be generated by the application of general rules for the combination of the words. In these approaches, 'doing linguistics' consists, precisely, in discovering and formulating these general rules.

Idioms (broadly understood) do not fit neatly into this model. Suppose you refer to a piece of irrelevant information as a 'red herring'. Syntactically, this expression is a perfectly regular and unexceptional Adj-N combination. Nevertheless, the expression is not created by assembling its components in accordance with a syntactic rule. This is because its meaning cannot be derived from the meanings of its components, *red* and *herring*. The expression has to be listed as an item in a person's knowledge of their language. Since the lexicon is taken to be the repository of the idiosyncratic, the expression will have to be included in the lexicon. Doing so, however, upsets the neat compartmentalization of lexicon and syntax. As mentioned, from a syntactic point of view, *red herring* is unexceptional.

Take, as another example, setting-subject clauses, of the kind *The fifth day saw our departure* and *The cottage sleeps six*. Although setting-subject expressions are not uncommon in English (section 21.2.3), it is not the case that any verb can participate in this kind of clause. We cannot say *The fifth day heard the explosion*, or *The cottage lives six*. While the syntactic form of the acceptable clauses might be brought under a syntactic rule, the rule will have to make reference to those verbs that are able to appear in the clauses and to the semantic role of their subject nominals. Alternatively—or contemporaneously—the lexical entries for *see* and *sleep* will need to state the availability of these verbs for the syntactic structures in question. This means that the distinction between the lexicon (the repository of the particular and idiosyncratic) and the syntax (the domain of the regular and predictable) can no longer be maintained. The syntax makes reference to lexical peculiarities, while the lexicon makes reference to syntactic generalities.

Neither is it the case that idioms (broadly understood) are always characterized by idiosyncrasies, whether syntactic or semantic. Suppose I ask a guest, *Would you like some more coffee?* In both its formal and semantic aspects the expression is unremarkable. However, it is implausible to maintain that whenever I ask this question I am assembling it from its component units in accordance with syntactic principles. The expression is a pre-formed unit, which I have used (and heard used) on innumerable occasions. Knowledge of the expression is part of my knowledge of English. A linguistic theory which compartmentalizes syntax and lexicon has no way of accommodating ready-made expressions of this nature. It would not be possible to assign a syntactically regular expression to the syntax—the syntax is the domain of general rules, not of specific expressions. Neither could a syntactically and semantically unexceptional expression be assigned to the lexicon—the lexicon is the repository of idiosyncratic facts, not of regular expressions.

These kinds of problems do not arise in Cognitive Grammar. The key to the Cognitive Grammar approach lies in the notion of the symbolic unit. Symbolic units comprise not only the sound-meaning associations of lexical items, but also the formal and semantic aspects of constructional schemas. (Lexicon and syntax differ merely with respect to the schematicity and internal complexity of the semantic and phonological units that are associated.) The notion of symbolic unit is easily able to accommodate idioms—that is, multi-word expressions that speakers have learned as conventionalized associations of a phonological form with a semantic representation, irrespective of the 'regularity' of such expressions; irrespective, that is, of whether the expressions may be brought under schemas of varying levels of generality. Once due cognizance is taken of constructions—the topic of the next chapter—and once it is recognized that constructions, too, are a kind of idiom (albeit at a schematic level), it becomes possible to turn the mainstream view of idioms on its head. Rather than being peripheral to the 'core' of a language, it becomes possible to argue that idioms *are* the core. A person's knowledge of a language consists, precisely, in knowledge of idioms, that is, conventionalized form-meaning relations, at varying levels of generality. Everything turns out to be idiomatic, to a greater or lesser extent.

27.2 The scope of the phenomenon

Here is a list of multi-word expressions, compiled at random, which exemplify the category of 'idioms, formulas, and fixed expressions':

(1) How do you do?, as far as I'm concerned, have the time of one's life, to the best of one's ability, gimme a break!, shut up!, a sea change, all's well that ends well, don't say a word to anyone, scarcely a week goes by without . . . , bang goes my weekend!, he has what it takes, to coin a phrase, the more the merrier, it ain't over till the fat lady sings, kill two birds with one stone, the ambulance at the bottom of the cliff, I wouldn't hold my breath, think outside the square, it's nothing to jump up and down about, etc., etc.

The reader will be able, without difficulty, to extend this list many times over. In fact, the first observation that we need to make about idioms is how many of them there are. Open any newspaper or magazine and select a random paragraph. You will be sure to find, in almost every line of print, at least one group of words that has an idiomatic feel to it.

A language typically contains many thousands, if not many tens of thousands, of units of the kind exemplified in (1). While native speakers may

> **The *Wheel of Fortune***
>
> Jackendoff (1997) elegantly illustrated the scope of idioms and fixed expressions in English by reference to the television game show, *Wheel of Fortune*.
>
> Participants win prizes by guessing the identity of a phrase. The phrases are presented initially as a series of blanks, one for each letter, with spaces separating the words. The 'wheel of fortune' spins, and comes to rest on a letter of the alphabet, which, if present in the phrase, is inserted into the appropriate blanks. The winner is the one who first guesses the identity of the phrase. Players can often identity the mystery phrase with only minimal linguistic cues, something which would hardly be possible unless the phrases are stored, ready-made, in memory.
>
> Jackendoff remarks on the enormous number of idioms and fixed expressions which exist in the language and which speakers must have stored in long-term memory:
>
> The existence of such 'fixed expressions' is well known; but what struck me in watching *Wheel of Fortune* is how many there are. Consider that the show presents about five puzzles a day and is shown six times a week, and that it has been on the air for over ten years. This comes to something on the order of ten to fifteen thousand puzzles with little if any repetition, and no sense of strain—no worry that the show is going to run out of puzzles, or even that the puzzles are becoming especially obscure. (Jackendoff 1997: 155–6).

not be immediately aware of the role of idioms in their language, foreign learners usually are acutely conscious of this aspect of a target language. Indeed, there is a sense in which, once the basic syntactic structures and the inflection classes of a language have been mastered, intermediate and advanced learners of a language do not need any further instruction in formal aspects of the language, or even in vocabulary acquisition; what they need is to extend their knowledge of idioms. What marks a proficient second or foreign language speaker is their command of idioms and other fixed expressions.[1]

Let us survey the kinds of phenomena that come under 'idioms', broadly construed. The following list is not meant as a definitive or scientific classification, neither are the categories mutually exclusive. Its purpose is merely to give an idea of the range of different things in a language that might reasonably be said to be 'idiomatic'.

27.2.1 Idioms

First, there is the category of 'idioms', narrowly construed. We can distinguish two respects in which an expression can be regarded as idiomatic.

---

[1] It is significant that much of the descriptive work on idioms and formulaic language over the past decades has been conducted by researchers in second- and foreign-language pedagogy. See Further reading for some references.

(i) The idiomatic character of an expression resides in its semantic value. Prototypical examples easily come to mind: *kick the bucket* ('die'), *spill the beans* ('reveal confidential information'), *red herring* ('piece of irrelevant and misleading information'), *cook someone's goose* ('frustrate a person's plans'), *pull someone's leg* ('tease a person'), *burn the candle at both ends* ('exhaust oneself trying to do too many things at the same time').

The syntax of these expressions is unexceptional. What renders them idiomatic is that their meanings cannot be predicted from the meanings which the component words have elsewhere in the language. As a consequence, the expressions are open to two kinds of interpretation—the 'literal' interpretation, and the 'idiomatic' interpretation. The latter has to be learned as a specific property of each of the expressions.

A notable feature of many idioms of this kind is their picturesque character; they often evoke a concrete and easily imageable scene. One might, in some cases, be inclined to interpret the concrete images in metaphorical terms. However, even the metaphorical mappings turn out to be 'idiomatic'. While one might identify the beans in *spill the beans* as a metaphor for confidential information, there is no schematic conceptual metaphor in English which construes information as legumes. Equally, there is no conceptual metaphor which maps information into fish, or the relevance of information into a colour (red or otherwise). Even if one were to take *red herring* to be a metaphor, we are dealing with an 'idiomatic' metaphor.

(ii) For a large number of expressions, the idiomaticity resides, not so much in the special meaning which attaches—unpredictably—to a syntactically regular phrase, but in the formal aspects of the expressions. The syntax may be somewhat deviant vis-à-vis more regular patterns prevailing in the language, or the idiomaticity may reside in a collocational requirement which is not fully predictable from general principles. Idioms of this kind do not normally have a 'picturesque' quality, nor do they allow a 'literal' interpretation alongside their 'idiomatic' interpretation. In fact, the meanings of this kind of idiom are often fairly transparent, and could be guessed at even by a learner who is encountering the expression for the first time. Nevertheless, because of their formal properties, the expressions have to be learned as such.

Examples of syntactically deviant idioms are *by and large*, *in short*, *for better or for worse*, *at once*, *not at all*. *By and large* is unusual, syntactically, in that the expression coordinates a preposition (*by*) and an adjective (*large*), something which is not sanctioned by general principles. There are no other expressions constructed on the same pattern—**by and small*, **out and large*, and such like, are horribly ungrammatical. *By and large* is rigidly fixed, in that none of its component units could be replaced by other units. Similarly, *in short* is syntactically unusual in that the preposition takes as its complement what looks like an adjective. Here, some limited variation is tolerated: *in brief*, *for short*, *(not) for long*. Nevertheless, there are still very tight restrictions on which prepositions can occur with which adjective-like complements. There is no *in long*, **for brief*, **by short*, etc.

Examples of idioms with strict collocational requirements are *to the best of my ability, have the time of one's life, take advantage of (a situation)*. *To the best of my ability* requires the introductory preposition *to* (**I did the best of my ability*), and *best* needs to co-occur with *ability* (or, alternatively, *knowledge*). Prepositions, in particular, are liable to have a large number of uses which are idiomatic with respect to the items with which they co-occur. Consider, for example, the contrast between <u>on</u> *my birthday*, <u>at</u> *Easter*, <u>in</u> *the afternoon*. It is an idiosyncratic ('idiomatic') fact about English that days go with the preposition *on*, cyclic occasions with *at*, and parts of the day with *in*.[2]

It will be appreciated that the boundary between the idiomatic (in the sense intended here) and the non-idiomatic is fuzzy in the extreme. One could, for example, claim that standard collocations are examples of idioms (*heavy smoker, heavy drinker*, but not **heavy eater*). The sequence of items in binominals (section 5.4.1) might also come under the rubric of the idiomatic: *It's a matter of life and death* vs. **It's a matter of death and life, People were coming and going* vs. **People were going and coming*.

27.2.2 Formulas

Formulas can be characterized as expressions which have a conventionalized function within the language. We can distinguish a number of subcategories:

(i) A multi-word expression may be conventionally associated with certain kinds of situation. To be included here are various greeting formulas (*How do you do? How are things?*), various ritualistic expressions which close an inter- action (*Have a nice day, Bye-bye, I'll be seeing you, Take care*), the formulaic salutations which close a letter (*Yours sincerely*), ritual expressions of thanks (*Thank you*) and the responses thereto (*Don't mention it*), and the cricketer's appeal to the umpire *How's that?*

There is no reason to restrict the class of situationally bound expressions to multi-word formulas. If the cricketer's *How's that?* counts as a formula because of its conventionalized value within the game, we should need to say the same of the chess-player's *Check!* and the bingo-player's *Bingo!* A similar status attaches to *Boo!*, said by a child who peeks out from behind a curtain pretending to frighten people. Perhaps even *Yes* and *No*, as conventionalized expressions of assent and dissent, should also be regarded as formulas.

(ii) If the above examples are tied to special kinds of situations, other ex- pressions have a distinctive discourse-structuring function. Examples include *by the way, as I was saying, in the first place, to sum up, last but not least*.

---

[2] There would be little to gain, I think, from attempting to explain the prepositional uses by refer- ence to underlying spatial metaphors (cf. Radden 1989), according to which days of the week are conceptualized as 'areas', cyclic occasions as 'points', and parts of the day as 'containers'.

Again, there is no reason why the category of discourse-structuring elements should be restricted to multi-word expressions. If *by the way* is a discourse-functioning expression, then so too is the single word *anyway*. If *in the first place* counts as a formula, then so too do *firstly*, *secondly*, and *finally*.

(iii) A further group comprises conventionalized ways of expressing speaker attitude. On hearing some unlikely piece of news, a person might comment *Is that a fact?* In its formal aspects, this is a perfectly regular polarity question. Its formulaic quality lies in its value as a conventionalized expression of surprise. Although interrogative in form, *Is that a fact?* would probably not be intended, or taken, as a request for information—the hearer, for example, would not feel obliged to respond 'Yes, that's a fact'. Some further examples are listed in (2).

(2) Would you believe it?
     I wouldn't do that if I were you.
     You've got to be joking.
     That's easier said than done.
     Over my dead body!

27.2.3 'Pre-formed' language

A third category of idioms, broadly construed, consists of pre-formed chunks of language which speakers have committed to memory. We can distinguish three subcategories:

(i) Texts and text fragments. At issue here are memorized literary texts (or fragments of texts), memorized religious texts, nursery rhymes, book and film titles, song lyrics, and the like. There will obviously be differences between speakers with respect to which chunks have been committed to memory. Nevertheless, within a given speech community, there will be significant overlap with respect to what has been memorized. Indeed, there is a sense in which the sharing of a culture may be characterized by a shared knowledge of texts (and text fragments). The texts may pertain to 'high' literature (Shakespeare, in particular), to religious texts (verses from the Bible, prayers, hymns), or to popular texts (television series, comedy shows, films, song lyrics, cartoon series). Speakers can express their cultural solidarity by peppering their speech with quotations (accurate or inaccurate) from, or allusions to, the texts which define their culture. On the following page are some examples of pre-formed language chunks which would probably be immediately recognized as such by modern English speakers.[3]

---

[3] The first four examples are Shakespeare quotations, the fifth is from a nursery rhyme, the sixth alludes to the title of Solzhenitsyn's *One Day in the Life of Ivan Denisovich*, while the last alludes to a Monty Python comedy sketch.

(3) To be or not to be
All's well that ends well
My kingdom for a horse
Lead on, Macduff!
Three blind mice
a day in the life of . . .
an ex-parrot

   (ii) A second category of multi-word, ready-made expressions is proverbs, sayings, and all manner of pithy aphorisms: *Too many cooks spoil the broth*, *Make hay while the sun shines*, *Shut the stable door after the horse has bolted*, *Kill the goose that lays the golden eggs*. Since these are usually well known (or are assumed to be well known) in a speech community, it is often possible to allude to the saying by mention of a prominent part of it: *That's a case of too many cooks*, *Now's the time to make hay*, *Don't kill the proverbial goose*, etc.

   (iii) Catchphrases and clichés. From actual quotations and allusions it is a short step to catchphrases and clichés. Partridge, who compiled the remarkable *Dictionary of Catch Phrases* (1977), characterized a catchphrase as a saying that has 'caught on', and which 'pleases the public' (p. xi). Catchphrases are expressions that are generally known, and are used with the expectation that the hearer will be familiar with them, even though their origin might be obscure. Some examples are listed in (4).

(4) Don't do anything that I wouldn't do.
What's a nice girl like you doing in a place like this?
That's the sixty-four thousand dollar question.
It ain't over till the fat lady sings.
Some of my best friends are Jews.

Mostly, these are fairly jocular in tone, though some, such as the last one in (4), are deadly serious in their import.
   Clichés are similar, in that an expression is regarded as a cliché only if it is recognized as a conventional expression. But whereas catchphrases are appreciated because of the shared cultural background that they evoke, clichés tend to be negatively evaluated, in that they are felt to display a lack of originality on the part of the speaker, with respect to both the thought that is being expressed and the speaker's way of expressing it. *We're all getting older*, *We're not getting any younger*, *Nobody's perfect* are examples of clichés.

27.2.4 Idioms of encoding

No survey of idiomatic expressions would be complete without mention of what Makkai (1972) has called 'idioms of encoding', in contrast to 'idioms of decoding'. Idioms are often thought of in terms of the special knowledge that a hearer must bring to bear on their interpretation. Without this special knowledge, a statement that someone 'spilled the beans' would be uninterpretable. Idioms of encoding view the matter from the perspective of the speaker. Idioms of encoding have to do with the speaker's knowledge of the conventionalized way of saying something.

To be sure, a full knowledge of the idioms surveyed above will comprise both the decoding and the encoding perspectives. A speaker not only needs to know the conventional meaning of *spill the beans*, she also has to know the circumstances in which the expression can be appropriately used. A focus on encoding, however, greatly expands the range of things that can appropriately be said to be idiomatic. This is because the conventionalized way of saying something may not, in itself, be in any way 'idiomatic', from a decoding perspective. The idiomaticity resides in the fact that *this* happens to be the conventionalized way to say something, rather than some other, equally plausible way.

Consider the example cited earlier in this chapter. I ask a guest *Would you like some more coffee?* There are, to be sure, other conventional ways of making the offer. Some of these are given in (5a). In principle, however, the offer could be made in other ways, as suggested in (5b).

(5) a. May I offer you some more coffee?
         May I pour you some more coffee?
         Would you care for some more coffee?

     b. Would you like to drink some more coffee?
         Shall I serve you some more coffee?
         Would you like me to serve you more of this coffee?
         Please may I give you another serving of coffee.
         Please let me know if it is your desire to drink more coffee.

The expressions in (5b)—though constructed fully in accordance with the syntactic and lexical resources of English—are increasingly 'unidiomatic' precisely because these are not the conventionalized ways of making the offer.

Once the category of idioms of encoding is recognized, idiomaticity threatens to take over quite a large part of the lexicon, in that the conventionalized way of naming an entity, or a type of entity, needs to be regarded as idiomatic. For many entities, or types of entity, there are usually a host of other, equally plausible names that could have been given, but which were not.

For example, the document that certifies a person as competent to drive a motorized vehicle could have been called many things. It could have been called a 'driving permit', a 'steering licence', or a 'driver's document'. It could even have become known as a 'DD' (an abbreviation of 'driver's document'), similar to the way in which 'identity document' has been abbreviated to 'ID'. None of these is a conventionalized name for the document in question. I note that the device on my laptop which allows me to move the cursor is called a 'touchpad'. It could just as easily have been called a 'fingerpad'. And what about all the possible (but non-conventionalized) designations for 'laptop'? A list of 'idioms of encoding' is endless.[4]

Idioms of silence

Idiomaticity, on the broad understanding of the concept that I adopt here, involves not just knowledge of the conventional things to say, and of the conventionalized ways of saying them, it also involves knowledge of what not to say. Whereas Germans, when beginning a meal, wish each other *guten Appetit*, it is a peculiarity of Anglo culture that no such greeting is expected. The English idiom consists, precisely, in the absence of a conventional formula.

Consider also the thanking routines in different cultures. English speakers are taught, from a very early age, always to say *Thank you* when they receive something from another person, however trivial it may be. Thus it is that customers at a supermarket checkout will say *Thank you* when they are given their change or their till slip. To receive one's change in stony silence would, I imagine, be perceived as rude by many English speakers. Contrast this with German usage. A German would not feel obliged to express thanks when receiving their change. The cashier has not performed any act of personal generosity towards the customer, but has simply handed the customer what they are entitled to.

If there are conventions about when to express thanks, there are also conventions for acknowledging thanks. Again, English and German differ. In English, one responds to a 'thank you' only when an act of personal generosity is involved. The conventional acknowledgements include *Don't mention it*, *Not at all*, or the laconic *That's OK*. The supermarket cashier would certainly not feel obliged to acknowledge a customer's 'thank you' in this way. However, when I, as a well-trained Englishman, instinctively say *Danke schön* at a German supermarket checkout, the cashier responds, also instinctively, and also, I suspect, a little uneasily, *Bitte sehr*. If Germans reserve *Danke schön* for situations in which there is a genuine reason to express gratitude, they are also meticulous in acknowledging an expression of thanks.

27.3 Semantic and formal characteristics of idioms

It will be clear from the above survey that a very wide range of phenomena come under the rubric of the idiomatic, in a broad sense of the term. In this section, I turn to the question, whether there are any general properties of idioms (broadly understood) which distinguish the category from the non-idiomatic rest of the language.

---

[4] The idiomatic character of names of things (and types of things) becomes apparent whenever we discover that different dialects of a language have different conventionalized names. British *drawing pin* corresponds to American *thumb tack* (Nunberg *et al.* 1994: 495), the things that elsewhere are called 'traffic lights' are called, in South Africa, 'robots'.

I have already drawn attention to two ways in which an expression might be regarded as idiomatic. First, idiomaticity may reside in the expression's semantics; an expression is idiomatic to the extent that its meaning cannot be worked out from the meanings of its parts and the manner in which they are combined. From this perspective, idioms are characterized by semantic non-compositionality. Alternatively, the idiomaticity of an expression resides in its formal aspects. Unlike non-idiomatic expressions, idioms are not freely assembled by the application of general syntactic rules.

Each of these approaches rests on problematic assumptions. The first rests on the assumption that expressions can be cleanly divided into those which exhibit semantic compositionality and those which do not. The second rests on the assumption that syntactic rules are indeed general in their application and operate independently of 'idiomatic' considerations.

Both of these assumptions turn out to be false. Once this is recognized, we will need to question whether it is indeed useful, or even possible, to distinguish the idiomatic from the non-idiomatic.

27.3.1 Idiomaticity of meaning

Nunberg *et al.* (1994: 498) assembled several definitions which appealed to the semantic peculiarities of idioms. They cite the following passage from Katz and Postal's early work on semantics:

> The essential feature of an idiom is that its full meaning . . . is not a compositional function of the meanings of the idiom's elementary parts (Katz and Postal 1964: 275)

They also cite Chomsky's (1980: 149) remark that the expressions *take care of*, *take advantage of*, *make much of*, and *kick the bucket* 'are idiomatic in the sense that their meaning is noncompositional'. It is interesting to note that the Collins *Dictionary of the English Language* takes a similar tack:[5]

> Idiom: A group of words whose meaning cannot be predicted from the meanings of the constituent words, as for example *(It was raining) cats and dogs.*

This aspect certainly does look like a salient property, if not of all idiomatic expressions, then at least of a significant proportion of them. There are, however, some fundamental problems associated with this approach.

A first problem was identified in Chapter 6. The compositionality principle rests on the assumption that each component of an expression can be assigned a fixed, determinate, and context-independent meaning. As discussed in Chapter 6 and in more detail in Chapters 22 and 23, this assumption has to be

---

[5] The dictionary gives a second definition, which comes closer to the usage-based account I endorse here: 'linguistic usage that is grammatical and natural to native speakers of a language'.

queried. Consequently, there are no grounds for asserting that, in contrast to idioms (whose meaning is non-compositional), there exists the rest of the language, where the meanings of complex expressions *are* compositionally derived. Strict compositionality is rarely, if ever, encountered. Most expressions (I am tempted to say: *all* expressions), when interpreted in the context in which they are uttered, are non-compositional to some degree.

Attempts to characterize idioms in terms of their non-compositionality (in contrast to the rest of the language) run into some further difficulties. Consider the case of idioms which contain a word which has no uses outside the idiom itself. Since the word is restricted to occurring within the idiom, there can be no basis for ascertaining what the 'basic', 'non-idiomatic' meaning of the word might be. One cannot claim that *take umbrage (at someone or something)* is idiomatic because its meaning (roughly, 'take offence') cannot be computed from the 'literal' meaning of *umbrage*, if by 'literal meaning' one understands the meaning that *umbrage* has when it is not being used idiomatically. The example is not at all exceptional. There are, in fact, quite a few expressions which contain what we might call a 'cranberry word'.[6] Here are some examples. The cranberry words have been italicized.

(6) give someone the *once-over*, under the *auspices* of, it's not all it's *cracked up* to be, in *cahoots* with, by *dint* of, *tit* for *tat*, *wheeling* and dealing, keep *tabs* on someone, to all *intents* and purposes, much of a *muchness*, *wend* one's way, in one *fell* swoop, be taken *aback*, be at *loggerheads* with someone, they are just *raring* to go, be *riven* with dissension

Whether a word counts as a cranberry word or not will depend on the extent of a speaker's linguistic knowledge. I dare say that most speakers will have encountered the word *hatchet* predominantly in the context of the idiom *bury the hatchet*. For a speaker who does not know that a hatchet is a kind of axe, *bury the hatchet* will contain a cranberry word. Many speakers may not recognize the names of parts of gun in *lock, stock, and barrel*, they may not be aware of the nautical metaphor in *change tack*, or the names of weaving instruments in *by hook or by crook*.

Borderline cases of cranberry words include words whose use is restricted to one or two collocations. *Wreak* is restricted, virtually, to the collocations *wreak havoc*, *wreak revenge*, and *wreak destruction*. *Wrought* is largely restricted to the collocation *wrought iron*. *Addled* applies mainly to eggs and to brains, *rancid* is used predominantly of cooking oil and butter.

A second problem with compositionality was pointed out by Cruse (1986: 37). Even in cases where the component words of an idiom are used in other contexts, Cruse argued that an appeal to non-compositionality as a defining feature of idioms is ultimately circular, in that it rests on the prior distinction

---

[6] Cf. 'cranberry morpheme' (section 14.2), i.e. a morpheme that is attested in only one word.

between those uses that we want to characterize as 'idiomatic', and those uses which we have recognized as 'non-idiomatic':

> A traditional definition of idiom runs as follows: an idiom is an expression whose meaning cannot be inferred from the meanings of its parts. Although at first sight straightforward, there is a curious element of circularity in this definition. Does it indicate that the meaning of an idiom cannot be inferred from (or, more precisely, cannot be accounted for as a compositional function of) the meanings the parts carry IN THAT EXPRESSION? Clearly not—so it must be a matter of their meanings in other expressions. But equally clearly, these 'other expressions' must be chosen with care: in considering *to pull someone's leg*, for instance, there is little point in referring to *pull* in *to pull a fast one*, or *leg* in *He hasn't got a leg to stand on*. The definition must be understood as stating that an idiom is an expression whose meaning cannot be accounted for as a compositional function of the meanings its parts have when they are not parts of idioms. The circularity is now plain: to apply the definition, we must already be in a position to distinguish idiomatic from non-idiomatic expressions. (Cruse 1986: 37)

If we cannot give much credence[7] to the theory of idioms as non-compositional (in contrast to the rest of the language, which *is* compositional), we also cannot accept the view that idioms are semantically unanalysable. Such, for example, was the approach taken by Cruse (1986), who characterizes idioms as (i) lexically complex, that is, they consist of more than one word, and (ii) semantically simplex, that is, their meaning constitutes 'a single minimal semantic constituent'. Thus, according to Cruse, the idiom *to cook (somebody's) goose* corresponds to the 'simplex' semantic unit 'to frustrate a person's plans'. In another context, Cruse (2000b: 73) asserts that an idiom is equivalent to a single lexical item; *pull someone's leg* is equivalent to 'tease':

> Although it is not true of all idioms, it seems fruitless to ask what *pull* and *leg* mean in *to pull someone's leg*: they do not mean anything at all, just as the *m-* of *mat* does not mean anything—all the meaning of the phrasal unit attaches to the phrase, and none to its parts. (Cruse 2000: 73)

The problem with this approach is that the meaning of *cook somebody's goose* can certainly be distributed over its parts. The goose corresponds to a person's pet idea, which, once 'cooked', is no longer viable. Moreover, speakers are able to play on the semantic analysability of idioms. The following dialogue fragment is easily interpreted:

(7) a. Did they cook his goose?
     b. He doesn't have a goose to cook.

For quite a large number of idioms it is possible to map components of the

---

[7] Note that *credence* is restricted, for most speakers, to the contexts *give credence to* and *lend credence to*.

idiom into components of its semantic interpretation as the following examples illustrate:

(8) to pull strings ('to exert influence')
    to take the bull by the horns ('to tackle a difficult situation at its core')
    The buck stops here. ('The responsibility lies here')
    to let the cat out of the bag ('to reveal a secret')
    to bury the hatchet ('to agree to forget an old dispute')
    That really gets my goat. ('that disturbs my composure')
    to have a bee in one's bonnet ('to have an obsessive idea in one's head')

While metaphor might seem to be involved in these cases, it is remarkable that the metaphorical mapping is in most cases not sanctioned by a more general conceptual metaphor. (This, no doubt, is the reason why we should say that the expressions in (8) are idioms, rather than run-of-the mill metaphors.) There is no conceptual metaphor in English which sanctions the mapping of a dispute into a chopping instrument (as in *bury the hatchet*), or which maps a state of mind into a farm animal (the goat in *That gets my goat*).

However, for quite a number of idioms (including some of those mentioned already) a rather different mechanism seems to be involved. The idiom invokes a concrete and easily imageable scene, which is taken as emblematic of the situation which it is used to refer to. Some examples are cited in (9).

(9) to paint the town red.
    to bend over backwards (trying to help someone)
    to burn the candle at both ends
    to have one foot in the grave.
    to dig one's own grave
    Butter wouldn't melt in his mouth.
    The bottom fell out of the market.

To paint the town red means, roughly, to have a riotously good time. The town, the painting of it, and the colour red do not necessarily map into any aspects of the situation to which the idiom might be applied. The idiom refers— somewhat like a proverb—to any situation in which high-spirited people do outrageous things. Similarly, the kinds of things that you do or say when you 'bend over backwards to help someone' are not understood as metaphorical mappings from the activity of 'bending over backwards'. The idiom cites an unusual physical contortion as representative of the effort that a person has put into an ultimately fruitless activity.

Some idioms resist even this kind of interpretation. Consider the curious expression *That's the bee's knees* (and its variants, such as *That's the cat's pyjamas*). Since bees do not have knees, one might suppose that the expression refers to the impossibility of a situation. In point of fact, it means just the opposite—it refers approvingly to a situation that is just as it should be.

With these examples we approach the limits of the semantic interpretability of idioms. We should not, however, lose sight of the other extreme, namely, fixed expressions whose meanings are not at all unexceptional. *He has what it takes* means, more or less, just what it says—the person in question has the characteristics that are necessary for the task in hand. *Have a nice day* expresses the wish that the person addressed should 'have a nice day'. The 'idiomatic' character of these expressions resides in their fixed form and their conventionalized use.

27.3.2 Idiomaticity of form

Some idioms are rigidly fixed. *How do you do?* tolerates no formal variation whatsoever. Formulaic expressions are formulaic, precisely because of their fixed form. Nevertheless, a large number of expressions which fall under the general rubric of the idiomatic do permit some degree of syntactic and lexical variation.

Particularly numerous are idioms which contain a 'slot' which can be filled by items of a particular kind. *Do (one's) best*, *pull (someone's) leg*, *have the time of (one's) life* contain a slot for the possessor (as well as for the subject nominal). *Take advantage of (something/someone)*, *give (someone) a wide berth*, *poke fun at (someone)* contain a slot for a nominal, *The buck stops (here)* contains a slot for a place expression. In these cases, it could be argued that the 'idiomatic' part of the idiom resides in the fixed components, the slots being extrinsic to the idiom as such. It has been noted (O'Grady 1998) that the 'idiomatic' part mostly concerns a dependency relation between a head and its complement, in many cases between a verb and its direct object. On this account, the filling of the 'slots' is handled by general syntactic principles. It should be observed, however, that even the 'idiomatic' part of an idiom often places quite severe restrictions on which items can fill the slots. The place expression that completes *The buck stops (here)* has to refer to the locus of responsibility: *The buck stops with me*, *The buck stops at the White House*, or (assuming that the CEO of a company has his office on the eleventh floor), *The buck stops on the eleventh floor*. Examples like this suggest that a differentiation between the 'idiomatic' and the 'non-idiomatic' part of an expression is not a clear-cut matter—the idiomatic character of the idiom is not confined to the idiomatic 'core'. Moreover, some idioms permit a limited amount of lexical variation, even with respect to their 'idiomatic' parts. You can *put a pistol to someone's head*, or you can *hold a gun to someone's head*; you can *add oil/fuel to the flames/fire*; and you can *hit the hay* or *hit the sack* (i.e. drop exhausted into bed). In a sense, these idioms also contain 'slots'—the slots, however, can be filled only by items selected from a very small set of possibilities.

A second respect in which idioms exhibit formal variation consists in the possibility that parts of the idiom can be modified and that the idiom can appear in different syntactic configurations. Here are some examples based on the idioms *do (one's) best*, *poke fun at (someone)*, *cook (someone's) goose*, and *Every dog has its day*.

(10) a. I did my very best.
        It was the best that I could do.
     b. They poked malicious fun at him.
        Nobody likes being poked fun at.
     c. He cooked his own goose.
        His goose has been well and truly cooked.
     d. Even this old dog will have his day.
        Every dog hopes, eventually, to have its day.

The possibilities of formal variation vary considerably from case to case, an important factor being the extent to which an idiom is analysable into components which themselves can be assigned meanings. In terms of the syntactic configurations in which it can occur, a transparent idiom like *do the dishes* is to all intents and purposes indistinguishable from the non-idiomatic *wash the dishes*. It is the relatively opaque idioms which tend to be fairly rigid in their form. *Kick the bucket* does not allow internal modification (**He kicked the old bucket*), nor can the idiom be made passive (**The bucket was finally kicked by the old man*), the reason, clearly, being that there is no conceptual unit which can be mapped on to the nominal *the bucket*. Even so, it is remarkable how even a relatively opaque idiom like *pull (someone's) leg* allows some degree of elaboration. True, one cannot say **They pulled my left leg*. But it would certainly be possible that, having had one of my legs pulled, I should challenge the leg-puller with *Go on, pull the other one!*

We have seen, in this section, that quite of a number of multi-word units that we should want to characterize as idioms are not at all rigidly fixed. Idioms cannot therefore be characterized in terms of their fixed form. I have not yet, however, fulfilled a promise that I made at the beginning of this section, namely, that a closer examination of the thesis that idioms can be characterized in terms of their syntactic peculiarities will show that the thesis is based on a false presupposition. The error lies in assuming that the syntax is the domain of the fully regular and predictable. I address this aspect in the next section.

27.4 The idiomatic vs. the predictable

The recognition of idioms as a distinct category presupposes a distinction between the idiomatic and the non-idiomatic, between the idiosyncratic and the regular, or, as Fillmore *et al.* (1988: 502) put it, between 'what it is that speakers of a language know outright about their language and what it is that they have to be able to figure out'. A speaker of English is able to 'figure out' what *red box* means, given that they know what *box* and *red* mean, together with the knowledge that *box* is a noun and *red* is (or can be used as) an adjective, in association with general principles for constructing and interpreting Adj-N combinations. Speakers of English are also able to figure out what *black box* means—at least, when the expression is being used in its non-idiomatic sense. The idiomatic senses—'flight-recorder', or 'mental module whose internal workings are unknown'—have to be learned. As an idiomatic expression, *black box* is 'something a language user could fail to know while knowing everything else in the language' (Fillmore *et al.* 1988: 504).[8]

The distinction that Fillmore *et al.* make seems reasonable enough. Nevertheless, if we pursue the distinction further we come up against a major problem. This is, that the general principles that allow speakers to 'figure out' what complex expressions mean are general only to a degree. General principles (i.e. 'rules') have peripheral applications, as well as outright exceptions. The range of application of even the most general principles therefore has to be learned, and to this extent even general statements are tinged with idiomaticity. On the other hand, it is rarely the case that the idiomatic and the exceptional totally lack rhyme or reason. The exceptions are subject to minor regularities, they are often analysable to some degree, and the idiomatic is rarely lacking in any kind of motivation.

We have encountered this kind of situation in morphology. There is a regular way of forming plural nouns in English, namely, through addition of [s] (or one of its variants). An English speaker can 'figure out' what the plural of *portcullis* (to take a fairly rare word, which will probably have been encountered only in the singular) is likely to be (namely, *portcullises*). One can figure out what the noun derived from *bizarre* (the noun with the meaning 'the property of being bizarre') is likely to be, namely *bizarreness*. Nevertheless, there are quite a few nouns which have 'irregular' plurals—that is, plurals which are 'exceptions' to the general rule—and which therefore have to be 'learned outright'. *Men, mice, theses,* and *loaves* are 'idiomatic' plurals. The formation of nouns from adjectives is subject to a much higher degree of idiomaticity. One has to 'learn outright' that the noun meaning 'the quality of being arrogant' is *arrogance*, not **arrogantness*, or **arrogancy*. Even so, these 'idiomatic' forms can often be brought under low-level schemas. This topic was addressed in Chapter 16.

We find a similar state of affairs in syntax. One generally thinks of the syntax of a language as the province of the regular and predictable. This, I think, misrepresents the situation. I examine this topic in more detail in

---

[8] Quine's (1987: 92) definition, though phrased differently from that of Fillmore *et al.*, amounts to much the same: 'Our word *idiom* is used to refer to a linguistic singularity: to a turn of phrase whose mode of use is not evident from broader regularities of the language nor from the use of its component words in other contexts.'

the next chapter, where I look at the properties of a range of syntactic constructions exhibiting varying degrees of productivity. In the meantime, let us consider some examples of what Goldberg (1995: ch. 8) calls the 'resultative construction' in English:

(11) They shot him dead.
      They painted the house green.
      I wiped the table clean.
      I squashed the insect flat.
      They beat her unconscious.
      They stripped him naked.
      He pushed the door open.
      He slammed the door shut.
      We cut the prisoner free.

There are some obvious similarities across these sentences. In each case the subject nominal designates an Agent who performs some activity with respect to a Patient, designated by the direct object of the verb, such that the Patient comes to be in a certain state, designated by the adjective. We appear to be in the realm of the regular and the predictable. Once a person is familiar with this kind of syntactic structure, it is possible to 'figure out' what *They shot him dead* means, or, taking an encoding perspective, to predict that such an expression will be fully grammatical in English.

However, the syntactic construction illustrated in (11) is not fully productive, in the sense that situations which appear to conform with the schematic characterization of the construction cannot always be described using the construction. One might suppose that if it is possible to 'shoot a person dead', it will also be possible to 'shoot a person wounded', where 'wounded' designates the state of the Patient resulting from the Agent's shooting of the Patient. Yet *shoot someone wounded* is unacceptable. Similarly, if it is possible to 'shoot a person dead', one might expect that one could also 'beat a person dead'. Yet *beat someone dead* is also ungrammatical. Some examples of 'impossible' resultatives are given in (12).

(12) *They shot him wounded.
      *They beat her dead.
      *They poisoned him dead.
      *They stabbed him dead.
      *They robbed him penniless.
      *They undressed him naked.
      *The doctor treated him healthy.
      *They fed the child obese.

In his *Aspects of the Theory of Syntax*—a book which was to set the agenda for linguistic research for several decades, and whose influence is still to be felt—Chomsky stated that 'the general rules of a grammar are not invalidated by the existence of exceptions' (Chomsky 1965: 218). The aim of linguistic research is to discover the general rules, not to list the idiosyncratic and the irregular. A generalization may be abandoned

only if a more highly valued grammar can be constructed that does not contain it. It is for this reason that the discovery of peculiarities and exceptions (which are rarely lacking, in a system of the complexity of a natural language) is generally so unrewarding and, in itself, has so little importance for the study of the grammatical structure of the language in question, unless, of course, it leads to the discovery of deeper generalizations. (Chomsky 1965: 218)

Applying this agenda to the resultative construction, one might search for semantic or other constraints on the construction's acceptability. If the enterprise is successful, we will be able to maintain that the construction is fully productive within the bounds set by the constraints. In this way, we will have arrived at a 'deeper generalization' concerning the construction. Several such constraints are discussed by Goldberg. One constraint she proposes is that the result must occur simultaneously with the end-point of the activity designated by the verb—*They shot him dead* means that the victim died instantly when shot, not that he died some time later as a result of his wounds. Still, this does not explain why *They beat him dead* is unacceptable—one can imagine a situation in which they beat him until he was dead. A second constraint is that the adjective designates the 'end-of-a-scale'—the Patient 'goes over the edge' (Goldberg 1995: 196). This may be a reason why *wounded* and *obese* do not sit comfortably with the construction—one can be wounded or obese to a degree. Still, it is not clear why *penniless* fails to appear as a resultative. Goldberg also observes that adjectives derived from participles are excluded from the construction; you cannot 'kick the door opened'. While this might cover the impossibility of *wounded* appearing in the construction, the semantic motivation for this restriction is not at all obvious. Moreover, *shut*, in *slam the door shut*, might well be regarded as derived from the past participle of the verb *shut*.

The example of the resultative construction (the example, by the way, is not at all untypical; practically any syntactic phenomenon could have been taken as an illustration) demonstrates that even syntax (traditionally thought of as the province of the regular and the predictable) is not untainted by the idiomatic. True, one would not normally think of *shoot someone dead* or *strip someone naked* as idioms—there is, after all, a general syntactic pattern to which the expressions conform, and the component words mean more or less what they mean elsewhere in the language. Nevertheless, the expressions *are* idiomatic in the sense that their grammaticality cannot be 'figured out' solely by reference to general principles. A speaker of English has to know that *shoot someone dead*, *beat someone unconscious*, and *paint the house green* are acceptable instances of the construction. As the examples in (12) suggest, the community of English speakers has been somewhat reluctant to extend the regularities manifested in (11) beyond the 'idiomatic' instances that they have encountered.

As Chomsky observed, the 'discovery of peculiarities and exceptions' may well be intrinsically unrewarding. The study of the idiomatic is worth pursuing only if it leads to 'deeper generalizations'. I suggest that the study of the idiomatic does indeed lead to a deeper understanding of the nature of language, but probably not one that Chomsky envisaged. The grammar comes to be characterized, not in terms of ever more general rules and principles, but as a huge inventory of rather particular facts, interrelated by schemas of varying levels of schematicity. Far from being marginal to the grammar, the idiomatic occupies the central place.

Study questions

1. Select at random a passage of prose from a newspaper, magazine, novel, etc. Identify the conventionalized expressions in the passage. Pay attention to the various dimensions of idiomaticity discussed in this chapter, including preferred collocations, formulas, and clichéd turns of phrase. The idiomatic character of an expression often becomes apparent if one tries to replace it by a different wording; although the different wording might well make sense in the context, it may not sound quite as natural as the original.

   On the basis of your observations, estimate the extent to which speakers and writers are activating pre-formed chunks of language.

2. Here are some Dutch idioms (from Geeraerts 1995):

   de pijp uitgaan 'to finish the pipe'
   met de meeste hoogachting 'with the highest esteem'
   iemand iets op de mouw spelden 'to pin something on someone's sleeve'
   met spek schieten 'to shoot with bacon'
   spekverkoper 'bacon-seller'
   aan de weg timmeren 'to practise carpentry by the roadside'
   de lakens uitdelen 'to hand out the sheets, to hand out the linen'
   uit z'n vel springen 'to jump out of one's skin'
   Abraham gezien hebben 'to have seen Abraham'

   If you do not know Dutch, try to work out what the conventionalized meanings of the idioms might be. What strategies did you use in the process?

   The idiomatic meanings are given in the Appendix, p. 586. How successful were your guesses? To what extent, and in what respects, are the Dutch idioms semantically transparent?

3. 'Creative idiomaticity' is the title of a paper by He (1989). In some linguistic theories, the notion of 'creative idiomaticity' would be an oxymoron — idioms, by definition, lie outside the bounds of linguistic creativity. Explain

why 'creative idiomaticity' would be a contradiction in some theories, and why the notion should be perfectly natural in Cognitive Grammar.

According to He, (i) and (v) are standard idioms in Chinese. The remaining examples are creative extensions from these. What do you think the extensions might mean? (See pp. 586–7 for He's suggestions.) What are the processes of idiomatic extension? Can you think of examples of idiom extension in English?

(i) zǒu hòu mén
     go by back door
     'use one's influential connections to gain an objective'

(ii) kāi hòu mén
     open back door

(iii) dǔ   hòu mén
     block back door

(iv) kāi qián mén
     open front door

(v) shā jı   gěi hóu   kàn
     kill chicken for monkey see
     'kill the chicken for the monkey(s) to see', i.e. 'punish one person as a warning to others'

(vi) shā hóu   gěi jī   kàn
     kill monkey for chicken see

(vii) shā hóu   gěi hóu   kàn
     kill monkey for monkey see

4. **Use-by dates.** The date by which a packaged foodstuff should be consumed is stated, in English, by means of the expression *Best before . . . .* Although this does not look like an idiomatic expression, it is interesting to note that the use-by date is formulated differently in different languages. Examine some foodstuff packagings for the conventionalized formulas that are used in French, Italian, German, etc.

   Consider how the following public notices are expressed in other languages: *No exit, No smoking, Keep out, Give way, Mind the step, Keep off the grass.* To what extent can the expressions in English and the other languages be regarded as idiomatic?

5. *Kick the bucket* is often cited as a classic example of a non-compositional idiom, in that the meaning 'die' does not appear to be distributed over the idiom's parts. Neither can the scene of a person (literally) 'kicking a bucket' be related in any obvious way to their death.

   In spite of the expression's apparent lack of motivation, it is not the case that *kick the bucket* can refer to any instance of dying. Consider the appropriateness of the idiom with respect to the death of a household pet (Can your poodle 'kick the bucket'?), the slaughter of farm animals, a person's death in a road accident or a plane crash, a person's death through murder, execution, euthanasia, or the discontinuation of a life-support system. Is the age of the person relevant? What about the cause of death? Is it equally appropriate to say of an old man and a young child that they 'kicked the bucket'? Are various adverbials (*finally*, *suddenly*, *unexpectedly*, *slowly*, *gradually*, *unfortunately*, etc.) equally appropriate?

On the basis of these considerations, sketch the prototypical usage of the idiom. Are there aspects of the prototypical usage that might be motivated in any way?

You might also care to check out the etymology of the expression (e.g. Ayto 1990: 83). Are any aspects of the expression's origins preserved in modern usage?

Further reading

On the role of idioms and formulas in language knowledge, see Pawley and Syder (1983).

An important survey of idioms and their semantic and formal characteristics is Nunberg *et al.* (1994). An older, but still useful overview is Makkai (1972). Collections of papers, representing different theoretical approaches, are Cacciari and Tabossi (1993) and Everaert *et al.* (1995). Idioms receive a prominent treatment in Jackendoff's more recent work; see Jackendoff (1997: ch. 7). For a survey of French idioms, see Gross (1982). On the processing of idioms and figurative language in general, see Gibbs (1994: chs 3 and 6). Partridge's *Dictionary of Catch Phrases* (1977) is a veritable mine of information.

Idioms and formulaic expressions have been an important topic in second-language acquisition research. See Cowie (1992), Nattinger and DeCarrico (1992), Weinert (1995), and Howarth (1998).

Constructions

On several occasions already in this book I have emphasized that Cognitive Grammar does not recognize a distinct level of syntactic organization. The combination of words into larger configurations is handled, not by a special syntactic component of the grammar, but in terms of constructions. A study of constructions reinforces many of the points made in the last chapter, concerning, for example, the absence of a clear-cut distinction between the idiomatic and the regular, and the impossibility, in principle, of separating facts pertaining to the lexicon from facts pertaining to the syntax.

28.1 Constructions and constructional schemas

A construction may be defined, very generally, as any linguistic structure that is analysable into component parts. Three kinds of entity are recognized in Cognitive Grammar—phonological structures, semantic structures, and symbolic structures. We can identify constructions in each of the three domains:

(i) phonological constructions; [kæt] constitutes a phonological construction, in that the complex structure can be analysed into three component segments, namely [k], [æ], and [t];

(ii) semantic constructions; [BLACK CAT] constitutes a semantic construction, which can be analysed into two component semantic units, namely [BLACK] and [CAT];

(iii) symbolic constructions; [BLACK CAT]/[blæk kæt] constitutes a symbolic construction, in that two component symbolic units can be identified, namely [BLACK]/[blæk] and [CAT]/[kæt].

In investigating constructions, whether these be phonological, semantic, or symbolic, we can appeal to many of the constructs that have proved useful in our study of other entities in a language. First, various kinds of relation can hold between constructions (section 2.1.1). One construction can be schematic for another construction; a construction can have, as one of its parts, a smaller construction; and constructions can be related through similarity. Secondly, constructions can vary according to their degree of entrenchment (section 14.3). In the case of schematic constructions, the question of productivity also arises: how readily do speakers of a language create expressions that instantiate the constructional schema (section 15.3)?

The constructions that were mentioned above—[kæt], [BLACK CAT], and [BLACK CAT]/[blæk kæt]—are specified in considerable detail. There are grounds for proposing schematic constructions of which these specific constructions are instances. Let us consider, first, the case of phonological constructions.

Alongside the phonological construction [kæt] there exist a large number of constructions which exhibit a similar internal structure: [sæt], [sɛt], [kæp], [kɪt], and countless more. This state of affairs suggests that we recognize a more schematic construction, namely the syllable construction $[CVC]_\sigma$, of which [kæt], [sæt], [sɛt], etc., are instances. The schema $[CVC]_\sigma$ specifies the kinds of units that are eligible to occur in the construction, namely, units of the kind 'consonant' (C) and 'vowel' (V), as well as the manner in which they are combined. The schema also characterizes the complex structure as a 'syllable'. Each of these aspects deserves closer examination.

As just noted, the schema $[CVC]_\sigma$ makes reference to entities of the kinds 'vowel' and 'consonant'. There may certainly be independent grounds for categorizing segments as vowels or consonants, in terms of their inherent sonority and phonological dependence, for example. Other things being equal, more sonorous (and phonologically autonomous) units will be eligible to fill the V slot in the syllable construction, less sonorous (and phonologically dependent) units will be restricted to the C slots. At the same time, there is an important sense in which the categories of vowel and consonant emerge as functions of the roles which segments play within the schematic construction. A segment counts as a vowel or as a consonant, not only because of its inherent phonetic properties, but in virtue of the slot which it fills in the syllable schema. In fact, strictly speaking, it is only with reference to the syllable schema that the phonetic aspects of a segment (sonority and phonological dependence) become relevant at all.

A second feature of the $[CVC]_\sigma$ schema is that the complex structure is characterized as a syllable. As was the case with the categories of vowels and consonants, there may well be independent grounds for defining and identifying syllables, in terms of variations in sonority, for example. Nevertheless, a particular sequence of sounds in a given language counts as a syllable, not only because of its inherent phonetic properties, but also because it conforms with (i.e., it can be regarded as an instance of) a schematically characterized syllable construction in the language. In other words, the notion of syllable emerges at the level of the constructional schema, not at the level of the instances. The schematic construction captures the commonalities of a vast range of specific constructions which share a similar internal structure. It is in virtue of these commonalities that a unit of the kind 'syllable' can be postulated. Constructions such as [kæt], [sæt], etc., count as syllables because they instantiate the construction.

These observations on phonological constructions can be brought to bear on semantic and symbolic constructions. Expressions such as *black cat, red box, tall tree*, and indefinitely many more, exemplify, and justify the recognition of, an [ADJ N] schema for combining a symbolic unit of the adjective category with a symbolic unit of the noun category. The schema specifies the manner in which the component phonological units are combined (in particular, the fact that the adjective is spoken before the noun) as well as the manner in which the component semantic units are combined. An important aspect of semantic combination is that the adjectival and nominal concepts are not simply lined up, one after the other, but are integrated into a modifier-head relation (section 12.2).

As was the case with vowels and consonants, there is an important sense in which the categories of adjective and noun (and indeed the other word classes) must be understood with respect to the constructional schemas in which they occur (Croft 1999). This is not to deny the possibility of entertaining construction-independent characterizations of the word classes, in terms of the nature of the concepts that the words designate, for example (Chapter 9). Ultimately, however, a word class emerges as a function of its role within a constructional schema. For example, adjectives (more precisely, attributive adjectives) have to be defined in terms of their possibility of combining with a noun in accordance with the phonological and semantic specifications of the attributive adjective construction [ADJ N]. Similarly, we identify a verb as transitive, not only because of its inherent semantic properties (it designates a temporal relation between a tr and a lm), but also because of its eligibility to occur in the transitive clause construction [NP$_{Subject}$ V$_{Transitive}$ NP$_{Direct Object}$]. Moreover, just as 'syllable' emerges as a schematic property of its instances, so also the notion of 'transitive clause' emerges as a generalization over expressions of the kind *The farmer shot the rabbit*.

28.1.1 Schema-instance relations among constructions

Constructional schemas can themselves stand in a schema-instance relation. A set of constructional schemas may be brought under an even more schematic construction, while a schematic construction can have, as its instances, a number of more specific constructional schemas.

A few examples will illustrate these relations. A phonological schema for a stressed syllable in English will have, as its instances, a schema for syllables containing a short vowel and a schema for syllables containing a long vowel (section 8.1.2). A syntactic schema for a grounded nominal ('noun phrase') will have, as its instances, a large number of sub-schemas for the different ways in which noun concepts can be quantified and grounded. The semantic schema for combining an adjectival and a nominal concept can be brought under a more general schema for a head-modifier construction, which will have, as its instances, not only the adjective-noun construction, but also adverb-verb constructions.

Although highly schematic constructions may well be justified in order to capture broad patterns in a language, low-level constructional schemas will still be needed in order to account for the special properties of individual items. While $[CVC]_\sigma$ captures the commonality of a large number of syllables in English, the schema wrongly predicts that [ŋæh] is a possible syllable in the language. While [h] and [ŋ] are certainly instances of the schematic unit [C], they are eligible to fill only the onset and coda positions, respectively, of the syllable construction. These facts need to be captured in low-level syllable schemas which make specific reference to the segments [h] and [ŋ].

Similar remarks apply to the behaviour of individual lexical items. A 'cran-berry word' (section 27.3.1) such as *auspices* is virtually restricted to occurring in the expression *under the auspices of NP* (where NP is the name of some authoritative entity). The expression instantiates the very same prepositional construction as countless other expressions (*by the side of the river*, *under the surface of the water*, etc.). Yet *auspices* is not able to occur with other prepositions in the prepositional construction, nor can it occur in other constructions which contain a nominal slot. You cannot perform some activity 'with the auspices' of some authority, nor can you 'query the auspices', 'recognize the auspices', or 'commend the auspices', nor say of auspices that they are invalid, fraudulent, or whatever. A characterization of the word *auspices* needs to make reference to the prepositional phrase construction in which it occurs. At the same time, we need to recognize, as an instance of the prepositional phrase construction, the specific expression *under the auspices of NP*. Collocations require a similar treatment. *Heavy smoker* and *heavy drinker* are acceptable collocations, whereas **heavy eater* is not. *Heavy smoker* and *heavy drinker* need to be listed as specific instantiations of the [ADJ N] schema. At the same time, a full characterization of *heavy* needs to include a reference to those [ADJ N] expressions in which the word may occur.

At a sufficiently fine-grained level of analysis, it could well turn out that every unit in a language has a distinct distribution with respect to the constructions in which it can occur. I have already hinted at this possibility in the phonological domain. In examining the distributional profile of the six stop consonants in English (see Study question 1 of Chapter 13) you may well have concluded that no two consonants share exactly the same distribution. Gross discovered a similar state of affairs in the domain of syntax. After examining the syntactic distributions of some 2,000 verbs in French, Gross (1994) found that no two verbs share exactly the same properties (see also Gross 1979). In a similar vein, after surveying the distributional properties of the English determiners and quantifiers, Culicover (1999: 64) observed that 'there seem to be almost as many patterns as there are elements'.

28.1.2 Constructions as parts of constructions

Given that constructions, by definition, are complex entities which can be analysed into component parts, it is to be expected that a construction can have, as one of its parts, another construction. When we define a phonological foot with reference to strong and weak syllables (section 5.2), we are recognizing phonological constructions (syllables) as parts of another phonological construction (the foot). (We might note in passing that the distinction between strong and weak syllables is itself a function of the role these play within the larger construction, namely, the foot.) Likewise, if we characterize a transitive clause as [NP$_{Subject}$ V$_{Transitive}$ NP$_{Direct Object}$], we do so by reference to noun phrase constructions.

It is sometimes possible for a construction of a certain type to contain, as one of its parts, a construction of the same type. A noun phrase can itself contain a noun phrase, a clause can be contained within a clause. Consider the prenominal possessive construction. A prenominal possessive has the schematic structure [NP-POSS N]$_{NP}$, where POSS is the possessive morpheme. Instances of the construction include *the man's hat, the neighbours' car, some students' essays*. Given that the prenominal possessive is itself an NP, we should expect a prenominal possessive to be able to occupy the NP slot within a larger prenominal possessive. This is indeed the case. In *the boy's father's boat*, the prenominal possessive *the boy's father* functions as the possessor within the larger construction. The embedding processes can be iterated: *the boy's father's friend's boat*. This aspect of constructions effectively handles what generative linguists have always proclaimed to be a defining property of human languages, namely, 'recursion' (Radford 1988: 128). A finite number of 'rules' (or, in Cognitive Grammar, constructions) is able to generate an infinite number of sentences (or, in Cognitive Grammar terms, is able to sanction an infinite number of instances).

28.1.3 The productivity of constructional schemas

Issues which we have already encountered in previous discussions of schemas come to bear also on constructional schemas. Of special importance is the question of productivity. A schema captures the commonalities over its instances. At the same time, the schema may be able to sanction new instances which conform with its specifications, and to this extent the schema may be said to be productive. In discussing morphology (Chapters 14 and 15) we saw that productivity is a function of a number of aspects, involving the entrenchment of the schema (itself a function of the type frequency of the instances) and the entrenchment of the instances. Thus (to recapitulate the earlier discussion), a schema which abstracts over a very large number of different instances, none of which, individually, is particularly frequent, is likely to be highly entrenched, and therefore liable to sanction new instances. A schema which abstracts over a relatively small number of different instances, some of which may individually be quite frequent, is not likely to be highly entrenched, and is therefore unlikely to be very productive. Highly entrenched instances, especially if they share few commonalities with other expressions in the language, are not likely to be subsumed under a schema at all, so productivity is hardly an issue.

For an example of a highly productive constructional schema we need look no further than the schema for a transitive clause. The schema [NP$_{Subject}$ V$_{Transitive}$ NP$_{Direct Object}$] is entrenched by the large number of different instances which speakers of English encounter just about every day of their lives; moreover, there do not seem to be any individual instances which are particularly entrenched. In view of its productivity, the transitive schema tends to be accorded the status of a 'core' element of English syntax. Somewhat less productive is the resultative construction discussed in the last chapter. The construction has the form [NP$_{Subject}$ V$_{Transitive}$ NP$_{Direct Object}$ ADJ], where the adjective designates the state of the direct object entity which results from the action of the subject entity. This construction is associated with a relatively small number of instances involving specific lexical items and speakers are somewhat reluctant to create new expressions on the same pattern. Finally, expressions such as *by and large* can hardly be brought under a constructional schema at all; these are fixed idioms, unable to be modified in any way.

28.2 Constructional idioms

As the name for a pattern for the combination of smaller units into larger syntactic configurations, the term 'construction' is well established in traditional grammar, as well as in some older linguistic theories (e.g. Bloomfield 1933). Nevertheless, constructions have a somewhat ambivalent status in many

Goldberg on constructions

My definition of construction, namely, as any linguistic structure which is analysable into component parts, differs from that adopted by Goldberg (1995). Goldberg's definition runs as follows:

C is a CONSTRUCTION iff$_{def}$ C is a form-meaning pair ‹F$_i$, S$_i$› such that some aspect of F$_i$ or some aspect of S$_i$ is not strictly predictable from C's component parts or from other previously established constructions. (Goldberg 1995: 4)

Goldberg's definition refers specifically to symbolic constructions, i.e. to associations of a phonological and a semantic structure. Moreover, only symbolic associations whose properties are not fully predictable from other form-meaning associations count as constructions. On Goldberg's definition, the lexical item *dog*—understood as the association of the phonological form [dɒg] with the concept [DOG]—turns out to be a construction, in that this specific association is not predictable from other symbolic associations in English. On the other hand, the expression *The farmer shot the rabbit* would not be regarded, on Goldberg's definition, as a construction, since the properties of this expression are derivable from the properties of the transitive clause construction in association with the properties of the symbolic units which make up the expression.

  Goldberg's emphasis, therefore, is on the idiosyncratic (or 'idiomatic') character of established form-meaning relations; my criterion for identifying a construction concerns only an expression's internal structure, irrespective of the schematicity with which the construction is specified, and also irrespective of whether the properties of the construction are predictable (or, conversely, idiosyncratic). In spite of these differences, the kinds of entities that Goldberg in her 1995 book regards as constructions—such as the schema for resultative clauses—also count as constructions on my understanding of the term.

contemporary theories. Many contemporary theories, especially those of a formalist or generativist inspiration, seek general principles of syntactic organization, whose interaction determines the grammaticality of an expression. On such a view, constructions are of little interest in themselves; they are, as Chomsky (1991: 417) put it, 'taxonomic epiphenomena', which emerge as the product of what are presumed to be more basic principles.[1] Such an approach entails that speakers of a language do not need to learn the constructions in their language, they need only know the general principles which determine their grammaticality (see Lakoff 1987: 467). Especially in Chomskyan theories, these 'general principles' are assumed to derive from a genetically inherited 'universal grammar'.

---

[1] It is interesting to note that phonological constructions have enjoyed a different fate. I doubt whether there are any modern phonologists, of whatever theoretical persuasion, who would dismiss syllables and feet as 'taxonomic epiphenomena'.

Evidence against such a 'reductionist', and even 'innatist' approach to syntax would come from constructions whose properties—indeed, whose very existence in a language—cannot be derived from more general principles. Fillmore *et al.* (1988) drew attention to quite a number of constructions in English which have just this property. They referred to these constructions as 'formal idioms'. Formal idioms are idiomatic in the sense just stated—their properties cannot be derived from more general principles. Unlike 'lexical idioms', of the kind *kick the bucket*, formal idioms are characterized in terms of a constructional schema with slots that can be filled by any items which match the construction's specifications.

I discuss an example of a formal idiom in some detail, in order to illustrate both its 'formal' and its 'idiomatic' character.

28.2.1 The incredulity response construction

I have selected for discussion, from among many possible candidates, the 'incredulity response construction'.[2] The construction is exemplified in (1).

(1) (What?!) Him write a novel?! (You must be joking.)

The expression *Him write a novel* has a distinct semantic-pragmatic value. It would be used in a situation in which the idea of a certain person writing a novel has already been brought up, or hinted at, in previous discourse. The speaker takes up this idea and dismisses it as absurd. Typically, the expression would be introduced by an exclamation of surprise and followed up by a remark emphasizing the proposition's absurdity. In (1), these additional components are placed in parentheses.

The special semantics of *Him write a novel* goes with a distinctive syntax. The expression consists of a verb phrase (*write a novel*) which occurs in association with a subject nominal (*him*). We note, however, that the subject nominal fails to appear in the nominative form *he* while the verb lacks the third-person *-s* inflection. The verb can also not occur with a past-tense inflection or with a modal: *What?! Him {*wrote / *can write / *must write} a novel?!* These facts point to the status of *Him write a novel* as an ungrounded clause.

The clause has some noteworthy phonological properties. In order for it to have the intended interpretation ('the idea of him writing a novel is absurd') the clause has to be spoken with a distinctive intonation. First, the subject nominal *him* and the verb phrase *write a novel* need to be spoken as two phonological phrases. Secondly, both phonological phrases need to be spoken

---

[2] The term is taken from Fillmore *et al.* (1988: 511), where the construction is briefly discussed. For more detailed analysis, see Lambrecht (1990). The subtitle of Lambrecht's paper—'"Mad Magazine sentences" revisited'—may puzzle some readers. The title alludes to *Mad Magazine*, an American publication in which the incredulity response construction is supposed to feature with particular frequency. (I must add, though, that having browsed through some issues of the magazine, I failed to find a single instance of the construction.)

with a rising intonation. If these conditions are not satisfied, (1) fails to have the semantic-pragmatic force that we described. There is in addition the possibility of associating an utterance of (1) with distinctive 'paralinguistic' features—a 'sneering' tone of voice, or a sneering facial gesture, for example. The reader may also have noticed that my orthographic representation in (1) is associated with a distinctive punctuation, namely '?!'.

In summary, the constructional idiom needs to be characterized in both its formal and semantic aspects:

- Formal aspects: the expression consists of an ungrounded clause. The subject nominal is in the oblique form and the verb phrase lacks tense and agreement markers. Subject and verb phrase constitute separate phonological phrases, each associated with a rising intonation. Optionally, the expression is spoken with 'sneering' paralinguistic features; in its written form, it may be associated with a distinctive punctuation.
- Semantic aspects: the ungrounded clause refers to a situation that has already been mentioned, or that was hinted at, in previous discourse. The possibility of this situation being true is dismissed as absurd.

The above characterization is not restricted to the specific expression in (1). As the reader can easily verify, very many expressions exhibit this same association of formal and semantic properties: *What?! Me worry?!*, *My boss give me a raise?!*, *Fred want to marry Louise?!* (However, see Study question 1 on the need for a more refined account of the construction's formal aspects.)

The question we need to address is whether the particular cluster of formal and semantic properties exhibited by (1) can be derived from more general principles. It is apparent that the construction is not totally encapsulated from other facts about the English language. The subject and direct object of the verb in (1) designate, respectively, the tr and the lm of the ungrounded process; both subject and object have the form of perfectly ordinary noun phrases; while a 'sneering' voice quality is in general likely to be associated with a dismissive attitude towards an expression's semantic content. Beyond this, however, the combination of properties exhibited by the incredulity response expressions turns out to be largely unique to this construction. While a rising intonation contour is likely to be associated with the speaker's uncertainty *vis-à-vis* the truth of a proposition (Taylor 1995a: 160–7), this fact fails to predict the association of rising intonation with an expression of incredulity. The same goes for the use of an ungrounded clause. In terms of general principles an ungrounded clause is just that—it is a clause which designates a situation which is not anchored in time or reality from the perspective of the speech–act situation. While this characterization may be consistent with an attitude of incredulity, the special semantic nuances associated with the ungrounded clause in (1) are specific to the construction. There is no way of predicting from general principles that an ungrounded clause will express speaker incredulity *vis-à-vis* a previously mentioned situation. Moreover, it is not a general property of clauses that the subject nominal and the verb phrase have to be spoken as separate phonological phrases.

Contrary to the reductionist approach, the particular cluster of formal and semantic properties of the incredulity response construction cannot be derived from general principles. This aspect becomes even more apparent when one considers translation equivalents in other languages. In German, for example, the incredulity response has a quite different syntactic form (Lambrecht 1990: 219):

(2) Was?! Er   und einen   Roman schreiben?!
    what   he-NOM and a-ACC novel   write-INF

As in English, the verb phrase *einen Roman schrieben* 'write a novel' lacks a grounding element. The subject nominal, though, appears in the nominative form *er* 'he' and is linked to the verb phrase by means of *und* 'and'.[3] This particular cluster of formal and semantic properties has to be learned. A speaker of German who had never before encountered the construction would not be able to predict that (2) was the appropriate way of expressing incredulity.

28.2.2 More constructional idioms

In this section I briefly survey a number of other 'formal idioms' that have attracted the attention of linguists in recent years.

(i) Negative polarity questions.[4] A polarity question, such as *Did Harry leave?*, invites the hearer to specify the polarity of the proposition 'Harry left'. One might suppose that a negative polarity question—*Didn't Harry leave?*— invites the hearer to specify the polarity of the negated proposition 'Harry didn't leave', whereby a negative response to the former ('No, it is not the case that Harry left') ought to be equivalent to an affirmative response to the latter ('Yes, it is the case that Harry didn't leave'), and vice versa. Yet negative polarity questions have a special value that cannot be derived from the addition of clausal negation to a polarity question. Whereas *Did Harry leave?* is a genuine request for information ('Tell me, is it or is it not the case that Harry left'), *Didn't Harry leave?* has the force of a hedged assertion ('I believe that it is the case that Harry left; please confirm this'). The assertive character shows up in the fact that negative questions can occur in environments which are reserved for assertions. *Because* introduces an assertive clause (3a) and is

---

[3] Lambrecht (1990: 227) refers also to the Latin construction, in which the verb appears in the subjunctive form: *Ego tibi irascar* 'Me be angry with you?!' This usage is commonly known as the 'repudiating subjunctive' (Palmer 1954: 312). According to John Barsby (personal communication), the repudiating subjunctive was especially frequent in Roman comedy. There is an intriguing parallel here with the supposedly frequent use of the English construction in the American humorous magazine.

[4] See Lakoff (1987: 533).

incompatible with a genuine interrogative (3b). In keeping with its basically assertive character, however, a negative polarity question can appear as the complement of *because* (3c).

(3) a. I'm surprised that you ask about Harry, because Harry left.
      b. *I'm surprised that you ask about Harry, because did Harry leave?
      c. I'm surprised that you ask about Harry, because didn't Harry leave?

(ii) *What's X doing Y?*[5] There is a corny joke in which a diner asks the waiter, 'What's this fly doing in my soup?' and the waiter responds, 'I think it's trying to swim to dry land, Madam'. The point of the joke is that the waiter interprets the question 'literally', that is, as a request for information on the current activity of the fly ('The fly is doing something; tell me what it is') and responds by describing the activity. The diner's question, though, has another value, roughly: 'There's a fly in my soup; this situation is contrary to what I expect to be the case; please give an explanation.' The 'X' in the construction is typically a referential nominal, while Y is an adjunct which characterizes the situation in which X is involved. The adjunct might be a locative phrase, as in the example just discussed, an *-ing* phrase (*What are you doing lying on the floor?*), or other kind of descriptive phrase (*What are the flags doing at half mast?*). Fixed elements of the construction are the items *what* and *doing*, as well as the verb *be*, which can occur in any of its present- or past-tense forms.

(iii) *The X-er the Y-er.*[6] The correlative construction is illustrated by familiar phrases such as *The more the merrier, the fewer the better, the bigger they come the further they fall*. The general meaning is 'more/less of X correlates with more/less of Y'. A notable feature is that the morpheme *the*, which introduces each of the correlated phrases, has little in common, semantically, with the definite determiner *the*. Another feature is that the construction lacks a main verb and is therefore 'timeless'. This no doubt contributes to the aphoristic flavour of correlative expressions. To this extent, the construction has affinities to other bipartite verbless expressions such as *Out of the frying pan into the fire, Easy come easy go, Penny wise pound foolish*.

(iv) *One more X and Y.*[7] Examples include *One more beer and I'll be off, One more botch-up like that and you're fired*. The construction conveys that the occurrence of event Y is dependent on, or will follow naturally from, a prior and not yet actualized event involving entity X. The construction therefore has the character of a conditional; event Y will ensue if an event involving X should take place. If Y is something the hearer does not want to happen, an utterance of the *one more* construction is likely to have the force of a threat or a warning.

[5] See Kay and Fillmore (1999); for an earlier account, see Pullum (1973).
[6] See Fillmore *et al.* (1988); also Culicover and Jackendoff (1999) and Culicover (1999: 83–5).
[7] Discussed—albeit from the point of view of autonomous syntax—in Culicover and Jackendoff (1997).

An interesting aspect of the construction is the function of the word *and*. Normally, *and* serves to conjoin two expressions of equivalent status, but in the *one more* construction it conjoins a nominal and a clause. Moreover, the 'conditional' character of the construction suggests a relation of subordination of the first event (the one involving X) to the second. Yet *and* could hardly be analysed as a subordinating conjunction. For one thing, it occurs before the main clause, not before the subordinated constituent.

'Conditional' *and* also occurs in expressions in which the first constituent has the form of an imperative: *Come one step closer and I'll shoot, Botch this up and you're fired*. Here, we note that what looks like an imperative clause (*come one step closer, botch this up*) does not have the force of a directive. Rather, it states the condition under which the second event will occur. Again, *and* introduces what is conceptually the main clause, not the subordinated condition.

(v) The *may* construction, exemplified by *He máy be a professor, but he sure is dumb*.[8] (Note that the construction requires primary stress on *may*.) Here, the speaker concedes the truth of a certain state of affairs, but dismisses the fact as not pertinent to some more important consideration. At issue is not the probability of a situation being true—the 'basic' sense of deontic *may*— but its relevance.

(vi) Various clefting and focusing constructions. These involve directing attention to certain constituents of a clause, often by means of a structure involving the copula *be*. Corresponding to the 'neutral' clause *I don't like cheese* are the 'clefted' constructions *It's cheese that I don't like* and *It's me that doesn't like cheese*, and the 'pseudocleft' *What I don't like is cheese*. (For a recent discussion, see Lambrecht 2001.) Perhaps the most remarkable of the focusing constructions is the double-*be* construction, illustrated by the title of a paper which Tuggy (1996) devotes to its analysis: 'The thing is is that people talk that way. The question is is why?'[9]

(vii) The *way* construction.[10] One of the uses of *way* is to designate the path along which a person moves towards a destination: *I took the shortest way home, I lost my way, What's the best way to the station?* It is also possible to 'make one's way' to, or towards, a destination—a person, in proceeding to their destination, makes, or creates, the path along which they proceed. The following sentence, therefore, does not appear to be in any way remarkable.

(4) I made my way to the exit.

What is interesting is that the syntactic form of (4) provides the prototype for a very productive constructional schema. The construction may be

---

[8] The construction is briefly mentioned in Fillmore *et al.* (1988).
[9] The construction has also been analysed by Massam (1999), who appears to have been unaware of Tuggy (1996).
[10] See Goldberg (1995: ch. 9), Jackendoff (1990: 211–23), and Israel (1996).

characterized as [V one's way PP], where [PP] designates a path or goal and V designates the activity the subject referent performs in order to create a path to the goal. A large number of verbs can occur in the construction—(5), though 'pure' motion verbs, such as *come* and *go*, and verbs designating a manner of motion, such as *walk* and *run*, seem not to be possible—(6).

(5) a. I had to fight my way to the exit.
    b. He lied his way into their confidence.
    c. She slept her way to the top.
    d. We can't legislate our way out of the drug problem.
    e. The government wants to spend its way out of recession.

(6) a. *We went our way home.
    b. *I ran my way to the exit.
    c. *I rushed my way to the airport.
    d. *I flew my way to London.

The *way* construction illustrates an important property of constructional schemas. In Chapter 16 I drew attention to the distinction between 'source-oriented rules' and 'product-oriented rules', claiming that morphological schemas (for a plural noun, or a past-tense verb, for example) state the properties of the complex form which a speaker needs to retrieve or create. They are not to be thought of in terms of operations that a speaker performs on a simpler form in order to get the complex form.

It is clear that the *way* construction must be thought of in similar terms. Consider the fact that in the construction *way* functions as the direct object of the verb. This is true even of verbs such as *sleep* and *lie* which are not inherently transitive. As for the verbs in (5) which are basically transitive, these are able to take *way* as their direct object only if the prepositional phrase is present: *The government spent its way*, *He fought his way*, etc. are unacceptable. It is therefore the construction itself, with its specific association of formal and semantic properties, which sanctions the transitive use of the verbs. A verb can occur in the construction, not because of its ability to take *way* as a direct object, nor because it can take a directional phrase, but because it is compatible with the overall specifications of the construction. *Way* expressions are created as a 'gestalt', in conformity with the constructional schema, they are not assembled by a process of successively adding constituents to, say, a verb.[11]

28.3 Constructional idioms in the grammar at large

One might be inclined to regard constructional idioms of the kind discussed above as fairly peripheral to the language system. Symptomatic of their

---

[11] A few verbs are largely restricted to occurring in the construction: *worm one's way* (into someone's confidence), *elbow one's way* (towards the door). These 'cranberry' verbs can only be described with reference to the construction in which they occur.

marginal status could be the fact that they are typically associated with rather special semantic and/or pragmatic values. Indeed, one can imagine vast stretches of discourse in which instances of the constructions never occur. To be sure, a speaker needs to specifically learn the constructions, in both their formal and their semantic/pragmatic aspects. Knowing such constructions could be an additional refinement to a person's language knowledge—useful, certainly, but outside of the 'core' linguistic system.

Such a view would be legitimate, were it the case that constructional idioms indeed occupied a marginal position within the language system, and could be cleanly distinguished from facts of a language which pertain to (i) the lexicon and (ii) the syntax. But this is not the case. Constructional idioms are Janus-like entities, which face towards both the lexicon and the syntax.

28.3.1 Constructional idioms and the lexicon

A constructional schema specifies, among other things, the kinds of items which are eligible to occur in it. In the case of the incredulity response construction, the slots are syntactic categories, namely, a nominal and a verb phrase, whereas in the case of the *What's X doing Y?* construction, the construction already specifies some of the lexical items that occur in it. One might say, therefore, that the construction exemplifies 'idiomatic' uses of the lexical items *what* and *do*. Similarly, the correlative *the X-er the Y-er* construction exemplifies a special use of *the*, the *one more* construction special uses of *one*, *more*, and *and*, and so on.

As a matter of fact, for a very large number of idiomatic expressions, it is a moot point whether they should be analysed in terms of special properties of the lexical items they contain or in terms of the constructions in which the lexical items occur.[12] At issue are idioms which are partially fixed, lexically, but which contain slots which can be filled by items of the appropriate category. Examples include *day in day out*, *yours sincerely*, *what on earth (are you doing)?*, *on and on*, *It's up to you*, to mention just a few. Consider, by way of illustration, expressions of the form *one by one*, *day by day*, *word by word*, briefly discussed in section 6.1.2. These exemplify a special use of *by*, but also point to the existence of a constructional idiom of the form [X by X]. The construction designates the rate at which some process unfolds, with X being the unit by which the unfolding of the process is measured. There are perhaps a dozen or so quite well-entrenched instances of this construction. At the same time, the construction is moderately productive. *Atom by atom* is definitely not an entrenched locution. Yet we can easily see how the [X by X] construction sanctions the expression in (7):

---

[12] In fact, I would maintain that both approaches need to be used, complementarily. The special use of *by* exemplified in *day by day* needs to be characterized with reference to the construction in which it occurs; conversely, a characterization of the construction necessarily refers to the lexical item *by*.

(7) Radiation is actually eroding the planet's surface atom by atom. (Cited in
     COBUILD)

The limiting case of a lexically specified construction would be an expression whose lexical content is fully fixed. An example is the introduction formula *How do you do?* The difference between this fully fixed expression and constructions whose lexical content is only partially fixed is a matter of degree, it is not of difference in character.

28.3.2 Constructional idioms and the syntax

While the idiomatic nature of constructional idioms is not in doubt, one might still feel that there is a qualitative difference between, say, the incredulity response construction and the major syntactic constructions in a language, between, for example, (8a) and (8b).

(8) a. What?! Him write a novel?!
     b. He wrote a novel.

The expression in (8a)—as well as the constructional schema of which it is an instance—is idiomatic in ways we have discussed. The clause in (8b) lacks any obviously idiomatic features. On the contrary, it appears to be assembled in accordance with very general syntactic principles, of the kind that were discussed in Chapter 12. The verb *write* designates a process involving a tr and a lm; tr and lm are elaborated by nominals which function as the complements of the verb; the lm stands as the direct object of the verb, the tr as its subject; the clause is grounded in the usual way and lacks any special pragmatic values—it merely reports an occurrence of the event at a time prior to the time of utterance.

I would like to suggest, however, that the difference between the two expressions in (8) is again a matter of degree, it does not point to a fundamental difference in character between the idiomatic and the regular. In both cases, an expression is sanctioned by the existence of a constructional schema. The schema for the transitive clause is perceived to be 'regular', no doubt because the schema is able to be applied to a very large and open-ended number of instances and is not associated with any special conditions of use.

As a matter of fact, it is not quite true to say that the schema for a transitive clause is fully regular and lacking any idiomatic aspects.[13] Consider, for example, the range of verbs which are eligible to fill the verb slot in the

---

[13] I find it difficult to imagine what a 'fully regular' construction would look like and doubt whether the concept is a useful one. Presumably, a fully regular construction would be one whose slots can be filled by any item meeting the construction's structural description. However, to the extent that the structural description defines the classes of items that can fill the constructional slots, claims about regularity are vacuous.

construction and the kinds of situations that the construction can designate. The prototype of a transitive clause involves an event in which an Agent affects a Patient. Prototypical transitive verbs include *kill*, *hit*, *push*, and *kick*. However, as is well known, the transitive construction in English may be used of situations which deviate considerably from the prototype. Verbs of perception and cognitive processes, such as *see*, *hear*, *know*, and *remember*, are eligible to occur in the construction, even though the subject referent of these verbs does not act on, or affect, a Patient. Some languages, in fact, do not allow a transitive construal in these cases. French *Je me souviens de ça* 'I remember that' does not construe the process as something that the tr does to the lm, rather, the agentive role of the tr is de-emphasized through the use of a reflexive. Extending the net even wider, we encounter transitive clauses in which the subject nominal designates the 'location', or the 'setting', for a process (section 21.4.2):

(9) a. My car burst a tyre.
     b. The tent sleeps six.
     c. The fifth day saw our departure.
     d. The book sold over a million copies.

These clauses are indeed 'idiomatic' in the sense that there are very tight restrictions on the kinds of items that can occur in setting-subject expressions. We cannot say, for example, that the next day 'heard the explosion', nor that a house 'lives two families', nor that a book 'translated twenty languages'. The examples in (9) are also idiomatic in that they fail to exhibit the full range of properties normally associated with transitive predications. Unlike 'regular' transitives, of the kind *He wrote a book*, the clauses in (9) may not be made passive: *A tyre was burst (by my car)*, *Our departure was seen (by the fifth day)*.

The transitive construction turns out to consist of a prototypical 'core' and an increasingly idiomatic periphery. The core encodes what Goldberg has called a 'humanly relevant scene' (1995: 39). All languages, we may assume, have the means for encoding scenes that are fundamental to human experience, such as that of an Agent consciously acting on and affecting a Patient. Languages may differ, though, with respect to the syntactic resources that are available to encode humanly relevant scenes, also with respect to the range of situations which can be encoded by these resources.

Consider the case of the ditransitive construction (Goldberg 1995: ch. 6), exemplified by *I gave the child a present*. The scene is one of transfer of ownership; an Agent causes a person to come to be in possession of an entity. Jackendoff (1996) has used this example in support of the theory of autonomous syntax. That English has the ditransitive construction whereas French (for example) does not, is, for Jackendoff, a syntactic fact (p. 99), not to be confused with semantic facts, concerning the possible uses to which the ditransitive construction may be used. For my part, I would see this availability of the ditransitive construction in English as an idiomatic fact about the language; the ditransitive is a constructional idiom, the structural and semantic aspects of which speakers have to learn.

28.3.3 Developmental aspects

The claim that even the transitive construction constitutes a constructional idiom is supported by research in language acquisition. Suppose that a two-year-old utters the three-word sentence *I kick ball*. We might take this as evidence that the child has acquired a basic sentence pattern of English (following, some would say, from the setting of parameters of Universal Grammar). Alternatively, it could be that the child has learned an idiosyncratic fact about the word *kick*, namely, that the word can be used in an [N₁ kick N₂] construction, where N₁ designates the kicker and N₂ the thing kicked. Tomasello and Brooks (1998) argue for the latter interpretation. They showed children between the ages of two and two-and-a-half highly transitive situations, involving, for example, a puppet doing something to a small object, and described the situations using novel verbs. In one condition the novel verbs occurred in the transitive construction (*The puppet is meeking the ball*), in the other condition the verbs were introduced in an intransitive construction (*The ball is meeking*). It was found that the children who had learned a new verb in the one construction were very reluctant to use it in the other. Tomasello and Brooks concluded that children learn the transitive and intransitive constructions on a verb-by-verb basis; or, to put it another way, they learn each verb in association with the construction in which it occurs. It is only some years later, when a significant number of lexically specified constructions have been learned, that the child abstracts a schematic representation which generalizes over the instances and it is only then that the construction is used productively.

An 'item-based' acquisition process has been observed for a number of basic syntactic patterns, including the passive (Brooks and Tomasello 1999), complementation patterns (Diessel and Tomasello 2001), and interrogatives (Dąbrowska 2001). Tomasello draws the following conclusion:

The findings . . . are best explained by a usage-based model in which children's early linguistic competence is organized as an inventory of item-based constructions. . . . Fluency with a construction is a function of its token frequency in the child's experience (entrenchment); creativity with a construction emanates from the child's experience of type variation in one or more of the constituents (abstraction). In this way, children build up in their linguistic inventories a very diverse set of constructions—concrete, abstract, and mixed—to call upon as needed in particular usage events. (Tomasello 2000: 76–7)

28.4 The ecology of constructions: 'Bang goes my weekend'

Langacker characterized a grammar as a 'structured inventory of linguistic units'. The presentation of Cognitive Grammar in this book may be seen as an extended exegesis of this statement. We have not only studied the kinds of units (phonological, semantic, and symbolic) which comprise the grammar, we have also explored what it means to say that the inventory of units is 'structured'. It is rarely the case that a linguistic unit is totally encapsulated from everything else that a person knows about the language.[14] Normally, each individual unit is related, in numerous and intricate ways, to other units. Adopting a metaphor of Lakoff's (1987: 492), we can say that each unit has its 'ecological niche' in a complex network of units.

In this section I exemplify this aspect of linguistic knowledge with reference to a constructional idiom of English. Consider the following expression:

(10) Bang goes my weekend!

A preliminary analysis of example (10) proceeds in the familiar way. Let us consider, first, the semantics of the expression. It conjures up a rather specific scenario. You have planned some activity for the weekend and are looking forward to it. Just before the weekend, something comes up which interferes with your plans. It could be that your boss requires you to submit a report first thing on Monday, or that family commitments require you to attend to an ailing relative. The interfering activity takes precedence and you need to cancel your plans. You feel annoyed, but cannot reasonably renege on your duties. The expression has a familiar, somewhat jocular tone—nothing of great importance is actually at stake. If your grandmother had died and the funeral was on Saturday, it would be in very bad taste to utter (10). It would also be inappropriate, on learning that your spouse, whom you love dearly, has set up home with another person, to comment: *Bang goes my marriage!* or, on learning that you have a terminal illness, to declare: *Bang goes my life!*

The possibility of substituting *my weekend* with other nominals—*Bang goes my Saturday afternoon!*, *Bang goes my nice new theory!*, *Bang go our chances of making a million!*—suggests the schematic characterization [bang go NP$_{Subj}$], where NP designates the cherished object. This NP functions as the subject of the verb, as shown by number agreement on *go*. There are, however, some marked preferences regarding the characteristics of the nominal and the tense of the verb. An Internet search, conducted on the search engine www.AlltheWeb.com, scored 4,072 hits for the collocation 'bang goes' against only 587 for 'bang go' and 1,012 for 'bang went'.[15] Table 28.1 summarizes

---

[14] Perhaps the only examples of fully encapsulated units would be phrases borrowed from a foreign language which a speaker does not know.

[15] It is likely that not all the Internet hits pertain to the *bang goes* construction. However, there is no reason to doubt that the numbers reflect real patterns in the construction's use.

Table 28.1 Number of Internet hits for collocations involving *bang* (*go*).

Singular		Plural	
bang goes my	132	bang goes our	31
bang go my	22	bang go our	2
bang goes your	2,626		
bang go your	9		
bang goes his	31	bang goes their	8
bang go his	3	bang go their	1
bang goes her	2		
bang go her	0		
bang goes its	1		
bang go its	0		
bang goes the	604		
bang go the	191		
bang went my	42	bang went our	10
bang went your	0		
bang went his	59	bang went their	3
bang went her	8		
bang went its	0		
bang went the	493		

Number of hits exemplifying

Unambiguously singular subjects:	3,435
Unambiguously plural subjects:	228
Subjects with 1st person possessors:	239
Subjects with 2nd person possessors:	2,635
Subjects with 3rd person possessors:	117
Subjects with definite article:	1,288
Present tense verb:	3,663
Past tense verb:	615

Source: Internet search engine **www.AlltheWeb.com**.

the number of hits for collocations suggestive of different kinds of subject nominals. It will be noted that singulars far outnumber plurals, also that the cherished object is overwhelmingly associated with a speech act participant (mainly the addressee) rather than with a third party. The preference for the present tense is also apparent. Not shown in the Table is the fact that perfective 'bang has/have gone', future 'bang will go', and various modals, e.g. 'bang might go', as well as negated expressions, scored no hits at all.

These features of the *bang goes* construction confirm that the construction is anchored in the speech act situation. The speaker expresses her current annoyance at the prospect of having to abandon a cherished plan, or empathizes—somewhat ironically, perhaps—with the addressee at their having to abandon their plans. Past tense is appropriate to the extent that a speaker reports a past experience. Other tenses, the various modalities, and of course negatives, would be incompatible with this characterization.

Let us next consider the place of the construction within a broader linguistic context. A notable feature is that the subject nominal follows the verb. Some other constructions in English share this property, including the deictic constructions in (11), preposed directionals in (12), and preposed locatives in (13).

(11) a. There's Harry with his red coat on.
     b. There goes Harry, with his new girlfriend.
     c. Here comes the bus.

(12) a. Away ran the children.
     b. Out of the hole crept a timid mouse.
     c. Along this road marched the army.

(13) a. Up on the hill used to stand the governor's residence.
     b. On the bed was lying the sleeping child.
     c. On the other side of the lake stands the war memorial

The deictics in (11) are introduced by *here* or *there* and serve to direct the hearer's attention to an entity currently in the speaker's perceptual field; the verb is one of *be*, *come*, and *go*, and in the present tense. The directionals in (12) designate the path of a moving entity; they are introduced by a directional phrase while the verb designates motion or manner of motion (*run*, *climb*, *crawl*, etc.). Directionals are typically used in narratives, therefore, unlike the deictics, they can be associated with the past tense. The locatives in (13) are introduced by an expression of place, while the verb is typically *be*, *stand*, or *lie*. Since the locative constructions serve to describe the place of an entity, they are compatible with a variety of tenses.

These examples suggest the existence of a schematic subject-final construction in English, [X V NP$_{Subj}$]. The deictic, directional, and locative constructions differ, however, with respect both to their semantics and to the kinds of items that are eligible to fill the X and V slots. The *bang goes* construction also instantiates the subject-final construction, specifying the initial constituent as the lexical item *bang* and the verb as *go*, in either the present or the past tense.

The *bang goes* construction is special in another way. The constructions in (11)–(13) may take a pronominal subject, in which case the subject appears in its normal position before the verb: *There he is*, *Away they ran*, *On the bed he lay*. The position of a pronominal subject does not arise with the *bang goes* construction since the construction seems not to tolerate a pronominal subject at all: *Bang it goes, *Bang goes it.

The fact that the *bang goes* construction permits only the verb *go* invites us to look more closely at this word. Why should just this verb be appropriate to the construction? After all, motion (presumably, the 'basic' sense of *go*) is not an issue in the construction.

The discussion in Chapter 25 suggested a more schematic meaning of *go*, involving change of state over time: *The milk went sour, The light went red.* A further use involves 'abstract motion', where a conceptualizer scans an elongated object through conceived time: *The road goes from Denver to Indianapolis.* As an extension, possibly, of the abstract motion sense, *go* can designate the sequential structure of a text, either a linguistic text, such as a poem or a joke, or a musical text.

(14) a. Do you know how the poem goes?
     b. I forget how the joke went.
     c. The tune goes like this.

Observe that (14c) would normally be followed up by the speaker actually humming or singing the tune in question. This brings us to the 'quotative' use of *go*. The verb introduces a mention of a perceptible event, whether acoustic or visual (15a); it cannot, however, introduce a report or a description (15b). The quoted event can be a linguistic utterance (15c); moreover, as this example shows, the quoted element can be fronted.

(15) a. He went {'sh' / [obscene gesture] / [shake of head]}.
     b. *He went {a hushing sound / an obscene gesture / a shake of the head}.
     c. 'Yes, of course,' went the young man.

When the quoted element is fronted, as in (15c), the expression instantiates the [X V NP$_{Subj}$] schema that we invoked in connection with the *bang goes* construction. Interestingly, quotative *go* can be associated, not only with a quotation as such, but with an ideophone—that is, with a word which conventionally designates an audible event. Ideophones which are compatible with *go* include *pop, crash, crack, bump, thud, slap, whoosh, whiz, swish,* as well as *bang.* The ideophone can be in initial or final position.

(16) a. The light bulb went pop.
     b. Crash went the Heffalump's head against the tree-root.
     c. Whoosh, whoosh, whoosh went the blood through her veins.
     d. The balloon went bang when it burst.

This brings us to the word *bang* itself. Like *go*, the word has a variety of uses (Riemer 1998). As a noun it designates a kind of sound (*There was a loud bang*), either the sound of an explosion or the sound of one object coming into sudden contact with another. The idea of a sudden and noisy impact predominates in verbal uses: *They banged on the door* (i.e. knocked loudly on it), *He banged the door shut* (i.e. closed it noisily). A further use of *bang* is as a kind of adverbial modifier (*It was bang on target*; *Your remark was bang on*). Here, the idea is of precision—a projectile hit the target at the precise intended point, the remark was highly relevant to the discussion in progress.

No doubt because *bang* is perceived to be onomatopoeically imitating the sound that it designates (see the Box on p. 583), the word also functions as an ideophone. As noted, the ideophone can occur with quotative *go*, with either a preposed or a postposed subject nominal.

(**17**) a. He shut the door, bang!
 b. The balloon went bang, when it burst.
 c. Bang went the balloon, when it burst.

It looks as if we have come full circle—*Bang went the balloon* exhibits exactly the same structure as *Bang goes my weekend*. Semantically, however, the expressions differ in important respects. *Bang* in *Bang went the balloon* represents the sound that the balloon made as it burst, but there is no suggestion that my weekend makes a sound when my plans for the weekend have to be abandoned. The two uses of *bang* are not entirely unrelated, however. If something 'goes bang' it is destroyed, through either an explosion or a sudden impact. The *bang goes* construction puts this aspect into perspective—my plans for the weekend are destroyed by obligations which interfere with those plans. The constructions also differ in their formal aspects. The ideophone can occur after quotative *go* (*The balloon went bang*), a possibility not available for *bang goes* expressions (**My weekend went bang*). The quotative construction is also compatible with a pronominal subject (*It went bang*, *Bang it went*), something which is again not possible with the *bang goes* construction.

These considerations point to the need to recognize the *bang goes* construction as a distinct constructional idiom in English. The discussion also shows, however, that in spite of its idiosyncratic properties, the construction is motivated in numerous ways by affinities, both formal and semantic, with other units in the language. The construction exists, and survives, because of the ecological niche which it occupies in the inventory of linguistic units which constitute the English language.

Bang as onomatopoeic?

English speakers may feel that *bang* is an onomatopoeic word, whose pronunciation iconically resembles the sound that the word designates. Yet does the word's pronunciation *really* resemble a banging sound? I don't think so.

How, then, can we account for the very strong intuition that the word *is* imitative? The reason, I suggest, lies in the phonetic and semantic associations triggered by the word. There are quite a few monosyllable words designating a noisy impact and/or sudden movement which contain the [æ] vowel:

slam, slap, crack, clap, flap, crash, bash, clang, spank, smack, wham, prang

There are several words commencing in [b] which are associated with a sudden event:

boo, beat, bat, batter, bump, bingo

In a number of words a final nasal (especially a velar nasal) is associated with sound or movement:

sing, ring, ping, zing, fling, sling, dong, gong, hum, vroom

All these associations serve to reinforce the appropriateness of the sound-meaning relation symbolized by the word *bang*. It is because of this network of associations, I suggest, that English speakers perceive the phonetic form [bæŋl] to be an appropriate word to designate the sound of sudden impact.

The situation is not all that dissimilar from that of the *bang goes* construction itself. Although idiomatic—its formal and semantic aspects have to be specifically learned—the construction is not totally encapsulated from other facts about the English language. Affinities between aspects of construction and other facts about the language motivate the formal and semantic properties of the construction and guarantee its 'ecological niche' within the language system. *Bang* also has its ecological niche among the cluster of words designating movement, sound, and impact.

Study questions

1. The incredulity response construction. In the text, I characterized the construction as consisting of a subject nominal followed by an ungrounded verb phrase. According to this analysis, any finite clause could be converted into an incredulity response simply by removing the grounding elements. This analysis needs to be refined. Consider whether, and how, the following can be responded to with incredulity:

Sally is a good cook.
Louise is going to marry Ferdinand.

Under the bed wasn't a good place to hide it.
There's somebody at the door.
It looks like rain.

Experiment with a wider range of finite clauses, involving different kinds of subject nominals in association with different tenses, verbs, and modalities. On the basis of these results, attempt a more precise characterization of the formal aspects of the incredulity response construction. To what extent can these formal aspects be related to the construction's semantics?

You might also want to consider the possibility that the elements in the construction can appear in a different order, e.g. *What?! Write a novel?! Me?!*

2. Lamb (2001) suggests that learning the syntax of a language is mostly a matter of learning the lexicon. What is meant by this claim and how might it be substantiated? And is it necessary to hedge the claim, as Lamb did, with 'mostly'?

3. Partially specified constructional idioms. The following expressions instantiate constructional idioms whose lexical content is partially specified. Consider (a) the range of lexical variation that is tolerated, (b) the schematic meaning of the idioms, and (c) the extent to which the schematic constructional meaning motivates the range of lexical variation.

on and on; to and fro; Have a drink!; Not in my house you won't!; my first cousin twice removed; Yours sincerely; Thanks very much; Long live the Queen!; Like hell I will!; on the face of it.

4. A lexicographer's dilemma. Constructional idioms which are in part lexically specified present a problem to lexicographers. Where, in a dictionary, should a lexicographer list information about *day by day*, *word by word*, etc. —under the content words *day* and *word*, or under the function word *by*?

5. Idioms with unusual syntax. Here are some idioms (cf. Nunberg *et al.* 1994: 515) whose structure cannot easily be assimilated to general syntactic patterns:

by and large; No can do; trip the light fantastic; till kingdom come; believe you me; in short; happy go lucky

Substantiate the claim that these expressions do indeed exhibit an idiomatic syntactic structure. Can you find other expressions in English which have an unusual syntax? (See Appendix, p. 586 for some suggestions.)

6. Optional parts of constructions. Just about any clause can be extended through specification of time, place, manner, or purpose, and by various combinations of these. Alongside *The farmer shot the rabbit* we can have *The farmer shot the rabbit on Sunday*, *The farmer shot the rabbit with his rifle*, *The farmer shot the rabbit with his rifle on Sunday*, and so on. Here are three ways in which the facts could be handled with respect to the corrections which they instantiate:

(i) We propose distinct constructional schemas for every possible clause + adjunct(s) pattern.

(ii) We include within the 'basic' clause schema a number of slots for the optional elements.

(iii) The descriptive burden is placed on the representation of the adjuncts, for example, temporal expressions (*on Sunday*, etc.) are characterized with reference to the kinds of items — nominal or clausal — which they are able to modify.

Evaluate these three possibilities.

7. Constructional schemas as product-oriented schemas. I suggested, on the evidence of the *way* construction, that constructional schemas characterize the product, they should not be thought of in terms of operations that a speaker performs on a simpler 'input' form in order to build up the complex 'output' (section 28.2.2). Consider the following resultative expressions. Do these expressions also point to the product-oriented nature of the resultative construction?

I painted the house green.
They shot him dead.
The noise is driving me insane.
The new system rendered my software obsolete.
I talked myself hoarse.
They cut him free.
He cut himself free.

Further reading

The foundational text on constructions is Goldberg (1995). Recognition of the primacy of constructions has given birth to so-called Construction Grammar; see Fillmore *et al.* (1988) and Kay and Fillmore (1999). Perhaps the most extensive analysis of a construction (or, rather, cluster of constructions) is Lakoff's account of deictic *there* (Lakoff 1987: 462–585). For the role of constructions in acquisition, see Tomasello (1998, 2000) and Tomasello and Brooks (1999).

Appendix

Answers to Study questions 2 and 3

Study question 2: Meanings of the Dutch idioms

de pijp uitgaan 'to finish the pipe'
'To die, to kick the bucket'

met de meeste hoogachting 'with the highest esteem'
'yours sincerely'

iemand iets op de mouw spelden 'to pin something on someone's sleeve'
'to fool someone, to tell someone tales'

met spek schieten 'to shoot with bacon'
'to tell a tall story, to boast'

spekverkoper 'bacon-seller'
'boastful person'

aan de weg timmeren 'to practise carpentry on the roadside'
'to work in public, to attract attention by one's activities, to put oneself in the limelight'

de lakens uitdelen 'to hand out the sheets, to hand out the linen'
'to run the show, to play first fiddle, to be in charge'

uit z'n vel springen 'to jump out of one's skin'
'to be beside oneself with rage'

Abraham gezien hebben 'to have seen Abraham'
'to be over 50 years old'

Study question 3: Chinese idioms

He (1989) gives the following glosses to the extended examples:

(ii) *kāi hòu mén* 'open the back door' i.e. 'use one's influence to let someone gain his objective'

(iii) *dǔ hòu mén* 'block the back door', i.e. 'impede the channel whereby people gain their objectives through influential connections'

(iv) *kāi qián mén* 'open the front door', i.e. 'open up the channel through which people can gain their objectives properly and fairly'

(vi) *shā hóu gěi jī kàn* 'kill the monkey for the chickens to see', i.e. 'punish an official as a warning to the people'

(vii) *shā hóu gěi hóu kàn* 'kill the monkey for the monkeys to see': 'punish an official as a warning to all other officials.

He's discussion of (vi) and (vii) refers to an article in the *People's Daily*, in which the author suggests strategies for eliminating official corruption. A correspondence is established between the monkeys and the chickens on the one hand, and the officials and common people on the other. Given this correspondence, the standard idiom, according to the author, is not appropriate. There is little point in punishing an innocent low-status chicken as an example to a corrupt, high-status monkey. Variant (vi) fares better, since the punishment is meted out to the official. But since the punishment is meant to deter the officials, not the common people, variant (vii) is to be preferred.

Answer to Study question 5 (Chapter 28)

Here is a sample of expressions with unusual syntax:

Far be it from me to (criticize, but . . .); Till death us do part; Easy come, easy go; penny wise, pound foolish; let go (of something); the long and the short of it; for better or for worse; (all) at once; for once; once upon a time; all of a sudden; for the most part; at most; not in the least; It's for keeps; Steady as she goes!; Take it easy!; at the ready; none the less; as sure as eggs is eggs; One swallow does not a summer make; No way!; Never mind!

Glossary

Active zone. When an entity participates in a relation, normally only some facets of the entity (the active zone) are directly involved. In *the book on the table*, the surface of the table is the table's active zone.

Apposition. In an expression [XY], X and Y are in apposition if X and Y both profile the same entity. Example: *My neighbour the butcher*.

Autonomy/autonomous. A unit is autonomous if its conceptualization does not make intrinsic reference to other entities. A dependent unit can only be conceptualized with reference to other entities. Autonomy and dependence form a continuum, they are not complementary opposites. The concept [BOOK] is (relatively) autonomous, the concept [ON] is dependent. In phonology, vowels are (relatively) autonomous *vis-à-vis* consonants.

Base. The conceptual structure which provides the essential context for the conceptualization of a profiled entity. The concept [ISLAND] consists in the profiling of a land mass against the base of the surrounding water.

Basic level. That level in a taxonomy which is most salient; the level at which entities are most likely to be named. *Chair, hammer, dog* are basic level terms; *furniture, tool, animal, artefact*, and *creature* are superordinate to the basic level; *upholstered chair, claw hammer*, and *Scottish Terrier* are terms subordinate to the basic level.

Blending. The process by which selected elements of two (or more) mental spaces are incorporated in a third space, the blend, which may have properties not derivable from either of the input spaces. Our understanding of *That surgeon is a butcher* incorporates elements from input spaces pertaining to the activities of, respectively, surgeons and butchers, resulting, in the blend, in the interpretation that the surgeon is incompetent.

Bondedness. When units combine into a complex expression—especially when the composite form is entrenched and is characterized by coercion—it may be difficult to identify the expression's component units. The units become 'bonded' in a relatively unanalysable structure. For example, the presence of the base morpheme *preside* is not particularly evident in the word *president*.

Categorization triangle. The relation between a schema [A] and its instances [B] and [C], where [B] and [C] are related by similarity. Typically, one of the instances, e.g. [B], will be the prototype; similarity to the prototype enables a new unit, e.g. [C], to be brought under the schema.

Coercion. The phenomenon whereby one unit forces a change in the specification of a unit with which it combines. Coercion can occur at both the semantic and the phonological levels. In *drop a book*, *drop* coerces the material-object reading of *book*, in *translate a book*, *translate* coerces the conceptualization of a book as a linguistic text. The suffix—*ic* [ɪk] coerces the phonological shape of its host: *atom* ['ætəm], but *atomic* [ə'tɒmɪk].

Cognitive Grammar. The term is used in this book to refer to the linguistic theory of Ronald Langacker (Langacker 1987*a*, 1991)

Cognitive Linguistics/cognitive linguistics. Cognitive Linguistics (with capitals) is used in this book to refer to an approach to language study which situates language within more general cognitive capacities; cognitive linguistics (with small letters) refers to any linguistic theory which claims that language knowledge is represented in the mind.

Collocation. A typical pattern of co-occurrence of words. *Heavy drinker* is an established collocation, *heavy eater* is not.

Complement. In an expression [XY], which is headed by X, Y is the complement of X if Y elaborates an entity that is prominent in the semantic structure of X. In *leave the office*, *the office* is the complement of *leave*.

Compositionality. According to the compositionality principle, the properties of a complex expression can be fully computed from the properties of its component parts and the manner of their combination (= strict compositionality). Partial compositionality requires only that the component units contribute to the properties of the whole, without, however, fully determining the properties of the whole.

Conceptual metaphor. A schematic mapping relation between two domains, usually stated in the form X IS Y, where X is the target domain, Y is the source domain. Examples: THEORIES ARE BUILDINGS, STATES ARE LOCATIONS. Specific metaphorical expressions (e.g. *This theory has shaky foundations*) elaborate the conceptual metaphors.

Construal. The process whereby a given state of affairs is structured by a language user for purposes of its linguistic expression. Typically, a state of affairs can be construed in alternate ways.

Construction. Any linguistic structure, whether phonological, semantic, or symbolic, that can be analysed into component parts. Constructions can be specified with varying degrees of schematicity. A schematic construction (also known as a constructional schema) captures a general pattern for the combination of smaller units into a larger assembly.

Dependence/dependent. *See* **Autonomy.**

Domain/domain matrix. A domain is any knowledge configuration which provides the context for a conceptualization. The term is somewhat broader in its application than base. Typically, several domains are relevant to a concept; these constitute the domain matrix.

Drift. The process whereby a complex expression can, over time, or in specific contexts of use, acquire properties in addition to, or at variance with, those which it inherited from its component units and the schema for their combination. *Dishes* can refer, not only to a plural number of entities of the kind 'dish', it can also (as in *wash the dishes*) refer to cooking and eating implements of various kinds, not only to 'dishes'.

Elaborate/elaboration. *See* **Schema.**

Elaborative distance. The term refers to the 'distance' between a schema and an instance, that is, to the amount of content that needs to be added to the schema in order to specify the instance. The elaborative distance between $[CVC]_\sigma$ and [kæt] is shorter than the elaborative distance between [SYLLABLE] and [kæt].

Encyclopaedic semantics. The claim that the meaning of a linguistic expression potentially reaches into any aspect of a person's conceptual life. Meaning cannot be restricted to a tightly circumscribed 'linguistic-semantic' definition.

Entrenchment. A unit is entrenched, that is, its mental representation is strengthened, to the extent to which it has been successfully used.

Ground/grounding. The ground is the circumstances of the speech event; a conceptualization is grounded if it is anchored with respect to the ground. Grounding is effected, in nominals, by determiners and (sometimes) by quantifiers; in clauses, by markers of tense and (in English) by modal verbs.

Head. The head of an expression is that constituent whose profile is inherited by the expression. *On the table* is headed by *on*, since the relational character of the phrase is inherited from the preposition.

Homonymy. The phenomenon whereby two (or more) linguistic units share the same phonological form. Their semantic structures, however, are perceived as being unrelated.

Instance. *See* **Schema.**

Landmark (lm). *See* **Trajector.**

Mental space. A conceived situation, populated with elements and relations between them. A mental space may be assumed to be veridical, that it, it is taken to be an accurate model of (some fragment of) reality. Mental spaces can also be hypothetical, fictional, or counterfactual, or may represent the desires or hopes of a speaker. A *would-be actor* is an actor only in the mental space of the person's conception of themselves.

Metonymy. The process by which an expression which 'basically' designates entity *e*, comes to be used of an entity closely associated with *e*, within a given domain, as in *I* (= my name and phone number) *am in the telephone book*.

Modifier. In an expression [XY], which is headed by X, Y is a modifier of X if X elaborates an entity that is prominent in the semantic structure of Y. In *book on the table*, *on the table* is a modifier of *book*.

Monosemy. Said of a symbolic unit whose semantic pole is represented by a single (possibly, schematic) representation. Contrasts with polysemy. Also referred to as vagueness.

Natural class. In phonology, a set of elements (usually: segments) which share similarities with respect to their articulation, and which behave in similar ways with respect to their participation in the phonological constructions of a language. In English, the voiceless stops [p, t, k] constitute a natural class, in virtue of their distributional similarities, also because the three units have aspirated variants in the onset position of stressed syllables. A natural class is represented by an appropriate schema, which captures the commonality of its members.

Polysemy. The phenomenon whereby two or more semantic values attach to a single phonological representation.

Productivity. A schema is productive to the extent that it is able to sanction new instances meeting its specifications.

Profile. The profile of an expression is what the expression designates. Profiling takes place against a domain, or domain matrix, some aspects of which may be intrinsic to the conceptualization, and which therefore constitute the base. *Island* profiles a mass of land; its base is the surrounding water; general notions of the Earth's geophysical structure constitute the domain.

Promiscuity/choosiness. An item is promiscuous if its characterization imposes relatively few restrictions on the kinds of items with which it can combine. A choosy item can only combine with items of a specified kind. The plural morpheme [s] is choosy—it can only attach to singular count nouns. The possessive morpheme [s] is promiscuous—it attaches to whatever element stands at the end of a possessor nominal.

Prototype. A prototype is the most representative, or most salient, instance of a schema. In terms of the categorization triangle, the prototype is the unit with respect to which new units can be brought under the schema, in virtue of their similarity to the prototype.

Schema. A schema is an 'abstract', or 'course-grained' representation *vis-à-vis* its more fully specified instances. The instances elaborate the schema in contrasting ways. The phonological unit [VOWEL] is schematic for [LONG VOWEL] and [SHORT VOWEL]. In turn, [SHORT VOWEL] is schematic for [æ], [ɛ], etc. A taxonomy results from recursive application of the schema-instance relation.

Schematic. A unit may be said to be schematic if it is specified in rather general terms, lacking specific detail. [VOWEL] is a schematic phonological unit; [DO] is a schematic semantic unit.

Source-oriented vs. product-oriented rules. A source-oriented rule states the ways in which component units combine to form a complex expression. A product-oriented rule states the characteristics of the complex expression.

Specification. With respect to nominals and clauses, the process whereby the type of entity designated by a bare noun or a bare verb is given more conceptual substance.

In the case of nominals, specification involves the use of adjectival and relative clause modifiers; in the case of clauses, specification involves a statement of the participants and circumstances.

Symbolic thesis. The claim that language is essentially a means for relating phonological structures (that is, language in its perceptible form) with semantic structures (that is, meanings, or conceptualizations). Accordingly, a language can be exhaustively described by reference only to (i) phonological structures, (ii) semantic structures, and (iii) symbolic relations between (i) and (ii).

Symbolic unit. A conventionalized association of a phonological structure with a semantic structure. Symbolic units can vary with respect to their degree of schematicity and their internal complexity.

Taxonomy. *See* **Schema.**

Trajector (tr). The trajector is the more prominent participant in a relation; the less prominent participant is the landmark (lm).

Type frequency vs. token frequency. With respect to a schema and its instances, token frequency refers to the frequency of occurrence of an instance, type frequency refers to the number of different instances which elaborate the schema. The schema for plural formation in *-s* has a very high type frequency in English—there are very many instances which elaborate the schema. The schema for vowel-change plurals (*man ~ men, goose ~ geese*, etc.) has a very low type frequency. The token frequency of a vowel-changing plural (such as *men*) can be quite high, while the token frequency of a plural in *-s* can be quite low (e.g. *portcullises*).

Universal Grammar. The claim that the general 'architecture' of a grammar is genetically inherited, and therefore does not have to be learned. Exposure to linguistic data merely serves to 'set the parameters' left open in the inherited architecture.

Usage-based approach. The claim that linguistic knowledge is acquired 'bottom-up', on the basis of encounters with the language, from which schematic representations are abstracted. Also: that knowledge of a language might consist very largely in knowledge of low-level generalizations, even, in knowledge of specific expressions, even if these conform with more general schemas.

Valence. An item's valence is its disposition to combine with other items. Typically, the characterization of an item will make reference to the kinds of items with which it is eligible to combine. Thus, a preposition—which designates a relation between a (schematic) trajector and a (schematic) landmark—can combine with nominals which elaborate these schematic entities.

References

ABNEY, S. P. (1987). The English noun phrase in its sentential aspect. Ph.D. dissertation, MIT.

ACHARD, M. (1998). *Representation of Cognitive Structures: Syntax and Semantics of French Sentential Complements*. Berlin: Mouton de Gruyter.

ACUÑA-FARIÑA, J. C. (1999). 'On apposition', *English Language and Linguistics* 3: 59–81.

ALEGRE, M., and GORDON, P. (1999). 'Frequency effects and the representational status of regular inflections', *Journal of Memory and Language* 40: 41–61.

ALLAN, K. (1986). *Linguistic Meaning*. London: Routledge & Kegan Paul.

ANDERSON, R. C., and ORTONY, A. (1975). 'On putting apples into bottles—A problem of polysemy', *Cognitive Psychology* 7: 167–80.

ANGLIN, J. M. (1986). 'Semantic and conceptual knowledge underlying the child's words'. In Kuczaj and Barrett (eds) (1986), 83–97.

ANTTILA, R. (1989). *Historical and Comparative Linguistics*. Amsterdam: Benjamins.

ARONOFF, M. (1994). *Morphology by Itself: Stems and Inflectional Classes*. Cambridge, Mass.: MIT Press.

ASKE, J. (1989). 'Path predicates in English and Spanish: A closer look', *BLS* 15: 1–14.

ATHANASIADOU, A., and TABAKOWSKA, E. (eds) (1998). *Speaking of Emotions: Conceptualisation and Expression*. Berlin: Mouton de Gruyter.

ATKINS, B. T. S., and ZAMPOLLI, A. (1994). *Computational Approaches to the Lexicon*, Oxford: Oxford University Press.

AUSTIN, J. L. (1979). *Philosophical Papers*. Oxford: Clarendon Press. 3rd edition. First published 1961.

—— (1980). *How to do Things with Words*. Oxford: Oxford University Press.

AYTO, J. (1990). *Bloomsbury Dictionary of Word Origins*. London: Bloomsbury.

BAAYEN, H., and LIEBER, R. (1991). 'Productivity and English derivation: A corpus-based study', *Linguistics* 29: 801–43.

——, ——, and SCHREUDER, R. (1997). 'The morphological complexity of simplex nouns', *Linguistics* 35: 861–77.

BARCLAY, J. R., BRANSFORD, J. D., FRANKS, J. J., McCARREL, N. S., and NITSCH, K. (1974). 'Comprehension and semantic flexibility', *Journal of Verbal Learning and Verbal Behavior* 13: 471–81.

BAR-HILLEL, Y. (1960). 'The present status of automatic translation in language'. In F. L. Alt (ed.), *Advances in Computers*, Appendix III, 158–63. New York: Academic Press.

BARLOW, M. (2000). 'Usage, blends and grammar'. In Barlow and Kemmer (eds) (2000), 315–45.

——, and KEMMER, S. (eds) (2000). *Usage-Based Models of Language*. Stanford, Cal.: CSLI Publications.

BARON-COHEN, S., LESLIE, A. M., and FRITH, U. (1985). 'Does the autistic child have a "theory of mind"?', *Cognition* 21: 37–46.

BARRETT, M. D. (1986). 'Early semantic representation and early word-usage'. In Kuczaj and Barrett (eds) (1986), 39–67.

—— (1995). 'Early lexical development'. In Fletcher and MacWhinney (eds) (1995), 362–92.

—— (ed.) (1999). *The Development of Language*. Hove: Psychology Press.

BARSALOU, L. W. (1983). 'Ad hoc categories', *Memory & Cognition* 11: 211–27.

—— (1987). 'The instability of graded structure: Implications for the nature of concepts'. In U. Neisser (ed.), *Concepts and Conceptual Development: Ecological and Intellectual Factors in Categorization*, 101–40. Cambridge: Cambridge University Press.

—— (1992). 'Frames, concepts, and conceptual fields'. In Lehrer and Kittay (eds) (1992), 21–74.

BATES, E. (to appear). 'On the nature and nurture of language'. Available at http://crl.ucsd.edu/~bates/

——, and GOODMAN, J. (1999). 'On the emergence of grammar from the lexicon'. In B. MacWhinney (ed.), *The Emergence of Language*, 29–79. Mahwah, N.J.: Lawrence Erlbaum.

——, and MacWHINNEY, B. (1982). 'Functionalist Approaches to Grammar'. In E. Wanner and L. R. Gleitman (eds), *Language Acquisition: The State of the Art*, 173–218. Cambridge: Cambridge University Press.

BERG, T. (1993). 'On the relationship between voice and word class in English', *Zeitschrift für Anglistik und Amerikanistik* 41: 198–212.

—— (2000). 'The position of adjectives on the noun-verb continuum', *English Language and Linguistics* 4: 269–93.

BERKO, J. (1958). 'The child's learning of English morphology', *Word* 14: 150–77.

BICKERTON, D. (1995). *Language and Human Behavior*. Seattle: University of Washington Press.

BLOOMFIELD, L. (1933). *Language*. New York: Henry Holt.

BOAS, F. (1911). 'Introduction'. In F. Boas, *Handbook of American Indian Languages*, 1–83. Washington, D.C.: Government Printing Office.

BOLINGER, D. (1962). 'Binomials and pitch accent', *Lingua* 11: 34–44.

—— (1967). 'Adjectives in English: Attribution and predication', *Lingua* 18: 1–34.

BORSLEY, R. (1999). *Syntactic Theory: A Unified Approach*. London: Arnold.

BOWERMAN, M. (1996). 'The origins of children's spatial semantic categories: Cognitive versus linguistic determinants'. In J. J. Gumperz and S. C. Levinson (eds), *Rethinking Linguistic Relativity*, 145–76. Cambridge: Cambridge University Press.

BOYSSON-BARDIES, B. de. (1999). *How Language Comes to Children: From Birth to Two Years*. Cambridge, Mass.: MIT Press. English translation of *Comment la parole vient aux enfants*, Paris: Odile Jacob, (1996). Trans. by M. B. DeBevoise.

BROOKS, P., and TOMASELLO, M. (1999). 'Young children learn to produce passives with nonce verbs', *Developmental Psychology* 35, 29–44.

BROWN, R. (1958*a*). 'How shall a thing be called?', *Psychological Review* 65: 14–21.

—— (1958*b*). *Words and Things: An Introduction to Language*. Glencoe, Ill.: Free Press.

BRUGMAN, C. (1981). Story of 'over'. MA thesis, University of California, Berkeley. Reprinted (1988) as *The Story of Over: Polysemy, Semantics, and the Structure of the Lexicon*. New York: Garland.

—— (1990). 'What is the Invariance Hypothesis?', *Cognitive Linguistics* 1: 257–66.

BYBEE, J. (1985). *Morphology: A Study of the Relation between Meaning and Form*. Philadelphia: Benjamins.

—— (1994). 'A view of phonology from a cognitive and functional perspective', *Cognitive Linguistics* 5: 285–305.

—— (1995). 'Regular morphology and the lexicon', *Language and Cognitive Processes* 10: 425–55.

—— (2000). 'The phonology of the lexicon: Evidence from lexical diffusion'. In Barlow and Kemmer (eds) (2000), 65–85.

—— (2001). 'Frequency effects on French liaison'. In J. Bybee and P. Hopper (eds), *Frequency and the Emergence of Linguistic Structure*, 337–59. Amsterdam: Benjamins.

——, and SCHEIBMAN, J. (1999). 'The effect of usage on degrees of constituency: The reduction of *don't* in English', *Linguistics* 37: 575–96.

——, and SLOBIN, D. I. (1982). 'Rules and schemas in the development and use of the English past tense', *Language* 58: 265–89.

CACCIARI, C., and TABOSSI, P. (eds) (1993). *Idioms: Processing, Structure, and Interpretation*. Hillsdale, N.J.: Lawrence Erlbaum.

CANN, R. (1993). *Formal Semantics: An Introduction*. Cambridge, Cambridge University Press.

CARSTAIRS-McCARTHY, A. (1992). *Current Morphology*. London: Routledge.

—— (1999). *The Origins of Complex Language: An Inquiry into the Evolutionary Beginnings of Sentences, Syllables, and Truth*. Oxford: Oxford University Press.

CASAD, E. (1995). 'Seeing it in more than one way'. In Taylor and MacLaury (eds) (1995), 23–49.

—— (ed.) (1996). *Cognitive Linguistics in the Redwoods: The Expansion of a New Paradigm in Linguistics*. Berlin: Mouton de Gruyter.

CASSIDY, K. W., and KELLY, M. H. (1991). 'Phonological information for grammatical category assignments', *Journal of Memory and Language* 30: 348–69.

CHOMSKY, N. (1957). *Syntactic Structures*. The Hague: Mouton.

—— (1959). 'Review of B. F. Skinner, *Verbal Behavior* (New York: Appleton-Century Crofts, 1957)', *Language* 35: 26–58.

—— (1965). *Aspects of the Theory of Syntax*. Cambridge, Mass.: MIT Press.

—— (1966). *Cartesian Linguistics*. New York: Harper and Row.

—— (1970). 'Remarks on nominalization'. In R. Jacobs and P. Rosenbaum (eds), *Readings in English Transformational Grammar*, 182–221. Waltham, Mass.: Ginn.

—— (1980). *Rules and Representations*. New York: Columbia University Press.

Chomsky, N. (1991). 'Some notes on economy of derivation and representation'. In R. Freidin (ed.), *Principles and Parameters in Comparative Grammar*, 417–54. Cambridge, Mass.: MIT Press.

—— (2000). *New Horizons in the Study of Language and Mind*. Cambridge: Cambridge University Press.

CIENKI, A. (1998). 'STRAIGHT: An image schema and its metaphorical extensions', *Cognitive Linguistics* 9: 107–49.

CLAHSEN, H., ROTHWEILER, M., WOERST, A., and MARCUS, G. (1992). 'Regular and irregular inflection in the acquisition of German plural nouns', *Cognition* 45: 225–55.

CLARK, E. (1973). 'What's in a word? On the child's acquisition of semantics in his first language'. In T. E. Moore (ed.), *Cognitive Development and the Acquisition of Language*, 65–110. New York: Academic Press.

—— (1993). *The Lexicon in Acquisition*. Cambridge: Cambridge University Press.

CLAUSNER, T., and CROFT, W. (1997). 'Productivity and schematicity in metaphors', *Cognitive Science* 21: 247–82.

COOPER, W. E., and ROSS, J. R. (1975). 'World order'. In R. E. Grossman, L. J. San, and T. J. Vance (eds), *Papers from the Parasession on Functionalism*, 63–111. Chicago: Chicago Linguistic Society.

CORBETT, G. (1991). *Gender*. Cambridge: Cambridge University Press.

COSERIU, E. (1977). 'L'Étude fonctionnelle du vocabulaire: Précis de lexématique', *Cahiers de Léxicologie* 29: 5–23.

—— (2000). 'Structural semantics and "cognitive" semantics', *Logos and Language: Journal of General Linguistics and Language Theory* 1: 19–42.

COULSON, S., and OAKLEY, T. (2000). 'Blending basics', *Cognitive Linguistics* 11: 175–96.

COWIE, A. P. (1992). 'Multiword lexical units and communicative language teaching'. In P. J. Arnaud and H. Béjoint (eds), *Vocabulary and Applied Linguistics*, 1–12. Basingstoke: MacMillan.

CROFT, W. (1991). *Syntactic Categories and Grammatical Relations*. Chicago: University of Chicago Press.

—— (1993). 'The role of domains in the interpretation of metaphors and metonymies', *Cognitive Linguistics* 4: 335–70.

—— (1998). 'Linguistic evidence and mental representations', *Cognitive Linguistics* 9: 151–73.

—— (1999). 'Some contributions of typology to cognitive linguistics, and vice versa'. In Janssen and Redeker (eds) (1999), 61–93.

——, and CLAUSNER, T. (1999). 'Domains and image schemas', *Cognitive Linguistics* 10: 1–31.

CRUSE, D. A. (1986). *Lexical Semantics*. Cambridge: Cambridge University Press.

—— (1992). 'Antonymy revisited: Some thoughts on the relationship between words and concepts'. In Lehrer and Kittay (eds) (1992), 289–306.

—— (1994). 'Prototype theory and lexical relations', *Rivista di Linguistica* 6: 167–88.

—— (2000). *Meaning in Language: An Introduction to Semantics and Pragmatics*. Oxford: Oxford University Press.

CRYSTAL, D. (1980). *A First Dictionary of Linguistics and Phonetics*. London: André Deutsch.

CULICOVER, P. (1999). *Syntactic Nuts: Hard Cases, Syntactic Theory, and Language Acquisition.* Oxford: Oxford University Press.

CULICOVER, P., and JACKENDOFF, R. (1997). 'Semantic subordination despite syntactic coordination', *Linguistic Inquiry* 28: 195–217.

——, —— (1999). 'The view from the periphery: The English correlative conditional', *Linguistic Inquiry* 30: 543–71.

CULLER, J. (1976). *Saussure.* London: Fontana.

CUTLER, A. (1990). 'Exploiting prosodic probabilities in speech segmentation'. In G. Altmann (ed.), *Cognitive Models of Speech Processing: Psycholinguistic and Computational Perspectives*, 105–21. Cambridge, Mass.: MIT Press.

—— and NORRIS, D. (1988). 'The role of strong syllables in segmentation for lexical access', *Journal of Experimental Psychology: Human Performance and Perception* 14, 113–21.

DĄBROWSKA, E. (2001). 'From formula to schema: The acquisition of English questions', *Cognitive Linguistics* 11: 83–102.

DEACON, T. (1997). *The Symbolic Species: The Co-Evolution of Language and the Human Brain.* Harmondsworth: Penguin.

DEANE, P. (1988). 'Polysemy and cognition', *Lingua* 75: 325–61.

—— (1992). *Grammar in Mind and Brain: Explorations in Cognitive Syntax.* Berlin: Mouton de Gruyter.

—— (1993). *Multimodal Spatial Representation: On the Semantic Unity of 'over' and Other Polysemous Prepositions.* Duisburg: LAUD (= Linguistic Agency, University of Duisburg).

DENNETT, D. C. (1996). *Kinds of Minds: Towards an Understanding of Consciousness.* London: Weidenfeld & Nicolson.

DEWELL, R. (1994). '*Over* again: Image-schema transformations in semantic analysis', *Cognitive Linguistics* 5: 351–80.

DIESSEL, M., and TOMASELLO, M. (2001). 'The acquisition of finite complement clauses in English: A corpus-based analysis', *Cognitive Linguistics* 12: 97–141.

DILLON, G. L. (1977). *Introduction to Contemporary Linguistic Semantics.* Englewood Cliffs, N.J.: Prentice Hall.

DIRVEN, R., (1989a). 'Space preposition'. In Dirven (1989b), 519–50.

—— (ed.) (1989b). *A User's Grammar of English: Word, Sentence, Text, Interaction.* Frankfurt: Lang.

—— (1994). *Metaphor and Nation: Metaphors Afrikaners Live By.* Frankfurt: Lang.

DIRVEN, R., and PÖRINGS, R. (eds) (2002). *Metaphor and Metonymy in Comparison and Contrast.* Berlin: Mouton de Gruyter.

——, and RADDEN, G. (in press). *Cognitive English Grammar.* Amsterdam: Benjamins.

——, and TAYLOR, J. (1988). 'The conceptualization of vertical space in English: The case of "tall"'. In Rudzka-Ostyn (ed.), (1988), 379–407.

——, —— (1994). 'English modality: A cognitive-didactic approach'. In K. Carlson, K. Davidse, and B. Rudzka-Ostyn (eds), *Perspectives on English: Studies in Honour of Professor Emma Vorlat*, 542–56. Leuven: Peeters.

——, and VERSPOOR, M. (eds) (1998). *Cognitive Exploration of Language and Linguistics.* Amsterdam: John Benjamins.

DOKE, C. M. (1981). *Textbook of Zulu Grammar.* Longman: Cape Town. First published 1927.

DOWTY, D. (2000). '"The garden swarms with bees" and the fallacy of "argument alternation"'. In Ravin and Leacock (eds) (2000), 111–28.

ECO, U. (1986). 'Dictionary vs. encyclopedia'. In *Semiotics and the Philosophy of Language*, 46–86. Bloomington: Indiana University Press.

—— (1995). *The Search for the Perfect Language*. Oxford: Blackwell.

—— (2000). *Kant and the Platypus: Essays In Language and Cognition*. London: Vintage.

ENDRESEN, R. T., and SIMONSEN, H. G. (2001). 'The Norwegian verb'. In Simonsen and Endresen (eds) (2001), 73–94.

EVERAERT, M., VAN DER LINDEN, E.-J., SCHENK, A., and SCHREUDER, R. (eds), (1995). *Idioms: Structural and Psychological Perspectives*. Hillsdale, N.J.: Lawrence Erlbaum.

FAUCONNIER, G. (1990). 'Domains and connections', *Cognitive Linguistics*, 151–74.

—— (1994). *Mental Spaces: Aspects of Meaning Construction in Natural Languages*. Cambridge: Cambridge University Press. First published 1985 by MIT Press. Translation of *Espaces mentaux*. Paris: Minuit (1984).

—— (1997). *Mappings in Thought and Language*. Cambridge: Cambridge University Press.

——, and TURNER, M. (1996). 'Blending as a central process of grammar'. In A. Goldberg (ed.), *Conceptual Structure, Discourse, and Language*, 113–31. Stanford, Cal.: CSLI Publications.

——, —— (1998). 'Conceptual integration networks', *Cognitive Science* 22: 133–87.

FEHR, B., and RUSSEL, J. (1984). 'Concepts of emotion viewed from a prototype perspective', *Journal of Experimental Psychology: General* 113: 464–86.

FILLMORE, C. J. (1968). 'The case for case'. In E. Bach and R. T. Harms (eds), *Universals in Linguistic Theory*, 1–88. New York: Holt, Rinehart & Winston.

—— (1979). 'On fluency'. In C. J. Fillmore, D. Kempler, and N. S.-Y. Wang (eds), *Individual Differences in Language Ability and Language Behavior*, 85–101. New York: Academic Press.

—— (1985). 'Frames and the semantics of understanding', *Quaderni di Semantica* 6: 222–53.

—— (1986). 'Pragmatically controlled zero anaphora', *BLS* 12: 95–107.

—— (1997). *Lectures on Deixis*. Stanford, Cal.: CSLI Publications.

——, and ATKINS, B. T. S. (1992). 'Towards a frame-based lexicon: the semantics of RISK and its neighbors'. In A. Lehrer and E. Kittay (eds) (1992), 75–102.

——, —— (1994). 'Starting where the dictionaries stop: The challenge of corpus lexicography'. In Atkins and Zampolli (eds) (1994), 349–93.

——, —— (2000). 'Describing polysemy: The case of "crawl"'. In Ravin and Leacock (eds) (2000), 91–110.

——, KAY, P., and O'CONNOR, M. C. (1988). 'Regularity and idiomaticity in grammatical constructions: The case of *Let alone*', *Language* 64: 501–38.

FLETCHER, P., and MACWHINNEY, B. (eds) (1995). *The Handbook of Child Language*. Oxford: Blackwell.

FODOR, J. (1980). 'The present status of the innateness controversy'. In *Representations: Philosophical Essays on the Foundations of Cognitive Science*, 257–316. Cambridge, Mass.: MIT Press.

—— (1998). *Concepts: Where Cognitive Science Went Wrong*. Oxford: Oxford University Press.

FOLEY, W. A. (1997). *Anthropological Linguistics: An Introduction*. Oxford: Blackwell.

FRANCIS, E. (2000). 'Two perspectives on the grammar of possession', *Language Sciences* 22: 87–107.

FROMKIN, V., and RODMAN, R. (1997). *An Introduction to Language*. San Diego: Harcourt Brace Jovanovich. 6th edition. First edition 1974.

GAZDAR, G. (1987). 'Generative Grammar'. In J. Lyons, R. Coates, M. Deuchar, and G. Gazdar (eds), *New Horizons in Linguistics 2*, 122–51. Harmondsworth: Penguin.

GEERAERTS, D. (1992). 'The semantic structure of Dutch *over*', *Leuvense Bijdragen* 81: 205–30.

—— (1993). 'Vagueness's puzzles, polysemy's vagaries', *Cognitive Linguistics* 4: 223–72.

—— (1995). 'Specialization and reinterpretation in idioms'. In Everaert *et al.* (eds) (1995), 57–73.

—— (1997). *Diachronic Prototype Semantics: A Contribution to Historical Lexicology*. Oxford: Oxford University Press.

—— (1999). 'Idealistic tendencies in Cognitive Linguistics'. In Janssen and Redeker (eds) (1999), 163–94.

—— (2000). 'Salience phenomena in the lexicon: A typology'. In L. Albertazzi (ed.), *Meaning and Cognition*, 79–101. Amsterdam: Benjamins.

——, and GRONDELAERS, S. (1995). 'Looking back at anger: Cultural traditions and metaphorical patterns'. In Taylor and MacLaury (eds) (1995), 153–79.

——, ——, and BAKEMA, P. (1994). *The Structure of Lexical Variation: Meaning, Naming, and Context*. Berlin: Mouton de Gruyter.

GIBBS, R. W. (1994). *The Poetics of Mind: Figurative Thought, Language, and Understanding*. Cambridge: Cambridge University Press.

—— (1996). 'What's cognitive about cognitive linguistics?' In Casad (ed.) (1996), 27–53.

——, and O'BRIEN, J. (1990). 'Idioms and mental imagery: The metaphorical motivation for idiomatic meaning', *Cognition* 36: 35–68.

——, and COLSTON, H. L. (1995). 'The cognitive psychological reality of image schemas and their transformations', *Cognitive Linguistics* 6: 347–78.

——, and STEEN, G. (eds) (1999). *Metaphor in Cognitive Linguistics*. Amsterdam: Benjamins.

GIEGERICH, H. (1992). *English Phonology: An Introduction*. Cambridge: Cambridge University Press.

GIVÓN, T. (1984). *Syntax: A Functional-Typological Introduction*, Vol. 1. Amsterdam: John Benjamins.

—— (1989). *Mind, Code and Context: Essays in Pragmatics*. Hillsdale, N.J.: Lawrence Erlbaum.

GLEASON, J. B., and RATNER, N. B. (1998). 'Language Acquisition'. In J. B. Gleason and N. B. Ratner (eds), *Psycholinguistics*, 347–407. Fort Worth: Harcourt Brace Jovanovich. 2nd edition. First published 1993.

GLUCKSBERG, S., and KEYSAR, B. (1993). 'How metaphors work'. In Ortony (ed.) (1993), 401–24.

GODDARD, C. (1998). *Semantic Analysis: A Practical Introduction*. Oxford: Oxford University Press.

GOLDBERG, A. (1995). *Constructions: A Construction Grammar Approach to Argument Structure*. Chicago: University of Chicago Press.

GORDON, P. (1985). 'Evaluating the semantic categories hypothesis: The case of the count/mass distinction', *Cognition* 20: 209–242.

GRADY, J. (1997a). Foundations of meaning: Primary metaphors and primary scene. Ph.D. dissertation, University of California, Berkeley.

—— (1997b). 'THEORIES ARE BUILDINGS revisited', *Cognitive Linguistics* 8: 267–90.

GREENSPAN, S. L. (1986). 'Semantic flexibility and referential specificity of concrete nouns', *Journal of Memory and Language* 25: 539–57.

GROSS, M. (1979). 'On the failure of generative grammar', *Language* 55, 859–885.

—— (1982). 'Une classification des phrases "figées" du français', *Revue Québécoise de linguistique* 11: 151–85.

—— (1994). 'Constructing lexicon-grammars'. In Atkins and Zampolli (eds) (1994), 213–63.

GUNDERSEN, H. (2001). 'Building blocks or network relations: Problems of morphological segmentation'. In Simonsen and Endresen (eds) (2001), 95–127.

GUY, G. (1980). 'Variation in the group and the individual: The case of final stop deletion'. In W. Labov (ed.), *Locating Language in Time and Space*, 1–36. New York: Academic Press.

HAIMAN, J. (1985). *Natural Syntax: Iconicity and Erosion*. Cambridge: Cambridge University Press.

HALLIDAY, M. A. K. (1973). *Explorations in the Functions of Language*. London: Edward Arnold.

HARRIS, R. (1981). *The Language Myth*. London: Duckworth.

—— (1987). *Reading Saussure: A Critical Commentary on the Cours de linguistique générale*. London: Duckworth.

HARRIS, R. A. (1993). *The Linguistics Wars*. New York: Oxford University Press.

HAWKINS, B. (1984). The semantics of English spatial prepositions. Ph.D. dissertation, University of California, San Diego.

HE, Z. (1989). 'Creative idiomaticity', *BLS* 15: 150–60.

HEINE, B. (1997a). *Cognitive Foundations of Grammar*. New York, Oxford University Press.

—— (1997b). *Possession: Cognitive Sources, Forces, and Grammaticalization*. Cambridge: Cambridge University Press.

HERSKOVITS, A. (1986). *Language and Spatial Cognition. An Interdisciplinary Study of the Prepositions in English*. Cambridge: Cambridge University Press.

HEWSON, J. (1991). 'Determiners as heads', *Cognitive Linguistics* 2: 317–37.

HINTON, L., NICHOLS, J., and OHALA, J. J. (eds) (1994). *Sound Symbolism*. Cambridge: Cambridge University Press.

HOCKETT, C. (1967). *The State of the Art*. Amsterdam: Benjamins.

—— (1987). *Refurbishing our Foundations: Elementary Linguistics from an Advanced Point of View*. Amsterdam: Benjamins.

HOWARTH, P. (1998). 'Phraseology and second language proficiency', *Applied Linguistics* 19: 24–44.

HUDSON, G. (2000). *Essential Introductory Linguistics*. Oxford: Blackwell.

HUDSON, R. (1984). *Word Grammar*. Oxford: Blackwell.

—— (1990). *English Word Grammar*. Oxford: Blackwell.

—— (1997). 'Inherent variability and linguistic theory', *Cognitive Linguistics* 8: 73–108.

IMAI, M., and GENTNER, D. (1997). 'A cross-linguistic study of early word meaning: Universal ontology and linguistic influence', *Cognition* 62: 169–200.

INGRAM, D. (1989). *First Language Acquisition: Method, Description and Explanation*. Cambridge: Cambridge University Press.

—— (1999). 'Phonological acquisition'. In Barrett (ed.) (1999), 73–97.

ISRAEL, M. (1996). 'The *way* constructions grow'. In A. Goldberg (ed.), *Conceptual Structure, Discourse and Language*, 217–30. Stanford, Cal.: CSLI Publications.

JACKENDOFF, R. (1983). *Semantics and Cognition*. Cambridge, Mass.: MIT Press.

—— (1990). *Semantic Structures*. Cambridge, Mass.: MIT Press.

—— (1996). 'Conceptual semantics and cognitive linguistics', *Cognitive Linguistics* 7: 93–129.

—— (1997). *The Architecture of the Language Faculty*. Cambridge, Mass.: MIT Press.

——, and AARON, D. (1991). Review of Lakoff and Turner (1989), *Language* 67: 320–38.

JÄKEL, O. (1995). 'The metaphorical conception of mind: "Mental activity is manipulation" '. In Taylor and MacLaury (eds) (1995), 197–229.

JAKOBSON, R. (1960). 'Linguistics and Poetics'. In T. A. Sebeok (ed.), *Style in Language*, 350–77. Cambridge, Mass.: MIT Press. Reprinted in 1981 in his *Selected Writings*, vol. III: 18–51. The Hague: Mouton.

—— (1971). 'The phonetic and grammatical aspects of language in their interrelations'. In his *Selected Writings*, vol. II: 103–14. The Hague: Mouton.

JANSSEN, T., and REDEKER, G. (eds) (1999). *Cognitive Linguistics: Foundations, Scope, and Methodology*. Berlin: Mouton de Gruyter.

JOHANSSON, S., and HOFLAND, K. (1989). *Frequency Analysis of English Vocabulary and Grammar, Based on the LOB Corpus*. Oxford: Clarendon Press.

JOHNSON, M. (1987). *The Body in the Mind: The Bodily Basis of Meaning, Imagination, and Reason*. Chicago: University of Chicago Press.

—— (1993). *Moral Imagination: Implications of Cognitive Science for Ethics*. Chicago: University of Chicago Press.

KATAMBA, F. (1989). *Introduction to Phonology*. London: Longman.

KATZ, J. J. and POSTAL, P. M. (1964). *An Integrated Theory of Linguistic Descriptions*. Cambridge, Mass.: MIT Press.

KAY, P., and FILLMORE, C. (1999). 'Grammatical constructions and linguistic generalizations: The *What's X doing Y?* construction', *Language* 75: 1–33.

KELLER, R. (1998). *A Theory of Linguistic Signs*. Oxford: Oxford University Press.

KELLY, M. H. (1992). 'Using sound to solve syntactic problems: The role of phonology in grammatical category assignment', *Psychological Review* 99: 349–64.

——, and BOCK, J. K. (1988). 'Stress in time', *Journal of Experimental Psychology: Human Perception and Performance* 14: 389–403.

KEMPSON, R. (1977). *Semantic Theory*. Cambridge: Cambridge University Press.

KIRSNER, R. S. (1993). 'From meaning to message in two theories: Cognitive and Saussurian views of the Modern Dutch demonstratives'. In R. Geiger and B. Rudzka-Ostyn (eds) (1993), *Conceptualizations and Mental Processing in Language*, 81–114. Berlin: Mouton de Gruyter.

KLAUSENBURGER, K. 1984. *French Liaison and Linguistic Theory*. Wiesbaden: Franz Steiner.

KLEIN, W., and PURDUE, C. (1997). 'The basic variety, or Couldn't languages be much simpler?', *Second Language Research* 13: 301–47.

KOMATSU, L. (1992). 'Recent views of conceptual structure', *Psychological Bulletin* 12: 500–26.

KÖPCKE, K.-M. (1988). 'Schemas in German plural formation', *Lingua* 74: 303–35.

—— (1998). 'The acquisition of plural marking in English and German revisited: Schemata versus rules', *Journal of Child Language* 25: 293–319.

——, and ZUBIN, D. A. (1983). 'Die kognitive Organisation der Genuszuweisung zu den einsilbigen Nomen der deutschen Gegenwartssprache', *Zeitschrift für germanistische Linguistik* 11: 166–82.

——, —— (1984). 'Sechs Prinzipien für die Genuszuweising im Deutschen: Ein Beitrag zur natürlichen Klassifikation', *Linguistische Berichte* 93: 26–50.

KÖVECSES, Z. (1986). *Metaphors of Anger, Pride, and Love*. Amsterdam: Benjamins.

—— (1990). *Emotion Concepts*. New York: Springer.

KREITZER, A. (1997). 'Multiple levels of schematization: A study in the conceptualization of space', *Cognitive Linguistics* 8: 291–325.

KUCZAJ, S. A., and BARRETT, M. D. (eds) (1986). *The Development of Word Meaning: Progress in Cognitive Development Research*. New York: Springer.

KUHL, P. (1994). 'Speech perception'. In F. D. Minifie (ed.) (1994), *Introduction to Communication Sciences and Disorders*, 77–148. San Diego: Singular Publishing.

KUMASHIRO, F. (2000). Phonotactic interactions: A non-reductionist approach to phonology. Ph.D. dissertation, University of California, San Diego.

LABOV, W. (1972). *Sociolinguistic Patterns*. Philadelphia: University of Pennsylvania Press.

LADEFOGED, P. (1975). *A Course in Phonetics*. New York: Harcourt Brace Jovanovich.

LAKOFF, G. (1987). *Women, Fire, and Dangerous Things: What Categories Reveal about the Mind*. Chicago: Chicago University Press.

—— (1990). 'The Invariance Hypothesis: Is abstract reason based on image-schemas?', *Cognitive Linguistics* 1: 39–74.

—— (1993). 'The contemporary theory of metaphor'. In Ortony (ed.) (1993), 202–51.

—— (1996). *Moral Politics: What Conservatives Know that Liberals Don't*. Chicago: University of Chicago Press.

——, and JOHNSON, M. (1980). *Metaphors We Live By*. Chicago: University of Chicago Press.

——, —— (1999). *Philosophy in the Flesh: The Embodied Mind and its Challenge to Western Thought*. New York: Basic Books.

——, and TURNER, M. (1989). *More than Cool Reason*. Chicago: University of Chicago Press.

LAMB, S. (1998). *Pathways of the Brain: The Neurocognitive Basis of Language*. Amsterdam: Benjamins.

—— (2001). 'Learning syntax—a neurocognitive approach'. In Pütz *et al.* (eds) (2001), Vol. 1, 167–91.

LAMBRECHT, K. (1984). 'Formulaicity, frame semantics, and pragmatics in German binominal expressions', *Language* 60: 753–96.

—— (1990). '"What, me worry?"—"Mad Magazine sentences" revisited', *BLS*, 16, 215–28.

—— (2001). 'A framework for the analysis of cleft constructions', *Linguistics* 39: 463–516.

LANGACKER, R. W. (1982). 'Space grammar, analyzability, and the English passive', *Language* 58, 22–80. Reprinted as 'The English passive'. In Langacker (1990), 101–47.

—— (1984). 'Active zones', *BLS* 10: 177–88. Reprinted in Langacker (1990), 189–201.

—— (1986). 'Abstract motion', *BLS* 12: 455–71. Reprinted in Langacker (1990), 149–63.

—— (1987a). *Foundations of Cognitive Grammar. Vol. 1. Theoretical Prerequisites.* Stanford, Cal.: Stanford University Press. Cited in the text as FCG1.

—— (1987b). 'Nouns and verbs', *Language* 63: 53–97. Reprinted in Langacker (1990), 59–100.

—— (1988a). 'An overview of cognitive grammar'. In Rudzka-Ostyn (ed.) (1988), 3–48.

—— (1988b). 'A view of linguistic semantics'. In Rudzka-Ostyn (ed.) (1988), 49–90.

—— (1990). *Concept, Image, and Symbol: The Cognitive Basis of Grammar.* Berlin: Mouton de Gruyter.

—— (1991). *Foundations of Cognitive Grammar. Vol. 2. Descriptive Application.* Stanford: Stanford University Press. Cited in the text as FCG2.

—— (1993). 'Reference point constructions', *Cognitive Linguistics* 4: 1–38. Reprinted with revisions in Langacker (1999), 171–202.

—— (1995). 'Raising and transparency', *Language* 71: 1–62. Reprinted with revisions in Langacker (1999), 317–60.

—— (1999). *Grammar and Conceptualization.* Berlin: Mouton de Gruyter.

LASS, R. (1984). *Phonology: An Introduction to Basic Concepts.* Cambridge: Cambridge University Press.

——, and WRIGHT, S. M. (1985). 'The South African chain shift'. In R. Eaton, O. Fischer, W. Koopman, and F. van der Leek (eds) (1985), *Papers from the 4th International Conference on English Historical Linguistics, Amsterdam, 10–13 April 1985,* 137–62. Amsterdam: Benjamins.

LEHRER, A., and KITTAY, E. (eds) (1992). *Frames, Fields, and Contrasts: New Essays in Semantic and Lexical Organization.* Hillsdale, N.J.: Lawrence Erlbaum.

LEVINSON, S. (1983). *Pragmatics.* Cambridge: Cambridge University Press.

LEVY, Y. (1983). 'It's frogs all the way down', *Cognition* 15: 75–93.

LIBERMAN, A. M., COOPER, F. S., HARRIS, K. S., and MacNEILAGE, P. J. (1967). Perception of the speech code', *Psychological Review* 74: 431–61.

LIEBERMAN, P. (1991). *Uniquely Human: The Evolution of Speech, Thought, and Selfless Behaviour.* Cambridge, Mass.: Harvard University Press.

LINDNER, S. (1981). A lexico-semantic analysis of English verb-particle constructions with UP and OUT. Ph.D. dissertation, University of California, San Diego.

LOCKE, J. (1995). 'Development of the capacity for spoken language'. In Fletcher and MacWhinney (eds) (1995), 278–302.

LOSIEWICZ, B. (1992). The effect of frequency on linguistic morphology. Ph.D. dissertation, University of Texas, Austin.

LYONS, J. (1968). *Introduction to Theoretical Linguistics*. Cambridge: Cambridge University Press.

—— (1977). *Semantics*. 2 vols. Cambridge: Cambridge University Press.

McCARTHY, J. (1982). 'Prosodic structure and expletive infixation', *Language* 58: 574–90.

MacLAURY, R. (1987). 'Coextensive semantic ranges: Different names for distinct vantages of one category', *CLS* 23/1: 268–82.

—— (1995a). *Color Categorization in Mesoamerica: A Cross-Linguistic Survey and a Cognitive Model*. Austin: University of Texas Press.

—— (1995b). 'Vantage theory'. In Taylor and MacLaury (eds) (1995), 231–76.

McLEOD, P., PLUNKETT, K., and ROLLS, E. T. (1998). *Introduction to Connectionist Modelling of Cognitive Processes*. Oxford: Oxford University Press.

MAKKAI, A. (1972). *Idiom Structure in English*. The Hague: Mouton.

MALKIEL, Y. (1959). 'Studies in irreversible binominals', *Lingua*, 8: 113–60.

MANDLER, J. (1992). 'How to build a baby: II. Conceptual primitives', *Psychological Review* 99, 587–604.

MARCUS, G., BRINKMAN, U., CLAHSEN, H., WIESE, R., and PINKER, S. (1995). 'German inflection: The exception that proves the rule', *Cognitive Psychology* 29: 189–256.

MARKMAN, E. M. (1989). *Categorization and Naming in Children: Problems of Induction*. Cambridge, Mass.: MIT Press.

MASSAM, D. (1999). '*Thing is* constructions: the thing is, is what's the right analysis?', *English Language and Linguistics* 3: 335–52.

MATSUKI, K. (1995). 'Metaphors of anger in Japanese'. In Taylor and MacLaury (eds) (1995), 137–51.

MATTHEWS, P. H. (1981). *Syntax*. Cambridge; Cambridge University Press.

MATTINGLY, I. (1972). 'Reading, the linguistic process, and linguistic awareness'. In J. Kavanagh and I. Mattingly (eds), *Language by Ear and by Eye: The Relationships between Speech and Reading*, 133–47. Cambridge, Mass.: MIT Press.

MENN, L. (1971). 'Phonotactic rules in beginning speech', *Lingua* 26: 582–92.

MIKOŁAJCZUK, A. (1998) 'The metonymic and metaphorical conceptualization of anger in Polish'. In A. Athanasiadou and E. Tabakowska (eds) (1998), *Speaking of Emotions: Conceptualisation and Expression*, 153–90. Berlin: Mouton de Gruyter.

MILLER, G. A., and CHARLES, W. G. (1991). 'Contextual correlates of semantic similarity', *Language and Cognitive Processes* 6: 1–28.

MINTZ, M. W. (1994). *A Student's Grammar of Malay & Indonesian*. Singapore: EPB Publishers.

MORGAN, P. S. (1997). 'Figuring out *figure out*: Metaphor and the semantics of the English verb-particle construction', *Cognitive Linguistics* 8: 327–57.

MORRIS, D., COLLETT, P., MARSH, P., and O'SHAUGHNESSY, M. (1979). *Gestures:*

Their Origins and Distribution: A New Look at the Human Animal. London: Jonathan Cape.

MURPHY, G. (1988). 'Comprehending complex concepts', *Cognitive Science* 12: 529–62.

——, and MEDIN, D. (1985). 'The role of theories in conceptual coherence', *Psychological Review* 92: 289–316.

MYLNE, T. (1995). 'Grammatical category and world view: Western colonization of the Dyirbal language', *Cognitive Linguistics* 6: 379–404.

NATHAN, G. (1986). 'Phonemes as mental categories', *BLS* 12: 212–23.

—— (1989). 'Preliminaries to a theory of phonological substance: The substance of sonority'. In Corrigan and Noonan (eds) (1989), 55–67.

—— (1994). 'How the phoneme inventory gets its shape: Cognitive grammar's view of phonological systems', *Rivista di Linguistica* 6: 275–87.

—— (1996). 'Steps towards a cognitive phonology'. In B. Hurch and R. A. Rhodes (eds) (1996), *Natural Phonology: The State of the Art. Papers from the Bern Workshop on Natural Phonology*, 107–20. Berlin: Mouton de Gruyter.

NATTINGER, J. R., and DeCARRICO, J. S. (1992). *Lexical Phrases and Language Teaching*. Oxford: Oxford University Press.

NESPOR, M., and VOGEL, I. (1986). *Prosodic Phonology*. Dordrecht: Foris.

NEWMEYER, F. (1986). *Linguistic Theory in America*. New York: Academic Press.

NIKIFORIDOU, K. (1991). 'The meanings of the genitive: A case study in semantic structure and semantic change', *Cognitive Linguistics* 2: 149–205.

NOBLE, W., and DAVIDSON, I. (1996). *Human Evolution, Language and Mind: A Psychological and Archaeological Inquiry*. Cambridge: Cambridge University Press.

NUNBERG, G. (1979). 'The non-uniqueness of semantic solutions: Polysemy', *Linguistics and Philosophy* 3: 143–84.

——, and ZAENEN, A. (1992). 'Systematic polysemy in lexicology and lexicography'. In H. Tommola, K. Varantola, T. Salmi-Tolonen, and J. Schopp (eds) (1992), *Euralex '92 Proceedings*, Part 11, 387–96. Tampere: University of Tampere.

——, SAG, I., and WASOW, T. (1994). 'Idioms'. *Language* 70: 491–538.

OAKESHOTT-TAYLOR, J. (1984). 'Phonetic factors in word order', *Phonetica* 41: 226–37.

O'GRADY, W. (1998). 'The syntax of idioms'. *Natural Language and Linguistic Theory* 16: 279–312.

OHALA, J. J. (1990). 'The phonetics and phonology of aspects of assimilation'. In J. Kingston and M. Beckman (eds) (1990), *Papers in Laboratory Phonology I: Between the Grammar and the Physics of Speech*, 258–75. Cambridge: Cambridge University Press.

ORTONY, A. (ed.) (1993). *Metaphor and Thought*. Cambridge: Cambridge University Press. First edition, 1979.

PALMER, F. (1971). *Grammar*. Harmondsworth: Penguin.

PALMER, G. B. (1996). *Toward a Theory of Cultural Linguistics*. Austin: University of Texas Press.

PALMER, L. R. (1954). *The Latin Language*. London: Faber and Faber.

PANTHER, K.-U., and THORNBURG, L. (2001). 'A Conceptual Analysis of English -er Nominals'. In Pütz *et al.* (eds) (2001), Vol. 11.

PARTRIDGE, E. (1977). *A Dictionary of Catch Phrases: British and American from the Sixteenth Century to the Present Day*. London: Routledge & Kegan Paul.

PAWLEY, A., and SYDER, F. (1983). 'Two puzzles for linguistic theory: Nativelike selection and nativelike fluency'. In J. C. Richards and R. W. Schmidt (eds) (1983), *Language and Communication*, 191–225. London: Longman.

PEETERS, B. (1998). 'Cognitive musings: Review of Rudzka-Ostyn (1993)', *Word* 49: 225–237.

—— (2000). 'Does Cognitive Linguistics live up to its name?' In R. Dirven, B. Hawkins, and E. Sandikcioglu (eds), *Language and Ideology: Cognitive Theoretical Approaches*, 83–106. Amsterdam: Benjamins.

PIAGET, J. (1952). *The Origins of Intelligence in Children*. New York: International Universities Press.

PIERREHUMBERT, J. (1994). 'Syllable structure and word structure: A study of triconsonantal clusters in English'. In P. Keating (ed.), *Papers in Laboratory Phonology III: Phonological Structure and Phonetic Form*, 168–88. Cambridge: Cambridge University Press.

PINKER, S. (1984). *Language Learnability and Language Development*. Cambridge, Mass.: Harvard University Press.

—— (1989). *Learnability and Cognition: The Acquisition of Argument Structure*. Cambridge, Mass.: MIT Press.

—— (1994). *The Language Instinct: How the Mind Creates Language*. New York: William Morrow.

—— (1999). *Words and Rules: The Ingredients of Language*. New York: Basic Books.

——, and PRINCE, A. (1988). 'On language and connectionism: Analysis of a parallel distribution processing model of language acquisition', *Cognition* 28: 73–193.

——, —— (1991). 'Regular and irregular morphology and the psychological status of rules of grammar', *BLS* 17: 230–51.

PLATTS, M. (1997). *Ways of Meaning: An Introduction to a Philosophy of Language*. Cambridge, Mass.: MIT Press. Second edition. First edition: London: Routledge & Kegan Paul (1979).

PLUNKETT, K. (1995). 'Connectionist approaches to language acquisition'. In Fletcher and MacWhinney (eds) (1995), 36–72.

——, and MARCHMAN, V. A. (1993). 'From rote learning to system building: Acquiring verb morphology in children and connectionist nets', *Cognition* 48: 21–69.

——, —— (1996). 'Learning from a connectionist model of the acquisition of the English past tense', *Cognition* 61: 299–308.

PORPHYRY THE PHOENICIAN (1975). *Isagoge*. Trans. by Edward W. Warren. Toronto: The Pontifical Institute of Mediaeval Studies.

PULLUM, G. (1973). 'What's a sentence like this doing showing up in a language like English?', *York Papers in Linguistics* 3: 113–5.

—— (1989). 'The great Eskimo vocabulary hoax', *Natural Language and Linguistic Theory* 7: 275–81. Reprinted in G. K. Pullum (1991), *The Great Eskimo Vocabulary Hoax and Other Irreverent Essays on the Study of Language*, 159–71. Chicago: University of Chicago Press.

PUSTEJOVSKY, J. (1991). 'The generative lexicon', *Computational Linguistics* 17: 409–41.

—— (1995). *The Generative Lexicon*. Cambridge, Mass.: MIT Press.

Pütz, M., Niemeier, S., and Dirven, R. (eds) (2001). *Applied Cognitive Linguistics. Vol. I, Theory and Language Aquisition; Vol. II Language Pedagogy.* Berlin: Mouton de Gruyter.

Queller, K. (2001). 'A usage-based approach to modeling and teaching the phrasal lexicon'. In Pütz *et al.* (eds) (2001), Vol. 11, 55–83.

Quine, W. V. O. (1960). *Word & Object.* Cambridge, Mass.: MIT Press.

—— (1987). *Quiddities: An Intermittently Philosophical Dictionary.* Cambridge, Mass.: Harvard University Press.

Radden, G. (1989). 'Figurative uses of prepositions'. In Dirven (1989b), 551–76.

—— (1996). 'Motion metaphorized: The case of *coming* and *going*'. In Casad (ed.) (1996), 423–58.

——, and Kövecses, Z. (1999). 'Towards a theory of metonymy'. In K.-U. Panther and G. Radden (eds) (1999), *Metonymy in Language and Thought,* 17–59. Amsterdam: Benjamins.

Radford, A. (1988). *Transformational Grammar: A First Course.* Cambridge: Cambridge University Press.

—— (1997). *Syntax: A Minimalist Introduction.* Cambridge: Cambridge University Press.

—— Atkinson, M. A., Britain, D., Clahsen, H., and Spencer, A. (1999). *Linguistics: An Introduction.* Cambridge: Cambridge University Press.

Ravin, Y., and Leacock, C. (eds) (2000). *Polysemy: Theoretical and Computational Approaches.* Oxford: Oxford University Press.

Reddy, M. (1993). 'The conduit metaphor: A case of frame conflict in our language about language'. In Ortony (ed.) (1993), 164–201. (Also in Ortony (ed.), first edition, 1979).

Rhodes, R. A. (1994). 'Aural images'. In Hinton *et al.* (eds), (1994), 276–92.

——, and Lawler, J. M. (1981). 'Athematic metaphors'. *CLS* 17: 318–42.

Riemer, N. (1998). 'The grammaticalization of impact: *Bang* and *slap* in English', *Australian Journal of Linguistics* 18: 169–83.

Robins, R. H. (1964). *General Linguistics: An Introductory Survey.* London: Longman.

——, and Johnson, W. (1999). *A Course in Phonology.* Oxford: Blackwell.

Rohrer, T. (2000). 'Even the Interface is for Sale: Metaphors, Visual Blends and the Hidden Ideology of the Internet'. In R. Dirven, R. Frank and C. Ilie (eds), *Language and Ideology: Descriptive Cognitive Approaches,* 189–214. Amsterdam: Benjamins.

Rosch, E. (1975). 'Universals and cultural specifics in human categorization'. In R. W. Brislin, S. Bochner, and W. J. Lonner (eds), *Cross-cultural Perspectives on Learning,* 177–206. New York: Wiley.

——, and Mervis, C. B. (1975). 'Family resemblances: Studies in the internal structure of categories', *Cognitive Psychology* 7: 573–605.

Rubba, J. (1993). Discontinuous morphology in modern Aramaic. Ph.D. dissertation, University of California, San Diego.

Rudzka-Ostyn, B. (ed.) (1988). *Topics in Cognitive Linguistics.* Amsterdam: Benjamins.

Rumelhart, D., and McClelland, J. (1986). 'On learning the past tenses of English verbs: Implicit rules or parallel distributed processing?' In J. McClelland,

D. Rumelhart, and the PDP Research Group (eds) (1986), *Parallel Distributed Processing: Explorations in the Microstructure of Cognition*, Vol. 2, 216–71. Cambridge, Mass.: MIT Press.

RUWET, N. (1986). 'On weather verbs', *CLS* 22: 195–215.

SAMPSON, G. (1985). *Writing Systems: A Linguistic Introduction*. Stanford, Cal.: Stanford University Press.

SANDRA, D. (1998). 'What linguists can and can't tell you about the human mind: A reply to Croft', *Cognitive Linguistics* 9: 361–78.

——, and RICE, S. (1995). 'Network analyses of prepositional meanings: Mirroring whose mind—the linguist's or language user's?', *Cognitive Linguistics* 6: 89–130.

SAPIR, E. (1921). *Language: An Introduction to the Study of Speech*. New York: Harcourt, Brace, and Company.

SAUSSURE, F. de (1964). *Cours de linguistique générale*. Paris: Payot. First published 1916. Translated by R. Harris, as *Course in General Linguistics*. London: Duckworth (1983).

SCHANK, R., and ABELSON, R. (1977). *Scripts, Plans, Goals and Understanding*. Hillsdale, N.J.: Lawrence Erlbaum.

SCHÜTZE, H. (2000). 'Disambiguation and connectionism'. In Ravin and Leacock (eds) (2000), 205–19.

SEARLE, J. (1969). *Speech Acts: An Essay in the Philosophy of Language*. Cambridge: Cambridge University Press.

—— (1979). *Expression and Meaning*. Cambridge: Cambridge University Press.

—— (1992). *The Rediscovery of the Mind*. Cambridge, Mass.: MIT Press.

—— (1993). 'Metaphor'. In Ortony (ed.) (1993), 83–111.

SERENO, J. A. (1994). 'Phonosyntactics'. In Hinton *et al.* (eds) (1994), 267–75.

——, and JONGMAN, A. (1990). 'Phonological and form class relations in the lexicon', *Journal of Psycholinguistic Research* 19: 387–404.

——, —— (1997). 'Processing of English inflectional morphology', *Memory & Cognition* 25: 425–37.

SHAVER, P., SCHWARTZ, J., KIRSON, D., and O'CONNOR, C. (1987). 'Emotion knowledge: Further exploration of a prototype approach', *Journal of Personality and Social Psychology* 52: 1061–86.

SIMONSEN, H. G., and ENDRESEN, R. T. (eds), (2001). *A Cognitive Approach to the Verb. Morphological and Constructional Perspectives*. Berlin: Mouton de Gruyter.

SKINNER, B. F. (1993). *About Behaviorism*. Harmondsworth: Penguin. First published 1974 by Alfred A. Knopf.

SLOBIN, D. (1996). 'Two ways to travel: Verbs of motion in English and Spanish'. In M. Shibatani and S. A. Thompson (eds), *Grammatical Constructions: Their Form and Meaning*, 195–219. Oxford: Oxford University Press.

SMITH, E. E., and MEDIN, D. L. (1981). *Categories and Concepts*. Cambridge, Mass.: Harvard University Press.

SNEDDON, J. N. (1996). *Indonesian: A Comprehensive Grammar*. London: Routledge.

SOJA, N. N., CAREY, S., and SPELKE, E. (1991). 'Ontological categories guide children's inductions of word meaning', *Cognitive Development* 7: 29–45.

SOLOMON, M. (1972). 'Stem endings and the acquisition of inflections', *Language Learning* 22: 43–50.

SPERBER, D., and WILSON, D. (1986). *Relevance: Communication and Cognition*. Oxford: Blackwell.

STUBBS, M. (1995). 'Collocations and semantic profiles: On the cause of the trouble with quantitative studies', *Functions of Language* 2: 23–55.

SWEETSER, E. (1990). *From Etymology to Pragmatics: Metaphorical and Cultural Aspects of Semantic Structure*. Cambridge: Cambridge University Press.

—— (1999). 'Compositionality and blending: Semantic composition in a cognitive realistic framework'. In Janssen and Redeker (eds) (1999), 129–62.

SWIGGERS, P. (1985). 'How to order eggs in French', *Folia Linguistica* 19: 63–8.

TALMY, L. (1983). 'How language structures space'. In H. Pick and L. Acredolo (eds), *Spatial Orientation: Theory, Research and Application*, 225–82. New York: Plenum Press.

—— (1985). 'Lexicalization patterns: Semantic structure in lexical forms'. In T. Shopen (ed.), *Language Typology and Syntactic Description*, vol. 3, 36–149. Cambridge: Cambridge University Press.

—— (1988). 'Force dynamics in language and cognition', *Cognitive Science* 12: 49–100.

—— (1996). 'Fictive motion in language and "ception"'. In P. Bloom, M. Peterson, L. Nadel, and M. Garrett (eds), *Language and Space*, 211–76. Cambridge, Mass.: MIT Press.

TANNEN, D. (1982). 'Ethnic style in male-female conversation'. In J. J. Gumperz (ed.), *Language and Social Identity*, 217–31. Cambridge: Cambridge University Press.

TAYLOR, J. (1987). 'Metaphors of communication and the nature of listening and reading comprehension', *Interface: A Journal of Applied Linguistics* 1: 119–34.

—— (1988). 'Contrasting prepositional categories: English and Italian'. In Rudzka-Ostyn (ed.) (1988), 299–326.

—— (1991). 'Remarks on the PIN–KIN vowels in South African English', *English World-Wide* 12: 75–85.

—— (1992). 'Old problems: Adjectives in Cognitive Grammar', *Cognitive Linguistics* 3: 1–46.

—— (1993). 'Prepositions: Patterns of polysemisation and strategies of disambiguation'. In C. Zelinski-Wibbelt (ed.), *The Semantics of Prepositions: From Mental Processing to Natural Language Processing*, 151–75. Berlin: Mouton de Gruyter.

—— (1995a). *Linguistic Categorization: Prototypes in Linguistic Theory*. Oxford: Clarendon Press. First edition, 1989.

—— (1995b). 'Models of word meaning in comparison: The two-level model (Manfred Bierwisch) and the network model (Ronald Langacker)'. In J. Vanparys and R. Dirven (eds), *Current Approaches to the Lexicon*, 3–26. Frankfurt: Lang.

—— (1996). *Possessives in English: An Exploration in Cognitive Grammar*. Oxford: Clarendon Press.

—— (1997). 'Double object constructions in Zulu'. In J. Newman (ed.), *The Linguistics of Giving*, 67–96. Amsterdam: Benjamins.

—— (1999). 'Cognitive semantics and structuralist semantics'. In A. Blank and P. Koch (eds), *Historical Semantics and Cognition*, 17–48. Berlin: Mouton de Gruyter.

——, and DIRVEN, R. (1991). *Complementation*, Paper A303. Duisburg: LAUD (= Linguistic Agency, University of Duisburg).

TAYLOR, J. , and MacLAURY, R. (eds) (1995). *Language and the Cognitive Construal of the World*. Berlin: Mouton de Gruyter.

——, and MBENSE, Th. (1998). 'Red dogs and rotten mealies: How Zulus talk about anger'. In Athanasiadou and Tabakowska (eds) (1998), 191–226.

THORNDIKE, E. L., and LORGE, I. (1944). *The Teacher's Word Book of 30,000 Words*. New York: Teachers College Press.

TOMASELLO, M. (1995). 'Language is not an instinct'. Review of Pinker (1994), *Cognitive Development* 10: 131–56.

—— (1998). 'The return of constructions', *Journal of Child Language* 25: 431–42.

—— (2000). 'First steps toward a usage-based theory of language acquisition', *Cognitive Linguistics* 11: 61–82.

——, and BROOKS, P. J. (1998). 'Young children's earliest transitive and intransitive constructions', *Cognitive Linguistics* 9: 379–95.

——, —— (1999). 'Early syntactic development: A construction grammar approach'. In Barrett (ed.) (1999), 161–90.

TRAUGOTT, E. C. (1985). '"Conventional" and "dead" metaphors revisited'. In W. Paprotté and R. Dirven (eds), *The Ubiquity of Metaphor: Metaphor in Language and Thought*, 17–56. Amsterdam: Benjamins.

TUGGY, D. (1988). 'Nahuatl causative/applicatives in cognitive grammar'. In Rudzka-Ostyn (ed.) (1988), 587–618.

—— (1992). 'The affix-stem distinction: A Cognitive Grammar analysis of data from Orizaba Nahuatl', *Cognitive Linguistics* 3: 237–300.

—— (1993). 'Ambiguity, polysemy, and vagueness', *Cognitive Linguistics* 4: 273–90.

—— (1996). 'The thing is is that people talk that way. The question is is why?' In Casad (ed.) (1996), 713–52.

—— (1999). 'Linguistic evidence for polysemy in the mind: A response to William Croft and Dominiek Sandra', *Cognitive Linguistics* 10: 343–68.

TURNER, M. (1987). *Death is the Mother of Beauty*. Chicago: University of Chicago Press.

—— (1996). *The Literary Mind*. New York: Oxford University Press.

TYLER, A., and EVANS, V. (2001a). 'Reconsidering prepositional polysemy networks: The case of *over*'. *Language* 77: 724–65.

——, —— (2001b). 'The Relation between Experience, Conceptual Structure and Meaning: Non-temporal Uses of Tense and Language Teaching'. In Pütz *et al.* (eds) (2001), Vol. 1, 63–105.

UNGERER, F., and SCHMID, H.-J. (1996). *An Introduction to Cognitive Linguistics*. London: Longman.

VANDELOISE, C. (1990). 'Representation, prototypes, and centrality'. In Tsohatzidis (ed.) (1990), 403–37.

VAN HOEK, K. (1997). *Anaphora and Conceptual Structure*. Chicago: University of Chicago Press.

VAN LANGENDONCK, W. (1994). 'Determiners as heads?', *Cognitive Linguistics* 5: 43–59.

VAN OOSTEN, J. (1986). *The Nature of Subjects, Topics and Agents: A Cognitive Explanation*. Bloomington: Indiana University Linguistics Club.

VENDLER, Z. (1967). *Linguistics in Philosophy*, Ithaca, N.Y.: Cornell University Press.

WALSH, T., and PARKER, F. (1983). 'The duration of morphemic and non-morphemic /s/ in English', *Journal of Phonetics* 11: 201–16.

WEINERT, R. (1995). 'The role of formulaic language in second language acquisition research: A review', *Applied Linguistics* 16: 180–205.

WELLS, J. C. (1982). *Accents of English*. 3 vols. Cambridge: Cambridge University Press.

WHEELER, C. J., and SCHUMSKY, D. A. (1980). 'The morpheme boundaries of some English derivational suffixes', *Glossa* 14: 3–34.

WHORF, B. L. (1956). *Language, Thought, and Reality: Selected Essays of Benjamin Lee Whorf*. Ed. J. B. Carroll. Cambridge, Mass.: MIT Press.

WIERZBICKA, A. (1985). 'Oats and wheat: the fallacy of arbitrariness'. In John Haiman (ed.), *Iconicity in Language*, 311–42. Amsterdam: Benjamins. Revised version in Wierzbicka (1988), 499–560.

—— (1986). 'Metaphors Linguists Live By: Lakoff & Johnson contra Aristotle'. Review of Lakoff and Johnson 1980, *Papers in Linguistics* 19: 287–313.

—— (1988). *The Semantics of Grammar*. Amsterdam: John Benjamins.

—— (1991). 'Semantic rules know no exceptions', *Studies in Language* 15: 371–98.

—— (1994). 'The universality of taxonomic categorization and the indispensability of the concept "kind"', *Rivista di Linguistica*, 6: 347–64.

—— (1996). *Semantics: Primes and Universals*. Oxford: Oxford University Press.

WILLIAMS, E. (1981). 'On the notions "lexically related" and "head of a word"', *Linguistic Inquiry* 12: 245–74.

WITTGENSTEIN, L. (1958). *The Blue and Brown Books*. Oxford: Blackwell.

—— (1978). *Philosophical Investigations*. Tr. G. E. M. Anscombe. Oxford: Blackwell.

WUNDERLICH, D. (1993). 'On German *um*: Semantic and conceptual aspects', *Linguistics* 31: 111–33.

YOSHIMURA, K. (to appear). 'Middle expressions in English: An encyclopaedically-based account of their viability'.

Name index

Subject index